TODAY'S MORAL ISSUES

Classic and Contemporary Perspectives

Second Edition

Daniel Bonevac
The University of Texas at Austin

Mayfield Publishing Company
London • Toronto
Mountain View, California

Library of Congress Cataloging-in-Publication Data

Today's moral issues : classic and contemporary perspectives / [edited by] Daniel Bonevac. — 2nd ed.

p. cm.

Includes bibliographical references and index.

ISBN 1-55934-513-6

1. Ethical problems. 2. Applied ethics. I. Bonevac, Daniel A.

BJ1031.T63 1995 95-33959

CIP

Manufactured in the United States of America

10 9 8 7 6 5 4 3 2 1

Mayfield Publishing Company
1280 Villa Street
Mountain View, California 94041

Sponsoring editor, James Bull; production, Robin Lockwood & Associates; manuscript editor, Jennifer Gordon; text and cover designer, Donna Davis; art director, Jeanne M. Schreiber; manufacturing manager, Randy Hurst. Cover image: Paul Klee (1879–1940), *Scheidung abends.* Privatbesitz Schweiz. Copyright © by ARS, New York. The text was set in 10/12 ITC Berkeley Oldstyle Book and Berkeley Oldstyle Medium by TBH Typecast, Inc., and printed on 50# Ecolocote by Malloy Lithographing, Inc.

This book is printed on recycled paper.

Contents

PART III. Rights and Responsibilities 275

PART IV. Justice 407

Classic Texts

Preface

This book is designed as a text for courses on contemporary moral issues. Such courses assume that philosophy has something important to contribute to the discussion of today's moral problems, and that the contribution can be communicated to college students—usually, freshmen and sophomores. I believe that both assumptions are true. But it is hard to demonstrate that in the classroom. It isn't easy to use theory and practice to illumine each other.

Textbooks on contemporary moral issues generally consist of selections on current moral problems such as abortion, euthanasia, capital punishment, and similar topics, written by professional philosophers for a professional audience. I have found it difficult to teach from such texts. Students understandably have trouble following arguments from professional journals. More fundamentally, students have trouble abstracting ethical principles and methods from treatments of particular issues. Even students with a good command of arguments about some issues flounder when faced with an issue that has not been treated explicitly in class.

This poses a dilemma for instructors. If students are left to themselves to generalize from treatments of particular problems, almost all emerge with only the vaguest idea of what ethical thinking is. If instructors supply an ethical framework for thinking about moral issues, as most do, then the course falls into two parts that are very hard to unify. The theoretical part strikes most students as dry and irrelevant, while the practical part remains confusing or, at best, an exercise in applying theory.

The resolution to the dilemma, I am convinced, consists in tying theoretical and practical considerations together. *Today's Moral Issues* combines classic and contemporary readings on each of four themes: liberty, first principles, rights and responsibilities, and justice. The classic readings relate closely to the contemporary readings that follow. I have found that using the classic texts themselves helps students to connect theory and practice, for writers such as Locke, Burke, and Mill tend to be more concrete and practical in outlook than most summaries or secondary discussions of their thought. Their motivations are not difficult for most students to understand.

Moreover, the classical sources constitute a foundation for reasoning about contemporary issues. Combining classic texts and contemporary issues lets students see the dialectic between theoretical and practical concerns in ethics. When confronted by practical dilemmas and disagreements, it is easy to see why ethical thinkers have sought to construct theories. And the issues provide opportunities to test theories as well as to apply them. Good students, I have found, not only attain a superior understanding of the theories, the issues, and how they relate, but also a real sense of what ethical thinking is all about. The text is organized to combine classical source materials with the contemporary readings to which they are most relevant. And the contemporary readings that have been chosen focus on key dimensions of the issues that relate particularly well to the general philosophical concerns of the classic texts.

Today's Moral Issues is also unique in treating contemporary topics in the context of political philosophy as well as ethics. Issues such as abortion, euthanasia, and the environment have political as well as personal dimensions. Others, such as capital punishment, freedom of speech, welfare, and affirmative action, are almost entirely political. It is impossible to treat these issues adequately without considering, for example, the bounds of legitimate state action and the proper ends of government.

New Features

The organization of the second edition differs slightly from that of the first. The "Utility" part has become "First Principles," with the addition of Kant, to allow instructors to contrast consequentialist and deontological approaches more clearly. The "Rights" part is now entitled "Rights and Responsibilities," to emphasize that rights and obligations are intimately connected.

The selections from philosophical classics have changed little since the first edition. The Kant placement has changed, and there is much more Aristotle. Otherwise, there has been only some light editing.

The selections on contemporary issues, in contrast, have changed considerably. More than half are new to this edition. Like the readings from the first edition, they reflect many different perspectives. Some of the writers represented here are philosophers, but many are journalists, public figures, public policy researchers, economists, and scientists. The readings argue from different principles at various levels of sophistication.

There are also new issues: "Health Care" and "Sexual Behavior." Racial harassment has been broadened to "Offensive Speech and Behavior," and "Welfare" and "World Hunger" receive their own sections. Students are likely to be well-informed on some of the issues included here; others will challenge them to become more informed.

Acknowledgments

This book has evolved over many years in the classroom. I am grateful to the many instructors, teaching assistants, and students who have used earlier versions and helped me refine them. I especially want to thank Nicholas Asher and Stephen Phillips, who have team-taught courses on contemporary moral problems with me. Their ideas have found expression here in more ways than I can distinguish. I would like to thank the reviewers whose comments have helped me clarify my own ideas and decide what issues and readings to include: for the first edition, L. E. Andrade, Illinois State University; Linda Bomstad, California State University, Sacramento; Karen Hanson, Indiana University; and Anita Silvers, San Francisco State University; for the second edition, Stephanie Beardman, Rutgers University–New Brunswick; Ray Cebik, University of Tennessee, Knoxville; Richard Eggerman, Oklahoma State University; Deirdre Golash, American University; Patrick Lee, Franciscan University of Steubenville; Aaron Meskin, Rutgers University–New Brunswick; Nathan Tierney, California Lutheran University; and Sharon Sytsma, Northern Illinois University.

I am grateful to Jim Bull for his support of this project, and to April Wells-Hayes and Robin Lockwood for their work in producing it.

PART I Liberty

The central problem of political philosophy is the relation between people and their governments—between the rulers and the ruled. When rulers acquire power through force or inheritance, there is little need to take the interests of the people into account. In a democracy, however, the rulers acquire power through elections and therefore must consider the interests of the people to some degree. But even if the rulers follow the will of the majority perfectly, the possibility of conflict remains. Rule by the people, as John Stuart Mill points out, is really rule of each by all the rest. Nothing in the concept of democracy itself protects the minority from the majority's power. Edmund Burke therefore warned of the "oppression of the minority"; Alexis de Tocqueville similarly foresaw "the tyranny of the majority." Both generalize Aristotle's worry that "If justice is the will of the majority, . . . they will unjustly confiscate the property of the wealthy minority" (*Politics* VI, 3).

Two kinds of issues arise here. First, certain distinct and unpopular or disadvantaged groups may consistently lose elections to a more powerful majority. Democracy, unembellished, does little to protect their rights. Usually, factions shift from issue to issue; a group on the losing side of one issue often comes out on the winning side on the next. Groups may have interests that vary so greatly, however, that the electoral balance of power is stable. Some may consistently win while others consistently lose. Second, individuals have little protection from the majority's power. Voters out of step with the majority may find themselves without any rights at all.

The American Bill of Rights—the first ten amendments to the United States Constitution—attempts to protect people from the unfettered power of undemocratic minorities and democratic majorities. By delineating people's rights, it carves out a sphere of individual liberty that government may not transgress. Philosophers such as John Stuart Mill seek to distinguish a sphere of personal liberty in a different way. A law is *paternalistic* if it restricts a person's liberty for his or her own good. Mill argues, with some important qualifications, that such laws are illegitimate. Mill's *harm principle* asserts that government may restrict a person's liberty only to prevent harm to others. To restrict liberty to prevent people from harming themselves or to promote their own good, Mill contends, goes beyond the proper bounds of government authority.

Many countries have a wide variety of paternalistic laws. They tend to fall into three categories:

1. *Laws promoting morality:* Laws regulating religious practices, diet, and various forms of sexual behavior—adultery, polygamy, polyandry, sodomy, prostitution, premarital sex, pornography, and miscegenation (interracial marriage).
2. *Laws promoting health and safety:* Laws regulating alcohol, drugs (both medical and recreational), suicide, self-mutilation, voluntary euthanasia, working conditions, and the use of motorcycle helmets and seat belts.
3. *Laws promoting economic welfare:* Laws regulating wages, working hours, shopping hours (for example, "blue laws"), gambling, investments, and retirement (for example, Social Security).

Few people would accept all laws of this kind as legitimate, but just as few would find all objectionable. How can we distinguish legitimate from illegitimate paternalistic laws?

One way incorporates Mill's distinction between *self-regarding* and *other-regarding* actions. Roughly, a self-regarding action affects only the agent or agents of the action; an other-regarding action affects others. Mill's harm principle, in these terms, rules out government restriction of self-regarding actions.

There are several complications. Some self-regarding actions involve only a single agent—taking a drug or failing to wear a seat belt, for example. Others involve a group of agents; it takes at least two agents to indulge in prostitution, sodomy, gambling, or employment, for example. In either case, Mill says, we can consider the act self-regarding only if several conditions are satisfied. First, every agent must be acting freely; there must be no coercion. Everyone involved must consent to the action. We can treat ordinary, consensual sexual activity as self-regarding, but rape is clearly other-regarding. Second, every agent must be acting voluntarily. If any participant is in any way incapable of choosing—if he or she is a child, for example, or mentally incapacitated, drugged, or insane—then the action is other-regarding. Third, every agent must be reasonably well-informed about the action. There must be no ignorance or deception about any important and relevant matters. Someone taking a dangerous drug while believing it to be aspirin is not exercising liberty in any meaningful sense. If any participant is ignorant or deceived about an important feature of the action, then, it counts as other-regarding. The harm principle protects from government intrusion only those actions that are undertaken freely and voluntarily by informed agents and that affect nobody but themselves.

Mill's harm principle has met with wide acceptance in certain realms, but it has also met serious objections. Aristotle, for example, holds a completely opposed view of liberty. He contends that the best government is that which produces the best citizens. The chief task of government, in his view, is to promote the good of its citizens by helping to educate and guide them. Edmund Burke and others take a more moderate view. They maintain that individual liberty is only one among many important and competing values. A society should value the individual liberty of its citizens, these philosophers charge, but it should also value harmony, order, justice, and equality, among others. These various values often come into conflict, both in our individual lives and in the political arena. The harm principle tries to resolve all such conflicts in favor of liberty. But, Burke holds, it is not obvious that any value wins out all of the time. Politics, in his view, is an art of balancing values, reconciling them when possible, seeking compromises between them when possible, and, if all else fails, resolving conflicts between them by appeal to analogy and the wisdom we have accumulated from the past.

The Supreme Court and various political philosophers of the twentieth century have responded to Mill's principle by distinguishing civil from economic liberties. Civil liberties—in the original sense of the term, liberties granted by society—have been interpreted as liberties relating in some way to a person's sense of identity or to the political process. It is not clear whether this distinction makes sense. In what category, for example, is the freedom to place an advertisement or produce a commercial in favor of a certain political position? Whatever the answer, Mill means his principle to apply to both civil and economic liberties. Some twentieth-century thinkers, however, have sought to apply it only to civil liberties, contending that liberty does take precedence over other values in such matters, whereas justice, equality, and other concerns often take precedence over liberty in economic matters.

Questions concerning freedom of speech have a central place in democratic societies. Democracies depend on informed and involved citizens. Citizens can be informed, however, only if they have access to information. Political argument and the supporting information it requires therefore need protection. Types of speech that have little in common with political discussion and debate, however, provoke greater controversy. Some issues concerning freedom of speech—pornography, for example—fall under the general topic of paternalism, for both speaker and listener are voluntary, informed, consenting adults. Other kinds of speech do not.

John Milton advances an early and sophisticated argument for freedom of the press. In brief, he contends that restrictions on publishing and printing interfere with the search for truth, inevitably fail to restrict what they are meant to restrict because of practical difficulties, insult citizens and prevent them from developing their own powers of judgment, and are in any case unnecessary, for truth will conquer falsehood in a free contest of ideas. John Stuart Mill adds to the arguments of Milton. An opinion may be true or contain some elements of truth. Even if it is false, only by battling such falsehoods can the truth remain vibrant and meaningful. Mill thus concludes that the content of an opinion can never justify suppressing it. Nor, he contends, can its manner of expression. Only circumstances in which an utterance might cause serious harm (for example, start a riot) can justify prohibiting it in those circumstances.

ARISTOTLE

from *Nicomachean Ethics*

Aristotle (384–322 B.C.E.), born in Stagira, was the son of Nicomachus, the court physician to Amyntas II, the king of Macedon. Nicomachus died when Aristotle was a boy. After training in medicine, Aristotle entered Plato's Academy in Athens at the age of seventeen. He stayed twenty years, until Plato's death. In 342, he became the tutor of Alexander the Great, Amyntas's grandson, who was thirteen; Aristotle stayed at the Macedonian court as Alexander's teacher for three years, until Alexander was appointed regent. In 335, Aristotle returned to Athens to establish his own school, the Lyceum. When Alexander died in 323, Athenians became suspicious of Aristotle's links to Macedonia. Fearing that he might be executed, as Socrates had been, he fled Athens, "lest the Athenians sin twice against philosophy." He died a year later in Chalcis of chronic indigestion brought about by overwork.

Aristotle's influence on intellectual history has been immense. He wrote treatises on physics, biology, astronomy, psychology, logic, metaphysics, poetry, rhetoric, ethics, and politics. Through the Middle Ages, in Europe and the Islamic world, Aristotle was known simply as "the philosopher." His philosophy is still important; most Western and Islamic thought is to some degree Aristotelian. His scientific work, though now chiefly of historical interest, was remarkably sophisticated. It was not superseded for more than 1500 years.

The Nicomachean Ethics *addresses the basic questions of moral philosophy: What is the good? What is virtue? What is happiness? Aristotle believes that the good, for human beings—what humans properly desire for its own sake—is happiness, which he thinks has its highest form in contemplative activity. Aristotle holds that people can attain virtue and happiness, however, only in the context of a good state governed in the proper way. Aristotle thus believes that ethics and politics are intertwined. (Source: Reprinted from* Aristotle's Nichomachean Ethics, *translated by W. D. Ross. Most notes have been omitted. [1925], by permission of Oxford University Press.)*

QUESTIONS FOR REFLECTION

1. How does Aristotle argue that happiness is the highest human good?
2. What is virtue, according to Aristotle?
3. How may a person become virtuous?
4. Paternalistic laws restrict a person's freedom for that person's own good. What justification does Aristotle present for paternalistic laws?
5. What is it to be a good person, according to Aristotle? What does this mean for legislation?

BOOK I

4

Let us resume our inquiry and state, in view of the fact that all knowledge and every pursuit aims at some good, what it is that we say political science aims at and what is the highest of all goods achievable by action. Verbally there is very general agreement; for both the general run of men and people of superior refinement say that it is happiness, and identify living well and doing well with being happy; but with regard to what happiness is they differ, and the many do not give the same account as the wise. . . .

7

Let us again return to the good we are seeking, and ask what it can be. It seems different in different actions and arts; it is different in medicine, in strategy, and in the other arts likewise. What then is the good of each? Surely that for whose sake everything else is done. In medicine this is health, in strategy victory, in architecture a house, in any other sphere something else, and in every action and pursuit the end; for it is for the sake of this that all men do whatever else they do. Therefore, if there is an end for all that we do, this will be the good achievable by action, and if there are more than one, these will be the goods achievable by action.

So the argument has by a different course reached the same point; but we must try to state this even more clearly. Since there are evidently more than one end, and we choose some of these (e.g. wealth, flutes, and in general instruments) for the sake of something else, clearly not all ends are final ends; but the chief good is evidently something final. Therefore, if there is only one final end, this will be what we are seeking, and if there are more than one, the most final of these will be what we are seeking. Now we call that which is in itself worthy of pursuit more final than that which is worthy of pursuit for the sake of something else, and that which is never desirable for the sake of something else more final than the things that are desirable both in themselves and for the sake of that other thing, and therefore we call final without qualification that which is always desirable in itself and never for the sake of something else.

Now such a thing happiness, above all else, is held to be; for this we choose always for itself and never for the sake of something else, but honour, pleasure, reason, and every virtue we choose indeed for themselves (for if nothing resulted from them we should still choose each of them), but we choose them also for the sake of happiness, judging that by means of them we shall be happy. Happiness, on the other hand, no one chooses for the sake of these, nor, in general, for anything other than itself.

From the point of view of self-sufficiency the same result seems to follow; for the final good is thought to be self-sufficient. Now by self-sufficient we do not mean that which is sufficient for a man by himself, for one who lives a solitary life, but also for parents, children, wife, and in general for his friends and fellow citizens, since man is born for citizenship. But some limit must be set to this; for if we extend our requirement to ancestors and descendants and friends' friends we are in for an infinite series. Let us examine this question, however, on another occasion; the self-sufficient we now define as that which when isolated makes life desirable and lacking in nothing; and such we think happiness to be; and further we think it most desirable of all things, without being counted as one good thing among others—if it were so counted it would clearly be made more desirable by the addition of even the least of goods; for that which is added becomes an excess of goods, and of goods the greater is always more desirable. Happiness, then, is something final and self-sufficient, and is the end of action.

Presumably, however, to say that happiness is the chief good seems a platitude, and a clearer account of what it is is still desired. This might perhaps be given, if we could first ascertain the function of man. For just as for a flute-player, a sculptor, or any artist, and, in general, for all things that have a function or activity, the good and the "well" is thought to reside in the function, so would it seem to be for man, if he has a function. Have the carpenter, then, and the tanner certain functions or activities, and has man none? Is he born without a function? Or as eye, hand, foot, and in general each of the parts evidently has a function, may one lay it down that man similarly has a function apart from all these? What then can this be? Life seems to be common even to plants, but we are seeking what is peculiar to man. Let us exclude, therefore, the life of nutrition and growth. Next there would be a life of perception, but *it* also seems to be common even to the horse, the ox, and every animal. There remains, then, an active life of the element that has a rational principle; of this, one part has such a principle in the sense of being obedient to one, the other in the sense of possessing one and exercising thought. And, as "life of the rational element" also has two meanings, we must state that life in the sense of activity is what we mean; for this seems to be the more proper sense of the term. Now if the function of man is an activity of soul which follows or implies a rational principle, and if we say "a so-and-so" and "a good so-and-so" have a function which is the same in kind, e.g. a lyre-player and a good lyre-player, and so without qualification in all cases, eminence in respect of goodness being added to the name of the function (for the function of a lyre-player is to play the lyre, and that of a good lyre-player is to do so well): if this is the case, [and we state the function of man to be a certain kind of life, and this to be an activity or actions of the soul implying a rational principle, and the function of a good man to be the good and noble performance of these, and if any action is well performed when it is performed in accordance with the appropriate excellence: if this is the case,] human good turns out to be activity of soul in accordance with virtue, and if there are more than one virtue, in accordance with the best and most complete.

But we must add "in a complete life." For one swallow does not make a summer, nor does one day; and so too one day, or a short time, does not make a man blessed and happy. . . .

BOOK II

1

Virtue, then, being of two kinds, intellectual and moral, intellectual virtue in the main owes both its birth and its growth to teaching (for which reason it requires experience and time), while moral virtue comes about as a result of habit, whence also its name (ἠθική) is one that is formed by a slight variation from the word ἔθος (habit). From this it is also plain that none of the moral virtues arises in us by nature; for nothing that exists by nature can form a habit contrary to its nature. For instance the stone which by nature moves downwards cannot be habituated to move upwards, not even if one tries to train it by throwing it up ten thousand times; nor can fire be habituated to move downwards, nor can anything else that by nature behaves in one way be trained to behave in another. Neither by nature, then, nor contrary to nature do the virtues arise in us; rather we are adapted by nature to receive them, and are made perfect by habit.

Again, of all the things that come to us by nature we first acquire the potentiality and later exhibit the activity (this is plain in the case of the senses; for it was not by often seeing or often hearing that we got these senses, but on the contrary we had them before we used them, and did not come to have them by using them); but the virtues we get by first exercising them, as also happens in the case of the arts as well. For the things we have to learn before we can do them, we learn by doing them, e.g. men become builders by building and lyre-players by playing the lyre; so too we become just by doing just acts, temperate by doing temperate acts, brave by doing brave acts.

This is confirmed by what happens in states; for legislators make the citizens good by forming habits in them, and this is the wish of every legislator, and those who do not effect it miss their mark, and it is in this that a good constitution differs from a bad one.

Again, it is from the same causes and by the same means that every virtue is both produced and destroyed, and similarly every art; for it is from playing the lyre that both good and bad lyre-players are produced. And the corresponding statement is true of builders and of all the rest; men will be good or bad builders as a result of building well or badly. For if this were not so, there would have been no need of a teacher, but all men would have been born good or bad at their craft. This, then, is the case with the virtues also; by doing the acts that we do in our transactions with other men we become just or unjust, and by doing the acts that we do in the presence of danger, and being habituated to feel fear or confidence, we become brave or cowardly. The same is true of appetites and feelings of anger; some men become temperate and good-tempered, others self-indulgent and irascible, by behaving in one way or the other in the appropriate circumstances. Thus, in one word, states of character arise out of like activities. This is why the activities we exhibit must be of a certain kind; it is because the states of character correspond to the differences between these. It makes no small difference, then, whether we form habits of one kind or of another from our very youth; it makes a very great difference, or rather *all* the difference.

2

Since, then, the present inquiry does not aim at theoretical knowledge like the others (for we are inquiring not in order to know what virtue is, but in order to become good, since otherwise our inquiry would have been of no use), we must examine the nature of actions, namely how we ought to do them; for these determine also the nature of the states of character that are produced, as we have said. Now, that we must act according to the right rule is a common principle and must be assumed—it will be discussed later, i.e. both what the right rule is, and how it is related to the other virtues. But this must be agreed upon beforehand, that the whole account of matters of conduct must be given in outline and not precisely, as we said at the very beginning that the accounts we demand must be in accordance with the subject-matter; matters concerned with conduct and questions of what is good for us have no fixity, any more than matters of health. The general account being of this nature, the account of particular cases is yet more lacking in exactness; for they do not fall under any art or precept but the agents themselves must in each case consider what is appropriate to the occasion, as happens also in the art of medicine or of navigation.

But though our present account is of this nature we must give what help we can. First, then, let us consider this, that it is the nature of such things to be destroyed by defect and excess, as we see in the case of strength and of health (for to gain light on things imperceptible we must use the evidence of sensible things); both excessive and defective exercise destroys the strength, and similarly drink or food which is above or below a certain amount destroys the health, while that which is proportionate both produces and increases and preserves it. So too is it, then, in the case of temperance and courage and the other virtues. For the man who flies from and fears everything and does not stand his ground against anything becomes a coward, and the man who fears nothing at all but goes to meet every danger becomes rash; and similarly the man who indulges in every pleasure and abstains from none becomes self-indulgent, while the man who shuns every pleasure, as boors do, becomes in a way insensible; temperance and courage, then, are destroyed by excess and defect, and preserved by the mean.

But not only are the sources and causes of their origination and growth the same as those of their destruction, but also the sphere of their actualization will be the same; for this is also true of the things which are more evident to sense, e.g. of strength; it is produced by taking much food and undergoing much exertion, and it is the strong man that will be most able to do these things. So too is it with the virtues; by abstaining from pleasures we become temperate, and it is when we have become so that we are most able to abstain from them; and similarly too in the case of courage; for by being habituated to despise things that are terrible and to stand our ground against them we become brave, and it is when we have become so that we shall be most able to stand our ground against them. . . .

4

The question might be asked, what we mean by saying that we must become just by doing just acts, and temperate by doing temperate acts; for if men do just and temperate acts, they are already just and temperate, exactly as, if they do what is in accordance with the laws of grammar and of music, they are grammarians and musicians.

Or is this not true even of the arts? It is possible to do something that is in accordance with the laws of grammar, either by chance or at the suggestion of another. A man will be a grammarian, then, only when he has both done something grammatical and done it grammatically; and this means doing it in accordance with the grammatical knowledge in himself.

Again, the case of the arts and that of the virtues are not similar; for the products of the arts have their goodness in themselves, so that it is enough that they should have a certain character, but if the acts that are in accordance with the virtues have themselves a certain character it does not follow that they are done justly or temperately. The agent also must be in a certain condition when he does them; in the first place he must have knowledge, secondly he must choose the acts, and choose them for their own sakes, and thirdly his action must proceed from a firm and unchangeable character. These are not reckoned in as conditions of the possession of the arts, except the bare knowledge; but as a condition of the possession of the virtues knowledge has little or no weight, while the other conditions count not for a little but for everything, i.e. the very conditions which result from often doing just and temperate acts.

Actions, then, are called just and temperate when they are such as the just or the temperate man would do; but it is not the man who does these that is just and temperate, but the man who also does them *as* just and temperate men do them. It is well said, then, that it is by doing just acts that the just man is produced, and by doing temperate acts the temperate man; without doing these no one would have even a prospect of becoming good.

But most people do not do these, but take refuge in theory and think they are being philosophers and will become good in this way, behaving somewhat like patients who listen attentively to their doctors, but do none of the things they are ordered to do. As the latter will not be made well in body by such a course of treatment, the former will not be made well in soul by such a course of philosophy. . . .

6

We must, however, not only describe virtue as a state of character, but also say what sort of state it is. We may remark, then, that every virtue or excellence both brings into good condition the thing of which it is the excellence and makes the work of that thing be done well; e.g. the excellence of the eye makes both the eye and its work good; for it is by the excellence of the eye that we see well. Similarly the excellence of the horse makes a horse both good in itself and good at running and at carrying its rider and at awaiting the attack of the enemy. Therefore, if this is true in every case, the virtue of man also will be the state of character which makes a man good and which makes him do his own work well.

How this is to happen we have stated already, but it will be made plain also by the following consideration of the specific nature of virtue. In everything that is continuous and divisible it is possible to take more, less, or an equal amount, and that either in terms of the thing itself or relatively to us; and the equal is an intermediate between excess and defect. By the intermediate in the object I mean that which is equidistant from each of the extremes, which is one and the same for all men; by the intermediate relatively to us that which is neither too much nor too little—and this is not one, nor the same for all. For instance, if ten is many and two is few, six is the intermediate, taken in terms of the object; for it exceeds and is exceeded by an equal amount; this is intermediate according to arithmetical proportion. But the intermediate relatively to us is not to be taken so; if ten pounds are too much for a particular person to eat and two too little, it does not follow that the trainer will order six pounds; for this also is perhaps too much for the person who is to take it, or too little—too little for Milo,* too much for the beginner in athletic exercises. The same is true of running and wrestling. Thus a master of any art avoids excess and defect, but seeks the intermediate and chooses this—the intermediate not in the object but relatively to us.

If it is thus, then, that every art does its work well—by looking to the intermediate and judging its works by this standard (so that we often say of good works of art that it is not possible either to

* A famous wrestler.

take away or to add anything, implying that excess and defect destroy the goodness of works of art, while the mean preserves it; and good artists, as we say, look to this in their work), and if, further, virtue is more exact and better than any art, as nature also is, then virtue must have the quality of aiming at the intermediate. I mean moral virtue; for it is this that is concerned with passions and actions, and in these there is excess, defect, and the intermediate. For instance, both fear and confidence and appetite and anger and pity and in general pleasure and pain may be felt both too much and too little, and in both cases not well; but to feel them at the right times, with reference to the right objects, towards the right people, with the right motive, and in the right way, is what is both intermediate and best, and this is characteristic of virtue. Similarly with regard to actions also there is excess, defect, and the intermediate. Now virtue is concerned with passions and actions, in which excess is a form of failure, and so is defect, while the intermediate is praised and is a form of success; and being praised and being successful are both characteristics of virtue. Therefore virtue is a kind of mean, since, as we have seen, it aims at what is intermediate.

Again, it is possible to fail in many ways (for evil belongs to the class of the unlimited, as the Pythagoreans conjectured, and good to that of the limited), while to succeed is possible only in one way (for which reason also one is easy and the other difficult—to miss the mark easy, to hit it difficult); for these reasons also, then, excess and defect are characteristic of vice, and the mean of virtue;

> For men are good in but one way, but bad in many.

Virtue, then, is a state of character concerned with choice, lying in a mean, i.e. the mean relative to us, this being determined by a rational principle, and by that principle by which the man of practical wisdom would determine it. Now it is a mean between two vices, that which depends on excess and that which depends on defect; and again it is a mean because the vices respectively fall short of or exceed what is right in both passions and actions, while virtue both finds and chooses that which is intermediate. Hence in respect of its substance and the definition which states its essence virtue is a mean, with regard to what is best and right an extreme.

But not every action nor every passion admits of a mean; for some have names that already imply badness, e.g. spite, shamelessness, envy, and in the case of actions adultery, theft, murder; for all of these and suchlike things imply by their names that they are themselves bad, and not the excesses or deficiencies of them. It is not possible, then, ever to be right with regard to them; one must always be wrong. Nor does goodness or badness with regard to such things depend on committing adultery with the right woman, at the right time, and in the right way, but simply to do any of them is to go wrong. It would be equally absurd, then, to expect that in unjust, cowardly, and voluptuous action there should be a mean, an excess, and a deficiency; for at that rate there would be a mean of excess and of deficiency, and excess of excess, and a deficiency of deficiency. But as there is no excess and deficiency of temperance and courage because what is intermediate is in a sense an extreme, so too of the actions we have mentioned there is no mean nor any excess and deficiency, but however they are done they are wrong; for in general there is neither a mean of excess and deficiency, nor excess and deficiency of a mean. . . .

BOOK X

9

. . . Surely, as the saying goes, where there are things to be done the end is not to survey and recognize the various things, but rather to do them; with regard to virtue, then, it is not enough to know, but we must try to have and use it, or try any other way there may be of becoming good. Now if arguments were in themselves enough to make men good, they would justly, as Theognis says, have won very great rewards, and such rewards should have been provided; but as things are, while they seem to have power to encourage and stimulate the generous-minded among our youth, and to make a character which is gently born, and a true lover of what is noble, ready to be possessed by virtue, they are not able to encourage the many to nobility and goodness. For these do not by nature obey the sense of shame, but only fear, and do not abstain from bad acts because of their baseness but through fear of punishment; living by passion they pursue their own pleasures and the means to them, and avoid the opposite pains, and have not even a conception of what is noble and truly pleasant, since they have never tasted it. What argument would remould such people? It is hard, if not impossible, to remove by argument the traits that have long since been incorporated in the character; and perhaps we must be content if, when all the influences by which we are thought to become good are present, we get some tincture of virtue.

Now some think that we are made good by nature, others by habituation, others by teaching. Nature's part evidently does not depend on us, but as a result of some divine causes is present in those who are truly fortunate; while argument and teaching, we may suspect, are not powerful with all men, but the soul of the student must first have been cultivated by means of habits for noble joy and noble hatred, like earth which is to nourish the seed. For he who lives as passion directs will not hear argument that dissuades him, nor understand it if he does; and how can we persuade one in such a state to change his ways? And in general passion seems to yield not to argument but to force. The character, then, must somehow be there already with a kinship to virtue, loving what is noble and hating what is base.

But it is difficult to get from youth up a right training for virtue if one has not been brought up under right laws; for to live temperately and hardily is not pleasant to most people, especially when they are young. For this reason their nurture and occupations should be fixed by law; for they will not be painful when they have become customary. But it is surely not enough that when they are young they should get the right nurture and attention; since they must, even when they are grown up, practise and be habituated to them, we shall need laws for this as well, and generally speaking to cover the whole of life; for most people obey necessity rather than argument, and punishments rather than the sense of what is noble.

This is why some think that legislators ought to stimulate men to virtue and urge them forward by the motive of the noble, on the assumption that those who have been well advanced by the formation of habits will attend to such influences; and that punishments and penalties should be imposed on those who disobey and are of inferior nature, while the incurably bad should be completely banished. A good man (they think), since he lives with his mind fixed on what is noble, will submit to argument, while a bad man, whose desire is for pleasure, is corrected by pain like a beast of burden. This is, too, why they say the pains inflicted should be those that are most opposed to the pleasures such men love.

However that may be, if (as we have said) the man who is to be good must be well trained and habituated, and go on to spend his time in worthy occupations and neither willingly nor unwillingly do bad actions, and if this can be brought about if men live in accordance with a sort of reason and right order, provided this has force—if this be so, the paternal command indeed has not the required force or compulsive power (nor in general has the command of one man, unless he be a king or something similar), but the law *has* compulsive power, while it is at the same time a rule proceeding from a sort of practical wisdom and reason. And while people hate *men* who oppose their impulses, even if they oppose them rightly, the law in its ordaining of what is good is not burdensome.

In the Spartan state alone, or almost alone, the legislator seems to have paid attention to questions of nurture and occupations; in most states such matters have been neglected, and each man lives as he pleases, Cyclops-fashion, "to his own wife and children dealing law." Now it is best that there should be a public and proper care for such matters; but if they are neglected by the community it would seem right for each man to help his children and friends towards virtue, and that they should have the power, or at least the will, to do this.

It would seem from what has been said that he can do this better if he makes himself capable of legislating. For public control is plainly effected by laws, and good control by good laws; whether written or unwritten would seem to make no difference, nor whether they are laws providing for the education of individuals or of groups—any more than it does in the case of music or gymnastics and other such pursuits. For as in cities laws and prevailing types of character have force, so in households do the injunctions and the habits of the father, and these have even more because of the tie of blood and the benefits he confers; for the children start with a natural affection and disposition to obey. Further, private education has an advantage over public, as private medical treatment has; for while in general rest and abstinence from food are good for a man in a fever, for a particular man they may not be; and a boxer presumably does not prescribe the same style of fighting to all his pupils. It would seem, then, that the detail is worked out with more precision if the control is private; for each person is more likely to get what suits his case.

But the details can be best looked after, one by one, by a doctor or gymnastic instructor or any one else who has the general knowledge of what is good for every one or for people of a certain kind (for the sciences both are said to be, and are, concerned with what is universal); not but what some particular detail may perhaps be well looked after by an unscientific person, if he has studied accurately in the light of experience what happens in each case, just as some people seem to be their own best doctors, though they could give no help to any one else. None the less, it will perhaps be agreed that if a man does wish to become master of an art or science he must go to the universal, and come to know it as well as possible; for, as we have said, it is with this that the sciences are concerned.

And surely he who wants to make men, whether many or few, better by his care must try to become capable of legislating, if it is through laws that we can become good. For to get any one whatever—any one who is put before us—into the right condition is not for the first chance comer; if any one can do it, it is the man who knows, just as in medicine and all other matters which give scope for care and prudence. . . .

JOHN MILTON

from *Areopagitica* (1644)

John Milton (1608–1674) is one of the great figures of English literature. Born in London, the son of a prosperous scribe, he was educated at St. Paul's School in London and at Christ's College, Cambridge, where he received an M.A. in 1632. He traveled widely after receiving his degree, meeting Galileo in Italy in 1638–1639. Many of Milton's early writings are political tracts. He published Areopagitica*, a ringing defense of freedom of the press, when he was thirty-six.*

A year earlier, Parliament had passed an order complaining of the "many false . . . scandalous, seditious, and libellous" works that were being published in England "to the great defamation of Religion and government." It required that all books printed or sold must first be "approved of and licensed by" censors appointed by Parliament. The order moreover gave police the right to search for unlicensed presses and destroy them; to search for unlicensed books and confiscate them; and to arrest authors, publishers, and others involved in publishing unlicensed books. Areopagitica *was Milton's eloquent response.*

In 1652, at the age of forty-four, Milton became totally blind. He nevertheless continued writing, producing Paradise Lost *in 1667 and both* Paradise Regained *and* Samson Agonistes *in 1671. (Source: Oxford, Clarendon Press, 1898.)*

QUESTIONS FOR REFLECTION

1. Milton contends that people should be trusted to distinguish good from harmful publications; if people are not trusted, he says, they cannot develop certain virtues. What virtues does Milton have in mind? Why would they remain undeveloped?
2. Milton argues that "this Order avails nothing to the suppressing of scandalous, seditious, and libellous books"; in other words, that Parliament's action would not succeed in banning harmful works. Why does he believe that censorship will be ineffective? What are his arguments? Do they apply to any act of censorship, or are they limited to this case? If you were an advocate of censorship, could you devise a scheme that would overcome any of Milton's arguments?
3. Milton believes that Parliament's action will discourage learning and make truth harder to attain. Why? Do you find his arguments persuasive?
4. Milton bases several arguments on the observation that censorship requires censors. Who will decide what should be licensed? Milton denies that this question has any adequate answer. Why?

A Speech for the Liberty of Unlicensed Printing, to the Parliament of England (1644)

. . . that . . . clause of Licensing Books . . . I shall now attend with such a homily, as shall lay before ye, first the inventors of it to be those whom ye will be loth to own; next what is to be thought in general of reading, whatever sort the books be; and that this Order avails nothing to the suppressing of scandalous, seditious, and libellous books, which were mainly intended to be suppressed. Last, that it will be primely to the discouragement of all learning, and the stop of Truth, not only of disexercising and blunting our abilities in what we know already, but by hindering and cropping the discovery that might be yet further made both in religious and civil Wisdom.

I deny not, but that it is of greatest concernment in the Church and Commonwealth, to have a vigilant eye how books demean themselves as well as men; and thereafter to confine, imprison, and do sharpest justice on them as malefactors. For books are not absolutely dead things, but do contain a potency of life in them to be as active as that soul was whose progeny they are; nay, they do preserve as in a vial the purest efficacy and extraction of that living intellect that bred them. I know they are as lively, and as vigorously productive, as those fabulous dragon's teeth; and being sown up and down, may chance to spring up armed men. And yet, on the other hand, unless wariness be used, as good almost kill a man as kill a good book. Who kills a man kills a reasonable creature, God's image; but he who destroys a good book, kills reason itself, kills the image of God, as it were in the eye. Many a man lives a burden to the earth; but a good book is the precious life-blood of a master spirit, embalmed and treasured up on purpose to a life beyond life. 'Tis true, no age can restore a life, whereof perhaps there is no great loss; and revolutions of ages do not oft recover the loss of a rejected truth, for the want of which whole nations fare the worse.

We should be wary therefore what persecution we raise against the living labours of public men, how we spill that seasoned life of man, preserved and stored up in books; since we see a kind of homicide may be thus committed, sometimes a martyrdom, and if it extend to the whole impression, a kind of massacre; whereof the execution ends not in the slaying of an elemental life, but strikes at that ethereal and fifth essence, the breath of reason itself, slays an immortality rather than a life. . . .

Good and evil we know in the field of this world grow up together almost inseparably; and the knowledge of good is so involved and interwoven with the knowledge of evil, and in so many cunning resemblances hardly to be discerned, that those confused seeds which were imposed upon Psyche as an incessant labour to cull out, and sort asunder, were not more intermixed. It was from out the rind of one apple tasted, that the knowledge of good and evil, as two twins cleaving together, leaped forth into the world. And perhaps this is that doom which Adam fell into of knowing good and evil, that is to say of knowing good by evil. As therefore the state of man now is; what wisdom can there be to choose, what continence to forbear without the knowledge of evil? He that can apprehend and consider vice with all her baits and seeming pleasures, and yet abstain, and yet distinguish, and yet prefer that which is truly better, he is the true wayfaring Christian.

I cannot praise a fugitive and cloistered virtue, unexercised and unbreathed, that never sallies out and sees her adversary, but slinks out of the race, where that immortal garland is to be run for, not without dust and heat. Assuredly we bring not innocence into the world, we bring impurity much rather; that which purifies us is trial, and trial is by what is contrary. That virtue therefore which is but a youngling in the contemplation of evil, and knows not the utmost that vice promises to her followers, and rejects it, is but a blank virtue, not a pure; her whiteness is but an excremental whiteness. Which was the reason why our sage and serious poet Spenser, whom I dare be known to think a better teacher than Scotus or Aquinas, describing true temperance under the person of Guion, brings him in with his palmer through the cave of Mammon, and the bower of earthly bliss, that he might see and know, and yet abstain. Since therefore the knowledge and survey of vice is in this world so necessary to the constituting of human virtue, and the scanning of error to the confirmation of truth, how can we more safely, and with less danger, scout into the regions of sin and falsity than by reading all manner of tractates and hearing all manner of reason? And this is the benefit which may be had of books promiscuously read.

But of the harm that may result hence three kinds are usually reckoned. First, is feared the infection that may spread; but then all human learning and controversy in religious points must remove out of the world, yea the Bible itself; for that ofttimes relates blasphemy not nicely, it describes the carnal sense of wicked men not unelegantly, it brings in holiest men passionately murmuring against Providence through all the arguments of Epicurus: in other great disputes it answers dubiously and darkly to the common reader. . . .

Seeing, therefore, that those books, and those in great abundance, which are likeliest to taint both life and doctrine, cannot be suppressed without the fall of learning and of all ability in disputation, and that these books of either sort are most and soonest catching to the learned, from whom to the common people whatever is heretical or dissolute may quickly be conveyed, and that evil manners are as perfectly learnt without books a thousand other ways which cannot be stopped, and evil doctrine not with books can propagate, except a teacher guide, which he might also do without writing, and so beyond prohibiting, I am not able to unfold, how this cautelous [cunning] enterprise of licensing can be exempted from the number of vain and impossible attempts. And he who were pleasantly disposed could not well avoid to liken it to the exploit of that gallant man who thought to pound up the crows by shutting his park gate.

Besides another inconvenience, if learned men be the first receivers out of books and dispreaders both of vice and error, how shall the licensers themselves be confided in, unless we can confer upon them, or they assume to themselves above all others in the land, the grace of infallibility and uncorruptedness? And again, if it be true that a wise man, like a good refiner, can gather gold out of the drossiest volume, and that a fool will be a fool with the best book, yea or without book; there is no reason that we should deprive a wise man of any advantage to his wisdom, while we seek to restrain from a fool, that which being restrained will be no hindrance to his folly. For if there should be so much exactness always used to keep that from him which is unfit for his reading, we should in the judgment of Aristotle not only, but of Solomon and of our Saviour, not vouchsafe him good precepts, and by consequence not willingly admit him to good books; as being certain that a wise man will make better use of an idle pamphlet, than a fool will do of sacred Scripture.

'Tis next alleged we must not expose ourselves to temptations without necessity, and next to that, not employ our time in vain things. To both these objections one answer will serve, out of the grounds already laid, that to all men such books are not temptations, nor vanities, but useful drugs and materials wherewith to temper and compose effective and strong medicines, which man's life cannot want. The rest, as children and childish men, who have not the art to qualify and prepare these working minerals, well may be exhorted to forbear, but hindered forcibly they cannot be by all the licensing that Sainted Inquisition could ever yet contrive. Which is what I promised to deliver next, That this order of licensing conduces nothing to the end for which it was framed; and hath almost prevented me by being clear already while thus much hath been explaining. See the ingenuity of Truth, who, when she gets a free and willing hand, opens herself faster than the pace of method and discourse can overtake her. . . .

. . . For if they fell upon one kind of strictness, unless their care were equal to regulate all other things of like aptness to corrupt the mind, that single endeavour they knew would be but a fond labour; to shut and fortify one gate against corruption, and be necessitated to leave others round about wide open.

If we think to regulate printing, thereby to rectify manners, we must regulate all recreations and pastimes, all that is delightful to man. No music must be heard, no song be set or sung, but what is grave and Doric. There must be licensing dancers, that no gesture, motion, or deportment be taught our youth but what by their allowance shall be thought honest; for such Plato was provided of; it will ask more than the work of twenty licensers to examine all the lutes, the violins, and the guitars in every house; they must not be suffered to prattle as they do, but must be licensed what they may say. And who shall silence all the airs and madrigals that whisper softness in chambers? The windows also, and the balconies must be thought on; there are shrewd books, with dangerous frontispieces, set to sale; who shall prohibit them, shall twenty licensers? The villages also must have their visitors to inquire what lectures the bagpipe and the rebeck reads, even to the ballatry and the gamut of every municipal fiddler, for these are the countryman's Arcadias, and his Monte Mayors.

Next, what more national corruption, for which England hears ill abroad, than household gluttony: who shall be the rectors of our daily rioting? And what shall be done to inhibit the multitudes that frequent those houses where drunkenness is sold and harboured? Our garments also should be referred to the licensing of some more sober work-masters to see them cut into a less wanton garb. Who shall regulate all the mixed conversation of our youth, male and female together, as is the fashion of this country? Who shall still appoint what shall be discoursed, what presumed, and no further? Lastly, who shall forbid and separate all idle resort, all evil company? These things will be, and must be; but how they shall be least hurtful, how least enticing, herein consists the grave and governing wisdom of a state.

To sequester out of the world into Atlantic and Utopian polities which never can be drawn into use, will not mend our condition; but to ordain wisely as in this world of evil, in the midst whereof God hath placed us unavoidably. Nor is it Plato's licensing of books will do this, which necessarily pulls along with it so many other kinds of licensing, as will make us all both ridiculous and weary, and yet frustrate; but those unwritten, or at least unconstraining, laws of virtuous education, religious and civil nurture, which Plato there mentions as the bonds and ligaments of the commonwealth, the pillars and the sustainers of every written statute; these they be which will bear chief sway in such matters as these, when all licensing will be easily eluded. Impunity and remissness, for certain, are the bane of a commonwealth; but here the great art lies, to discern in what the law is to bid restraint and punishment, and in what things persuasion only is to work.

If every action, which is good or evil in man at ripe years, were to be under pittance and prescription and compulsion, what were virtue but a name, what praise could be then due to well-doing, what gramercy to be sober, just, or continent? Many there be that complain of Divine Providence for suffering Adam to transgress; foolish tongues! When God gave him reason, He gave him freedom to choose, for reason is but choosing; he had been else a mere artificial Adam, such an Adam as he is in the motions. We ourselves esteem not of that obedience, or love, or gift, which is of force: God therefore left him free, set before him a provoking object, ever almost in his eyes; herein consisted his merit, herein the right of his reward, the praise of his abstinence. Wherefore did He create passions within us, pleasures round about us, but that these rightly tempered are the very ingredients of virtue?

They are not skilful considerers of human things, who imagine to remove sin by removing the matter of sin; for, besides that it is a huge heap increasing under the very act of diminishing, though some part of it may for a time be withdrawn from some persons, it cannot from all, in such a universal thing as books are; and when this is done, yet the sin remains entire. Though ye take from a covetous man all his treasure, he has yet one jewel left, ye cannot bereave him of his covetousness. Banish all objects of lust, shut up all youth into the severest discipline that can be exercised in any hermitage, ye cannot make them chaste, that came not thither so: such great care and wisdom is required to the right managing of this point. Suppose we could expel sin by this means; look how much we thus expel of sin, so much we expel of virtue: for the matter of them both is the same; remove that, and ye remove them both alike.

This justifies the high providence of God, who, though He commands us temperance, justice, continence, yet pours out before us, even to a profuseness, all desirable things, and gives us minds that can wander beyond all limit and satiety. Why should we then affect a rigour contrary to the manner of God and of nature, by abridging or scanting those means, which books freely permitted are, both to the trial of virtue and the exercise of truth? It would be better done, to learn that the law must needs be frivolous, which goes to restrain things, uncertainly and yet equally working to good and to evil. And were I the chooser, a dram of well-doing should be preferred before many times as much the forcible hindrance of evil-doing. For God sure esteems the growth and completing of one virtuous person more than the restraint of ten vicious.

And albeit whatever thing we hear or see, sitting, walking, travelling, or conversing, may be fitly called our book, and is of the same effect that writings are, yet grant the thing to be prohibited were only books, it appears that this order hitherto is far insufficient to the end which it intends. Do we not see, not once or oftener, but weekly, that continued court-libel against the Parliament and City, printed, as the wet sheets can witness, and dispersed among us, for all that licensing can do? yet this is the prime service a man would think, wherein this Order should give proof of itself. If it were executed, you'll say. But certain, if execution be remiss or blindfold now, and in this particular, what will it be hereafter and in other books? If then the Order shall not be vain and frustrate, behold a new labour, Lords and Commons, ye must repeal and proscribe all scandalous and unlicensed books already printed and divulged; after ye have drawn them up into a list, that all may know which are condemned, and which not; and ordain that no foreign books be delivered out of custody, till they have been read over. This office will require the whole time of not a few overseers, and those no vulgar men. There be also books which are partly useful and excellent, partly culpable and pernicious; this work will ask as many more officials, to make expurgations and expunctions, that the Commonwealth of Learning be not damnified. In fine, when the multitude of books increase upon their hands, ye must be fain to catalogue all those printers who are found frequently offending, and forbid the importation of their whole suspected typography. In a word, that this your Order may be exact and not deficient, ye must reform it perfectly according to the model of Trent and Seville, which I know ye abhor to do.

Yet though ye should condescend to this, which God forbid, the Order still would be but fruitless and defective to that end whereto ye meant it. If to prevent sects and schisms, who is so unread or so uncatechised in story, that hath not heard of many sects refusing books as a hindrance, and preserving their doctrine unmixed for many ages, only by unwritten traditions? The Christian faith, for that was once a schism, is not unknown to have spread all over Asia, ere any Gospel or Epistle was seen in writing. If the amendment of manners be aimed at, look into Italy and Spain, whether these places be one scruple the better, the honester, the wiser, the chaster, since all the inquisitional rigour that hath been executed upon books.

Another reason, whereby to make it plain that this Order will miss the end it seeks, consider by the quality which ought to be in every licenser. It cannot be denied but that he who is made judge to sit upon the birth or death of books, whether they may be wafted into this world or not, had need to be a man above the common measure, both studious, learned, and judicious; there may be else no mean mistakes in the censure of what is passable or not; which is also no mean injury. If he be of such worth as behoves him, there cannot be a more tedious and unpleasing journey-work, a greater loss of time levied upon his head, than to be made the perpetual reader of unchosen books and pamphlets, ofttimes huge volumes. There is no book that is acceptable unless at certain seasons; but to be enjoined the reading of that at all times, and in a hand scarce legible, whereof three pages would not down at any time in the fairest print, is an imposition which I cannot believe how he that values time and his own studies, or is but of a sensible nostril, should be able to endure. In this one thing I crave leave of the present licensers to be pardoned for so thinking; who doubtless took this office up, looking on it through their obedience to the Parliament, whose command perhaps made all things seem easy and unlaborious to them; but that this short trial hath wearied them out already, their own expressions and excuses to them who make so many journeys to solicit their licence are testimony enough. Seeing therefore those who now possess the employment by all evident signs wish themselves well rid of it; and that no man of worth, none that is not a plain unthrift of his own hours is ever likely to succeed them, except he mean to put himself to the salary of a press corrector; we may easily foresee what kind of licensers we are to expect hereafter, either ignorant, imperious, and remiss, or basely pecuniary. This is what I had to show, wherein this Order cannot conduce to that end whereof it bears the intention.

I lastly proceed from the no good it can do, to the manifest hurt it causes, in being first the greatest discouragement and affront that can be offered to learning, and to learned men.

It was the complaint and lamentation of prelates, upon every least breath of a motion to remove pluralities, and distribute more equally Church revenues, that then all learning would be for ever dashed and discouraged. But as for that opinion, I never found cause to think that the tenth part of learning stood or fell with the clergy: nor could I ever but hold it for a sordid and unworthy speech of any churchman who had a competency left him. If therefore ye be loth to dishearten heartily and discontent, not the mercenary crew of false pretenders to learning, but the free and ingenuous sort of such as evidently were born to study, and love learning for itself, not for lucre or any other end but the service of God and of truth, and perhaps that lasting fame and perpetuity of praise which God and good men have consented shall be the reward of those whose published labours advance the good of mankind, then know that, so far to distrust the judgment and the honesty of one who hath but a common repute in learning, and never yet offended, as not to count him fit to print his mind without a tutor and examiner, lest he should drop a schism, or something of corruption, is the greatest displeasure and indignity to a free and knowing spirit that can be put upon him.

What advantage is it to be a man over it is to be a boy at school, if we have only escaped the ferula to come under the fescue of an Imprimatur, if serious and elaborate writings, as if they were no more than the theme of a grammar-lad under his pedagogue, must not be uttered without the cursory eyes of a temporising and extemporising licenser? He who is not trusted with his own actions, his drift not being known to be evil, and standing to the hazard of law and penalty, has no great argument to think himself reputed in the Commonwealth, wherein he was born, for other than a fool or a foreigner. When a man writes to the world, he summons up all his reason and deliberation to assist him; he searches, meditates, is industrious, and likely consults and confers with his judicious friends; after all which done he takes himself to be informed in what he writes, as well as any that writ before him. If, in this the most consummate act of his fidelity and ripeness, no years, no industry, no former proof of his abilities can bring him to that state of maturity, as not to be still mistrusted and suspected, unless he carry all his considerate diligence, all his midnight watchings and expense of Palladian oil, to the hasty view of an unleisured licenser, perhaps much his younger, perhaps far his inferior in judgment, perhaps one who never knew the labour of book-writing, and if he be not repulsed or slighted, must appear in print like a puny with his guardian, and his censor's hand on the back of his title to be his bail and surety that he is no idiot or seducer, it cannot be but a dishonour and derogation to the author, to the book, to the privilege and dignity of Learning.

And what if the author shall be one so copious of fancy, as to have many things well worth the adding come into his mind after licensing, while the book is yet under the press, which not seldom happens to the best and diligentest writers; and that perhaps a dozen times in one book? The printer dares not go beyond his licensed copy; so often then must the author trudge to his leave-giver, that those his new insertions may be reviewed; and many a jaunt will be made, ere that licenser, for it must be the same man, can either be found, or found at leisure; meanwhile either the press must stand still, which is no small damage, or the author lose his accuratest thoughts, and send the book forth worse than he had made it, which to a diligent writer is the greatest melancholy and vexation that can befall.

And how can a man teach with authority, which is the life of teaching, how can he be a doctor in his book as he ought to be, or else had better be silent, whenas all he teaches, all he delivers, is but under the tuition, under the correction of his patriarchal licensor to blot or alter what precisely accords not with the hidebound humour which he calls his judgment? When every acute reader, upon the first sight of a pedantic licence, will be ready with these like words to ding the book a quoit's distance from him: I hate a pupil teacher, I endure not an instructor that comes to me under the wardship of an overseeing fist. I know nothing of the licenser, but that I have his own hand here for his arrogance; who shall warrant me his judgment? The State, sir, replies the stationer, but has a quick return: The State shall be my governors, but not my critics; they may be mistaken in the choice of a licenser, as easily as this licenser may be mistaken in an author; this is some common stuff; and he might add from Sir Francis Bacon, That such authorised books are but the language of the times. For though a licenser should happen to be judicious more than ordinary, which will be a great jeopardy of the next succession, yet his very office and his commission enjoins him to let pass nothing but what is vulgarly received already.

Nay, which is more lamentable, if the work of any deceased author, though never so famous in his lifetime and even to this day, come to their hands for licence to be printed, or reprinted, if there be found in his book one sentence of a venturous edge, uttered in the height of zeal and who knows whether it might not be the dictate of a divine spirit, yet not suiting with every low decrepit humour of their own, though it were Knox himself, the Reformer of a Kingdom, that spake it, they will not pardon him their dash: the sense of that great man shall to all posterity be lost, for the fearfulness or the presumptuous rashness of a perfunctory licenser. And to what an author this violence hath been lately done, and in what book of greatest consequence to be faithfully published, I could now instance, but shall forbear till a more convenient season.

Yet if these things be not resented seriously and timely by them who have the remedy in their power, but that such iron-moulds as these shall have authority to gnaw out the choicest periods of exquisitest books, and to commit such a treacherous fraud against the orphan remainders of worthiest men after death, the more sorrow will belong to that hapless race of men, whose misfortune it is to have understanding. Henceforth let no man care to learn, or care to be more than worldly-wise; for certainly in higher matters to be ignorant and slothful, to be a common steadfast dunce, will be the only pleasant life, and only in request.

And as it is a particular disesteem of every knowing person alive, and most injurious to the written labours and monuments of the dead, so to me it seems an undervaluing and vilifying of the whole Nation. I cannot set so light by all the invention, the art, the wit, the grave and solid judgment which is in England, as that it can be comprehended in any twenty capacities how good soever, much less that it should not pass except their superintendence be over it, except it be sifted and strained with their strainers, that it should be uncurrent without their manual stamp. Truth and understanding are not such wares as to be monopolised and traded in by tickets and statutes and standards. We must not think to make a staple commodity of all the knowledge in the land, to mark and licence it like our broadcloth and our woolpacks. . . .

. . . this obstructing violence meets for the most part with an event utterly opposite to the end which it drives at: instead of suppressing sects and schisms, it raises them and invests them with a reputation. "The punishing of wits enhances their authority," said the Viscount St. Albans; "and a forbidden writing is thought to be a certain spark of truth that flies up in the faces of them who seek to tread it out." This Order, therefore, may prove a nursing-mother to sects, but I shall easily show how it will be a step-dame to Truth: and first by disenabling us to the maintenance of what is known already.

Well knows he who uses to consider, that our faith and knowledge thrives by exercise, as well as our limbs and complexion. Truth is compared in Scripture to a streaming fountain; if her waters flow not in a perpetual progression, they sicken into a muddy pool of conformity and tradition. A man may be a heretic in the truth; and if he believe things only because his Pastor says so, or the Assembly so determines, without knowing other reason, though his belief be true, yet the very truth he holds becomes his heresy. . . .

There is yet behind of what I proposed to lay open, the incredible loss and detriment that this plot of incensing puts us to; more than if some enemy at sea should stop up all our havens and ports and creeks, it hinders and retards the importation of our richest Merchandise, Truth; nay, it was first established and put in practice by Antichristian malice and mystery on set purpose to extinguish, if it were possible, the light of Reformation, and to settle falsehood; little differing from that policy wherewith the Turk upholds his Alcoran, by the prohibition of Printing. 'Tis not denied, but gladly confessed, we are to send our thanks and vows to Heaven louder than most of nations, for that great measure of truth which we enjoy, especially in those main points between us and the Pope, with his appurtenances the Prelates: but he who thinks we are to pitch our tent here, and have attained the utmost prospect of reformation that the mortal glass wherein we contemplate can show us, till we come to beautific vision, that man by this very opinion declares that he is yet far short of Truth.

Truth indeed came once into the world with her Divine Master, and was a perfect shape most glorious to look on: but when He ascended, and His Apostles after Him were laid asleep, then straight arose a wicked race of deceivers, who, as that story goes of the Egyptian Typhon with his conspirators, how they dealt with the good Osiris, took the virgin Truth, hewed her lovely form into a thousand pieces, and scattered them to the four winds. From that time ever since, the sad friends of Truth, such as durst appear, imitating the careful search that Isis made for the mangled body of Osiris, went up and down gathering up limb by limb, still as they could find them. We have not yet found them all, Lords and Commons, nor ever shall do, till her Master's second coming; He shall bring together every joint and member, and shall mould them into an immortal feature of loveliness and perfection. Suffer not these licensing prohibitions to stand at every place of opportunity, forbidding and disturbing them that continue seeking, that continue to do our obsequies to the torn body of our martyred saint.

We boast our light; but if we look not wisely on the Sun itself, it smites us into darkness. Who can discern those planets that are oft combust, and those stars of brightest magnitude that rise and set with the Sun, until the opposite motion of their orbs bring them to such a place in the firmament, where they may be seen evening or morning? The light which we have gained was given us, not to be ever staring on, but by it to discover onward things more remote from our knowledge. It is not the unfrocking of a priest, the unmitring of a bishop, and the removing him from off the presbyterian shoulders, that will make us a happy Nation. No, if other things as great in the Church, and in the rule of life both economical and political, be not looked into and reformed, we have looked so long upon the blaze the Zuinglius and Calvin hath beaconed up to us, that we are stark blind. There be who perpetually complain of schisms and sects, and make it such a calamity that any man dissents from their maxims. 'Tis their own pride and ignorance which causes the disturbing, who neither will hear with meekness, nor can convince; yet all must be suppressed which is not found in their Syntagma.* They are the troublers, they are the dividers of unity, who neglect and permit not others to unite those dissevered pieces which are yet wanting to the body of Truth. To be still searching what we know not by what we know, still closing up truth to truth as we find it (for all her body is homogeneal and proportional), this is the golden rule in theology as well as in arithmetic, and makes up the best harmony in a Church; not the forced and outward union of cold and neutral, and inwardly divided minds. . . .

Where there is much desire to learn, there of necessity will be much arguing, much writing, many opinions; for opinion in good men is but knowledge in the making. . . .

What would ye do then? should ye suppress all this flowery crop of knowledge and new light sprung up and yet springing daily in this city? should ye set an oligarchy of twenty engrossers over it, to bring a famine upon our minds again, when we shall know nothing but what is measured to us by their bushel? Believe it, Lords and Commons, they who counsel ye to such a suppressing

* Systematically arranged treatise. —Ed.

do as good as bid ye suppress yourselves; and I will soon show how. If it be desired to know the immediate cause of all this free writing and free speaking, there cannot be assigned a truer than your own mild and free and humane government. It is the liberty, Lords and Commons, which your own valorous and happy counsels have purchased us, liberty which is the nurse of all great wits; this is that which hath rarefied and enlightened our spirits like the influence of heaven; this is that which hath enfranchised, enlarged and lifted up our apprehensions degrees above themselves.

Ye cannot make us now less capable, less knowing, less eagerly pursuing of the truth, unless ye first make yourselves, that made us so, less the lovers, less the founders of our true liberty. We can grow ignorant again, brutish, formal and slavish, as ye found us; but you then must first become that which ye cannot be, oppressive, arbitrary and tyrannous, as they were from whom ye have freed us. That our hearts are now more capacious, our thoughts more erected to the search and expectation of greatest and exactest things, is the issue of your own virtue propagated in us; ye cannot suppress that, unless ye reinforce an abrogated and merciless law, that fathers may despatch at will their own children. And who shall then stick closest to ye, and excite others? not he who takes up arms for coat and conduct, and his four nobles of Danegelt.* Although I dispraise not the defence of just immunities, yet love my peace better, if that were all. Give me the liberty to know, to utter, and to argue freely according to conscience, above all liberties. . . .

And now the time in special is, by privilege to write and speak what may help to the further discussing of matters in agitation. The temple of Janus with his two controversial faces might now not unsignificantly be set upon. And though all the winds of doctrine were let loose to play upon the earth, so Truth be in the field, we do injuriously, by licensing and prohibiting, to misdoubt her strength. Let her and Falsehood grapple; who ever knew Truth put to the worse, in a free and open encounter? Her confuting is the best and surest suppressing. He who hears what praying there is for light and clearer knowledge to be sent down among us, would think of other matters to be constituted beyond the discipline of Geneva, framed and fabricked already to our hands. Yet when the new light which we beg for shines in upon us, there be who envy and oppose, if it come not first in at their casements. What a collusion is this, whenas we are exhorted by the wise man to use diligence, to seek for wisdom as for hidden treasures early and late, that another order shall enjoin us to know nothing but by statute? When a man hath been labouring the hardest labour in the deep mines of knowledge; hath furnished out his findings in all their equipage; drawn forth his reasons as it were a battle ranged; scattered and defeated all objections in his way; calls out his adversary into the plain, offers him the advantage of wind and sun, if he please, only that he may try the matter by dint of argument: for his opponents then to skulk, to lay ambushments, to keep a narrow bridge of licensing where the challenger should pass, though it be valour enough in soldiership, is but weakness and cowardice in the wars of Truth.

For who knows not that Truth is strong, next to the Almighty? She needs no policies, nor stratagems, nor licensings to make her victorious; those are the shifts and the defences that error uses against her power. Give her but room, and do not bind her when she sleeps, for then she speaks not true, as the old Proteus did who spake oracles only when he was caught and bound, but then rather she turns herself into all shapes, except her own, and perhaps tunes her voice according to the time, as Micaiah did before Ahab, until she be adjured into her own likeness. Yet is it not impossible that she may have more shapes than one. What else is all that rank of things indifferent, wherein Truth may be on this side or on the other, without being unlike herself? What but a vain shadow else is the abolition of those ordinances, that hand-writing nailed to the cross? What great purchase is this Christian liberty which Paul so often boasts of? His doctrine is, that he who eats or eats not,

* An annual tax imposed around 1000 C.E. to protect England from the Danes and continued thereafter. —ED.

regards a day or regards it not, may do either to the Lord. How many other things might be tolerated in peace, and left to conscience, had we but charity, and were it not the chief stronghold of our hypocrisy to be ever judging one another? . . .

. . . if it come to prohibiting, there is not aught more likely to be prohibited than truth itself; whose first appearance to our eyes, bleared and dimmed with prejudice and custom, is more unsightly and unplausible than many errors, even as the person is of many a great man slight and contemptible to see to. . . .

EDMUND BURKE

from *Reflections on the Revolution in France* (1790)

Edmund Burke (1729–1797) was born in Ireland to a Protestant family of modest means that had recently converted from Catholicism. Educated at a Quaker school and at Trinity College, Dublin, he took a first-class honors degree in classics, and proceeded to study law in London. He did not, however, practice law. Instead, he became a "man of letters": he edited the Annual Register *(a political journal) and belonged to Samuel Johnson's literary club. Burke's first two books appeared when he was twenty-seven; at thirty-seven, he became a member of the House of Commons. Eventually, he became paymaster-general.*

Burke was sixty when the French Revolution began in 1789. King Louis XVI, an absolute monarch, had summoned the largely advisory States General, had lost control of it, and had seen it transform itself into the National Assembly. That body had abolished feudalism, seized the lands of the French church, and inspired the capture and imprisonment of the royal family. A young Frenchman, Charles-François Depont, wrote Burke to ask his opinion of the Revolution. His response was Reflections on the Revolution in France, *which has become a classic of European political thought. The book is sharply critical of the Revolution. Burke's worries about the extremism of the revolutionaries were soon justified. The Reign of Terror led to the execution of thousands, including the king, his family, and much of the French aristocracy.*

Burke is a thoroughly practical thinker. He rejects the Enlightenment view that a change in the social or political order can perfect human nature and society. More fundamentally, he rejects all attempts to analyze human problems in terms of a few basic principles. Profoundly skeptical of philosophical theorizing, Burke stresses the complexity of real ethical problems. Solving a moral or political problem, he believes, involves balancing various moral considerations—various kinds of goods and evils—in light of features of the particular situation giving rise to it. Liberty, in Burke's view, is one kind of good, but there are many others; liberty does not always take precedence. There is no theory, method, or set of rules for achieving a proper balance between liberty and other goods. Instead, Burke urges, we should reason by analogy, clinging to social mechanisms that have stood the test of time.

QUESTIONS FOR REFLECTION

1. What does Burke mean by a "manly, moral, regulated liberty"?
2. Burke is a pluralist—he believes that there are fundamentally different kinds of moral value. What are some of these kinds? What kind of value is liberty? Is it unequivocally good?
3. Burke points out that "liberty, when men act in bodies, is *power*." What does he deduce from this? What, in your view, does Burke's observation imply about liberty?
4. Burke thinks that it is very important "to derive all we possess as *an inheritance from our forefathers*." Why does Burke place such an emphasis on tradition?
5. Burke worries that democracy allows the "oppression of the minority." Why? What can be done to guard against it?

. . . I flatter myself that I love a manly, moral, regulated liberty as well as any gentleman of that society, be he who he will; and perhaps I have given as good proofs of my attachment to that cause in the whole course of my public conduct. I think I envy liberty as little as they do to any other nation. But I cannot stand forward and give praise or blame to anything which relates to human actions, and human concerns, on a simple view of the object, as it stands stripped of every relation, in all the nakedness and solitude of metaphysical abstraction. Circumstances (which with some gentlemen pass for nothing) give in reality to every political principle its distinguishing color and discriminating effect. The circumstances are what render every civil and political scheme beneficial or noxious to mankind. Abstractedly speaking, government, as well as liberty, is good; yet could I, in common sense, ten years ago, have felicitated France on her enjoyment of a government (for she then had a government) without inquiry what the nature of that government was, or how it was administered? Can I now congratulate the same nation upon its freedom? Is it because liberty in the abstract may be classed amongst the blessings of mankind, that I am seriously to felicitate a madman, who has escaped from the protecting restraint and wholesome darkness of his cell, on his restoration to the enjoyment of light and liberty? Am I to congratulate a highwayman and murderer who has broke prison upon the recovery of his natural rights? This would be to act over again the scene of the criminals condemned to the galleys, and their heroic deliverer, the metaphysic Knight of the Sorrowful Countenance.*

When I see the spirit of liberty in action, I see a strong principle at work; and this, for a while, is all I can possibly know of it. The wild *gas,* the fixed air, is plainly broke loose; but we ought to suspend our judgment until the first effervescence is a little subsided, till the liquor is cleared, and until we see something deeper than the agitation of a troubled and frothy surface. I must be tolerably sure, before I venture publicly to congratulate men upon a blessing, that they have really received one. Flattery corrupts both the receiver and the giver, and adulation is not of more service to the people than to kings. I should, therefore, suspend my congratulations on the new liberty of France until I was informed how it had been combined with government, with public force, with the discipline and obedience of armies, with the collection of an effective and well-distributed revenue, with morality and religion, with the solidity of property, with peace and order, with civil and social manners. All these (in their way) are good things, too, and without them liberty is not a benefit whilst it lasts, and is not likely to continue long. The effect of liberty to individuals is that they may do what they please; we ought to see what it will please them to do, before we risk congratulations which may be soon turned into complaints. Prudence would dictate this in the case of separate, insulated, private men, but liberty, when men act in bodies, is *power.* Considerate people, before they declare themselves, will observe the use which is made of *power,* and particularly of so trying a thing as *new* power in *new* persons of whose principles, tempers, and dispositions they have little or no experience, and in situations where those who appear the most stirring in the scene may possibly not be the real movers.

. . . .

. . . The Revolution was made to preserve our *ancient,* indisputable laws and liberties and that *ancient* constitution of government which is our only security for law and liberty. If you are desirous of knowing the spirit of our constitution and the policy which predominated in that great period which has secured it to this hour, pray look for both in our histories, in our records, in our acts of parliament, and journals of parliament, and not in the sermons of the Old Jewry† and the after-dinner toasts of the Revolution Society. In the former you will find other ideas and another language. Such a claim is as ill-suited to our temper and wishes as it is unsupported by any appearance of authority.

* A reference to Don Quixote, who set criminals free only to be beaten by them. —Ed.

† The courthouse, so-called because it was built on the site of a former synagogue.—Ed.

The very idea of the fabrication of a new government is enough to fill us with disgust and horror. We wished at the period of the Revolution, and do now wish, to derive all we possess as *an inheritance from our forefathers*. Upon that body and stock of inheritance we have taken care not to inoculate any cyon* alien to the nature of the original plant. All the reformations we have hitherto made have proceeded upon the principle of reverence to antiquity; and I hope, nay, I am persuaded, that all those which possibly may be made hereafter will be carefully formed upon analogical precedent, authority, and example. . . .

You will observe that from Magna Charta to the Declaration of Right it has been the uniform policy of our constitution to claim and assert our liberties as an *entailed inheritance* derived to us from our forefathers, and to be transmitted to our posterity—as an estate specially belonging to the people of this kingdom, without any reference whatever to any other more general or prior right. By this means our constitution preserves a unity in so great a diversity of its parts. We have an inheritable crown, an inheritable peerage, and a House of Commons and a people inheriting privileges, franchises, and liberties from a long line of ancestors.

This policy appears to me to be the result of profound reflection, or rather the happy effect of following nature, which is wisdom without reflection, and above it. A spirit of innovation is generally the result of a selfish temper and confined views. People will not look forward to posterity, who never look backward to their ancestors. Besides, the people of England well know that the idea of inheritance furnishes a sure principle of conservation and a sure principle of transmission, without at all excluding a principle of improvement. It leaves acquisition free, but it secures what it acquires. Whatever advantages are obtained by a state proceeding on these maxims are locked fast as in a sort of family settlement, grasped as in a kind of mortmain† forever. By a constitutional policy, working after the pattern of nature, we receive, we hold, we transmit our government and our privileges in the same manner in which we enjoy and transmit our property and our lives. The institutions of policy, the goods of fortune, the gifts of providence are handed down to us, and from us, in the same course and order. Our political system is placed in a just correspondence and symmetry with the order of the world and with the mode of existence decreed to a permanent body composed of transitory parts, wherein, by the disposition of a stupendous wisdom, molding together the great mysterious incorporation of the human race, the whole, at one time, is never old or middle-aged or young, but, in a condition of unchangeable constancy, moves on through the varied tenor of perpetual decay, fall, renovation, and progression. Thus, by preserving the method of nature in the conduct of the state, in what we improve we are never wholly new; in what we retain we are never wholly obsolete. By adhering in this manner and on those principles to our forefathers, we are guided not by the superstition of antiquarians, but by the spirit of philosophic analogy. In this choice of inheritance we have given to our frame of polity the image of a relation in blood, binding up the constitution of our country with our dearest domestic ties, adopting our fundamental laws into the bosom of our family affections, keeping inseparable and cherishing with the warmth of all their combined and mutually reflected charities our state, our hearths, our sepulchres, and our altars.

Through the same plan of a conformity to nature in our artificial institutions, and by calling in the aid of her unerring and powerful instincts to fortify the fallible and feeble contrivances of our reason, we have derived several other, and those no small, benefits from considering our liberties in the light of an inheritance. Always acting as if in the presence of canonized forefathers, the spirit of freedom, leading in itself to misrule and excess, is tempered with an awful gravity. This idea of a liberal descent inspires us with a sense of habitual native dignity which prevents that upstart insolence almost inevitably adhering to and disgracing those who are the first acquirers of any distinction. By this means our liberty becomes a noble

* A shoot, twig, or graft; old form of *scion*. —Ed.

† Literally "dead hand," a legal device to make a corporation possess something in perpetuity; or, the condition of lands held in perpetuity. —Ed.

freedom. It carries an imposing and majestic aspect. It has a pedigree and illustrating ancestors. It has its bearings and its ensigns armorial. It has its gallery of portraits, its monumental inscriptions, its records, evidences, and titles. We procure reverence to our civil institutions on the principle upon which nature teaches us to revere individual men: on account of their age and on account of those from whom they are descended. All your sophisters cannot produce anything better adapted to preserve a rational and manly freedom than the course that we have pursued, who have chosen our nature rather than our speculations, our breasts rather than our inventions, for the great conservatories and magazines of our rights and privileges.

You might, if you pleased, have profited of our example and have given to your recovered freedom a correspondent dignity. Your privileges, though discontinued, were not lost to memory. Your constitution, it is true, whilst you were out of possession, suffered waste and dilapidation; but you possessed in some parts the walls and in all the foundations of a noble and venerable castle. You might have repaired those walls; you might have built on those old foundations. Your constitution was suspended before it was perfected, but you had the elements of a constitution very nearly as good as could be wished. In your old states you possessed that variety of parts corresponding with the various descriptions of which your community was happily composed; you had all that combination and all that opposition of interests; you had that action and counteraction which, in the natural and in the political world, from the reciprocal struggle of discordant powers, draws out the harmony of the universe. These opposed and conflicting interests which you considered as so great a blemish in your old and in our present constitution interpose a salutary check to all precipitate resolutions. They render deliberation a matter, not of choice, but of necessity; they make all change a subject of *compromise,* which naturally begets moderation; they produce *temperaments* preventing the sore evil of harsh, crude, unqualified reformations, and rendering all the headlong exertions of arbitrary power, in the few or in the many, for ever impracticable. Through that diversity of members and interests, general liberty had as many securities as there were separate views in the several orders, whilst, by pressing down the whole by the weight of a real monarchy, the separate parts would have been prevented from warping and starting from their allotted places.

You had all these advantages in your ancient states, but you chose to act as if you had never been molded into civil society and had everything to begin anew. You began ill, because you began by despising everything that belonged to you.

. . . .

. . . I reprobate no form of government merely upon abstract principles. There may be situations in which the purely democratic form will become necessary. There may be some (very few, and very particularly circumstanced) where it would be clearly desirable. This I do not take to be the case of France or of any other great country. Until now, we have seen no examples of considerable democracies. The ancients were better acquainted with them. Not being wholly unread in the authors who had seen the most of those constitutions, and who best understood them, I cannot help concurring with their opinion that an absolute democracy, no more than absolute monarchy, is to be reckoned among the legitimate forms of government. They think it rather the corruption and degeneracy than the sound constitution of a republic. If I recollect rightly, Aristotle observes that a democracy has many striking points of resemblance with a tyranny. Of this I am certain, that in a democracy the majority of the citizens is capable of exercising the most cruel oppressions upon the minority whenever strong divisions prevail in that kind of polity, as they often must; and that oppression of the minority will extend to far greater numbers and will be carried on with much greater fury than can almost ever be apprehended from the dominion of a single scepter. In such a popular persecution, individual sufferers are in a much more deplorable condition than in any other. Under a cruel prince they have the balmy compassion of mankind to assuage the smart of their wounds;

they have the plaudits of the people to animate their generous constancy under their sufferings; but those who are subjected to wrong under multitudes are deprived of all external consolation. They seem deserted by mankind, overpowered by a conspiracy of their whole species.

. . . .

. . . A brave people will certainly prefer liberty accompanied with a virtuous poverty to a depraved and wealthy servitude. But before the price of comfort and opulence is paid, one ought to be pretty sure it is real liberty which is purchased, and that she is to be purchased at no other price. I shall always, however, consider that liberty as very equivocal in her appearance which has not wisdom and justice for her companions and does not lead prosperity and plenty in her train.

. . . .

The effects of the incapacity shown by the popular leaders in all the great members of the commonwealth are to be covered with the "all-atoning name" of liberty. In some people I see great liberty indeed; in many, if not in the most, an oppressive, degrading servitude. But what is liberty without wisdom and without virtue? It is the greatest of all possible evils; for it is folly, vice, and madness, without tuition or restraint. Those who know what virtuous liberty is cannot bear to see it disgraced by incapable heads on account of their having high-sounding words in their mouths. Grand, swelling sentiments of liberty I am sure I do not despise. They warm the heart; they enlarge and liberalize our minds; they animate our courage in time of conflict. Old as I am, I read the fine raptures of Lucan and Corneille with pleasure. Neither do I wholly condemn the little arts and devices of popularity. They facilitate the carrying of many points of moment; they keep the people together; they refresh the mind in its exertions; and they diffuse occasional gaiety over the severe brow of moral freedom. Every politician ought to sacrifice to the graces, and to join compliance with reason. But in such an undertaking as that in France, all these subsidiary sentiments and artifices are of little avail. To make a government requires no great prudence. Settle the seat of power, teach obedience, and the work is done. To give freedom is still more easy. It is not necessary to guide; it only requires to let go the rein. But to form a *free government,* that is, to temper together these opposite elements of liberty and restraint in one consistent work, requires much thought, deep reflection, a sagacious, powerful, and combining mind. This I do not find in those who take the lead in the National Assembly. Perhaps they are not so miserably deficient as they appear. I rather believe it. It would put them below the common level of human understanding. But when the leaders choose to make themselves bidders at an auction of popularity, their talents, in the construction of the state, will be of no service. They will become flatterers instead of legislators, the instruments, not the guides, of the people. If any of them should happen to propose a scheme of liberty, soberly limited and defined with proper qualifications, he will be immediately outbid by his competitors who will produce something more splendidly popular. Suspicions will be raised of his fidelity to his cause. Moderation will be stigmatized as the virtue of cowards, and compromise as the prudence of traitors, until, in hopes of preserving the credit which may enable him to temper and moderate, on some occasions, the popular leader is obliged to become active in propagating doctrines and establishing powers that will afterwards defeat any sober purpose at which he ultimately might have aimed. . . .

. . . I wish my countrymen rather to recommend to our neighbors the example of the British constitution than to take models from them for the improvement of our own. In the former, they have got an invaluable treasure. They are not, I think, without some causes of apprehension and complaint, but these they do not owe to their constitution but to their own conduct. I think our happy situation owing to our constitution, but owing to the whole of it, and not to any part singly, owing in a great measure to what we have left standing in our several reviews and reformations as well as to what we have altered or superadded. Our people will find employment enough for a truly patriotic, free, and independent spirit in guarding what they possess from violation. I would not exclude alteration neither, but even when I changed, it should be to preserve. I should be led to my remedy by a great grievance. In what I did, I should follow the example of our ancestors. I would make the reparation as nearly as possible in the style of the building. A politic caution, a guarded circumspection, a moral rather than a complexional timidity were among the ruling principles of our forefathers in their most decided conduct. Not being illuminated with the light of which the gentlemen of France tell us they have got so abundant a share, they acted under a strong impression of the ignorance and fallibility of mankind. He that had made them thus fallible rewarded them for having in their conduct attended to their nature. Let us imitate their caution if we wish to deserve their fortune or to retain their bequests. Let us add, if we please, but let us preserve what they have left; and, standing on the firm ground of the British constitution, let us be satisfied to admire rather than attempt to follow in their desperate flights the aeronauts of France. . . .

JOHN STUART MILL

from *On Liberty* (1859)

John Stuart Mill (1806–1873), born in London, was the most influential philosopher of the English-speaking world during the nineteenth century. His father, James Mill (1773–1836), was the son of a Scottish shoemaker who had become a prominent supporter of philosophical radicalism, a school of thought that advocated representative democracy, universal suffrage, and a scientific approach to philosophy. The elder Mill had a highly unusual and ambitious plan for educating his son at home. Consequently, John Stuart Mill never attended any school or college. He learned to read Greek at three and Latin just a few years later; he was well-read in classical literature and history by eight and studied philosophy, mathematics, and economics before reaching his teens. At seventeen, he became a clerk in the East India Company, which governed India under charter from the British government. He eventually became chief of his department and worked at the company until 1858. In that year, Harriet Taylor, Mill's wife of six years—whom in the dedication of On Liberty *he calls "the inspirer, and in part the author, of all that is best in my writings"—died while they were traveling together in France. Mill decided to devote his time fully to writing the works they had discussed together. The next few years saw the publication of Mill's most influential ethical works:* On Liberty *(1859),* Utilitarianism *(1861), and* On the Subjection of Women *(1869). In 1865, Mill won election to Parliament, despite his refusal to campaign or defend his views.*

On Liberty *is a classic statement of the importance of individual liberty. Its chapter "Of the Liberty of Thought and Discussion" is probably the most famous and influential defense of freedom of speech ever written. Mill was a staunch advocate of democracy but saw that majority rule, in itself, could allow the oppression of the minority. Mill wrote* On Liberty *to outline a realm of freedom that not even democratic majorities may transgress. (Source: London: Parker, 1859.)*

QUESTIONS FOR REFLECTION

1. What is the "one very simple principle"—usually called the *harm principle*—that Mill's essay aims to assert? What does it mean? What conditions and qualifications does Mill place on it? How does it counteract the "tyranny of the majority"?
2. Later philosophers have often stated Mill's harm principle in terms of a distinction between self-regarding and other-regarding actions. How might this distinction be drawn? How can Mill's principle be stated in terms of that distinction?

CHAPTER I / INTRODUCTORY

. . . The object of this essay is to assert one very simple principle, as entitled to govern absolutely the dealings of society with the individual in the way of compulsion and control, whether the means used be physical force in the form of legal penalties or the moral coercion of public opinion. That principle is that the sole end for which mankind are warranted, individually or collectively, in interfering with the liberty of action of any of their number is self-protection. That the only purpose for which power can be rightfully exercised over any member of a civilized community, against his will, is to prevent harm to others. His own good, either physical or moral, is not a sufficient warrant. He cannot rightfully be compelled to do or forbear because it will be better for him to do so, because it will make him happier, because, in the opinions of others, to do so would be wise or even right. These are good reasons for remonstrating with him, or reasoning with him, or persuading him, or entreating him, but not for compelling him or visiting him with any evil in case he do otherwise. To justify that, the conduct from which it is desired to deter him must be calculated to produce evil to someone else. The only part of the conduct of anyone for which he is amenable to society is that which concerns others. In the part which merely concerns himself, his independence is, of right, absolute. Over himself, over his own body and mind, the individual is sovereign.

It is, perhaps, hardly necessary to say that this doctrine is meant to apply only to human beings in the maturity of their faculties. We are not speaking of children or of young persons below the age which the law may fix as that of manhood or womanhood. Those who are still in a state to require being taken care of by others must be protected against their own actions as well as against external injury. . . . But as soon as mankind have attained the capacity of being guided to their own improvement by conviction or persuasion (a period long since reached in all nations with whom we need here concern ourselves), compulsion, either in the direct form or in that of pains and penalties for noncompliance, is no longer admissible as a means to their own good, and justifiable only for the security of others.

It is proper to state that I forego any advantage which could be derived to my argument from the idea of abstract right as a thing independent of utility. I regard utility as the ultimate appeal on all ethical questions; but it must be utility in the largest sense, grounded on the permanent interests of man as a progressive being. Those interests, I contend, authorize the subjection of individual spontaneity to external control only in respect to those actions of each which concern the interest of other people. If anyone does an act hurtful to others, there is a *prima facie* case for punishing him by law or, where legal penalties are not safely applicable, by general disapprobation. There are also many positive acts for the benefit of others which he may rightfully be compelled to perform, such as to give evidence in a court of justice, to bear his fair share in the common defense or in any other joint work necessary to the interest of the society of which he enjoys the protection, and to perform certain acts of individual beneficence, such as saving a fellow creature's life or interposing to protect the defenseless against ill usage—things which whenever it is obviously a man's duty to do he may rightfully be made responsible to society for not doing. A person may cause evil to others not only by his actions but by his inaction, and in either case he is justly accountable to them for the injury. The latter case, it is true, requires a much more cautious exercise of compulsion than the former. To make anyone answerable for doing evil to others is the rule; to make him answerable for not preventing evil is, comparatively speaking, the exception. Yet there are many cases clear enough and grave enough to justify that exception. In all things which regard the external relations of the individual, he is *de jure* amenable to those whose interests are concerned, and, if need be, to society as their protector. There are often good reasons for not holding him to the responsibility; but these reasons must arise from the special expediencies of the case: either because it is a kind of case in which he is on the whole likely to act better when left to his own discretion than when controlled in any way in which society have it in their power to control him; or because the attempt to exercise control would produce other evils, greater than those which it would prevent. When such reasons as these preclude the enforcement of responsibility, the conscience of the agent himself should step into the vacant judgment seat and protect those interests of others which have no external protection; judging himself all the more rigidly, because the case does not admit of his being made accountable to the judgment of his fellow creatures.

But there is a sphere of action in which society,

as distinguished from the individual, has, if any, only an indirect interest: comprehending all that portion of a person's life and conduct which affects only himself or, if it also affects others, only with their free, voluntary, and undeceived consent and participation. When I say only himself, I mean directly and in the first instance; for whatever affects himself may affect others through himself: and the objection which may be grounded on this contingency will receive consideration in the sequel. This, then, is the appropriate region of human liberty. It comprises, first, the inward domain of consciousness, demanding liberty of conscience in the most comprehensive sense, liberty of thought and feeling, absolute freedom of opinion and sentiment on all subjects, practical or speculative, scientific, moral, or theological. The liberty of expressing and publishing opinions may seem to fall under a different principle, since it belongs to that part of the conduct of an individual which concerns other people, but, being almost of as much importance as the liberty of thought itself and resting in great part on the same reasons, is practically inseparable from it. Secondly, the principle requires liberty of tastes and pursuits, of framing the plan of our life to suit our own character, of doing as we like, subject to such consequences as may follow, without impediment from our fellow creatures, so long as what we do does not harm them, even though they should think our conduct foolish, perverse, or wrong. Thirdly, from this liberty of each individual follows the liberty, within the same limits, of combination among individuals; freedom to unite for any purpose not involving harm to others: the persons combining being supposed to be of full age and not forced or deceived.

No society in which these liberties are not, on the whole, respected is free, whatever may be its form of government; and none is completely free in which they do not exist absolute and unqualified. The only freedom which deserves the name is that of pursuing our own good in our own way, so long as we do not attempt to deprive others of theirs or impede their efforts to obtain it. Each is the proper guardian of his own health, whether bodily *or* mental and spiritual. Mankind are greater gainers by suffering each other to live as seems good to themselves than by compelling each to live as seems good to the rest. . . .

QUESTIONS FOR REFLECTION

1. How does Mill's defense of freedom of thought and discussion fit into the overall scheme of *On Liberty*? Is speech self-regarding or other-regarding? Is his defense an application of the harm principle or an extension of it?
2. "All silencing of discussion is an assumption of infallibility," Mill contends. How does he argue for this claim? Do you agree?
3. Why does Mill think that the expression even of obviously false opinions should be protected?
4. Some contemporary advocates of controlling certain forms of expression argue that although the government cannot ban the expression of certain views, it can ban certain ways of expressing them—ways involving pornography, say, or the use of racial epithets. What is Mill's view about such restrictions? What arguments does he advance in support of his position? Do you find his arguments persuasive?
5. Mill mentions one exception to freedom of speech: inciting a mob to violence. What general principle lies behind this exception? What other exceptions might Mill be willing to accept?

CHAPTER II / OF THE LIBERTY OF THOUGHT AND DISCUSSION

. . . Let us suppose . . . that the government is entirely at one with the people, and never thinks of exerting any power of coercion unless in agreement with what it conceives to be their voice. But I deny the right of the people to exercise such coercion, either by themselves or by their government. The power itself is illegitimate. The best government has no more title to it than the worst. It is as noxious, or more noxious, when exerted in accordance with public opinion than when in opposition to it. If all mankind minus one were of one opinion, mankind would be no more justified in silencing that one person than he, if he had the power, would be justified in silencing mankind. Were an opinion a personal possession of no value except to the owner, if to be obstructed in the enjoyment of it were simply a private injury, it would make some difference whether the injury was inflicted only on a few persons or on many. But the peculiar evil of silencing the expression of an opinion is that it is robbing the human race, posterity as well as the existing generation—those who dissent from the opinion, still more than those who hold it. If the opinion is right, they are deprived of the opportunity of exchanging error for truth; if wrong, they lose, what is almost as great a benefit, the clearer perception and livelier impression of truth produced by its collision with error.

It is necessary to consider separately these two hypotheses, each of which has a distinct branch of the argument corresponding to it. We can never be sure that the opinion we are endeavoring to stifle is a false opinion; and if we were sure, stifling it would be an evil still.

First, the opinion which it is attempted to suppress by authority may possibly be true. Those who desire to suppress it, of course, deny its truth; but they are not infallible. They have no authority to decide the question for all mankind and exclude every other person from the means of judging. To refuse a hearing to an opinion because they are sure that it is false is to assume that *their* certainty is the same thing as *absolute* certainty. All silencing of discussion is an assumption of infallibility. . . .

The objection likely to be made to this argument would probably take some such form as the following. There is no greater assumption of infallibility in forbidding the propagation of error than in any other thing which is done by public authority on its own judgment and responsibility. Judgment is given to men that they may use it. Because it may be used erroneously, are men to be told that they ought not to use it at all? To prohibit what they think pernicious is not claiming exemption from error, but fulfilling the duty incumbent on them, although fallible, of acting on their conscientious conviction. If we were never to act on our opinions, because those opinions may be wrong, we should leave all our interests uncared for, and all our duties unperformed. An objection which applies to all conduct can be no valid objection to any conduct in particular. It is the duty of governments, and of individuals, to form the truest opinions they can; to form them carefully, and never impose them upon others unless they are quite sure of being right. But when they are sure (such reasoners may say), it is not conscientiousness but cowardice to shrink from acting on their opinions and allow doctrines which they honestly think dangerous to the welfare of mankind, either in this life or in another, to be scattered abroad without restraint, because other people, in less enlightened times, have persecuted opinions now believed to be true. Let us take care, it may be said, not to make the same mistake; but governments and nations have made mistakes in other things which are not denied to be fit subjects for the exercise of authority: they have laid on bad taxes, made unjust wars. Ought we therefore to lay on no taxes and, under whatever provocation, make no wars? Men and governments must act to the best of their ability. There is no such thing as absolute certainty, but there is assurance sufficient for the purposes of human life. We may, and must, assume our opinion to be true for the guidance of our own conduct; and it is assuming no more when we forbid bad men to pervert society by the propagation of opinions which we regard as false and pernicious.

I answer, that it is assuming very much more. There is the greatest difference between presuming an opinion to be true because, with every opportunity for contesting it, it has not been refuted, and assuming its truth for the purpose of not permitting its refutation. Complete liberty of contradicting and disproving our opinion is the very condition which justifies us in assuming its truth for purposes of action; and on no other terms can a being with human faculties have any rational assurance of being right.

When we consider either the history of opinion or the ordinary conduct of human life, to what is it to be ascribed that the one and the other are no worse than they are? Not certainly to the inherent force of the human understanding, for on any matter not self-evident there are ninety-nine persons totally incapable of judging of it for one who is capable; and the capacity of the hundredth person is only comparative, for the majority of the eminent men of every past generation held many opinions now known to be erroneous, and did or approved numerous things which no one will now justify. Why is it, then, that there is on the whole a preponderance among mankind of rational opinions and rational conduct? If there really is this preponderance—which there must be unless human affairs are, and have always been, in an almost desperate state—it is owing to a quality of the human mind, the source of everything respectable in man either as an intellectual or as a moral being, namely, that his errors are corrigible. He is capable of rectifying his mistakes by discussion and experience. Not by experience alone. There must be discussion to show how experience is to be interpreted. Wrong opinions and practices gradually yield to fact and argument; but facts and arguments, to produce any effect on the mind, must be brought before it. Very few facts are able to tell their own story, without comments to bring out their meaning. The whole strength and value, then, of human judgment depending on the one property, that it can be set right when it is wrong, reliance can be placed on it only when the means of setting it right are kept constantly at hand. In the case of any person whose judgment is really deserving of confidence, how has it become so? Because he has kept his mind open to criticism of his opinions and conduct. Because it has been his practice to listen to all that could be said against him; to profit by as much of it as was just, and to expound to himself, and upon occasion to others, the fallacy of what was fallacious. Because he has felt that the only way in which a human being can make some approach to knowing the whole of a subject is by hearing what can be said about it by persons of every variety of opinion, and studying all modes in which it can be looked at by every character of mind. No wise man ever acquired his wisdom in any mode but this; nor is it in the nature of human intellect to become wise in any other manner. The steady habit of correcting and completing his own opinion by collating it with those of others, so far from causing doubt and hesitation in carrying it into practice, is the only stable foundation for a just reliance on it; for, being cognizant of all that can, at least obviously, be said against him and having taken up his position against all gainsayers—knowing that he has sought for objections and difficulties instead of avoiding them, and has shut out no light which can be thrown upon the subject from any quarter—he has a right to think his judgment better than that of any person, or any multitude, who have not gone through a similar process. . . .

Let us now pass to the second division of the argument, and dismissing the supposition that any of the received opinions may be false, let us assume them to be true and examine into the worth of the manner in which they are likely to be held when their truth is not freely and openly canvassed. However unwillingly a person who has a strong opinion may admit the possibility that his opinion may be false, he ought to be moved by the consideration that, however true it may be, if it is not fully, frequently, and fearlessly discussed, it will be held as a dead dogma, not a living truth.

There is a class of persons (happily not quite so numerous as formerly) who think it enough if a person assents undoubtingly to what they think true, though he has no knowledge whatever of the grounds of the opinion and could not make a tenable defense of it against the most superficial objections. Such persons, if they can once get their creed taught from authority, naturally think that no good, and some harm, comes of its being allowed to be questioned. Where their influence prevails, they make it nearly impossible for the received opinion to be rejected wisely and considerately, though it may still be rejected rashly and ignorantly; for to shut out discussion entirely is seldom possible, and when it once gets in, beliefs not grounded on conviction are apt to give way before the slightest semblance of an argument. Waiving, however, this possibility—assuming that the true opinion abides in the mind, but abides as a prejudice, a belief independent of, and proof against, argument—this is not the way in which truth ought to be held by a rational being. This is not knowing the truth. Truth, thus held, is but one superstition the more, accidentally clinging to the words which enunciate a truth. . . .

If, however, the mischievous operation of the absence of free discussion, when the received opinions are true, were confined to leaving men ignorant of the grounds of those opinions, it might be thought that this, if an intellectual, is no moral evil and does not affect the worth of the opinions, regarded in their influence on the character. The fact, however, is that not only the grounds of the opinion are forgotten in the absence of discussion, but too often the meaning of the opinion itself. The words which convey it cease to suggest ideas, or suggest only a small portion of those they were originally employed to communicate. Instead of a vivid conception and a living belief, there remain only a few phrases retained by rote; or, if any part, the shell and husk only of the meaning is retained, the finer essence being lost. The great chapter in human history which this fact occupies and fills cannot be too earnestly studied and meditated on.

It is illustrated in the experience of almost all ethical doctrines and religious creeds: They are all full of meaning and vitality to those who originate them, and to the direct disciples of the originators. Their meaning continues to be felt in undiminished strength, and is perhaps brought out into even fuller consciousness, so long as the struggle lasts to give the doctrine or creed an ascendancy over other creeds. At last it either prevails and becomes the general opinion, or its progress stops; it keeps possession of the ground it has gained, but ceases to spread further. When either of these results has become apparent, controversy on the subject flags, and gradually dies away. The doctrine has taken its place, if not as a received opinion, as one of the admitted sects or divisions of opinion; those who hold it have generally inherited, not adopted it; and conversion from one of these doctrines to another, being now an exceptional fact, occupies little place in the thoughts of their professors. Instead of being, as at first, constantly on the alert either to defend themselves against the world or to bring the world over to them, they have subsided into acquiescence and neither listen, when they can help it, to arguments against their creed, nor trouble dissentients (if there be such) with arguments in its favor. From this time may usually be dated the decline in the living power of the doctrine. . . .

. . . There are many reasons, doubtless, why doctrines which are the badge of a sect retain more of their vitality than those common to all recognized sects, and why more pains are taken by teachers to keep their meaning alive; but one reason certainly is that the peculiar doctrines are more questioned and have to be oftener defended against open gainsayers. Both teachers and learners go to sleep at their post as soon as there is no enemy in the field. . . .

It still remains to speak of one of the principal causes which make diversity of opinion advantageous, and will continue to do so until mankind shall have entered a stage of intellectual advancement which at present seems at an incalculable distance. We have hitherto considered only two possibilities: that the received opinion may be false, and some other opinion, consequently, true; or that, the received opinion being true, a conflict with the opposite error is essential to a clear apprehension and deep feeling of its truth. But there is a commoner case than either of these: when the conflicting doctrines, instead of being one true and the other false, share the truth between them, and the nonconforming opinion is needed to supply the remainder of the truth of which the received doctrine embodies only a part. Popular opinions, on subjects not palpable to sense, are often true, but seldom or never the whole truth. They are a part of the truth, sometimes a greater, sometimes a smaller part, but exaggerated, distorted, and disjointed from the truths by which they ought to be accompanied and limited. Heretical opinions, on the other hand, are generally some of these suppressed and neglected truths, bursting the bonds which kept them down, and either seeking reconciliation with the truth contained in the common opinion, or fronting it as enemies, and setting themselves up, with similar exclusiveness, as the whole truth. The latter case is hitherto the most frequent, as, in the human mind, one-sidedness has always been the rule, and many-sidedness the exception. Hence, even in revolutions of opinion, one part of the truth usually sets while another rises. Even progress, which ought to superadd, for the most part only substitutes one partial and incomplete truth for another; improvement consisting chiefly in this, that the new fragment of truth is more wanted, more adapted to the needs of the time than that which it displaces. Such being the partial character of prevailing opinions, even when resting on a true foundation, every opinion which embodies somewhat of the portion of truth which the common opinion omits ought to be considered precious, with whatever amount of error and confusion that truth may be blended. No sober judge of human affairs will feel bound to be indignant because those who force on our notice truths which we should otherwise have overlooked, overlook some of those which we see. Rather, he will think that so long as popular truth is one-sided, it is more desirable than otherwise that unpopular truth should have one-sided assertors, too, such being usually the most energetic and the most likely to compel reluctant attention to the fragment of wisdom which they proclaim as if it were the whole. . . .

. . . only through diversity of opinion is there, in the existing state of human intellect, a chance of fair play to all sides of the truth. When there are persons to be found who form an exception to the apparent unanimity of the world on any subject, even if the world is in the right, it is always probable that dissentients have something worth hearing to say for themselves, and that truth would lose something by their silence. . . .

We have now recognized the necessity to the mental well-being of mankind (on which all their other well-being depends) of freedom of opinion, and freedom of the expression of opinion, on four distinct grounds, which we will now briefly recapitulate:

First, if any opinion is compelled to silence, that opinion may, for aught we can certainly know, be true. To deny this is to assume our own infallibility.

Secondly, though the silenced opinion be an error, it may, and very commonly does, contain a portion of truth; and since the general or prevailing opinion on any subject is rarely or never the whole truth, it is only by the collision of adverse opinions that the remainder of the truth has any chance of being supplied.

Thirdly, even if the received opinion be not only true, but the whole truth; unless it is suffered to be, and actually is, vigorously and earnestly contested, it will, by most of those who receive it, be held in the manner of a prejudice, with little comprehension or feeling of its rational grounds. And not only this, but, fourthly, the meaning of the doctrine itself will be in danger of being lost or enfeebled, and deprived of its vital effect on the character and conduct: the dogma becoming a mere formal profession, inefficacious for good, but cumbering the ground and preventing the growth of any real and heartfelt conviction from reason or personal experience. . . .

CHAPTER III / OF INDIVIDUALITY, AS ONE OF THE ELEMENTS OF WELL-BEING

. . . No one pretends that actions should be as free as opinions. On the contrary, even opinions lose their immunity when the circumstances in which they are expressed are such as to constitute their expression a positive instigation to some mischievous act. An opinion that corn dealers are starvers of the poor, or that private property is robbery, ought to be unmolested when simply circulated through the press, but may justly incur punishment when delivered orally to an excited mob assembled before the house of a corn dealer, or when handed about among the same mob in the form of a placard. Acts of whatever kind, which without justifiable cause do harm to others may be, and in the more important cases absolutely require to be, controlled by the unfavorable sentiments, and, when needful, by the active interference of mankind. The liberty of the individual must be thus far limited; he must not make himself a nuisance to other people. But if he refrains from molesting others in what concerns them, and merely acts according to his own inclination and judgment in things which concern himself, the same reasons which show that opinion should be free prove also that he should be allowed, without molestation, to carry his opinions into practice at his own cost. . . .

QUESTIONS FOR REFLECTION

1. To what extent may people be punished by the opinions or behavior of others, independent of any legal coercion? Is Mill's view compatible with his analysis of the social stigma attending the expression of unpopular opinions?
2. Mill admits that distinguishing self-regarding from other-regarding actions is a matter of degree, for virtually every action affects someone other than the agent who performs it. What is Mill's criterion for determining whether an act affects others enough to count as other-regarding and, so, to be subject to government interference?
3. What arguments does Mill advance in this section in favor of the harm principle?

CHAPTER IV / OF THE LIMITS TO THE AUTHORITY OF SOCIETY OVER THE INDIVIDUAL

What, then, is the rightful limit to the sovereignty of the individual over himself? Where does the authority of society begin? How much of human life should be assigned to individuality, and how much to society?

Each will receive its proper share if each has that which more particularly concerns it. To individuality should belong the part of life in which it is chiefly the individual that is interested; to society, the part which chiefly interests society.

Though society is not founded on a contract, and though no good purpose is answered by inventing a contract in order to deduce social obligations from it, everyone who receives the protection of society owes a return for the benefit, and the fact of living in society renders it indispensable that each should be bound to observe a certain line of conduct toward the rest. This conduct consists, first, in not injuring the interests of one another, or rather certain interests which, either by express legal provision or by tacit understanding, ought to be considered as rights; and secondly, in each person's bearing his share (to be fixed on some equitable principle) of the labors and sacrifices incurred for defending the society or its members from injury and molestation. These conditions society is justified in enforcing at all costs to those who endeavor to withhold fulfillment. Nor is this all that society may do. The acts of an individual may be hurtful to others or wanting in due consideration for their welfare, without going to the length of violating any of their constituted rights. The offender may then be justly punished by opinion, though not by law. As soon as any part of a person's conduct affects prejudicially the interests of others, society has jurisdiction over it, and the question whether the general welfare will or will not be promoted by interfering with it becomes open to discussion. But there is no room for entertaining any such question when a person's conduct affects the interests of no persons besides himself, or needs not affect them unless they like (all the persons concerned being of full age and the ordinary amount of understanding). In all such cases, there should be perfect freedom, legal and social, to do the action and stand the consequences. . . .

The distinction here pointed out between the part of a person's life which concerns only himself and that which concerns others, many persons will refuse to admit. How (it may be asked) can any part of the conduct of a member of society be a matter of indifference to the other members? No person is an entirely isolated being; it is impossible for a person to do anything seriously or permanently hurtful to himself without mischief reaching at least to his near connections, and often far beyond them. If he injures his property, he does harm to those who directly or indirectly derived support from it, and usually diminishes, by a greater or less amount, the general resources of the community. If he deteriorates his bodily or mental faculties, he not only brings evil upon all who depended upon him for any portion of their happiness, but disqualifies himself for rendering the services which he owes to his fellow creatures generally, perhaps becomes a burden on their affection or benevolence; and if such conduct were very frequent hardly any offense that is committed would detract more from the general sum of good. Finally, if by his vices or follies a person does no direct harm to others, he is nevertheless (it may be said) injurious by his example, and ought to be compelled to control himself for the sake of those whom the sight or knowledge of his conduct might corrupt or mislead.

And even (it will be added) if the consequences of misconduct could be confined to the vicious or thoughtless individual, ought society to abandon to their own guidance those who are manifestly unfit for it? If protection against themselves is confessedly due to children and persons under age, is not society equally bound to afford it to persons of mature years who are equally incapable of self-government? If gambling, or drunkenness, or incontinence, or idleness, or uncleanliness are as injurious to happiness, and as great a hindrance to improvement, as many or most of the acts prohibited by law, why (it may be asked) should not law, so far as is consistent with practicability and social convenience, endeavor to repress these also? And as a supplement to the unavoidable imperfections of law, ought not opinion at least to organize a powerful police against these vices and visit rigidly with social penalties those who are known to practice them? There is no question here (it may be said) about restricting individuality, or impeding the trial of new and original experiments in living. The only things it is sought to prevent are things which have been tried and condemned from the beginning of the world until now—things which experience has shown not to be useful or suitable to any person's individuality. There must be some length of time and amount of experience after which a moral or prudential truth may be regarded as established; and it is merely desired to prevent generation after generation from falling over the same precipice which has been fatal to their predecessors.

I fully admit that the mischief which a person does to himself may seriously affect, both through their sympathies and their interests, those nearly connected with him and, in a minor degree, society at large. When, by conduct of this sort, a person is led to violate a distinct and assignable obligation to any other person or persons, the case is taken out of the self-regarding class and becomes amenable to moral disapprobation in the proper sense of the term. If, for example, a man, through intemperance or extravagance, becomes unable to pay his debts, or, having undertaken the moral responsibility of a family, becomes from the same cause incapable of supporting or educating them, he is deservedly reprobated and might be justly punished; but it is for the breach of duty to his family or creditors, not for the extravagance. If the resources which ought to have been devoted to them had been diverted from them for the most prudent investment, the moral culpability would have been the same. George Barnwell murdered his uncle to get money for his mistress, but if he had done it to set himself up in business, he would equally have been hanged. Again, in the frequent case of a man who causes grief to his family by addiction to bad habits, he deserves reproach for his unkindness or ingratitude; but so he may for cultivating habits not in themselves vicious, if they are painful to those with whom he passes his life, or who from personal ties are dependent on him for their comfort. Whoever fails in the consideration generally due to the interests and feelings of others, not being compelled by some more imperative duty, or justified by allowable self-preference, is a subject of moral disapprobation for that failure, but not for the cause of it, nor for the errors, merely personal to himself, which may have remotely led to it. In like manner, when a person disables himself, by conduct purely self-regarding, from the performance of some definite duty incumbent on him to the public, he is guilty of a social offense. No person ought to be punished simply for being drunk; but a soldier or policeman should be punished for being drunk on duty. Whenever, in short, there is a definite damage, or a definite risk of damage, either to an individual or to the public, the case is taken out of the province of liberty and placed in that of morality or law.

But with regard to the merely contingent or, as it may be called, constructive injury which a person causes to society by conduct which neither violates any specific duty to the public, nor occasions perceptible hurt to any assignable individual except himself, the inconvenience is one which society can afford to bear, for the sake of the greater good of human freedom. . . .

But the strongest of all the arguments against the interference of the public with purely personal conduct is that, when it does interfere, the odds are that it interferes wrongly and in the wrong place. On questions of social morality, of duty to others, the opinion of the public, that is, of an overruling majority, though often wrong, is likely to be still oftener right, because on such questions they are only required to judge of their own interests, of the manner in which some mode of conduct, if allowed to be practiced, would affect themselves. But the opinion of a similar majority, imposed as a law on the minority, on questions of self-regarding conduct is quite as likely to be wrong as right, for in these cases public opinion means, at the best, some people's opinion of what is good or bad for other people, while very often it does not even mean that—the public, with the most perfect indifference, passing over the pleasure or convenience of those whose conduct they censure and considering only their own preference. There are many who consider as an injury to themselves any conduct which they have a distaste for, and resent it as an outrage to their feelings; as a religious bigot, when charged with disregarding the religious feelings of others, has been known to retort that they disregard his feelings by persisting in their abominable worship or creed. But there is no parity between the feeling of a person for his own opinion and the feeling of another who is offended at his holding it, no more than between the desire of a thief to take a purse and the desire of the right owner to keep it. And a person's taste is as much his own peculiar concern as his opinion or his purse. It is easy for anyone to imagine an ideal public which leaves the freedom and choice of individuals in all uncertain matters undisturbed and only requires them to abstain from modes of conduct which universal experience has condemned. But where has there been seen a public which set any such limit to its censorship? Or when does the public trouble itself about universal experience? In its interferences with personal conduct it is seldom thinking of anything but the enormity of acting or feeling differently from itself; and this standard of judgment, thinly disguised, is held up to mankind as the dictate of religion and philosophy by nine-tenths of all moralists and speculative writers. These teach that things are right because they are right; because we feel them to be so. They tell us to search in our own minds and hearts for laws of conduct binding on ourselves and on all others. What can the poor public do but apply these instructions and make their own personal feelings of good and evil, if they are tolerably unanimous in them, obligatory on all the world? . . .

QUESTIONS FOR REFLECTION

1. Between 1905 and 1937, a period known as the *Lochner* era, the U.S. Supreme Court used a form of the harm principle to strike down laws regulating economic activity: laws setting a minimum wage, for example, or regulating working hours and conditions. Does the harm principle, in Mill's view, apply to economic transactions? How does the harm principle relate to what he calls the doctrine of "free trade"?
2. What is the point of Mill's example of someone about to cross an unsafe bridge? What does it indicate about the harm principle?
3. The United States, like many other countries, regulates advertising. Is such regulation compatible with Mill's position in *On Liberty*? What kinds of regulation, if any, might Mill be willing to accept?
4. Many governments impose "sin taxes" on items such as alcohol and cigarettes. What is Mill's criterion for determining whether such taxes are acceptable?
5. Mill insists that voluntary slavery ought to be prohibited, although it might appear to fall into

the realm of individual liberty. Why? Is Mill's support for this prohibition consistent with the harm principle?

CHAPTER V /APPLICATIONS

Again, trade is a social act. Whoever undertakes to sell any description of goods to the public does what affects the interest of other persons, and of society in general; and thus his conduct, in principle, comes within the jurisdiction of society; accordingly, it was once held to be the duty of governments, in all cases which were considered of importance, to fix prices and regulate the process of manufacture. But it is now recognized, though not till after a long struggle, that both the cheapness and the good quality of commodities are most effectually provided for by leaving the producers and sellers perfectly free, under the sole check of equal freedom to the buyers for supplying themselves elsewhere. This is the so-called doctrine of "free trade," which rests on grounds different from, though equally solid with, the principle of individual liberty asserted in this essay. Restrictions on trade, or on production for purposes of trade, are indeed restraints; and all restraint, *qua* restraint, is an evil; but the restraints in question affect only that part of conduct which society is competent to restrain, and are wrong solely because they do not really produce the results which it is desired to produce by them. As the principle of individual liberty is not involved in the doctrine of free trade, so neither is it in most of the questions which arise respecting the limits of that doctrine, as, for example, what amount of public control is admissible for the prevention of fraud by adulteration; how far sanitary precautions, or arrangements to protect workpeople employed in dangerous occupations, should be enforced on employers. Such questions involve considerations of liberty only in so far as leaving people to themselves is better, *caeteris paribus*, than controlling them; but that they may be legitimately controlled for these ends is in principle undeniable. On the other hand, there are questions relating to interference with trade which are essentially questions of liberty, such as the Maine Law, already touched upon: the prohibition of the importation of opium into China; the restriction of the sale of poisons—all cases, in short, where the object of the interference is to make it impossible or difficult to obtain a particular commodity. These interferences are objectionable, not as infringements on the liberty of the producer or seller, but on that of the buyer.

One of these examples, that of the sale of poisons, opens a new question: the proper limits of what may be called the functions of police; how far liberty may legitimately be invaded for the prevention of crime, or of accident. It is one of the undisputed functions of government to take precautions against crime before it has been committed, as well as to detect and punish it afterwards. The preventive function of government, however, is far more liable to be abused, to the prejudice of liberty, than the punitory function; for there is hardly any part of the legitimate freedom of action of a human being which would not admit of being represented, and fairly, too, as increasing the facilities for some form or other of delinquency. Nevertheless, if a public authority, or even a private person, sees anyone evidently preparing to commit a crime, they are not bound to look on inactive until the crime is committed, but may interfere to prevent it. If poisons were never bought or used for any purpose except the commission of murder, it would be right to prohibit their manufacture and sale. They may, however, be wanted not only for innocent but for useful purposes, and restrictions cannot be imposed in the one case without operating in the other. Again, it is a proper office of public authority to guard against accidents. If either a public officer or anyone else saw a person attempting to cross a bridge which had been ascertained to be unsafe, and there were no time to warn him of his danger, they might seize him and turn him back, without any real infringement of his liberty; for liberty consists in doing what one desires, and he does not desire to fall into the river. Nevertheless, when there is not a certainty, but only a danger of mischief, no one but the person himself can judge of the sufficiency of the motive which may prompt him to incur the risk; in this case, therefore (unless he is a child, or delirious, or in some state of excitement or absorption incompatible with the full use of the reflecting faculty), he ought, I conceive, to be only warned of the danger; not forcibly prevented from exposing himself to it. Similar considerations, applied to such a question as the sale of poisons, may enable us to decide which among the possible modes of regulation are or are not contrary to principle. Such a precaution, for example, as that of labeling the drug with some word expressive of its dangerous character may be enforced without violation of liberty: the buyer cannot wish not to know that the thing he possesses has poisonous qualities. . . .

The right inherent in society to ward off crimes against itself by antecedent precautions suggests the obvious limitations to the maxim that purely self-regarding misconduct cannot properly be meddled with in the way of prevention or punishment. Drunkenness, for example, in ordinary cases, is not a fit subject for legislative interference, but I should deem it perfectly legitimate that a person who had once been convicted of any act of violence to others under the influence of drink should be placed under a special legal restriction, personal to himself; that if he were afterwards found drunk, he should be liable to a penalty, and that if, when in that state, he committed another offense, the punishment to which he would be liable for that other offense should be increased in severity. The making himself drunk, in a person whom drunkenness excites to do harm to others, is a crime against others. So, again, idleness, except in a person receiving support from the public, or except when it constitutes a breach of contract, cannot without tyranny be made a subject of legal punishment; but if, either from idleness or from any other avoidable cause, a man fails to perform his legal duties to others, as for instance to support his children, it is no tyranny to force him to fulfill that obligation by compulsory labor if no other means are available.

Again, there are many acts which, being directly injurious only to the agents themselves, ought not to be legally interdicted, but which, if done publicly, are a violation of good manners and, coming thus within the category of offenses against others, may rightly be prohibited. Of this kind are offenses against decency; on which it is unnecessary to dwell, the rather as they are only connected indirectly with our subject, the objection to publicity being equally strong in the case of many actions not in themselves condemnable, nor supposed to be so. . . .

A further question is whether the State, while it permits, should nevertheless indirectly discourage conduct which it deems contrary to the best interests of the agent; whether, for example, it should take measures to render the means of drunkenness more costly, or add to the difficulty of procuring them by limiting the number of the places of sale. On this, as on most other practical questions, many distinctions require to be made. To tax stimulants for the sole purpose of making them more difficult to be obtained is a measure differing only in degree from their entire prohibition, and would be justifiable only if that were justifiable. Every increase of cost is a prohibition to those whose means do not come up to the augmented price; and to those who do, it is a penalty laid on them for gratifying a particular taste. Their choice of pleasures and their mode of expending their income, after satisfying their legal and moral obligations to the State and to individuals, are their own concern and must rest with their own judgment. These considerations may seem at first sight to condemn the selection of stimulants as special subjects of taxation for purposes of revenue. But it must be remembered that taxation for fiscal purposes is absolutely inevitable; that in most countries it is necessary that a considerable part of that taxation should be indirect; that the State, therefore, cannot help imposing penalties, which to some persons may be prohibitory, on the use of some articles of consumption. It is hence the duty of the State to consider, in the imposition of taxes, what commodities the consumers can best spare; and *a fortiori*, to select in preference those of which it deems the use, beyond a very moderate quantity, to be positively injurious. Taxation, therefore, of stimulants up to the point which produces the largest amount of revenue (supposing that the State needs all the revenue which it yields) is not only admissible, but to be approved of. . . .

It was pointed out in an early part of this essay that the liberty of the individual, in things wherein the individual is alone concerned, implies a corresponding liberty in any number of individuals to regulate by mutual agreement such things as regard them jointly, and regard no persons but themselves. This question presents no difficulty so long as the will of all the persons implicated remains unaltered; but since that will may change it is often necessary, even in things in which they alone are concerned, that they should enter into engagements with one another; and when they do, it is fit, as a general rule, that those engagements should be kept. Yet, in the laws, probably, of every country, this general rule has some exceptions. Not only persons are not held to engagements which violate the rights of third parties, but it is sometimes considered a sufficient reason for releasing them from an engagement that it is injurious to themselves. In this and most other civilized countries, for example, an engagement by which a person should sell himself, or allow himself to be sold, as a slave would be null and void, neither enforced by law nor by opinion. The ground for thus limiting his power of voluntarily disposing of his own lot in life is apparent, and is very clearly seen in this extreme case. The reason for not interfering, unless for the sake of others, with a person's voluntary acts is consideration for his liberty. His voluntary choice is evidence that what he so chooses is desirable, or at least endurable, to him, and his good is on the whole best provided for by allowing him to take his own means of pursuing it. But by selling himself for a slave, he abdicates his liberty; he foregoes any future use of it beyond that single act. He therefore defeats, in his own case, the very purpose which is the justification of allowing him to dispose of himself. He is no longer free, but is thenceforth in a position which has no longer the presumption in its favor that would be afforded by his voluntarily remaining in it. The principle of freedom cannot require that he should be free not to be free. It is not freedom to be allowed to alienate his freedom. These reasons, the force of which is so conspicuous in this peculiar case, are evidently of far wider application, yet a limit is everywhere set to them by the necessities of life, which continually require, not indeed that we should resign our freedom, but that we should consent to this and the other limitation of it. The principle, however, which demands uncontrolled freedom of action in all that concerns only the agents themselves requires that those who have become bound to one another, in things which concern no third party, should be able to release one another from the engagement; and even without such voluntary release there are perhaps no contracts or engagements, except those that relate to money or money's worth, of which one can venture to say that there ought to be no liberty whatever of retraction. Baron Wilhelm von Humboldt . . . states it as his conviction that engagements which involve personal relations or services should never be legally binding beyond a limited duration of time; and that the most important of these engagements, marriage, having the peculiarity that its objects are frustrated unless the feelings of both the parties are in harmony with it, should require nothing more than the declared will of either party to dissolve it. This subject is too important and too complicated to be discussed in a parenthesis, and I touch on it only so far as is necessary for purposes of illustration. If the conciseness and generality of Baron Humboldt's dissertation had not obliged him in this instance to content himself with enunciating his conclusion without discussing the premises, he would doubtless have recognized that the question cannot be decided on grounds so simple as those to which he confines himself. When a person, either by express promise or by conduct, has encouraged another to rely on his continuing to act in a certain way—to build expectations and calculations, and stake any part of his plan of life upon that supposition—a new series of moral obligations arises on his part toward that person, which may possibly be overruled, but cannot be ignored. And again, if the relation between two contracting parties has been followed by consequences to others; if it has placed third parties in any peculiar position, or, as in the case of marriage, has even called third parties into existence, obligations arise on the part of both the contracting parties toward those third persons, the fulfillment of which, or at all events the mode of fulfillment, must be greatly affected by the continuance or disruption of the relation between the original parties to the contract. It does not follow, nor can I admit, that these obligations extend to requiring the fulfillment of the contract at all costs to the happiness of the reluctant party; but they are a necessary element in the question; and, even if, as von Humboldt maintains, they ought to make no difference in the *legal* freedom of the parties to release themselves from the engagement (and I also hold that they ought not to make *much* difference), they necessarily make a great difference in the *moral* freedom. A person is bound to take all these circumstances into account before resolving on a step which may affect such important interests of others; and if he does not allow proper weight to those interests, he is morally responsible for the wrong. . . .

Drug Legalization

Over the past several decades, drug use has grown from a fashion among a small collection of bohemian artists and musicians into a major social problem. The use of illegal and seriously harmful drugs can be found in almost any high school, college, or university in the United States; scores of cities routinely witness drug-related shootings and other forms of violence. Several times the government has declared a "war on drugs," but the result has seemed, at best, a stalemate. Frustration with this state of affairs has led some to call for the legalization of drugs.

Drug use may appear to be a self-regarding act that may harm the drug user but that has little effect on anyone else. Few contemporary advocates of legalization, however, have rested their case solely on Mill's harm principle. Many writers on both sides of the issue believe that nonusers suffer significant harms that must be taken into account; they have debated whether criminal penalties reduce or add to the harms to nonusers. Moreover, addictive drugs pose problems related to those Mill confronts in discussing voluntary slavery; people may initially choose, freely and voluntarily, to take an addictive drug, but their freedom does not last long. As Mill asks, do people have the freedom to surrender their freedom? Many contemporary writers share Mill's conviction that they do not and thus include harms to users of addictive drugs as morally relevant. This does not mean, however, that philosophical attitudes toward liberty are unrelated to discussions of the drug problem. Some writers clearly presuppose something akin to Mill's harm principle. Others assume the opposed principle of moral paternalism, holding that a government should promote the moral well-being of its citizens. Still others treat harms to users and harms to nonusers as morally equivalent, in effect denying the significance of the distinction between self-regarding and other-regarding actions.

Milton Friedman, a respected economist, argues that the war on drugs has been a costly failure. He urges decriminalization of drugs, that is, removing criminal penalties against their sale and use. He advocates treating drugs much as we now treat alcohol and cigarettes—as substances that should be regulated and whose users should be treated rather than jailed.

William Bennett, "drug czar" under Presidents Reagan and Bush, maintains that Friedman's proposal is flawed and even reckless. Bennett defends criminal penalties for drug use by arguing that they reduce harms both to drug users and to others. He contends that "government has a responsibility to craft and uphold laws that help educate citizens about right and wrong."

Ethan Nadelmann argues Friedman's case in greater detail. He holds that drug legalization would produce significant economic benefits, reduce crime, and revitalize the inner cities. Douglas Husak argues, from a more theoretical perspective, that laws against drug use violate fundamental liberties. James Q. Wilson further articulates Bennett's case, contending that the war on drugs is justifiable and moderately successful. He holds that enforcing criminal penalties has helped to confine the drug problem to a relatively small portion of the population while sheltering most people from harms associated with the drug trade. Legalization, he believes, would greatly increase drug use and the attendant harms to users and nonusers alike.

MILTON FRIEDMAN

An Open Letter to Bill Bennett

Milton Friedman is Senior Research Fellow at the Hoover Institution at Stanford University and Professor Emeritus of Economics at the University of Chicago. He was awarded the Nobel Prize in economics in 1976. (Source: Reprinted from The Wall Street Journal, *September 7, 1989, p. A14. Copyright © 1989 by Dow Jones and Company, Inc.)*

QUESTIONS FOR REFLECTION

1. Asserting that government prohibition of drug use is illegitimate in itself differs from asserting that it is a bad idea in practice. Certainly Friedman asserts the latter. How does he argue for this position? Does he also assert the former?
2. Friedman claims that the drug war undermines "human liberty and individual freedom." What is Friedman's conception of liberty? Is Friedman's argument compatible with Mill's harm principle?

DEAR BILL:

In Oliver Cromwell's eloquent words, "I beseech you, in the bowels of Christ, think it possible you may be mistaken" about the course you and President Bush urge us to adopt to fight drugs. The path you propose of more police, more jails, use of the military in foreign countries, harsh penalties for drug users, and a whole panoply of repressive measures can only make a bad situation worse. The drug war cannot be won by those tactics without undermining the human liberty and individual freedom that you and I cherish.

You are not mistaken in believing that drugs are a scourge that is devastating our society. You are not mistaken in believing that drugs are tearing asunder our social fabric, ruining the lives of many young people, and imposing heavy costs on some of the most disadvantaged among us. You are not mistaken in believing that the majority of the public share your concerns. In short, you are not mistaken in the end you seek to achieve.

Your mistake is failing to recognize that the very measures you favor are a major source of the evils you deplore. Of course the problem is demand, but it is not only demand, it is demand that must operate through repressed and illegal channels. Illegality creates obscene profits that finance the murderous tactics of the drug lords; illegality leads to the corruption of law enforcement officials; illegality monopolizes the efforts of honest law forces so that they are starved for resources to fight the simpler crimes of robbery, theft and assault.

Drugs are a tragedy for addicts. But criminalizing their use converts that tragedy into a disaster for society, for users and non-users alike. Our experience with the prohibition of drugs is a replay of our experience with the prohibition of alcoholic beverages.

I append excerpts from a column that I wrote in 1972 on "Prohibition and Drugs." The major problem then was heroin from Marseilles; today, it is cocaine from Latin America. Today, also, the problem is far more serious than it was 17 years ago: more addicts, more innocent victims; more drug pushers, more law enforcement officials; more money spent to enforce prohibition, more money spent to circumvent prohibition.

Had drugs been decriminalized 17 years ago, "crack" would never have been invented (it was invented because the high cost of illegal drugs made it profitable to provide a cheaper version) and there would today be far fewer addicts. The lives of thousands, perhaps hundreds of thousands of innocent victims would have been saved, and not only in the U.S. The ghettos of our major cities would not be drug-and-crime-infested no-man's lands. Fewer people would be in jails, and fewer jails would have been built.

Colombia, Bolivia and Peru would not be suffering from narco-terror, and we would not be distorting our foreign policy because of narco-terror. Hell would not, in the words with which Billy Sunday welcomed Prohibition, "be forever for rent," but it would be a lot emptier.

Decriminalizing drugs is even more urgent now than in 1972, but we must recognize that the harm done in the interim cannot be wiped out, certainly not immediately. Postponing decriminalization will only make matters worse, and make the problem appear even more intractable.

Alcohol and tobacco cause many more deaths in users than do drugs. Decriminalization would not prevent us from treating drugs as we now treat alcohol and tobacco: prohibiting sales of drugs to minors, outlawing the advertising of drugs and similar measures. Such measures could be enforced, while outright prohibition cannot be. Moreover, if even a small fraction of the money we now spend on trying to enforce drug prohibition were devoted to treatment and rehabilitation, in an atmosphere of compassion not punishment, the reduction in drug usage and in the harm done to the users could be dramatic.

This plea comes from the bottom of my heart. Every friend of freedom, and I know you are one, must be as revolted as I am by the prospect of turning the United States into an armed camp, by the vision of jails filled with casual drug users and of an army of enforcers empowered to invade the liberty of citizens on slight evidence. A country in which shooting down unidentified planes "on suspicion" can be seriously considered as a drug-war tactic is not the kind of United States that either you or I want to hand on to future generations.

Milton Friedman
Senior Research Fellow
Hoover Institution
Stanford University

Flashback

This is a truncated version of a column by Mr. Friedman in Newsweek's *May 1, 1972, issue, as President Nixon was undertaking an earlier "drug war":*

"The reign of tears is over. The slums will soon be only a memory. We will turn our prisons into factories and our jails into storehouses and corncribs. Men will walk upright now, women will smile, and the children will laugh. Hell will be forever for rent."

That is how Billy Sunday, the noted evangelist and leading crusader against Demon Rum, greeted the onset of Prohibition in early 1920.

We know now how tragically his hopes were doomed.

Prohibition is an attempted cure that makes matters worse—for both the addict and the rest of us.

Consider first the addict. Legalizing drugs might increase the number of addicts, but it is not clear that it would. Forbidden fruit is attractive, particularly to the young. More important, many drug addicts are deliberately made by pushers, who give likely prospects that first few doses free. It pays the pusher to do so because, once hooked, the addict is a captive customer. If drugs were legally available, any possible profit from such inhumane activity would disappear, since the addict could buy from the cheapest source.

Whatever happens to the number of addicts, the individual addict would clearly be far better off if drugs were legal. Addicts are driven to associate with criminals to get the drugs, become criminals themselves to finance the habit, and risk constant danger of death and disease.

Consider next the rest of us. The harm to us from the addiction of others arises almost wholly from the fact that drugs are illegal. It is estimated that addicts commit one third to one half of all street crime in the U.S.

Legalize drugs, and street crime would drop dramatically.

Moreover, addicts and pushers are not the only ones corrupted. Immense sums are at stake. It is inevitable that some relatively low-paid police and other government officials—and some high-paid ones as well—will succumb to the temptation to pick up easy money.

Legalizing drugs would simultaneously reduce the amount of crime and raise the quality of law enforcement. Can you conceive of any other measure that would accomplish so much to promote law and order?

In drugs, as in other areas, persuasion and example are likely to be far more effective than the use of force to shape others in our image.

WILLIAM J. BENNETT

A Response to Milton Friedman

William J. Bennett is Research Fellow at the American Enterprise Institute. He has served as Director of the Office of National Drug Control Policy and as U.S. Secretary of Education. (Source: Reprinted from The Wall Street Journal, *September 19, 1989, p. A30. Copyright © 1989 by Dow Jones and Company, Inc.)*

QUESTIONS FOR REFLECTION

1. Bennett contends that legalizing drugs would increase harms to nonusers. How does he argue this position?
2. Part of Bennett's case rests on his view that enforcing criminal penalties against drug use decreases harms done by drugs to drug users themselves. What is his argument? Is Bennett's use of this argument compatible with Mill's harm principle?
3. Friedman claims that the drug war undermines "human liberty and individual freedom." How does Bennett respond to this allegation, if at all? What does this indicate about Bennett's conception of freedom and of the proper bounds of government authority?

DEAR MILTON:

There was little, if anything, new in your open letter to me calling for the legalization of drugs (The Wall Street Journal, Sept. 7). As the excerpt from your 1972 article made clear, the legalization argument is an old and familiar one, which has recently been revived by a small number of journalists and academics who insist that the only solution to the drug problem is no solution at all. What surprises me is that you would continue to advocate so unrealistic a proposal without pausing to consider seriously its consequences.

If the argument for drug legalization has one virtue it is its sheer simplicity. Eliminate laws against drugs, and street crime will disappear. Take the profit out of the black market through decriminalization and regulation, and poor neighborhoods will no longer be victimized by drug dealers. Cut back on drug enforcement, and use the money to wage a public health campaign against drugs, as we do with tobacco and alcohol.

Counting Costs

The basic premise of all these propositions is that using our nation's laws to fight drugs is too costly. To be sure, our attempts to reduce drug use do carry with them enormous costs. But the question that must be asked—and which is totally ignored by the legalization advocates—is what are the costs of *not* enforcing laws against drugs?

In my judgment, and in the judgment of virtually every serious scholar in this field, the potential costs of legalizing drugs would be so large as to make it a public policy disaster.

Of course, no one, including you, can say with certainty what would happen in the U.S. if drugs were suddenly to become a readily purchased product. We do know, however, that wherever drugs have been cheaper and more easily obtained, drug use — and addiction — has skyrocketed. In opium and cocaine producing countries, addiction is rampant among the peasants involved in drug production.

Professor James Q. Wilson tells us that during the years in which heroin could be legally prescribed by doctors in Britain, the number of addicts increased forty-fold. And after the repeal of Prohibition—an analogy favored but misunderstood by legalization advocates—consumption of alcohol soared by 350%.

Could we afford such dramatic increases in drug use? I doubt it. Already the toll of drug use on American society—measured in lost productivity, in rising health insurance costs, in hospitals flooded with drug overdose emergencies, in drug caused accidents, and in premature death—is surely more than we would like to bear.

You seem to believe that by spending just a little more money on treatment and rehabilitation, the costs of increased addiction can be avoided. That hope betrays a basic misunderstanding of the problems facing drug treatment. Most addicts don't suddenly decide to get help. They remain addicts either because treatment isn't available or because they don't seek it out. The National Drug Control Strategy announced by President Bush on Sept. 5 goes a long way in making sure that more treatment slots are available. But the simple fact remains that many drug users won't enter treatment until they are forced to—often by the very criminal justice system you think is the source of the problem.

As for the connection between drugs and crime, your unswerving commitment to a legalization solution prevents you from appreciating the complexity of the drug market. Contrary to your claim, most addicts do not turn to crime to support their habit. Research shows that many of them were involved in criminal activity before they turned to drugs. Many former addicts who have received treatment continue to commit crimes during their recovery. And even if drugs were legal, what evidence do you have that the habitual drug user wouldn't continue to rob and steal to get money for clothes, food or shelter? Drug addicts always want more drugs than they can afford, and no legalization scheme has yet come up with a way of satisfying that appetite.

The National Drug Control Strategy emphasizes the importance of reclaiming the streets and neighborhoods where drugs have wrought havoc because, I admit, the price of having drug laws is having criminals who will try to subvert them. Your proposal might conceivably reduce the amount of gang- and dealer-related crime, but it is fanciful to suggest that it would make crime vanish. Unless you are willing to distribute drugs freely and widely, there will always be a black market to undercut the regulated one. And as for the potential addicts, for the school children and for the pregnant mothers, all of whom would find drugs more accessible and legally condoned, your proposal would offer nothing at all.

So I advocate a larger criminal justice system to take drug users off the streets and deter new users from becoming more deeply involved in so hazardous an activity. You suggest that such policies would turn the country "into an armed camp." Try telling that to the public housing tenants who enthusiastically support plans to enhance security in their buildings, or to the residents who applaud police when a local crack house is razed. They recognize that drug use is a threat to the individual liberty and domestic tranquility guaranteed by the Constitution.

I remain an ardent defender of our nation's laws against illegal drug use and our attempts to enforce them because I believe drug use is wrong. A true friend of freedom understands that government has a responsibility to craft and uphold laws that help educate citizens about right and wrong. That, at any rate, was the Founders' view of our system of government.

Liberal Ridicule

Today this view is much ridiculed by liberal elites and entirely neglected by you. So while I cannot doubt the sincerity of your opinion on drug legalization, I find it difficult to respect. The moral cost of legalizing drugs is great, but it is a cost that apparently lies outside the narrow scope of libertarian policy prescriptions.

I do not have a simple solution to the drug problem. I doubt that one exists. But I am committed to fighting the problem on several fronts through imaginative policies and hard work over a long period of time. As in the past, some of these efforts will work and some won't. Your response, however, is to surrender and see what happens. To my mind that is irresponsible and reckless public policy. At a time when national intolerance for drug use is rapidly increasing, the legalization argument is a political anachronism. Its recent resurgence is, I trust, only a temporary distraction from the genuine debate on national drug policy.

William J. Bennett
Director
Office of National Drug Control Policy

ETHAN A. NADELMANN

The Case for Legalization

Ethan A. Nadelmann is Assistant Professor of Politics and Public Affairs at the Woodrow Wilson School of Public and International Affairs at Princeton University. (Source: Public Interest *92 [Summer 1988]. Notes have been omitted.)*

QUESTIONS FOR REFLECTION

1. Why, according to Nadelmann, have current drug policies failed?
2. In Nadelmann's view, what harms does drug prohibition produce?
3. How does Nadelmann relate drug use and drug prohibition to crime? Do you find his analysis persuasive? Why or why not?

What can be done about the "drug problem"? Despite frequent proclamations of war and dramatic increases in government funding and resources in recent years, there are many indications that the problem is not going away and may even be growing worse. During the past year alone, more than thirty million Americans violated the drug laws on literally billions of occasions. Drug-treatment programs in many cities are turning people away for lack of space and funding. In Washington, D.C., drug-related killings, largely of one drug dealer by another, are held responsible for a doubling in the homicide rate over the past year. In New York and elsewhere, courts and prisons are clogged with a virtually limitless supply of drug-law violators. In large cities and small towns alike, corruption of policemen and other criminal-justice officials by drug traffickers is rampant. . . .

If there were a serious public debate on this issue, far more attention would be given to one policy option that has just begun to be seriously considered but that may well prove more successful than anything currently being implemented or proposed: legalization. . . .

There is, of course, no single legalization strategy. At one extreme is the libertarian vision of virtually no government restraints on the production and sale of drugs or any psychoactive substances, except perhaps around the fringes, such as prohibiting sales to children. At the other extreme is total government control over the production and sale of these goods. In between lies a strategy that may prove more successful than anything yet tried in stemming the problems of drug abuse and drug-related violence, corruption, sickness, and suffering. It is one in which government makes most of the substances that are now banned legally available to competent adults, exercises strong regulatory powers over all large-scale production and sale of drugs, makes drug-treatment programs available to all who need them, and offers honest drug-education programs to children. This strategy, it is worth noting, would also result in a net benefit to public treasuries of at least ten billion dollars a year, and perhaps much more.

There are three reasons why it is important to think about legalization scenarios, even though most Americans remain hostile to the idea. First, current drug-control policies have failed, are failing, and will continue to fail, in good part because they are fundamentally flawed. Second, many drug-control efforts are not only failing but also proving highly costly and counterproductive; indeed, many of the drug-related evils that Americans identify as part and parcel of the "drug problem" are in fact caused by our drug-prohibition policies. Third, there is good reason to believe that repealing many of the drug laws would not lead, as many people fear, to a dramatic rise in drug abuse. In this essay I expand on each of these reasons for considering the legalization option. Government efforts to deal with the drug problem will succeed only if the rhetoric and crusading mentality that now dominate drug policy are replaced by reasoned and logical analysis.

Why Current Drug Policies Fail

Most proposals for dealing with the drug problem today reflect a desire to point the finger at those most removed from one's home and area of expertise. New York Mayor Ed Koch, Florida Congressman Larry Smith, and Harlem Congressman Charles Rangel, who recognize government's inability to deal with the drug problem in the cities, are among the most vocal supporters of punishing foreign drug-producing countries and stepping up interdiction efforts. Foreign leaders and U.S. State Department and drug-enforcement officials stationed abroad, on the other hand, who understand all too well why it is impossible to crack down successfully on illicit drug production outside the United States, are the most vigorous advocates of domestic enforcement and demand-reduction efforts within the United States. In between, those agencies charged with drug interdiction, from the Coast Guard and U.S. Customs Service to the U.S. military, know that they will never succeed in capturing more than a small percentage of the illicit drugs being smuggled into the United States. Not surprisingly, they point their fingers in both directions. The solution, they promise, lies in greater source-control efforts abroad and greater demand-reduction efforts at home.

Trying to pass the buck is always understandable. But in each of these cases, the officials are half right and half wrong—half right in recognizing that they can do little to affect their end of the drug problem, given the suppositions and constraints of current drug-control strategies; half wrong (if we assume that their finger pointing is sincere) in expecting that the solution lies elsewhere. It would be wrong, however, to assume that the public posturing of many officials reflects their real views. Many of them privately acknowledge the futility of all current drug-control strategies and wonder whether radically different options, such as legalization, might not prove more successful in dealing with the drug problem. The political climate pervading this issue is such, however, that merely to ask that alternatives to current policies be considered is to incur a great political risk.

By most accounts, the dramatic increase in drug-enforcement efforts over the past few years has had little effect on the illicit drug market in the United States. The mere existence of drug-prohibition laws, combined with a minimal level of law-enforcement resources, is sufficient to maintain the price of illicit drugs at a level significantly higher than it would be if there were no such laws. Drug laws and enforcement also reduce the availability of illicit drugs, most notably in parts of the United States where demand is relatively limited to begin with. Theoretically, increases in drug-enforcement efforts should result in reduced availability, higher prices, and lower purity of illegal drugs. That is, in fact, what has happened to the domestic marijuana market (in at least the first two respects). But in general the illegal drug market has not responded as intended to the substantial increases in federal, state, and local drug-enforcement efforts.

Cocaine has sold for about a hundred dollars a gram at the retail level since the beginning of the 1980s. The average purity of that gram, however, has increased from 12 to 60 percent. Moreover, a growing number of users are turning to "crack," a potent derivative of cocaine that can be smoked; it is widely sold in ghetto neighborhoods now for five to ten dollars per vial. Needless to say, both crack and the 60 percent pure cocaine pose much greater threats to users than did the relatively benign powder available eight years ago. Similarly, the retail price of heroin has remained relatively constant even as the average purity has risen from 3.9 percent in 1983 to 6.1 percent in 1986. Throughout the southwestern part of the United States, a particularly potent form of heroin known as "black tar" has become increasingly prevalent. And in many cities, a powerful synthetic opiate, Dilaudid, is beginning to compete with heroin as the preferred opiate. The growing number of heroin-related hospital emergencies and deaths is directly related to these developments.

All of these trends suggest that drug-enforcement efforts are not succeeding and may even be backfiring. There are numerous indications, for instance, that a growing number of marijuana dealers in both the producer countries and the United States are switching to cocaine dealing, motivated both by the promise of greater profits and by government drug-enforcement efforts that place a premium on minimizing the bulk of the illicit product (in order to avoid detection). It is possible, of course, that some of these trends would be even more severe in the absence of drug laws and enforcement. At the same time, it is worth observing that the increases in the potency of illegal drugs have coincided with decreases in the potency of legal substances. Motivated in good part by health concerns, cigarette smokers are turning increasingly to lower-tar and lower-nicotine tobacco products, alcohol drinkers from hard liquor to wine and beer, and even coffee drinkers from regular to decaffeinated coffee. This trend may well have less to do with the nature of the substances than with their legal status. It is quite possible, for instance, that the subculture of illicit-drug use creates a bias or incentive in favor of riskier behavior and more powerful psychoactive effects. If this is the case, legalization might well succeed in reversing today's trend toward more potent drugs and more dangerous methods of consumption.

The most "successful" drug-enforcement operations are those that succeed in identifying and destroying an entire drug-trafficking organization. Such operations can send dozens of people to jail and earn the government millions of dollars in asset forfeitures. Yet these operations have virtually no effect on the availability or price of illegal drugs throughout much of the United States. During the past few years, some urban police departments have devoted significant manpower and financial resources to intensive crackdowns on street-level drug dealing in particular neighborhoods. Code-named Operation Pressure Point, Operation Clean Sweep, and so on, these massive police efforts have led to hundreds, even thousands, of arrests of low-level dealers and drug users and have helped improve the quality of life in the targeted neighborhoods. In most cases, however, drug dealers have adapted relatively easily by moving their operations to nearby neighborhoods. In the final analysis, the principal accomplishment of most domestic drug-enforcement efforts is not to reduce the supply or availability of illegal drugs, or even to raise their price; it is to punish the drug dealers who are apprehended, and cause minor disruptions in established drug markets.

The Failure of International Drug Control

Many drug-enforcement officials and urban leaders recognize the futility of domestic drug-enforcement efforts and place their hopes in international control efforts. Yet these too are doomed to fail—for numerous reasons. First, marijuana and opium can be grown almost anywhere, and the coca plant, from which cocaine is derived, is increasingly being cultivated successfully in areas that were once considered inhospitable environments. Wherever drug-eradication efforts succeed, other regions and countries are quick to fill the void; for example, Colombian marijuana growers rapidly expanded production following successful eradication efforts in Mexico during the mid-1970s. Today, Mexican growers are rapidly taking advantage of recent Colombian government successes in eradicating marijuana in the Guajira peninsula. Meanwhile, Jamaicans and Central Americans from Panama to Belize, as well as a growing assortment of Asians and Africans, do what they can to sell their own marijuana in American markets. And within the United States, domestic marijuana production is believed to be a multi-billion-dollar industry, supplying between 15 and 50 percent of the American market. . . .

Beyond the push-down/pop-up factor, international source-control efforts face a variety of other obstacles. In many countries, governments with limited resources lack the ability to crack down on drug production in the hinterlands and other poorly policed regions. In some countries, ranging from Colombia and Peru to Burma and Thailand, leftist insurgencies are involved in drug production for either financial or political profit and may play an important role in hampering government drug-control efforts. With respect to all three of the illicit crops, poor peasants with no comparable opportunities to earn as much money growing legitimate produce are prominently involved in the illicit business. In some cases, the illicit crop is part of a traditional, indigenous culture. Even where it is not, peasants typically perceive little or nothing immoral about taking advantage of the opportunity to grow the illicit crops. Indeed, from their perspective their moral obligation is not to protect the foolish American consumer of their produce but to provide for their families' welfare. And even among those who do perceive participation in the illicit drug market as somewhat unethical, the temptations held out by the drug traffickers often prove overwhelming.

No illicit drug is as difficult to keep out of the United States as heroin. The absence of geographical limitations on where it can be cultivated is just one minor obstacle. American heroin users consume an estimated 6 tons of heroin each year. The 60 tons of opium required to produce that heroin represent just 2 or 3 percent of the estimated 2,000 to 3,000 tons of illicit opium produced during each of the past few years. Even if eradication efforts combined with what often proves to be the opium growers' principal nemesis—bad weather—were to eliminate three-fourths of that production in one year, the U.S. market would still require just 10 percent of the remaining crop. Since U.S. consumers are able and willing to pay more than any others, the chances are good that they would still obtain their heroin. In any event, the prospects for such a radical reduction in illicit opium production are scanty indeed.

As Peter Reuter argues, interdiction, like source control, is largely unable to keep illicit drugs out of the United States. Moreover, the past twenty years' experience has demonstrated that even dramatic increases in interdiction and source-control efforts have little or no effect on the price and purity of drugs. The few small successes, such as the destruction of the Turkish-opium "French Connection" in the early 1970s and the crackdown on Mexican marijuana and heroin in the late 1970s, were exceptions to the rule. The elusive goal of international drug control since then has been to replicate those unusual successes. It is a strategy that is destined to fail, however, as long as millions of Americans continue to demand the illicit substances that foreigners are willing and able to supply.

The Costs of Prohibition

The fact that drug-prohibition laws and policies cannot eradicate or even significantly reduce drug abuse is not necessarily a reason to repeal them. They do, after all, succeed in deterring many people from trying drugs, and they clearly reduce the availability and significantly increase the price of illegal drugs. These accomplishments alone might warrant retaining the drug laws, were it not for the fact that these same laws are also responsible for much of what Americans identify as the "drug problem." Here the analogies to alcohol and tobacco are worth noting. There is little question that we could reduce the health costs associated with use and abuse of alcohol and tobacco if we were to criminalize their production, sale, and possession. But no one believes that we could eliminate their use and abuse, that we could create an "alcohol-free" or "tobacco-free" country. Nor do most Americans believe that criminalizing the alcohol and tobacco markets would be a good idea. Their opposition stems largely from two beliefs: that adult Americans have the right to choose what substances they will consume and what risks they will take and that the costs of trying to coerce so many Americans to abstain from those substances would be enormous. It was the strength of these two beliefs that ultimately led to the repeal of Prohibition, and it is partly due to memories of that experience that criminalizing either alcohol or tobacco has little support today.

Consider the potential consequences of criminalizing the production, sale, and possession of all tobacco products. On the positive side, the number of people smoking tobacco would almost certainly decline, as would the health costs associated with tobacco consumption. Although the "forbidden fruit" syndrome would attract some people to cigarette smoking who would not otherwise have smoked, many more would likely be deterred by the criminal sanction, the moral standing of the law, the higher cost and unreliable quality of the illicit tobacco, and the difficulties involved in acquiring it. Non-smokers would rarely if ever be bothered by the irritating habits of their fellow citizens. The anti-tobacco laws would discourage some people from ever starting to smoke and would induce others to quit.

On the negative side, however, millions of Americans, including both tobacco addicts and recreational users, would no doubt defy the law, generating a massive underground market and billions in profits for organized criminals. Although some tobacco farmers would find other work, thousands more would become outlaws and continue to produce their crops covertly. Throughout Latin America, farmers and gangsters would rejoice at the opportunity to earn untold sums of gringo greenbacks, even as U.S. diplomats pressured foreign governments to cooperate with U.S. laws. Within the United States, government helicopters would spray herbicides on illicit tobacco fields; people would be rewarded by the government for informing on their neighbors who grow, sell, and smoke tobacco; urine tests would be employed to identify violators of the anti-tobacco laws; and a Tobacco Enforcement Administration (the T.E.A.) would employ undercover agents, informants, and wiretaps to uncover tobacco-law violators. Municipal, state, and federal judicial systems would be clogged with tobacco traffickers and "abusers." "Tobacco-related murders" would increase dramatically as criminal organizations competed with one another for turf and markets. Smoking would become an act of youthful rebellion, and no doubt some users would begin to experiment with more concentrated, potent, and dangerous forms of tobacco. Tobacco-related corruption would infect all levels of government, and respect for the law would decline noticeably. Government expenditures on tobacco-law enforcement would climb rapidly into the billions of dollars, even as budget balancers longingly recalled the almost ten billion dollars per year in tobacco taxes earned by the federal and state governments prior to prohibition. Finally, the state of North Carolina might even secede again from the Union.

This seemingly far-fetched tobacco-prohibition scenario is little more than an extrapolation based on the current situation with respect to marijuana, cocaine, and heroin. In many ways, our predicament resembles what actually happened during Prohibition. Prior to Prohibition, most Americans hoped that alcohol could be effectively banned by passing laws against its production and supply. During the early years of Prohibition, when drinking declined but millions of Americans nonetheless continued to drink, Prohibition's supporters placed their faith in tougher laws and more police and jails. After a few more years, however, increasing numbers of Americans began to realize that laws and policemen were unable to eliminate the smugglers, bootleggers, and illicit producers, as long as tens of millions of Americans continued to want to buy alcohol. At the same time, they saw that more laws and policemen seemed to generate more violence and corruption, more crowded courts and jails, wider disrespect for government and the law, and more power and profits for the gangsters. Repeal of Prohibition came to be seen not as a capitulation to Al Capone and his ilk but as a means of both putting the bootleggers out of business and eliminating most of the costs associated with the prohibition laws.

Today, Americans are faced with a dilemma similar to that confronted by our forebears sixty years ago. Demand for illicit drugs shows some signs of abating but no signs of declining significantly. Moreover, there are substantial reasons to doubt that tougher laws and policing have played an important role in reducing consumption. Supply, meanwhile, has not abated at all. Availability of illicit drugs, except for marijuana in some locales, remains high. Prices are dropping, even as potency increases. And the number of drug producers, smugglers, and dealers remains sizable, even as jails and prisons fill to overflowing. As was the case during Prohibition, the principal beneficiaries of current drug policies are the new and old organized-crime gangs. The principal victims, on the other hand, are not the drug dealers but the tens of millions of Americans who are worse off in one way or another as a consequence of the existence and failure of the drug-prohibition laws.

All public policies create beneficiaries and victims, both intended and unintended. When a public policy results in a disproportionate magnitude of unintended victims, there is good reason to reevaluate the assumptions and design of the policy. In the case of drug-prohibition policies, the intended beneficiaries are those individuals who would become drug abusers but for the existence and enforcement of the drug laws. The intended victims are those who traffic in illicit drugs and suffer the legal consequences. The unintended beneficiaries, conversely, are the drug producers and traffickers who profit handsomely from the illegality of the market, while avoiding arrest by the authorities and the violence perpetrated by other criminals. The unintended victims of drug-prohibition policies are rarely recognized as such, however. Viewed narrowly, they are the thirty million Americans who use illegal drugs, thereby risking loss of their jobs, imprisonment, and the damage done to health by ingesting illegally produced drugs; viewed broadly, they are all Americans, who pay the substantial costs of our present ill-considered policies, both as taxpayers and as the potential victims of crime. These unintended victims are generally thought to be victimized by the unintended beneficiaries (i.e., the drug dealers), when in fact it is the drug-prohibition policies themselves that are primarily responsible for their plight.

If law-enforcement efforts could succeed in significantly reducing either the supply of illicit drugs or the demand for them, we would probably have little need to seek alternative drug-control policies. But since those efforts have repeatedly failed to make much of a difference and show little indication of working better in the future, at this point we must focus greater attention on their costs. Unlike the demand and supply of illicit drugs, which have remained relatively indifferent to legislative initiatives, the costs of drug-enforcement measures can be affected—quite dramatically—by legislative measures. What tougher criminal sanctions and more police have failed to accomplish, in terms of reducing drug-related violence, corruption, death, and social decay, may well be better accomplished by legislative repeal of the drug laws and adoption of less punitive but more effective measures to prevent and treat substance abuse.

Costs to the Taxpayer

Since 1981, federal expenditures on drug enforcement have more than tripled—from less than one billion dollars a year to about three billion. According to the National Drug Enforcement Policy Board, the annual budgets of the Drug Enforcement Administration (DEA) and the Coast Guard have each risen during the past seven years from about \$220 million to roughly \$500 million. During the same period, FBI resources devoted to drug enforcement have increased from \$8 million a year to over \$100 million, U.S. Marshals resources from \$26 million to about \$80 million, U.S. Attorney resources from \$20 million to about \$100 million, State Department resources from \$35 million to \$100 million, U.S. Customs resources from \$180 million to over \$400 million, and Bureau of Prison resources from \$77 million to about \$300 million. Expenditures on drug control by the military and the intelligence agencies are more difficult to calculate, although by all accounts they have increased by at least the same magnitude and now total hundreds of millions of dollars per year. Even greater are the expenditures at lower levels of government. In a 1987 study for the U.S. Customs Service by Wharton Econometrics, state and local police were estimated to have devoted 18 percent of their total investigative resources, or close to five billion dollars, to drug-enforcement activities in 1986. This represented a 19 percent increase over the previous year's expenditures. All told, 1987 expenditures on all aspects of drug enforcement, from drug eradication in foreign countries to imprisonment of drug users and dealers in the United States, totaled at least ten billion dollars.

Of course, even ten billion dollars a year pales in comparison with expenditures on military defense. Of greater concern than the actual expenditures, however, has been the diversion of limited resources—including the time and energy of judges, prosecutors, and law-enforcement agents, as well as scarce prison space—from the prosecution and punishment of criminal activities that harm far more innocent victims than do violations of the drug laws. Drug-law violators account for approximately 10 percent of the roughly 800,000 inmates in state prisons and local jails and more than one-third of the 44,000 federal prison inmates. These proportions are expected to increase in coming years, even as total prison populations continue to rise dramatically. Among the 40,000 inmates in New York State prisons, drug-law violations surpassed first-degree robbery in 1987 as the number one cause of incarceration, accounting for 20 percent of the total prison population. The U.S. Sentencing Commission has estimated that, largely as a consequence of the Anti-Drug Act passed by Congress in 1986, the proportion of federal inmates incarcerated for drug violations will rise from one-third of the 44,000 prisoners sentenced to federal-prison terms today to one-half of the 100,000 to 150,000 federal prisoners anticipated in fifteen years. The direct costs of building and maintaining enough prisons to house this growing population are rising at an astronomical rate. The opportunity costs, in terms of alternative social expenditures forgone and other types of criminals not imprisoned, are perhaps even greater.

During each of the last few years, police made about 750,000 arrests for violations of the drug laws. Slightly more than three-quarters of these have not been for manufacturing or dealing drugs but solely for possession of an illicit drug, typically marijuana. (Those arrested, it is worth noting, represent little more than 2 percent of the thirty million Americans estimated to have used an illegal drug during the past year.) On the one hand, this has clogged many urban criminal-justice systems: in New York City, drug-law violations last year accounted for more than 40 percent of all felony indictments—up from 25 percent in 1985; in Washington, D.C., the figure was more than 50 percent. On the other hand, it has distracted criminal-justice officials from concentrating greater resources on violent offenses and property crimes. In many cities, law enforcement has become virtually synonymous with drug enforcement.

Drug laws typically have two effects on the market in illicit drugs. The first is to restrict the general availability and accessibility of illicit drugs, especially in locales where underground drug markets are small and isolated from the community. The second is to increase, often significantly, the price of illicit drugs to consumers. Since the costs of producing most illicit drugs are not much different from the costs of alcohol, tobacco, and coffee, most of the price paid for illicit substances is in effect a value-added tax created by their criminalization, which is enforced and supplemented by the law-enforcement establishment but collected by the drug traffickers. A report by Wharton Econometrics for the President's Commission on Organized Crime identified the sale of illicit drugs as the source of more than half of all organized-crime revenues in 1986, with the marijuana and heroin business each providing over seven billion dollars and the cocaine business over thirteen billion. By contrast, revenues from cigarette bootlegging, which persists principally because of differences among the states in their cigarette-tax rates, were estimated at 290 million dollars. If the marijuana, cocaine, and heroin markets were legal, state and federal governments would collect billions of dollars annually in tax revenues. Instead, they expend billions on what amounts to a subsidy of organized crime and unorganized criminals.

Drugs and Crime

The drug/crime connection is one that continues to resist coherent analysis, both because cause and effect are so difficult to distinguish and because the role of the drug-prohibition laws in causing and labeling "drug-related crime" is so often ignored. There are four possible connections between drugs and crime, at least three of which would be much diminished if the drug-prohibition laws were repealed. First, producing, selling, buying, and consuming strictly controlled and banned substances are crimes that occur billions of times each year in the United States alone. In the absence of drug-prohibition laws, these activities would obviously cease to be crimes. Selling drugs to children would, of course, continue to be criminal, and other evasions of government regulation of a legal market would continue to be prosecuted; but by and large the drug/crime connection that now accounts for all of the criminal-justice costs noted above would be severed.

Second, many illicit-drug users commit crimes such as robbery and burglary, as well as drug dealing, prostitution, and numbers running, to earn enough money to purchase the relatively high-priced illicit drugs. Unlike the millions of alcoholics who can support their habits for relatively modest amounts, many cocaine and heroin addicts spend hundreds and even thousands of dollars a week. If the drugs to which they are addicted were significantly cheaper—which would be the case if they were legalized—the number of crimes committed by drug addicts to pay for their habits would, in all likelihood, decline dramatically. Even if a legal-drug policy included the imposition of relatively high consumption taxes in order to discourage consumption, drug prices would probably still be lower than they are today.

The third drug/crime connection is the commission of crimes—violent crimes in particular—by people under the influence of illicit drugs. This connection seems to have the greatest impact upon the popular imagination. Clearly, some drugs do "cause" some people to commit crimes by reducing normal inhibitions, unleashing aggressive and other anti-social tendencies, and lessening the sense of responsibility. Cocaine, particularly in the form of crack, has gained such a reputation in recent years, just as heroin did in the 1960s and 1970s and marijuana did in the years before that. Crack's reputation for inspiring violent behavior may or may not be more deserved than those of marijuana and heroin; reliable evidence is not yet available. No illicit drug, however, is as widely associated with violent behavior as alcohol. According to Justice Department statistics, 54 percent of all jail inmates convicted of violent crimes in 1983 reported having used alcohol just prior to committing their offense. The impact of drug legalization on this drug/crime connection is the most difficult to predict. Much would depend on overall rates of drug abuse and changes in the nature of consumption, both of which are impossible to predict. It is worth noting, however, that a shift in consumption from alcohol to marijuana would almost certainly contribute to a decline in violent behavior.

The fourth drug/crime link is the violent, intimidating, and corrupting behavior of the drug traffickers. Illegal markets tend to breed violence—not only because they attract criminally minded individuals but also because participants in the market have no resort to legal institutions to resolve their disputes. During Prohibition, violent struggles between bootlegging gangs and hijackings of booze-laden trucks and sea vessels were frequent and notorious occurrences. Today's equivalents are the booby traps that surround some marijuana fields, the pirates of the Caribbean looking to rip off drug-laden vessels en route to the shores of the United States, and the machine-gun battles and executions carried out by drug lords—all of which occasionally kill innocent people. Most law-enforcement officials agree that the dramatic increases in urban murder rates during the past few years can be explained almost entirely by the rise in drug-dealer killings.

Perhaps the most unfortunate victims of the drug-prohibition policies have been the law-abiding residents of America's ghettos. These policies have largely proven futile in deterring large numbers of ghetto dwellers from becoming drug abusers, but they do account for much of what ghetto residents identify as the drug problem. In many neighborhoods, it often seems to be the aggressive gun-toting drug dealers who upset law-abiding residents far more than the addicts nodding out in doorways. Other residents, however, perceive the drug dealers as heroes and successful role models. In impoverished neighborhoods, they often stand out as symbols of success to children who see no other options. At the same time, the increasingly harsh criminal penalties imposed on adult drug dealers have led to the widespread recruitment of juveniles by drug traffickers. Formerly, children started dealing drugs only after they had been using them for a while; today the sequence is often reversed: many children start using illegal drugs now only after working for older drug dealers. And the juvenile-justice system offers no realistic options for dealing with this growing problem.

The conspicuous failure of law-enforcement agencies to deal with this drug/crime connection is probably most responsible for the demoralization of neighborhoods and police departments alike. Intensive police crackdowns in urban neighborhoods do little more than chase the menace a short distance away to infect new areas. By contrast, legalization of the drug market would drive the drug-dealing business off the streets and out of apartment buildings and into legal, government-regulated, tax-paying stores. It would also force many of the gun-toting dealers out of business and would convert others into legitimate businessmen. Some, of course, would turn to other types of criminal activities, just as some of the bootleggers did following Prohibition's repeal. Gone, however, would be the unparalleled financial temptations that lure so many people from all sectors of society into the drug-dealing business.

The Costs of Corruption

All vice-control efforts are particularly susceptible to corruption, but none so much as drug enforcement. When police accept bribes from drug dealers, no victim exists to complain to the authorities. Even when police extort money and drugs from traffickers and dealers, the latter are in no position to report the corrupt officers. What makes drug enforcement especially vulnerable to corruption are the tremendous amounts of money involved in the business. Today, many law-enforcement officials believe that police corruption is more pervasive than at any time since Prohibition. In Miami, dozens of law-enforcement officials have been charged with accepting bribes, stealing from drug dealers, and even dealing drugs themselves. Throughout many small towns and rural communities in Georgia, where drug smugglers en route from Mexico, the Caribbean, and Latin America drop their loads of cocaine and marijuana, dozens of sheriffs have been implicated in drug-related corruption. In New York, drug-related corruption in one Brooklyn police precinct has generated the city's most far-reaching police-corruption scandal since the 1960s. More than a hundred cases of drug-related corruption are now prosecuted each year in state and federal courts. Every one of the federal law-enforcement agencies charged with drug-enforcement responsibilities has seen an agent implicated in drug-related corruption.

It is not difficult to explain the growing pervasiveness of drug-related corruption. The financial temptations are enormous relative to other opportunities, legitimate or illegitimate. Little effort is required. Many police officers are demoralized by the scope of the drug traffic, their sense that many citizens are indifferent, and the fact that many sectors of society do not even appreciate their efforts —as well as the fact that many of the drug dealers who are arrested do not remain in prison. Some police also recognize that enforcing the drug laws does not protect victims from predators so much as it regulates an illicit market that cannot be suppressed but can be kept underground. In every respect, the analogy to Prohibition is apt. Repealing the drug-prohibition laws would dramatically reduce police corruption. By contrast, the measures currently being proposed to deal with the growing problem, including better funded and more aggressive internal investigations, offer relatively little promise.

Among the most difficult costs to evaluate are those that relate to the widespread defiance of the drug-prohibition laws: the effects of labeling as criminals the tens of millions of people who use drugs illicitly, subjecting them to the risks of criminal sanction, and obligating many of these same people to enter into relationships with drug dealers (who may be criminals in many more senses of the word) in order to purchase their drugs; the cynicism that such laws generate toward other laws and the law in general; and the sense of hostility and suspicion that many otherwise law-abiding individuals feel toward law-enforcement officials. It was costs such as these that strongly influenced many of Prohibition's more conservative opponents.

Physical and Moral Costs

Perhaps the most paradoxical consequence of the drug laws is the tremendous harm they cause to the millions of drug users who have not been deterred from using illicit drugs in the first place. Nothing resembling an underground Food and Drug Administration has arisen to impose quality control on the illegal drug market and provide users with accurate information on the drugs they consume. Imagine that Americans could not tell whether a bottle of wine contained 6 percent, 30 percent, or 90 percent alcohol, or whether an aspirin tablet contained 5 or 500 grams of aspirin. Imagine, too, that no controls existed to prevent winemakers from diluting their product with methanol and other dangerous impurities and that vineyards and tobacco fields were fertilized with harmful substances by ignorant growers and sprayed with poisonous herbicides by government agents. Fewer people would use such substances, but more of those who did would get sick. Some would die.

The above scenario describes, of course, the current state of the illicit drug market. Many marijuana smokers are worse off for having smoked cannabis that was grown with dangerous fertilizers, sprayed with the herbicide paraquat, or mixed with more dangerous substances. Consumers of heroin and the various synthetic substances sold on the street face even severer consequences, including fatal overdoses and poisonings from unexpectedly potent or impure drug supplies. More often than not, the quality of a drug addict's life depends greatly upon his or her access to reliable supplies. Drug-enforcement operations that succeed in temporarily disrupting supply networks are thus a double-edged sword: they encourage some addicts to seek admission into drug-treatment programs, but they oblige others to seek out new and hence less reliable suppliers; the result is that more, not fewer, drug-related emergencies and deaths occur.

Today, over 50 percent of all people with AIDS in New York City, New Jersey, and many other parts of the country, as well as the vast majority of AIDS-infected heterosexuals throughout the country, have contracted the disease directly or indirectly through illegal intravenous drug use. Reports have emerged of drug dealers' beginning to provide clean syringes together with their illegal drugs. But even as other governments around the world actively attempt to limit the spread of AIDS by and among drug users by instituting free syringe-exchange programs, state and municipal governments in the United States resist following suit, arguing that to do so would "encourage" or "condone" the use of illegal drugs. Only in January 1988 did New York City approve such a program on a very limited and experimental basis. At the same time, drug-treatment programs remain notoriously underfunded, turning away tens of thousands of addicts seeking help, even as billions of dollars more are spent to arrest, prosecute, and imprison illegal drug sellers and users. In what may represent a sign of shifting priorities, the President's Commission on AIDS, in its March 1988 report, emphasized the importance of making drug-treatment programs available to all in need of them. In all likelihood, however, the criminal-justice agencies will continue to receive the greatest share of drug-control funds.

Most Americans perceive the drug problem as a moral issue and draw a moral distinction between use of the illicit drugs and use of alcohol and tobacco. Yet when one subjects this distinction to reasoned analysis, it quickly disintegrates. The most consistent moral perspective of those who favor drug laws is that of the Mormons and the Puritans, who regard as immoral any intake of substances to alter one's state of consciousness or otherwise cause pleasure: they forbid not only the illicit drugs and alcohol but also tobacco, caffeine, and even chocolate. The vast majority of Americans are hardly so consistent with respect to the propriety of their pleasures. Yet once one acknowledges that there is nothing immoral about drinking alcohol or smoking tobacco for non-medicinal purposes, it becomes difficult to condemn the consumption of marijuana, cocaine, and other substances on moral grounds. The "moral" condemnation of some substances and not others proves to be little more than a prejudice in favor of some drugs and against others.

The same false distinction is drawn with respect to those who provide the psychoactive substances to users and abusers alike. If degrees of immorality were measured by the levels of harm caused by one's products, the "traffickers" in tobacco and alcohol would be vilified as the most evil of all substance purveyors. That they are perceived instead as respected members of our community, while providers of the no more dangerous illicit substances are punished with long prison sentences, says much about the prejudices of most Americans with respect to psychoactive substances but little about the morality or immorality of purveyors' activities.

Much the same is true of gun salesmen. Most of the consumers of their products use them safely; a minority, however, end up shooting either themselves or someone else. Can we hold the gun salesman morally culpable for the harm that probably would not have occurred but for his existence? Most people say no, except perhaps where the salesman clearly knew that his product would be used to commit a crime. Yet in the case of those who sell illicit substances to willing customers, the providers are deemed not only legally guilty but also morally reprehensible. The law does not require any demonstration that the dealer knew of a specific harm to follow; indeed, it does not require any evidence at all of harm having resulted from the sale. Rather, the law is predicated on the assumption that harm will inevitably follow. Despite the patent falsity of that assumption, it persists as the underlying justification for the drug laws.

Although a valid moral distinction cannot be drawn between the licit and the illicit psychoactive substances, one can point to a different kind of moral justification for the drug laws: they arguably reflect a paternalistic obligation to protect those in danger of succumbing to their own weaknesses. If drugs were legally available, most people would either abstain from using them or would use them responsibly and in moderation. A minority without self-restraint, however, would end up harming themselves if the substances were more readily available. Therefore, the majority has a moral obligation to deny itself legal access to certain substances because of the plight of the minority. This obligation is presumably greatest when children are included among the minority.

At least in principle, this argument seems to provide the strongest moral justification for the drug laws. But ultimately the moral quality of laws must be judged not by how those laws are intended to work in principle but by how they function in practice. When laws intended to serve a moral end inflict great damage on innocent parties, we must rethink our moral position.

Because drug-law violations do not create victims with an interest in notifying the police, drug-enforcement agents rely heavily on undercover operations, electronic surveillance, and information provided by informants. These techniques are indispensable to effective law enforcement, but they are also among the least palatable investigative methods employed by the police. The same is true of drug testing: it may be useful and even necessary for determining liability in accidents, but it also threatens and undermines the right of privacy to which many Americans believe they are entitled. There are good reasons for requiring that such measures be used sparingly.

Equally disturbing are the increasingly vocal calls for people to inform not only on drug dealers but also on neighbors, friends, and even family members who use illicit drugs. Government calls on people not only to "just say no" but also to report those who have not heeded the message. Intolerance of illicit-drug use and users is heralded not only as an indispensable ingredient in the war against drugs but also as a mark of good citizenship. Certainly every society requires citizens to assist in the enforcement of criminal laws. But societies—particularly democratic and pluralistic ones—also rely strongly on an ethic of tolerance toward those who are different but do no harm to others. Overzealous enforcement of the drug laws risks undermining that ethic and encouraging the creation of a society of informants. This results in an immorality that is far more dangerous in its own way than that associated with the use of illicit drugs.

The Benefits of Legalization

Repealing the drug-prohibition laws promises tremendous advantages. Between reduced government expenditures on enforcing drug laws and new tax revenue from legal drug production and sales, public treasuries would enjoy a net benefit of at least ten billion dollars a year, and possibly much more. The quality of urban life would rise significantly. Homicide rates would decline. So would robbery and burglary rates. Organized criminal groups, particularly the newer ones that have yet to diversify out of drugs, would be dealt a devastating setback. The police, prosecutors, and courts would focus their resources on combatting the types of crimes that people cannot walk away from. More ghetto residents would turn their backs on criminal careers and seek out legitimate opportunities instead. And the health and quality of life of many drug users—and even drug abusers—would improve significantly. . . .

JAMES Q. WILSON

Against the Legalization of Drugs

James Q. Wilson is Collins Professor of Management and Public Policy at the University of California at Los Angeles. (Source: Reprinted from Commentary *[February 1990], by permission; all rights reserved.)*

QUESTIONS FOR REFLECTION

1. Wilson contends that the war on drugs has been successful. What evidence does he adduce in support of this claim?
2. Wilson believes that legalizing drugs would increase drug use significantly, and he supports his view with an economic argument. What is that argument? Do you find it persuasive?
3. Wilson talks about heroin and cocaine, but not marijuana. Which of his arguments would apply to marijuana, in your view? Which would not?
4. Wilson rejects the view that cocaine use is a "victimless crime," that is, a self-regarding act. Why?
5. Wilson does not accept Mill's harm principle; he advocates a rather different conception of individual liberty and societal responsibility. What is Wilson's conception? What role does it play in his argument? Compare Wilson's conception to that of Burke.
6. Many advocates of legalization recommend treatment over incarceration. Wilson, however, is skeptical of drug treatment, at least in the absence of laws outlawing drug use. Why? Do you find his arguments persuasive?

In 1972, the President appointed me chairman of the National Advisory Council for Drug Abuse Prevention. Created by Congress, the Council was charged with providing guidance on how best to coordinate the national war on drugs. (Yes, we called it a war then, too.) In those days, the drug we were chiefly concerned with was heroin. When I took office, heroin use had been increasing dramatically. Everybody was worried that this increase would continue. Such phrases as "heroin epidemic" were commonplace.

That same year, the eminent economist Milton Friedman published an essay in *Newsweek* in which he called for legalizing heroin. His argument was on two grounds: as a matter of ethics, the government has no right to tell people not to use heroin (or to drink or to commit suicide); as a matter of economics, the prohibition of drug use imposes costs on society that far exceed the benefits. Others, such as the psychoanalyst Thomas Szasz, made the same argument.

We did not take Friedman's advice. (Government commissions rarely do.) I do not recall that we even discussed legalizing heroin, though we did discuss (but did not take action on) legalizing a drug, cocaine, that many people then argued was benign. Our marching orders were to figure out how to win the war on heroin, not to run up the white flag of surrender.

That was 1972. Today, we have the same number of heroin addicts that we had then—half a million, give or take a few thousand. Having that many heroin addicts is no trivial matter; these people deserve our attention. But not having had an increase in that number for over fifteen years is also something that deserves our attention. What happened to the "heroin epidemic" that many people once thought would overwhelm us?

The facts are clear: a more or less stable pool of heroin addicts had been getting older, with relatively few new recruits. In 1976 the average age of heroin users who appeared in hospital emergency rooms was about twenty-seven; ten years later it was thirty-two. More than two-thirds of all heroin users appearing in emergency rooms are now over the age of thirty. Back in the early 1970's, when heroin got onto the national political agenda, the typical heroin addict was much younger, often a teenager. Household surveys show the same thing—the rate of opiate use (which includes heroin) has been flat for the better part of two decades. More fine-grained studies of inner-city neighborhoods confirm this. John Boyle and Ann Brunswick found that the percentage of young blacks in Harlem who used heroin fell from 8 percent in 1970–71 to about 3 percent in 1975–76.

Why did heroin lose its appeal for young people? When the young blacks in Harlem were asked why they stopped, more than half mentioned "trouble with the law" or "high cost" (and high cost is, of course, directly the result of law enforcement). Two-thirds said that heroin hurt their health; nearly all said they had had a bad experience with it. We need not rely, however, simply on what they said. In New York City in 1973–75, the street price of heroin rose dramatically and its purity sharply declined, probably as a result of the heroin shortage caused by the success of the Turkish government in reducing the supply of opium base and of the French government in closing down heroin-processing laboratories located in and around Marseilles. These were short-lived gains for, just as Friedman predicted, alternative sources of supply—mostly in Mexico—quickly emerged. But the three-year heroin shortage interrupted the easy recruitment of new users.

Health and related problems were no doubt part of the reason for the reduced flow of recruits. Over the preceding years, Harlem youth had watched as more and more heroin users died of overdoses, were poisoned by adulterated doses, or acquired hepatitis from dirty needles. The word got around: heroin can kill you. By 1974 new hepatitis cases and drug-overdose deaths had dropped to a fraction of what they had been in 1970.

Alas, treatment did not seem to explain much of the cessation in drug use. Treatment programs can and do help heroin addicts, but treatment did not explain the drop in the number of *new* users (who by definition had never been in treatment) nor even much of the reduction in the number of experienced users.

No one knows how much of the decline to attribute to personal observation as opposed to high prices or reduced supply. But other evidence suggests strongly that price and supply played a large role. In 1972 the National Advisory Council was especially worried by the prospect that U.S. servicemen returning to this country from Vietnam would bring their heroin habits with them. Fortunately, a brilliant study by Lee Robins of Washington University in St. Louis put that fear to rest. She measured drug use of Vietnam veterans shortly after they had returned home. Though many had used heroin regularly while in Southeast Asia, most gave up the habit when back in the United States. The reason: here, heroin was less available and sanctions on its use were more pronounced. Of course, if a veteran had been willing to pay enough—which might have meant traveling to another city and would certainly have meant making an illegal contact with a disreputable dealer in a threatening neighborhood in order to acquire a (possibly) dangerous dose—he could have sustained his drug habit. Most veterans were unwilling to pay this price, and so their drug use declined or disappeared.

Reliving the Past

Suppose we had taken Friedman's advice in 1972. What would have happened? We cannot be entirely certain, but at a minimum we would have placed the young heroin addicts (and, above all, the prospective addicts) in a very different position from the one in which they actually found themselves. Heroin would have been legal. Its price would have been reduced by 95 percent (minus whatever we chose to recover in taxes). Now that it could be sold by the same people who make aspirin, its quality would have been assured—no poisons, no adulterants. Sterile hypodermic needles would have been readily available at the neighborhood drugstore, probably at the same counter where the heroin was sold. No need to travel to big cities or unfamiliar neighborhoods—heroin could have been purchased anywhere, perhaps by mail order.

There would no longer have been any financial or medical reason to avoid heroin use. Anybody could have afforded it. We might have tried to prevent children from buying it, but as we have learned from our efforts to prevent minors from buying alcohol and tobacco, young people have a way of penetrating markets theoretically reserved for adults. Returning Vietnam veterans would have discovered that Omaha and Raleigh had been converted into the pharmaceutical equivalent of Saigon.

Under these circumstances, can we doubt for a moment that heroin use would have grown exponentially? Or that a vastly larger supply of new users would have been recruited? Professor Friedman is a Nobel Prize-winning economist whose understanding of market forces is profound. What did he think would happen to consumption under his legalized regime? Here are his words: "Legalizing drugs might increase the number of addicts, but it is not clear that it would. Forbidden fruit is attractive, particularly to the young."

Really? I suppose that we should expect no increase in Porsche sales if we cut the price by 95 percent, no increase in whiskey sales if we cut the price by a comparable amount—because young people only want fast cars and strong liquor when they are "forbidden." Perhaps Friedman's uncharacteristic lapse from the obvious implications of price theory can be explained by a misunderstanding of how drug users are recruited. In his 1972 essay he said that "drug addicts are deliberately made by pushers, who give likely prospects their first few doses free." If drugs were legal it would not pay anybody to produce addicts, because everybody would buy from the cheapest source. But as every drug expert knows, pushers do not produce addicts. Friends or acquaintances do. In fact, pushers are usually reluctant to deal with non-users because a non-user could be an undercover cop. Drug use spreads in the same way any fad or fashion spreads: somebody who is already a user urges his friends to try, or simply shows already-eager friends how to do it.

But we need not rely on speculation, however plausible, that lowered prices and more abundant supplies would have increased heroin usage. Great Britain once followed such a policy and with almost exactly those results. Until the mid-1960's, British physicians were allowed to prescribe heroin to certain classes of addicts. (Possessing these drugs without a doctor's prescription remained a criminal offense.) For many years this policy worked well enough because the addict patients were typically middle-class people who had become dependent on opiate painkillers while undergoing hospital treatment. There was no drug culture. The British system worked for many years, not because it prevented drug abuse, but because there was no problem of drug abuse that would test the system.

All that changed in the 1960's. A few unscrupulous doctors began passing out heroin in wholesale amounts. One doctor prescribed almost 600,000 heroin tablets—that is, over thirteen pounds—in just one year. A youthful drug culture emerged with a demand for drugs far different from that of the older addicts. As a result, the British government required doctors to refer users to government-run clinics to receive their heroin.

But the shift to clinics did not curtail the growth in heroin use. Throughout the 1960's the number of addicts increased—the late John Kaplan of Stanford estimated by fivefold—in part as a result of the diversion of heroin from clinic patients to new users on the streets. An addict would bargain with the clinic doctor over how big a dose he would receive. The patient wanted as much as he could get, the doctor wanted to give as little as was needed. The patient had an advantage in this conflict because the doctor could not be certain how much was really needed. Many patients would use some of their "maintenance" dose and sell the remaining part to friends, thereby recruiting new addicts. As the clinics learned of this, they began to shift their treatment away from heroin and toward methadone, an addictive drug that, when taken orally, does not produce a "high" but will block the withdrawal pains associated with heroin abstinence.

Whether what happened in England in the 1960's was a mini-epidemic or an epidemic depends on whether one looks at numbers or at rates of change. Compared to the United States, the numbers were small. In 1960 there were 68 heroin addicts known to the British government; by 1968 there were 2,000 in treatment and many more who refused treatment. (They would refuse in part because they did not want to get methadone at a clinic if they could get heroin on the street.) Richard Hartnoll estimates that the actual number of addicts in England is five times the number officially registered. At a minimum, the number of British addicts increased by thirtyfold in ten years; the actual increase may have been much larger.

In the early 1980's the numbers began to rise again, and this time nobody doubted that a real epidemic was at hand. The increase was estimated to be 40 percent a year. By 1982 there were thought to be 20,000 heroin users in London alone. Geoffrey Pearson reports that many cities—Glasgow, Liverpool, Manchester, and Sheffield among them—were now experiencing a drug problem that once had been largely confined to London. The problem, again, was supply. The country was being flooded with cheap, high-quality heroin, first from Iran and then from Southeast Asia.

The United States began the 1960's with a much larger number of heroin addicts and probably a bigger at-risk population than was the case in Great Britain. Even though it would be foolhardy to suppose that the British system, if installed here, would have worked the same way or with the same results, it would be equally foolhardy to suppose that a combination of heroin available from leaky clinics and from street dealers who faced only minimal law-enforcement risks would not have produced a much greater increase in heroin use than we actually experienced. My guess is that if we had allowed either doctors or clinics to prescribe heroin, we would have had far worse results than were produced in Britain, if for no other reason than the vastly larger number of addicts with which we began. We would have had to find some way to police thousands (not scores) of physicians and hundreds (not dozens) of clinics. If the British civil service found it difficult to keep heroin in the hands of addicts and out of the hands of recruits when it was dealing with a few hundred people, how well would the American civil service have accomplished the same tasks when dealing with tens of thousands of people?

Back to the Future

Now cocaine, especially in its potent form, crack, is the focus of attention. Now as in 1972 the government is trying to reduce its use. Now as then some people are advocating legalization. Is there any more reason to yield to those arguments today than there was almost two decades ago?

I think not. If we had yielded in 1972 we almost certainly would have had today a permanent population of several million, not several hundred thousand, heroin addicts. If we yield now we will have a far more serious problem with cocaine.

Crack is worse than heroin by almost any measure. Heroin produces a pleasant drowsiness and, if hygienically administered, has only the physical side effects of constipation and sexual impotence. Regular heroin use incapacitates many users, especially poor ones, for any productive work or social responsibility. They will sit nodding on a street corner, helpless, but at least harmless. By contrast, regular cocaine use leaves the user neither helpless nor harmless. When smoked (as with crack) or injected, cocaine produces instant, intense, and short-lived euphoria. The experience generates a powerful desire to repeat it. If the drug is readily available, repeat use will occur. Those people who progress to "bingeing" on cocaine become devoted to the drug and its effects to the exclusion of almost all other considerations—job, family, children, sleep, food, even sex. Dr. Frank Gawin at Yale and Dr. Everett Ellinwood at Duke report that a substantial percentage of all high-dose, binge users become uninhibited, impulsive, hypersexual, compulsive, irritable, and hyperactive. Their moods vacillate dramatically, leading at times to violence and homicide.

Women are much more likely to use crack than heroin, and if they are pregnant, the effects on their babies are tragic. Douglas Besharov, who has been following the effects of drugs on infants for twenty years, writes that nothing he learned about heroin prepared him for the devastation of cocaine. Cocaine harms the fetus and can lead to physical deformities or neurological damage. Some crack babies have for all practical purposes suffered a disabling stroke while still in the womb. The long-term consequences of this brain damage are lowered cognitive ability and the onset of mood disorders. Besharov estimates that about 30,000 to 50,000 such babies are born every year, about 7,000 in New York City alone. There may be ways to treat such infants, but from everything we now know the treatment will be long, difficult, and expensive. Worse, the mothers who are most likely to produce crack babies are precisely the ones who, because of poverty or temperament, are least able and willing to obtain such treatment. In fact, anecdotal evidence suggests that crack mothers are likely to abuse their infants.

The notion that abusing drugs such as cocaine is a "victimless crime" is not only absurd but dangerous. Even ignoring the fetal drug syndrome, crack-dependent people are, like heroin addicts, individuals who regularly victimize their children by neglect, their spouses by improvidence, their employers by lethargy, and their coworkers by carelessness. Society is not and could never be a collection of autonomous individuals. We all have a stake in ensuring that each of us displays a minimal level of dignity, responsibility, and empathy. We cannot, of course, coerce people into goodness, but we can and should insist that some standards must be met if society itself—on which the very existence of the human personality depends—is to persist. Drawing the line that defines those standards is difficult and contentious, but if crack and heroin use do not fall below it, what does?

The advocates of legalization will respond by suggesting that my picture is overdrawn. Ethan Nadelmann of Princeton argues that the risk of legalization is less than most people suppose. Over 20 million Americans between the ages of eighteen and twenty-five have tried cocaine (according to a government survey), but only a quarter million use it daily. From this Nadelmann concludes that at most 3 percent of all young people who try cocaine develop a problem with it. The implication is clear: make the drug legal and we only have to worry about 3 percent of our youth.

The implication rests on a logical fallacy and a factual error. The fallacy is this: the percentage of occasional cocaine users who become binge users *when the drug is illegal* (and thus expensive and hard to find) tells us nothing about the percentage who will become dependent when the drug is legal (and thus cheap and abundant). Drs. Gawin and Ellinwood report, in common with several other researchers, that controlled or occasional use of cocaine changes to compulsive and frequent use "when access to the drug increases" or when the user switches from snorting to smoking. More cocaine more potently administered alters, perhaps sharply, the proportion of "controlled" users who become heavy users.

The factual error is this: the federal survey Nadelmann quotes was done in 1985, *before* crack had become common. Thus the probability of becoming dependent on cocaine was derived from the responses of users who snorted the drug. The speed and potency of cocaine's action increases dramatically when it is smoked. We do not yet know how greatly the advent of crack increases the risk of dependency, but all the clinical evidence suggests that the increase is likely to be large.

It is possible that some people will not become heavy users even when the drug is readily available in its most potent form. So far there are no scientific grounds for predicting who will and who will not become dependent. Neither socioeconomic background nor personality traits differentiate between casual and intensive users. Thus, the only way to settle the question of who is correct about the effect of easy availability on drug use, Nadelmann or Gawin and Ellinwood, is to try it and see. But that social experiment is so risky as to be no experiment at all, for if cocaine is legalized and if the rate of its abusive use increases dramatically, there is no way to put the genie back in the bottle, and it is not a kindly genie.

Have We Lost?

Many people who agree that there are risks in legalizing cocaine or heroin still favor it because, they think, we have lost the war on drugs. "Nothing we have done has worked" and the current federal policy is just "more of the same." Whatever the costs of greater drug use, surely they would be less than the costs of our present, failed efforts.

That is exactly what I was told in 1972—and heroin is not quite as bad a drug as cocaine. We did not surrender and we did not lose. We did not win, either. What the nation accomplished then was what most efforts to save people from themselves accomplish: the problem was contained and the number of victims minimized, all at a considerable cost in law enforcement and increased crime. Was the cost worth it? I think so, but others may disagree. What are the lives of would-be addicts worth? I recall some people saying to me then, "Let them kill themselves." I was appalled. Happily, such views did not prevail.

Have we lost today? Not at all. High-rate cocaine use is not commonplace. The National Institute of Drug Abuse (NIDA) reports that less than 5 percent of high-school seniors used cocaine within the last thirty days. Of course this survey misses young people who have dropped out of school and miscounts those who lie on the questionnaire, but even if we inflate the NIDA estimate by some plausible percentage, it is still not much above 5 percent. Medical examiners reported in 1987 that about 1,500 died from cocaine use; hospital emergency rooms reported about 30,000 admissions related to cocaine abuse.

These are not small numbers, but neither are they evidence of a nationwide plague that threatens to engulf us all. Moreover, cities vary greatly in the proportion of people who are involved with cocaine. To get city-level data we need to turn to drug tests carried out on arrested persons, who obviously are more likely to be drug users than the average citizen. The National Institute of Justice, through its Drug Use Forecasting (DUF) project, collects urinalysis data on arrests in 22 cities. As we have already seen, opiate (chiefly heroin) use has been flat or declining in most of these cities over the last decade. Cocaine use has gone up sharply, but with great variation among cities. New York, Philadelphia, and Washington, D.C., all report that two-thirds or more of their arrestees tested positive for cocaine, but in Portland, San Antonio, and Indianapolis the percentage was one-third or less.

In some neighborhoods, of course, matters have reached crisis proportions. Gangs control the streets, shootings terrorize residents, and drug-dealing occurs in plain view. The police seem barely able to contain matters. But in these neighborhoods—unlike at Palo Alto cocktail parties—the people are not calling for legalization, they are calling for help. And often not much help has come. Many cities are willing to do almost anything about the drug problem except spend more money on it. The federal government cannot change that; only local voters and politicians can. It is not clear that they will.

It took about ten years to contain heroin. We have had experience with crack for only about three or four years. Each year we spend perhaps $11 billion on law enforcement (and some of that goes to deal with marijuana) and perhaps $2 billion on treatment. Large sums, but not sums that should lead anyone to say, "We just can't afford this any more."

The illegality of drugs increases crime, partly because some users turn to crime to pay for their habits, partly because some users are stimulated by certain drugs (such as crack or PCP) to act more violently or ruthlessly than they otherwise would, and partly because criminal organizations seeking to control drug supplies use force to manage their markets. These also are serious costs, but no one knows how much they would be reduced if drugs were legalized. Addicts would no longer steal to pay black-market prices for drugs, a real gain. But some, perhaps a great deal, of that gain would be offset by the great increase in the number of addicts. These people, nodding on heroin or living in the delusion-ridden high of cocaine, would hardly be ideal employees. Many would steal simply to support themselves, since snatch-and-grab, opportunistic crime can be managed even by people unable to hold a regular job or plan an elaborate crime. Those British addicts who get their supplies from government clinics are not models of law-abiding decency. Most are in crime, and though their per-capita rate of criminality may be lower thanks to the cheapness of their drugs, the total volume of crime they produce may be quite large. Of course, society could decide to support all unemployable addicts on welfare, but that would mean that gains from lowered rates of crime would have to be offset by large increases in welfare budgets.

Proponents of legalization claim that the costs of having more addicts around would be largely if not entirely offset by having more money available with which to treat and care for them. The money would come from taxes levied on the sale of heroin and cocaine.

To obtain this fiscal dividend, however, legalization's supporters must first solve an economic dilemma. If they want to raise a lot of money to pay for welfare and treatment, the tax rate on the drugs will have to be quite high. Even if they themselves do not want a high rate, the politicians' love of "sin taxes" would probably guarantee that it would be high anyway. But the higher the tax, the higher the price of the drug, and the higher the price the greater the likelihood that addicts will turn to crime to find the money for it and that criminal organizations will be formed to sell tax-free drugs at below-market rates. If we managed to keep taxes (and thus prices) low, we would get that much less money to pay for welfare and treatment and more people could afford to become addicts. There may be an optimal tax rate for drugs that maximizes revenue while minimizing crime, bootlegging, and the recruitment of new addicts, but our experience with alcohol does not suggest that we know how to find it.

The Benefits of Illegality

The advocates of legalization find nothing to be said in favor of the current system except, possibly, that it keeps the number of addicts smaller than it would otherwise be. In fact, the benefits are more substantial than that.

First, treatment. All the talk about providing "treatment on demand" implies that there is a demand for treatment. That is not quite right. There are some drug-dependent people who genuinely want treatment and will remain in it if offered; they should receive it. But there are far more who want only short-term help after a bad crash; once stabilized and bathed, they are back on the street again, hustling. And even many of the addicts who enroll in a program honestly wanting help drop out after a short while when they discover that help takes time and commitment. Drug-dependent people have very short time horizons and a weak capacity for commitment. These two groups—those looking for a quick fix and those unable to stick with a long-term fix—are not easily helped. Even if we increase the number of treatment slots—as we should—we would have to do something to make treatment more effective.

One thing that can often make it more effective is compulsion. Douglas Anglin of UCLA, in common with many other researchers, has found that the longer one stays in a treatment program, the better the chances of a reduction in drug dependency. But he, again like most other researchers, has found that drop-out rates are high. He has also found, however, that patients who enter treatment under legal compulsion stay in the program longer than those not subject to such pressure. His research on the California civil-commitment program, for example, found that heroin users involved with its required drug-testing program had over the long term a lower rate of heroin use than similar addicts who were free of such constraints. If for many addicts compulsion is a useful component of treatment, it is not clear how compulsion could be achieved in a society in which purchasing, possessing, and using the drug were legal. It could be managed, I suppose, but I would not want to have to answer the challenge from the American Civil Liberties Union that it is wrong to compel a person to undergo treatment for consuming a legal commodity.

Next, education. We are now investing substantially in drug-education programs in the schools. Though we do not yet know for certain what will work, there are some promising leads. But I wonder how credible such programs would be if they were aimed at dissuading children from doing something perfectly legal. We could, of course, treat drug education like smoking education: inhaling crack and inhaling tobacco are both legal, but you should not do it because it is bad for you. That tobacco is bad for you is easily shown; the Surgeon General has seen to that. But what do we say about crack? It is pleasurable, but devoting yourself to so much pleasure is not a good idea (though perfectly legal)? Unlike tobacco, cocaine will not give you cancer or emphysema, but it will lead you to neglect your duties to family, job, and neighborhood? Everybody is doing cocaine, but you should not?

Again, it might be possible under a legalized regime to have effective drug-prevention programs, but their effectiveness would depend heavily, I think, on first having decided that cocaine use, like tobacco use, is purely a matter of practical consequences; no fundamental moral significance attaches to either. But if we believe—as I do—that dependency on certain mind-altering drugs is a moral issue and that their illegality rests in part on their immorality, then legalizing them undercuts, if it does not eliminate altogether, the moral message.

That message is at the root of the distinction we now make between nicotine and cocaine. Both are highly addictive; both have harmful physical effects. But we treat the two drugs differently, not simply because nicotine is so widely used as to be beyond the reach of effective prohibition, but because its use does not destroy the user's essential humanity. Tobacco shortens one's life, cocaine debases it. Nicotine alters one's habits, cocaine alters one's soul. The heavy use of crack, unlike the heavy use of tobacco, corrodes those natural sentiments of sympathy and duty that constitute our human nature and make possible our social life. To say, as does Nadelmann, that distinguishing morally between tobacco and cocaine is "little more than a transient prejudice" is close to saying that morality itself is but a prejudice.

The Alcohol Problem

Now we have arrived where many arguments about legalizing drugs begin: is there any reason to treat heroin and cocaine differently from the way we treat alcohol?

There is no easy answer to that question because, as with so many human problems, one cannot decide simply on the basis either of moral principles or of individual consequences; one has to temper any policy by a common-sense judgment of what is possible. Alcohol, like heroin, cocaine, PCP, and marijuana, is a drug—that is, a mood-altering substance—and consumed to excess it certainly has harmful consequences: auto accidents, barroom fights, bedroom shootings. It is also, for some people, addictive. We cannot confidently compare the addictive powers of these drugs, but the best evidence suggests that crack and heroin are much more addictive than alcohol.

Many people, Nadelmann included, argue that since the health and financial costs of alcohol abuse are so much higher than those of cocaine or heroin abuse, it is hypocritical folly to devote our efforts to preventing cocaine or drug use. But as Mark Kleiman of Harvard has pointed out, this comparison is quite misleading. What Nadelmann is doing is showing that a *legalized* drug (alcohol) produces greater social harm than *illegal* ones (cocaine and heroin). But of course. Suppose that in the 1920's we had made heroin and cocaine legal and alcohol illegal. Can anyone doubt that Nadelmann would now be writing that it is folly to continue our ban on alcohol because cocaine and heroin are so much more harmful?

And let there be no doubt about it—widespread

heroin and cocaine use are associated with all manner of ills. Thomas Bewley found that the mortality rate of British heroin addicts in 1968 was 28 times as high as the death rate of the same age group of non-addicts, even though in England at the time an addict could obtain free or low-cost heroin and clean needles from British clinics. Perform the following mental experiment: suppose we legalized heroin and cocaine in this country. In what proportion of auto fatalities would the state police report that the driver was nodding off on heroin or recklessly driving on a coke high? In what proportion of spouse-assault and child-abuse cases would the local police report that crack was involved? In what proportion of industrial accidents would safety investigators report that the forklift or drill-press operator was in a drug-induced stupor or frenzy? We do not know exactly what the proportion would be, but anyone who asserts that it would not be much higher than it is now would have to believe that these drugs have little appeal except when they are illegal. And that is nonsense.

An advocate of legalization might concede that social harm—perhaps harm equivalent to that already produced by alcohol—would follow from making cocaine and heroin generally available. But at least, he might add, we would have the problem "out in the open" where it could be treated as a matter of "public health." That is well and good, *if* we knew how to treat—that is, cure—heroin and cocaine abuse. But we do not know how to do it for all the people who would need such help. We are having only limited success in coping with chronic alcoholics. Addictive behavior is immensely difficult to change, and the best methods for changing it—living in drug-free therapeutic communities, becoming faithful members of Alcoholics Anonymous or Narcotics Anonymous—require great personal commitment, a quality that is, alas, in short supply among the very persons—young people, disadvantaged people—who are often most at risk for addiction.

Suppose that today we had, not 15 million alcohol abusers, but half a million. Suppose that we already knew what we have learned from our long experience with the widespread use of alcohol. Would we make whiskey legal? I do not know, but I suspect there would be a lively debate. The Surgeon General would remind us of the risks alcohol poses to pregnant women. The National Highway Traffic Safety Administration would point to the likelihood of more highway fatalities caused by drunk drivers. The Food and Drug Administration might find that there is a non-trivial increase in cancer associated with alcohol consumption. At the same time the police would report great difficulty in keeping illegal whiskey out of our cities, officers being corrupted by bootleggers, and alcohol addicts often resorting to crime to feed their habits. Libertarians, for their part, would argue that every citizen has a right to drink anything he wishes and that drinking is, in any event, a "victimless crime."

However the debate might turn out, the central fact would be that the problem was still, at that point, a small one. The government cannot legislate away the addictive tendencies in all of us, nor can it remove completely even the most dangerous addictive substances. But it can cope with harms when the harms are still manageable.

Science and Addiction

One advantage of containing a problem while it is still containable is that it buys time for science to learn more about it and perhaps to discover a cure. Almost unnoticed in the current debate over legalizing drugs is that basic science has made rapid strides in identifying the underlying neurological processes involved in some forms of addiction. Stimulants such as cocaine and amphetamines alter the way certain brain cells communicate with one another. That alteration is complex and not entirely understood, but in simplified form it involves modifying the way in which a neurotransmitter called dopamine sends signals from one cell to another.

When dopamine crosses the synapse between two cells, it is in effect carrying a message from the first cell to activate the second one. In certain parts of the brain that message is experienced as pleasure. After the message is delivered, the dopamine returns to the first cell. Cocaine apparently blocks this return, or "reuptake," so that the excited cell and others nearby continue to send pleasure messages. When the exaggerated high produced by cocaine-influenced dopamine finally ends, the brain cells may (in ways that are still a matter of dispute) suffer from an extreme lack of dopamine, thereby making the individual unable to experience any pleasure at all. This would explain why cocaine users often feel so depressed after enjoying the drug. Stimulants may also affect the way in which other neurotransmitters, such as serotonin and noradrenaline, operate.

Whatever the exact mechanism may be, once it is identified it becomes possible to use drugs to block either the effect of cocaine or its tendency to produce dependency. There have already been experiments using desipramine, imipramine, bromocriptine, carbamazepine, and other chemicals. There are some promising results.

Tragically, we spend very little on such research, and the agencies funding it have not in the past occupied very influential or visible posts in the federal bureaucracy. If there is one aspect of the "war on drugs" metaphor that I dislike, it is its tendency to focus attention almost exclusively on the troops in the trenches, whether engaged in enforcement or treatment, and away from the research-and-development efforts back on the home front where the war may ultimately be decided.

I believe that the prospects of scientists in controlling addiction will be strongly influenced by the size and character of the problem they face. If the problem is a few hundred thousand chronic, high-dose users of an illegal product, the chances of making a difference at a reasonable cost will be much greater than if the problem is a few million chronic users of legal substances. Once a drug is legal, not only will its use increase but many of those who then use it will prefer the drug to the treatment: they will want the pleasure, whatever the cost to themselves or their families, and they will resist—probably successfully—any effort to wean them away from experiencing the high that comes from inhaling a legal substance.

If I Am Wrong . . .

No one can know what our society would be like if we changed the law to make access to cocaine, heroin, and PCP easier. I believe, for reasons given, that the result would be a sharp increase in use, a more widespread degradation of the human personality, and a greater rate of accidents and violence.

I may be wrong. If I am, then we will needlessly have incurred heavy costs in law enforcement and some forms of criminality. But if I am right, and the legalizers prevail anyway, then we will have consigned millions of people, hundreds of thousands of infants, and hundreds of neighborhoods to a life of oblivion and disease. To the lives and families destroyed by alcohol we will have added countless more destroyed by cocaine, heroin, PCP, and whatever else a basement scientist can invent.

Human character is formed by society; indeed, human character is inconceivable without society, and good character is less likely in a bad society. Will we, in the name of an abstract doctrine of radical individualism, and with the false comfort of suspect predictions, decide to take the chance that somehow individual decency can survive amid a more general level of deregulation?

I think not. The American people are too wise for that, whatever the academic essayists and cocktail-party pundits may say. But if Americans today are less wise than I suppose, then Americans at some future time will look back on us now and wonder, what kind of people were they that they could have done such a thing?

DOUGLAS HUSAK

from *Drugs and Rights*

Douglas Husak is Associate Professor of Philosophy at Rutgers University. (Source: From Drugs and Rights, *Cambridge University Press. Copyright © 1992 by Cambridge University Press. Reprinted by permission. Notes have been omitted.)*

QUESTIONS FOR REFLECTION

1. Evaluate Husak's analogy between drug use and other recreational activities.
2. How does Husak argue that addiction does not undermine autonomy?
3. Husak rejects voluntary slavery as a model for addiction. Why? Do you agree?

DRUGS AND HARM TO USERS

. . . The paternalistic case for LAD* can be compared and contrasted with the paternalistic case for other recreational activities that pose significant risks to adults who engage in them. These activities include boxing, mountain climbing, race car driving, skiing, eating fatty foods, playing football, driving a car with or without a seat belt, riding a motorcycle with or without a helmet, sunbathing, playing "Russian roulette," consuming saccharin, participating in rodeos, bungee-jumping, and a host of others. At present, some but not all of these activities are and ought to be prohibited by law. Does the principle of autonomy apply to and protect the decision to engage in any of these risky behaviors? If so, defenders of LAD can be asked to point to a morally relevant difference between drug use and the recreational activities that autonomy protects. But if the principle of autonomy does not apply to or protect the decision to engage in any of these risky behaviors, this strategy fails to offer much insight into the justifiability of LAD. All analogical arguments are limited in this respect.

Suppose that autonomy does not apply to or protect any of these recreational activities. According to this school of thought, . . . adults do not have a moral *right* to eat ice cream after all. Instead, adults are merely *permitted* to eat ice cream, but their behavior is unprotected by a right derived from the principle of autonomy. Again, rights are important because they cannot be defeated by ordinary utilitarian reasons. In other words, a utilitarian rationale would be sufficient to justify prohibiting eating ice cream, if persons were merely permitted to do so. A utilitarian rationale would be insufficient, however, to justify prohibiting eating ice cream, if this behavior were protected by a right. If this account of the significance of rights is correct, it would be crucial to decide whether persons have a moral right to eat ice cream, in the event that its consumption turned out to cause a substantial risk to health and a net balance of disutility.

Examples of behavior that is and is not protected by a moral right are easy to provide. The

* LAD stands for "laws against drugs."—ED.

behavior governed by most traffic regulations is unprotected by a right. Suppose that persons are initially permitted to drive in either direction along Euclid Avenue but that subsequent studies conclude that highway safety would be facilitated, and congestion relieved, by making the avenue one-way east. Almost everyone believes that these ordinary utilitarian reasons would be sufficient to prohibit persons from driving west along Euclid Avenue. But many other examples are not comparable to traffic regulations. Suppose that the practice of a religion or the exercise of speech produced a net balance of disutility. This supposition would not justify prohibiting them. Unlike the behavior governed by traffic regulations, speech and religious expression are protected by moral rights. . . .

Perhaps the most familiar reason that will be given to differentiate the use of illegal drugs from many other recreational activities is that drug use is *more* risky than members of the comparison class that are and ought to be permitted. According to version (a) of this response, the principle of autonomy applies to and protects the decision to take a risk, unless the extent of this risk exceeds a given critical threshold. No protection is afforded after the amount of a risk exceeds this threshold. According to version (b) of this response, the principle of autonomy applies to and protects the decision to take any risk, however great. But after the extent of a risk exceeds a given critical threshold, the protection afforded by the principle of autonomy is outweighed by the need to prevent persons from harming themselves.

Neither strategy to exempt very risky behavior from the scope of protection by the principle of autonomy is very plausible. One would anticipate that the principle of autonomy would allow adults to decide for themselves what extent of risk to assume. Still, the perception that drugs are especially harmful to users has contributed greatly to public hostility toward them. At least two questions must be confronted if this defense of LAD is to have any prospects for success. First, how should this critical threshold of risk be characterized? Second, which drugs, if any, create risks to users that exceed this critical threshold? These questions cannot be answered with any precision. But enough progress can be made to indicate that this strategy is unlikely to support anything remotely resembling the status quo about LAD.

A common standard to compare the extent of risk of very different kinds of activities is not easily constructed. Some risky activities result in broken bones that usually heal; others cause a deterioration in mental functions that may or may not be reversed; still others progressively damage soft tissue. No single statistic can reduce the extent of risk to a common denominator, and I do not pretend to do so here.

Yet insight can be gained by a quick comparison of the fatality records for legal and illegal drugs. These data, long available, should surprise only those who have succumbed to drug hysteria without bothering to examine the empirical evidence. There seems to be no correlation (except perhaps an inverse one) between the illegality of a drug and the likelihood that it will cause death. Nicotine causes many more deaths (between 350,000 and 430,000 annually) than all other drugs combined, both legal and illegal, and the toll is still rising. Next highest in number of fatalities is alcohol (between 50,000 and 200,000 annual deaths). These data become only slightly less alarming when adjusted for the fact that nicotine and alcohol are used more widely than illegal drugs. When the risk of a given drug is expressed as a ratio of the number of fatalities per weekly users, nicotine (83.3 deaths per 10,000 weekly users) is still far and away the most deadly drug. About 25 percent of all adolescents who smoke a pack of cigarettes daily lose, on average, ten to fifteen years of their lives. Illegal drugs seem benign by comparison, although the data on their long-term effects are less reliable. Significantly, no known fatalities have ever been attributed to the consumption of marijuana, despite its use by 51 million Americans in the past fifteen years. Cocaine, even when smoked in the form of crack, was cited as the primary cause of death in only 2,496 cases in 1989, and there is reason to suspect that this figure may be exaggerated. Since 862,000 Americans reported using cocaine weekly in 1988, the number of deaths per

10,000 weekly users is about 29. This figure is roughly comparable to alcohol (perhaps 20.6 deaths per 10,000 weekly users).

If the rationale for LAD is to prevent persons from killing themselves, it seems apparent that the state has made the wrong recreational drugs illegal. Any number of commentators have concluded that "the data demonstrate that for the population as a whole, the health problems caused by the currently legal recreational drugs are far more serious than those caused by the currently illegal recreational drugs."

It is unlikely that anyone would react to these statistics by demanding that the use of both nicotine and alcohol should be punished. Even though some historical revisionists have begun to pronounce the country's past experiment with the prohibition of alcohol as "a success," no leading figure has recommended a return to that era. What is less clear is whether the universal unwillingness to reinstate the prohibition of alcohol is based on the perception that the experiment "failed" as social policy or is due to the conviction that adults have a moral right to drink. Many theorists would adopt both positions. After all, a constitutional amendment was required to ban alcohol in 1919, suggesting that prohibition could not be implemented by ordinary democratic procedures.

When placed in perspective, illegal drug use is not an extraordinarily dangerous recreational activity. The risk of fatality encountered by users of illegal recreational drugs is not unlike that faced in many permitted recreational pursuits. About 4,200 Americans died in motorcycle accidents in 1987, even though there are fewer motorcycles than cocaine users. The risk of recreational drug use may be roughly comparable to that of mountain climbing in general, but it is far smaller than the risk of an assault on the Himalayas in particular (which killed 47 of the 1,609 non-Nepalese who attempted it). Furthermore, illegal drug use is probably a good deal less hazardous than race car driving or boxing.

Surely it is possible to imagine a recreational drug that poses a greater risk of death to users than any of these activities. Sometimes drugs are likened to the Sirens described in Homer's *Odyssey*, who lured all sailors to their doom until Odysseus devised a clever scheme to listen to their songs while avoiding harm. But no such drug exists today. If such a recreational drug were to be created, and the principle of autonomy did not apply to or protect activities that exceed a given critical threshold of risk, prohibitions of such a drug would be justifiable. . . .

Addiction, Slavery, and Autonomy

Prohibitions of addictive substances that give rise to severe withdrawal symptoms are not the only instances in which philosophers have argued that the need to protect autonomy justifies paternalistic interference. John Stuart Mill denied that a voluntary agreement to sell oneself into slavery should be enforceable, because it would involve a total forfeiture of autonomy. Mill concluded that

> by selling himself for a slave, [the individual] abdicates his liberty. . . . He therefore defeats, in his own case, the very purpose which is the justification of allowing him to dispose of himself. . . . The principle of freedom cannot require that he should be free not to be free. It is not freedom, to be allowed to alienate his freedom. These reasons, the force of which is so conspicuous in this peculiar case, are evidently of far wider application.

Mill's example of voluntary slavery has generated far more theoretical discussion than is warranted by its practical significance. To the best of my knowledge, no one has ever attempted to enforce such a bizarre agreement. Yet this example is important because it is "of far wider application." Even the most confirmed critics of paternalism might balk at enforcing this agreement. If paternalistic interference with a voluntary choice is ever justified to protect autonomy, it is justified here.

For present purposes, voluntary slavery agreements are significant because of their alleged affinities with decisions to use addictive drugs. According to Goodin,

> If the product is truly addictive, then we have no more reason to respect a person's voluntary choice (however well-informed) to abandon his future volition than we have for respecting a person's voluntary choice (however well-informed) to sell himself into slavery.

Goodin concludes that the desirability of safeguarding autonomy provides no reason to protect either decision.

In this section I will argue that the case for prohibiting the use of addictive drugs is much weaker than the case for prohibiting voluntary slavery. If I am correct, those who are persuaded by Mill's example might still reject LAD, in virtue of their several differences. And those who are unpersuaded by Mill's example should be even more resistant to LAD.

It is helpful to make the examples that I will contrast more believable. First, suppose that a wealthy Legree offers Smith one million dollars to become his slave. Smith, a person of moderate means, is inclined to accept this offer because of his beneficence and generosity; he would like to provide a first-rate education and upscale life-style for each of his several children. If it is clear that Smith is sane and that his consent is truly voluntary, should the state prevent him from binding himself for his own good? The second example, to be contrasted with the first, is more familiar. Jones would like to use an addictive recreational drug. If he is sane and his consent is truly voluntary, should the state prevent him from using the drug for his own good?

Feinberg would not create an exception to his opposition to paternalism in the case of the voluntary slave. According to Feinberg, the fact that a voluntary decision to become a slave involves a permanent, irrevocable, and total forfeiture of autonomy is not a sufficient reason to prohibit it. He observes, "If one is not in principle 'free not to be free' then he does not enjoy de jure autonomy." Analogously, the supposed loss of autonomy involved in addiction is not a sufficient reason to support LAD.

Feinberg may be correct. But I am less interested in addressing the more basic question of whether the law should enforce the agreement between Legree and Smith than in differentiating this issue from the justifiability of LAD. The point of this section is to describe both the conceptual and empirical differences between these two examples. I will argue that addiction and voluntary slavery seem comparable only when the addictive process is misdescribed. I will attempt to characterize what addiction would have to be like before the two examples become relevantly similar. In other words, I will attempt to identify the properties a drug would have to possess before the reasons to prohibit it are as strong as those against voluntary slavery. Alternatively, I will modify the slavery example to make it more like addiction. When the slavery example is modified in these respects, reservations about enforcing Smith's agreement are weakened. Whatever is said about the justifiability of preventing Smith from enslaving himself, I will conclude that the case against allowing Jones to use an addictive drug is much weaker.

Notice that this argument again presupposes that drugs are addictive in a sense in which other recreational activities are not. Although a few other recreational activities are said to be addictive, they are never portrayed as reducing participants to a state of slavery. No one suggests that skiing should be prohibited because, if permitted, it would enslave many adults who tried it. Anyone who endorses this argument as a justification for LAD must describe what is unique about drug addiction that makes the slavery metaphor so compelling.

Feinberg notes two significant differences between the slavery example and *any* instance of criminal paternalism. First, the slavery example does not involve criminal penalties. Neither Smith nor Legree is punished for having made their agreement. Instead, the state simply refuses to enforce their promise in the event of a breach. Jones, in contrast, is punished for his choice. Surely a much higher standard of justification is required to warrant the use of the penal sanction than to make contractual remedies unavailable. Second, the failure of the state to enforce their agreement does not prevent either Smith or Legree from acting according to his preferences by establishing a de facto arrangement of slavery. Smith is free to obey Legree's orders, and Legree is free to command him. However, the state will not compel Smith to continue as a slave should he change his mind. Jones, in contrast, is prohibited by LAD from acting according to his preferences.

Other important differences between these two examples are not common to each instance of criminal paternalism. I will explore six of these differences at greater length. The first difference has already been discussed, and I will only summarize it here. Many of the evils of addiction that invite comparisons with slavery are a product of the illegality of drugs and not of their pharmacology. Persons addicted to illegal drugs deplete their bank accounts to pay for their supplies, go to extraordinary lengths to locate dealers, and avoid whatever medical treatment they might need for fear that their condition will come to the attention of authorities. If drugs were readily available, no one would think of addicts as enslaved to them.

The second significant difference between these examples is that the decision to sell oneself into voluntary slavery involves an *immediate* surrender of autonomy. In other words, autonomy is lost at the instant the agreement becomes effective. Smith is not given the opportunity to experiment with slavery for a while and postpone his final decision about whether to become enslaved. If Smith were afforded this opportunity, and allowed to enter into slavery gradually, there would be somewhat less reason not to enforce his agreement.

But addiction is not similarly instantaneous. Jones will not become addicted upon his initial use of a drug. This point is both conceptual and empirical. Many criteria of addiction (or of the "dependence syndrome") as construed in the preceding section cannot be satisfied by a single incidence of drug use. A drug user cannot "desire to stop drug use in the face of continued use," or display "a relatively stereotyped pattern of drug-taking behavior," or "[reinstate] the syndrome after a period of abstinence" by using a drug for the first time. A person might exhibit a few of the remaining criteria of addiction after a single exposure to a drug. Jones might immediately acquire a tolerance, afford drugs a psychological centrality relative to his other interests, or experience withdrawal after the effects of the drug recede. He would probably be unaware that he has developed a tolerance, or is prepared to make great sacrifices to obtain the drug again, or is undergoing withdrawal. Nonetheless, each of these criteria might be satisfied.

I have argued that most of the criteria of addiction that can be present after a single episode of drug use are irrelevant to the question of how the use of an addictive drug affects autonomy. The phenomena of tolerance and psychological dependence are not grounds for concluding that behavior is nonautonomous. However, there is no conceptual reason why the pain of withdrawal could not be so severe after a single incident that persons would be powerless to resist further use. If so, addiction would be immediate.

As a matter of fact, however, no existing recreational drug creates such extreme withdrawal symptoms so quickly. I have already expressed doubts that withdrawal symptoms from drugs that have been used over long periods of time are sufficiently severe to warrant the judgment that continued use is nonautonomous. Withdrawal symptoms after a single episode of drug use are practically nonexistent. If a new drug were created that triggered terrible withdrawal symptoms after a single use, the case for prohibiting Jones from taking it would be comparable, ceteris paribus, to the case for not enforcing Smith's agreement. However, existing recreational drugs addict persons much more slowly.

Many persons try drugs and conclude that they do not want to try them again. Some persons do not enjoy their experience enough to repeat it. Others have satisfied their curiosity and have no further motive to persist. Still others abstain from additional experimentation because they enjoyed their initial exposure too much and do not want to run the risk of addiction. But whatever their motives for failing to continue, no comparable opportunity is available to Smith.

Goodin appears to recognize this difference between Jones's choice and Smith's agreement. He concedes that the initial decision of the recreational drug user might be autonomous. Subsequent decisions, however, are said not to be comparable. Goodin contends: "The real force of the addiction findings . . . is to undercut the claim that there is any *continuing* consent to the risks involved. . . . Once you were hooked, you lost the capacity to consent in any meaningful sense on a continuing basis."

But Goodin has overlooked a crucial series of points. Admittedly, Smith and Jones are similarly situated at the time that they decide whether to take their initial steps. Suppose also that their positions are comparable after Smith has become enslaved and Jones has become "hooked." But what about the intermediary stages, when Jones decides whether to use a drug for a second, ninth, or twentieth time? Notice that the same question cannot be raised about Smith; there *are* no intermediary stages to examine. One simply cannot compare the beginning point, at which the agent contemplates becoming a slave or using an addictive substance, with the end point, at which he has become a slave or an addict, and conclude that there are no important differences between the two. The crucial difference is that there are any number of intermediate points in the drug example but not in the slavery case.

A third important difference between LAD and the prohibition of voluntary slavery is that Smith's decision is *irrevocable*. This fact is crucial to the unwillingness to enforce his promise. If Smith were able to reconsider his decision and resume a normal life, reservations about allowing him to be enslaved would all but vanish.

Addiction, however, can be temporary. Although addictions are notoriously difficult to break, persons can and do overcome them every day. Few individuals who are addicted to an illegal drug remain addicts for the duration of their lives. Many heroin addicts permanently give up heroin after a relatively brief period of addiction. Even the most committed heroin users frequently "mature out" of addiction after a few years. Many crack addicts quit because they do not want to lose their jobs, alienate their friends, neglect their children, or ruin their social status.

The fact that many addicts "kick" their habits is well-known. Why, then, would anyone compare addiction to a permanent state of slavery? Perhaps there are misconceptions about the difficulty in overcoming addiction. It might be thought that just as slaves can be emancipated, so too can addiction be overcome, but only with the help of treatment.

This preconception cannot withstand empirical scrutiny, however. Because of their concern with health, the importance of a personal relationship, or their perception that they have "hit bottom," large numbers of addicts succeed in quitting even the most addictive drugs. Many persons "revoke" their addiction without the benefit of a treatment program. "Spontaneous" recoveries from addiction to opiates, alcohol, tobacco, and cocaine are well documented. Some of the more spectacular examples were provided by Vietnam War veterans who had been heroin addicts during the war. The vast majority of these addicts did not continue their use of heroin upon returning home, and only a handful required treatment to quit. In addition, only a tiny percentage of hospital patients who regularly receive more powerful doses of opiates than those available on the streets ever become addicted or remain addicted after release. Quite simply, addiction need not be a permanent condition.

A fourth important difference between slavery and addiction involves the probability of the undesirable outcome in each example. The use of addictive substances does not create a certainty of addiction. Many studies have shown that persons (sometimes called "chippers") are able to use addictive drugs over long periods of time in a controlled, non-abusive way, without ever becoming addicted. Although the percentages differ for various drugs, most users of what are generally considered to be the most addictive and dangerous substances do not become addicts. A majority of the persons who have ever tried *any* illegal drug have stopped using it. Perhaps these facts have not been widely publicized because of a fear that knowledge among prospective users would reduce their inhibitions against experimentation.

Consider cocaine. Empirical studies indicate that most persons control their intake, using cocaine during leisure hours or on special occasions. Statistics reinforce this finding. Few of the 21 to 25 million Americans who have tried cocaine have become addicts. Although 8 million people reported using cocaine at least once in 1988, only

862,000 used the drug at least once a week, and a mere 320,000 reported using it daily. Thus, daily users of cocaine constitute less than 5 percent of all persons who use it annually and less than 2 percent of persons who have ever tried it. These are not the statistics one would expect if cocaine addicted everyone who sampled it.

These figures do not seem to differ radically when cocaine is smoked in the form of crack. According to one estimate, approximately one of every six persons who tries crack becomes a crack addict. According to another survey, about 9 percent of current crack users (persons who have used crack in the last month) are heavy users (persons who have used crack twenty or more times in the last month). Some theorists contend that at any given time about 10 percent of cocaine and heroin users can be classified as addicts, that is, about the same percentage as drinkers of alcohol who can be classified as alcoholics. Nicotine is the drug with the highest percentage of current users who are addicts; the figure may be as high as 90 percent. The exact ratio of addicts to users, however, is less important than the general conclusion to be drawn from this figure. The use of addictive recreational drugs creates only a possibility, not a probability, and clearly not a certainty, that addiction will result.

Mark Kleiman and Aaron Saiger reach a more pessimistic conclusion from these same data. They maintain that the ratio of one crack addict for every six users is "about as bad as it could be." They reason that if the ratio were higher, fewer persons would experiment and run the risk of addiction; if the ratio were lower, crack would be less socially disruptive. But whether this figure is "as bad as it could be" depends on the argumentative purpose for which it is employed. A ratio of one to six is not so bad in the context of comparing crack use to slavery. The comparable ratio in the slavery example is six times worse: Every person who enters into a slavery agreement becomes enslaved. Smith's consent does not merely create a possibility that Legree will enslave him; it creates a certainty.

Opinions about the legitimacy of the slavery example might change if it were modified to reflect this fact. Suppose that Smith were offered one million dollars in exchange for a 5 percent or 10 percent chance that he would become enslaved. This gamble appears more rational, and less repugnant. I am unclear about whether this modification is persuasive in allowing Legree to enforce his agreement, but surely it is a relevant factor.

A fifth difference is that Smith's agreement subjects him to a *continuous* state of slavery. His status as a slave is uninterrupted. Had Smith negotiated permission from Legree to take several extended vacations, his agreement would seem less objectionable. He might have agreed to become a slave only on weekends or holidays, otherwise leading a relatively normal life. Again, I am unclear about how much of a difference this modification makes to the judgment about whether Smith's agreement should be enforceable, but I am confident that it has importance.

Addiction, by way of contrast, is seldom continuous. Heroin addicts commonly undergo periods of semivoluntary abstinence. Less than one-half of the addicts on the street for a year will have used an opiate daily throughout that period. Sometimes addicts interrupt their heroin use to lower their tolerance, so that they can eventually resume consumption at a lower, cheaper, and more euphoric level. This behavior has no analogue in the case of slavery.

A sixth and final difference between these two examples contrasts the plight of the slave with that of the addict. Slavery is a dreadful state. We are loathe to allow Legree to enslave Smith because we imagine that slavery may include torture, humiliation, and working conditions that no person should be made to endure. After all, Smith has given Legree carte blanche to subject him to every kind of indignity. If we could be assured that Legree's treatment of Smith would be humane, involving working conditions no more terrible than those in typical factories, we would become more willing to enforce their agreement.

Comparisons between addiction and enslavement to a sadistic Legree become apt only when the horrors of addiction are grossly exaggerated. The zombielike image of the addict has been perpetuated by our government. Time and time again, the judiciary has presented a parody of the drug addict. Perhaps the most extreme example is the caricature described by Justice Douglas in 1962:

> To be a confirmed drug addict is to be one of the walking dead. . . . The teeth have rotted out; the appetite is lost and the stomach and intestines don't function properly. . . . Good traits of character disappear and bad ones emerge. Sex organs become affected. Veins collapse and livid purplish scars remain. Boils and abscesses plague the skin; gnawing pain racks the body. Nerves snap; vicious twitching develops. Imaginary and fantastic fears blight the mind and sometimes complete insanity results. Often times, too, death comes—much too early in life. . . . Such is the torment of being a drug addict; such is the plague of being one of the walking dead.

Small wonder that the Court concluded that punishment for such a condition was tantamount to punishment for a disease and thus was unconstitutional according to the Eighth Amendment's prohibition of cruel and unusual punishment. If typical cases of drug addiction conformed to this pathetic description, sympathies for paternalistic restrictions on drug use would be overwhelming.

Media portrayals of heavy drug users reinforce this dreadful stereotype. Television and movie depictions of recreational drug use follow a predictable script. Users initially believe that drugs are "cool," are confident that they can quit anytime, become helplessly addicted, squander their fortunes, turn to crime, abandon their loved ones, and either die a miserable death or are miraculously saved by heroic efforts. These case histories exist. But no effort is made to inform the public that these scenarios are atypical. No media exposure is afforded to moderate, successful, long-term drug users. This media bias is not inadvertent. Lorne Michaels, the producer of the irreverent "Saturday Night Live," admits that "the policy of NBC now is that the only references to drugs must be negative."

Even so, the public has ample reason to abandon this exaggerated stereotype of drug addiction. Many professional athletes have been exposed as drug addicts, and few remind anyone of a zombie. No one can know whether George Rogers was realizing his full potential during the football season in which his staggering cocaine habit came to the attention of the press. But his opponents did not confuse him with one of the walking dead while Rogers led the National Football League in rushing that year.

Empirical research simply does not support this terrible stereotype of drug addiction. Most drug addicts lead relatively normal lives. According to the U.S. Department of Labor, 77 percent of "serious cocaine users" are regularly employed. Bennett has cited this statistic to urge business leaders to join the "front" in the "fight" against drugs. But this statistic can also be used to undermine the dreadful portrayal of drug addiction. It is hard to imagine how the caricature of the drug addict described by Justice Douglas could be gainfully employed.

Despite these six important differences between drug use and slavery, one remaining dissimilarity between Jones's use of an addictive drug and Smith's attempt to enslave himself seems to provide a better reason to oppose the former than the latter. Smith, it will be recalled, gains one million dollars if he is allowed to act according to his preference. Everyone should understand why he is at least tempted by Legree's offer. But what has Jones gained of comparable value? A new pleasurable experience? Is this trivial gain sufficient to run the risk of addiction?

These questions illustrate the importance of the earlier distinction between formal and substantive conceptions of autonomy. Much of the point of opposing paternalism is to prevent the state, through the coercive apparatus of the criminal law, from deciding what persons should value. Jones, like Smith, would prefer to be free to decide for himself whether the prospective gains of his choice outweigh its disadvantages. Suppose that the original slavery example is altered so that Smith's family is not rewarded in exchange for Smith's agreement to become enslaved. Instead, Smith attempts to enslave himself to express his unbounded loyalty to Legree. To what extent is this modification significant? Once it is clear that Smith is sane and his agreement is voluntary, I doubt that the details of his motive should matter much in deciding whether the state should allow him to be bound by his agreement.

If the examples of Smith and Jones are really as dissimilar as I have indicated, why has drug addiction been misleadingly portrayed as an immediate, irrevocable, certain, continuous, and awful state? No single answer is satisfactory. The entire field of drug research has frequently subordinated scientific objectivity to political agendas in the effort to prove preconceived biases and justify punitive responses. In addition, the nonusing public, health care professionals, and law enforcement officials gain most of their experience with drug use by dealing with worst-case scenarios. Addicts who do not conform to this extreme stereotype are less likely to come to the attention of health practitioners or police, and they are rarely identified as heavy drug users by ordinary citizens. Studies of drug addicts have tended to focus on persons with the greatest problems. Because of the tremendous stigma associated with drug use, addicts who depart from this worst-case scenario are inhibited from discussing how their experience with drugs may have been favorable.

The contrasts between the addiction and slavery examples indicate the several respects in which decisions about the justifiability of LAD require sensitivity to the delicate process of drawing lines. Several questions are unresolved. How quickly must withdrawal symptoms become severe before a given drug should be prohibited? What percentage of addicts must be unable to overcome their addictions before a drug should be banned? How many users of an addictive substance must become addicts before criminal penalties are justifiable? To what extent must addiction to a drug be continuous before its use is outlawed? How terrible must addiction be before it is so bad that persons should be protected from it? I have no precise answers. These questions identify what pharmacological and sociological evidence about drugs and drug users is relevant to issues about moral rights.

No drug prohibitionist has indicated, to my knowledge, that any of these issues is important to the case in favor of LAD. It would be too charitable to conclude that the prohibitionists' thinking about LAD fails to take moral rights seriously. More accurately, their thinking about LAD fails to take account of moral rights at all.

I have argued that any support for LAD drawn from comparisons between addiction and slavery depends on controversial empirical assumptions that are seldom articulated and generalizes from worst-case scenarios that fail to conform to the reality of typical drug use. Even if the autonomy principle does not protect an adult's "freedom to be unfree," the attempt to exempt drug use from the scope of the principle of autonomy by regarding it as a form of slavery is a gross distortion. The genuine struggles of real slaves throughout history are demeaned by this comparison. . . .

Pornography

Most philosophers defend freedom of thought, of speech, and of the press. Some, like Milton and Mill, are strongly committed to these freedoms; others, like Burke, acknowledge that they are goods, but believe that they must be balanced against other goods. Nevertheless, virtually no one believes that these freedoms are completely unrestricted. Slander, libel, false advertising, harassment, inciting to riot, and public endangerment—shouting "Fire!" in a crowded theater, for example—have often been held up as exceptions. Thus the problem of determining the proper limits of these freedoms arises.

Pornography raises especially difficult questions about limits on freedom of thought, speech, and the press. The exceptions mentioned above are often thought to be exceptions because they risk or cause harm that outweighs their values as communications. Many people believe pornography to be harmful and base their opposition to it on that ground. But any harms caused by pornography are subtler and harder to detect than those of inciting to riot, for example. Consequently, the question of whether pornography is harmful has become an important focus of debate.

Also, the harm done by a speaker is usually weighed against the value of the communication. It is harder to slander a public official than a private citizen, for example, because the public's need for information about officials of government is much greater than its need for information about you or me; communication about the beliefs and behavior of public officials has greater value than communications about the rest of us. But what does pornography communicate? Often, it is hard to discern any message at all. Is pornography ever communication? These problems make weighing the value of a piece of pornography against its harmful effects very difficult.

Moreover, most of the arguments that Milton and Mill advance in favor of free speech rest on the supposition that speech communicates something that might be true or false. Mill argues that an opinion might be true; that, even if false, it might contain part of the truth; and that, even if totally false, its combat with the truth helps keep the truth alive. This argument makes sense for opinions, for propositions or bits of information that might be true or false. But does it make any sense applied to *Sex Orgies Illustrated?* Or *Deep Throat?* Or a *Playboy* centerfold? If not, on what does the case for freedom of pornographic speech rest?

The United States Supreme Court, in *Miller* v. *California,* decided that the government may regulate pornographic materials, banning those that are obscene. The Court moreover proposed criteria for determining whether something is obscene: (a) it must, judged by the average person applying contemporary community standards, appeal to a prurient (that is, arousing and unwholesome) interest in sex; (b) it must depict or describe sexual conduct in a patently offensive way; and (c) it must lack serious literary, artistic, political, or scientific value. The first two criteria pertain to harm; the third, to lack of any positive communicative value that might balance the harm.

Dissenters to the decisions have argued that sexual expression deserves protection against government interference. Some hold that such an expression may have positive value for individuals that outweighs any harm it causes; some claim that freedoms of thought, speech, and the press are all forms of freedom of expression, which is what properly defines the limits of government authority. Others believe that there is no fair and accurate way to distinguish obscene from nonobscene materials.

Jeff Rosen points to the difficulties the Court has faced in implementing the *Miller* criteria, which require that police officers, jurors, and judges determine whether works have serious artistic value. Rosen finds such aesthetic issues undecidable and argues that they have no place in a court of law. Catharine MacKinnon asserts that pornography is a practice of sex discrimination and thus a violation of women's civil rights. She argues for the constitutionality of ordinances that prohibit pornography.

In the final selection, the Attorney General's Commission on Pornography argues at length that certain kinds of pornography, particularly those involving violence, are harmful and ought to be restricted. The commission argues that these forms of pornography harm not only the "users," the viewers of the material, but also others with whom the users come into contact. The commission holds, however, that other forms of pornography seem relatively harmless and should escape any government restrictions.

Miller v. *California* (1973)

(Source: Miller v. California *413 U.S. [1973]. Most legal references have been omitted.)*

QUESTIONS FOR REFLECTION

1. Explain the obscenity test proposed by the Court.
2. Many critics, including Justice Douglas, have attacked the Court's test for obscenity as vague. What sources of vagueness do you see in the Court's criteria? How might they be eliminated? Should they be eliminated?
3. Justice Brennan complains that it is impossible to distinguish obscene from nonobscene materials accurately. How does the majority defend its view against this complaint?
4. Why does the majority believe that obscenity is not protected by freedom of speech?
5. How does Justice Douglas argue for his contention that "obscenity cases . . . have no business being in the courts"? Do you agree?
6. Offensiveness forms part of the test of obscenity. Justice Douglas contends that offense does not justify government restriction. What are his arguments? How would Mill recommend treating offensive material? What is the difference between offense and harm?

. . . Mr. Chief Justice Burger delivered the opinion of the Court. . . .

I

This case involves the application of a State's criminal obscenity statute to a situation in which sexually explicit materials have been thrust by aggressive sales action upon unwilling recipients who had in no way indicated any desire to receive such materials. This Court has recognized that the States have a legitimate interest in prohibiting dissemination or exhibition of obscene material when the mode of dissemination carries with it a significant danger of offending the sensibilities of unwilling recipients or of exposure to juveniles. It is in this context that we are called on to define the standards which must be used to identify obscene material that a State may regulate without infringing on the First Amendment as applicable to the States through the Fourteenth Amendment. . . .

Apart from the initial formulation in the *Roth* case, no majority of the Court has at any given time been able to agree on a standard to determine what constitutes obscene, pornographic material subject to regulation under the States' police power. We have seen "a variety of views among the members of the Court unmatched in any other course of constitutional adjudication." This is not remarkable, for in the area of freedom of speech and press the courts must always remain sensitive to any infringement on genuinely serious literary, artistic, political, or scientific expression. This is an area in which there are few eternal verities. . . .

II

This much has been categorically settled by the Court, that obscene material is unprotected by the First Amendment. We acknowledge, however, the inherent dangers of undertaking to regulate any form of expression. State statutes designed to regulate obscene materials must be carefully limited. As a result, we now confine the permissible scope of such regulation to works which depict or describe sexual conduct. That conduct must be specifically defined by the applicable state law, as written or authoritatively construed. A state offense must also be limited to works which, taken as a whole, appeal to the prurient interest in sex, which portray sexual conduct in a patently offensive way, and which, taken as a whole, do not have serious literary, artistic, political, or scientific value.

The basic guidelines for the trier of fact must be: (a) whether "the average person, applying contemporary community standards" would find that the work, taken as a whole, appeals to the prurient interest; (b) whether the work depicts or describes, in a patently offensive way, sexual conduct specifically defined by the applicable state law; and (c) whether the work, taken as a whole, lacks serious literary, artistic, political, or scientific value. We do not adopt as a constitutional standard the "*utterly* without redeeming social value" test of *Memoirs* v. *Massachusetts;* that concept has never commanded the adherence of more than three Justices at one time.

We emphasize that it is not our function to propose regulatory schemes for the States. That must await their concrete legislative efforts. It is possible, however, to give a few plain examples of what a state statute could define for regulation under part (b) of the standard announced in this opinion:

(a) Patently offensive representations or descriptions of ultimate sexual acts, normal or perverted, actual or simulated.

(b) Patently offensive representations or descriptions of masturbation, excretory functions, and lewd exhibition of the genitals.

Sex and nudity may not be exploited without limit by films or pictures exhibited or sold in places of public accommodation any more than live sex and nudity can be exhibited or sold without limit in such public places. At a minimum, prurient, patently offensive depiction or description of sexual conduct must have serious literary, artistic, political, or scientific value to merit First Amendment protection. For example, medical books for the education of physicians and related personnel necessarily use graphic illustrations and descriptions of human anatomy. In resolving the inevitably sensitive questions of fact and law, we must continue to rely on the jury system, accompanied by the safeguards that judges, rules of evidence, presumption of innocence, and other protective features provide, as we do with rape, murder, and a host of other offenses against society and its individual members.

Mr. Justice Brennan, author of the opinions of the Court, or the plurality opinions, in *Roth* v. *United States; Jacobellis* v. *Ohio; Ginzburg* v. *United States* (1966); *Mishkin* v. *New York* (1966); and *Memoirs* v. *Massachusetts,* has abandoned his former position and now maintains that no formulation of this Court, the Congress, or the States can adequately distinguish obscene material unprotected by the First Amendment from protected expression. Paradoxically, Mr. Justice Brennan indicates that suppression of unprotected obscene material is permissible to avoid exposure to unconsenting adults, as in this case, and to juveniles, although he gives no indication of how the division between protected and unprotected materials may be drawn with greater precision for these purposes than for regulation of commercial exposure to consenting adults only. Nor does he indicate where in the Constitution he finds the authority to distinguish between a willing "adult" one month past the state law age of majority and a willing "juvenile" one month younger.

Under the holdings announced today, no one will be subject to prosecution for the sale or exposure of obscene materials unless these materials depict or describe patently offensive "hard core" sexual conduct specifically defined by the regulating state law, as written or construed. We are satisfied that these specific prerequisites will provide fair notice to a dealer in such materials that his public and commercial activities may bring prosecution. If the inability to define regulated materials with ultimate, god-like precision altogether removes the power of the States or the Congress to regulate, then "hard core" pornography may be exposed without limit to the juvenile, the passerby, and the consenting adult alike, as, indeed, Mr. Justice Douglas contends. In this belief, however, Mr. Justice Douglas now stands alone.

Mr. Justice Brennan also emphasizes "institutional stress" in justification of his change of view. Noting that "[t]he number of obscenity cases on our docket gives ample testimony to the burden that has been placed upon this Court," he quite rightly remarks that the examination of contested materials "is hardly a source of edification to the members of this Court." He also notes, and we agree, that "uncertainty of the standards creates a continuing source of tension between state and federal courts. . . ." "The problem is . . . that one cannot say with certainty that material is obscene until at least five members of this Court, applying inevitably obscure standards, have pronounced it so." . . .

It is certainly true that the absence, since *Roth,* of a single majority view of this Court as to proper standards for testing obscenity has placed a strain on both state and federal courts. But today, for the first time since *Roth* was decided in 1957, a majority of this Court has agreed on concrete guidelines to isolate "hard core" pornography from expression protected by the First Amendment. . . .

III

Under a National Constitution, fundamental First Amendment limitations on the powers of the States do not vary from community to community, but this does not mean that there are, or should or can be, fixed, uniform national standards of precisely what appeals to the "prurient interest" or is "patently offensive." These are essentially questions of fact, and our Nation is simply too big and too diverse for this Court to reasonably expect that such standards could be articulated for all 50 States in a single formulation, even assuming the prerequisite consensus exists. When triers of fact are asked to decide whether "the average person, applying contemporary community standards" would consider certain materials "prurient," it would be unrealistic to require that the answer be based on some abstract formulation. The adversary system, with lay jurors as the usual ultimate factfinders in criminal prosecutions, has historically permitted triers of fact to draw on the standards of their community, guided always by limiting instructions on the law. To require a State to structure obscenity proceedings around evidence of a *national* "community standard" would be an exercise in futility. . . .

It is neither realistic nor constitutionally sound to read the First Amendment as requiring that the people of Maine or Mississippi accept public depiction of conduct found tolerable in Las Vegas, or New York City. People in different States vary in their tastes and attitudes, and this diversity is not to be strangled by the absolutism of imposed uniformity. As the Court made clear in *Mishkin* v. *New York,* the primary concern with requiring a jury to apply the standard of "the average person, applying contemporary community standards" is to be certain that, so far as material is not aimed at a deviant group, it will be judged by its impact on an average person, rather than a particularly susceptible or sensitive person—or indeed a totally insensitive one. . . . We hold that the requirement that the jury evaluate the materials with reference to "contemporary standards of the State of California" serves this protective purpose and is constitutionally adequate.

IV

The dissenting Justices sound the alarm of repression. But, in our view, to equate the free and robust exchange of ideas and political debate with commercial exploitation of obscene material demeans the grand conception of the First Amendment and its high purposes in the historic struggle for freedom. It is a "misuse of the great guarantees of free speech and free press. . . ." The First Amendment protects works which, taken as a whole, have serious literary, artistic, political, or scientific value, regardless of whether the government or a majority of the people approve of the ideas these works represent. "The protection given speech and press was fashioned to assure unfettered interchange of *ideas* for the bringing about of political and social changes desired by the people" (emphasis added). But the public portrayal of hard-core sexual conduct for its own sake, and for the ensuing commercial gain, is a different matter.

There is no evidence, empirical or historical, that the stern 19th century American censorship of public distribution and display of material relating to sex in any way limited or affected expression of serious literary, artistic, political, or scientific ideas. On the contrary, it is beyond any question that the era following Thomas Jefferson to Theodore Roosevelt was an "extraordinarily vigorous period," not just in economics and politics, but in *belles lettres* and in "the outlying fields of social and political philosophies." We do not see the harsh hand of censorship of ideas—good or bad, sound or unsound—and "repression" of political liberty lurking in every state regulation of commercial exploitation of human interest in sex.

Mr. Justice Brennan finds "it is hard to see how state-ordered regimentation of our minds can ever be forestalled." These doleful anticipations assume that courts cannot distinguish commerce in ideas, protected by the First Amendment, from commercial exploitation of obscene material. Moreover, state regulation of hard-core pornography so as to make it unavailable to nonadults, a regulation which Mr. Justice Brennan finds constitutionally permissible, has all the elements of "censorship" for adults; indeed even more rigid enforcement techniques may be called for with such dichotomy of regulation. One can concede that the "sexual revolution" of recent years may have had useful byproducts in striking layers of prudery from a subject long irrationally kept from needed ventilation. But it does not follow that no regulation of patently offensive "hard core" materials is needed or permissible; civilized people do not allow unregulated access to heroin because it is a derivative of medicinal morphine.

In sum, we (a) reaffirm the *Roth* holding that obscene material is not protected by the First Amendment; (b) hold that such material can be regulated by the States, subject to the specific safeguards enunciated above, without a showing that the material is "*utterly* without redeeming social value"; and (c) hold that obscenity is to be determined by applying "contemporary community standards," not "national standards." The judgment of the Appellate Department of the Superior Court, Orange County, California, is vacated and the case remanded to that court for further proceedings not inconsistent with the First Amendment standards established by this opinion. . . .

Mr. Justice Douglas, dissenting.

I

Today we leave open the way for California to send a man to prison for distributing brochures that advertise books and a movie under freshly written standards defining obscenity which until today's decision were never the part of any law.

The Court has worked hard to define obscenity and concededly has failed. In *Roth* v. *United States*, it ruled that "[o]bscene material is material which deals with sex in a manner appealing to prurient interest." Obscenity, it was said, was rejected by the First Amendment because it is "utterly without redeeming social importance." The presence of a "prurient interest" was to be determined by "contemporary community standards." That test, it has been said, could not be determined by one standard here and another standard there, but "on the basis of a national standard." My Brother Stewart in *Jacobellis* commented that the difficulty of the Court in giving content to obscenity was that it was "faced with the task of trying to define what may be indefinable."

In *Memoirs* v. *Massachusetts*, the *Roth* test was elaborated to read as follows: "[T]hree elements must coalesce: it must be established that (a) the dominant theme of the material taken as a whole appeals to a prurient interest in sex; (b) the material is patently offensive because it affronts contemporary community standards relating to the description or representation of sexual matters; and (c) the material is utterly without redeeming social value."

In *Ginzburg* v. *United States,* a publisher was sent to prison, not for the kind of books and periodicals he sold, but for the manner in which the publications were advertised. The "leer of the sensualist" was said to permeate the advertisements. The Court said, "Where the purveyor's sole emphasis is on the sexually provocative aspects of his publications, that fact may be decisive in the determination of obscenity." As Mr. Justice Black said in dissent, " . . . Ginzburg . . . is now finally and authoritatively condemned to serve five years in prison for distributing printed matter about sex which neither Ginzburg nor anyone else could possibly have known to be criminal." That observation by Mr. Justice Black is underlined by the fact that the *Ginzburg* decision was five to four.

A further refinement was added by *Ginzburg* v. *New York,* where the Court held that "it was not irrational for the legislature to find that exposure to material condemned by the statute is harmful to minors."

But even those members of this Court who had created the new and changing standards of "obscenity" could not agree on their application. Some condemn it if its "dominant tendency might be to `deprave or corrupt' a reader." Others look not to the content of the book but to whether it is advertised "`to appeal to the erotic interests of customers.'" Some condemn only "hard-core pornography"; but even then a true definition is lacking. It has indeed been said of that definition, "I could never succeed in [defining it] intelligibly," but "I know it when I see it."

Today we would add a new three-pronged test: "(a) whether 'the average person, applying contemporary community standards' would find that the work, taken as a whole, appeals to the prurient interest, . . . (b) whether the work depicts or describes, in a patently offensive way, sexual conduct specifically defined by the applicable state law, and (c) whether the work, taken as a whole, lacks serious literary, artistic, political, or scientific value."

Those are the standards we ourselves have written into the Constitution. Yet how under these vague tests can we sustain convictions for the sale of an article prior to the time when some court has declared it to be obscene?

Today the Court retreats from the earlier formulations of the constitutional test and undertakes to make new definitions. This effort, like the earlier ones, is earnest and well intentioned. The difficulty is that we do not deal with constitutional terms, since "obscenity" is not mentioned in the Constitution or Bill of Rights. And the First Amendment makes no such exception from "the press" which it undertakes to protect nor, as I have said on other occasions, in an exception necessarily implied, for there was no recognized exception to the free press at the time the Bill of Rights was adopted which treated "obscene" publications differently from other types of papers, magazines, and books. So there are no constitutional guidelines for deciding what is and what is not "obscene." The Court is at large because we deal with tastes and standards of literature. What shocks me may be sustenance for my neighbor. What causes one person to boil up in rage over one pamphlet or movie may reflect only his neurosis, not shared by others. We deal here with a regime of censorship which, if adopted, should be done by constitutional amendments after full debate by the people.

Obscenity cases usually generate tremendous emotional outbursts. They have no business being in the courts. If a constitutional amendment authorized censorship, the censor would probably be an administrative agency. Then criminal prosecutions could follow as, if, and when publishers defied the censor and sold their literature. Under that regime a publisher would know when he was on dangerous ground. Under the present regime—whether the old standards or the new ones are used—the criminal law becomes a trap. A brand new test would put a publisher behind bars under a new law improvised by the courts after the publication. That was done in *Ginzburg* and has all the evils of an *ex post facto* law.

My contention is that until a civil proceeding

has placed a tract beyond the pale, no criminal prosecution should be sustained. For no more vivid illustration of vague and uncertain laws could be designed than those we have fashioned. As Mr. Justice Harlan has said:

> "The upshot of all this divergence in viewpoint is that anyone who undertakes to examine the Court's decisions since *Roth* which have held particular material obscene or not obscene would find himself in utter bewilderment." *Interstate Circuit, Inc.* v. *Dallas.*

. . . In any case—certainly when constitutional rights are concerned—we should not allow men to go to prison or be fined when they had no "fair warning" that what they did was criminal conduct.

[II . . .]

III

While the right to know is the corollary of the right to speak or publish, no one can be forced by government to listen to disclosure that he finds offensive. That was the basis of my dissent in *Public Utilities Comm'n* v. *Pollak,* where I protested against making streetcar passengers a "captive" audience. There is no "captive audience" problem in these obscenity cases. No one is being compelled to look or to listen. Those who enter newsstands or bookstalls may be offended by what they see. But they are not compelled by the State to frequent those places; and it is only state or governmental action against which the First Amendment, applicable to the States by virtue of the Fourteenth, raises a ban.

The idea that the First Amendment permits government to ban publications that are "offensive" to some people puts an ominous gloss on freedom of the press. That test would make it possible to ban any paper or any journal or magazine in some benighted place. The First Amendment was designed "to invite dispute," to induce "a condition of unrest," to "create dissatisfaction with conditions as they are," and even to stir "people to anger." The idea that the First Amendment permits punishment for ideas that are "offensive" to the particular judge or jury sitting in judgment is astounding. No greater leveler of speech or literature has even been designed. To give the power to the censor, as we do today, is to make a sharp and radical break with the traditions of a free society. The First Amendment was not fashioned as a vehicle for dispensing tranquilizers to the people. Its prime function was to keep debate open to "offensive" as well as to "staid" people. The tendency throughout history has been to subdue the individual and to exalt the power of government. The use of the standard "offensive" gives authority to government that cuts the very vitals out of the First Amendment. As is intimated by the Court's opinion, the materials before us may be garbage. But so is much of what is said in political campaigns, in the daily press, on TV, or over the radio. By reason of the First Amendment—and solely because of it—speakers and publishers have not been threatened or subdued because their thoughts and ideas may be "offensive" to some.

The standard "offensive" is unconstitutional in yet another way. In *Coates* v. *City of Cincinnati,* we had before us a municipal ordinance that made it a crime for three or more persons to assemble on a street and conduct themselves "in a manner annoying to persons passing by." We struck it down, saying: "If three or more people meet together on a sidewalk or street corner, they must conduct themselves so as not to annoy any police officer or other person who should happen to pass by. In our opinion this ordinance is unconstitutionally vague because it subjects the exercise of the right of assembly to an unascertainable standard, and unconstitutionally broad because it authorizes the punishment of constitutionally protected conduct.

"Conduct that annoys some people does not annoy others. Thus, the ordinance is vague, not in the sense that it requires a person to conform his conduct to an imprecise but comprehensive normative standard, but rather in the sense that no standard of conduct is specified at all."

How we can deny Ohio the convenience of punishing people who "annoy" others and allow California power to punish people who publish materials "offensive" to some people is difficult to square with constitutional requirements.

If there are to be restraints on what is obscene, then a constitutional amendment should be the way of achieving the end. There are societies where religion and mathematics are the only free segments. It would be a dark day for America if that were our destiny. But the people can make it such if they choose to write obscenity into the Constitution and define it.

We deal with highly emotional, not rational, questions. To many the Song of Solomon is obscene. I do not think we, the judges, were ever given the constitutional power to make definitions of obscenity. If it is to be defined, let the people debate and decide by a constitutional amendment what they want to ban as obscene and what standards they want the legislatures and the courts to apply. Perhaps the people will decide that the path towards a mature, integrated society requires that all ideas competing for acceptance must have no censor. Perhaps they will decide otherwise. Whatever the choice, the courts will have some guidelines. Now we have none except our own predilections. . . .

JEFF ROSEN

"Miller" Time

Jeff Rosen is a lawyer and staff writer for The New Republic. *(Source: Reprinted by permission of* The New Republic, *October 1, 1990, pp. 17–19. Copyright © 1990 by the New Republic, Inc.)*

QUESTIONS FOR REFLECTION

1. How, according to the *Miller* test, should art be distinguished from obscenity? To what extent does the test require jurors, judges, and police officers to make aesthetic judgments about art?
2. Rosen plainly despairs of devising any test for determining whether a work has serious artistic value. What is the rationale for his despair? Do you share it?
3. How might the *Miller* test be revised so that tests of artistic seriousness are unnecessary?
4. Rosen makes several arguments for overturning *Miller* that are independent of his worries about judging serious artistic value. What are they? Do you find them convincing?

This fall a Cincinnati curator is facing a federal judge for having displayed the photographs of Robert Mapplethorpe. Luther Campbell of 2 Live Crew will appeal his Florida conviction for having produced *As Nasty As They Wanna Be*. And Karen Finley may challenge her grant denial from the National Endowment for the Arts. All three will use the Supreme Court's obscenity test to defend their work as "serious" art. But in a perverse betrayal of its purpose, the Supreme Court's test, properly applied, may threaten naughty artists more than it protects them.

When the test was announced in *Miller* v. *California* in 1973, it promised to distinguish art from obscenity by protecting sexually explicit work that had "serious" artistic value. (The more lenient previous test said obscenity had to be "utterly without redeeming social value.") But over the years, art has become more sexually explicit, the line between high art and low has been increasingly blurred, and artists have come to question the idea of artistic "seriousness." Now the *Miller* test measures art by a standard that many artists are unwilling to meet and that jurors are unable to identify. For different reasons, unlikely allies such as William Brennan, Antonin Scalia, and movie czar Jack Valenti agree that it's time to take aesthetic decisions out of the courtrooms.

In *Miller* the Court said that judges and juries should ask themselves three questions when attempting to distinguish between art and obscenity: first, "whether 'the average person, applying contemporary community standards' would find that the work, taken as a whole, appeals to the prurient interest"; second, "whether the work depicts or describes, in a patently offensive way, sexual conduct specifically defined by the applicable state law"; and, third, "whether the work, taken as a whole, lacks serious literary, artistic, political, or scientific value." If the answer to all three questions is yes, then the work can be banned; if not, then the work must be protected.

From the moment it was conceived, the test seemed ambiguous. "To be prurient and offensive, a work has to turn you on and gross you out at the same time," says Kathleen Sullivan of Harvard Law School. But during the 1980s the ambiguous test became unintelligible as changes in art and law eliminated "serious" artistic values as a viable distinction between art and obscenity. First, artistic goals changed. As Amy Adler argues in a student note in a recent issue of *The Yale Law Journal,* postmodernism rebelled against the modernist demand that art should be "serious," or that it should have any traditional "value" at all. "Bad" painters like David Salle juxtaposed images from art history and pornography. Sculptors like Jeff Koons created what *New York Times* critic Michael Brenson called "art that looks like trash and trashes high art," including a porcelain bust of Italian porn star Cicciolina. And rappers like 2 Live Crew mixed scatology with Muddy Waters. As a result, the *Miller* test has come to evaluate postmodern art by the very standard that postmodern art seeks to defy.

Second, the *Miller* test itself changed. Three years ago, in *Pope* v. *Illinois,* the Supreme Court decided that courts should ask whether a "reasonable person" would find serious value in the suspect art. It is hard to imagine a more philistine and less appropriate test for artistic value than the aesthetic sensibility of the "reasonable person." Reasonable people attacked Manet's *Déjeuner Sur L'Herbe* and Beethoven's "Ode to Joy" as indecent. And reasonable people are even less likely to find serious value in artists like Mapplethorpe and Finley, who go out of their way to offend reasonable tastes. When the "reasonable person" standard was announced, liberals like Brennan cringed at the bewildering union of law and aesthetics. But they were joined by the conservative Scalia, who is wary of judicial subjectivity wherever it occurs. "[I]t is quite impossible," wrote Scalia, "to come to an objective assessment of (at least) literary or artistic value. . . . Since ratiocination has little to do with esthetics, the fabled 'reasonable man' is of little help in the inquiry. . . . For the law courts to decide 'What is Beauty' is novelty even by today's standards."

The changes in art and law left artists vulnerable to prosecution when local authorities decided to crack down in 1990. As a result, the artists who face federal judges this fall have no way of predicting with confidence whether they have broken the law. To appreciate their predicament, pretend you are a juror at an obscenity trial and try to apply the *Miller* test to the work of Mapplethorpe, 2 Live Crew, and Finley.

Start with Mapplethorpe's photograph of the man with the bullwhip up his ass. Would an average person in our community find that it appeals to the prurient interest? The Supreme Court complicates matters by defining "prurient" not only as "material having a tendency to excite lustful thoughts," but also as material that shows a "shameful or morbid interest in nudity, sex, or excretion." An expert witness may be helpful. "The male genitals are often presented . . . as surrogates for the face," write the poet Richard Howard in a tribute to Mapplethorpe. Sounds like an interest in nudity, which might even be shameful, depending on what your neighbors are used to. Is the simulation of sodomy patently offensive? Again, your community is the judge. As for the third criterion, wouldn't someone like Dennis Barrie, the director of the Contemporary Arts Center of Cincinnati, know "serious" artistic value when he sees it? Other art experts, though, doubt Mapplethorpe's seriousness. Robert Hughes calls Mapplethorpe an "overrated photographer." And Hilton Kramer of *The New Criterion* detects no serious artistic value. "Are these disputed pictures works of art?" Kramer asks. "Alas, I suppose they are," but they do not "belong to the highest levels of art." Who is a more reasonable person, Barrie or Kramer? Would a reasonable person find either of them reasonable?

Now try the same exercise with 2 Live Crew. Assume, as Judge Jose A. Gonzalez did, that *As Nasty As They Wanna Be* appeals to lustful thoughts (it doesn't; it's boring), and that it is patently offensive in some parts of Florida (Gonzalez justified his knowledge of community standards by noting that he had "attended public functions and events" throughout the community). Scholars and journalists have been properly ridiculed for defending 2 Live Crew by exaggerating their artistic, literary, even scientific seriousness. . . . But the legal test requires no less, refusing to protect pop culture unless it masquerades as high culture.

It is hard to conclude, as Gonzalez did (using the wrong test), that *Nasty* is "utterly without any redeeming social value." You don't have to compare the rappers' braggadocio in the call and response form to duets from Wagner's Siegfried ("The boy is fearless and his sword is sharp") to recognize that boasting about sex in rhyme is part of the black oral tradition. If dirty rap can be banned, suggests Bruce Jackson, an English professor at the State University of New York at Buffalo, then so can hundreds of equally filthy verses dating back to the nineteenth century. And a quick skim of his anthology of black narrative poetry, *Get Your Ass in the Water and Swim Like Me,* proves the point.

But if a nineteenth-century pedigree suggests that scatology in rhyme may have *some* literary or artistic value, how is anyone, reasonable or not, to decide whether the value is "serious"? In a relativistic age, that is a judgment that even the defenders of rap are reluctant to make. To complicate matters, black culture, from novels to jazz, has long rejected the distinction between popular art and serious art. Gonzalez's analysis is embarrassing ("Obscenity? Yes!" his opinion shrieked), but 2 Live Crew leaves the *Miller* test at a loss.

Finally, consider a performance artist like Finley, whose angry, scatological feminism is intended to be *anti*-pornographic. "If a woman can't talk about rape or sexual violence in the language she was abused in," Finley said in 1988, "it's against our First Amendment rights." But it may not be if our First Amendment rights are defined by *Miller.* Prurient interest? Finley says, "There's nothing sexually exciting about my work"; but remember that prurient also means "a shameful or morbid interest in nudity, sex, or excretion." That, suggests Adler, sounds like an apt description of Finley's oeuvre, as she smears food into her genitals, defecates onstage, and describes graphic sex acts with priests and the handicapped. Patently offensive? That's Finley's goal. Which leaves "serious artistic value" as the only way of distinguishing Finley from the pornography she abhors. But performance art was designed to mock the idea of artistic seriousness. "This is work that sends up the notion of art taking itself seriously," says Barbara Tsumagari, executive director of the Kitchen, a performance space in New York where Finley has performed. Does that effort itself have serious artistic value? "It's a very postmodern question. We need a postmodern test," says Tsumagari.

Until we get one, sexually explicit artists will continue to be suppressed. But that can't be constitutional if the First Amendment protects self-expression regardless of its political value, as the Supreme Court has repeatedly held. In other words, if art can't be cleanly distinguished from obscenity, as more than thirty years of failed Supreme Court tests make clear, then private consumption of obscenity must be endured so that art can be protected.

Justices Brennan and Scalia, who rarely agreed on anything, have said that the *Miller* test should be reconsidered, although they disagree about appropriate alternatives. In a little noticed concurrence last January, Scalia suggested that courts should focus on the intention of the distributors, rather than on the intention of the creators, of sexually explicit material. He would prohibit communities from suppressing particular books or films, but would allow them to close down adult bookstores and theaters that specialize in pandering sex for profit. Scalia's solution has the clear advantage of taking the courts out of aesthetics and guaranteeing that individual works of literature or art (or pornography for that matter) could never be banned in America again. At the same time, Scalia would allow communities to reduce access to soft-core porn, which is constitutionally protected, as well as hard-core porn, which is not. But Mapplethorpe, Campbell, and Finley would be safe.

Justice Brennan's alternative—no obscenity test at all—fell one vote short of a Supreme Court majority in 1973 and is likely to fall shorter today. But it remains the solution of choice for First Amendment absolutists, and it would allow communities to focus their attention on the problem at hand: keeping sexually explicit material away from children and unwilling adults in an increasingly explicit age. Until the *Miller* test exposed itself this year, the most important pornography cases over the past two decades concerned zoning regulations rather than aesthetic decisions. In 1976, and again in 1986, the Supreme Court gave local communities broad discretion to concentrate red light districts or to disperse them in the interest of preserving the "quality of urban life." Liberals like Brennan dissented from the zoning decisions, criticizing them as speech discrimination masquerading as urban renewal. But zoning regulations would seem much less threatening if the states were denied the draconian power to ban obscenity entirely.

In addition to zoning regulations, voluntary self-regulation of movies and records can reduce the need for state regulation. And the recent efforts of Jack Valenti for the Motion Picture Association and Tipper Gore for the Parents' Music Resource Center on behalf of voluntary warning labels have been in precisely the right direction. Valenti has resisted calls for an "A" rating between R and X to distinguish sexually explicit "art" films from soft-core porn. The purpose of ratings, he says, is to warn parents, not to identify art. And he recognizes that ratings boards are no more qualified than judges to specify the mystic point at which an "artistic" portrayal of cannibalism, for example, becomes, for some, obscene.

As for explicit records, 2 Live Crew vindicates Gore as a civil libertarian and a prophet as well. In 1985 she predicted that if liberals didn't embrace voluntary warning labels, "extremists" would resort to bans, which she opposes unequivocally. And her efforts on behalf of voluntary labels helped to preempt legislation requiring labels in twenty-two states.

Reversing *Miller* would also focus the debate over congressional subsidies on aesthetics rather than law. The current debate over reauthorizing the NEA is harping obsessively on the *Miller* test: liberals, having accepted some legal restrictions as inevitable, want to limit them to the language of *Miller;* conservatives want broader restrictions. "I think there is an enormous irony that the artistic community is embracing *Miller* so ardently today," says Floyd Abrams, who is representing the New School in its challenge to NEA chairman John Frohnmayer's loyalty oaths.

The legalistic squabbles, suggests Michael McConnell of Chicago Law School, obscure the distinction between criminalization and refusal to fund. When the NEA is saddled with congressional restrictions, a sensible grant refusal can look like an obscenity charge. By legislating aesthetics, and making heroes out of refuseniks, Congress reduces, rather than enhances, the Endowment's ability to discriminate on the basis of artistic merit. Even if the *Miller* test is not overturned, an NEA reauthorized without *Miller*'s restrictions would have a freer hand to reject art that lacked "serious" value. And artistic value is a more appropriate test for public subsidy than for criminal punishment.

Abandoning *Miller,* finally, would protect our judges from the scourge of pornography. There has been something sordid over the past thirty years about Supreme Court justices peering at skin flicks in the dark basement of the Court. (Justice Harlan, almost blind, asked his clerks to narrate as the action unfolded.) David Souter seems like an ascetic and upright man. For his own sake, he should join Scalia, persuade the liberals, and remove aesthetics from the courts.

CATHARINE MACKINNON

Pornography, Civil Rights, and Speech

Catharine MacKinnon is Professor of Law at the University of Michigan. (Source: Reprinted by permission of the Harvard Civil Rights/Civil Liberties Law Review. *Copyright © 1985 by the President and Fellows of Harvard College.)*

QUESTIONS FOR REFLECTION

1. What is feminism, according to MacKinnon?
2. Why, in MacKinnon's view, is pornography discriminatory?
3. What are MacKinnon's arguments against the *Miller* decision? How might a defender of *Miller* respond?

... There is a belief that this is a society in which women and men are basically equals. Room for marginal corrections is conceded, flaws are known to exist, attempts are made to correct what are conceived as occasional lapses from the basic condition of sex equality. Sex discrimination law has concentrated most of its focus on these occasional lapses. It is difficult to overestimate the extent to which this belief in equality is an article of faith for most people, including most women, who wish to live in self-respect in an internal universe, even (perhaps especially) if not in the world. It is also partly an expression of natural law thinking: if we are inalienably equal, we can't "really" be degraded.

This is a world in which it is worth trying. In this world of presumptive equality, people make money based on their training or abilities or diligence or qualifications. They are employed and advanced on the basis of merit. In this world of just deserts, if someone is abused, it is thought to violate the basic rules of the community. If it doesn't, victims are seen to have done something they could have chosen to do differently, by exercise of will or better judgment. Maybe such people have placed themselves in a situation of vulnerability to physical abuse. Maybe they have done something provocative. Or maybe they were just unusually unlucky. In such a world, if such a person has an experience, there are words for it. When they speak and say it, they are listened to. If they write about it, they will be published. If certain experiences are never spoken about, if certain people or issues are seldom heard from, it is supposed that silence has been chosen. The law, including much of the law of sex discrimination and the First Amendment, operates largely within the realm of these beliefs.

Feminism is the discovery that women do not live in this world, that the person occupying this realm is a man, so much more a man if he is white and wealthy. This world of potential credibility, authority, security, and just rewards, recognition of one's identity and capacity, is a world that some people do inhabit as a condition of birth, with variations among them. It is not a basic condition accorded humanity in this society, but a prerogative of status, a privilege, among other things, of gender.

I call this a discovery because it has not been an assumption. Feminism is the first theory, the first practice, the first movement, to take seriously the situation of all women from the point of view of all women, both on our situation and on social life as a whole. The discovery has therefore been made that the implicit social content of humanism, as well as the standpoint from which legal method has been designed and injuries have been defined, has not been women's standpoint. Defining feminism in a way that connects epistemology with power as the politics of women's point of view, this discovery can be summed up by saying that women live in another world: specifically, a world of *not* equality, a world of inequality. . . .

. . . In pornography, there it is, in one place, all of the abuses that women had to struggle so long even to begin to articulate, all the *unspeakable* abuse: the rape, the battery, the sexual harassment, the prostitution, and the sexual abuse of children. Only in the pornography it is called something else: sex, sex, sex, sex, and sex, respectively. Pornography sexualizes rape, battery, sexual harassment, prostitution, and child sexual abuse; it thereby celebrates, promotes, authorizes, and legitimizes them. More generally, it eroticizes the dominance and submission that is the dynamic common to them all. It makes hierarchy sexy and calls that "the truth about sex" or just a mirror of reality. Through this process pornography constructs what a woman is as what men want from sex. This is what the pornography means.

Pornography constructs what a woman is in terms of its view of what men want sexually, such that acts of rape, battery, sexual harassment, prostitution, and sexual abuse of children become acts of sexual equality. Pornography's world of equality is a harmonious and balanced place. Men and women are perfectly complementary and perfectly bipolar. . . .

. . . There, women substantively desire dispossession and cruelty. We desperately want to be bound, battered, tortured, humiliated, and killed. Or, to be fair to the soft core, merely taken and used. This is erotic to the male point of view. Subjection itself, with self-determination ecstatically relinquished, is the content of women's sexual desire and desirability. Women are there to be violated and possessed, men to violate and possess us, either on screen or by camera or pen on behalf of the consumer. On a simple descriptive level, the inequality of hierarchy, of which gender is the primary one, seems necessary for sexual arousal to work. Other added inequalities identify various pornographic genres or subthemes, although they are always added through gender: age, disability, homosexuality, animals, objects, race (including anti-Semitism), and so on. Gender is never irrelevant.

What pornography *does* goes beyond its content: it eroticizes hierarchy, it sexualizes inequality. It makes dominance and submission into sex. Inequality is its central dynamic; the illusion of freedom coming together with the reality of force is central to its working. Perhaps because this is a bourgeois culture, the victim must look free, appear to be freely acting. Choice is how she got there. Willing is what she is when she is being equal. It seems equally important that then and there she actually be forced and that forcing be communicated on some level, even if only through still photos of her in postures of receptivity and access, available for penetration. Pornography in this view is a form of forced sex, a practice of sexual politics, an institution of gender inequality.

From this perspective, pornography is neither harmless fantasy nor a corrupt and confused misrepresentation of an otherwise natural and healthy sexual situation. It institutionalizes the sexuality of male supremacy, fusing the erotization of dominance and submission with the social construction of male and female. To the extent that gender is sexual, pornography is part of constituting the meaning of that sexuality. Men treat women as who they see women as being. Pornography constructs who that is. Men's power over women means that the way men see women defines who women can be. Pornography is that way. Pornography is not imagery in some relation to a reality elsewhere constructed. It is not a distortion, reflection, projection, expression, fantasy, representation, or symbol either. It is a sexual reality.

. . . Pornography *participates* in its audience's eroticism through creating an accessible sexual object, the possession and consumption of which *is* male sexuality, as socially constructed; to be consumed and possessed as which, *is* female sexuality, as socially constructed; pornography is a process that constructs it that way.

The object world is constructed according to how it looks with respect to its possible uses. Pornography defines women by how we look according to how we can be sexually used. Pornography codes how to look at women, so you know what you can do with one when you see one. Gender is an assignment made visually, both originally and in everyday life. A sex object is defined on the basis of its looks, in terms of its usability for sexual pleasure, such that both the looking—the quality of the gaze, including its point of view—and the definition according to use become eroticized as part of the sex itself. This is what the feminist concept "sex object" means. In this sense, sex in life is no less mediated than it is in art. Men have sex with their image of a woman. It is not that life and art imitate each other; in this sexuality, they *are* each other.

To give a set of rough epistemological translations, to defend pornography as consistent with the equality of the sexes is to defend the subordination of women to men as sexual equality. What in the pornographic view is love and romance looks a great deal like hatred and torture to the feminist. Pleasure and eroticism become violation. Desire appears as lust for dominance and submission. The vulnerability of women's projected sexual availability, that acting we are allowed (that is, asking to be acted upon), is victimization. Play conforms to scripted roles. Fantasy expresses ideology, is not exempt from it. Admiration of natural physical beauty becomes objectification. Harmlessness becomes harm. Pornography is a harm of male supremacy made difficult to see because of its pervasiveness, potency, and, principally, because of its success in making the world a pornographic place. Specifically, its harm cannot be discerned, and will not be addressed, if viewed and approached neutrally, because it *is* so much of "what is." In other words, to the extent pornography succeeds in constructing social reality, it becomes invisible as harm. If we live in a world that pornography creates through the power of men in a male-dominated situation, the issue is not what the harm of pornography is, but how that harm is to become visible.

Obscenity law provides a very different analysis and conception of the problem of pornography. In 1973 the legal definition of obscenity became that which the average person, applying contemporary community standards, would find that, taken as a whole, appeals to the prurient interest; that which depicts or describes in a patently offensive way—you feel like you're a cop reading someone's *Miranda* rights—sexual conduct specifically defined by the applicable state law; and that which, taken as a whole, lacks serious literary, artistic, political or scientific value. Feminism doubts whether the average person gender-neutral exists; has more questions about the content and process of defining what community standards are than it does about deviations from them; wonders why prurience counts but powerlessness does not and why sensibilities are better protected from offense than women are from exploitation; defines sexuality, and thus its violation and expropriation, more broadly than does state law; and questions why a body of law that has not in practice been able to tell rape from intercourse should, without further guidance, be entrusted with telling pornography from anything less. Taking the work "as a whole" ignores that which the victims of pornography have long known: legitimate settings diminish the perception of injury done to those whose trivialization and objectification they contextualize. Besides, and this is a heavy one, if a woman is subjected, why should it matter that the work has other value? Maybe what redeems the work's value is what enhances its injury to women, not to mention that existing standards of literature, art, science, and politics, examined in a feminist light, are remarkably consonant with pornography's mode, meaning, and message. And finally—first and foremost, actually—although the subject of these materials is overwhelmingly women, their contents almost entirely made up of women's bodies, our invisibility has been such, our equation as a sex *with* sex has been such, that the law of obscenity has never even considered pornography a women's issue.

Obscenity, in this light, is a moral idea, an idea about judgments of good and bad. Pornography, by contrast, is a political practice, a practice of power and powerlessness. Obscenity is ideational and abstract; pornography is concrete and substantive. The two concepts represent two entirely different things. Nudity, excess of candor, arousal or excitement, prurient appeal, illegality of the acts depicted, and unnaturalness or perversion are all qualities that bother obscenity law when sex is depicted or portrayed. Sex forced on real women so that it can be sold at a profit and forced on other real women; women's bodies trussed and maimed and raped and made into things to be hurt and obtained and accessed, and this presented as the nature of women in a way that is acted on and acted out, over and over; the coercion that is visible and the coercion that has become invisible—this and more bothers feminists about pornography. Obscenity as such probably does little harm. Pornography is integral to attitudes and behaviors of violence and discrimination that define the treatment and status of half the population. . . .

ATTORNEY GENERAL'S COMMISSION ON PORNOGRAPHY

The Question of Harm

(Source: from the United States Attorney General's Commission on Pornography, Attorney General's Commission on Pornography: Final Report *[Washington: U.S. Department of Justice, 1986].)*

QUESTIONS FOR REFLECTION

1. In answering the question "What is a harm?" the commission distinguishes primary from secondary harm. Explain this distinction. What, according to the commission, is its moral significance?
2. Why does the commission believe that sexually violent material is harmful?
3. The commission holds that nonviolent but degrading material is also harmful. What is "degrading" material? Why is it harmful?
4. What is the commission's opinion of nonviolent, nondegrading pornography? Is it harmful in any way? Should the government attempt to restrict access to such material, according to the commission? Do you agree?
5. Does the test for obscenity in *Miller* correspond to the distinction the commission makes between harmful and (largely) harmless pornography? If not, how might the test be revised to make it correspond?

5.1.2 What Counts as a Harm?

What is a harm? And why focus on harm at all? We do not wish in referring repeatedly to "harm" to burden ourselves with an unduly narrow conception of harm. To emphasize in different words what we said in the previous section, the scope of identifiable harms is broader than the scope of that with which government can or should deal. We refuse to truncate our consideration of the question of harm by defining harms in terms of possible government regulation. And we certainly reject the view that the only noticeable harm is one that causes physical or financial harm to identifiable individuals. An environment, physical, cultural, moral, or aesthetic, can be harmed, and so can a community, organization, or group be harmed independent of identifiable harms to members of that community.

Most importantly, although we have emphasized in our discussion of harms the kinds of harms that can most easily be observed and measured, the idea of harm is broader than that. To a number of us, the most important harms must be seen in moral terms, and the act of moral condemnation of that which is immoral is not merely important but essential. From this perspective there are acts that need be seen not only as causes of immorality but as manifestations of it. Issues of human dignity and human decency, no less real for their lack of scientific measurability, are for many of us central to thinking about the question of harm. And when we think about harm in this way, there are acts that must be condemned not because the evils of the world will thereby be eliminated, but because conscience demands it.

We believe it useful in thinking about harms to note the distinction between harm and offense.

Although the line between the two is hardly clear, most people can nevertheless imagine things that offend them, or offend others, that still would be hard to describe as harms. . . .

In thinking about harms, it is useful to draw a rough distinction between primary and secondary harms. Primary harms are those in which the alleged harm is commonly taken to be intrinsically harmful, even though the precise way in which the harm is harmful might yet be further explored. Nevertheless, murder, rape, assault, and discrimination on the basis of race and gender are all examples of primary harms in this sense. We treat these acts as harms not because of where they will lead, but simply because of what they are.

In other instances, however, the alleged harm is secondary, not in the sense that it is in any way less important, but in the sense that the concern is not with what the act *is*, but where it will lead. Curfews are occasionally imposed not because there is anything wrong with people being out at night, but because in some circumstances it is thought that being out at night in large groups may cause people to commit other crimes. Possession of "burglar tools" is often prohibited because of what those tools may be used for. Thus, when it is urged that pornography is harmful because it causes some people to commit acts of sexual violence, because it causes promiscuity, because it encourages sexual relations outside of marriage, because it promotes so-called "unnatural" sexual practices, or because it leads men to treat women as existing solely for the sexual satisfaction of men, the alleged harms are secondary, again not in any sense suggesting that the harms are less important. The harms are secondary here because the allegation of harm presupposes a causal link between the act and the harm, a causal link that is superfluous if, as in the case of primary harms, the act quite simply *is* the harm.

Thus we think it important, with respect to every area of possible harm, to focus on whether the allegation relates to a harm that comes from the sexually explicit material itself, or whether it occurs *as a result* of something the material does. If it is the former, then the inquiry can focus directly on the nature of the alleged harm. But if it is the latter, then there must be a two-step inquiry. First it is necessary to determine if some hypothesized result is in fact harmful. In some cases, where the asserted consequent harm is unquestionably a harm, this step of the analysis is easy. With respect to claims that certain sexually explicit material increases the incidence of rape or other sexual violence, for example, no one could plausibly claim that such consequences were not harmful, and the inquiry can then turn to whether the causal link exists. In other cases, however, the harmfulness of the alleged harm is often debated. With respect to claims, for example, that some sexually explicit material causes promiscuity, encourages homosexuality, or legitimizes sexual practices other than vaginal intercourse, there is serious societal debate about whether the consequences themselves are harmful.

Thus, the analysis of the hypothesis that pornography causes harm must start with the identification of hypothesized harms, proceed to the determination of whether those hypothesized harms are indeed harmful, and then conclude with the examination of whether a causal link exists between the material and the harm. When the consequences of exposure to sexually explicit material are not harmful, or when there is no causal relationship between exposure to sexually explicit material and some harmful consequence, then we cannot say that the sexually explicit material is harmful. But if sexually explicit material of some variety is causally related to, or increases the incidence of, some behavior that *is* harmful, then it is safe to conclude that the material is harmful. . . .

5.2.1 Sexually Violent Material

The category of material on which most of the evidence has focused is the category of material featuring actual or unmistakably simulated or unmistakably threatened violence presented in sexually explicit fashion with a predominant focus on the sexually explicit violence. Increasingly, the most prevalent forms of pornography, as well as an increasingly prevalent body of less sexually explicit material, fit this description. Some of this material involves sado-masochistic themes, with the standard accoutrements of the genre, including whips, chains, devices of torture, and so on. But another theme of some of this material is not sado-masochistic, but involves instead the recurrent theme of a man making some sort of sexual advance to a woman, being rebuffed, and then raping the woman or in some other way violently forcing himself on the woman. In almost all of this material, whether in magazine or motion picture form, the woman eventually becomes aroused and ecstatic about the initially forced sexual activity, and usually is portrayed as begging for more. There is also a large body of material, more "mainstream" in its availability, that portrays sexual activity or sexually suggestive nudity coupled with extreme violence, such as disfigurement or murder. The so-called "slasher" films fit this description, as does some material, both in films and in magazines, that is less or more sexually explicit than the prototypical "slasher" film. . . .

When clinical and experimental research has focused particularly on sexually violent material, the conclusions have been virtually unanimous. In both clinical and experimental settings, exposure to sexually violent materials has indicated an increase in the likelihood of aggression. More specifically, the research . . . shows a causal relationship between exposure to material of this type and aggressive behavior towards women.

Finding a link between aggressive behavior towards women and sexual violence, whether lawful or unlawful, requires assumptions not found exclusively in the experimental evidence. We see no reason, however, not to make these assumptions. The assumption that increased aggressive behavior towards women is causally related, for an aggregate population, to increased sexual violence is significantly supported by the clinical evidence, as well as by much of the less scientific evidence. They are also to all of us assumptions that are plainly justified by our own common sense. This is not to say that all people with heightened levels of aggression will commit acts of sexual violence. But it is to say that over a sufficiently large number of cases we are confident in asserting that an increase in aggressive behavior directed at women will cause an increase in the level of sexual violence directed at women.

Thus we reach our conclusions by combining the results of the research with highly justifiable assumptions about the generalizability of more limited research results. Since the clinical and experimental evidence supports the conclusion that there is a causal relationship between exposure to sexually violent materials and an increase in aggressive behavior directed towards women, and since we believe that an increase in aggressive behavior towards women will in a population increase the incidence of sexual violence in that population, we have reached the conclusion, unanimously and confidently, that the available evidence strongly supports the hypothesis that substantial exposure to sexually violent materials as described here bears a causal relationship to antisocial acts of sexual violence and, for some subgroups, possibly to unlawful acts of sexual violence.

Although we rely for this conclusion on significant scientific empirical evidence, we feel it worthwhile to note the underlying logic of the conclusion. The evidence says simply that the images that people are exposed to bears a causal relationship to their behavior. This is hardly surprising. What would be surprising would be to find otherwise, and we have not so found. We have not, of course, found that the images people are exposed to are a greater cause of sexual violence than all or even many other possible causes the investigation of which has been beyond our mandate. Nevertheless, it would be strange indeed if graphic representations of a form of behavior, especially in a form that almost exclusively portrays such behavior as desirable, did not have at least some effect on patterns of behavior.

Sexual violence is not the only negative effect reported in the research to result from substantial exposure to sexually violent materials. The evidence is also strongly supportive of significant attitudinal changes on the part of those with substantial exposure to violent pornography. These attitudinal changes are numerous. Victims of rape and other forms of sexual violence are likely to be perceived by people so exposed as more responsible for the assault, as having suffered less injury, and as having been less degraded as a result of the experience. Similarly, people with a substantial exposure to violent pornography are likely to see the rapist or other sexual offender as less responsible for the act and as deserving of less stringent punishment.

These attitudinal changes have been shown experimentally to include a larger range of attitudes than those just discussed. The evidence also strongly supports the conclusion that substantial exposure to violent sexually explicit material leads to a greater acceptance of the "rape myth" in its broader sense—that women enjoy being coerced into sexual activity, that they enjoy being physically hurt in sexual context, and that as a result a man who forces himself on a woman sexually is in fact merely acceding to the "real" wishes of the woman, regardless of the extent to which she seems to be resisting. The myth is that a woman who says "no" really means "yes," and that men are justified in acting on the assumption that the "no" answer is indeed the "yes" answer. We have little trouble concluding that this attitude is both pervasive and profoundly harmful, and that any stimulus reinforcing or increasing the incidence of this attitude is for that reason alone properly designated as harmful.

Two vitally important features of the evidence supporting the above conclusions must be mentioned here. The first is that all of the harms discussed here, including acceptance of the legitimacy of sexual violence against women but not limited to it, are more pronounced when the sexually violent materials depict the woman as experiencing arousal, orgasm, or other form of enjoyment as the ultimate result of the sexual assault. This theme, unfortunately very common in the materials we have examined, is likely to be the major, albeit not the only, component of what it is in the materials in this category that causes the consequences that have been identified.

The second important clarification of all of the above is that the evidence lends some support to the conclusion that the consequences we have identified here *do not vary with the extent of sexual explicitness so long as the violence is presented in an undeniably sexual context.* Once a threshold is passed at which sex and violence are plainly linked, increasing the sexual explicitness of the material, or the bizarreness of the sexual activity, seems to bear little relationship to the extent of the consequences discussed here. Although it is unclear whether sexually violent material makes a substantially greater causal contribution to sexual violence itself than does material containing violence alone, it appears that increasing the amount of violence after the threshold of connecting sex with violence is more related to increase in the incidence or severity of harmful consequences than is increasing the amount of sex. As a result, the so-called "slasher" films, which depict a great deal of violence connected with an undeniably sexual theme but less sexual explicitness than materials that are truly pornographic, are likely to produce the consequences discussed here to a greater extent than most of the materials available in "adults only" pornographic outlets.

Although we have based our findings about material in this category primarily on evidence presented by professionals in the behavioral sciences, we are confident that it is supported by the less scientific evidence we have consulted, and we are each personally confident on the basis of our own knowledge and experiences that the conclusions are justified. None of us has the least doubt that sexual violence is harmful, and that general acceptance of the view that "no" means "yes" is a consequence of the most serious proportions. We have found a causal relationship between sexually explicit materials featuring violence and these consequences, and thus conclude that the class of such materials, although not necessarily every individual member of that class, is on the whole harmful to society.

5.2.2 Nonviolent Materials Depicting Degradation, Domination, Subordination, or Humiliation

Current research has rather consistently separated out violent pornography, the class of materials we have just discussed, from other sexually explicit materials. With respect to further subdivision the process has been less consistent. A few researchers have made further distinctions, while most have merely classed everything else as "non-violent." We have concluded that more subdivision than that is necessary. Our examination of the variety of sexually explicit materials convinces us that once again the category of "non-violent" ignores significant distinctions within this category, and thus combines classes of material that are in fact substantially different.

The subdivision we adopt is one that has surfaced in some of the research. And it is also one that might explain a significant amount of what would otherwise seem to be conflicting research results. Some researchers have found negative effects from non-violent material, while others report no such negative effects. But when the stimulus material these researchers have used is considered, there is some suggestion that the presence or absence of negative effects from non-violent material might turn on the non-violent material being considered "degrading," a term we shall explain shortly. It appears that effects similar to although not as extensive as that involved with violent material can be identified with respect to such degrading material, but that these effects are likely absent when neither degradation nor violence is present.

An enormous amount of the most sexually explicit material available, as well as much of the material that is somewhat less sexually explicit, is material that we would characterize as "degrading," the term we use to encompass the undeniably linked characteristics of degradation, domination, subordination, and humiliation. The degradation we refer to is degradation of people, most often women, and here we are referring to material that, although not violent, depicts people, usually women, as existing solely for the sexual satisfaction of others, usually men, or that depicts people, usually women, in decidedly subordinate roles in their sexual relations with others, or that depicts people engaged in sexual practices that would to most people be considered humiliating. Indeed, forms of degradation represent the largely predominant proportion of commercially available pornography.

With respect to material of this variety, our conclusions are substantially similar to those with respect to violent material, although we make them with somewhat less confidence and our making of them requires more in the way of assumption than was the case with respect to violent material. The evidence, scientific and otherwise, is more tentative, but supports the conclusion that the material we describe as degrading bears some causal relationship to the attitudinal changes we have previously identified. That is, substantial exposure to material of this variety is likely to increase the extent to which those exposed will view rape or other forms of sexual violence as less serious than they otherwise would have, will view the victim of rape and other forms of sexual violence as significantly more responsible, and will view the offenders as significantly less responsible. We also conclude that the evidence supports the conclusion that substantial exposure to material of this type will increase acceptance of the proposition that women like to be forced into sexual practices, and, once again, that the woman who says "no" really means "yes."

With respect to material of this type, there is less evidence causally linking the material with sexual aggression, but this may be because this is a category that has been isolated in only a few studies, albeit an increasing number. The absence of evidence should by no means be taken to deny the existence of the causal link. But because the causal link is less the subject of experimental studies, we have been required to think more carefully here about the assumptions necessary to causally connect increased acceptance of rape myths and other attitudinal changes with increased sexual aggression and sexual violence. And on the basis of all the evidence we have considered, from all sources, and on the basis of our own insights and experiences, we believe we are justified in drawing the following conclusion: Over a large enough sample a population that believes that many women like to be raped, that believes that sexual violence or sexual coercion is often desired or appropriate, and that believes that sex offenders are less responsible for their acts, will commit more acts of sexual violence or sexual coercion than would a population holding these beliefs to a lesser extent.

We should make clear what we have concluded here. We are not saying that everyone exposed to material of this type had his attitude about sexual violence changed. We are saying only that the evidence supports the conclusion that substantial exposure to degrading material increases the likelihood for an individual and the incidence over a large population that these attitudinal changes will occur. And we are not saying that everyone with these attitudes will commit an act of sexual violence or sexual coercion. We are saying that such attitudes will increase the likelihood for an individual and the incidence for a population that acts of sexual violence, sexual coercion, or unwanted sexual aggression will occur. Thus, we conclude that substantial exposure to materials of this type bears some causal relationship to the level of sexual violence, sexual coercion, or unwanted sexual aggression in the population so exposed.

We need mention as well that our focus on these more violent or more coercive forms of actual subordination of women should not diminish what we take to be a necessarily incorporated conclusion: Substantial exposure to materials of this type bears some causal relationship to the incidence of various non-violent forms of discrimination against or subordination of women in our society. To the extent that these materials create or reinforce the view that women's function is disproportionately to satisfy the sexual needs of men, then the materials will have pervasive effects on the treatment of women in society far beyond the incidence of identifiable acts of rape or other sexual violence. We obviously cannot here explore fully all of the forms in which women are discriminated against in contemporary society. Nor can we explore all of the causes of that discrimination against women. But we feel confident in concluding that the view of women as available for sexual domination is one cause of that discrimination, and we feel confident as well in concluding that degrading material bears a causal relationship to the view that women ought to subordinate their own desires and beings to the sexual satisfaction of men.

Although the category of the degrading is one that has only recently been isolated in some research, in the literature generally, and in public discussion of the issue, it is not a small category. If anything, it constitutes somewhere between the predominant and the overwhelming portion of what is currently standard fare heterosexual pornography, and is a significant theme in a broader range of materials not commonly taken to be sexually explicit enough to be pornographic. But as with sexually violent materials, the extent of the effect of these degrading materials may not turn substantially on the amount of sexual explicitness once a threshold of undeniable sexual content is surpassed. The category therefore includes a great deal of what would now be considered to be pornographic, and includes a great deal of what would now be held to be legally obscene, but it includes much more than that. Since we are here identifying harms for a class, rather than identifying harms caused by every member of that class, and since we are here talking about the identification of harm rather than making recommendations for legal control, we are not reluctant to identify harms for a class of material considerably wider than what is or even should be regulated by law.

5.2.3 Non-Violent and Non-Degrading Materials

Our most controversial category has been the category of sexually explicit materials that are not violent and are not degrading as we have used that term. They are materials in which the participants appear to be fully willing participants occupying substantially equal roles in a setting devoid of actual or apparent violence or pain. This category is in fact quite small in terms of currently available materials. There is some, to be sure, and the amount may increase as the division between the degrading and the non-degrading becomes more accepted, but we are convinced that only a small amount of currently available highly sexually explicit material is neither violent nor degrading. We thus talk about a small category, but one that should not be ignored. . . .

. . . Although the social science evidence is far from conclusive, we are on the current state of the evidence persuaded that material of this type does not bear a causal relationship to rape and other acts of sexual violence. . . .

A larger issue is the very question of promiscuity. Even to the extent that the behavior depicted is not inherently condemned by some or any of us, the manner of presentation almost necessarily suggests that the activities are taking place outside of the context of marriage, love, commitment, or even affection. Again, it is far from implausible to hypothesize that materials depicting sexual activity without marriage, love, commitment, or affection bear some causal relationship to sexual activity without marriage, love, commitment, or affection. There are undoubtedly many causes for what used to be called the "sexual revolution," but it is absurd to suppose that depictions or descriptions of uncommitted sexuality were not among them. Thus, once again our disagreements reflect disagreements in society at large, although not to as great an extent. Although there are many members of this society who can and have made affirmative cases for uncommitted sexuality, none of us believes it to be a good thing. A number of us, however, believe that the level of commitment in sexuality is a matter of choice among those who voluntarily engage in the activity. Others of us believe that uncommitted sexual activity is wrong for the individuals involved and harmful to society to the extent of its prevalence. Our view of the ultimate harmfulness of much of this material, therefore, is reflective of our individual views about the extent to whether sexual commitment is purely a matter of individual choice.

Even insofar as sexually explicit material of the variety being discussed here is not perceived as harmful for the messages it carries or the symbols it represents, the very publicness of what is commonly taken to be private is cause for concern. Even if we hypothesize a sexually explicit motion picture of a loving married couple engaged in mutually pleasurable and procreative vaginal intercourse, the depiction of that act on a screen or in a magazine may constitute a harm in its own right (a "primary harm" in the terminology introduced earlier in this Chapter) solely by virtue of being shown. Here the concern is with the preservation of sex as an essentially private act, in conformity with the basic privateness of sex long recognized by this and all other societies. The alleged harm here, therefore, is that as soon as sex is put on a screen or put in a magazine it changes its character, regardless of what variety of sex is portrayed. And to the extent that the character of sex as public rather than private is the consequence here, then that to many would constitute a harm. . . .

A number of witnesses have testified about the effects on their own sexual relations, usually with their spouses, of the depiction on the screen and in magazines of sexual practices in which they had not previously engaged. A number of these witnesses, *all women,* have testified that men in their lives have used such material to strongly encourage, or coerce, them into engaging in sexual practices in which they do not choose to engage. To the extent that such implicit or explicit coercion takes place as a result of these materials, we all agree that it is a harm. There has been other evidence, however, about the extent to which such material might for some be a way of revitalizing their sex lives, or, more commonly, simply constituting a part of a mutually pleasurable sexual experience for both partners. On this we could not agree. For reasons relating largely to the question of publicness in the first sense discussed above, some saw this kind of use as primarily harmful. Others saw it as harmless and possibly beneficial in contexts such as this. Some professional testimony supported this latter view, but we have little doubt that professional opinion is also divided on the issue. . . .

Offensive Speech and Behavior

In response to racial incidents, colleges and universities across the country have been enacting speech codes to limit what can be said on campus. Some are narrow, proscribing only repeated harassment of individuals; others are broad, prohibiting "insensitive" speech and behavior. At least one restriction has been struck down by a court as unconstitutional. Off campus, legal scholars have proposed new rules for civil lawsuits related to racial insults, and complaints and lawsuits concerning sexual harassment have become commonplace. Many companies now have sexual harassment policies and complaint procedures. Many states have passed laws giving stiffer penalties to criminals motivated by prejudice.

Advocates of these changes point to equality, the protection of rights, and the benefits of a more inclusive social environment. Critics, however, see restrictions on speech that are hard to justify.

Freedoms of thought, speech, and the press have well-recognized exceptions. One may not slander a person, incite a mob to riot, or shout "Fire!" in a crowded theater that is not on fire. In Mill's words, "Acts, of whatever kind, which without justifiable cause do harm to others may be, and in the more important cases absolutely require to be, controlled by the unfavorable sentiments, and, when needful, by the active interference of mankind." In cases of the kinds just mentioned, the harm done to particular people outweighs any possible value the speech possesses.

Is that true of racial insults, sexual harassment, and other offensive speech? Undoubtedly, harassment of various kinds can cause harm. But often offensive speech is just that—offensive. If someone insults me, or makes lewd remarks to me, or makes an obscene gesture toward me, I am probably going to be offended. But it is not so clear that I will suffer harm. There seems to be a big difference between an obscene gesture and a punch in the nose. The childhood rhyme says, "Sticks and stones will break my bones, but words will never hurt me." This seems wrong—words can hurt—but it nevertheless makes an important point: There are differences between offense and harm.

The most important case concerning racial or ethnic harassment is *Collin* v. *Smith.* It arose when the American Nazi Party asked for a permit to march through Skokie, Illinois, home to many survivors of the Holocaust. The Nazis, with the support of the American Civil Liberties Union, argued that freedom of speech protected their right to march, displaying Nazi uniforms and swastikas, through the Chicago suburb. Skokie refused to grant the permit.

In *Offense to Others,* Joel Feinberg considers a wide variety of offensive situations, asking which ought to be prohibited by law. Warning: Many are offensive to encounter even in print! Feinberg points out that there are different kinds of offensive behaviors, and different kinds of offense, in addition to different degrees of offense. Some, in his view, justify restrictions, but none constitute harms.

Stanley Fish argues that speech is never really free; all defenses of freedom of speech make exceptions. The exceptions, Fish contends, are based not on principle but on politics. Deciding what speech to allow is deciding what will be politically favored. Fish concludes by defending speech codes and other restrictions, maintaining that they produce social benefits.

Jonathan Rauch sees in arguments such as Fish's a humanitarian threat to freedom. People restrict offensive speech for good, humanitarian reasons—to protect people from offense and harm. But, Rauch thinks, the restrictions threaten the entire institution of liberal science. Seeking the truth requires not only free inquiry but free intellectual battle, which may sometimes include offensive speech and behavior. Liberal science, Rauch insists, is the best method we have for determining truth. And it punishes those who are wrong by ridiculing them and their ideas. This is not an unfortunate accident, Rauch believes; it is essential to the scientific process.

Collin v. *Smith* (1978)

(Source: Collin *v.* Smith *578 F.2d 1197 [1978]. Most legal references have been omitted.)*

QUESTIONS FOR REFLECTION

1. What were the important provisions of Skokie's ordinances banning the Nazi march? How similar are they to university rules against racist speech?
2. Why does the Court refuse to consider the Nazi march as analogous to "fighting words"? Do you agree with this justification?
3. What is Skokie's fourth argument? Why does the Court reject it? Do you agree?
4. What is Judge Sprecher's basis for dissent? How does Judge Pell respond to the arguments he raises?

PELL, Circuit Judge.

Plaintiff-appellee, the National Socialist Party of America (NSPA) is a political group described by its leader, plaintiff-appellee Frank Collin, as a Nazi party. Among NSPA's more controversial and generally unacceptable beliefs are that black persons are biologically inferior to white persons, and should be expatriated to Africa as soon as possible; that American Jews have "inordinate . . . political and financial power" in the world and are "in the forefront of the international Communist revolution." NSPA members affect a uniform reminiscent of those worn by members of the German Nazi Party during the Third Reich, and display a swastika thereon and on a red, white, and black flag they frequently carry.

The Village of Skokie, Illinois, a defendant-appellant, is a suburb north of Chicago. It has a large Jewish population, including as many as several thousand survivors of the Nazi holocaust in Europe before and during World War II. Other defendants-appellants are Village officials.

When Collin and NSPA announced plans to march in front of the Village Hall in Skokie on May 1, 1977, Village officials responded by obtaining in state court a preliminary injunction against the demonstration. After state courts refused to stay the injunction pending appeal, the United States Supreme Court ordered a stay, *National Socialist Party of America v. Village of Skokie* (1977). The injunction was subsequently reversed first in part, *Village of Skokie v. National Socialist Party of America* (1977), and then in its entirety (1978). On May 2, 1977, the Village enacted three ordinances to prohibit demonstrations such as the one Collin and NSPA had threatened. This lawsuit seeks declaratory and injunctive relief against enforcement of the ordinances.

Village Ordinance No. 77–5–N–994 (hereinafter designated, for convenience of reference, as 994) is a comprehensive permit system for all parades or public assemblies of more than 50 persons. It requires permit applicants to obtain $300,000 in public liability insurance and $50,000 in property damage insurance. One of the prerequisites for a permit is a finding by the appropriate official(s) that the assembly

> will not portray criminality, depravity or lack of virtue in, or incite violence, hatred, abuse or hostility toward a person or group of persons by reason of reference to religious, racial, ethnic, national or regional affiliation.

Another is a finding that the permit activity will not be conducted "for an unlawful purpose." None of this ordinance applies to activities by the Village itself or of a governmental agency, and any provision of the ordinance may be waived by unanimous consent of the Board of Trustees of the Village. To parade or assemble without a permit is a crime, punishable by fines from $5 to $500.

Village Ordinance No. 77–5–N–995 (995) prohibits

> [t]he dissemination of any materials within the Village of Skokie which promotes and incites hatred against persons by reason of their race, national origin, or religion, and is intended to do so.

"Dissemination of materials" includes

> publication or display or distribution of posters, signs, handbills, or writings and public display of markings and clothing of symbolic significance.

Violation is a crime punishable by fine of up to $500, or imprisonment of up to six months. Village Ordinance No. 77–5–N–996 (996) prohibits public demonstrations by members of political parties while wearing "military-style" uniforms, and violation is punishable as in 995.

Collin and NSPA applied for a permit to march on July 4, 1977, which was denied on the ground the application disclosed an intention to violate 996. The Village apparently applies 994 so that an intention to violate 995 or 996 establishes an "unlawful purpose" for the march or assembly. The permit application stated that the march would last about a half hour, and would involve 30 to 50 demonstrators wearing uniforms including swastikas and carrying a party banner with a swastika and placards with statements thereon such as "White Free Speech," "Free Speech for the White Man," and "Free Speech for White America." A single file sidewalk march that would not disrupt traffic was proposed, without speeches or the distribution of handbills or literature. Counsel for the Village advises us that the Village does not maintain that Collin and NSPA will behave other than as described in the permit application(s).

The district court, after considering memoranda, exhibits, depositions, and live testimony, issued a comprehensive and thorough opinion granting re-relief to Collin and NSPA. The insurance requirements of 994 were invalidated as insuperable obstacles to free speech in Skokie, and [other sections] were adjudged impermissible prior restraints. Ordinance 995 was determined to be fatally vague and overbroad, and 996 was invalidated as overbroad and patently unjustified.

On its appeal, the Village concedes the invalidity of the insurance requirements as applied to these plaintiffs and of the uniform prohibition of 996.

I

The conflict underlying this litigation has commanded substantial public attention, and engendered considerable and understandable emotion. We would hopefully surprise no one by confessing personal views that NSPA's beliefs and goals are repugnant to the core values held generally by residents of this country, and, indeed, to much of what we cherish in civilization. As judges sworn to defend the Constitution, however, we cannot decide this or any case on that basis. Ideological tyranny, no matter how worthy its motivation, is forbidden as much to appointed judges as to elected legislators.

The record in this case contains the testimony of a survivor of the Nazi holocaust in Europe. Shortly before oral argument in this case, a lengthy and highly publicized citizenship revocation trial of an alleged Nazi war criminal was held in a federal court in Chicago, and in the week immediately after argument here, a four-part "docudrama" on the holocaust was nationally televised and widely observed. We cannot then be unmindful of the horrors associated with the Nazi regime of the Third Reich, with which to some real and apparently intentional degree appellees associate themselves. Nor does the record allow us to ignore the certainty that appellees know full well that, in light of their views and the historical associations they would bring with them to Skokie, many people would find their demonstration extremely mentally and emotionally disturbing, or the suspicion that such a result may be relished by appellees.

But our tasks here is to decide whether the First Amendment protects the activity in which appellees wish to engage, not to render moral judgment on their views or tactics. No authorities need be cited to establish the proposition, which the Village does not dispute, that First Amendment rights are truly precious and fundamental to our national life. Nor is this truth without relevance to the saddening historical images this case inevitably arouses. It is, after all, in part the fact that our constitutional system protects minorities unpopular at a particular time or place from governmental harassment and intimidation, that distinguishes life in this country from life under the Third Reich.

Before undertaking specific analysis of the clash between the Village ordinances and appellees' desires to demonstrate in Skokie, it will be helpful to establish some general principles of pertinence to the decision required of us. Putting to one side for the moment the question of whether the content of appellees' views and symbols makes a constitutional difference here, we find we are unable to deny that the activities in which the appellees wish to engage are within the ambit of the First Amendment.

These activities involve the "cognate rights" of free speech and free assembly. "[T]he wearing of an armband for the purpose of expressing certain views is the type of symbolic act that is within the Free Speech Clause of the First Amendment." *Tinker v. Des Moines Independent Community School District* (1969). Standing alone, at least, it is "closely akin to 'pure speech' which, we have repeatedly held, is entitled to comprehensive protection under the First Amendment." The same thing can be said of NSPA's intended display of a party flag and of the messages intended for the placards party members would carry. Likewise, although marching, parading, and picketing, because they involve conduct implicating significant interests in maintaining public order, are less protected than pure speech, they are nonetheless subject to significant First Amendment protection. Indeed, an orderly and peaceful demonstration, with placards, in the vicinity of a seat of government, is "an exercise of [the] basic constitutional rights of [speech, assembly, and petition] in their most pristine and classic form."

No doubt, the Nazi demonstration could be subjected to reasonable regulation of its time, place, and manner. Although much of the permit system of 994 is of that nature, the provisions attacked here are not. No objection is raised by the Village, in ordinances or in their proofs and arguments in this case, to the suggested time, place, or manner of the demonstration, except the general assertion that in the place of Skokie, in these times, *given the content of appellees' views and symbols,* the demonstration and its symbols and speech should be prohibited. Because the ordinances turn on the content of the demonstration, they are necessarily not time, place, or manner regulations.

Legislating against the content of First Amendment activity, however, launches the government on a slippery and precarious path:

> [A]bove all else, the First Amendment means that government has no power to restrict expression because of its messages, its ideas, its subject matter, or its content. To permit the continued building of our politics and culture, and to assure self-fulfillment for each individual, our people are guaranteed the right to express any thought, free from government censorship. The essence of this forbidden censorship is content control. Any restriction on expressive activity because of its content would completely undercut the "profound national commitment to the principle that debate on public issues should be uninhibited, robust, and wide-open." *New York Times Co. v. Sullivan* [1964]. *Mosley* [1972].

This is not to say, of course, that content legislation is *per se* invalid. Chief Justice Burger concurred in *Mosley* just to point out the established exceptions to such a rule, namely obscenity, fighting words, and, as limited by constitutional requirements, libel. Likewise, in very narrow circumstances, a government may proscribe content on the basis of imminent danger of a grave substantive evil. But analysis of content restrictions must begin with a healthy respect for the truth that they are the most direct threat to the vitality of First Amendment rights.

II

We first consider ordinance 995, prohibiting the dissemination of materials which would promote hatred towards persons on the basis of their heritage. The Village would apparently apply this provision to NSPA's display of swastikas, their uniforms, and, perhaps, to the content of their placards.

The ordinance cannot be sustained on the basis of some of the more obvious exceptions to the rule against content control. While some would no doubt be willing to label appellees' views and symbols obscene, the constitutional rule that obscenity is unprotected applies only to material with erotic content. Furthermore, although the Village introduced evidence in the district court tending to prove that some individuals, at least, might have difficulty restraining their reactions to the Nazi demonstration, the Village tells us that it does not rely on a fear of responsive violence to justify the ordinance, and does not even suggest that there will be any physical violence if the march is held. This confession takes this case out of the scope of *Brandenburg v. Ohio* and *Feiner v. New York* (1951) (intentional "incitement to riot" may be prohibited). The Village does not argue otherwise.

The concession also eliminates any argument based on the fighting words doctrine of *Chaplinsky v. New Hampshire* (1942). The Court in *Chaplinsky* affirmed a conviction under a statute that, as authoritatively construed, applied only to words with a direct tendency to cause violence by the persons to whom, individually, the words were addressed. A conviction for less than words that at least tend to incite an immediate breach of the peace cannot be justified under *Chaplinsky*. The Illinois Supreme Court, in *Village of Skokie v. National Socialist Party of America* has squarely ruled that responsive violence fears and the fighting words doctrine could not support the prohibition of appellees' demonstration. Although that decision was in a prior restraint context, and we are here considering only the post facto criminal aspects of 995, the decision does buttress our conclusion that *Chaplinsky* does not cover this case. Again, the Village does not seriously contest this point.

Four basic arguments are advanced by the Village to justify the content restrictions of 995. First, it is said that the content criminalized by 995 is "totally lacking in social content," and that it consists of "false statements of fact" in which there is "no constitutional value." *Gertz v. Robert Welch, Inc.* (1974). We disagree that, if applied to the proposed demonstration, the ordinance can be said to be limited to "statements of fact," false or otherwise. No handbills are to be distributed; no speeches are planned. To the degree that the symbols in question can be said to assert anything specific, it must be the Nazi ideology, which cannot be treated as a mere false "fact."

We may agree with the district court that

> if any philosophy should be regarded as completely unacceptable to civilized society, that of plaintiffs, who, while disavowing on the witness stand any advocacy of genocide, have nevertheless deliberately identified themselves with a regime whose record of brutality and barbarism is unmatched in modern history, would be a good place to start.

But there can be no legitimate start down such a road.

> Under the First Amendment there is no such thing as a false idea. However pernicious an opinion may seem, we depend for its correction not on the conscience of judges and juries but on the competition of other ideas.

Gertz. In the words of Justice Jackson, "every person must be his own watchman for truth, because the forefathers did not trust any government to separate the true from the false for us." *Thomas v. Collins* [1945]. The asserted falseness of Nazi dogma, and, indeed, its general repudiation, simply do not justify its suppression.

The Village's second argument, and the one on which principal reliance is placed, centers on

Beauharnais v. Illinois (1952). There a conviction was upheld under a statute prohibiting, in language substantially (and perhaps not unintentionally) similar to that used in the ordinance here, the dissemination of materials promoting racial or religious hatred. The closely-divided Court stated that the criminal punishment of libel of an *individual* raised no constitutional problems, relying on *Chaplinsky v. New Hampshire:*

> There are certain well-defined and narrowly limited classes of speech, the prevention and punishment of which have never been thought to raise any Constitutional problem. These include the lewd and obscene, the profane, the libelous, and the insulting or "fighting" words. . . . [S]uch utterances are no essential part of any exposition of ideas, and are of such slight social value as a step to truth that any benefit that may be derived from them is clearly outweighed by the social interest in order and morality.

That being so, the Court reasoned that the state could constitutionally extend the prohibition to utterances aimed at groups.

In our opinion *Beauharnais* does not support ordinance 995, for two independent reasons. First, the rationale of that decision turns quite plainly on the strong tendency of the prohibited utterances to cause violence and disorder. The Illinois Supreme Court had so limited the statute's application, as the United States Supreme Court noted. The latter Court also pointed out that the tendency to induce breach of the peace was the traditional justification for the criminal libel laws which had always been thought to be immune from the First Amendment. After stating the issue (whether Illinois could extend criminal libel to groups) the Court turned to Illinois' history of racial strife "and its frequent obligato of extreme racial and religious propaganda" and concluded that the Illinois legislature could reasonably connect the strife and the propaganda and criminalize the latter to prevent the former. *Cantwell v. Connecticut* (1940) was quoted:

> The danger in these times from the coercive activities of those who in the delusion of racial or religious conceit *would incite violence and breaches of the peace* in order to deprive others of their equal right to the exercise of their liberties, is emphasized by events familiar to all. These and other transgressions of [the limits to First Amendment rights] the States appropriately may punish. [Emphasis added.]

It may be questioned . . . whether the *tendency to induce violence* approach sanctioned implicitly in *Beauharnais* would pass constitutional muster today. Assuming that it would, however, it does not support ordinance 995, because the Village, as we have indicated, does not assert appellees' possible violence, an audience's possible responsive violence, or possible violence against third parties by those incited by appellees, as justifications for 995. Ordinance 995 would apparently be applied in the absence of any such threat. The rationale of *Beauharnais,* then, simply does not apply here.

Further, when considering the application of *Beauharnais* to the present litigation, we cannot be unmindful of the "package" aspects of the ordinances and that the "insulting" words are to be made public only after a 30-day permit application waiting period. Violence occurring under such a circumstance would have such indicia of premeditation as to seem inconsistent with calling into play any remaining vitality of the *Beauharnais* rationale.

The Village asserts that *Beauharnais* implicitly sanctions prohibiting the use of First Amendment rights to invoke racial or religious hatred *even without reference to fears of violence.* In the light of our discussion of *Beauharnais'* premises, we do not find the case susceptible of this interpretation. Even if it were, however, we agree with the district court that decisions in the quarter-century since *Beauharnais* have abrogated the *Chaplinsky* dictum, made one of the premises of *Beauharnais,* that the punishment of libel "has never been thought to raise any Constitutional problem." *New York Times Co. v. Sullivan* (1964); *Garrison v. Louisiana* (1964) (criminal libel); and *Gertz v. Robert Welch, Inc.* are indisputable evidence that libel does indeed now raise serious and knotty First Amendment problems, sufficient as a matter of constitutional law to require the substantial rewriting of both criminal and civil state libel laws.

The Eighth Circuit and Judge Wright of the District of Columbia Circuit have expressed doubt, which we share, that *Beauharnais* remains good law at all after the constitutional libel cases. We agree at least this far: If 995 is to be sustained, it must be done on the basis of the Village's interest asserted, and the conduct to which 995 applies, not on the basis of blind obeisance to uncertain implications from an opinion issued years before the Supreme Court itself rewrote the rules.

The Villages' third argument is that it has a policy of fair housing, which the dissemination of racially defamatory material could undercut. We reject this argument without extended discussion. That the effective exercise of First Amendment rights may undercut a given government's policy on some issue is, indeed, one of the purposes of those rights. No distinction is constitutionally admissible that turns on the intrinsic justice of the particular policy in issue.

The Village's fourth argument is that the Nazi march, involving as it does the display of uniforms and swastikas, will create a substantive evil that it has a right to prohibit: the infliction of psychic trauma on resident holocaust survivors and other Jewish residents. The Village points out that Illinois recognizes the "new tort" of intentional infliction of severe emotional distress, the coverage of which may well include personally directed racial slurs. Assuming that specific individuals could proceed in tort under this theory to recover damages provably occasioned by the proposed march, and that a First Amendment defense would not bar the action, it is nonetheless quite a different matter to criminalize protected First Amendment conduct in anticipation of such results.

It would be grossly insensitive to deny, as we do not, that the proposed demonstration would seriously disturb, emotionally and mentally, at least some, and probably many of the Village's residents. The problem with engrafting an exception on the First Amendment for such situations is that they are indistinguishable in principle from speech that "invite[s] dispute . . . induces a condition of unrest, creates dissatisfaction with conditions as they are, or even stirs people to anger." *Terminiello v. Chicago* (1949). Yet these are among the "high purposes" of the First Amendment. It is perfectly clear that a state many not "make criminal the peaceful expression of unpopular views." *Edwards v. South Carolina* [1963]. Likewise, "mere public intolerance or animosity cannot be the basis for abridgement of these constitutional freedoms." *Coates v. City of Cincinnati* (1971). Where, as here, a crime is made of a silent march, attended only by symbols and not by extrinsic conduct offensive in itself, we think the words of the Court in *Street v. New York* are very much on point:

> [A]ny shock effect . . . must be attributed to the content of the ideas expressed. It is firmly settled that under our Constitution the public expression of ideas may not be prohibited merely because the ideas are themselves offensive to some of their hearers. [Citations omitted.]

It is said that the proposed march is not speech, or even "speech plus," but rather an invasion, intensely menacing no matter how peacefully conducted. The Village's expert psychiatric witness, in fact, testified that the effect of the march would be much the same regardless of whether uniforms and swastikas were displayed, due to the intrusion of self-proclaimed Nazis into what he characterized as predominately Jewish "turf." There is room under the First Amendment for the government to protect targeted listeners from offensive speech, but only when the speaker intrudes on the privacy of the home, or a captive audience cannot practically avoid exposure.

> The Supreme Court has consistently stressed that "we are often 'captives' outside the sanctuary of the home and subject to objectionable speech." The ability of government, consonant with the Constitution, to shut off discourse solely to protect others from hearing it is, in other words, dependent upon a showing that substantial privacy interests are being invaded in an essentially intolerable manner. *Any broader view of this authority would effectively*

empower a majority to silence dissidents simply as a matter of personal predilections. [Emphasis added.]

Cohen v. California [1971].

This case does not involve intrusion into people's homes. There *need be* no captive audience, as Village residents may, if they wish, simply avoid the Village Hall for thirty minutes on a Sunday afternoon, which no doubt would be their normal course of conduct on a day when the Village Hall was not open in the regular course of business. Absent such intrusion or captivity, there is no justifiable substantial privacy interest to save 995 from constitutional infirmity, when it attempts, by fiat, to declare the entire Village, at all times, a privacy zone that may be sanitized from the offensiveness of Nazi ideology and symbols.

We conclude that 995 may not be applied to criminalize the conduct of the proposed demonstration. Because it is susceptible to such an application, we also conclude that it suffers from substantial overbreadth, even if some of the purposes 995 is said to serve might constitutionally be protected by an appropriate and narrower ordinance. The latter conclusion is also supported by the fact that the ordinances could conceivably be applied to criminalize dissemination of *The Merchant of Venice* or a vigorous discussion of the merits of reverse racial discrimination in Skokie. Although there is reason to think, as the district court concluded, that the ordinance is fatally vague as well, because it turns in part on subjective reactions to prohibited conduct, we do not deem it necessary to rest our decision on that ground.

III

Our decision that 995 cannot constitutionally be applied to the proposed march necessarily means that a permit for the march may not be denied on the basis of anticipated violations thereof. We turn to the question of whether the similar provision built into 994 by §27–56(c) can be the basis of a permit denial.

The answer really follows with even greater strength from our conclusion on 995. Because 994 §27–56(c) gives to Village "officials the power to deny use of a forum in advance of actual expression," *Southeastern Promotions, Ltd. v. Conrad* (1975), it is a prior restraint, which thus "comes to this Court with a 'heavy presumption' against its constitutional validity." *Organization for a Better Austin v. Keefe* (1971).

> The presumption against prior restraints is heavier—and the degree of protection broader—than that against limits on expression imposed by criminal penalties. Behind the distinction is a theory deeply etched in our law: a free society prefers to punish the few who abuse rights of speech *after* they break the law than to throttle them and all others beforehand.

Southeastern Promotions. The slightly more specific language of §27–56(c) than that which 995 contains might cut against finding the former provision unconstitutionally vague, but there is otherwise no meaningful difference between the two provisions except the element of prior restraint. The requested parade permit cannot be denied on the basis of §27–56(c). . . .

SPRECHER, Circuit Judge, concurring in part and dissenting in part.

The basic situation in this case—the efforts of avowed and uniformed Hitlerian Nazis to demonstrate without municipal regulations in the streets of a predominantly Jewish village housing some 7,000 Jewish survivors of World War II and their families—conjures up a unique amalgam of complex First Amendment concepts such as prior restraint, group libel, fighting words and hostile audiences, incitement to riot, and shouting "fire" in a crowded theater. Seldom before has a federal court been faced with a situation raising such powerful cross-pressures as have been created in this case. For instance, the fact that it now seems to be instilled in Jewish culture to confront threatened oppression with active resistance and aggressive retaliation differentiates this case factually from *Terminiello v. Chicago* (1949). With a situation that is so unique, it is important to keep in mind Mr. Justice Stevens's admonition from one of the most recent First Amendment cases that "[e]ven within the area of protected speech, a difference in content may require a different governmental response." *Young v. American Mini Theatres, Inc.* (1976). There may very well be a necessity for a new balancing of values in these circumstances as opposed to the immediate governmental paralysis which is supposed to occur when the rubric of "prior restraint" is sounded. . . .

[I . . .]

[II . . .]

III

. . . We must first examine whether plaintiffs' proposed conduct falls within the scope of the First Amendment. We are dealing with a proposed march through a predominantly Jewish community. The plaintiffs would wear nazi-style uniforms and swastika armbands or emblems and carry written signs. No speeches were to be made. Plaintiffs' handbills had been distributed in the Village and a number of Skokie residents with Jewish surnames had received "offensive and threatening telephone calls." The portent of this action and the proposed march could not be lost on anyone familiar with the methods of Hitler's Nazis in Germany.

Under these circumstances, the appearance of plaintiffs' group in Skokie may be so extremely offensive and of such little social utility as to be beyond the protection of the First Amendment. In this sense the present case does not differ greatly from *Chaplinsky v. New Hampshire* (1942), where the Court upheld the conviction of a Jehovah's Witness for calling complainant a "God damned racketeer" and "a damned fascist." The analysis the Court used there applies with equal force here to the activities proposed by plaintiffs:

> Allowing the broadest scope to the language and purpose of the Fourteenth Amendment, it is well understood that the right of free speech is not absolute at all times and under all circumstances. There are certain well-defined and narrowly limited classes of speech, the prevention and punishment of which have never been thought to raise any Constitutional problem. These include . . . "fighting" words—those which by their very utterance inflict injury or tend to incite an immediate breach of the peace. It has been well observed that such utterances are no essential part of any exposition of ideas, and are of such slight social value as a step to truth that any benefit that may be derived from them is clearly outweighed by the social interest in order and morality. "Resort to epithets or personal abuse is not in any proper sense communication of information or opinion safeguarded by the Constitution. . . . "

Another basis on which to conclude that plaintiffs' proposed conduct falls outside the protection of the First Amendment is that under the circumstances it constitutes a pernicious form of group libel. In *Beauharnais v. Illinois* (1952), the Court upheld a statute which is strikingly similar to those attacked here. The Court there declared:

> It is not within our competence to confirm or deny claims of social scientists as to the dependence of the individual on the position of his racial or religious group in the community. It would, however, be arrant dogmatism, quite outside the scope of our authority in passing on the powers of a State, for us to deny that the Illinois legislature may warrantably believe that a man's job and his educational opportunities and the dignity accorded him may depend as much on the reputation of the racial and religious group to which he willy-nilly belongs, as on his own merits. This being so, we are precluded from saying that speech concededly punishable when immediately directed at individuals cannot be outlawed if directed at groups with whose position and esteem in society the affiliated individuals may be inextricably involved.

Nor do we need to back away from this analysis merely because the Supreme Court has substantially modified the law of libel insofar as it relates to public officials or public figures as opposed to the minor backtracking concerning libel of private individuals. Moreover, although *Beauharnais* is said to have been scarcely noted since 1952, neither has it been overruled.

It appears to me that plaintiffs' proposed activities, under the circumstances presented here, might reasonably be viewed as not within the area of constitutionally protected activity. At least the question seems close enough to warrant serious concern and analysis within the factual situation presented. Plaintiffs' proposed actions in this case arguably "are no essential part of any exposition of ideas, and are of such slight social value as a step to truth that any benefit that may be derived from them is clearly outweighed by the social interest in order and morality." *Chaplinsky v. New Hampshire.* This conclusion supports a finding at the very least of the validity of the challenged insurance ordinance.

IV

Concerning the assumption that the content of speech or conduct is an impermissible consideration when regulation of those activities are proposed, we note that regulation of First Amendment activities never has been and never can be "content blind." As early as 1919, the Supreme Court in *Schenck v. United States* declared through Mr. Justice Holmes:

> The question in every case is whether the words used are used in such circumstances and are of such a nature as to create a clear and present danger that they will bring about the substantive evils that Congress has a right to prevent. It is a question of proximity and degree.

There is no dispute that speech may not be suppressed merely because it offends its listeners. At some point, however, considerations of a neutral desire to maintain the public peace and general welfare come into play in determining whether activities should be allowed. Where the activity is, as here, by its nature and by the circumstances, a threat to a reasonable attempt to maintain the public order, it cannot claim to go unregulated under the auspices that content may not properly be considered. . . .

JOEL FEINBERG

A Ride on the Bus

Joel Feinberg is Professor of Philosophy at the University of Arizona. (Source: From Offense to Others *[New York: Oxford, 1985]. Notes have been omitted.*

QUESTIONS FOR REFLECTION

1. Which of Feinberg's examples would you consider least offensive? Why?
2. Which would you consider most offensive? What makes them particularly bad? Would you evaluate them as harmful to you? Why, or why not?
3. How does Feinberg distinguish offense from harm?

A Ride on the Bus

There is a limit to the power of abstract reasoning to settle questions of moral legitimacy. The question raised by this chapter is whether there are any human experiences that are harmless in themselves yet so unpleasant that we can rightly demand legal protection from them even at the cost of other persons' liberties. The best way to deal with that question at the start is to engage our imaginations in the inquiry, consider hypothetically the most offensive experiences we can imagine, and then sort them into groups in an effort to isolate the kernel of the offense in each category. Accordingly, this section will consist of a number of vividly sketched imaginary tales, and the reader is asked to project himself into each story and determine as best he can what his reaction would be. In each story the reader should think of himself as a passenger on a normally crowded public bus on his way to work or to some important appointment in circumstances such that if he is forced to leave the bus prematurely, he will not only have to pay another fare to get where he is going, but he will probably be late, to his own disadvantage. If he is not exactly a captive on the bus, then, he would nevertheless be greatly inconvenienced if he had to leave the bus before it reached his destination. In each story, another passenger, or group of passengers, gets on the bus, and proceeds to cause, by their characteristics or their conduct, great offense to *you*. The stories form six clusters corresponding to the kind of offense caused.

A. *Affronts to the senses*

Story 1. A passenger who obviously hasn't bathed in more than a month sits down next to you. He reeks of a barely tolerable stench. There is hardly room to stand elsewhere on the bus and all other seats are occupied.

Story 2. A passenger wearing a shirt of violently clashing orange and crimson sits down directly in your forward line of vision. You must keep your eyes down to avoid looking at him.

Story 3. A passenger sits down next to you, pulls a slate tablet from his brief case, and proceeds to scratch his fingernails loudly across the slate, sending a chill up your spine and making your teeth clench. You politely ask him to stop, but he refuses.

Story 4. A passenger elsewhere in the bus turns on a portable radio to maximum volume. The sounds it emits are mostly screeches, whistles, and static, but occasionally some electronically amplified rock and roll music blares through.

B. *Disgust and revulsion*

Story 5. This is much like story 1 except that the malodorous passenger in the neighboring seat continually scratches, drools, coughs, farts, and belches.

Story 6. A group of passengers enters the bus and shares a seating compartment with you. They spread a table cloth over their laps and proceed to eat a picnic lunch that consists of live insects, fish heads, and pickled sex organs of lamb, veal, and pork, smothered in garlic and onions. Their table manners leave almost everything to be desired.

Story 7. Things get worse and worse. The itinerant picnickers practice gluttony in the ancient Roman manner, gorging until satiation and then vomiting on to their table cloth. Their practice, however, is a novel departure from the ancient custom in that they eat their own and one another's vomit along with the remaining food.

Story 8. A coprophagic sequel to story 7.

Story 9. At some point during the trip the passenger at one's side quite openly and nonchalantly changes her sanitary napkin and drops the old one into the aisle.

C. *Shock to moral, religious, or patriotic sensibilities*

Story 10. A group of mourners carrying a coffin enter the bus and share a seating compartment with you. Although they are all dressed in black their demeanor is by no means funereal. In fact they seem more angry than sorrowful, and refer to the deceased as "the old bastard," and "the bloody corpse." At one point they rip open the coffin with hammers and proceed to smash the corpse's face with a series of hard hammer blows.

Story 11. A strapping youth enters the bus and takes a seat directly in your line of vision. He is wearing a T-shirt with a cartoon across his chest of Christ on the cross. Underneath the picture appear the words "Hang in there, baby!"

Story 12. After taking the seat next to you a passenger produces a bundle wrapped in a large American flag. The bundle contains, among other things, his lunch, which he proceeds to eat. Then he spits into the star-spangled corner of the flag and uses it first to clean his mouth and then to blow his nose. Then he uses the main striped part of the flag to shine his shoes.

D. *Shame, embarrassment (including vicarious embarrassment), and anxiety*

Story 13. The passenger who takes the seat directly across from you is entirely naked. On one version of the story, he or she is the same sex as you; on the other version of the story, he or she is the opposite sex.

Story 14. The passenger in the previous story proceeds to masturbate quietly in his or her seat.

Story 15. A man and woman, more or less fully clothed to start, take two seats directly in front of you, and then begin to kiss, hug, pet, and fondle one another to the accompaniment of loud sighs and moans of pleasure. They continue these activities throughout the trip.

Story 16. The couple of the previous story, shortly before the bus reaches their destination, engage in acts of mutual masturbation, with quite audible instructions to each other and other sound effects.

Story 17. A variant of the previous story which climaxes in an act of coitus, somewhat acrobatically performed as required by the crowded circumstances.

Story 18. The seat directly in front of you is occupied by a youth (of either sex) wearing a T-shirt with a lurid picture of a copulating couple across his or her chest.

Story 19. A variant of the previous story in which the couple depicted is recognizable (in virtue of conventional representations) as Jesus and Mary.

Story 20. The couple in stories 15–17 perform a variety of sadomasochistic sex acts with appropriate verbal communications ("Oh, that hurts so sweet! Hit me again! Scratch me! Publicly humiliate me!").

Story 21. The two seats in front of you are occupied by male homosexuals. They flirt and tease at first, then kiss and hug, and finally perform mutual fellatio to climax.

Story 22. This time the homosexuals are both female and they perform cunnilingus.

Story 23. A passenger with a dog takes an aisle seat at your side. He or she keeps the dog calm at first by petting it in a familiar and normal way, but then petting gives way to hugging, and gradually goes beyond the merely affectionate to the unmistakably erotic, culminating finally with oral contact with the canine genitals.

E. *Annoyance, boredom, frustration*

Story 24. A neighboring passenger keeps a portable radio at a reasonably low volume, and the sounds it emits are by no means offensive to the senses. Nor is the content of the program offensive to the sensibilities. It is, however, a low quality "talk show" which you find intensely boring, and there is no possible way for you to disengage your attention.

Story 25. The two seats to your left are occupied by two persons who put on a boring "talk show" of their own. There is no way you can avoid hearing every animated word of their inane conversation, no way your mind can roam to its own thoughts, problems, and reveries.

Story 26. The passenger at your side is a friendly bloke, garrulous and officious. You quickly tire of his conversation and beg leave to read your newspaper, but he persists in his chatter despite repeated requests to desist. The bus is crowded and there are no other empty seats.

F. *Fear, resentment, humiliation, anger* (from empty threats, insults, mockery, flaunting, or taunting)

Story 27. A passenger seated next to you reaches into a military kit and pulls out a "hand grenade" (actually only a realistic toy), and fondles and juggles it throughout the trip to the accompaniment of menacing leers and snorts. Then he pulls out a (rubber) knife and "stabs" himself and others repeatedly to peals of maniacal laughter. He turns out to be harmless enough. His whole intent was to put others in apprehension of harm.

Story 28. A passenger sits next to you wearing a black arm band with a large white swastika on it.

Story 29. A passenger enters the bus straight from a dispersed street rally. He carries a banner with a large and abusive caricature of the Pope and an anti-Catholic slogan. (You are a loyal and pious Catholic.)

Story 30. Variants of the above. The banner displays a picture of a black according to some standard offensive stereotype (Step 'n Fetchit, Uncle Tom, etc.) with an insulting caption, or a picture of a sneering, sniveling, hook-nosed Fagin or Shylock, with a scurrilous anti-Jewish caption, or a similar offensive denunciation or lampooning of groups called "Spicks," "Dagos," "Polacks," etc.

Story 31. Still another variant. A counter-demonstrator leaves a feminist rally to enter the bus. He carries a banner with an offensive caricature of a female and the message, in large red letters: "Keep the bitches barefoot and pregnant."

. . . The Modes and Meaning of "Offense"

I have tried to make a number of different points by telling these bloodcurdling tales: that there are at least six distinguishable classes of offended states that can be caused by the blamable conduct of others; that to suffer such experiences, at least in their extreme forms, is an evil; but that to the normal person (like the reader) such experiences, unpleasant as they are, do not cause or constitute harm. It is very important that the reader put himself on the bus and imagine his own reactions, for no amount of abstract argument can convince him otherwise that the represented experiences are in principle of a kind that the state can legitimately make its business to prevent.

When I imagine myself on the bus in these various stories, I find that one of the least unsettling experiences is that of the otherwise well-behaved nude passenger (story 13). Needless to say, I have never seen a nude person on a public bus, so I cannot be certain what my reaction would be. But I know that the sight of a nude body as such never did a normal person any harm, and as for the "unsettling experience" itself, one might escape it, I suppose, by turning one's eyes elsewhere, or escaping into one's private reveries. For all that, however, I suspect that I would be made at least vaguely ill at ease by the nude body (for reasons that urgently require examination—see below, . . .), and perhaps less stable persons in such a situation would be thrown into the kind of inner turmoil to which even the reader and I would be subject in most of the other situations.

The examples of "affronts to the senses" are all cases where the gratingly unpleasant experience derives entirely from its sound, color, or odor, and not at all from any symbolic representation, or recognized object. The shirt in story 2 "offends the eye" not because it is recognized as a shirt or because it symbolically asserts or suggests any proposition about shirts or any other subject. It is the sensuous garb of the experience rather than any cognitively mediated content that directly assails the eye, and that is the very feature that distinguishes affronts to the *senses* from shock to the *sensibilities*. That most of us are more disturbed emotionally by assaults on our sensibilities than by direct affronts to our senses is a contingent fact about our psyches and our common culture that could well have been other than it is without violating any law of nature. Story 3 (fingernails scratching slate) is designed to show, moreover, that affronts to senses can be so intensely unpleasant as to be nearly unbearable, even when they do not involve the cognitive faculties (and hence the sensibilities) in the offense. On the other hand, it is likely that the offense in story 1 (a passenger's odor) is influenced to some extent by one's awareness of its source as an unwashed human being, and the revulsion attendant upon that recognition. Precisely the same odor, if it were recognized as one's own, for example, would not be quite an equal offense, presumably, in one's own nostrils. Indeed, the unpleasantness of smells (perhaps more than that of other senses) is very difficult to separate from associated beliefs and sensibilities. The smell of freshly baked macaroni and cheese smells very little different from that of much human vomit, yet the latter but not the former, when mediated by recognition, is offensive. A carton of rotten eggs, however, would smell no worse for being recognized as such, or as some particular person's property, and it may well be a transcultural truth that no one finds sulphurous oxide or the smell of skunk in high concentration very pleasant. These examples suggest that some affronts to the olfactory sense may be less dependent on cognition than others.

Another fact suggested by the stories in group A is that offensive sounds and smells can reach much greater extremes of intensity than directly offensive shapes and colors. Quite apart from the point that visual affronts are more easily avoided (we can shut our eyes more easily than our noses and ears), the visual sense seems less vulnerable to affront than the others, a purely neurological fact that has certain obvious implications for the legislator who employs an offense principle mediated by the kind of balancing tests used in the law of nuisance. Eyesores, so called, are for the most part not as great nuisances as noisome stenches and loud or grating sounds.

Disgust and revulsion, as illustrated by the stories in group B, differ from mere sensuous assaults in two important respects. In the first place, their impact on the offended person, while not *always* more intense, is less localized and more profound. Indeed, the etymology of the word "disgust" (from the Latin for "bad taste") suggests that the condition it designates is more likely to involve the digestive tract than the organs of perception. The first definition of the word in *Webster's New International Dictionary* (Third Edition, 1961) presumably captures something like its original sense: "marked aversion or repugnance toward food or toward a particular dish or kind of food . . . " In a second, more generalized definition, disgust is an extremely disagreeable emotional reaction "excited by exposure to something [anything] highly distasteful or loathesome," for example, the sight of a patient's festering wounds. Whatever the object of the disgust, the term is distinguished only in degree from its near synonyms "sicken" ("a disgust so strong that one is affected physically as by a turning of the stomach") and "nausea" ("stronger still, suggesting a loathesomeness that provokes vomiting"). To be acutely disgusted is to suffer as disagreeable a state of mind and body as is possible below the threshold of actual harm, since to be sickened or nauseated is, in most cases, to cross that threshold.

In the second place, disgust—unlike sensuous affront—is always mediated by recognition or belief. What turns the spectator's stomach when he sees the itinerant picnickers in stories 6–8 consume their unusual "food" is not the color, shape, touch, sound—not even the smell—of the objects of their appetite (although these may be independently offensive to the senses), but rather the recognition of those things as objects of a certain kind—live insects, slugs, sex organs, feces, vomit, etc. If the spectator mistakenly believed that the picnickers were eating eggplant, macaroni and cheese, and sweetbreads, he might still experience some aversion in the circumstances, but it would not amount to disgust or revulsion of the near-sickening kind. Disgust then is an offense not merely to sense but rather to *sensibility,* that susceptibility to offense from witnessing objects or events which, because of the observer's recognition of them as objects of a certain kind, are painful for him to behold.

The sensibilities offended in the stories of group B might be called "lower order sensibilities," and as such they can be contrasted with the moral, religious, and patriotic sensibilities in group C. We are disgusted at the sight of a person eating a dripping, wriggling, live sea slug, simply because we recognize it to be such, and given the character of our gastronomic sensibility, that recognition is quite sufficient to induce disgust. It is not necessary to the process that we hold a moral principle, or even a specific moral conviction, that eating sea slugs is cruel, sinful, or wicked. It is simply disgusting in some pre-rational, nondiscursive way, and that is an end to the matter. An additional step is involved in the production of disgust by offense to higher level sensibilities. When we see a strapping young man arrogantly push aside an aged lady in his haste to occupy the only remaining seat on the bus, we recognize the items in our experience as *young man, aged lady, push,* and *seat,* and that brings to mind a moral principle prescribing the proper conduct of persons of the type perceived. Then, in virtue of the perceived gross violation of that principle, we are disgusted. Similarly, the sight of a person wantonly desecrating a crucifix offends the religious sensibility not simply because the abused object is recognized as a wooden object in the shape of a cross, but because of the conventional symbolism of such shapes, and a whole complex of religious convictions, commitments, and emotions directed to the objects symbolized.

The examples of indecorous sexual conduct in group D include some extreme deviations from prevailing standards of "normalcy" (stories 20–23), but they also include examples of perfectly ordinary and acceptable ways of deriving sexual pleasure when done in private (stories 14–17) and at least one commonplace state of being in which almost everyone in the world participates daily in private (story 13). Why should examples of the latter kinds be so upsetting? Why should conduct perfectly acceptable in itself become "indecent" when performed in public? These examples are not like the instances of disgusting eating in group B. Rather they would seem analogous to examples of "normal eating" in a public place, for example, munching peanuts or eating sandwiches, alone or with a friend, on a bus, activities which are not generally thought shameful, embarrassing, or indecent, but are at the very most, minor violations of etiquette.

Our culture, of course, is far more uptight about sexual pleasures than about "harmless" pleasures of any other kind, which is easy enough to understand given the danger in, and harmful consequences of, sexual behavior in the past—disease, personal exploitation, unwanted pregnancy, etc.—and the intricate association of sexual taboos with rules of property transfer, legitimacy, marriage, and the like. Perhaps our abundant anxieties and our susceptibilities to shock will all fade away in the future, as improved contraceptive techniques reduce dangers of disease and unwanted pregnancy, and candid treatments of sexual themes in public forums and private conversations become more common still. But that day, despite recent relaxations of attitudes, still seems far off.

The disquietude caused in captive observers by public nudity and sexual behavior is a complicated psychological phenomenon, difficult to explain not only because of wide individual differences, but also because so many psychic elements are involved, and combine in so many possible ways. To begin with, nude bodies and copulating couples, like all forms of nuisance, have the power of preempting the attention and absorbing the reluctant viewer, whatever his preferences in the matter. The presence of such things in one's field of perception commands one's notice; they are distractions that must be attended to and coped with whatever one might prefer to be doing or thinking. Moreover, the problem of coping, for many persons at least, is a bit of a difficult one, not insurmountable, but something of an unpleasant strain. Part, but only part, of the explanation of that displeasure, no doubt rests on the fact that nudity and sex acts have an irresistible power to draw the eye and focus the thoughts on matters that are normally repressed. Indeed, most of us spend an inordinate amount of time and energy, even without provocation, in sexual fantasies and the repression of lust. The unresolved conflict between instinctual desires and cultural taboos leaves many people in a state of unstable equilibrium and a readiness to be wholly fascinated, in an ambivalent sort of way, by any suggestion of sexuality in their perceptual fields. There is a temptation to see and savour all, and to permit oneself to become sexually stimulated, as by a pornographic film, but instantly the temptations of voyeurism trigger the familiar mechanism of inhibition and punishment in the form of feelings of shame. The primary basis of one's "offended state" then is this tension between attracting and repressing forces, against a psychic background of total fascination, a combination which can be at once exciting, upsetting, and anxiety-producing. When the precipitating experience is not mere nudity, but actual sexual activity, even of a "normal" kind, it will create a kind of inner agitation at best, and at worst that experience of exposure to oneself of one's "peculiarly sensitive, intimate, vulnerable aspects" which is called *shame*. When one has not been able to prepare one's defenses, "one's feeling is involuntarily exposed openly in one's face. . . . We are . . . caught unawares, made a fool of." For some relatively unenlightened persons the result will be a severe psychic jolt; those of us who are better able to cope with our feelings might well resent the necessity to do so and regard it as an irritating distraction and a bore, much the same as any other nuisance.

Understandable doubt has been expressed by some writers over the contention that the public nudity or sexual behavior of others can produce something called "shameful embarrassment" in oneself. Michael Bayles has effectively entered a challenge to that way of describing matters:

> It is difficult to understand how the public nudity of others invades one's privacy or causes one embarrassment. Surely the privacy involved is the nude's, but one has not invaded it. For one to be ashamed of something, it must have a relation to oneself, be something for which one takes responsibility. One can be ashamed of the conduct of one's friends, for one may take vicarious responsibility for their conduct or consider oneself responsible for who one's friends are . . .

Shame, in the relevant sense, is "a painful emotion caused by consciousness of guilt, shortcoming, or impropriety in one's own behavior or position, or in the behavior or position of a closely associated person or group." It is, therefore, difficult to understand how the painful emotion felt by the captive observer of nudity or sex play on the bus could possibly be shame, for *he* is not the one who is behaving improperly or indecorously. If the nude passenger or lewd lovers were his fellow countrymen in a foreign country, his children, friends, or business partners, he might well feel ashamed of *them*, but in our hypothetical story, the offending persons are total strangers and the offended observer is in his own country.

Still, for all of that, it does seem natural to describe the offended reaction of the observer as "shame." After all, the unexpected apprehension of nudity or "indecency" can be expected to bring a blush to the face of the observer, which is a recognized symptom both of intense self-consciousness and "shame, modesty, or confusion." How then could the reaction to another's misconduct be shameful embarrassment? There are at least two answers to this question. First, the "guilt, shortcoming, or impropriety of one's own" that is the object of the shame may well be the instantaneous reaction of one's own to the offending experience, a sudden loss of control, soon recovered, over impulses normally restrained by the firmest reins. One reacts in a certain way and then is immediately ashamed of that reaction. Second, one can feel shame or embarrassment vicariously in a way other than that which Bayles acknowledges. Bayles accounts for those cases where one person is ashamed of or *because of* another person with whom he is closely associated or for whom he is responsible. In those cases some of the other's shame "rubs off" on him, so to speak. But there are other cases in which the improper or inept actions of a total stranger can induce shame or embarrassment in an observer. In these cases, the observer, by a kind of sympathetic identification with the other party that comes naturally to sensitive and imaginative people, feels ashamed or embarrassed *for* the other party. In these cases the observer feels the shame he would feel were he in the other's place. In many cases, an observer's painful emotion is complex and contains elements of shame of both the personal and vicarious kinds.

And sometimes the offended mental state is still more complex. When the observer can perceive the whole embarrassing situation not only from his own vantage point, but also imaginatively from the point of view of the offenders, he comes to feel that whatever *they* may think about it, his own presence is a jarring foreign element in their privacy. His own witness then seems a part of their humiliation, and since they neither know nor care about their own public disgrace, their human dignity is further diminished in his eye, to his further distress. Still another quite independent element in the unwilling observer's painful emotion may be the feeling that he is threatened by what is happening, that either the unrestrained public performers or his own stirred up feelings may surge out of control. Thus one becomes anxiously apprehensive, and concerned lest unwilling revelations of one's own feeling discredit or embarrass one at any moment. Another element may be a response to the whole spectacle, performance *and* audience, not merely the performers themselves. What may seem obscene to the observer is not simply that the offenders are there nude or tumescent in his eye, but that they stand (or lie) revealed to many other eyes. . . . The obscenity consists not in the object of observation but in the fact that many people are looking and "collectively" experiencing their own inadmissible feelings. The observer might thus feel embarrassed to be part of the spectacle perceived by the other members of the observing audience and also vicariously embarrassed on *their* behalf. And so, a final element steals into the complex mental state of the offended observer: a near total confusion and disarray of feeling.

The stories of abnormal sexual acts (numbers 20–23) provide examples of public behavior that would be even more disagreeable to witness. Two elements are present in the painful feelings induced in these stories that are rarely present to the same degree in mere nudity and ordinary sex: (1) The witnessed incidents are taken to be immediately and powerfully *threatening*, and (2) "lower-level sensibilities" are shocked so that a spontaneous *disgust* arises to mingle with the other painful elements in the experience. The point about threats is best illustrated by the example of male homosexuality. The general nervousness about this subject is even reflected in the way it is treated in the most iconoclastic pornographic films. The celebrated film *Emmanuelle*, for example, included numerous scenes of female homosexuality (not very graphically displayed) presumably because such scenes are thought to be especially titillating to the males who constitute the bulk of the audience for those films. But there was not so much as a suggestion of male homosexuality, a practice which many males loathe and execrate, and hold in considerable terror. Not only do homosexual acts violate powerful taboos in our culture; they also threaten the "ego ideals" of heterosexual men. Homosexuals are the objects of near universal contempt and ridicule, and their peculiar practice is held inconsistent with the ideals of genuine manhood. Hatred of homosexuality, therefore is a part of the psychic fortress many men build around their self-esteem. The point about disgust is best illustrated by the story about bestiality (number 23). Not even the story of the feces-and-vomit-eating picnickers in group B is more disgusting to most of us than that.

After considering such jolts to sensibility, it may seem altogether anticlimactic to turn to the offenses in group E, for the boredom of radio shows and dull conversation are of such a common type that we suffer from it to some degree almost every day of our lives. At their extremes, however, the mental states they induce can be almost as intensely disliked and difficult to tolerate as fingernails on a slate board or unavoidable witness to homosexual couplings. Boredom is sometimes conceived as mere listless aimlessness or ennui, the state of a solitary person who cannot think of anything to do. That condition is unhappy enough, but there is nothing acute or piercing about it, and it is not necessarily an "offense" directly caused by another person. When one is button-holed by a "cocktail party bore," or a "discussion-period bore," on the other hand, the displeasure can be so sharp and penetrating as to suggest the pointed revolving tool that "bores" holes in firmly held objects. The bore is persistent and undivertable; he *will* command your attention; there is no escape. The offended state he produces results from another kind of tense inner conflict: one is trying desperately to escape by thinking up stratagems, excuses, and diversions, but clear thinking is impossible in the face of the bore's peremptory demands on one's attention. Often there is no escape possible without unacceptable rudeness, so one resigns oneself in depressed and weary annoyance. At that point one is "crushed with irksome tediousness." The boring people on the bus are surely not that bad, however, if only because (stories 24 and 25) they do not attempt to exact responses from you, whereas in story 26, the officious talker can in the end be requested, without rudeness, to be quiet. But insofar as the boring passengers commandeer one's attention irresistibly, they are nuisances in the same manner, even if to a lesser degree, as their disgusting, shocking, embarrassing, and threatening counterparts in the other stories.

The group insults issued by passengers in the stories in group F, the contemptuous mockery, the deliberate baiting and taunting through the display of offensive signs and symbols, can be the most disturbing behavior of all in its effects on members of the insulted groups, and even on others to whom such conduct is odious. In these cases, as in the others, disagreeable emotions are aroused that have to be coped with, but it is distinctive of these cases that the emotion is the most difficult of all to handle, namely sudden violent anger, conjoined with anxious fear, and a feeling of humiliation and impugned "honor." Again, as soon as the emotion flares it is likely to be followed by a feeling of shame and worry over its presence and a desperate effort at repression. But the offending symbols are still there in one's visual field, still mocking and threatening, nagging and tugging at one's attention, like another kind of efficient boring tool. And attendant upon one's shame is a new anxiety: fear of making a fool of oneself by losing control. These conflicting elements pull a person in all directions and throw him into confusion. Despite the legal doctrine of "fighting words" which permits states to ban "personally abusive epithets . . . that are inherently likely to provoke violent reaction," it is unlikely that present laws would permit one who is personally insulted to accept what he takes to be a challenge and vent his anger in retaliatory aggression, any more than it would permit the sexually excited witness of nudity or indecency on the bus to force his lust on the provoking person. But again, having to cope with one's rage is as burdensome a bore as having to suffer shame, or disgust, or noisome stenches, something unpleasant to experience and inconvenient to accommodate, even when it causes one no harm. . . .

It should be clear at this point that despite the miscellaneous character of "offended states" they have some important characteristics in common. They are at the very least unpleasant to the one who suffers them, though the mode of displeasure varies from case to case. With the exception of irritations to the senses, and only some of these, they are complex states whose unpleasantness is in part a function of the tension between conflicting elements. And, most importantly from the legislative point of view, they are nuisances, making it difficult for one to enjoy one's work or leisure in a locality which one cannot reasonably be expected to leave in the circumstances. In extreme cases, the offending conduct commandeers one's attention from the outside, forcing one to relinquish control of one's inner state, and drop what one was doing in order to cope, when it is greatly inconvenient to do so. . . .

STANLEY FISH

There's No Such Thing as Free Speech, and It's a Good Thing, Too

Stanley Fish is Professor of English at Duke University. (Source: There's No Such Thing as Free Speech, and It's a Good Thing, Too *[New York: Oxford, 1994]. Copyright © 1994 by Oxford University Press. Reprinted by permission.)*

QUESTIONS FOR REFLECTION

1. Why, according to Fish, does freedom of speech always have exceptions?
2. Fish rejects the distinction between speech and action. Why? Do you agree?
3. How does Fish defend campus speech codes?
4. What does Fish mean when he says, "There's no such thing as free speech"? Why does he think "it's a good thing, too"?

Nowadays the First Amendment is the First Refuge of Scoundrels.

—S. Johnson and S. Fish

Lately, many on the liberal and progressive left have been disconcerted to find that words, phrases, and concepts thought to be their property and generative of their politics have been appropriated by the forces of neoconservatism. This is particularly true of the concept of free speech, for in recent years First Amendment rhetoric has been used to justify policies and actions the left finds problematical if not abhorrent: pornography, sexist language, campus hate speech. How has this happened? The answer I shall give in this essay is that abstract concepts like free speech do not have any "natural" content but are filled with whatever content and direction one can manage to put into them. "Free speech" is just the name we give to verbal behavior that serves the substantive agendas we wish to advance; and we give our preferred verbal behaviors *that* name when we can, when we have the power to do so, because in the rhetoric of American life, the label "free speech" is the one you want your favorites to wear. Free speech, in short, is not an independent value but a political prize, and if that prize has been captured by a politics opposed to yours, it can no longer be invoked in ways that further your purposes, for it is now an obstacle to those purposes. This is something that the liberal left has yet to understand, and what follows is an attempt to pry its members loose from a vocabulary that may now be a disservice to them.

Not far from the end of his *Areopagitica,* and after having celebrated the virtues of toleration and unregulated publication in passages that find their way into every discussion of free speech and the First Amendment, John Milton catches himself up short and says, of course I didn't mean Catholics, them we exterminate:

> I mean not tolerated popery, and open superstition, which as it extirpates all religious and civil supremacies, so itself should be extirpate . . . that also which is impious or evil absolutely against faith or manners no law can possibly permit that intends not to unlaw itself.

Notice that Milton is not simply stipulating a single exception to a rule generally in place; the kinds of utterance that might be regulated and even prohibited on pain of trial and punishment constitute an open set; popery is named only as a particularly perspicuous instance of the advocacy that cannot be tolerated. No doubt there are other forms of speech and action that might be categorized as "open superstitions" or as subversive of piety, faith, and manners, and presumably these too would be candidates for "extirpation." Nor would Milton think himself culpable for having failed to provide a list of unprotected utterances. The list will fill itself out as utterances are put to the test implied by his formulation: would this form of speech or advocacy, if permitted to flourish, tend to undermine the very purposes for which our society is constituted? One cannot answer this question with respect to a particular utterance in advance of its emergence on the world's stage; rather, one must wait and ask the question in the full context of its production and (possible) dissemination. It might appear that the result would be ad hoc and unprincipled, but for Milton the principle inheres in the core values in whose name individuals of like mind came together in the first place. Those values, which include the search for truth and the promotion of virtue, are capacious enough to accommodate a diversity of views. But at some point—again impossible of advance specification—capaciousness will threaten to become shapelessness, and at that point fidelity to the original values will demand acts of extirpation.

I want to say that all affirmations of freedom of expression are like Milton's, dependent for their force on an exception that literally carves out the space in which expression can then emerge. I do not mean that expression (saying something) is a realm whose integrity is sometimes compromised by certain restrictions but that restriction, in the form of an underlying articulation of the world that necessarily (if silently) negates alternatively possible articulations, is constitutive of expression. Without restriction, without an inbuilt sense of what it would be meaningless to say or wrong to say, there could be no assertion and no reason for asserting it. The exception to unregulated expression is not a negative restriction but a positive hollowing out of value—we are for *this,* which means we are against *that*—in relation to which meaningful assertion can then occur. It is in reference to that value—constituted as all values are by an act of exclusion—that some forms of speech will be heard as (quite literally) intolerable. Speech, in short, is never a value in and of itself but is always produced within the precincts of some assumed conception of the good to which it must yield in the event of conflict. When the pinch comes (and sooner or later it will always come) and the institution (be it church, state, or university) is confronted by behavior subversive of its core rationale, it will respond by declaring "of course we mean not tolerated———, that we extirpate," not because an exception to a general freedom has suddenly and contradictorily been announced, but because the freedom has never been general and has always been understood against the background of an originary exclusion that gives it meaning.

This is a large thesis, but before tackling it directly I want to buttress my case with another example, taken not from the seventeenth century but from the charter and case law of Canada. Canadian thinking about freedom of expression departs from the line usually taken in the United States in ways that bring that country very close to the *Areopagitica* as I have expounded it. The differences are fully on display in a recent landmark case, *R. v. Keegstra.* James Keegstra was a high school teacher in Alberta who, it was established by evidence, "systematically denigrated Jews and Judaism in his classes." He described Jews as treacherous, subversive, sadistic, money loving, power hungry, and child killers. He declared them "responsible for depressions, anarchy, chaos, wars and revolution" and required his students "to regurgitate these notions in essays and examinations." Keegstra was indicted under Section 319(2) of the Criminal

Code and convicted. The Court of Appeal reversed, and the Crown appealed to the Supreme Court, which reinstated the lower court's verdict.

Section 319(2) reads in part, "Every one who, by communicating statements other than in private conversation, willfully promotes hatred against any identifiable group is guilty of . . . an indictable offense and is liable to imprisonment for a term not exceeding two years." In the United States, this provision of the code would almost certainly be struck down because, under the First Amendment, restrictions on speech are apparently prohibited without qualification. To be sure, the Canadian charter has its own version of the First Amendment, in Section 2(b): "Everyone has the following fundamental freedoms . . . (b) freedom of thought, belief, opinion, and expression, including freedom of the press and other media of communication." But Section 2(b), like every other section of the charter, is qualified by Section 1: "The Canadian Charter of Rights and Freedoms guarantees the rights and freedoms set out in it subject only to such reasonable limits prescribed by law as can be demonstrably justified in a free and democratic society." Or in other words, every right and freedom herein granted can be trumped if its exercise is found to be in conflict with the principles that underwrite the society.

This is what happens in *Keegstra* as the majority finds that Section 319(2) of the Criminal Code does in fact violate the right of freedom of expression guaranteed by the charter but is nevertheless a *permissible* restriction because it accords with the principles proclaimed in Section 1. There is, of course, a dissent that reaches the conclusion that would have been reached by most, if not all, U.S. courts; but even in dissent the minority is faithful to Canadian ways of reasoning. "The question," it declares, "is always one of balance," and thus even when a particular infringement of the charter's Section 2(b) has been declared unconstitutional, as it would have been by the minority, the question remains open with respect to the next case. In the United States the question is presumed closed and can only be pried open by special tools. In our legal culture as it is now constituted, if one yells "free speech" in a crowded courtroom and makes it stick, the case is over.

Of course, it is not that simple. Despite the apparent absoluteness of the First Amendment, there are any number of ways of getting around it, ways that are known to every student of the law. In general, the preferred strategy is to manipulate the distinction, essential to First Amendment jurisprudence, between speech and action. The distinction is essential because no one would think to frame a First Amendment that began "Congress shall make no law abridging freedom of action," for that would amount to saying "Congress shall make no law," which would amount to saying "There shall be no law," only actions uninhibited and unregulated. If the First Amendment is to make any sense, have any bite, speech must be declared not to be a species of action, or to be a special form of action lacking the aspects of action that cause it to be the object of regulation. The latter strategy is the favored one and usually involves the separation of speech from consequences. This is what Archibald Cox does when he assigns to the First Amendment the job of protecting "expressions separable from conduct harmful to other individuals and the community." The difficulty of managing this segregation is well known: speech always seems to be crossing the line into action, where it becomes, at least potentially, consequential. In the face of this categorical instability, First Amendment theorists and jurists fashion a distinction within the speech/action distinction: some forms of speech are not really speech because their purpose is to incite violence or because they are, as the court declares in *Chaplinsky v. New Hampshire* (1942), "fighting words," words "likely to provoke the average person to retaliation, and thereby cause a breach of the peace."

The trouble with this definition is that it distinguishes not between fighting words and words that remain safely and merely expressive but between words that are provocative to one group (the group that falls under the rubric "average person") and words that might be provocative to other groups, groups of persons not now considered average. And if you ask what words are likely to be provocative to those nonaverage groups, what are likely to be *their* fighting words, the answer is anything and everything, for as Justice Holmes said long ago (in *Gitlow v. New York*), every idea is an incitement to somebody, and since ideas come packaged in sentences, in words, every sentence is potentially, in some situation that might occur tomorrow, a fighting word and therefore a candidate for regulation.

This insight cuts two ways. One could conclude from it that the fighting words exception is a bad idea because there is no way to prevent clever and unscrupulous advocates from shoveling so many forms of speech into the excepted category that the zone of constitutionally protected speech shrinks to nothing and is finally without inhabitants. Or, alternatively, one could conclude that there was never anything in the zone in the first place and that the difficulty of limiting the fighting words exception is merely a particular instance of the general difficulty of separating speech from action. And if one opts for this second conclusion, as I do, then a further conclusion is inescapable: insofar as the point of the First Amendment is to identify speech separable from conduct and from the consequences that come in conduct's wake, there is no such speech and therefore nothing for the First Amendment to protect. Or, to make the point from the other direction, when a court invalidates legislation because it infringes on protected speech, it is not because the speech in question is without consequences but because the consequences have been discounted in relation to a good that is judged to outweigh them. Despite what they say, courts are never in the business of protecting speech per se, "mere" speech (a nonexistent animal); rather, they are in the business of classifying speech (as protected or regulatable) in relation to a value—the health of the republic, the vigor of the economy, the maintenance of the status quo, the undoing of the status quo—that is the true, if unacknowledged, object of their protection.

But if this is the case, a First Amendment purist might reply, why not drop the charade along with the malleable distinctions that make it possible, and declare up front that total freedom of speech is our primary value and trumps anything else, no matter what? The answer is that freedom of expression would only be a primary value if it didn't matter what was said, didn't matter in the sense that no one gave a damn but just liked to hear talk. There are contexts like that, a Hyde Park corner or a call-in talk show where people get to sound off for the sheer fun of it. These, however, are special contexts, artificially bounded spaces designed to assure that talking is not taken seriously. In ordinary contexts, talk is produced with the goal of trying to move the world in one direction rather than another. In these contexts—the contexts of everyday life—you go to the trouble of asserting that X is Y only because you suspect that some people are wrongly asserting that X is Z or that X doesn't exist. You assert, in short, because you give a damn, not about assertion—as if it were a value in and of itself—but about what your assertion is about. It may seem paradoxical, but free expression could only be a primary value if what you are valuing is the right to make noise; but if you are engaged in some purposive activity in the course of which speech happens to be produced, sooner or later you will come to a point when you decide that some forms of speech do not further but endanger that purpose.

Take the case of universities and colleges. Could it be the purpose of such places to encourage free expression? If the answer were "yes," it would be hard to say why there would be any need for classes, or examinations, or departments, or disciplines, or libraries, since freedom of expression requires nothing but a soapbox or an open telephone line. The very fact of the university's machinery—of the events, rituals, and procedures that fill its calendar—argues for some other, more substantive purpose. In relation to that purpose (which will be realized differently in different kinds of institutions), the flourishing of free expression will in almost all circumstances be an obvious good; but in some circumstances, freedom of expression may pose a threat to that purpose, and at that point it may be necessary to discipline or regulate speech, lest, to paraphrase Milton, the institution sacrifice itself to one of its *accidental* features.

Interestingly enough, the same conclusion is reached (inadvertently) by Congressman Henry Hyde, who is addressing these very issues in a recently offered amendment to Title VI of the Civil Rights Act. The first section of the amendment states its purpose, to protect "the free speech rights of college students" by prohibiting private as well as public educational institutions from "subjecting any student to disciplinary sanctions solely on the basis of conduct that is speech." The second section enumerates the remedies available to students whose speech rights may have been abridged; and the third, which is to my mind the nub of the matter, declares as an exception to the amendment's jurisdiction any "educational institution that is controlled by a religious organization," on the reasoning that the application of the amendment to such institutions "would not be consistent with the religious tenets of such organizations." In effect, what Congressman Hyde is saying is that at the heart of these colleges and universities is a set of beliefs, and it would be wrong to require them to tolerate behavior, including speech behavior, inimical to those beliefs. But insofar as this logic is persuasive, it applies across the board, for all educational institutions rest on some set of beliefs—no institution is "just there" independent of any purpose—and it is hard to see why the rights of an institution to protect and preserve its basic "tenets" should be restricted only to those that are religiously controlled. Read strongly, the third section of the amendment undoes sections one and two—the exception becomes, as it always was, the rule—and points us to a balancing test very much like that employed in Canadian law: given that any college or university is informed by a core rationale, an administrator faced with complaints about offensive speech should ask whether damage to the core would be greater if the speech were tolerated or regulated.

The objection to this line of reasoning is well known and has recently been reformulated by Benno Schmidt, former president of Yale University. According to Schmidt, speech codes on campuses constitute "well intentioned but misguided efforts to give values of community and harmony a higher place than freedom" (*Wall Street Journal*, May 6, 1991). "When the goals of harmony collide with freedom of expression," he continues, "freedom must be the paramount obligation of an academic community." The flaw in this logic is on display in the phrase "academic community," for the phrase recognizes what Schmidt would deny, that expression only occurs in communities—if not in an academic community, then in a shopping mall community or a dinner party community or an airplane ride community or an office community. In these communities and in any others that could be imagined (with the possible exception of a community of major league baseball fans), limitations on speech in relation to a defining and deeply assumed purpose are inseparable from community membership.

Indeed, "limitations" is the wrong word because it suggests that expression, as an activity and a value, has a pure form that is always in danger of being compromised by the urgings of special interest communities; but independently of a community context informed by interest (that is, purpose), expression would be at once inconceivable and unintelligible. Rather than being a value that is threatened by limitations and constraints, expression, in any form worth worrying about, is a *product* of limitations and constraints, of the already-in-place presuppositions that give assertions their very particular point. Indeed, the very act of thinking of something to say (whether or not it is subsequently regulated) is already constrained—rendered impure, and because impure, communicable —by the background context within which the thought takes its shape. (The analysis holds too for "freedom," which in Schmidt's vision is an entirely empty concept referring to an urge without direction. But like expression, freedom is a coherent notion only in relation to a goal or good that limits and, by limiting, shapes its exercise.)

Arguments like Schmidt's only get their purchase by first imagining speech as occurring in no context whatsoever, and then stripping particular speech acts of the properties conferred on them by contexts. The trick is nicely illustrated when Schmidt urges protection for speech "no matter how obnoxious in content." "Obnoxious" at once acknowledges the reality of speech-related harms and trivializes them by suggesting that they are *surface* injuries that any large-minded ("liberated and humane") person should be able to bear. The possibility that speech-related injuries may be grievous and *deeply* wounding is carefully kept out of sight, and because it is kept out of sight, the fiction of a world of weightless verbal exchange can be maintained, at least within the confines of Schmidt's carefully denatured discourse.

To this Schmidt would no doubt reply, as he does in his essay, that harmful speech should be answered not by regulation but by more speech; but that would make sense only if the effects of speech could be canceled out by additional speech, only if the pain and humiliation caused by racial or religious epithets could be ameliorated by saying something like "So's your old man." What Schmidt fails to realize at every level of his argument is that expression is more than a matter of proffering and receiving propositions, that words do work in the world of a kind that cannot be confined to a purely cognitive realm of "mere" ideas.

It could be said, however, that I myself mistake the nature of the work done by freely tolerated speech because I am too focused on short-run outcomes and fail to understand that the good effects of speech will be realized, not in the present, but in a future whose emergence regulation could only inhibit. This line of reasoning would also weaken one of my key points, that speech in and of itself cannot be a value and is only worth worrying about if it is in the service of something with which it cannot be identical. My mistake, one could argue, is to equate the something in whose service speech is with some locally espoused value (e.g., the end of racism, the empowerment of disadvantaged minorities), whereas in fact we should think of that something as a now-inchoate shape that will be given firm lines only by time's pencil. That is why the shape now receives such indeterminate characterizations (e.g., true self-fulfillment, a more perfect polity, a more capable citizenry, a less partial truth); we cannot now know it, and therefore we must not prematurely fix it in ways that will bind successive generations to error.

This forward-looking view of what the First Amendment protects has a great appeal, in part because it continues in a secular form the Puritan celebration of millenarian hopes, but it imposes a requirement so severe that one would except more justification for it than is usually provided. The requirement is that we endure whatever pain racist and hate speech inflicts for the sake of a future whose emergence we can only take on faith. In a specifically religious vision like Milton's, this makes perfect sense (it is indeed the whole of Christianity), but in the context of a politics that puts its trust in the world and not in the Holy Spirit, it raises more questions than it answers and could be seen as the second of two strategies designed to delegitimize the complaints of victimized groups. The first strategy, as I have noted, is to define speech in such a way as to render it inconsequential (on the model of "sticks and stones will break my bones, but . . ."); the second strategy is to acknowledge the (often grievous) consequences of speech but declare that we must suffer them in the name of something that cannot be named. The two strategies are denials from slightly different directions of the *present* effects of racist speech; one confines those effects to a closed and safe realm of pure mental activity; the other imagines the effects of speech spilling over into the world but only in an ever-receding future for whose sake we must forever defer taking action.

I find both strategies unpersuasive, but my own skepticism concerning them is less important than the fact that in general they seem to have worked; in the parlance of the marketplace (a parlance First Amendment commentators love), many in the society seemed to have bought them. Why? The answer, I think, is that people cling to First Amendment pieties because they do not wish to face what they correctly take to be the alternative. That alternative is *politics,* the realization (at which I have already hinted) that decisions about what is and is not protected in the realm of expression will rest not on principle or firm doctrine but on the ability of some persons to interpret—recharacterize or rewrite—principle and doctrine in ways that lead to the protection of speech they want heard and the regulation of speech they want silenced. (That is how George Bush can argue *for* flag-burning statutes and *against* campus hate-speech codes.) When the First Amendment is successfully invoked, the result is not a victory for free speech in the face of a challenge from politics but a *political victory* won by the party that has managed to wrap its agenda in the mantle of free speech.

It is from just such a conclusion—a conclusion that would put politics *inside* the First Amendment—that commentators recoil, saying things like "This could render the First Amendment a dead letter," or "This would leave us with no normative guidance in determining when and what speech to protect," or "This effaces the distinction between speech and action," or "This is incompatible with any viable notion of freedom of expression." To these statements (culled more or less at random from recent law review pieces) I would reply that the First Amendment has always been a dead letter if one understood its "liveness" to depend on the identification and protection of a realm of "mere" expression distinct from the realm of regulatable conduct; the distinction between speech and action has always been effaced in principle, although in practice it can take whatever form the prevailing political conditions mandate; we have never had any normative guidance for marking off protected from unprotected speech; rather, the guidance we have has been fashioned (and refashioned) in the very political struggles over which it then (for a time) presides. In short, the name of the game has always been politics, even when (indeed, especially when) it is played by stigmatizing politics as the area to be avoided.

In saying this, I would not be heard as arguing either for or against regulation and speech codes as a matter of general principle. Instead my argument turns away from general principle to the pragmatic (anti)principle of considering each situation as it emerges. The question of whether or not to regulate will always be a local one, and we can not rely on abstractions that are either empty of content or filled with the content of some partisan agenda to generate a "principled" answer. Instead we must consider in every case what is at stake and what are the risks and gains of alternative courses of action. In the course of this consideration many things will be of help, but among them will not be phrases like "freedom of speech" or "the right of individual expression," because, as they are used now, these phrases tend to obscure rather than clarify our dilemmas. Once they are deprived of their talismanic force, once it is no longer strategically effective simply to invoke them in the act of walking away from a problem, the conversation could continue in directions that are now blocked by a First Amendment absolutism that has only been honored in the breach anyway. To the student reporter who complains that in the wake of the promulgation of a speech code at the University of Wisconsin there is now something in the back of his mind as he writes, one could reply, "There was always something in the back of your mind, and perhaps it might be better to have this code in the back of your mind than whatever was in there before." And when someone warns about the slippery slope and predicts mournfully that if you restrict one form of speech, you never know what will be restricted next, one could reply, "Some form of speech is always being restricted, else there could be no meaningful assertion; we have always and already slid down the slippery slope; someone is always going to be restricted next, and it is your job to make sure that the someone is not you." And when someone observes, as someone surely will, that antiharassment codes chill speech, one could reply that since speech only becomes intelligible against the background of what isn't being said, the background of what has already been silenced, the only question is the political one of which speech is going to be chilled, and, all things considered, it seems a good thing to chill speech like "nigger," "cunt," "kike," and "faggot." And if someone then says, "But what happened to free-speech principles?" one could say what I have now said a dozen times, free-speech principles don't exist except as a component in a bad argument in which such principles are invoked to mask motives that would not withstand close scrutiny. . . .

Let me be clear. I am not saying that First Amendment principles are inherently bad (they are *inherently* nothing), only that they are not always the appropriate reference point for situations involving the production of speech, and that even when they are the appropriate reference point, they do not constitute a politics-free perspective because the shape in which they are invoked will always be political, will always, that is, be the result of having drawn the relevant line (between speech and action, or between high-value speech and low-value speech, or between words essential to the expression of ideas and fighting words) in a way that is favorable to some interests and indifferent or hostile to others. This having been said, the moral is not that First Amendment talk should be abandoned, for even if the standard First Amendment formulas do not and could not perform the function expected of them (the elimination of political considerations in decisions about speech), they still serve a function that is not at all negligible: they slow down outcomes in an area in which the fear of overhasty outcomes is justified by a long record of abuses of power. It is often said that history shows (itself a formula) that even a minimal restriction on the right of expression too easily leads to ever-larger restrictions; and to the extent that this is an empirical fact (and it is a question one could debate), there is some comfort and protection to be found in a procedure that requires you to jump through hoops—do a lot of argumentative work—before a speech regulation will be allowed to stand.

I would not be misunderstood as offering the notion of "jumping through hoops" as a new version of the First Amendment claim to neutrality. A hoop must have a shape—in this case the shape of whatever binary distinction is representing First Amendment "interests"—and the shape of the hoop one is asked to jump through will in part determine what kinds of jumps can be regularly made. Even if they are only mechanisms for slowing down outcomes, First Amendment formulas by virtue of their substantive content (and it is impossible that they be without content) will slow down some outcomes more easily than others, and that means that the form they happen to have at the present moment will favor some interests more than others. Therefore, even with a reduced sense of the effectivity of First Amendment rhetoric (it can not assure any particular result), the counsel with which I began remains relevant: so long as so-called free-speech principles have been fashioned by your enemy (so long as it is *his* hoops you have to jump through), contest their relevance to the issue at hand; but if you manage to refashion them in line with your purposes, urge them with a vengeance.

It is a counsel that follows from the thesis that there is no such thing as free speech, which is not, after all, a thesis as startling or corrosive as may first have seemed. It merely says that there is no class of utterances separable from the world of conduct and that therefore the identification of some utterances as members of that nonexistent class will always be evidence that a political line has been drawn rather than a line that denies politics entry into the forum of public discourse. It is the job of the First Amendment to mark out an area in which competing views can be considered without state interference; but if the very marking out of that area is itself an interference (as it always will be), First Amendment jurisprudence is inevitably self-defeating and subversive of its own aspirations. That's the bad news. The good news is that precisely *because* speech is never "free" in the two senses required—free of consequences and free from state pressure—speech always matters, is always doing work; because everything we say impinges on the world in ways indistinguishable from the effects of physical action, we must take responsibility for our verbal performances—*all* of them—and not assume that they are being taken care of by a clause in the Constitution. Of course, with responsibility comes risks, but they have always been our risks, and no doctrine of free speech has ever insulated us from them. They are the risks, respectively, of permitting speech that does obvious harm and of shutting off speech in ways that might deny us the benefit of Joyce's *Ulysses* or Lawrence's *Lady Chatterly's Lover* or Titian's paintings. Nothing, I repeat, can insulate us from those risks. (If there is no normative guidance in determining when and what speech to protect, there is no normative guidance in determining what is art—like free speech a category that includes everything and nothing—and what is obscenity.) Moreover, nothing can provide us with a principle for deciding which risk in the long run is the best to take. I am persuaded that at the present moment, right now, the risk of not attending to hate speech is greater than the risk that by regulating it we will deprive ourselves of valuable voices and insights or slide down the slippery slope toward tyranny. This is a judgment for which I can offer reasons but no guarantees. All I am saying is that the judgments of those who would come down on the other side carry no guarantees either. They urge us to put our faith in apolitical abstractions, but the abstractions they invoke—the marketplace of ideas, speech alone, speech itself—only come in political guises, and therefore in trusting to them we fall (unwittingly) under the sway of the very forces we wish to keep at bay. It is not that there are no choices to make or means of making them; it is just that the choices as well as the means are inextricable from the din and confusion of partisan struggle. There is no safe place.

JONATHAN RAUCH

The Humanitarian Threat

Jonathan Rauch is a Fellow of the Cato Institute. (Source: From Kindly Inquisitors: The New Attacks on Free Thought, *Chicago: University of Chicago Press, 1993. Notes have been omitted.*

QUESTIONS FOR REFLECTION

1. What are the basic features of liberal science, according to Rauch?
2. What is the fundamental argument for restrictions on speech? How does Rauch reply?
3. Which of the arguments outlined by Rauch do you find most persuasive? Evaluate his response to it.

As knowledge-making regimes go, nothing is as successful or as respectful of diversity or as humane as liberal science. The trouble is that liberal science often does not look very humane. It uses sticks as well as carrots. The carrots are the respectability, frequent use, and public credit that it bestows on the opinions that it validates; the sticks are the disrespect and the silent treatment that it inflicts on the opinions that fail. Those sticks are nonviolent, true. But it is unconscionable not to admit that denying respectability is a very serious matter indeed. It causes pain and outrage. . . . Here is where the door opens to the most formidable attack on the liberal science—the humanitarian attack.

"Well," goes the argument, "we must, it appears, have intellectual standards. But what should our standards be? Obviously it is desirable to have standards that minimize pain. And a lot of beliefs cause pain (that is, they hurt people's feelings). Racist beliefs cause pain. Anti-Semitic and sexist and homophobic beliefs cause pain. So do anti-American and anti-religious beliefs. So do beliefs which proclaim one ethnic group or culture to be better than another, or different from others in some way which carries social disapproval. If we're going to have a social system for weeding out beliefs, it should start by weeding out beliefs which cause pain. Thus it should weed out racist and anti-Semitic and ethnocentric and sexist beliefs. The first criterion for sorting worthy from unworthy beliefs should be: Cause no pain, and allow none to be caused—especially not to the politically vulnerable. Intellectuals should be like doctors. They should first do no harm."

The empathetic spirit from which that line of thinking springs is admirable. But the principle to which it leads is nothing but dreadful. The right principle, and the only one consonant with liberal science, is, Cause no pain solely in order to hurt. The wrong principle, but the one that has increasingly taken the place of the right one, is, Allow no pain to be caused.

The social system does not and never can exist which allows no harm to come to anybody. Conflict of impulse and desire is an inescapable fact of human existence, and where there is conflict there will always be losers and wounds. Utopian systems premised on a world of loving harmony—communism, for instance—fail because in the attempt to obliterate conflict they obliterate freedom. The chore of a social regime is not to obliterate conflict but to manage it, so as to put it to good use while causing a minimum of hurt and abuse. Liberal systems, although far from perfect, have at least two great advantages: they can channel conflict rather than obliterate it, and they give a certain degree of protection from centrally administered abuse. The liberal intellectual system is no exception. It causes pain to people whose views are criticized, still more to those whose views fail to check out and so are rejected. But there are two important consolations. First, no one gets to run the system to his own advantage or stay in charge for long. Whatever you can do to me, I can do to you. Those who are criticized may give as good as they get. Second, the books are never closed, and the game is never over. Sometimes rejected ideas (continental drift, for one) make sensational comebacks.

Humanitarians, though, remain unsatisfied. Their hope, which is no less appealing for being futile, is that somehow the harm can be prevented in the first place. Their worry is that the harm may emanate in two directions, one social and the other individual.

Social harm accrues to society as a whole from the spread of bad ideas; held to be especially vulnerable are minorities or groups seen as lacking power. "AIDS comes from homosexuals," "Jews fabricated the Holocaust," "Blacks are less intelligent than whites"—those ideas and others like them can do real mischief.

Though the special concern for minorities as groups is a new twist, this argument is an old and highly principled one. It was used, in all good conscience, by the Inquisition. The heretic, in those days, endangered the peace and stability of the whole society by challenging the rightful authority of the Church. The Inquisition was a policing action. But by its own lights it was a humanitarian action, too. The heretic endangered the faith of believers, and so threatened to drag others with him to an eternity of suffering in perdition; not least of all, he threw away his own soul. To allow such a person to destroy souls seemed at least as indecent as allowing racist hate speech seems today. "It is an error to think of the persecution of heretics as being forced by the Church upon unwilling or indifferent laity. The heretic was an unpopular person in the Middle Ages. There are, in fact, instances in the late eleventh century and early twelfth century of heretics being lynched by an infuriated mob, who regarded the clergy as too lenient." If you cared about the good of society and about the souls of your neighbors and friends, then you believed that the Inquisition's mission was at bottom humane, even if the inquisitorial methods sometimes were not.

Humane motives, however, could not save the Inquisition from the same problem that faces humanitarians today: although allowing mistakes is risky, suppressing them is much riskier, because then a "mistake" becomes whatever it is that the authorities don't like to hear. Suppressing offensiveness, too, comes at a high cost, since offensiveness is not the same thing as wrongness—often just the contrary. Sometimes patently "offensive" verbiage turns out to be telling the unpopular truth. As I am hardly the first to point out, practically all knowledge of any importance began as a statement which offended someone. "All the durable truths that have come into the world within historic times," said Mencken, "have been opposed as bitterly as if they were so many waves of smallpox." Many people were appalled by the notion that the earth was not at the center of the universe (to say so was hate speech—hateful of God), many other people by the proposition that man was created last rather than first, and still others by the exploding of the common "knowledge" that white people were inherently more intelligent than people of all other races.

Will someone's belief, if accepted, destroy society? Maybe. But more likely not. "Throughout history, scientists have been urged to suppress their views about nature for the sake of the public welfare," wrote David Hull. That the solar system is heliocentric, that species evolve, that genes influence mental traits—at one time or another people feared that those ideas and many others would destroy society if they became widely accepted. "Thus far, however, those who have urged the suppression of new views for the 'good of the people' have underestimated the ability of both societies and individual people to survive successive challenges to their conceptions of the world and how it works." So often have those who warned us about "dangerous" ideas been wrong, and so often have they abused whatever restraining power they possessed, that I have no hesitation in saying: it is better in every case to let critical public inquiry run its course than to try to protect society from it. If we have anything to learn from the progress of knowledge in the last few centuries, it is that to Peirce's injunction, "Do not block the way of inquiry," must be added, "And by no means should inquiry be blocked to 'save' society."

The other, and much newer, strand of intellectual humanitarianism is intuitively more appealing and emotionally harder to resist. It says that wrongheaded opinions and harsh words are hurtful, if not necessarily to society as a whole, then to *individuals*. And here liberal science has been put squarely on the defensive, for the first time in more than a hundred years; for here you have, not the cold-blooded public censor raising bureaucratic objections on behalf of "society," but an identifiable person saying "*I* am hurt" and speaking for his own dignity. In today's world the second kind of claim, like all human-rights claims, seems compelling. Facing it means owning up to the truth about knowledge and about the system which best produces it.

So let us be frank, once and for all: creating knowledge is painful, for the same reason that it can also be exhilarating. Knowledge does not come free to any of us; we have to suffer for it. We have to stand naked before the court of critical checkers and watch our most cherished beliefs come under fire. Sometimes we have to watch while our notion of evident truth gets tossed in the gutter. Sometimes we feel we are treated rudely, even viciously. As others prod and test and criticize our ideas, we feel angry, hurt, embarrassed.

We would all like to think that knowledge could be separated from hurt. We would all like to think that painful but useful and thus "legitimate" criticism is objectively distinguishable from criticism which is merely ugly and hurtful. Surely criticism is one thing, and "Hitler should have finished the job" is another. But what we would like to think is not so: the only such distinction is in the eye of the beholder. The fact is that even the most "scientific" criticism can be horribly hurtful, devastatingly so. The physicist Ludwig Boltzmann was so depressed by the harshness of F. W. Ostwald's and Ernst Mach's attacks on his ideas that he committed suicide. "And Georg Cantor, the originator of the modern theory of sets of points and of the orders of infinity, lost his mind because of the hatred and animosity against him and his ideas by his teacher Leopold Kronecker: he was confined to a mental hospital for many years at the end of his life." The medical researcher Robert Gallo wrote vividly about the pain and shock of what he believed to be viciously harsh criticism.

> What surprised me were not the findings—as I say, I was already developing my own doubts—but the vehemence with which they were delivered. More than one speaker used our misfortune to ridicule the very idea of a human retrovirus. . . . Even now I have difficulty thinking back to that day. I would be subjected to far more extensive, personal, and even vicious attacks years later when I entered AIDS research. . . . But nothing compared with the feelings that passed over me as I sat that day in Hershey, Pennsylvania, hearing not just HL-23 but much of my life's work—the search for tumor-causing RNA viruses in humans—systematically and disdainfully dismissed. . . . I was too old to cry, but it hurt too much to laugh.

I am certainly not saying that we should all go out and be offensive or inflammatory just for the sake of it. Please don't paint swastikas on the synagogue and say I gave my blessing. I am against offending people for fun. But I am also only too well aware that in the pursuit of knowledge many people—probably most of us at one time or another—will be hurt, and that this is a reality which no amount of wishing or regulating can ever change. It is not good to offend people, but it is necessary. A no-offense society is a no-knowledge society.

If you want an example from life, take the case of Japan. The Japanese have no tradition of open public criticism. In the traditional Japanese way of thinking, criticism was a mark of enmity; in fact, according to the intellectual historian Masao Maruyama, there was no word in Japanese for "opposition," as distinct from "enmity" or "antagonism," until one was imported from the West in the last century. That fact plus the society's emphasis on consensus and unanimity produced a climate in which people avoided criticizing each other. Pointing out someone's mistakes was considered rude, or worse. Change has been slow in coming. "An open debate is nearly impossible in this country," one Japanese economist told me when I visited Japan in 1990. A renowned political scientist said ruefully that the best policy toward ideas that you disagree with is one of benign neglect—to be mute. Criticism would be seen as an attack. Book reviewers typically don't review books they don't like. The result is that in Japan ideas tend to be traded on a kind of gray market. People criticize privately, exchanging gossip and asking each other "What did you think of so-and-so's new book on this or that?" Producing new ideas is hard, and testing ideas, sorting the useful from the empty, is harder. And so intellectual resources lie fallow.

The situation seems to be gradually improving. Yet there can be little doubt that the costs of the Japanese aversion to criticism have been enormous—not just for Japan but for the world. Japan is one of the world's largest, richest, best-educated, and hardest working nations. Yet she relies on outsiders to set her intellectual agenda; her universities are, by international standards, backwaters; her record on intellectual innovation is bleak. From 1901 to 1985 Japan won five Nobel Prizes in science—one twenty-eighth of America's share, one-tenth of Germany's. And has avoiding offense produced a better society? Not many American thinkers would want to live there, sitting expressionlessly through academic meetings. The price of the no-offense society is high.

Too many people today are forgetting this. They think you can keep knowledge and get rid of pain. They are epistemological pacifists, enjoying the products of critical inquiry while righteously condemning any unpleasantness which they see in the products' manufacture. A lot of them seem to think that intellectual goods grow on trees. A few years ago, a French course at Yale came under attack by a senior who brought it before the school's sexual harassment committee. Pierre Capretz, the designer of the course, had produced a kind of French-language TV soap opera ("French in Action"), which proved to be an immensely popular teaching aid; "dozens of public stations show it, and hundreds of universities use it as their basic French curriculum." But the student was offended by what she regarded as sexual stereotyping—for instance, "a big picture of a woman from a French advertisement with half her shirt on." The student said, "It just really offended me to be in a classroom being portrayed in a completely objectified way." A lesbian student complained that "to have to sit through a sexist heterosexual romance every day as a way of learning French is very offensive." The students said that men might also be offended; the senior said that she "felt sorry for one balding student when hair vocabulary was the topic." It never seemed to have occurred to any of those people that the show was effective because it was fun, and that it was fun because its maker had ventured to be innovative and idiosyncratic, and that if he had been obliged to pander to everybody's feelings he would have produced numbing drivel. Then a lot of people who wanted to learn French would have been hurt.

A liberal society stands on the proposition that we should all take seriously the idea that we might be wrong. That means we must place no one, including ourselves, beyond the reach of criticism (no final say); it means that we must allow people to err, even where the error offends and upsets, as it often will. But we also are not supposed to claim we have knowledge except where belief is checked by no one in particular (no personal authority).

In other words, liberal science is built on two pillars. One is the right to offend in pursuit of truth. The other is the responsibility to check and be checked. Here, and here alone, is the social morality which finds error as fast as possible while keeping hurt to a minimum: intellectual license checked by intellectual discipline. . . .

And what should we require be done to assuage

the feelings of people who have been offended, to recompense them for their hurt and punish their tormentors? This and only this: *absolutely nothing*. Nothing at all.

The standard answer to people who say they are offended should be: "Is there any casualty other than your feelings? Are you or others being threatened with violence or vandalism? No? Then it's a shame your feelings are hurt, but that's too bad. You'll live." If one is going to enjoy the benefits of living in a liberal society without being shamelessly hypocritical, one must try to be thick-skinned, since the way we make knowledge is by rubbing against one another. In a liberal culture, this is a matter of positive moral obligation. In practical terms, it means that people who get righteously offended twice every day before breakfast should learn to count to a hundred—granted, that takes discipline—and say to themselves, "Well, it's just that fellow's opinion," before they charge out the door crying for justice. (A sense of humor would help.) And it means that people receiving the complaints of the offended should count to a thousand before rushing out to do something about them. The alternative is to reward people for being upset. And as soon as people learn they can get something if they raise Cain about being offended, they go into the business of professional offendedness. Some people believe that the Russians are reading their minds with microwaves; other people fret about French classes that might inadvertently upset balding men. In a liberal society, the initial presumption ought to be that neither kind of concern deserves any better than to be politely ignored.

If that sounds callous, remember that the establishment of a right not to be offended would lead not to a more civil culture but to a lot of shouting matches over who was being offensive to whom, and who could claim to be more offended. All we will do that way is to shut ourselves up. The doctrine of Never Offend is the biggest reason so many Western intellectuals had so little to say when Khomeini went after Rushdie. The fundamentalists offended us, but one of our writers offended them first, so who's to blame? "We understand that the book itself has been found deeply offensive by people of the Muslim faith. It is a book that is offensive in many other ways as well. We can understand why it could be criticized," and so on.

In one sense the rise of intellectual humanitarianism represents an advance of honesty: it drops the pretense that liberal science is a painless and purely mechanistic process, like doing crossword puzzles. But the conclusion which the humanitarians draw—that the hurting must be stopped—is all wrong. Impelling them toward their wrong conclusion is a dreadful error: the notion that hurtful words are a form of violence. Offensive speech hurts, say the humanitarians; it constitutes "words that wound" (writes one law professor); it does "real harm to real people" who deserve protection and redress (writes another law professor). When a law student at Georgetown University published an article charging that the academic credentials of white and black students accepted at Georgetown were "dramatically unequal," a number of students demanded that the writer be punished. And note carefully the terms of the condemnation: "I think the article is assaultive. People were injured. I think that kind of speech is outrageous." The notion of "assaultive speech" is no rarity today. Stanley Fish, a professor at Duke University, has said that "the speech that is being assaulted [on college campuses] is itself assaultive speech."

A University of Michigan law professor said: "To me, racial epithets are not speech. They are bullets." This, finally, is where the humanitarian line leads: to the erasure of the distinction, in principle and ultimately also in practice, between discussion and bloodshed. My own view is that words are words and bullets are bullets, and that it is important to keep this straight. For you do not have to be Kant to see what comes after "offensive words are bullets": if you hurt me with words, I reply with bullets, and the exchange is even. Rushdie hurt fundamentalist Muslims with words; his book was every bit as offensive to them as any epithet or slogan you can imagine. So they set out to hurt him back. Words are bullets; fair is fair.

If you are inclined to equate verbal offense with physical violence, think again about the logic of your position. If hurtful opinions are violence, then painful criticism is violence. In other words, on the humanitarian premise, *science itself is a form of violence*. What do you do about violence? You establish policing authorities—public or private—to stop it and to punish the perpetrators. You set up authorities empowered to weed out hurtful ideas and speech. In other words: an inquisition.

It is bad enough to have to remind people that there is no right not to be offended, and that criticism is not the same as violence. It is deeply embarrassing to have to deliver this reminder to people at the center of American intellectual life. The last few years have witnessed a rash of attempts on university campuses to restrict offensive speech, both by punishing offenders after the fact and by establishing preemptive restrictions. Most of the universities—certainly the private ones—were within their legal rights to set standards for behavior on their campuses. But universities are neither churches nor finishing schools: their mission and moral charter, their reason for being, is not to convert errant minds or to teach good manners. Their mission is to advance knowledge by teaching and practicing public criticism. Alas, many of them are doing exactly what a university, of all institutions, should not do: defining offensive speech as quasi-violent behavior, and treating it accordingly.

In 1989 the University of Wisconsin revised its student-conduct code to say that students would be disciplined for comments which "demean the [victim's] race, sex, religion, color, creed, disability, sexual orientation, national origin, ancestry or age," or which created "an intimidating, hostile or demeaning environment for education." One student got seven months' probation for telling an Asian-American student, "It's people like you—that's the reason this country is screwed up," "You don't belong here," and "Whites are always getting screwed by minorities and someday the whites will take over." Such statements, as federal judge Robert W. Warren noted in striking down the rule, express opinions. The University of Michigan adopted a six-page anti-bias code, likewise found unconstitutional, which provided for punishment of students who engaged in conduct that "stigmatizes or victimizes an individual on the basis of race, ethnicity, religion, sex, sexual orientation, creed, national origin, ancestry, age, marital status, handicap, or Vietnam-era veteran status." It's hard to think what kind of social commentary might not be dragged in under one of those categories—especially given the university's enforcement guidelines, which gave as an example of discriminatory harassment, "A male student makes remarks in class like 'Women just aren't as good in this field as men,' thus creating a hostile learning atmosphere for female classmates." The guidelines said, "The University encourages open and vigorous intellectual discussion in the classroom. To reach this goal students must be free to participate in class discussion without *feeling* [my italics] harassed or intimidated by others' comments." In overturning the university's rule, federal judge Avern Cohn noted that there had been three cases in which students were disciplined or threatened with discipline for comments made in a classroom setting. The University of Pennsylvania forbade as harassment "any behavior, verbal or physical [note that speech has become "verbal behavior" here], that stigmatizes or victimizes individuals on the basis of race, ethnic or national origin . . . and that has the purpose or effect of interfering with an individual's academic or work performance; and/or creates an intimidating or offensive academic, living, or work environment."

In other words, anyone who might make anyone else angry or upset, even inadvertently ("that has . . . the effect"), had better watch out. Tufts University wrote a policy which created three levels of allowable speech. "Varying degrees of expression are permissible on campus, depending upon the ability of others to avoid 'offensive' speech." The University of Connecticut adopted rules punishing students for the use of "derogatory names, inappropriately directed laughter [!], inconsiderate jokes, and conspicuous exclusion [of another student] from conversation." One official at Emory University was quoted as saying, "I don't believe freedom of speech on campus was designed to allow people to demean others on campus." Rutgers University adopted a policy against "insult, defamation, and harassment," written so as to encompass "belittling comments" and enforced against, for example, a student who publicly used the word "fag." A student charging a Harvard Law

School professor with sexism in a contracts course wrote, "A professor in any position at any school has no right or privilege to use the classroom in such a way as to offend, at the very least, 40 percent of the students." (One wonders, would 10 percent be OK? How about 4 percent deeply offended, as against 40 percent mildly offended?) One can go on and on with the depressing litany. UCLA suspended a student editor when the paper ran a cartoon making fun of affirmative action; when a student editor at California State University, Northridge, ran an op-ed piece criticizing UCLA, he was suspended from the newspaper. At Stanford, a junior said, "We don't put as many restrictions on freedom of speech as we should." On and on.

It is important to see that the Constitution is not, in those cases, the main issue. The Constitution can stop government institutions (like public universities) from punishing speech, but it does not proscribe attempts by private organizations to patrol their membership for offensive beliefs. What proscribes that is the morality of liberal science, with its commitment to public criticism of each by any; but in the inner sanctum of our intellectual life, liberal morality is fast being eroded by a misguided humanitarianism. I called some professors I know to ask if there was really much to worry about. They said that there was. A political science department chairman at a leading public university said, "There are certain subjects which can't be seriously discussed." The commitment on campus, he said, is not to the free exchange of views, but "only to the free exchange of acceptable views." Another political scientist told me, "We have a freedom of speech problem on campus." At a prestigious private college on the East Coast, a philosophy professor told me, "There's an extreme chilling effect here among the faculty and the students on the idea, right or wrong, that some of these minorities may be responsible for some of their own problems." One side of a whole variety of arguments is simply left out, he said.

And how are restraints on offensive opinion justified? With arguments that are appealing on the surface but alarming down below. Trace their logic and you find that they all lead back to the same conclusion: freewheeling criticism (thus liberal science) is dangerous or hurtful and must be regulated by right-thinking people.

"Why tolerate bigotry?" A classic argument, framed today in terms like this: "Prohibiting racially and religiously bigoted speech is praiseworthy because it seeks to elevate, not to degrade, because it draws from human experience, not from woolly dogmas or academic slogans, because it salutes reason as the backbone of freedom and tolerance."

That kind of rhetoric, besides being almost completely empty of meaning, glides right around the important question: just who is supposed to decide what speech is "bigoted" and what speech is merely "critical"? What about the student at Michigan who was summoned to a disciplinary hearing for saying that homosexuality is a disease treatable with therapy? Why is that a "bigoted" suggestion rather than an unpopular opinion? What's the difference? And who is to say?

The anti-bigotry people never approach the question directly, because doing so would show them up. The answer is: *we*, the right-thinking, are the ones who will say who is and isn't bigoted.

Whenever anyone says that bigoted or offensive or victimizing or oppressing or vicious opinions should be suppressed, all he is really saying is, "Opinions which *I* hate should be suppressed." In other words, he is doing the same thing Plato did when he claimed that the philosopher (i.e., himself) should rule for the good of society: he is making a power grab. He wants to be the pope, the ayatollah, the philosopher-king.

The answer to the question "Why tolerate hateful or misguided opinions?" has been the same ever since Plato unveiled his ghastly utopia: because the alternative is worse.

"We don't want to block criticism and inquiry, just hate and intimidation." The trouble is the same: one person's hate speech is another person's sincerest criticism ("The Holocaust is an Israeli fabrication"). So who is to draw the line? Let's make up some examples. It is hard to see any redeeming social value in someone's saying "Niggers are stupid." But what about "On average, blacks are less

intelligent than whites"? Should people who say that be punished? Then what about "Blacks display less aptitude for math, on average, than Asians"? If you clamp down on the first of those opinions, what do you do when someone complains about the next, and the next? Who will draw the fine distinctions?

It's no good, either, to proscribe epithets. Is "boy" an epithet, if a white man uses it to address a black man? When is it an epithet, when a term of affection, when just a mannerism? If an Anti-Epithet Board tried to decide such questions by looking at the particulars of each case—and each is different—it would soon be hopelessly entangled in ad hoc distinctions, conflicting testimony, and political mare's nests. ("In this case the addressee who was called 'boy' is a casual and usually friendly acquaintance of the addresser and is two years over the legal drinking age but looks much younger, and therefore a mitigating element of affection as well as an element of literalism may have been present. . . .") The alternative is to draw up lists of proscribed words; but that's no better. Put "nigger" on the list and you have proscribed *Huckleberry Finn*—unless you decorate your list with endless baroque distinctions, in which case you are hopelessly entangled again. ("Persons shall not use the word 'nigger' in direct conversation with black persons, unless the word is being used demonstratively or illustratively or both parties to the conversation are black or dark-skinned or the intentions are friendly as evinced by signs or gestures attesting to the conversation's mutual congeniality such as smiles, handshakes, or affectionate language. . . . Nothing in these rules shall be interpreted as proscribing *Huckleberry Finn* except when it is read aloud to a black person or persons in a taunting or confrontational manner, as evinced by undue emphasis on words such as 'nigger,' 'slave,' 'owner,' or when it is read in other circumstances which a reasonable person might regard as prejudicial and offensive. . . .") Meanwhile, of course, people who want to hurl insults will be busy inventing new ways to do so. They can always stay a step or two ahead of the list. The epithet guidelines would soon collapse.

Suppose, for argument's sake, that someone managed to discover a distinction separating hate talk from criticism as definitively as zero separates negative numbers from positive ones. Even that would be no guarantee of anything. The distinction might (or might not) satisfy philosophers, but in the political world ambitious activists would have every reason to smudge the line, stretch it, blur it, erase it, move it, or cross over it outright. And if they had support in the voting booths or in the student senate or in the streets, they would succeed. In politics the only distinction, finally, is between what you can get away with and what you can't.

Already—right from the start, in fact—humanitarians have tried to regulate theories and hypotheses as well as jeers and shouted epithets. After all, a theory can be just as hurtful as a jeer. At the University of Michigan, one administrator called for prohibitions on professors as well as students, saying, "Harassment in classrooms is based on theories held by teachers, and that environment has prevented minorities from having the same advantages afforded others." In other words, hurtful theories should be suppressed.

The unhappy reality is that some people are always going to say gross and vicious things to hurt other people. If they don't destroy property or do violence, ignore them or criticize them. But do not set up an authority to punish them. Any guidelines elaborate enough to distinguish vicious opinions from unpopular ones will be too elaborate to work. In practice, the distinction will be between the opinions which the political authorities find congenial and those which they find inconvenient.

"In practice, we can distinguish verbal harassment from legitimate criticism by the hurtful intent of the speaker." No. In the first place, even the most "legitimate" criticism may be intended to hurt or discredit its target, as Robert Gallo, among many other scientists, knows well. In the second place, and more important: authorities that seek to punish the "intent" of criticism are even more dangerous than ones that seek to punish criticism itself. To establish the intent of words you must put the speaker's mind on trial. When the Michigan student said that homosexuality was a curable disease, did he intend to upset gay students, or not? That is the Inquisition indeed.

It is certainly true that the courts routinely

weigh motive and intent in establishing, for instance, whether a killing was murder or self-defense, intentional or accidental. That is necessary and proper. But in the case of someone's telling a Jew that the Holocaust is an Israeli fabrication, the "crime" established by the intent is merely speech—criticism—and not violence. To make speech punishable on grounds of intent is to give authorities the power to punish criticism whenever they are suspicious of the critic. We should know better than to give any authority such power, least of all at a university. Certainly, then, there is no excuse for a university code like Stanford's, which prohibits speech that "*is intended* [my italics] to insult or stigmatize."

"Real people are being hurt, and so protective action is morally imperative." That people's *feelings* are hurt is undeniable. But one of the glaring failings of the never-offend movement—the same failing that the anti-pornography movement always has to finesse—is its absolute inability to show any concrete, objective damage which offensive speech and opinions have actually done beyond damage to feelings. Nor have they been able to define how seriously one's feelings must be hurt to qualify one as verbally "wounded," or how to tell whether the victim of wounding words is really as badly hurt as he claims to be. How do you distinguish words that wound from words that annoy?

When pressed on this, humanitarians retreat to rhetoric about the way bigoted or vicious ideas are deeply repugnant, damage people's self-esteem, are a form of oppression, and the like. They argue that even to speak of hurtful words as "obnoxious" or "offensive" is to slight the words' damage. "'Obnoxious' suggests that the injury or offense is a surface one that a large-minded ('liberated and humane') person should be able to tolerate if not embrace," writes Stanley Fish. "The idea that the effects of speech can penetrate to the core—either for good or for ill—is never entertained; everything is kept on the level of weightless verbal exchange; there is no sense of the lacerating harms that speech of certain kinds can inflict." Note the retreat to the violence metaphor ("lacerating"). Note also the circularity: true, words "of certain kinds" *can* "penetrate to the core," but the whole question is *which* kinds and *which* words, and how do you tell, and how deep into the core is too deep? If we had an offendedness meter, then we might be able to solve that problem; as it is, the complaint that "real people are being hurt" does not begin to tell us who is being hurt, when, how badly, or how much is too much. Even if such a meter did exist, we would still have a problem: what about *true* words that "penetrate to the core"? What about useful but harsh criticisms that "penetrate to the core"? Suppose a creationist collapses in tears and drops out of college after a biology teacher declares that Darwin was right? Is that a "laceration"? Should it be stopped?

By and large, the humanitarians never even reach those questions, much less answer them. Beyond the rhetoric, all they are saying is this: "These ideas or words are very upsetting to me and to some others." Yes, they are upsetting. But if everyone has a right not to be upset, then all criticism, and therefore all scientific inquiry, is at best morally hazardous and at worst impossible. Even joking becomes impossible.

Faced with this problem, very often the humanitarians retreat to the position that *some* people—historically oppressed groups—have a special right not to be upset. That answer is no better. In the first place, it throws liberal science out the window, because it junks the empirical rule that anyone is allowed to criticize anyone, regardless of race or ethnic history or whatever. The fact that you're oppressed doesn't make you right. In the second place, who is going to decide who is allowed to upset whom? The only possible answer: a centralized political authority.

"It is hardly reasonable to justify here-and-now pain in the name of abstract principles or of knowledge which may or may not ever be produced." This is another humanitarian standby: hurting people in the name of abstract or future "freedom" or "knowledge" is like torturing people in the name of "God's word" or "your future salvation." "The requirement is that we endure whatever pain racist and hate speech inflicts for the sake of a future whose emergence we can only take on faith," writes Fish. "In a specifically religious vision like Milton's this makes perfect sense (it is indeed the whole of Christianity), but in the context of a politics that puts trust in the world and not in the Holy

Spirit, it raises more questions than it answers and could be seen as the other prong of a strategy designed to de-legitimize the complaints of victimized groups." In effect, abstract principles are all too often smoke screens for attacks on minorities.

Maybe they are; but we are not, in fact, talking about abstract principles or vague future gains. The trouble with the argument that real pain outweighs airy abstractions is that it leaves out one whole side of the equation: the pain is very real and very concrete for the "offensive" speaker who is sentenced by political authorities to prison, privation, or, as in Salman Rushdie's case, death. The whole point of liberal science is that it *substitutes* criticism for force and violence. That is to say, it substitutes the power of critics to select worthy ideas verbally for the power of political authorities to select "worthy" ideas forcibly. The false choice presented by humanitarians is between wounding people with words and not wounding people with words. The real choice is between hurtful words and billy clubs, jail cells, or worse. If you think that the right to offend is a mere "abstraction," ask Rushdie.

"We're making the intellectual climate more free not less free." The conventional wisdom now in many American universities seems to be that you can't have free thought or free speech where people, especially members of minority groups, feel intimidated, harassed, upset. Thus, if you get rid of talk which upsets or intimidates, you add to intellectual freedom.

Usually, that argument comes with high-sounding rhetoric of the following type. James T. Laney, the president of Emory University, was making the case for Emory's policy banning "discriminatory harassment," defined as "conduct (oral, written, graphic, or physical) directed against any person or group . . . that has the purpose or reasonably foreseeable effect of creating an offensive, demeaning, intimidating, or hostile environment." (Note, again, the implicit equivalence of speech and violence as two hurtful forms of conduct, "oral" and "physical.") Laney wrote: "Can the truth have its day in court when the courtroom is made into a mud-wrestling pit where vicious epithets are flung? And should the university be a place of such severe neutrality about values that mere volubility or numbers can carry the day?" He declared, "What we intend is not to curb free speech but to make it more probable."

Leave aside, for now, the question of whether you actually can get rid of "intimidating" speech by slapping controls on it. Look instead at the premise of the argument: that you can only do science where people feel good about each other, where they feel secure and unharassed—in other words, where they are exempt from upsetting criticism. Of course, that is dead wrong. A lot of researchers and theorists hate each other. The history of science is full of bitter criticism and hard feelings; there is simply no way around it. If you insist on an unhostile or nonoffensive environment, then you belong in a monastery, not a university.

Look also at the Orwellian nature of the attack. It basically says that the more you stifle upsetting (e.g., "intimidating," "demeaning") speech and thought, the more "free" everybody becomes—so that the most "free" intellectual regime is the one with the most taboos on criticism.

The arguments of people like Laney sound good, because they appeal to our gut instinct that false and offensive opinions are a kind of immoral spewage which no good society should put up with. But it is important to remember where we have heard such arguments before: Plato. Society is lost if people with wrong opinions are allowed to go around spreading them. Such opinions "are ugly things" that lead citizens astray from truth, which is why people who hold them must be excluded from debate. As with Plato's policy, so with Emory's. The agenda is always the same: stifle ideas you hate in the name of a higher social good.

A footnote on a common rhetorical sleight-of-hand that fools too many people. Laney asks, "Should the university be a place of such severe neutrality about values that mere volubility or numbers can carry the day?" That is either a trick or an appalling misunderstanding. Liberal inquiry *is* a value, and *it,* not the promulgation of some particular group's notion of "truth," is the university's highest value.

"Without regulation, bad criticism will drive out good." That is, bigoted and vicious attacks will make reasoned debate impossible. Thus, regula-

tion is needed to keep the critical discussion from blowing itself up.

Except in the very short run and among very small and confined groups, the truth is really just the other way around: good criticism drives out bad. If you want to be effective at the game of liberal science, you must persuade others that you are right; and, as a rule, abusive shouting is a poor way to make converts. For that reason, an epithet-shouting strategy is self-punishing except in the very short run. Why has science evolved such a mannerly demeanor? Not because scientists are better brought up than other people, but because thoughtful, systematic argument works better than "Nigger!" or "Faggot!"

What easily *can* blow up reasoned debate, of course, is the attempt to regulate it from the outside. If you think of cases in which critical argument really did break down—the Soviet Union, Nazi Germany, American McCarthyism, some American universities today on the subject of race—you realize that the reason was that someone powerful acted to protect the society forcibly from "disruptive," "subversive," or "oppressive" words.

"Equality in the marketplace of ideas must be attained before speech can be truly free or debate can be fair." The idea here is that, not only is bigoted or vicious speech hurtful, it also silences its target, thus violating the target's right to equal participation in debate. "Speakers too can perpetrate repression aimed at victims whose voices in turn are silenced, undermining equality and decreasing both individual liberty and democratic dialogue," writes Mary Ellen Gale, a law professor. Just as markets need antitrust laws to prevent monopoly and corruption, so debate needs equalizing measures, lest "dominant groups devalue and subordinate the speech of others [and thus] undercut any legitimate competition of ideas and stack the outcome in favor of existing power and privilege."

Even setting aside the constitutional issues—if Gale and others are right, then the Constitution positively *requires* that the government regulate speech—the problems here are endless. In the first place, there is no right to "equal speech." We say what we like and are able to say. Any other standard would require that the voluble be forcibly silenced and the shy forced to stick their necks out. The feisty, the keen, the aggressive and confident *will* talk more, but that doesn't necessarily mean they will be the most effective. And to stop them is to risk losing valuable criticism.

Second, the notion that criticism (as opposed to direct threats, which no one thinks should be allowed either by governments or by universities) silences its targets is flatly false. Some people, no doubt, just roll over or slink away. But, of course, many more get angry and argue back, far more strongly than if they had never been provoked. Harsh, even vicious, criticism spurs just the sort of debate which turns the heat of conflict into the light of knowledge. And so silencing strong criticism does not "balance" an argument; it eviscerates it.

Third, and most important, there is, as always, the problem of authority. Just who is supposed to say when speech is "equal"? Will there be affirmative action for historically "silenced" minorities? Does "equality" mean that blacks talk as much as whites, proportionately, or more? That they be taken more seriously? How about creationists? Do *they* get equal time? Who will decide? Obviously, an equal-speech regime inherently requires a strong regulative authority which can have no agreed-upon mission. So we are back, again, to the political regulation of inquiry on the behalf of the most politically powerful.

"The anti-harassment authorities will be neutral." In other words, if you establish a fair authority, criticism can be regulated fairly.

Sorry, but the hope is illusory and the record is abysmal. Does anyone seriously believe that today's university anti-discrimination committees would treat offended left-wingers and offended right-wingers the same way? Or that they would treat offended creationists and offended racial minorities the same way? The young editor at California State University at Northridge was suspended for running a cartoon critical of affirmative action; does anyone really think an editor would be suspended if he ran a cartoon critical of affirmative action's conservative opponents, even one depicting them as Neanderthals swinging from trees? Some people are offended by photos of white performers in blackface and others are offended by photos of gay sex; does anyone think that the antidiscrimination committees are equally likely to ban both from the university museum? And what about the day when right-wingers get the upper hand? Will *they* be "fair"? People who like authoritarianism always picture themselves running the show. But no one stays on top for long.

And what about people who are shocked and offended by charges that they are "bigoted" and "offensive"? They will come forward with their own claims. Any decision-making committee will inevitably have to favor one offended group over another. Neutrality is impossible even in principle.

Recognizing that, some of the never-offend people have already said flat out that restraints on criticism and opinion should protect only "historical victim groups," whoever they are. (Should Jews be included? rich blacks? gay Republicans? tenured female professors making $60,000 a year?) So much for neutrality. Now we're in an argument over who should control inquiry. No one wins that kind of argument. Knowledge loses.

"The anti-harassment authorities will be wise." Maybe, maybe not. More likely, they will be politically powerful and determined to stay in power. In any case, wisdom is a shabby substitute for public criticism. Most people would agree that Plato was among the wisest philosophers who ever lived, and look at what he wanted to do.

"Society will be better off with offensive and vicious opinions driven out." Many people say, "It's a shame we need to punish and drive out people who say and believe vicious things, but that is the price we pay to protect the civil from the uncivil and the oppressed from their would-be oppressors." In other words, you have to break a few eggs to make an omelet. The answer, as George Orwell said, is, yes, but where's the omelet?

The Inquisition failed to keep Copernicanism down. All it did was slow the progress of knowledge and kill people. The new inquisitions won't work any better. Attempts to suppress beliefs only succeed in calling attention to them and making them causes célèbres. The insistence that racist or homophobic or any other opinions not be tolerated only guarantees that any college sophomore can make the headlines by being outspokenly racist or homophobic, and for many sophomores the temptation is too much to resist. Nasty speech gets nastier as people get angry and start picking fights. Outrage escalates on every side. But nobody's mind is changed.

Every year hundreds of dense literary novels sell a few thousand copies and then sink into oblivion. Yet Ayatollah Khomeini managed to put one such novel on the best-seller lists. In America, thousands of scholars are working on thousands of research projects; most of them go unnoticed by everyone except specialists. Guess which scholar was the subject of a half-page, above-the-fold article in the *New York Times*? A researcher exploring "whether there are differences in intelligence between blacks and whites that help explain differences in their economic and social standing." Liberal science declares that the issue of race and intelligence should be explored by any researcher who cares to explore it and who will follow the rules. But liberal science cannot guarantee a researcher half-page newspaper coverage. Only bans and taboos can do that.

"But we must take collective action to eliminate prejudice and bigotry." No, no, a thousand times no. We must take collective action to *check* prejudice and bigotry, that is all. What I said before is worth repeating: liberal science requires not that we be unprejudiced, but that we have *different* prejudices. The authorities' role is not to get rid of prejudices but to protect criticism. The critical sorting system will do the rest. If central authorities care about advancing knowledge, as government and universities certainly should, then they may participate in public debate, but they must not try to regulate it.

It is, of course, admirable for *individuals* (as opposed to central authorities) to try to get rid of their prejudices. But there are two ways by which you absolutely cannot get rid of prejudice, even though both are very tempting. One, the method of Plato's philosopher, is to sit quietly in your room, thinking as carefully and objectively as you can and trying to clear your mind of prejudice. If you do that, you may feel that you are clearing your mind, but in fact you will be sinking deeper into your own stew. "Is it not a common experience," says Popper, "that those who are most convinced of having got rid of their prejudices are most prejudiced?" The second method, the political method of Plato's philosopher-king, is to find the most unprejudiced opinion in the land and instate it by force. Little more need be said about that method of eliminating prejudice.

The only reliable way to identify prejudice is through public critical exchange. If you want to think you're unprejudiced, you must *do* something: science. "What we call 'scientific objectivity,'" writes Popper, "is not a product of the individual scientist's impartiality, but a product of the social or public character of scientific method."

"But doesn't the First Amendment protect us?" From government regulation of inquiry, yes. But not from ourselves, if we come to accept an ethic which obliterates the line between criticism and violence and so makes liberal science immoral in principle. If we accept the moral rightness of the humanitarian attack on intellectual liberalism, or of the egalitarian attack, then no First Amendment can save us.

"You're not black, or gay, or Hispanic, or whatever; you wouldn't understand." Only outsiders, only the oppressed, can understand the hurt, so only they can really comprehend the need for restrictions on debate. White males have no standing to protest controls, because they haven't felt the pain.

That argument deserves a special place in the hall of shame. For one thing, it assumes that only members of certified minority groups know what pain is like. Much worse, though: the only-minorities-can-understand argument is anti-intellectualism at its most rancid. It is the age-old tribalist notion that, as Popper put it, "we think with our blood," "with our national heritage," or "with our class." White supremacists will always say that blacks shouldn't be in charge because they "can't understand" (they're too stupid), anti-Semites will say the same about Jews (too corrupt), and now, shamefully, some American minority activists are saying something similar about "in-groups" (too pampered, too blind). They are denying the very possibility of liberal science, whose premise is that knowledge is available to everyone and comes through public inquiry and criticism, not from the color of your skin or your ethnic heritage or your social class. Accept their credo, and you have a race war or a class war where liberal inquiry once was. . . .

PART II

First Principles

Most of our moral judgments concern particular things. We judge certain actions and certain people good or bad. There are many gradations: Acts and people may be heroic, splendid, admirable, acceptable, indifferent, unsatisfactory, despicable, or horrible, to mention just a few moral adjectives. There are also many dimensions of moral consideration: Acts or people may be honest, kind, loyal, trustworthy, noble, brave, generous, self-controlled, gentle, friendly, witty, pleasant, helpful, effective, efficient, or considerate, to mention just a few positive attributes. Usually, we apply these to particular actions or to particular people.

When people disagree about a moral judgment, they try to justify their own views. They do this by constructing an argument that appeals to moral principles. Suppose, for example, that Jennifer killed Michael by breaking a baseball bat over his head. And say that you and I disagree about the morality of the act. I think it was wrong; you think it was justifiable. I might try to justify my judgment by constructing a simple argument:

1. Jennifer's killing Michael was murder. (Fact)
2. Murder is always wrong. (Moral principle)
3. Therefore, Jennifer's killing Michael was wrong. (Moral conclusion)

An argument for a particular moral conclusion generally contains both factual and moral premises, just as this one does. The first premise is factual; it purports to describe the way the world is. The second premise, in contrast, is moral. It does not describe the world as it is but evaluates a general category of action. Assertions like the first premise are often called *factual* or *descriptive*. Those like the second premise or the conclusion are often called *evaluative, prescriptive,* or *normative.*

The distinction between these kinds of assertion matters, for we resolve disagreements about them in very different ways. Suppose, for example, that you challenge my first premise. You deny, in other words, that Jennifer committed a murder. We might resolve our disagreement by clarifying our use of words and investigating the facts. If I defend my premise with further premises:

4. Murder is killing a human being with malice aforethought.
5. Jennifer killed Michael.
6. Michael was human.
7. Jennifer intended to do Michael harm.

you might challenge my definition of murder (4) or my description of the facts (5, 6, and 7). We might proceed to investigate whether Jennifer was really the killer, and Michael really the victim; whether Jennifer intended to harm Michael or killed him accidentally; whether Michael was human or a robot; and whether my definition of murder is correct. All these issues concern definitions or matters of fact.

If you challenge my second premise, however, investigating matters of fact cannot resolve our disagreement. We differ not on how the world is, but on how it ought to be. To justify my premise, I must appeal to some broader moral principle—and, ultimately, many philosophers have thought, to a first, most fundamental moral principle from which all others follow. The thinkers of the Enlightenment, especially, saw that if we could establish and agree upon a first principle of morality, all our disagreements would concern definitions and matters of fact, and thus be resolvable by investigation. Morality would lend itself to scientific inquiry as much as anything else.

The search for a first principle of morality has other sources. One stems from the great variety of things we call good. We say that certain actions, people, and even qualities (such as honesty) are good. What makes them all good? What do they have in common? Similarly, we call things as diverse as the Kennedy assassination, Hitler, deception, and cruelty wrong. What makes them all wrong? What do they have in common? To answer would be to give the first principle of morality. Why couldn't there be several such principles? Because we could raise the question, What makes them fundamental principles of morality? What do they all have in common?

The Enlightenment produced two great and competing accounts of the foundations of morality. Immanuel Kant maintains that all of ethics reduces to a single principle, the categorical imperative. He articulates five versions of the principle, but he takes all to be equivalent. The two most important versions are:

I. Act so that the maxim of your action might be willed as universal law.
II. Treat everyone as a end, not merely as a means.

The first means that you must act on the basis of principle; you cannot make an exception for yourself. You must act, in other words, in such a way that everyone could act on your principles. The second means that every human being deserves to be treated with respect, as an independent moral agent; you must not use people as a means to your own ends.

Kant derives the categorical imperative from general considerations about morality. A first principle, he warns, must be necessarily true; it must hold no matter what the world is like, for, as a moral assertion, it does not describe the world. It must be something we can know *a priori,* independently of experience. It must therefore be universal, applying to all rational agents capable of thinking and acting morally. And it must be categorical, of the form "Everyone always ought to . . . ," rather than hypothetical (of the form "If you want . . . , you ought to . . ."), for it must not depend on the goals we adopt for ourselves, even general goals such as happiness. What all hypothetical imperatives have in common is simply the form of law, that is, the idea of acting on principle as a moral agent. That leads to his formulations of the categorical imperative. You must act on principle; you must respect yourself and others as moral agents.

The second great Enlightenment account of the foundations of morality rejects Kant's picture completely. Utilitarianism, a moral theory mentioned in Plato's dialogues, first advocated by Francis Hutcheson, and brought to full development by Jeremy Bentham and John Stuart Mill, can be summarized in two words: *Maximize good.* Utilitarians hold that all of ethics and political philosophy reduces to that one maxim, the principle of utility.

The principle seems simple but has a number of far-reaching consequences. First, utilitarians evaluate actions by the extent to which they maximize good. They evaluate actions, therefore, solely by examining their consequences. In determining whether an action or kind of action is right or wrong, we need to ask, Is it for the best? What effect does it have on the amount of good in the universe? Utilitarianism is thus a version of *consequentialism,* the view that the moral value of an action depends completely on its consequences.

Other moral philosophers contend that other features of actions are relevant to their moral value. Killing, for example, is generally a bad thing. But our judgment of a killer depends on other factors. Was the killing purely accidental, or did it result from negligence? Did it stem from a fit of rage, or was it premeditated? The prior actions, motives, intentions, and general state of mind of the agent, we think, make a moral difference. Utilitarians are committed to saying that all these things are irrelevant to evaluating the killing itself—but, they would say, they are highly relevant to evaluating the killer. Utilitarians need not banish motives, intentions, states of mind, and circumstances from ethics. But they must define their moral values ultimately in terms of the moral value of actions. We might say that an intention is good, for example, to the extent that it results in good actions; that a motive is good to the extent that it results in good intentions; that a character trait is good to the extent that it results in good motives; and so on.

Second, utilitarianism is a *universalist* theory: We must judge whether an action or kind of action maximizes the total amount of good in the universe. Thus, we must consider the consequences of the action on everyone it affects. We cannot consider ourselves alone, or just people in our community, or our fellow citizens; we must consider *everyone*. Most actions affect only a few people in any significant, identifiable way. Political decisions, however, often affect millions. In either case, we must be prepared to consider the effects on everyone affected.

Third, utilitarianism requires an independent theory of the good. The principle of utility tells us to maximize good, but it does not tell us what the good is. What, exactly, must we maximize? Bentham and Mill are *hedonists:* they believe that pleasure and pain are the only sources of value. The good, for both, is pleasure and the absence of pain. In the view of these philosophers, then, the principle of utility directs us to maximize the balance of pleasure over pain. Other utilitarians hold other theories of the good. Some, for example, identify the good with the satisfaction of desire. Some maintain that the good is indefinable and cannot be identified with anything else.

Whatever theory of the good a utilitarian holds, however, that theory must treat the good as a quantity to be maximized. The principle requires us to maximize good; good, therefore, must be the kind of thing that can be maximized. Certainly this means that we must be able to judge whether one circumstance contains more good than another. It probably also means that we must be able to quantify the amount of good in any given circumstance; that is, that we must be able to say how much good that circumstance contains—ideally, by assigning it a number.

Utilitarians tend to fall into two main varieties. Some, called *act-utilitarians,* take the evaluation of individual actions as primary. They judge an action by the effects it has on the amount of good. Others, *rule-utilitarians,* take the evaluation of kinds of actions as primary. They judge rules by the effects of following them and then judge individual actions by appealing to the recommended rules. Bentham is an act-utilitarian; Mill appears to be a rule-utilitarian, although it is possible to interpret him as an act-utilitarian.

In most cases, act- and rule-utilitarians agree in their moral evaluations of individual actions. They disagree, however, (*a*) when an action maximizes good while violating rules that usually—but not in a particular case—maximize good, and (*b*) when an action does not maximize good in a particular case but does follow those rules. Both situations involve a conflict between the principle of utility and a rule designed to maximize good in general. Act-utilitarians consider it bizarre to say that we should follow the rule instead of the principle of utility; according to rule-utilitarianism itself, the rule derives its force solely from the principle in the first place. But rule-utilitarians believe that rules are indispensable to moral thinking. We cannot calculate what to do in every individual case; we must think about kinds of actions, formulate rules that, if followed, maximize good, and then follow those rules.

Rule-utilitarians encounter a special difficulty: the rules justified by the principle of utility may come into conflict with each other. Among the good-maximizing rules, for example, are some commanding us to avoid murder and to save innocent lives. But there may be cases in which we can save lives only by committing a murder. Which rule takes precedence? Mill suggests that, in such cases, we appeal to the principle of utility itself. In his theory, then, the principle has two roles. It determines which rules we should adopt and resolves conflicts between them.

IMMANUEL KANT

from *Grounding of the Metaphysics of Morals* (1785)

Immanuel Kant (1724–1804) was born in Königsberg, in East Prussia (now Kaliningrad, part of the Russian republic). The son of a saddlemaker and grandson of a Scottish immigrant, Kant attended the University of Königsberg, from which he graduated at twenty-two. A year later he published his first philosophical work, a book on living forces. He was a private tutor for several years while continuing his studies. At twenty-nine he received a master's degree and began teaching at Königsberg as a Privatdozent*—roughly, an unpaid lecturer who collected fees from his students. He continued in that capacity for fifteen years. Finally, in 1770, he was appointed to a chair of logic and metaphysics at the University of Königsberg.*

At the age of fifty-seven, Kant published the Critique of Pure Reason, *a work that earned him fame and that contemporary philosophers regard as one of the greatest works of the Western philosophical tradition. The decade that followed was extremely productive for Kant.* Prolegomena to Any Future Metaphysics *appeared in 1783;* Grounding of the Metaphysics of Morals *in 1785; the second edition of the* Critique of Pure Reason *in 1787; the* Critique of Practical Reason *in 1788; and the* Critique of Judgment *in 1790. Kant continued writing well into his seventies.*

Though known for his wit and conversational skill as well as for his intellect, Kant never married and never traveled more than a few miles from the place of his birth. His habits were so regular that, according to legend, neighbors would set their clocks by his afternoon walks.

Kant's Grounding of the Metaphysics of Morals *argues that only one thing is good intrinsically, that is, in itself: a good will. He argues that rational beings will recognize that they are subject to the moral law, which he formulates in several versions of what he takes to be single moral principle: the categorical imperative. From it stem human rights, human dignity, and everything else essential to morality. (Source: Reprinted from* Grounding of the Metaphysics of Morals, *translated and edited by James A. Ellington. Copyright ©1987 by Hackett Publishing Company Inc., Indianapolis, IN, and Cambridge, MA.)*

QUESTIONS FOR REFLECTION

1. What is an imperative? What is the difference between hypothetical and categorical imperatives?
2. Why must a categorical imperative be established *a priori*, that is, independently of experience?
3. Kant gives several different formulations of the categorical imperative. What are they? Why does he take them to be equivalent?
4. Consider Kant's four examples. How does he apply the categorical imperative to each?
5. What is autonomy? How does it relate to dignity?

SECOND SECTION / TRANSITION FROM POPULAR MORALITY TO A METAPHYSICS OF MORALS

. . . Everything in nature works according to laws. Only a rational being has the power to act according to his conception of laws, i.e., according to principles, and thereby has he a will. Since the derivation of actions from laws requires reason, the will is nothing but practical reason. If reason infallibly determines the will, then in the case of such a being actions which are recognized to be objectively necessary are also subjectively necessary, i.e., the will is a faculty of choosing only that which reason, independently of inclination, recognizes as being practically necessary, i.e., as good. But if reason of itself does not sufficiently determine the will, and if the will submits also to subjective conditions (certain incentives) which do not always agree with objective conditions; in a word, if the will does not in itself completely accord with reason (as is actually the case with men), then actions which are recognized as objectively necessary are subjectively contingent, and the determination of such a will according to objective laws is necessitation. That is to say that the relation of objective laws to a will not thoroughly good is represented as the determination of the will of a rational being by principles of reason which the will does not necessarily follow because of its own nature.

The representation of an objective principle insofar as it necessitates the will is called a command (of reason), and the formula of the command is called an imperative.

All imperatives are expressed by an *ought* and thereby indicate the relation of an objective law of reason to a will that is not necessarily determined by this law because of its subjective constitution (the relation of necessitation). Imperatives say that something would be good to do or to refrain from doing, but they say it to a will that does not always therefore do something simply because it has been represented to the will as something good to do. That is practically good which determines the will by means of representations of reason and hence not by subjective causes, but objectively, i.e., on grounds valid for every rational being as such. It is distinguished from the pleasant as that which influences the will only by means of sensation from merely subjective causes, which hold only for this or that person's senses but do not hold as a principle of reason valid for everyone.

A perfectly good will would thus be quite as much subject to objective laws (of the good), but could not be conceived as thereby necessitated to act in conformity with law, inasmuch as it can of itself, according to its subjective constitution, be determined only by the representation of the good. Therefore no imperatives hold for the divine will, and in general for a holy will; the *ought* is here out of place, because the *would* is already of itself necessarily in agreement with the law. Consequently, imperatives are only formulas for expressing the relation of objective laws of willing in general to the subjective imperfection of the will of this or that rational being, e.g., the human will.

Now all imperatives command either hypothetically or categorically. The former represent the practical necessity of a possible action as a means for attaining something else that one wants (or may possibly want). The categorical imperative would be one which represented an action as objectively necessary in itself, without reference to another end.

Every practical law represents a possible action as good and hence as necessary for a subject who is practically determinable by reason; therefore all imperatives are formulas for determining an action which is necessary according to the principle of a will that is good in some way. Now if the action would be good merely as a means to something else, so is the imperative hypothetical. But if the action is represented as good in itself, and hence as necessary in a will which of itself conforms to reason as the principle of the will, then the imperative is categorical.

An imperative thus says what action possible by me would be good, and it presents the practical rule in relation to a will which does not forthwith perform an action simply because it is good, partly because the subject does not always know that the action is good and partly because (even if he does know it is good) his maxims might yet be opposed to the objective principles of practical reason.

A hypothetical imperative thus says only that an action is good for some purpose, either possible or actual. In the first case it is a problematic practical principal; in the second case an assertoric one. A categorical imperative, which declares an action to be of itself objectively necessary without reference to any purpose, i.e., without any other end, holds as an apodeictic practical principle.

Whatever is possible only through the powers of some rational being can be thought of as a possible purpose of some will. Consequently, there are in fact infinitely many principles of action insofar as they are represented as necessary for attaining a possible purpose achievable by them. All sciences have a practical part consisting of problems saying that some end is possible for us and of imperatives telling us how it can be attained. These can, therefore, be called in general imperatives of skill. Here there is no question at all whether the end is reasonable and good, but there is only a question as to what must be done to attain it. The prescriptions needed by a doctor in order to make his patient thoroughly healthy and by a poisoner in order to make sure of killing his victim are of equal value so far as each serves to bring about its purpose perfectly. Since there cannot be known in early youth what ends may be presented to us in the course of life, parents especially seek to have their children learn many different kinds of things, and they provide for skill in the use of means to all sorts of arbitrary ends, among which they cannot determine whether any one of them could in the future become an actual purpose for their ward, though there is always the possibility that he might adopt it. Their concern is so great that they commonly neglect to form and correct their children's judgment regarding the worth of things which might be chosen as ends.

There is, however, one end that can be presupposed as actual for all rational beings (so far as they are dependent beings to whom imperatives apply); and thus there is one purpose which they not merely can have but which can certainly be assumed to be such that they all do have by a natural necessity, and this is happiness. A hypothetical imperative which represents the practical necessity of an action as means for the promotion of happiness is assertoric. It may be expounded not simply as necessary to an uncertain, merely possible purpose, but as necessary to a purpose which can be presupposed a priori and with certainty as being present in everyone because it belongs to his essence. Now skill in the choice of means to one's own greatest well-being can be called prudence in the narrowest sense. And thus the imperative that refers to the choice of means to one's own happiness, i.e., the precept of prudence, still remains hypothetical; the action is commanded not absolutely but only as a means to a further purpose.

Finally, there is one imperative which immediately commands a certain conduct without having as its condition any other purpose to be attained by it. This imperative is categorical. It is not concerned with the matter of the action and its intended result, but rather with the form of the action and the principle from which it follows; what is essentially good in the action consists in the mental disposition, let the consequences be what they may. This imperative may be called that of morality. . . .

If I think of a hypothetical imperative in general, I do not know beforehand what it will contain until its condition is given. But if I think of a categorical imperative, I know immediately what it contains. For since, besides the law, the imperative contains only the necessity that the maxim should accord with this law, while the law contains no condition to restrict it, there remains nothing but the universality of a law as such with which the maxim of the action should conform. This conformity alone is properly what is represented as necessary by the imperative.

Hence there is only one categorical imperative and it is this: Act only according to that maxim whereby you can at the same time will that it should become a universal law.

Now if all imperatives of duty can be derived from this one imperative as their principle, then there can at least be shown what is understood by the concept of duty and what it means, even though there is left undecided whether what is called duty may not be an empty concept.

The universality of law according to which effects are produced constitutes what is properly called nature in the most general sense (as to form), i.e., the existence of things as far as determined by universal laws. Accordingly, the universal imperative of duty may be expressed thus: Act as if the maxim of your action were to become through your will a universal law of nature.

We shall now enumerate some duties, following the usual division of them into duties to ourselves and to others and into perfect and imperfect duties.

1. A man reduced to despair by a series of misfortunes feels sick of life but is still so far in possession of his reason that he can ask himself whether taking his own life would not be contrary to his duty to himself. Now he asks whether the maxim of his action could become a universal law of nature. But his maxim is this: from self-love I make as my principle to shorten my life when its continued duration threatens more evil than it promises satisfaction. There only remains the question as to whether this principle of self-love can become a universal law of nature. One sees at once a contradiction in a system of nature whose law would destroy life by means of the very same feeling that acts so as to stimulate the furtherance of life, and hence there could be no existence as a system of nature. Therefore, such a maxim cannot possibly hold as a universal law of nature and is, consequently, wholly opposed to the supreme principle of all duty.

2. Another man in need finds himself forced to borrow money. He knows well that he won't be able to repay it, but he sees also that he will not get any loan unless he firmly promises to repay it within a fixed time. He wants to make such a promise, but he still has conscience enough to ask himself whether it is not permissible and is contrary to duty to get out of difficulty in this way. Suppose, however, that he decides to do so. The maxim of his action would then be expressed as follows: when I believe myself to be in need of money, I will borrow money and promise to pay it back, although I know that I can never do so. Now this principle of self-love or personal advantage may perhaps be quite compatible with one's entire future welfare, but the question is now whether it is right. I then transform the requirement of self-love into a universal law and put the question thus: how would things stand if my maxim were to become a universal law? He then sees at once that such a maxim could never hold as a universal law of nature and be consistent with itself, but must necessarily be self-contradictory. For the universality of a law which says that anyone believing himself to be in difficulty could promise whatever he pleases with the intention of not keeping it would make promising itself and the end to be attained thereby quite impossible, inasmuch as no one would believe what was promised him but would merely laugh at all such utterances as being vain pretenses.

3. A third finds in himself a talent whose cultivation could make him a man useful in many respects. But he finds himself in comfortable circumstances and prefers to indulge in pleasure rather than to bother himself about broadening and improving his fortunate natural aptitudes. But he asks himself further whether his maxim of neglecting his natural gifts, besides agreeing of itself with his propensity to indulgence, might agree also with what is called duty. He then sees that a system of nature could indeed always subsist according to such a universal law, even though every man (like South Sea Islanders) should let his talents rust and resolve to devote his life entirely to idleness, indulgence, propagation, and, in a word, to enjoyment. But he cannot possibly will that this should become a universal law of nature or be implanted in us as such a law by a natural instinct. For as a rational being he necessarily wills that all his faculties should be developed, inasmuch as they are given him for all sorts of possible purposes.

4. A fourth man finds things going well for himself but sees others (whom he could help) struggling with great hardships; and he thinks: what does it matter to me? Let everybody be as happy as Heaven wills or as he can make himself; I shall take nothing from him nor even envy him; but I have no desire to contribute anything to his well-being or to his assistance when in need. If such a way of thinking were to become a universal law of nature, the human race admittedly could very well

subsist and doubtless could subsist even better than when everyone prates about sympathy and benevolence and even on occasion exerts himself to practice them but, on the other hand, also cheats when he can, betrays the rights of man, or otherwise violates them. But even though it is possible that a universal law of nature could subsist in accordance with that maxim, still it is impossible to will that such a principle should hold everywhere as a law of nature. For a will which resolved in this way would contradict itself, inasmuch as cases might often arise in which one would have need of the love and sympathy of others and in which he would deprive himself, by such a law of nature springing from his own will, of all hope of the aid he wants for himself.

These are some of the many actual duties, or at least what are taken to be such, whose derivation from the single principle cited above is clear. We must be able to will that a maxim of our action become a universal law; this is the canon for morally estimating any of our actions. Some actions are so constituted that their maxims cannot without contradition even be thought as a universal law of nature, much less be willed as what should become one. In the case of others this internal impossibility is indeed not found, but there is still no possibility of willing that their maxim should be raised to the universality of a law of nature, because such a will would contradict itself. There is no difficulty in seeing that the former kind of action conflicts with strict or narrow [perfect] (irremissible) duty, while the second kind conflicts only with broad [imperfect] (meritorious) duty. By means of these examples there has thus been fully set forth how all duties depend as regards the kind of obligation (not the object of their action) upon the one principle.

If we now attend to ourselves in any transgression of a duty, we find that we actually do not will that our maxim should become a universal law—because this is impossible for us—but rather that the opposite of this maxim should remain a law universally. We only take the liberty of making an exception to the law for ourselves (or just for this one time) to the advantage of our inclination. Consequently, if we weighed up everything from one and the same standpoint, namely, that of reason, we would find a contradiction in our own will, viz., that a certain principle be objectively necessary as a universal law and yet subjectively not hold universally but should admit of exceptions. But since we at one moment regard our action from the standpoint of a will wholly in accord with reason and then at another moment regard the very same action from the standpoint of a will affected by inclination, there is really no contradiction here. Rather, there is an opposition (*antagonismus*) of inclination to the precept of reason, whereby the universality (*universalitas*) of the principle is changed into a mere generality (*generalitas*) so that the practical principle of reason may meet the maxim halfway. Although this procedure cannot be justified in our own impartial judgment, yet it does show that we actually acknowledge the validity of the categorical imperative and (with all respect for it) merely allow ourselves a few exceptions which, as they seem to us, are unimportant and forced upon us.

We have thus at least shown that if duty is a concept which is to have significance and real legislative authority for our actions, then such duty can be expressed only in categorical imperatives but not at all in hypothetical ones. We have also—and this is already a great deal—exhibited clearly and definitely for every application what is the content of the categorical imperative, which must contain the principle of all duty (if there is such a thing at all). But we have not yet advanced far enough to prove a priori that there actually is an imperative of this kind, that there is a practical law which of itself commands absolutely and without any incentives, and that following this law is duty. . . .

The will is thought of as a faculty of determining itself to action in accordance with the representation of certain laws, and such a faculty can be found only in rational beings. Now what serves the will as the objective ground of its self-determination is an end; and if this end is given by reason alone, then it must be equally valid for all rational beings. On the other hand, what contains merely the ground of the possibility of the action, whose effect is an end, is called the means. The subjective ground of desire is the incentive; the objective ground of volition is the motive. Hence there arises the distinction between subjective ends, which rest on incentives, and objective ends, which depend on motives valid for every rational being. Practical principles are formal when they abstract from all subjective ends; they are material, however, when they are founded upon subjective ends, and hence upon certain incentives. The ends which a rational being arbitrarily proposes to himself as effects of this action (material ends) are all merely relative, for only their relation to a specially constituted faculty of desire in the subject gives them their worth. Consequently, such worth cannot provide any universal principles, which are valid and necessary for all rational beings and, furthermore, are valid for every volition, i.e., cannot provide any practical laws. Therefore, all such relative ends can be grounds only for hypothetical imperatives.

But let us suppose that there were something whose existence has in itself an absolute worth, something which as an end in itself could be a ground of determinate laws. In it, and in it alone, would there be the ground of a possible categorical imperative, i.e., of a practical law.

Now I say that man, and in general every rational being, exists as an end in himself and not merely as a means to be arbitrarily used by this or that will. He must in all his actions, whether directed to himself or to other rational beings, always be regarded at the same time as an end. All the objects of inclinations have only a conditioned value; for if there were not these inclinations and the needs founded on them, then their object would be without value. But the inclinations themselves, being sources of needs, are so far from having an absolute value such as to render them desirable for their own sake that the universal wish of every rational being must be, rather, to be wholly free from them. Accordingly, the value of any object obtainable by our action is always conditioned. Beings whose existence depends not on our will but on nature have, nevertheless, if they are not rational beings, only a relative value as means and are therefore called things. On the other hand, rational beings are called persons inasmuch as their nature already marks them out as ends in themselves, i.e., as something which is not to be used merely as means and hence there is imposed thereby a limit on all arbitrary use of such beings, which are thus objects of respect. Persons are, therefore, not merely subjective ends, whose existence as an effect of our actions has a value for us; but such beings are objective ends, i.e., exist as ends in themselves. Such an end is one for which there can be substituted no other end to which such beings should serve merely as means, for otherwise nothing at all of absolute value would be found anywhere. But if all value were conditioned and hence contingent, then no supreme practical principle could be found for reason at all.

If then there is to be a supreme practical principle and, as far as the human will is concerned, a categorical imperative, then it must be such that from the conception of what is necessarily an end for everyone because this end is an end in itself it constitutes an objective principle of the will and can hence serve as a practical law. The ground of such a principle is this: rational nature exists as an end in itself. In this way man necessarily thinks of his own existence; thus far is it a subjective principle of human actions. But in this way also does every other rational being think of his existence on the same rational ground that holds also for me; hence it is at the same time an objective principle, from which, as a supreme practical ground, all laws of the will must be able to be derived. The practical imperative will therefore be the following: Act in such a way that you treat humanity, whether in your own person or in the person of another, always at the same time as an end and never simply as a means. We now want to see whether this can be carried out in practice.

Let us keep to our previous examples.

First, as regards the concept of necessary duty to oneself, the man who contemplates suicide will ask himself whether his action can be consistent with the idea of humanity as an end in itself. If he destroys himself in order to escape from a difficult situation, then he is making use of his person merely as a means so as to maintain a tolerable condition till the end of his life. Man, however, is not a thing and hence is not something to be used merely as a means; he must in all his actions always be regarded as an end in himself. Therefore, I cannot dispose of man in my own person by mutilating, damaging, or killing him. (A more exact determination of this principle so as to avoid all misunderstanding, e.g., regarding the amputation of limbs in order to save oneself, or the exposure of one's life to danger in order to save it, and so on, must here be omitted; such questions belong to morals proper.)

Second, as concerns necessary or strict duty to others, the man who intends to make a false promise will immediately see that he intends to make use of another man merely as a means to an end which the latter does not likewise hold. For the man whom I want to use for my own purposes by such a promise cannot possibly concur with my way of acting toward him and hence cannot himself hold the end of this action. This conflict with the principle of duty to others becomes even clearer when instances of attacks on the freedom and property of others are considered. For then it becomes clear that a transgressor of the rights of men intends to make use of the persons of others merely as a means, without taking into consideration that, as rational beings, they should always be esteemed at the same time as ends, i.e., be esteemed only as beings who must themselves be able to hold the very same action as an end.

Third, with regard to contingent (meritorious) duty to oneself, it is not enough that the action does not conflict with humanity in our own person as an end in itself; the action must also harmonize with this end. Now there are in humanity capacities for greater perfection which belong to the end that nature has in view as regards humanity in our own person. To neglect these capacities might perhaps be consistent with the maintenance of humanity as an end in itself, but would not be consistent with the advancement of this end.

Fourth, concerning meritorious duty to others, the natural end that all men have is their own happiness. Now humanity might indeed subsist if nobody contributed anything to the happiness of others, provided he did not intentionally impair their happiness. But this, after all, would harmonize only negatively and not positively with humanity as an end in itself, if everyone does not also strive, as much as he can, to further the ends of others. For the ends of any subject who is an end in himself must as far as possible be my ends also, if that conception of an end in itself is to have its full effect in me.

This principle of humanity and of every rational nature generally as an end in itself is the supreme limiting condition of every man's freedom of action. This principle is not borrowed from experience, first, because of its universality, inasmuch as it applies to all rational beings generally, and no experience is capable of determining anything about them; and, secondly, because in experience (subjectively) humanity is not thought of as an end of men, i.e., as an object that we of ourselves actually make our end which as a law ought to constitute the supreme limiting condition of all subjective ends (whatever they may be); and hence this principle must arise from pure reason [and not from experience]. That is to say that the ground of all practical legislation lies objectively in the rule and in the form of universality, which (according to the first principle) makes the rule capable of being a law (say, for example, a law of nature). Subjectively, however, the ground of all practical legislation lies in the end; but (according to the second principle) the subject of all ends is every rational being as an end in himself. From this there now follows the third practical principle of the will as the supreme condition of the will's conformity with universal practical reason, viz., the idea of the will of every rational being as a will that legislates universal law.

According to this principle all maxims are rejected which are not consistent with the will's own legislation of universal law. The will is thus not merely subject to the law but is subject to the law in such a way that it must be regarded also as legislating for itself and only on this account as being subject to the law (of which it can regard itself as the author). . . .

When we look back upon all previous attempts that have been made to discover the principle of morality, these is no reason now to wonder why they one and all had to fail. Man was viewed as bound to laws by his duty; but it was not seen that man is subject only to his own, yet universal, legislation and that he is bound only to act in accordance with his own will, which is, however, a will purposed by nature to legislate universal laws. For when man is thought as being merely subject to a law (whatever it might be), then the law had to carry with it some interest functioning as an attracting stimulus or as a constraining force for obedience, inasmuch as the law did not arise as a law from his own will. Rather, in order that his will conform with law, it had to be necessitated by something else to act in a certain way. By this absolutely necessary conclusion, however, all the labor spent in finding a supreme ground for duty was irretrievably lost; duty was never discovered, but only the necessity of acting from a certain interest. This might be either one's own interest or another's, but either way the imperative had to be always conditional and could never possibly serve as a moral command. I want, therefore, to call my principle the principle of the autonomy of the will, in contrast with every other principle, which I accordingly count under heteronomy.

The concept of every rational being as one who must regard himself as legislating universal law by all his will's maxims, so that he may judge himself and his actions from this point of view, leads to another very fruitful concept, which depends on the aforementioned one, viz., that of a kingdom of ends.

By "kingdom" I understand a systematic union of different rational beings through common laws. Now laws determine ends as regards their universal validity; therefore, if one abstracts from the personal differences of rational beings and also from all content of their private ends, then it will be possible to think of a whole of all ends in systematic connection (a whole both of rational being as ends in themselves and also of the particular ends which each may set for himself); that is, one can think of a kingdom of ends that is possible on the aforesaid principles.

For all rational beings stand under the law that each of them should treat himself and all others never merely as means but always at the same time as an end in himself. Hereby arises a systematic union of rational beings through common objective laws, i.e., a kingdom that may be called a kingdom of ends (certainly only an ideal), inasmuch as these laws have in view the very relation of such beings to one another as ends and means.

A rational being belongs to the kingdom of ends as a member when he legislates in it universal laws while also being himself subject to these laws. He belongs to it as sovereign, when as legislator he is himself subject to the will of no other.

A rational being must always regard himself as legislator in a kingdom of ends rendered possible by freedom of the will, whether as member or as sovereign. The position of the latter can be maintained not merely through the maxims of his will but only if he is a completely independent being without needs and with unlimited power adequate to his will.

Hence morality consists in the relation of all action to that legislation whereby alone a kingdom of ends is possible. This legislation must be found in every rational being and must be able to arise from his will, whose principle then is never to act on any maxim except such as can also be a universal law and hence such as the will can thereby regard itself as at the same time the legislator of universal law. If now the maxims do not by their very nature already necessarily conform with this objective principle of rational beings as legislating universal laws, then the necessity of acting on that principle is called practical necessitation, i.e., duty. Duty does not apply to the sovereign in the kingdom of ends, but it does apply to every member and to each in the same degree.

The practical necessity of acting according to this principle, i.e., duty, does not rest at all on feelings, impulses, and inclinations, but only on the relation of rational beings to one another, a relation in which the will of a rational being must always be regarded at the same time as legislative, because otherwise he could not be thought of as an end in himself. Reason, therefore, relates every maxim of the will as legislating universal laws to every other will and also to every action toward oneself; it does so not on account of any other practical motive or future advantage but rather from the idea of the dignity of a rational being who obeys no law except what he at the same time enacts himself.

In the kingdom of ends everything has either a price or a dignity. Whatever has a price can be replaced by something else as its equivalent; on the other hand, whatever is above all price, and therefore admits of no equivalent, has a dignity.

Whatever has reference to general human inclinations and needs has a market price; whatever, without presupposing any need, accords with a certain taste, i.e., a delight in the mere unpurposive play of our mental powers, has an affective price; but that which constitutes the condition under which alone something can be an end in itself has not merely a relative worth, i.e., a price, but has an intrinsic worth, i.e., dignity.

Now morality is the condition under which alone a rational being can be an end in himself, for only thereby can he be a legislating member in the kingdom of ends. Hence morality and humanity, insofar as it is capable of morality, alone have dignity. Skill and diligence in work have a market price; wit, lively imagination, and humor have an affective price; but fidelity to promises and benevolence based on principles (not on instinct) have intrinsic worth. Neither nature nor art contain anything which in default of these could be put in their place; for their worth consists, not in the effects which arise from them, nor in the advantage and profit which they provide, but in mental dispositions, i.e., in the maxims of the will which are ready in this way to manifest themselves in action, even if they are not favored with success. Such actions also need no recommendation from any subjective disposition or taste so as to meet with immediate favor and delight; there is no need of any immediate propensity or feeling toward them. They exhibit the will performing them as an object of immediate respect; and nothing but reason is required to impose them upon the will, which is not to be cajoled into them, since in the case of duties such cajoling would be a contradiction. This estimation, therefore, lets the worth of such a disposition be recognized as dignity and puts it infinitely beyond all price, with which it cannot in the least be brought into competition or comparison without, as it were, violating its sanctity.

What then is it that entitles the morally good disposition, or virtue, to make such lofty claims? It is nothing less than the share which such a disposition affords the rational being of legislating universal laws, so that he is fit to be a member in a possible kingdom of ends, for which his own nature has already determined him as an end in himself and therefore as a legislator in the kingdom of ends. Thereby is he free as regards all laws of nature, and he obeys only those laws which he gives to himself. Accordingly, his maxims can belong to a universal legislation to which he at the same time subjects himself. For nothing can have any worth other than what the law determines. But the legislation itself which determines all worth must for that very reason have dignity, i.e., unconditional and incomparable worth; and the word "respect" alone provides a suitable expression for the esteem which a rational being must have for it. Hence autonomy is the ground of the dignity of human nature and of every rational nature. . . .

We can now end where we started in the beginning, viz., the concept of an unconditionally good will. That will is absolutely good which cannot be evil, i.e., whose maxim, when made into a universal law, can never conflict with itself. This principle is therefore also its supreme law: Act always according to that maxim whose universality as a law you can at the same time will. This is the only condition under which a will can never be in conflict with itself, and such an imperative is categorical. Inasmuch as the validity of the will as a universal law for possible actions is analogous to the universal connection of the existence of things in accordance with universal laws, which is the formal aspect of nature in general, the categorical imperative can also be expressed thus: Act according to maxims which can at the same time have for their object themselves as universal laws of nature. In this way there is provided the formula for an absolutely good will.

Rational nature is distinguished from the rest of nature by the fact that it sets itself an end. This end would be the matter of every good will. But in the idea of an absolutely good will—good without any qualifying condition (of attaining this or that end)—complete abstraction must be made from every end that has to come about as an effect (since such would make every will only relatively good). And so the end must here be conceived, not as an end to be effected, but as an independently existing end. Hence it must be conceived only negatively, i.e., as an end which should never be acted against and therefore as one which in all willing must never be regarded merely as means but must always be esteemed at the same time as an end. Now this end can be nothing but the subject of all possible ends themselves, because this subject is at the same time the subject of a possible absolutely good will; for such a will cannot without contradiction be subordinated to any other object. The principle: So act in regard to every rational being (yourself and others) that he may at the same time count in your maxim as an end in himself, is thus basically the same as the principle: Act on a maxim which at the same time contains in itself its own universal validity for every rational being. That in the use of means for every end my maxim should be restricted to the condition of its universal validity as a law for every subject says just the same as that a subject of ends, i.e., a rational being himself, must be made the ground for all maxims of actions and must thus be used never merely as means but as the supreme limiting condition in the use of all means, i.e., always at the same time as an end.

Now there follows incontestably from this that every rational being as an end in himself must be able to regard himself with reference to all laws to which he may be subject as being at the same time the legislator of universal law, for just this very fitness of his maxims for the legislation of universal law distinguishes him as an end in himself. There follows also that his dignity (prerogative) of being above all the mere things of nature implies that his maxims must be taken from the viewpoint that regards himself, as well as every other rational being, as being legislative beings (and hence are they called persons). In this way there is possible a world of rational beings (*mundus intelligibilis*) as a kingdom of ends, because of the legislation belonging to all persons as members. Therefore, every rational being must so act as if he were through his maxim always a legislating member in the universal kingdom of ends. The formal principle of these maxims is this: So act as if your maxims were to serve at the same time as a universal law (for all rational beings). Thus a kingdom of ends is possible only on the analogy of a kingdom of nature; yet the former is possible only through maxims, i.e., self-imposed rules, while the latter is possible only through laws of efficient causes necessitated from without. Regardless of this difference and even though nature as a whole is viewed as a machine, yet insofar as nature stands in a relation to rational beings as its ends, it is on this account given the name of a kingdom of nature. Such a kingdom of ends would actually be realized through maxims whose rule is prescribed to all rational beings by the categorical imperative, if these maxims were universally obeyed. But even if a rational being himself strictly obeys such a maxim, he cannot for that reason count on everyone else's being true to it, nor can he expect the kingdom of nature and its purposive order to be in harmony with him as a fitting member of a kingdom of ends made possible by himself, i.e., he cannot expect the kingdom of nature to favor his expectation of happiness. Nevertheless, the law: Act in accordance with the maxims of a member legislating universal laws for a merely possible kingdom of ends, remains in full force, since it commands categorically. And just in this lies the paradox that merely the dignity of humanity as rational nature without any further end or advantage to be thereby gained—and hence respect for a mere idea—should yet serve as an inflexible precept for the will; and that just this very independence of the maxims from all such incentives should constitute the sublimity of maxims and the worthiness of every rational subject to be a legislative member in the kingdom of ends, for otherwise he would have to be regarded as subject only to the natural law of his own needs. And even if the kingdom of nature as well as the kingdom of ends were thought of as both united under one sovereign so that the latter kingdom would thereby no longer remain a mere idea but would acquire true reality, then indeed the kingdom of ends would gain the addition of a strong incentive, but never any increase in its intrinsic worth. For this sole absolute legislator must, in spite of all this, always be thought of as judging the worth of rational beings solely by the disinterested conduct prescribed to themselves by means of this idea alone. The essence of things is not altered by their external relations; and whatever without reference to such relations alone constitutes the absolute worth of man is also what he must be judged by, whoever the judge may be, even the Supreme Being. Hence morality is the relation of actions to the autonomy of the will, i.e., to the possible legislation of universal law by means of the maxims of the will. That action which is compatible with the autonomy of the will is permitted; that which is not compatible is forbidden. That will whose maxims are necessarily in accord with the laws of autonomy is a holy, or absolutely good, will. The dependence of a will which is not absolutely good upon the principle of autonomy (i.e., moral necessitation) is obligation, which cannot therefore be applied to a holy will. The objective necessity of an action from obligation is called duty.

From what has just been said, there can now easily be explained how it happens that, although in the concept of duty we think of subjection to the law, yet at the same time we thereby ascribe a certain dignity and sublimity to the person who fulfills all his duties. For not insofar as he is subject to the moral law does he have sublimity, but rather has it only insofar as with regard to this very same law he is at the same time legislative, and only thereby is he subject to the law. We have also shown above how neither fear nor inclination, but solely respect for the law, is the incentive which can give an action moral worth. Our own will, insofar as it were to act only under the condition of its being able to legislate universal law by means of its maxims—this will, ideally possible for us, is the proper object of respect. And the dignity of humanity consists just in its capacity to legislate universal law, though with the condition of humanity's being at the same time itself subject to this very same legislation.

JEREMY BENTHAM

from *An Introduction to the Principles of Morals and Legislation* (1789)

Jeremy Bentham (1748–1832), an English utilitarian, was born in Houndsditch, London. He was a prodigious student, entering Queen's College, Oxford, at twelve and graduating at fifteen. He studied law at Lincoln's Inn and was admitted to the bar at nineteen. Bentham was so appalled by English law, however, that he never practiced it, even for a day. Instead, he devoted his life to legal reform.

Bentham wrote many thousands of pages of pamphlets, papers, and books, relatively few of which were published during his lifetime. He founded a group of powerful and ultimately very influential thinkers, the philosophical radicals, which included James Mill, economist David Ricardo, and legal theorist John Austin. Bentham also founded the Westminster Review, *a political journal, and University College, London, where his embalmed body still rests, seated, in a glass case in the library.*

Principles of Morals and Legislation, *the only major theoretical work of his own that Bentham saw in print, appeared in 1789, the year of the French Revolution. Bentham objects strongly to views of morality and politics that stress individual conscience or religious conviction; both, in his view, are little more than prejudice in disguise. Bentham also rejects doctrines of natural rights, such as those invoked by the French revolutionaries, calling them "nonsense on stilts." Instead, he proposes to base ethics and politics on a single principle, the principle of utility. Roughly, Bentham's version of this principle states that a good action increases the balance of pleasure over pain in the community of people affected by it; a bad action decreases the balance. From this principle, taken together with the facts about the effects of actions, Bentham maintains, all our correct moral and political judgments follow. (Source: Reprinted from Jeremy Bentham,* An Introduction to the Principles of Morals and Legislation. *London: Printed for T. Payne, 1789.)*

QUESTIONS FOR REFLECTION

1. What is Bentham's principle of utility? What is utility?
2. What does Bentham's principle imply about what ought to be done when (*a*) only one available option, on balance, augments the happiness of the community; (*b*) only one available option, on balance, diminishes the happiness of the community; (*c*) all available options augment, on balance, the happiness of the community; (*d*) all available options diminish, on balance, the happiness of the community? What, intuitively, ought to be done in such cases, from a utilitarian point of view? What does this indicate about Bentham's principle?
3. Actions that, on balance, augment the happiness of the community "ought to be done" or at least are not ones that "ought not to be done." Explain the difference. Why does Bentham waffle? (Consider the cases mentioned in the previous question.)
4. How does Bentham argue for the principle of utility?
5. What is the principle of sympathy and antipathy? Why does Bentham disapprove of it?
6. In Chapter IV, Bentham details the *moral calculus*, his method for computing the utility of actions. How does it work? What aspects of pleasure and pain does Bentham consider?

CHAPTER 1 / OF THE PRINCIPLE OF UTILITY

1. Nature has placed mankind under the governance of two sovereign masters, *pain* and *pleasure*. It is for them alone to point out what we ought to do, as well as to determine what we shall do. On the one hand the standard of right and wrong, on the other the chain of causes and effects, are fastened to their throne. They govern us in all we do, in all we say, in all we think: every effort we can make to throw off our subjection, will serve but to demonstrate and confirm it. In words a man may pretend to abjure their empire: but in reality he will remain subject to it all the while. The *principle of utility* recognises this subjection, and assumes it for the foundation of that system, the object of which is to rear the fabric of felicity by the hands of reason and of law. Systems which attempt to question it, deal in sounds instead of senses, in caprice instead of reason, in darkness instead of light.

But enough of metaphor and declamation: it is not by such means that moral science is to be improved.

2. The principle of utility is the foundation of the present work: it will be proper therefore at the outset to give an explicit and determinate account of what is meant by it. By the principle of utility is meant that principle which approves or disapproves of every action whatsoever; according to the tendency which it appears to have to augment or diminish the happiness of the party whose interest is in question: or, what is the same thing in other words, to promote or to oppose that happiness. I say of every action whatsoever, and therefore not only of every action of a private individual, but of every measure of government.

3. By utility is meant that property in any object, whereby it tends to produce benefit, advantage, pleasure, good, or happiness, (all this in the present case comes to the same thing) or (what comes again to the same thing) to prevent the happening of mischief, pain, evil, or unhappiness to the party whose interest is considered: if that party be the community in general, then the happiness of the community: if a particular individual, then the happiness of that individual.

4. The interest of the community is one of the most general expressions that can occur in the phraseology of morals: no wonder that the meaning of it is often lost. When it has a meaning, it is this. The community is a fictitious *body*, composed of the individual persons who are considered as constituting as it were its *members*. The interest of the community then is, what?—the sum of the interests of the several members who compose it.

5. It is in vain to talk of the interest of the community, without understanding what is the interest of the individual. A thing is said to promote the interest, or to be *for* the interest, of an individual, when it tends to add to the sum total of his pleasures: or, what comes to the same thing, to diminish the sum total of his pains.

6. An action then may be said to be comformable to the principle of utility, or, for shortness sake, to utility, (meaning with respect to the community at large) when the tendency it has to augment the happiness of the community is greater than any it has to diminish it.

7. A measure of government (which is but a particular kind of action, performed by a particular person or persons) may be said to be conformable to or dictated by the principle of utility, when in like manner the tendency which it has to augment the happiness of the community is greater than any which it has to diminish it.

8. When an action, or in particular a measure of government, is supposed by a man to be conformable to the principle of utility, it may be convenient, for the purposes of discourse, to imagine a kind of law or dictate, called a law or dictate of utility; and to speak of the action in question, as being conformable to such law or dictate.

9. A man may be said to be a partisan of the principle of utility, when the approbation or disapprobation he annexes to any action, or to any measure, is determined by and proportioned to the tendency which he conceives it to have to augment or to diminish the happiness of the community: or in other words, to its conformity or uncomformity to the laws or dictates of utility.

10. Of an action that is conformable to the principle of utility one may always say either that it is one that ought to be done, or at least that it is not one that ought not to be done. One may say also, that it is right it should be done; at least that it is not wrong it should be done: that it is a right action; at least that it is not a wrong action. When thus interpreted, the words *ought,* and *right* and *wrong,* and others of that stamp, have a meaning: when otherwise, they have none.

11. Has the rectitude of this principle been ever formally contested? It should seem that it had, by those who have not known what they have been meaning. Is it susceptible of any direct proof? it should seem not: for that which is used to prove every thing else, cannot itself be proved: a chain of proofs must have their commencement somewhere. To give such proof is as impossible as it is needless.

12. Not that there is or ever has been that human creature breathing, however stupid or perverse, who has not on many, perhaps on most occasions of his life, deferred to it. By the natural constitution of the human frame, on most occasions of their lives men in general embrace this principle, without thinking of it: if not for the ordering of their own actions, yet for the trying of their own actions, as well as of those of other men. There have been, at the same time, not many, perhaps, even of the most intelligent, who have been disposed to embrace it purely and without reserve. There are even few who have not taken some occasion or other to quarrel with it, either on account of their not understanding always how to apply it, or on account of some prejudice or other which they were afraid to examine into, or could not bear to part with. For such is the stuff that man is made of: in principle and in practice, in a right track and in a wrong one, the rarest of all human qualities is consistency.

13. When a man attempts to combat the principle of utility, it is with reasons drawn, without his being aware of it, from that very principle itself. His arguments, if they prove any thing, prove not that the principle is *wrong,* but that, according to the application he supposes to be made of it, it is *misapplied.* Is it possible for a man to move the earth? Yes; but he must first find out another earth to stand upon.

14. To disprove the propriety of it by arguments is impossible; but, from the causes that have been mentioned, or from some confused or partial view of it, a man may happen to be disposed not to relish it. Where this is the case, if he thinks the settling of his opinions on such a subject worth the trouble, let him take the following steps and at length, perhaps, he may come to reconcile himself to it.

1. Let him settle with himself, whether he would wish to discard this principle altogether; if so, let him consider what it is that all his reasonings (in matters of politics especially) can amount to?
2. If he would, let him settle with himself, whether he would judge and act without any principle, or whether there is any other he would judge and act by?
3. If there be, let him examine and satisfy himself whether the principle he thinks he has found is really any separate intelligible principle; or whether it be not a mere principle in words, a kind of phrase, which at bottom expresses neither more nor less than the mere averment of his own unfounded sentiments; that is, what in another person he might be apt to call caprice?
4. If he is inclined to think that his own approbation or disapprobation, annexed to the idea of an act, without any regard to its consequences, is a sufficient foundation for him to judge and act upon, let him ask himself whether his sentiment is to be a standard of right and wrong, with respect to every other man, or whether every other man's sentiment has the same privilege of being a standard to itself?
5. In the first case, let him ask himself whether his principle is not despotical, and hostile to all the rest of human race?
6. In the second case, whether it is not anarchical, and whether at this rate there are not as many different standards of right and wrong as there are men? and whether even to the same

man, the same thing, which is right to-day, may not (without the least change in its nature) be wrong to-morrow? and whether the same thing is not right and wrong in the same place at the same time? and in either case, whether all argument is not at an end? and whether, when two men have said, "I like this," and "I don't like it," they can (upon such a principle) have any thing more to say?

7. If he should have said to himself, No: for that the sentiment which he proposes as a standard must be grounded on reflection, let him say on what particulars the reflection is to turn? if on particulars having relation to the utility of the act, then let him say whether this is not deserting his own principle, and borrowing assistance from that very one in opposition to which he sets it up: or if not on those particulars, on what other particulars?

8. If he should be for compounding the matter, and adopting his own principle in part, and the principle of utility in part, let him say how far he will adopt it?

9. When he has settled with himself where he will stop, then let him ask himself how he justifies to himself the adopting it so far? and why he will not adopt it any farther?

10. Admitting any other principle than the principle of utility to be a right principle, a principle that it is right for a man to pursue; admitting (what is not true) that the word *right* can have a meaning without reference to utility, let him say whether there is any such thing as a *motive* that a man can have to pursue the dictates of it: if there is, let him say what that motive is, and how it is to be distinguished from those which enforce the dictates of utility: if not, then lastly let him say what it is this other principle can be good for? . . .

CHAPTER II / OF PRINCIPLES ADVERSE TO THAT OF UTILITY

. . . 11. Among principles adverse to that of utility, that which at this day seems to have most influence in matters of government, is what may be called the principle of sympathy and antipathy. By the principle of sympathy and antipathy, I mean that principle which approves or disapproves of certain actions, not on account of their tending to augment the happiness, nor yet on account of their tending to diminish the happiness of the party whose interest is in question, but merely because a man finds himself disposed to approve or disapprove of them: holding up that approbation or disapprobation as a sufficient reason for itself, and disclaiming the necessity of looking out for any extrinsic ground. Thus far in the general department of morals: and in the particular department of politics, measuring out the quantum (as well as determining the ground) of punishment, by the degree of the disapprobation.

12. It is manifest, that this is rather a principle in name than in reality: it is not a positive principle of itself, so much as a term employed to signify the negation of all principle. What one expects to find in a principle is something that points out some external consideration, as a means of warranting and guiding the internal sentiments of approbation and disapprobation: this expectation is but ill fulfilled by a proposition, which does neither more nor less than hold up each of those sentiments as a ground and standard for itself.

13. In looking over the catalogue of human actions (says a partisan of this principle) in order to determine which of them are to be marked with the seal of disapprobation, you need but to take counsel of your own feelings: whatever you find in yourself a propensity to condemn, is wrong for that very reason. For the same reason it is also meet for punishment: in what proportion it is adverse to utility, or whether it be adverse to utility at all, is a matter that makes no difference. In that same *proportion* also is it meet for punishment: if you hate much, punish much: if you hate little, punish little: punish as you hate. If you hate not at all, punish not at all: the fine feelings of the soul are not to be overborne and tyrannised by the harsh and rugged dictates of political utility.

14. The various systems that have been formed concerning the standard of right and wrong, may all be reduced to the principle of sympathy and

antipathy. One account may serve for all of them. They consist all of them in so many contrivances for avoiding the obligation of appealing to any external standard, and for prevailing upon the reader to accept of the author's sentiment or opinion as a reason for itself. The phrase is different, but the principle the same.

15. It is manifest, that the dictates of this principle will frequently coincide with those of utility, though perhaps without intending any such thing. Probably more frequently than not: and hence it is that the business of penal justice is carried on upon that tolerable sort of footing upon which we see it carried on in common at this day. For what more natural or more general ground of hatred to a practice can there be, than the mischievousness of such practice? What all men are exposed to suffer by, all men will be disposed to hate. It is far yet, however, from being a constant ground: for when a man suffers, it is not always that he knows what it is he suffers by. A man may suffer grievously, for instance, by a new tax, without being able to trace up the cause of his sufferings to the injustice of some neighbour, who has eluded the payment of an old one.

16. The principle of sympathy and antipathy is most apt to err on the side of severity. It is for applying punishment in many cases which deserve none: in many cases which deserve some, it is for applying more than they deserve. There is no incident imaginable, be it ever so trivial, and so remote from mischief, from which this principle may not extract a ground of punishment. Any difference in taste: any difference in opinion: upon one subject as well as upon another. No disagreement so trifling which perseverance and altercation will not render serious. Each becomes in the other's eyes an enemy, and if laws permit, a criminal. This is one of the circumstances by which the human race is distinguished (not much indeed to its advantage) from the brute creation.

17. It is not, however, by any means unexampled for this principle to err on the side of lenity. A near and perceptible mischief moves antipathy. A remote and imperceptible mischief, though not less real, has no effect. Instances in proof of this will occur in numbers in the course of the work. It would be breaking in upon the order of it to give them here. . . .

19. There are two things which are very apt to be confounded, but which it imports us carefully to distinguish:—the motive or cause, which, by operating on the mind of an individual, is productive of any act: and the ground or reason which warrants a legislator, or other by-stander, in regarding that act with an eye of approbation. When the act happens, in the particular instance in question, to be productive of effects which we approve of, much more if we happen to observe that the same motive may frequently be productive, in other instances, of the like effects, we are apt to transfer our approbation to the motive itself, and to assume, as the just ground for the approbation we bestow on the act, the circumstance of its originating from that motive. It is in this way that the sentiment of antipathy has often been considered as a just ground of action. Antipathy, for instance, in such or such a case, is the cause of an action which is attended with good effects: but this does not make it a right ground of action in that case, any more than in any other. Still farther. Not only the effects are good, but the agent sees beforehand that they will be so. This may make the action indeed a perfectly right action: but it does not make antipathy a right ground of action. For the same sentiment of antipathy, if implicitly deferred to, may be, and very frequently is, productive of the very worst effects. Antipathy, therefore, can never be a right ground of action. No more, therefore, can resentment, which, as will be seen more particularly hereafter, is but a modification of antipathy. The only right ground of action, that can possibly subsist, is, after all, the consideration of utility, which if it is a right principle of action, and of approbation, in any one case, is so in every other. Other principles in abundance, that is, other motives, may be the reasons why such and such an act *has* been done: that is, the reasons or causes of its being done: but it is this alone that can be the reason why it might or ought to have been done. Antipathy or resentment requires always to be regulated, to prevent its doing mischief: to be regulated by what? always by the principle of utility. The principle of utility neither

requires nor admits of any other regulator than itself.

[CHAPTER III . . .]

CHAPTER IV / VALUE OF A LOT OF PLEASURE OR PAIN, HOW TO BE MEASURED

1. Pleasures then, and the avoidance of pains, are the *ends* which the legislator has in view: it behooves him therefore to understand their *value.* Pleasures and pains are the *instruments* he has to work with: it behooves him therefore to understand their force, which is again, in other words, their value.

2. To a person considered *by himself,* the value of a pleasure or pain considered *by itself,* will be greater or less, according to the four following circumstances:

1. Its *intensity.*
2. Its *duration.*
3. Its *certainty* or *uncertainty.*
4. Its *propinquity* or *remoteness.*

3. These are the circumstances which are to be considered in estimating a pleasure or a pain considered each of them by itself. But when the value of any pleasure or pain is considered for the purpose of estimating the tendency of any *act* by which it is produced, there are two other circumstances to be taken into account; these are,

5. Its *fecundity,* or the chance it has of being followed by sensations of the *same* kind: that is, pleasures, if it be a pleasure: pain, if it be a pain.
6. Its *purity,* or the chance it has of *not* being followed by sensations of the *opposite* kind: that is, pains, if it be a pleasure: pleasures, if it be a pain.

These two last, however, are in strictness scarcely to be deemed properties of the pleasure or the pain itself; they are not, therefore, in strictness to be taken into the account of the value of that pleasure or that pain. They are in strictness to be deemed properties only of the act, or other event, by which such pleasure or pain has been produced; and accordingly are only to be taken into the account of the tendency of such act or such event.

4. To a *number* of persons, with reference to each of whom the value of a pleasure or a pain is considered, it will be greater or less, according to seven circumstances: to wit, the six preceding ones; *viz.*

1. Its *intensity.*
2. Its *duration.*
3. Its *certainty* or *uncertainty.*
4. Its *propinquity* or *remoteness.*
5. Its *fecundity.*
6. Its *purity.*

And one other; to wit:

7. Its *extent;* that is, the number of persons to whom it *extends;* or (in other words) who are affected by it.

5. To take an exact account then of the general tendency of any act, by which the interests of a community are affected, proceed as follows. Begin with any one person of those whose interests seem most immediately to be affected by it: and take an account,

1. Of the value of each distinguishable *pleasure* which appears to be produced by it in the *first* instance.
2. Of the value of each *pain* which appears to be produced by it in the *first* instance.
3. Of the value of each pleasure which appears to be produced by it *after* the first. This constitutes the *fecundity* of the first *pleasure* and the *impurity* of the first *pain.*
4. Of the value of each *pain* which appears to be produced by it after the first. This constitutes the *fecundity* of the first *pain,* and the *impurity* of the first pleasure.
5. Sum up all the values of all the *pleasures* on the one side, and those of all the pains on

the other. The balance, if it be on the side of pleasure, will give the *good* tendency of the act upon the whole, with respect to the interests of that *individual* person; if on the side of pain, the *bad* tendency of it upon the whole.

6. Take an account of the *number* of persons whose interests appear to be concerned; and repeat the above process with respect to each. *Sum up* the numbers expressive of the degrees of *good* tendency, which the act has, with respect to each individual, in regard to whom the tendency of it is *good* upon the whole: do this again with respect to each individual, in regard to whom the tendency of it is *bad* upon the whole. Take the *balance;* which, if on the side of *pleasure,* will give the general *good tendency* of the act, with respect to the total number or community of individuals concerned; if on the side of pain, the general *evil tendency,* with respect to the same community.

6. It is not to be expected that this process should be strictly pursued previously to every moral judgment, or to every legislative or judicial operation. It may, however, be always kept in view: and as near as the process actually pursued on these occasions approaches to it, so near will such process approach to the character of an exact one.

7. The same process is alike applicable to pleasure and pain, in whatever shape they appear: and by whatever denomination they are distinguished: to pleasure, whether it be called *good* (which is properly the cause or instrument of pleasure) or *profit* (which is distant pleasure, or the cause or instrument of distant pleasure,) or *convenience,* or *advantage, benefit, emolument, happiness,* and so forth: to pain, whether it be called *evil,* (which corresponds to *good*) or *mischief,* or *inconvenience,* or *disadvantage,* or *loss,* or *unhappiness,* and so forth.

8. Nor is this a novel and unwarranted, any more than it is a useless theory. In all this there is nothing but what the practice of mankind, wheresoever they have a clear view of their own interest, is perfectly conformable to. An article of property, an estate in land, for instance, is valuable, on what account? On account of the pleasures of all kinds which it enables a man to produce, and what comes to the same thing the pains of all kinds which it enables him to avert. But the value of such an article of property is universally understood to rise or fall according to the length or shortness of the time which a man has in it: the certainty or uncertainty of its coming into possession: and the nearness or remoteness of the time at which, if at all, it is to come into possession. As to the *intensity* of the pleasures which a man may derive from it, this is never thought of, because it depends upon the use which each particular person may come to make of it; which cannot be estimated till the particular pleasures he may come to derive from it, or the particular pains he may come to exclude by means of it, are brought to view. For the same reason, neither does he think of the *fecundity* or *purity* of those pleasures. . . .

JOHN STUART MILL

from *Utilitarianism* (1861)

(Source: Reprinted from John Stuart Mill, Utilitarianism. *London: Longman's, 1907.)*

QUESTIONS FOR REFLECTION

1. What is Mill's principle of utility? What does he mean by "utility"?
2. Mill distinguishes qualities, as well as quantities, of pleasures. Why? How does Mill rank pleasures in terms of quality?
3. People sometimes choose pleasures of lower quality over those of higher quality. How does Mill explain this?
4. Some philosophers have held that Mill's distinction between qualities of pleasures confronts him with a dilemma. Either differences in quality can be measured in terms of differences in quantity, in which case the distinction does not seem very important, or they cannot be, in which case the idea of maximizing the general happiness seems to make little sense. How do you think Mill might respond to this dilemma?
5. What objections against utilitarianism does Mill consider? How does he respond to them?
6. What are the roles of tradition and conscience in Mill's theory?
7. What are secondary principles? What role do they play in Mill's theory? How do we decide which secondary principles to adopt? What happens when these principles conflict?

CHAPTER II / WHAT UTILITARIANISM IS

. . . The creed which accepts as the foundation of morals "utility" or the "greatest happiness principle" holds that actions are right in proportion as they tend to promote happiness; wrong as they tend to produce the reverse of happiness. By happiness is intended pleasure and the absence of pain; by unhappiness, pain and the privation of pleasure. To give a clear view of the moral standard set up by the theory, much more requires to be said; in particular, what things it includes in the ideas of pain and pleasure, and to what extent this is left an open question. But these supplementary explanations do not affect the theory of life on which this theory of morality is grounded—namely, that pleasure and freedom from pain are the only things desirable as ends; and that all desirable things (which are as numerous in the utilitarian as in any other scheme) are desirable either for pleasure inherent in themselves or as means to the promotion of pleasure and the prevention of pain.

Now such a theory of life excites in many minds, and among them in some of the most estimable in feeling and purpose, inveterate dislike. To suppose that life has (as they express it) no higher end than pleasure—no better and nobler object of desire and pursuit—they designate as utterly mean and groveling, as a doctrine worthy only of swine, to whom the followers of Epicurus were, at a very early period, contemptuously likened; and modern holders of the doctrine are occasionally made the subject of equally polite comparison by its German, French, and English assailants.

When thus attacked, the Epicureans have always answered that it is not they, but their accusers, who represent human nature in a degrading light, since the accusation supposes human beings to be capable of no pleasures except those of which swine are capable. If this supposition were true, the charge could not be gainsaid, but would then be no longer an imputation; for if the sources of pleasure were precisely the same to human beings and to swine, the rule of life which is good enough for the one would be good enough for the other. The comparison of the Epicurean life to that of beasts is felt as degrading, precisely because a beast's pleasures do not satisfy a human being's conceptions of happiness. Human beings have faculties more elevated than the animal appetites and, when once made conscious of them, do not regard anything as happiness which does not include their gratification. I do not indeed, consider the Epicureans to have been by any means faultless in drawing out their scheme of consequences from the utilitarian principle. To do this in any sufficient manner, many Stoic, as well as Christian, elements require to be included. But there is no known Epicurean theory of life which does not assign to the pleasures of the intellect, of the feelings and imagination, and of the moral sentiments a much higher value as pleasures than to those of mere sensation. It must be admitted, however, that utilitarian writers in general have placed the superiority of mental over bodily pleasures chiefly in the greater permanency, safety, uncostliness, etc., of the former—that is, in their circumstantial advantages rather than in their intrinsic nature. And on all these points utilitarians have fully proved their case; but they might have taken the other and, as it may be called, higher ground with entire consistency. It is quite compatible with the principle of utility to recognize the fact that some kinds of pleasure are more desirable and more valuable than others. It would be absurd that, while in estimating all other things quality is considered as well as quantity, the estimation of pleasure should be supposed to depend on quantity alone.

If I am asked what I mean by difference of quality in pleasures, or what makes one pleasure more valuable than another, merely as a pleasure, except its being greater in amount, there is but one possible answer. Of two pleasures, if there be one to which all or almost all who have experience of both give a decided preference, irrespective of any feeling of moral obligation to prefer it, that is the more desirable pleasure. If one of the two is, by those who are competently acquainted with both, placed so far above the other that they prefer it, even though knowing it to be attended with a greater amount of discontent, and would not resign it for any quantity of the other pleasure which their nature is capable of, we are justified in ascribing to the preferred enjoyment a superiority in quality so far outweighing quantity as to render it, in comparison, of small account.

Now it is an unquestionable fact that those who are equally acquainted with and equally capable of appreciating and enjoying both do give a most marked preference to the manner of existence which employs their higher faculties. Few human creatures would consent to be changed into any of the lower animals for a promise of the fullest allowance of a beast's pleasures; no intelligent human being would consent to be a fool, no instructed person would be an ignoramus, no person of feeling and conscience would be selfish and base, even though they should be persuaded that the fool, the dunce, or the rascal is better satisfied with his lot than they are with theirs. They would not resign what they possess more than he for the most complete satisfaction of all the desires which they have in common with him. If they ever fancy they would, it is only in cases of unhappiness so extreme that to escape from it they would exchange their lot for almost any other, however undesirable in their own eyes. A being of higher faculties requires more to make him happy, is capable probably of more acute suffering, and certainly accessible to it at more points, than one of an inferior type; but in spite of these liabilities, he can never really wish to sink into what he feels to be a lower grade of existence. We may give what explanation we please of this unwillingness; we may attribute it to pride, a name which is given indiscriminately to some of the most and to some of the least estimable feelings of which mankind are capable; we may refer it to the love of liberty and personal independence, an appeal to which was with the Stoics one of the most effective means for the inculcation of it; to the love of power or to the love of excitement, both of which do really enter into and contribute to it; but its most appropriate appellation is a sense of dignity, which all human beings possess in one form or other, and in some, though by no means in exact, proportion to their higher faculties, and which is so essential a part of the happiness of those in whom it is strong that nothing which conflicts with it could be otherwise than momentarily an object of desire to them. Whoever supposes that this preference takes place at a sacrifice of happiness—that the superior being, in anything like equal circumstances, is not happier than the inferior—confounds the two very different ideas of happiness and content. It is indisputable that the being whose capacities of enjoyment are low has the greatest chance of having them fully satisfied; and a highly endowed being will always feel that any happiness which he can look for, as the world is constituted, is imperfect. But he can learn to bear its imperfections, if they are at all bearable; and they will not make him envy the being who is indeed unconscious of the imperfections, but only because he feels not at all the good which those imperfections qualify. It is better to be a human being dissatisfied than a pig satisfied; better to be Socrates dissatisfied than a fool satisfied. And if the fool, or the pig, are of a different opinion, it is because they only know their own side of the question. The other party to the comparison knows both sides.

It may be objected that many who are capable of the higher pleasures occasionally, under the influence of temptation, postpone them to the lower. But this is quite compatible with a full appreciation of the intrinsic superiority of the higher. Men often, from infirmity of character, make their election for the nearer good, though they know it to be the less valuable; and this no less when the choice is between two bodily pleasures than when it is between bodily and mental. They pursue sensual indulgence to the injury of health, though perfectly aware that health is the greater good. It may be further objected that many who begin with youthful enthusiasm for everything noble, as they advance in years, sink into indolence and selfishness. But I do not believe that those who undergo this very common change voluntarily choose the lower description of pleasures in preference to the higher. I believe that, before they devote themselves exclusively to the one, they have already become incapable of the other. Capacity for the nobler feelings is in most natures a very tender plant, easily killed, not only by hostile influences, but by mere want of sustenance; and in the majority of young persons it speedily dies away if the occupations to which their position in life has devoted them, and the society into which it has thrown them, are not favorable to keeping that higher capacity in exercise. Men lose their high aspirations as they lose their intellectual tastes, because they have not time or opportunity for indulging them; and they addict themselves to inferior pleasures, not because they deliberately prefer them, but because they are either the only ones to which they have access or the only ones which they are any longer capable of enjoying. It may be questioned whether anyone who has remained equally susceptible to both classes of pleasures ever knowingly and calmly preferred the lower, though many, in all ages, have broken down in an ineffectual attempt to combine both.

From this verdict of the only competent judges, I apprehend there can be no appeal. On a question which is the best worth having of two pleasures, or which of two modes of existence is the most grateful to the feelings, apart from its moral attributes, and from its consequences, the judgment of these who are qualified by knowledge of both, or, if they differ, that of the majority among them, must be admitted as final. And there needs be the less hesitation to accept this judgment respecting the quality of pleasures, since there is no other tribunal to be referred to even on the question of quantity. What means are there of determining which is the acutest of two pains, or the intensest of two pleasurable sensations, except the general suffrage of those who are familiar with both? Neither pains nor pleasures are homogeneous, and pain is always heterogeneous with pleasure. What is there to decide whether a particular pleasure is worth purchasing at the cost of a particular pain, except the feelings and judgment of the experienced? When, therefore, those feelings and judgment declare the pleasures derived from the higher faculties to be preferable *in kind,* apart from the question of intensity, to those of which the animal nature, disjoined from the higher faculties, is susceptible, they are entitled on this subject to the same regard.

I have dwelt on this point as being part of a perfectly just conception of utility or happiness considered as the directive rule of human conduct. But it is by no means an indispensable condition to the acceptance of the utilitarian standard; for that standard is not the agent's own greatest happiness, but the greatest amount of happiness altogether; and if it may possibly be doubted whether a noble character is always the happier for its nobleness, there can be no doubt that it makes other people happier, and that the world in general is immensely a gainer by it. Utilitarianism, therefore, could only attain its end by the general cultivation of nobleness of character, even if each individual were only benefited by the nobleness of others, and his own, so far as happiness is concerned, were a sheer deduction from the benefit. But the bare enunciation of such an absurdity as this last renders refutation superfluous.

According to the greatest happiness principle, as above explained, the ultimate end, with reference to and for the sake of which all other things are desirable—whether we are considering our own good or that of other people—is an existence exempt as far as possible from pain, and as rich as possible in enjoyments, both in point of quantity and quality; the test of quality and the rule for measuring it against quantity being the preference felt by those who, in their opportunities of experience, to which must be added their habits of self-consciousness and self-observation, are best furnished with the means of comparison. This, being according to the utilitarian opinion the end of human action, is necessarily also the standard of morality, which may accordingly be defined "the rules and precepts for human conduct," by the observance of which an existence such as has been described might be, to the greatest extent possible, secured to all mankind; and not to them only, but, so far as the nature of things admits, to the whole sentient creation. . . .

I must again repeat what the assailants of utilitarianism seldom have the justice to acknowledge, that the happiness which forms the utilitarian standard of what is right in conduct is not the agent's own happiness but that of all concerned. As between his own happiness and that of others, utilitarianism requires him to be as strictly impartial as a disinterested and benevolent spectator. In the golden rule of Jesus of Nazareth, we read the complete spirit of the ethics of utility. "To do as you would be done by," and "to love your neighbor as yourself," constitute the ideal perfection of utilitarian morality. As the means of making the nearest approach to this ideal, utility would enjoin, first, that laws and social arrangements should place the happiness or (as, speaking practically, it may be called) the interest of every individual as nearly as possible in harmony with the interest of the whole; and, secondly, that education and opinion, which have so vast a power over human character, should so use that power as to establish in the mind of every individual an indissoluble association between his own happiness and the good of the whole, especially between his own happiness and the practice of such modes of conduct, negative and positive, as regard for the universal happiness prescribes; so that not only he may be unable to conceive the possibility of happiness to himself, consistently with conduct opposed to the general good, but also that a direct impulse to promote the general good may be in every individual one of the habitual motives of action, and the sentiments connected therewith may fill a large and prominent place in every human being's sentient existence. If the impugners of the utilitarian morality represented it to their own minds in this its true character, I know not what recommendations possessed by any other morality they could possibly affirm to be wanting to it; what more beautiful or more exalted developments of human nature any other ethical system can be supposed to foster, or what springs of action, not accessible to the utilitarian, such systems rely on for giving effect to their mandates.

The objectors to utilitarianism cannot always be

charged with representing it in a discreditable light. On the contrary, those among them who entertain anything like a just idea of its disinterested character sometimes find fault with its standard as being too high for humanity. They say it is exacting too much to require that people shall always act from the inducement of promoting the general interest of society. But this is to mistake the very meaning of a standard of morals and confound the rule of action with the motive of it. It is the business of ethics to tell us what are our duties, or by what test we may know them; but no system of ethics requires that the sole motive of all we do shall be a feeling of duty; on the contrary, ninety-nine hundredths of all our actions are done from other motives, and rightly so done if the rule of duty does not condemn them. It is the more unjust to utilitarianism that this particular misapprehension should be made a ground of objection to it, inasmuch as utilitarian moralists have gone beyond almost all others in affirming that the motive has nothing to do with the morality of the action, though much with the worth of the agent. He who saves a fellow creature from drowning does what is morally right, whether his motive be duty or the hope of being paid for his trouble; he who betrays the friend that trusts him is guilty of a crime, even if his object be to serve another friend to whom he is under great obligations. But to speak only of actions done from the motive of duty, and in direct obedience to principle: it is a misapprehension of the utilitarian mode of thought to conceive it as implying that people should fix their minds upon so wide a generality as the world, or society at large. The great majority of good actions are intended not for the benefit of the world, but for that of individuals, of which the good of the world is made up; and the thoughts of the most virtuous man need not on these occasions travel beyond the particular persons concerned, except so far as is necessary to assure himself that in benefiting them he is not violating the rights, that is, the legitimate and authorized expectations, of anyone else. The multiplication of happiness is, according to the utilitarian ethics, the object of virtue: the occasions on which any person (except one in a thousand) has it in his power to do this on an extended scale—in other words, to be a public benefactor—are but exceptional; and on these occasions alone is he called on to consider public utility; in every other case, private utility, the interest or happiness of some few persons, is all he has to attend to. Those alone the influence of whose actions extends to society in general need concern themselves habitually about so large an object. In the case of abstinences indeed—of things which people forbear to do from moral considerations, though the consequences in the particular case might be beneficial—it would be unworthy of an intelligent agent not to be consciously aware that the action is of a class which, if practiced generally, would be generally injurious, and that this is the ground of the obligation to abstain from it. The amount of regard for the public interest implied in this recognition is no greater than is demanded by every system of morals, for they all enjoin to abstain from whatever is manifestly pernicious to society.

The same considerations dispose of another reproach against the doctrine of utility, founded on a still grosser misconception of the purpose of a standard of morality and of the very meaning of the words "right" and "wrong." It is often affirmed that utilitarianism renders men cold and unsympathizing; that it chills their moral feelings toward individuals; that it makes them regard only the dry and hard consideration of the consequences of actions, not taking into their moral estimate the qualities from which those actions emanate. If the assertion means that they do not allow their judgment respecting the rightness or wrongness of an action to be influenced by their opinion of the qualities of the person who does it, this is a complaint not against utilitarianism, but against any standard or morality at all; for certainly no known ethical standard decides an action to be good or bad because it is done by a good or bad man, still less because done by an amiable, a brave, or a benevolent man, or the contrary. These considerations are relevant, not to the estimation of actions, but of persons; and there is nothing in the utilitarian theory inconsistent with the fact that there are other things which interest us in persons besides the rightness and wrongness of their actions. The Stoics, indeed, with the paradoxical misuse of language which was part of their system, and by which they strove to raise themselves above all concern about anything but virtue, were fond of saying that he who has that has everything; that he, and only he, is rich, is beautiful, is a king. But no claim of this description is made for the virtuous man by the utilitarian doctrine. Utilitarians are quite aware that there are other desirable possessions and qualities besides virtue, and are perfectly willing to allow to all of them their full worth. They are also aware that a right action does not necessarily indicate a virtuous character, and that actions which are blamable often proceed from qualities entitled to praise. When this is apparent in any particular case, it modifies their estimation, not certainly of the act, but of the agent. I grant that they are, notwithstanding, of opinion that in the long run the best proof of a good character is good actions; and resolutely refuse to consider any mental disposition as good of which the predominant tendency is to produce bad conduct. This makes them unpopular with many people, but it is an unpopularity which they must share with everyone who regards the distinction between right and wrong in a serious light; and the reproach is not one which a conscientious utilitarian need be anxious to repel.

If no more be meant by the objection than that many utilitarians look on the morality of actions, as measured by the utilitarian standards, with too exclusive a regard, and do not lay sufficient stress upon the other beauties of character which go toward making a human being lovable or admirable, this may be admitted. Utilitarians who have cultivated their moral feelings, but not their sympathies, nor their artistic perceptions, do fall into this mistake; and so do all other moralists under the same conditions. What can be said in excuse for other moralists is equally available for them, namely, that, if there is to be any error, it is better that it should be on that side. As a matter of fact, we may affirm that among utilitarians, as among adherents of other systems, there is every imaginable degree of rigidity and of laxity in the application of their standard; some are even puritanically rigorous, while others are as indulgent as can possibly be desired by sinner or by sentimentalist. But on the whole, a doctrine which brings prominently forward the interest that mankind have in the repression and prevention of conduct which violates the moral law is likely to be inferior to no other in turning the sanctions of opinion against such violations. It is true, the question "What does violate the moral law?" is one on which those who recognize different standards of morality are likely now and then to differ. But difference of opinion on moral questions was not first introduced into the world by utilitarianism, while that doctrine does supply, if not always an easy, at all events a tangible and intelligible, mode of deciding such differences.

It may not be superfluous to notice a few more of the common misapprehensions of utilitarian ethics, even those which are so obvious and gross that it might appear impossible for any person of candor and intelligence to fall into them; since persons, even of considerable mental endowment, often give themselves so little trouble to understand the bearings of any opinion against which they entertain a prejudice, and men are in general so little conscious of this voluntary ignorance as a defect that the vulgarest misunderstandings of ethical doctrines are continually met with in the deliberate writings of persons of the greatest pretensions both to high principle and to philosophy. We not uncommonly hear the doctrine of utility inveighed against a *godless* doctrine. If it be necessary to say anything at all against so mere an assumption, we may say that the question depends upon what idea we have formed of the moral character of the Deity. If it be a true belief that God desires, above all things, the happiness of his creatures, and that this was his purpose in their creation, utility is not only not a godless doctrine, but more profoundly religious than any other. If it be meant that utilitarianism does not recognize the revealed will of God as the supreme law of morals, I answer that a utilitarian who believes in the perfect goodness and wisdom of *God* necessarily believes that whatever God has thought fit to reveal on the subject of morals must fulfill the requirements of utility in a supreme degree. But others besides utilitarians have been of opinion that the Christian revelation was intended, and is fitted, to inform the hearts and minds of mankind with a spirit which should enable them to find for themselves what is right, and incline them to do it when found, rather than to tell them, except in a very general way, what it is; and that we need a doctrine of ethics, carefully followed out, to *interpret* to us the will of God. Whether this opinion is correct or not, it is superfluous here to discuss; since whatever aid religion, either natural or revealed, can afford to ethical investigation is as open to the utilitarian moralist as to any other. He can use it as the testimony of God to the usefulness or hurtfulness of any given course of action by as good a right as others can use it for the indication of a transcendental law having no connection with usefulness or with happiness.

Again, utility is often summarily stigmatized as an immoral doctrine by giving it the name of "expediency," and taking advantage of the popular use of that term to contrast it with principle. But the expedient, in the sense in which it is opposed to the right, generally means that which is expedient for the particular interest of the agent himself; as when a minister sacrifices the interests of his country to keep himself in place. When it means anything better than this, it means that which is expedient for some immediate object, some temporary purpose, but which violates a rule whose observance is expedient in a much higher degree. The expedient, in this sense, instead of being the same thing with the useful, is a branch of the hurtful. Thus it would often be expedient, for the purpose of getting over some momentary embarrassment, or attaining some object immediately useful to ourselves or others, to tell a lie. But inasmuch as the cultivation in ourselves of a sensitive feeling on the subject of veracity is one of the most useful, and the enfeeblement of that feeling one of the most hurtful, things to which our conduct can be instrumental; and inasmuch as any, even unintentional, deviation from truth does that much toward weakening the trustworthiness of human assertion, which is not only the principal support of all present social well-being, but the insufficiency of which does more than any one thing that can be named to keep back civilization, virtue, everything on which human happiness on the largest scale depends—we feel that the violation, for a present advantage, of a rule of such transcendent expediency is not expedient, and that he who, for the sake of convenience to himself or to some other individual, does what depends on him to deprive mankind of the good, and inflict upon them the evil, involved in the greater or less reliance which they can place in each other's words, acts the part of one of their worst enemies. Yet that even this rule, sacred as it is, admits of possible exceptions is acknowledged by all moralists; the chief of which is when the withholding of some fact (as of information from a malefactor, or of bad news from a person dangerously ill) would save an individual (especially an individual other than oneself) from great and unmerited evil, and when the withholding can only be effected by denial. But in order that the exception may not extend itself beyond the need, and may have the least possible effect in weakening reliance on veracity, it ought to be recognized and, if possible, its limits defined; and, if the principle of utility is good for anything, it must be good for weighing these conflicting utilities against one another and marking out the region within which one or the other preponderates.

Again, defenders of utility often find themselves called upon to reply to such objections as this—that there is not time, previous to action, for calculating and weighing the effects of any line of conduct on the general happiness. This is exactly as if anyone were to say that it is impossible to guide our conduct by Christianity because there is not time, on every occasion on which anything has to be done, to read through the Old and New Testaments. The answer to the objection is that there has been ample time, namely, the whole past duration of the human species. During all that time mankind have been learning by experience the tendencies of actions; on which experience all the prudence as well as all the morality of life are dependent. People talk as if the commencement of this course of experience had hitherto been put off, and as if, at the moment when some man feels tempted to meddle with the property or life of another, he had to begin considering for the first time whether murder and theft are injurious to human happiness. Even then I do not think that he would find the question very puzzling; but, at all events, the matter is now done to his hand. It is truly a whimsical supposition that, if mankind were agreed in considering utility to be the test of morality, they would remain without any agreement as to what *is* useful, and would take no measures for having their notions on the subject taught to the young and enforced by law and opinion. There is no difficulty in proving any ethical standard whatever to work ill if we suppose universal idiocy to be conjoined with it; but on any hypothesis short of that, mankind must by this time have acquired positive beliefs as to the effects of some actions on their happiness; and the beliefs which have thus come down are the rules of morality for the multitude, and for the philosopher until he has succeeded in finding better. That philosophers might easily do this, even now, on many subjects; that the received code of ethics is by no means of divine right; and that mankind have still much to learn as to the effects of actions on the general happiness, I admit or rather earnestly maintain. The corollaries from the principle of utility, like the precepts of every practical art, admit of indefinite improvement, and, in a progressive state of the human mind, their improvement is perpetually going on. But to consider the rules of morality as improvable is one thing; to pass over the intermediate generalization entirely and endeavor to test each individual action directly by the first principle is another. It is a strange notion that the acknowledgment of a first principle is inconsistent with the admission of secondary ones. To inform a traveler respecting the place of his ultimate destination is not to forbid the use of landmarks and direction-posts on the way. The proposition that happiness is the end and aim of morality does not mean that no road ought to be laid down to that goal, or that persons going thither should not be advised to take one direction rather than another. Men really ought to leave off talking a kind of nonsense on this subject, which they would neither talk nor listen to on other matters of practical concernment. Nobody argues that the art of navigation is not founded on astronomy because sailors cannot wait to calculate the Nautical Almanac. Being rational creatures, they go to sea with it ready calculated; and all rational creatures go out upon the sea of life with their minds made up on the common questions of right and wrong, as well as on many of the far more difficult questions of wise and foolish. And this, as long as foresight is a human quality, it is to be presumed they will continue to do. Whatever we adopt as the fundamental principle of morality, we require subordinate principles to apply it by; the impossibility of doing without them, being common to all systems, can afford no argument against any one in particular; but gravely to argue as if no such secondary principles could be had, and as if mankind had remained till now, and always must remain, without drawing any general conclusions from the experience of human life is as high a pitch, I think, as absurdity has ever reached in philosophical controversy.

The remainder of the stock arguments against utilitarianism mostly consist in laying to its charge the common infirmities of human nature, and the general difficulties which embarrass conscientious persons in shaping their course through life. We are told that a utilitarian will be apt to make his own particular case an exception to moral rules, and, when under temptation, will see a utility in the breach of a rule, greater than he will see in its observance. But is utility the only creed which is able to furnish us with excuses for evil-doing and means of cheating our own conscience? They are afforded in abundance by all doctrines which recognize as a fact in morals the existence of conflicting considerations, which all doctrines do that have been believed by sane persons. It is not the fault of any creed, but of the complicated nature of human affairs, that rules of conduct cannot be so framed as to require no exceptions, and that hardly any kind of action can safely be laid down as either always obligatory or always condemnable. There is no ethical creed which does not temper the rigidity of its laws by giving a certain latitude, under the moral responsibility of the agent, for accommodation to peculiarities of circumstances; and under every creed, at the opening thus made, self-deception and dishonest casuistry get in. There exists no moral system under which there do not arise unequivocal cases of conflicting obligation. These are the real difficulties, the knotty points both in the theory of ethics and in the conscientious guidance of personal conduct. They are overcome practically, with greater or with less success, according to the intellect and virtue of the individual; but it can hardly be pretended that anyone will be the less qualified for dealing with them, from possessing an ultimate standard to which conflicting rights and duties can be referred. If utility is the ultimate source of moral obligations, utility may be invoked to decide between them when their demands are incompatible. Though the application of the standard may be difficult, it is better than none at all; while in other systems, the moral laws all claiming independent authority, there is no common umpire entitled to interfere between them; their claims to precedence one over another rest on little better than sophistry, and, unless determined, as they generally are, by the unacknowledged influence of consideration of utility, afford a free scope for the action of personal desires and partialities. We must remember that only in these cases of conflict between secondary principles is it requisite that first principles should be appealed to. There is no case of moral obligation in which some secondary principle is not involved; and if only one, there can seldom be any real doubt which one it is, in the mind of any person by whom the principle itself is recognized.

The Environment

Every living thing interacts with its environment. Humans have no choice, therefore, but to change the natural world. But two factors have turned such changes into a significant public policy issue. First, the world's population has grown rapidly during the past several centuries, greatly amplifying humanity's impact on the environment. Second, the technological advances of the industrial revolution have not only increased our ability to affect our surroundings but have brought about new kinds of effects that, even today, we only partially understand.

Utilitarians look at environmental questions in terms of consequences, that is, in terms of costs and benefits. Whether cost–benefit analysis is adequate to environmental issues, however, is itself subject to debate. One might argue that the interdependency of ecosystems makes consequences very difficult to predict. Small effects on one part of a system may produce large effects on another. Moreover, cost–benefit analyses usually omit various environmental effects that are difficult to quantify but nevertheless ecologically significant.

Paul and Anne Ehrlich point to other difficulties with utilitarian analysis. Environmental questions force us to assess difficult trade-offs between very different kinds of goods. How much money, for example, is a year of a human life worth? How much should society be willing to spend to keep, say, a hundred people from dying prematurely each year? Even this is too simple, for real-world issues involve questions of *risk* rather than cost. Actual trade-off questions are more like this: What should society be willing to spend to lower the probability of the average person's dying this year by, say, .00004%? And what if our confidence in that estimate of risk is itself low? The Ehrlichs argue for a policy of increasing humanity's margin for error, recognizing that our risk–benefit analyses are themselves highly uncertain.

Bill Devall and George Sessions raise other objections to utilitarian analysis. The natural world, they contend, deserves respect; it is not merely a tool for producing human pleasure and avoiding human pain.

Outlining a view known as *deep ecology,* they argue that all forms of life deserve equal respect. Other beings and species have intrinsic moral worth. Kant says that everything has a dignity or a price. To put the thesis in Kantian terms, Devall and Sessions maintain that everything in the natural environment has a dignity. Utilitarian calculations go wrong by assigning everything—including human beings—a price. They conclude that humanity must undertake a sweeping reevaluation of its place in the environment.

William Baxter defends risk–benefit calculations, contending that environmental decisions must be made by assessing the effects of actions and policies on human beings. People, he contends, are more important than penguins, and nobody is in a position to speak for the penguins' interests. Dr. Seuss's Lorax, who speaks for the trees, is fictional; we have no reason to accept anyone as entitled to speak for the natural world.

Baxter sees environmental problems as arising not from misguided calculations, but from what Garrett Hardin dubbed *the tragedy of the commons.* Often, each party to a collective decision has reason to pursue his/her self-interest, given what the others are doing. If everyone pursues self-interest, however, everyone becomes worse off. Each possible polluter, for example, may believe that his/her additional pollution will make no significant difference to the environment but will yield substantial economic rewards. This may be true. Yet if each potential polluter reasons similarly and pollutes, the resulting environmental degradation may make everyone worse off than before.

This is a special case of what has become known as a *prisoners' dilemma.* Suppose that the police catch two criminals, Mug and Thug. They immediately separate them and interrogate them independently. Having caught them on a minor violation, but lacking the evidence to be confident of obtaining a conviction on a major charge, the police offer Mug a deal: "You can make it easy for us, and on yourself, or you can make it tough. If you confess, and your testimony against Thug lets us get him on the major charge, you walk out of here. We bargain on the small stuff; you get probation. If you don't confess, you do time. You know we have you on the small stuff. If you don't work with us, we don't cut any deals. You go to jail. And if we get you on the big one, you go to jail for a long time. What do you say?" They offer the same deal to Thug.

We can represent the situation in a simple table, where Mug and Thug must choose to confess or remain silent, and where the outcomes are pairs [effect on Mug, effect on Thug]:

		Thug	
		Confess	Remain Silent
Mug	Confess	[–2, –2]	[0, –5]
	Remain Silent	[–5, 0]	[–1, –1]

That is, if both remain silent, they each get a year in jail on minor charges. If both confess, the police cut a deal for cooperation, but both are convicted of the serious offense, so each gets two years. If one confesses and the other doesn't, the one who confesses goes free, but the one who remains silent is convicted of everything, without any deals, and gets five years.

Mug and Thug can't communicate, and they aren't sure, let's assume, what the other will do. Mug might reason as follows: "If Thug confesses, I'm better off confessing. I'll get only two years instead of three. If Thug doesn't confess, I'm still better off confessing; I walk instead of getting a year. So, no matter what Thug does, I'm better off confessing." Mug therefore confesses. Thug reasons similarly, of course, and also confesses. So each criminal spends two years in jail. Their reasoning appears impeccable. Yet, if they had both remained silent, they would have cut their sentences in half.

Here's how the prisoners' dilemma applies to environmental problems and leads to the tragedy of the commons. Imagine that, in place of Mug and Thug, we have two companies, Vanishing, Inc., and Roco Co. Each faces a choice between polluting and installing pollution control equipment. Each reasons that its pollution will have minor effects on overall air and water quality, but that installing control equipment will have a big impact on its bottom line. So, each pollutes. But the result may be a lower quality of life for everyone, and even economic harm to the companies themselves (through additional costs required to clean the water to be used in their industrial processes, for example, or to replace equipment more frequently, or to attract workers to such an unpleasant community, or to pay increased health care costs).

Again, we can represent the choice in a table where the pairs are [effect on Vanishing, Inc., effect on Roco Co.]:

		Roco Co.	
		Pollute	Control
Vanishing, Inc.	Pollute	[2, 2]	[4, 1]
	Control	[1, 4]	[3, 3]

Each company can reason that it is better off polluting, no matter what the other does. Suppose that you are the CEO of Vanishing, Inc. If Roco Co. pollutes, you are better off polluting; you have to put up with the disadvantages of their pollution anyway, and the control equipment is expensive. If they control their pollution, you are still better off polluting, because you save the costs of the control equipment, and you gain the benefits of their clean-up efforts. But Roco Co. faces the same situation and reasons similarly. So, you both pollute. But this is the worst possible outcome: a tragedy of the commons. You would have been better off, jointly and singly, if you had both controlled your pollution. The two of you taken together would have been better off if even one of you had done so.

So far, prisoners' dilemmas make the point that people or companies acting independently and rationally to promote their own self-interest can produce substantial and avoidable harm to the community as a whole. But the point applies to act-utilitarians as well as to self-interested agents. Suppose that Mug and Thug are utilitarians and that no one else is affected by what happens to them, so that they are seeking to maximize their combined welfare. Summing their individual utilities to compute the effects on the two taken together, their choice becomes:

		Thug	
		Confess	Remain Silent
Mug	Confess	–4	–5
	Remain Silent	–5	–2

Mug, the utilitarian, sees that he should do whatever Thug does. Thug, the utilitarian, recognizes this too. So, Mug and Thug satisfy the demands of act-utilitarianism if they both remain silent *or if they both confess*. This shows that act-utilitarianism is *indeterminate*—it may be satisfied by different patterns of behavior with different utilities for the community as a whole.

If our companies act as utilitarians in the case outlined above, they solve their problem: Each maximizes welfare overall by controlling pollution, achieving the best outcome. (Vanishing, Inc., sees that the community is better off if it controls its pollution, no matter what Roco Co. does.) But small changes in the effects on the two companies change this:

		Roco Co.	
		Pollute	Control
Vanishing, Inc.	Pollute	[2.1, 2.1]	[4, 0]
	Control	[0, 4]	[3, 3]

Now, the choice is just like Mug and Thug's. Each company can reason, as an act-utilitarian, that it should do what the other company does. But that means that both can be good act-utilitarians even while polluting and achieving less than the best overall outcome.

This points to an important limitation of act-utilitarian (that is, cost–benefit or risk–benefit) analyses made by independent parties: Even when they accurately assess risks and benefits, different patterns of behavior with different implications for the community's welfare can pass all such tests. Only by cooperating can the criminals or the companies achieve the best combined outcome.

This might seem to be an argument for rule-utilitarianism. But it too can lead to suboptimal outcomes. Suppose that Pig, Inc., and Poke Co. each pollute slightly less than some threshold harmful amount. Then, if both pollute, they together produce significant harms. But the pollution of just one produces no harm at all. They seem to face the choice:

		Poke Co.	
		Pollute	Control
Pig, Inc.	Pollute	[2, 2]	[4, 3]
	Control	[3, 4]	[3, 3]

Self-interest and act-utilitarianism imply that exactly one company should pollute. The polluting company does better economically without producing any environmental harm. Yet rule-utilitarianism tells each company to follow the rule that will produce the best outcome overall. If both follow the rule "Pollute," the overall utility is 4; if they follow the rule "Don't pollute," it is 6. So, if the companies act as rule-utilitarians, they will both install controls, producing less than the best outcome for the community.

This has important implications for environmental problems, which Baxter adumbrates in a later chapter of this book. The traditional model of government regulation of the environment is one of law enforcement: determining what kinds of actions are tolerably safe and what kinds are environmentally dangerous, then banning the latter and prosecuting those who violate the law. In essence, the model is rule-utilitarian, requiring people to follow the best rules. In some circumstances, this may not lead to the best outcome, for it imposes uniformity: Everyone must follow the same rules. Free-market economists thus argue against governmental solutions to environmental problems and defend market-based solutions instead.

PAUL R. EHRLICH AND ANNE H. EHRLICH

Risks, Costs, and Benefits

Paul R. Ehrlich is Professor of Biological Sciences and Director of the Center for Conservation Biology at Stanford University. Anne H. Ehrlich, his wife, has collaborated with him on many works, including Ecoscience, Extinction, *and* The End of Affluence. *(Source: From* Healing the Planet: Strategies for Resolving the Environmental Crisis, *Reading, Mass.: Addison-Wesley Publishing Company, Inc. Notes have been omitted. Copyright © 1991 by Paul R. Ehrlich and Anne H. Ehrlich.)*

QUESTIONS FOR REFLECTION

1. What problems do the Ehrlichs see in applying risk–benefit analysis to environmental problems?
2. How do social risk–benefit analyses differ from individual risk–benefit analyses?
3. The Ehrlichs argue for increasing humanity's margin for error. Summarize the argument. Do you find it persuasive?
4. What do the Ehrlichs' conclusions imply about the application of utilitarianism to environmental issues?

Humanity clearly must make many decisions about the risks involved in present and future alterations of Earth's life support systems. What, if anything, should be done now to slow global warming? Are the ozone protocols tough enough, and what enforcement measures are justified? Is the damage done to natural ecosystems by acid precipitation sufficiently serious to justify the expenditure of billions of dollars in an attempt to reduce it by half? Would it be worthwhile for rich countries all to spend one half of one percent of their GNPs in attempts to foster ecologically sound agricultural development in poor nations? All such questions relating to the healing of Earth are difficult to answer, since they involve many uncertainties. Nonetheless, rational people and societies are (or ought to be) interested in comparing honestly and systematically the costs and benefits of actions they might take.

Throughout human history, people have had impacts on natural systems, and for millennia those impacts have generally increased Earth's long-term carrying capacity for people. The agricultural revolution some 10,000 years ago, when people first began to grow most of their food rather than hunt and gather it, was a prime example: it led to the transformation of huge tracts of grassland and forest into farmland. That eventually made it possible to support billions of people on Earth rather than millions.

In this century, humanity has become a truly planetary ecological force, its effects going far beyond the transformation of the landscape to include altering the composition of the atmosphere globally, interfering with planetary nutrient cycles, modifying climate, and exterminating other life forms. In historical perspective, the switch—from a modest to an overwhelming scale of impact, and from a positive to a negative impact on carrying capacity—was almost instantaneous and monumental: human activities now appear to be lowering the long-term carrying capacity and incurring risks on a scale unimaginable less than a lifetime ago.

All human activities have unavoidable effects on ecosystems. In order to remain alive, people must take in oxygen from the environment and release carbon dioxide to it. We must acquire energy directly or indirectly from the chemical bonds that plants manufacture in the process of photosynthesis, and we must return some of that energy to the environment in the form of waste heat. Every move you make changes your environment—sometimes the changes are not perceptible, but they happen. So there is no question as to whether or not we should affect our environment—the questions all center on the *scale and consequences* of our influence. These questions generally boil down to assessments of risks, costs, and benefits, as a basis for making decisions in the face of uncertainty. The penalties of making environmental mistakes plagued our ancestors at least since the first fire set to drive game toward hunters got out of control and killed someone. But until very recently, the penalties were borne by a few or a few million people, locally or regionally. Now they can be borne by billions of people globally.

In the modern era, people are constantly faced with decisions involving risks, costs, and benefits; and more and more of them are related to environmental issues. Faced with a plethora of environmental problems, societies must make all manner of decisions about which pose the greatest risks, which are most important to deal with first, how much effort (if any) to allocate to each, and so on. All such decisions involve trade-offs; for instance, money spent on scrubbers for factory smokestacks will not be available to improve the quality of the factory's waste-water effluents; scientists designing sophisticated weapons cannot spend their time designing energy-efficient automobiles. A society that subsidizes organ transplants and medical care for the aged will have fewer resources to spend on maternal and child health or family planning clinics.

Many decisions, unfortunately, are made without being informed by careful risk assessments or cost-benefit analyses. Of course, such evaluations add to the costs of decision making, and may be unnecessary when the choices are fairly clear. But every politician knows of cases where hindsight has revealed too late a need for careful study in advance. In the context here, though, familiarity with the nature of these evaluations could be particularly helpful in thinking about ways to heal the Earth.

"Risk" is sometimes used as a synonym for "probability" in insurance policies—the risk of a loss. In analyzing issues like those discussed in this chapter, "risk" means the consequences of an event multiplied by its probability (or frequency) of occurrence—or, to put it another way, risk is a probability times a bad consequence. For example, if the collapse of a particular dam would cause 5,000 deaths and the probability of such a collapse is 1 in 1,000 per year, then the associated risk is 5,000 deaths times 1/(1,000 years) = 5 deaths per year. Similarly, one measure of the risk of driving automobiles in the United States is 50,000 deaths per year. You can think of that risk as the average number of deaths per automobile accident multiplied by the probability or frequency of auto accidents (accidents per year).

If an activity can have more than one kind of adverse consequence, its risk can be measured in more than one way. For instance, the risk of automobile driving can be measured, in addition to deaths per year, by injuries per year or by property damage per year. Different risk measures also result from different formulations of the probability or frequency involved. One might be interested not in the total number of automobile deaths in the United States, but in the number per year in a particular state, or the number per million vehicle miles, or the number per hour of driving.

In comparing risks of different activities, one must take care that the measures of risk are really comparable with respect to both the consequences and the type of probability measure used. As an example of consequences that are not directly comparable, consider two different types of cancer. Suppose exposure to chemical A gives one chance in 10,000 of causing pancreatic cancer and chemical B one chance in 10,000 of causing the commonest form of skin cancer. The former almost always causes a rapid and painful death; the latter is very rarely fatal. Then the risks of the two exposures would be considered equal if expressed as cancer cases per year; but since the two cancer types are not equivalent in their implications, a more informative measure would be fatal cancers per year.

Very often the environmental and safety risks that one wishes to evaluate cannot easily be expressed in monetary terms—risks of loss of many human lives, of the extinction of a million species, or of increasing the speed of climatic change. In such cases, the risks and benefits of given decisions are compared in a "risk-benefit" analysis. If the risks can be expressed in monetary terms, then those are included with other costs in a more comprehensive "cost-benefit" analysis.

An important feature of risk-benefit and cost-benefit analyses is that often neither the risks nor the benefits of a particular decision are known with assurance. Therefore, while risk is a probability times a bad consequence, benefit is a probability times a good consequence. For instance, deciding whether or not to purchase a piece of land to make a reserve to protect a given species involves an assumed risk: the probability of the species going extinct if the reserve is not created times the seriousness of its loss to society. Costs would include the price of the land, the expenses of fencing and policing the reserve, and so forth. The benefits, too, must be calculated: the increased chance of the species' survival provided by the reserve (that is, the increased chance that the risk will be avoided) times the value to society of preserving the species (including esthetic values, possible direct economic values, possible values in helping to supply ecosystem services, and so forth). If the costs are less than the benefits, then creating the reserve would be a good decision economically.

Of course, quantifying the various factors in such an analysis can be difficult, but the exercise nevertheless can be extremely useful. Often, just analyzing the factors that can be readily quantified will provide the basis for a sound decision; many an environmentally unsound development project has been stopped by a "straightforward" economic cost-benefit analysis that neglected important considerations because they were difficult to quantify. But often such limited procedures can result in serious errors.

The trap of ignoring what can't easily be expressed in dollar costs has been described by economist Herman Daly as concentrating on things that are countable rather than things that count. Focusing on what can be quantified rather than what is important has become a major problem in the social sciences. It is essential to take care always to consider the qualitative (and ethical and moral) contexts in which risks, costs, and benefits are assessed. For instance, as Daly has pointed out, a key role in avoiding ethical responsibilities in quantitative analysis is played by the use of randomness. Somehow the deaths in auto accidents of 50,000 random, unknown people in the United States each year are generally acceptable. But if those people were predetermined and named, you can bet that the pressures for more auto safety would be enormously greater.

Neither Daly nor we would argue that such moral considerations should displace quantitative analysis—only that they must be explicitly included along with the results of the analyses when courses of action are determined. We can't say what is "acceptable"; that is a decision for society as a whole. We do personally believe that society would be better off if more effort were made to personalize the 50,000 American accident victims or the millions who die of malnutrition in poor countries each year. In schools and in the media, more attention to selected individual stories of those who are now just faceless statistics would help.

The other important problem with quantitative analyses is what energy analyst John Holdren calls "the tyranny of illusory precision"—using quantitative risk estimates, divorced from the underlying assumptions and the uncertainties associated with the estimates, to announce firm conclusions that are unjustified. A classic example was the "Rasmussen Report" on the safety of nuclear power plants. In that study 0.024 excess deaths per reactor-year of operation was publicized as a meaningful estimate of the risk of reactor accidents. Submerged in the fine print were the uncertainties associated with that estimate—according to the authors of the report, the risk could be twentyfold larger or smaller (and according to competent critics it could have been 100-fold larger or smaller). Also lost in the shuffle was any acknowledgment that critical components of risk, such as earthquakes and sabotage, were not included in the analysis at all.

A more recent occasion that presented elements of illusory precision was the pompous announcement of the conclusions of the 1990 National Acid Precipitation Assessment Program (NAPAP) by one of the key participants on the CBS television program *Sixty Minutes*. A precise (and small) number of lakes were stated to be at risk from acidification in the northeastern United States. The assessment itself, while containing some good science, was summarized so as to produce an illegitimately low evaluation of the threat by using data selectively and ignoring important dimensions of the problem.

Pancreatic cancer illustrates one of the most difficult aspects of risk analysis, a so-called zero-infinity problem. The probability that you will get the cancer is clearly very small—almost zero. The consequences, should that unlikely event occur, from the viewpoint of the affected individual, can be thought of as infinitely bad. But many voluntary activities involve trade-offs with the risk of a painful death. If people were unwilling to consider those trade-offs, every car would be a Sherman tank and the speed limit would be 15 miles per hour. People are unwilling to pay for a tank or to drive that slowly, so they accept what they perceive as a small risk of the infinitely bad.

In many people's judgment, the risk of a nuclear war is now moving into the zero-infinity area; the chances of such an event are dwindling, but the deaths of hundreds of millions of people are nonetheless likely if the event occurs. Other environmental risks seem to be moving toward what we would call a "likely-infinity" situation—one where the probabilities may be 20 to 50 percent or more, with hundreds of millions or even billions of lives hanging in the balance. Rapid climate change due to global warming is in this category, as ozone depletion will be if the recently agreed protocol to end the use of CFCs and halons is not complied with, or if some still-unknown factor in atmospheric chemistry (similar to the unexpected ice-cloud chemistry that created the Antarctic ozone hole) makes that protocol inadequate.

There are two other important issues related to the zero-infinity problem. One is that few people would judge as equal two risks measured as "one death per year" if in one case that risk were generated by a 1 in 10,000 chance of a disaster killing 10,000 people and in the other a 1 in 2 chance of killing 2 people per year. There is a soundly based aversion to running the risk of big, concentrated disasters (which are likely to have psychological and social consequences very different from risks causing gradual attrition). Most people consider some disasters too big to entertain the risk no matter how small the probabilities. If a nuclear reactor accident could kill everyone on Earth, few would deem it tolerable to generate electricity with nuclear power even if the annual accident probability were only one in a trillion. We suspect that if people were well informed on the consequences of very rapid climatic change or the extermination of most of Earth's life forms, they would find the activities promoting them intolerable as well.

The second issue is that people often find the infinity more believable than the zero. People understand that experts are more successful at estimating the consequences of big disasters than in estimating their probability. There was no question about the consequences of the *Titanic* sinking; it was the probability of its sinking that the experts miscalculated. So the public doesn't really believe that the risk stays constant as the consequences rise and the probability falls.

Evaluating Risk

At the personal level, risk-benefit decisions often involve the question of whether to avoid substances that may be harmful to health. Is the flavor of a steak well marbled with fat worth a possibly increased probability of dying of a heart attack? Is the relaxation, pleasure, and possible ease of weight control that accompanies smoking a sufficient benefit to counterbalance the substantially increased possibilities of dying young of lung cancer or circulatory disease? Do the benefits of using aerosol underarm deodorants or hair sprays compensate for possible health effects, which are certainly small (and may be zero), of inhaling them? People informally weigh such risks all the time, always in the face of uncertainty and often even without access to the basic information about the risks that society possesses.

Even when considerable information is available, and the power to act is in your hands, decisions may not be easy. Suppose it were announced that your town's drinking water contained that chemical that gives you a one in 10 million chance of dying of liver cancer if you drink that water for the rest of your life. Would you spend $10 a year on a filter to remove the material? $100 a year? $1,000? Your answer would obviously depend on many things, including your age and financial situation.

Consider a more familiar example. There are undeniable benefits to driving a private automobile—convenience being paramount among them. But when everybody is driving a private automobile and commuters spend hours daily in near gridlock, the convenience factor is reduced and the direct (accident) and indirect (air pollution) risks escalate. Even now the benefits of driving are difficult to balance against the escalating risks. How does one calculate into the conveniences and inconveniences of automobile commuting the risks of additional exposure to airborne carcinogens and heart-threatening carbon monoxide or the contribution that the automobile makes toward global warming? Is the residual convenience worth a month-shorter life expectancy? A year? Two years? Is it worth a 1-percent chance of subjecting your grandchildren to food shortages by contributing to future crop failures caused by global warming? A 2-percent chance? A 5-percent chance?

Both the risk of diminished life expectancy and the risk of starving your grandchildren are especially difficult to analyze because they contain both personal and social components. If you give up driving or riding in cars, the risk to your personal life expectancy from the use of automobiles will be reduced, but not to zero. You could still be run down as a pedestrian, or die of lung cancer caused by smog. Only if a substantial portion of society gave up driving would that component of risk decrease very much. The risk to your grandchildren from global warming is even more difficult to reduce by personal effort, so one is tempted to take no action because "it won't make any difference." On the other hand, one can always try to set an example, or even try to persuade society as a whole to make the "right" decision (as civil rights, peace, and environmental activists have done).

Probabilistic thinking, dealing with the odds rather than certainties, is both a pain and unavoidable in analyzing risks. Suppose (to pick a random example) you were a biologist at Stanford University. How should you react to the announcement that there is a 50 percent chance of a large earthquake on the San Francisco peninsula in the next 30 years? If you were 60 years old, you certainly might react differently than if you were 30. In practice, you presumably would want to estimate (that is, make an educated guess at) the probability of being hurt or killed in such an earthquake. That would involve estimating the strength of the building where you work, the degree of earthquake resistance of your house, the proportion of time you will spend in each place, and how much of the time you are likely to be out of town.

Then you might want to consider the new hazards you might expose yourself to should you move: tornadoes in Kansas, hurricanes in Florida, running out of water in Tucson, a smaller chance of a more catastrophic quake in St. Louis, a greater chance of being robbed or murdered in New York City, and so on. Of course, virtually no one actually sits down and tries to make this kind of calculation, but people nonetheless weigh these kinds of odds in a more casual way every day. And while the public perception of risks does correlate somewhat with the calculations of experts, a combination of lack of information and a much richer variety of elements entering the evaluation leads to some striking differences. Nuclear power, for instance, is generally considered much more risky by the public than by risk analysts. The former often weigh such factors as the potential for catastrophes or threats to future generations more heavily than the estimates of annual fatalities preferred by experts. In addition, people tend to view the world as already unacceptably risky.

The problems experts face in measuring both costs and benefits are even more difficult because costs and benefits are usually distributed so unevenly among individuals, because individuals differ in their responses to risk, and because people judge risks on criteria other than simple probability times consequences. For example, the statistical risks incurred by smoking are large—a smoker runs a yearly risk of around 1 in 300 of dying because of the habit—but many people still choose to smoke, and some heavy smokers enjoy the habit thoroughly and die of accidents at a ripe old age. Some individuals are probably genetically resistant to some of the deleterious consequences of smoking, and many individuals are virtually immune to propaganda attempting to persuade them to give it up.

Comparatively, the chance of getting liver cancer from a trace of a toxic chemical in the water supply may be one in a million annually, but that risk, unlike that of smoking, is taken involuntarily. Most people evaluate involuntarily assumed risks as much more serious than those assumed willingly. This difference in attitude about voluntarily and involuntarily assumed risks led to the rapid passage of antismoking legislation in many places when the hazards for nonsmokers from sidestream smoke became clear, even though that danger is small compared with the hazard to smokers themselves. No legislation has been proposed to prevent people from smoking in private.

There also may be serious problems of scale in assessing social risks; a behavior that may not be harmful for a small group of people may become extremely dangerous if practiced by a large group. For example, a town of 1,000 people piping its sewage a mile out to sea may not overwhelm the ocean's waste-disposal capability, and beaches may remain clean and safe. A city of one million doing the same may cause a high incidence of infection in swimmers and surfers who frequent its beaches.

Social risk-benefit choices are always made on the basis of incomplete information. Decisions to use novel chemicals or deploy new technologies are generally made to capture benefits already identified—killing insects that compete for our food, generating cheap energy, providing fast, convenient transportation, and so on. But the sizes of the benefits may be quite uncertain. Some risks can be identified early, but others may become manifest only after deployment of the technology. Thalidomide is a drug that was originally used widely for the benefits it provided as a sleeping pill and sedative, and it has proven helpful in the treatment of leprosy. It was readily available for a few years in Canada and some European countries and was taken by many pregnant women. We now know that it caused about 7,000 children to be born with unformed limbs. . . .

Our Values and Risk-Benefit Decisions by Society

We may be conservative in dealing with risks personally, but we are extremely conservative—that is, risk-averse—when considering the health of Earth's ecosystems. We believe great caution is called for when making potentially irreversible changes in humanity's only home or in taking chances with hundreds of millions or even billions of lives, including those of our own grandchildren. We don't agree with political scientist Aaron Wildavsky, who wrote in 1989 that "the secret of safety lies in danger." He sees the free market as an ideal mechanism for balancing risks and benefits. If an activity is too risky, he believes people will decide not to pay the costs and the activity will fade away. Wildavsky is very concerned about the possible risks of overestimating the dangers posed by new technologies (forgoing some or all of their potential benefits). He greatly downplays the risks that may be associated with the harm such technologies may do to people or ecosystems, basically claiming that rich nations can buy their way out of any unforeseen difficulties.

Wildavsky's predilections are widely shared in business and government, and even in some segments of the scientific community. It normally appears in the form of statements such as "If you can't *prove* that doing X will do serious harm to the environment, then we should go ahead and reap the vast benefits of doing X." Like the accused in our criminal justice system, technologies are innocent until proven guilty. In other words, wait until the existence of negative externalities is proven before taking action that would internalize them. That was the defense of the chemical industry, which managed to delay badly needed action on the ozone front for a decade and a half.

This type of reasoning applied to the pharmaceutical industry, for example, would change the standard for drug approval to one where the drug could be sold without testing until someone "proved" that it was deadly. It is not clear that we should have different standards for the health of the ecosphere than for human health. In either case, one needs to weigh the expected costs and benefits of any action, not simply apply either "zero tolerance" rules or laissez-faire.

Under a laissez-faire philosophy, it would have been folly to oppose the conversion of the United States to a nation dependent on the automobile for commuting. The technology provided the imperative; the market demanded it. Of course, automobile and tire manufacturers and oil companies lent the market a hand, but that is a detail. We have reaped the benefits in mobility, jobs, economic growth, and privacy on the way to work. It wasn't until the 1960s that some of the costs became apparent in the form of smog, loss of community, and traffic jams. While the potential of carbon dioxide for causing global warming had been known in the nineteenth century, the automobiles' contribution to the problem was not widely discussed until the 1980s. Now it is clear that allowing the automobile to dominate the structure of American society entailed many unforeseen costs, and the United States is faced with a potentially traumatic and extremely costly task of reversing its dependence on individual automotive transport.

The risk of global warming was anticipated but long ignored. One can imagine many ways to improve society's performance in dealing with such recognized risks. But what about risks that remain unknown long after the technologies generating them have been deployed? The time it takes for costs to appear after decisions are made can be impressive, as the history of CFCs clearly illustrates. Even when the risks are anticipated by a few people, they often remain unappreciated by decision makers for a long time, as in the cases of the AIDS epidemic and global warming.

Social Risk Assessments

"Societies" can't make the kinds of conscious risk assessments that informed individuals do. Instead, those decisions are made by small subsets of the society, with most individuals (including many leaders) unaware that they are being made. Furthermore, although questions of intergenerational equity do play a role in individual risk assessment (women will, for example, avoid consuming substances in pregnancy they think may later harm their children), we believe that it should play a much larger role in social risk-taking. Social systems have adapted to the consequences of inevitable individual deaths. But should our generation's "decision" to wipe out much of Earth's biodiversity be carried out, the consequences could plague our descendants for a hundred thousand generations or more.

The consequences of mistakes in social risk-taking can be therefore much more widespread and long-lasting than those of individual risk-taking. As has often been said about the extinction crisis, we are not just causing the deaths of many other organisms, we are causing an end to their births. To most people, the latter is a much grimmer consequence, be it for rhinos or for humanity. Since the probability of the extinction of many organisms is very high and the consequences are deemed very serious, the risk being run by not dealing effectively with the extinction crisis is gigantic.

Social risk-benefit decisions differ from personal ones in another important way. The kinds of risks one faces day to day tend to be familiar and easily perceived, as are the benefits. Most of us have seen many automobile accidents, if not in person, then on the evening news. The risks one runs in driving are part of everyday life, but so is the convenience of personal transportation. Virtually everyone over fifty has seen a friend or relative die miserably of cancer and has lost someone close from a heart attack. Costs that are thought to lie far in the future may be heavily discounted—the "getting lung cancer in my seventies is a small price to pay for the joy of smoking until then" syndrome. But easily perceived risks are often ignored if one values the benefits highly enough. Skydivers are in no doubt about the potential costs of the chute's not opening but know the exhilaration of the drop. Many regularly confront the zero-infinity dilemma of jumping out of an airplane for the fun of it and accept the risk.

In contrast, few people recognize the benefits of sharing Earth with millions of other organisms or think much about the importance of a reasonably stable climate. Furthermore, the most critical environmental risks are difficult to perceive. With the possible exception of a zoo keeper or someone else observing the death of Martha, the last passenger pigeon (or some other sole survivor) in captivity, no one has ever watched one species go extinct, let alone thousands. No one has ever observed the results of heating the planet by a half-dozen degrees over fifty years or so, either. The costs associated with individual risks are usually paid in minutes or months; those associated with environmental risks may be paid over millennia or more. The costs may be virtually infinite, but they are distant in time and amorphous, unlike those of hitting the ground at 100 miles an hour after your parachute has failed to open.

Environmental risks often do not present themselves in forms that are easily perceived by people. A car swerving toward our car or a snarling dog lunging at us are the sorts of stimuli that millions of years of biological and cultural evolution have prepared us to recognize as threats. But the gradually climbing zigzag line on Keeling's chart of the CO_2 concentration above Mauna Loa or statistics on habitat destruction are not. For most of human history, people could do nothing about environmental changes occurring over decades. People didn't cause them, and people couldn't stop them. Consequently, human beings evolved perceptual systems that were not good at focusing on gradual change in the environmental backdrop against which their lives were played out—in fact, they actually suppress detection of such change. With the background held constant, the sudden appearance of a hungry tiger or a tasty gazelle (or a speeding car) was all the more readily perceived and dealt with.

Despite all these difficulties in perception, society must constantly weigh risks and benefits. Suppose, as the Stanford computer study suggested, that very rapid climate change in the next century could result in hundreds of millions of premature human deaths? What costs should be incurred to slow that change if its probability were 1 percent? 5 percent? 25 percent? 50 percent? These are not easy questions to answer, and there is no *scientific* basis for answering them. Since most of the measures required to slow the warming, from greatly increasing energy efficiency to land reform in poor nations, would carry other great benefits, and since the probability of unprecedented change appears to be in the vicinity of 50 percent, a very large social effort, one incurring substantial costs, seems to us not simply justified but virtually mandatory. In our view, the delay in dealing with chemicals that attack the ozone layer was inexcusable when the principal costs to societies would have been those of a transition to substitutes, a move that could have brought out the best in industry's competitiveness and innovation.

The debate over the risks, costs, and benefits associated with society's possible responses to global warming has hardly begun, as we saw in the discussion of the Nordhaus analysis. It is clear that the social process will be fraught with disputes. For instance, Nordhaus approved of the Bush administration's inaction, saying it "should be commended for following a reasoned approach and avoiding measures that would lock the economy onto a path that could not respond flexibly to new information or emerging technologies." We, of course, strongly disagree and find the administration's behavior execrable. We also wonder how research and development of new technologies for alternative energy sources could make society less flexible!

We do not disagree with Nordhaus because we think slowing global warming will be cost-free. Very substantial costs will inevitably be incurred in solving the suite of environmental dilemmas now facing civilization. The monetary amount of those costs and the monetary benefits will be difficult to calculate and doubtless always partly in dispute. But even now rough orders of magnitude can be discussed. Suppose the economists who claim that it would cost a trillion dollars ($10 billion per year) over the next century for the United States to do its part in slowing global warming are correct. Suppose that slowing global warming would save 1 billion lives over that period (10 million per year). In that case, the American contribution to saving each life would be $1,000. If other nations contributed in proportion to their GNPs, the rough price paid to save each life would be about $3,000. Expressing the value of human life in dollars is difficult. By most of the criteria that can be used, however, from our own subjective judgments or jury awards for wrongful death to evaluations of productivity lost by premature demise or the amounts society is willing to pay to save lives, $3,000 is a few percent of the monetary value of a human life—which should probably be valued at least at $100,000. Now let's suppose that the chances of global warming costing 1 billion lives over the next century were 50-50. Clearly, inaction in the face of the threat of global warming would be difficult to defend, since we would be avoiding an "expected" loss of 50 trillion dollars (1 billion lives × 0.50 probability × [say] $100,000 per life) for an investment of 1 trillion dollars—a great bargain in cost-benefit terms.

Of course, the steps envisioned in the trillion-dollar estimate to abate global warming would not deal with all other environmental problems—although they *would* help ameliorate many (toxic air and water pollution, for example). To be conservative, let's suppose that to assure our environmental security comprehensively and effectively would cost ten times as much as just tackling the warming. In that case, the cost would be $100 billion annually. Could that be afforded? We think so; it represents about a third of that spent on military security, an expense that almost everyone believes should decline in the future. And, of course, just as military expenditures provide subsidiary benefits such as jobs and the development of technologies that also have nonmilitary uses, so one would expect subsidiary benefits from expenditures on environmental security. They would include having a more pleasant (not just more secure) environment, better health, and lower health care costs. In short, even without being able to calculate risks, costs, and benefits exactly, rough estimates indicate that *we can afford to insure ourselves against environmental catastrophe.* Not to do so would be bizarre for a society that routinely insures lives, limbs, homes, automobiles, and businesses against risks whose probabilities of occurrence are much smaller than those, say, of unprecedented climate change due to global warming.

We believe it is important to take out that insurance for another reason. Not all risk decisions are as straightforward as those involved in abating ozone destruction or even global warming. Yet in both cases, the risk-benefit question and decisions are coming much too late—when the problems are entering the "probable-infinity" range and may have so much inertia that avoiding serious consequences is impossible. The lesson of the unexpected depletion of Antarctic ozone due to previously unknown chemistry in stratospheric ice clouds is an important one. Insurance should be taken out *before* engaging in risk-taking. Once the parachute has failed to open, it's too late to call your insurance broker.

So we are convinced that a more conservative approach is needed in the environmental risk philosophy of our society. A primary component of that philosophy should be to *increase humanity's margin for error.* And the basic way to accomplish that is to reduce the scale of human activities. Lacking crystal balls, analysts cannot accurately judge all the possible hazards of our activities, much as they may try. But we could move to a situation where even serious technological errors (like the manufacture of CFCs) would be unlikely to overwhelm the capacity of the planet to heal itself before they are detected and corrected. So once again, we see that reduction of scale is the principal challenge for the next stage of human evolution.

BILL DEVALL AND GEORGE SESSIONS

from *Deep Ecology*

Bill Devall is Professor of Sociology at Humboldt State University. George Sessions is Professor of Humanities at Sierra College. (Source: From Deep Ecology, *Salt Lake City: Gibbs Smith. Notes have been omitted.*

QUESTIONS FOR REFLECTION

1. What is *deep ecology*? How does it differ from environmentalism in general?
2. What is *biocentric equality*? How do Devall and Sessions argue for it? What are its implications for environmental issues?
3. Do you accept the principle of biocentric equality? Why, or why not?
4. Do any basic principles of deep ecology contradict utilitarianism?
5. Analyze and critique the basic principles from a Kantian perspective.

The term *deep ecology* was coined by Arne Naess in his 1973 article, "The Shallow and the Deep, Long-Range Ecology Movements." Naess was attempting to describe the deeper, more spiritual approach to Nature exemplified in the writings of Aldo Leopold and Rachel Carson. He thought that this deeper approach resulted from a more sensitive openness to ourselves and nonhuman life around us. The essence of deep ecology is to keep asking more searching questions about human life, society, and Nature as in the Western philosophical tradition of Socrates. As examples of this deep questioning, Naess points out "that we ask why and how, where others do not. For instance, ecology as a science does not ask what kind of a society would be the best for maintaining a particular ecosystem—that is considered a question for value theory, for politics, for ethics." Thus deep ecology goes beyond the so-called factual scientific level to the level of self and Earth wisdom.

Deep ecology goes beyond a limited piecemeal shallow approach to environmental problems and attempts to articulate a comprehensive religious and philosophical worldview. The foundations of deep ecology are the basic intuitions and experiencing of ourselves and Nature which comprise ecological consciousness. Certain outlooks on politics and public policy flow naturally from this consciousness. . . .

Ecological consciousness and deep ecology are in sharp contrast with the dominant worldview of technocratic-industrial societies which regards humans as isolated and fundamentally separate from the rest of Nature, as superior to, and in charge of, the rest of creation. But the view of humans as separate and superior to the rest of Nature is only part of larger cultural patterns. For thousands of years, Western culture has become increasingly obsessed with the idea of *dominance:* with dominance of humans over nonhuman

Nature, masculine over the feminine, wealthy and powerful over the poor, with the dominance of the West over non-Western cultures. Deep ecological consciousness allows us to see through these erroneous and dangerous illusions.

For deep ecology, the study of our place in the Earth household includes the study of ourselves as part of the organic whole. Going beyond a narrowly materialist scientific understanding of reality, the spiritual and the material aspects of reality fuse together. While the leading intellectuals of the dominant worldview have tended to view religion as "just superstition," and have looked upon ancient spiritual practice and enlightenment, such as found in Zen Buddhism, as essentially subjective, the search for deep ecological consciousness is the search for a more objective consciousness and state of being through an active deep questioning and meditative process and way of life.

Many people have asked these deeper questions and cultivated ecological consciousness within the context of different spiritual traditions—Christianity, Taoism, Buddhism, and Native American rituals, for example. While differing greatly in other regards, many in these traditions agree with the basic principles of deep ecology.

Warwick Fox, an Australian philosopher, has succinctly expressed the central intuition of deep ecology: "It is the idea that we can make no firm ontological divide in the field of existence: That there is no bifurcation in reality between the human and the non-human realms . . . to the extent that we perceive boundaries, we fall short of deep ecological consciousness."

From this most basic insight or characteristic of deep ecological consciousness, Arne Naess has developed two *ultimate norms* or intuitions which are themselves not derivable from other principles or intuitions. They are arrived at by the deep questioning process and reveal the importance of moving to the philosophical and religious level of wisdom. They cannot be validated, of course, by the methodology of modern science based on its usual mechanistic assumptions and its very narrow definition of data. These ultimate norms are *self-realization* and *biocentric equality.*

I. Self-Realization

In keeping with the spiritual traditions of many of the world's religions, the deep ecology norm of self-realization goes beyond the modern Western *self* which is defined as an isolated ego striving primarily for hedonistic gratification or for a narrow sense of individual salvation in this life or the next. This socially programmed sense of the narrow self or social self dislocates us, and leaves us prey to whatever fad or fashion is prevalent in our society or social reference group. We are thus robbed of beginning the search for our unique spiritual/biological personhood. Spiritual growth, or unfolding, begins when we cease to understand or see ourselves as isolated and narrow competing egos and begin to identify with other humans from our family and friends to, eventually, our species. But the deep ecology sense of self requires a further maturity and growth, an identification which goes beyond humanity to include the nonhuman world. We must see beyond our narrow contemporary cultural assumptions and values, and the conventional wisdom of our time and place, and this is best achieved by the meditative deep questioning process. Only in this way can we hope to attain full mature personhood and uniqueness.

A nurturing nondominating society can help in the "real work" of becoming a whole person. The "real work" can be summarized symbolically as the realization of "self-in-Self" where "Self" stands for organic wholeness. This process of the full unfolding of the self can also be summarized by the phrase, "No one is saved until we are all saved," where the phrase "one" includes not only me, an individual human, but all humans, whales, grizzly bears, whole rain forest ecosystems, mountains and rivers, the tiniest microbes in the soil, and so on.

II. Biocentric Equality

The intuition of biocentric equality is that all things in the biosphere have an equal right to live and blossom and to reach their own individual forms of unfolding and self-realization within the larger Self-

FIGURE 5-1

Dominant Worldview	*Deep Ecology*
Dominance over Nature	Harmony with Nature
Natural environment as resource for humans	All nature has intrinsic worth/biospecies equality
Material/economic growth for growing human population	Elegantly simple material needs (material goals serving the larger goal of self-realization)
Belief in ample resource reserves	Earth "supplies" limited
High technological progress and solutions	Appropriate technology; nondominating science
Consumerism	Doing with enough/recycling
National/centralized community	Minority tradition/bioregion

realization. This basic intuition is that all organisms and entities in the ecosphere, as parts of the interrelated whole, are equal in intrinsic worth. Naess suggests that biocentric equality as an intuition is true in principle, although in the process of living, all species use each other as food, shelter, etc. Mutual predation is a biological fact of life, and many of the world's religions have struggled with the spiritual implications of this. Some animal liberationists who attempt to side-step this problem by advocating vegetarianism are forced to say that the entire plant kingdom including rain forests have no right to their own existence. This evasion flies in the face of the basic intuition of equality. Aldo Leopold expressed this intuition when he said humans are "plain citizens" of the biotic community, not lord and master over all other species.

Biocentric equality is intimately related to the all-inclusive Self-realization in the sense that if we harm the rest of Nature then we are harming ourselves. There are no boundaries and everything is interrelated. But insofar as we perceive things as individual organisms or entities, the insight draws us to respect all human and nonhuman individuals in their own right as parts of the whole without feeling the need to set up hierarchies of species with humans at the top.

The practical implications of this intuition or norm suggest that we should live with minimum rather than maximum impact on other species and on the Earth in general. Thus we see another aspect of our guiding principle: "simple in means, rich in ends." Further practical implications of these norms are discussed at length in chapters. . . .

A fuller discussion of the biocentric norm as it unfolds itself in practice begins with the realization that we, as individual humans, and as communities of humans, have vital needs which go beyond such basics as food, water, and shelter to include love, play, creative expression, intimate relationships with a particular landscape (or Nature taken in its entirety) as well as intimate relationships with other humans, and the vital need for spiritual growth, for becoming a mature human being.

Our vital material needs are probably more simple than many realize. In technocratic-industrial societies there is overwhelming propaganda and advertising which encourages false needs and destructive desires designed to foster increased production and consumption of goods. Most of this actually diverts us from facing reality in an objective way and from beginning the "real work" of spiritual growth and maturity. . . .

As a brief summary of our position thus far, figure 5-1 summarizes the contrast between the dominant worldview and deep ecology.

III. Basic Principles of Deep Ecology

. . .

Basic Principles

1. The well-being and flourishing of human and nonhuman Life on Earth have value in themselves (synonyms: intrinsic value, inherent value). These values are independent of the usefulness of the nonhuman world for human purposes.
2. Richness and diversity of life forms contribute to the realization of these values and are also values in themselves.
3. Humans have no right to reduce this richness and diversity except to satisfy *vital* needs.
4. The flourishing of human life and cultures is compatible with a substantial decrease of the human population. The flourishing of nonhuman life requires such a decrease.
5. Present human interference with the nonhuman world is excessive, and the situation is rapidly worsening.
6. Policies must therefore be changed. These policies affect basic economic, technological, and ideological structures. The resulting state of affairs will be deeply different from the present.
7. The ideological change is mainly that of appreciating *life quality* (dwelling in situations of inherent value) rather than adhering to an increasingly higher standard of living. There will be a profound awareness of the difference between big and great.
8. Those who subscribe to the foregoing points have an obligation directly or indirectly to try to implement the necessary changes.

Naess and Sessions Provide Comments on the Basic Principles:

RE (1). This formulation refers to the biosphere, or more accurately, to the ecosphere as a whole. This includes individuals, species, populations, habitat, as well as human and nonhuman cultures. From our current knowledge of all-pervasive intimate relationships, this implies a fundamental deep concern and respect. Ecological processes of the planet should, on the whole, remain intact. "The world environment should remain 'natural'" (Gary Snyder).

The term "life" is used here in a more comprehensive nontechnical way to refer also to what biologists classify as "nonliving"; rivers (watersheds), landscapes, ecosystems. For supporters of deep ecology, slogans such as "Let the river live" illustrate this broader usage so common in most cultures.

Inherent value as used in (1) is common in deep ecology literature. ("The presence of inherent value in a natural object is independent of any awareness, interest, or appreciation of it by a conscious being.")

RE (2). More technically, this is a formulation concerning diversity and complexity. From an ecological standpoint, complexity and symbiosis are conditions for maximizing diversity. So-called simple, lower, or primitive species of plants and animals contribute essentially to the richness and diversity of life. They have value in themselves and are not merely steps toward the so-called higher or rational life forms. The second principle presupposes that life itself, as a process over evolutionary time, implies an increase of diversity and richness. The refusal to acknowledge that some life forms have greater or lesser intrinsic value than others (see points 1 and 2) runs counter to the formulations of some ecological philosophers and New Age writers.

Complexity, as referred to here, is different from complication. Urban life may be more complicated than life in a natural setting without being more complex in the sense of multifaceted quality.

RE (3). The term "vital need" is left deliberately vague to allow for considerable latitude in judgment. Differences in climate and related factors, together with differences in the structures of societies as they now exist, need to be considered (for some Eskimos, snowmobiles are necessary today to satisfy vital needs).

People in the materially richest countries cannot be expected to reduce their excessive interference with the nonhuman world to a moderate level overnight. The stabilization and reduction of the human population will take time. Interim strategies need to be developed. But this in no way excuses the present complacency—the extreme seriousness of our current situation must first be realized. But the longer we wait the more drastic will be the measures needed. Until deep changes are made, substantial decreases in richness and diversity are liable to occur: the rate of extinction of species will be ten to one hundred times greater than any other period of earth history.

RE (4). The United Nations Fund for Population Activities in their State of World Population Report (1984) said that high human population growth rates (over 2.0 percent annum) in many developing countries "were diminishing the quality of life for many millions of people." During the decade 1974–1984, the world population grew by nearly 800 million—more than the size of India. "And we will be adding about one Bangladesh (population 93 million) per annum between now and the year 2000."

The report noted that "The growth rate of the human population has declined for the first time in human history. But at the same time, the number of people being added to the human population is bigger than at any time in history because the population base is larger."

Most of the nations in the developing world (including India and China) have as their official government policy the goal of reducing the rate of human population increase, but there are debates over the types of measures to take (contraception, abortion, etc.) consistent with human rights and feasibility.

The report concludes that if all governments set specific population targets as public policy to help alleviate poverty and advance the quality of life, the current situation could be improved.

As many ecologists have pointed out, it is also absolutely crucial to curb population growth in the so-called developed (i.e., overdeveloped) industrial societies. Given the tremendous rate of consumption and waste production of individuals in these societies, they represent a much greater threat and impact on the biosphere per capita than individuals in Second and Third World countries.

RE (5). This formulation is mild. For a realistic assessment of the situation, see the unabbreviated version of the I.U.C.N.'s *World Conservation Strategy*. There are other works to be highly recommended, such as Gerald Barney's *Global 2000 Report to the President of the United States*.

The slogan of "noninterference" does not imply that humans should not modify some ecosystems as do other species. Humans have modified the earth and will probably continue to do so. At issue is the nature and extent of such interference.

The fight to preserve and extend areas of wilderness or near-wilderness should continue and should focus on the general ecological functions of these areas (one such function: large wilderness areas are required in the biosphere to allow for continued evolutionary speciation of animals and plants). Most present designated wilderness areas and game preserves are not large enough to allow for such speciation.

RE (6). Economic growth as conceived and implemented today by the industrial states is incompatible with (1)–(5). There is only a faint resemblance between ideal sustainable forms of economic growth and present policies of the industrial societies. And "sustainable" still means "sustainable in relation to humans."

Present ideology tends to value things because they are scarce and because they have a commodity value. There is prestige in vast consumption and waste (to mention only several relevant factors).

Whereas "self-determination," "local community," and "think globally, act locally," will remain key terms in the ecology of human societies, nevertheless the implementation of deep changes requires increasingly global action—action across borders.

Governments in Third World countries (with

the exception of Costa Rica and a few others) are uninterested in deep ecological issues. When the governments of industrial societies try to promote ecological measures through Third World governments, practically nothing is accomplished (e.g., with problems of desertification). Given this situation, support for global action through nongovernmental international organizations becomes increasingly important. Many of these organizations are able to act globally "from grassroots to grassroots," thus avoiding negative governmental interference.

Cultural diversity today requires advanced technology, that is, techniques that advance the basic goals of each culture. So-called soft, intermediate, and alternative technologies are steps in this direction.

RE (7). Some economists criticize the term "quality of life" because it is supposed to be vague. But on closer inspection, what they consider to be vague is actually the nonquantitative nature of the term. One cannot quantify adequately what is important for the quality of life as discussed here, and there is no need to do so.

RE (8). There is ample room for different opinions about priorities: what should be done first, what next? What is most urgent? What is clearly necessary as opposed to what is highly desirable but not absolutely pressing? . . .

WILLIAM F. BAXTER

from *People or Penguins*

William F. Baxter is William Benjamin Scott and Luna M. Scott Professor of Law at Stanford University. (Source: From People or Penguins: The Case for Optimal Pollution, *New York: Columbia University Press. Copyright © 1974 by Columbia University Press. Reprinted by permission of the publisher.)*

QUESTIONS FOR REFLECTION

1. How does Baxter argue that only effects on humans should be counted in environmental calculations?
2. What is the problem of the commons?
3. What constraints should govern collective decisions about the environment, in Baxter's view?

. . . My criteria are oriented to people, not penguins. Damage to penguins, or sugar pines, or geological marvels is, without more, simply irrelevant. One must go further, by my criteria, and say: Penguins are important because people enjoy seeing them walk about rocks; and furthermore, the well-being of people would be less impaired by halting use of DDT than by giving up penguins. In short, my observations about environmental problems will be people-oriented, as are my criteria. I have no interest in preserving penguins for their own sake.

It may be said by way of objection to this position, that it is very selfish of people to act as if each person represented one unit of importance and nothing else was of any importance. It is undeniably selfish. Nevertheless I think it is the only tenable starting place for analysis for several reasons. First, no other position corresponds to the way most people really think and act—i.e., corresponds to reality.

Second, this attitude does not portend any massive destruction of nonhuman flora and fauna, for people depend on them in many obvious ways, and they will be preserved because and to the degree that humans do depend on them.

Third, what is good for humans is, in many respects, good for penguins and pine trees—clean air for example. So that humans are, in these respects, surrogates for plant and animal life.

Fourth, I do not know how we could administer any other system. Our decisions are either private or collective. Insofar as Mr. Jones is free to act privately, he may give such preferences as he wishes to other forms of life: he may feed birds in winter and do with less himself, and he may even decline to resist an advancing polar bear on the ground that the bear's appetite is more important than those portions of himself that the bear may choose to eat. In short my basic premise does not rule out private altruism to competing life-forms. It does rule out, however, Mr. Jones' inclination to feed Mr. Smith to the bear, however hungry the bear, however despicable Mr. Smith.

Insofar as we act collectively on the other hand, only humans can be afforded an opportunity to participate in the collective decisions. Penguins cannot vote now and are unlikely subjects for the franchise—pine trees more unlikely still. Again each individual is free to cast his vote so as to benefit sugar pines if that is his inclination. But many of the more extreme assertions that one hears from some conservationists amount to tacit assertions that they are specially appointed representatives of sugar pines, and hence that their preferences should be weighted more heavily than the preferences of other humans who do not enjoy equal rapport with "nature." The simplistic assertion that agricultural use of DDT must stop at once because it is harmful to penguins is of that type.

Fifth, if polar bears or pine trees or penguins, like men, are to be regarded as ends rather than means, if they are to count in our calculus of social organization, someone must tell me how much each one counts, and someone must tell me how these life-forms are to be permitted to express their preferences, for I do not know either answer. If the answer is that certain people are to hold their proxies, then I want to know how those proxy-holders are to be selected: self-appointment does not seem workable to me.

Sixth, and by way of summary of all the foregoing, let me point out that the set of environmental issues under discussion—although they raise very complex technical questions of how to achieve any objective—ultimately raise a normative question: what *ought* we to do. Questions of *ought* are unique to the human mind and world—they are meaningless as applied to a nonhuman situation.

I reject the proposition that we *ought* to respect the "balance of nature" or to "preserve the environment" unless the reason for doing so, express or implied, is the benefit of man.

I reject the idea that there is a "right" or "morally correct" state of nature to which we should return. The word "nature" has no normative connotation. Was it "right" or "wrong" for the earth's crust to heave in contortion and create mountains and seas? Was it "right" for the first amphibian to crawl up out of the primordial ooze? Was it "wrong" for plants to reproduce themselves and alter the atmospheric composition in favor of oxygen? For animals to alter the atmosphere in favor of carbon dioxide both by breathing oxygen and eating plants? No answers can be given to these questions because they are meaningless questions.

All this may seem obvious to the point of being tedious, but much of the present controversy over environment and pollution rests on tacit normative assumptions about just such nonnormative phenomena: that it is "wrong" to impair penguins with DDT, but not to slaughter cattle for prime rib roasts. That it is wrong to kill stands of sugar pines with industrial fumes, but not to cut sugar pines and build housing for the poor. Every man is entitled to his own preferred definition of Walden Pond, but there is no definition that has any moral superiority over another, except by reference to the selfish needs of the human race.

From the fact that there is no normative definition of the natural state, it follows that there is no normative definition of clean air or pure water—hence no definition of polluted air—or of pollution—except by reference to the needs of man. The "right" composition of the atmosphere is one which has some dust in it and some lead in it and some hydrogen sulfide in it—just those amounts that attend a sensibly organized society thoughtfully and knowledgeably pursuing the greatest possible satisfaction for its human members. . . .

3 / THE PROBLEM OF THE COMMONS AND ITS REGULATION

The problem of the commons is the primary source of our environmental and conservation difficulties. I want to develop that theme first with a particular historic example, and then with several current ones. The historic example has to do with the production of natural gas and petroleum. In the late 1920s and early 1930s there was widespread outcry about conservation practices in the petroleum industry—production rates were inordinately high and prices very depressed. These conditions then were widely thought to be just another aspect of the depression and that view still prevails in some quarters. However, I think these phenomena were largely independent of the depression, and I will offer you another view of them.

Natural Resources

Oil and gas are produced from underground pools subject to natural pressure that will drive the oil or gas up through the well once it has been drilled. If an individual or single company owned all the land overlying a petroleum pool, he would make certain calculations . . . about the rate at which he would produce from that pool. Basically, he would want to produce in a way that generated the largest possible difference between his costs and his revenues. How much oil should he take from the pool this year, how much next year, and so on, to attain this profit-maximizing goal? If too much oil is produced in the current year, the price will fall—eventually it will fall below the out-of-pocket costs of pumping it and getting it to market. Clearly production will be halted then. But there is a factor in addition to current market price and production costs that the owner will take into account. He would be foolish to produce and sell a barrel of oil this year for a dollar if he could sell that barrel next year for a substantially higher price—say, two dollars. Of course he would rather have a dollar of income this year than just a dollar of income next year; but depending on the level of prevailing interest rates, he would be indifferent between a dollar of income this year and perhaps $1.06 of income in the second year, and perhaps $1.13 of income in the third year, assuming a 6 percent interest rate. Thus he would leave oil in the ground whenever its future expected value exceeded present value by more than the interest rate.

In sum, such a unified producer would conserve his pool over time because he would recognize that there were two elements of cost to him of removing from the pool currently any given barrel of oil: (1) his out-of-pocket production cost; (2) a cost attributable to the foregone opportunity of selling that barrel at a subsequent point in time; and he would slow the rate of present exploitation so that the sum of these costs did not exceed prevailing price. Since the subsequent price will be higher than the present price in most extractive industries because of the expanding demands of the society for the minerals and because of the gradual depletion of our aggregate stock of minerals and the resultant scarcity, this consideration markedly reduces extraction rates. Since higher future market prices are discounted to present value by a compounded interest rate, current production occurs at a socially desirable rate if unified ownership exists.

However, at the time under consideration, it was not generally the case that a single individual or firm owned all of the surface rights that overlay the petroleum pool. It was far more common for a very large number of owners to have parcels overlying the pool. And the property laws of many of the states that were important petroleum producers at that time were not conducive to desirable rates of production. In effect the laws said that a man owned a barrel of petroleum when it came out of the ground through his well. Consequently, it was not sensible for any individual producer to think in terms of the foregone opportunity to produce a barrel of oil next year if he did not produce it this year. If he did not produce it this year, someone else was likely to pull it out through that person's well. And the consequence was a race among the competing producers overlying the field, each to produce as rapidly as possible and get as much as he could out through his well before others took it out through theirs.

The type of property rule involved in this situation is often referred to as a *rule of capture,* for obvious reasons. And as we shall see, a variant of the rule of capture continues to prevail in a large number of contexts. I think it is possible to make the general assertion that wherever a large number of independent persons or business entities, operating under a rule of capture, share in common access to a supply or inventory of an exhaustible resource, they will consume and exhaust that resource at an inappropriately rapid rate.

This particular aspect of the problem of the commons comes up in a variety of contexts, some profound and some mundane. Let me offer a trivial but, I think, amusing example. I have a perceptive colleague who takes some pleasure in finding earthy applications of important principles. I once heard him express the principle to which I have been referring in a form I now call "Barnett's Lunch Law." Barnett's Lunch Law goes as follows: If six or more people go to lunch, the bill is always divided evenly rather than apportioned on the basis of what each person actually ordered. Therefore if six or more people go to lunch, each, to assure that he is not cheated, will order the most expensive thing on the menu. As an aside I suggest to you that Barnett's Lunch Law has important application to the behavior of our state and federal legislatures, but elaboration of that application must await a differently titled publication.

Manufactured Goods

The preceding examples have shown that unduly high consumption rates are caused by common access to a stock of some natural resource. A different manifestation of the same basic problem appears where there is common access to a supply of goods which is not supplied by nature but must be brought into existence by private activity. In such circumstances, because the problem of the commons will operate after the supply is created, no one has adequate incentives to create the supply in the first place. Society's aggregate supply of knowledge or inventions is an example.

Compare the incentives confronting a man who has a choice between investing in a shoe factory and investing in research by which he hopes to discover a better mousetrap. If he invests in a shoe factory, there is no ambiguity about his ownership of the shoe factory, the shoes produced in it, and the proceeds that can be obtained by selling the shoes. He will invest $100 in a shoe factory if he expects that it will produce a stream of shoes that can be exchanged or sold for a stream of receipts that has a present value of more than $100. And that is also the socially optimum level of investment in shoe factories.

But if he considers investing $100 in discovering a better mousetrap, then in the absence of any special legal institution that will assist him, it is not at all clear that he will be able to produce mousetraps and exchange them for receipts, or other goods and services, that are commensurate with the value that other persons attach to having the better mousetrap that he has developed. The reason for this is that knowledge—knowledge in this case of how to build a better mousetrap—almost inevitably turns out to be something to which we all have common access. It will be difficult both to sell the new mousetrap and to keep his development secret; yet as soon as the secret is lost, others may copy his development and sell mousetraps in competition with him. Unlike him, however, the copiers will not have made the initial investment in development; competition will force prices down to the point where they are just adequate to cover his and his competitors' production costs. In all probability he will be unable to recover his development costs. This, of course, is precisely the problem to which our patent laws are addressed. There is every reason to expect, in a competitive economy, that the flow of investment into research and development would be far less than socially optimum unless we either had a patent system or, in the alternative, provided government subsidies for research and development.

This second aspect of the problem of commonality might be stated as follows: Where the fruits of investment will be commonly available for the benefit of all, then individual incentives to make such investments will be inadequate and the aggregate devotion of resources in the society to that form of investment will be less than optimum.

I do not mean to suggest that these two different aspects of the problem of the commons are profoundly different. They are opposite sides of the same coin, and in some contexts it is difficult to decide which is the more appropriate to describe the phenomenon that one is observing. Consider the use of the water in a lake, for example. There are many persons along its shores, each of whom is free to withdraw water for a variety of purposes. None has very strong incentives to conserve water, to use it sparingly. What one does not withdraw today someone may withdraw tomorrow. Neither does anyone have adequate incentives to invest in purification devices which would restore the water to its original clean state before it runs back into the lake by seepage or otherwise. Such an investment would be an investment in producing a clean lake, and a clean lake will be equally accessible to all so that the investor will experience private gains that are far less than the aggregate of the benefits that he has conferred upon the community as a whole by his investment in purification devices.

Let me try to state explicitly the point I have been driving at with this series of illustrations. Our environmental problems have many aspects. There are difficult scientific questions about what is harmful when it is dumped into our air or into our water. There are difficult medical and genetic questions involved in assessing the extent of harm caused by these agents even after they have been identified as harmful to some degree. There are enormously difficult engineering questions to be faced in altering the industrial or other processes by which those ingredients now are introduced in excessive amounts. But even after all these questions have been answered with as much certainty as will ever be possible, there remains the very difficult problem of creating adequate incentives on the part of individuals and companies to take full advantage of the knowledge that has been provided by the fields of science and engineering. This is so because invariably there will be substantial private costs that must be incurred in order to yield the benefits we desire, and yet the benefits will accrue to a very large number of very widely diversified individuals so that it will not be feasible to recover from each beneficiary a price that corresponds to the satisfaction conferred upon him. Therefore the person who engages in providing social benefits of this sort generally finds it impossible to gather for himself a revenue stream, to gather private benefits, adequate to compensate him for the private costs that he has incurred. The activity will take place to an insufficient extent.

Land Preservation

Let me take a series of contemporary environmental problems and offer more concrete illustrations of how these principles work out in practice. For a starter, take a problem that has no serious technological aspects: the question of preserving undeveloped some optimum amount of timber and grasslands in the foothills of the San Francisco peninsula. The case for having some quantity of such lands is very strong. All who live in the area derive aesthetic enjoyment from walking through them, even looking at them from our patios or as we drive past them on the highways. Such lands serve as sanctuaries for wildlife, which we enjoy in similar ways; and they help to preserve the equable climate of the area we all enjoy. But of course someone owns those lands and there are alternative uses to which they can be put. Let us assume that the alternative uses are less valuable to the community as a whole than is their retention in a wholly undeveloped state. The difficulty is that the private owners have practicable ways of obtaining a stream of private receipts from the lands when they are put into alternative uses, such as housing or industrial development, or even farming, or harvesting the timber that stands on the lands. But the owner has no practicable way of selling to each of us, i.e., exchanging for the goods and services that each of us produces, the benefits that would be conferred upon us if the lands were kept in the natural state—benefits we would happily pay for rather than forego. If there were some practicable way of billing each of us for the amount we would be willing to pay for those benefits, then our traditional market systems would make it privately profitable to retain the lands in the natural state precisely because, by our assumption, that is the use that creates the largest stream of benefits. But because of the enormous number of people involved, and because of the impossibility of denying benefits to those who do not pay, that possibility is purely theoretical.

In a situation such as this, collective action, generally through local government, is the only realistic alternative. No *precise* determination will ever be possible either of the amounts of lands, or which particular lands, should remain undeveloped. In principle development should be allowed to proceed until development of one more parcel would yield a stream of marketable benefits of lesser magnitude than the stream of unmarketable benefits that would be provided by keeping that next parcel undeveloped. When this point has been reached, development should be halted by governmental action since the interaction of market systems will not bring it to a halt. When that point has been reached must be determined by political means, and I say that with full recognition that such political determinations generally will yield far less accurate results than would private market exchanges if, contrary to fact, such exchanges represented a practicable possibility.

But these observations leave open some of the most important questions. How is development to be stopped? We must recognize that forbidding the development of land held by a private individual has the consequence of effecting an income transfer from him to all of the other members of the community who will enjoy the benefits of nondevelopment. Indeed, this is true even if we do not ordain complete nondevelopment but merely restrict the use to which he may put the land by zoning it. The situation is no different than if we took the land physically from him, perhaps to build a school, which would similarly confer benefits on the community as a whole as opposed to the prior landowner. We are accustomed to the notion that the community must condemn land, it must pay for the diminution of value it imposes on the prior owners, when it physically takes land for such purposes as school construction. Any other course is prohibited by one of the most fundamental and ancient of constitutional prohibitions: that property shall not be taken for public use without just compensation. The most obvious justification for that constitutional principle is to guard against the unfairness of substantial and selective income redistributions from particular individuals to members of the community as a whole.

But there is a second and in some ways even more important objective that underlies that constitutional provision: the basic justification for taking the land at all is that it is more valuable to the community (including the owner) in the new public use than it is to the community in the privately profitable use to which the owner would put it. If this justification is truly available with respect to a given parcel, then it follows that the community can afford to pay the owner the market value of the land. For by assumption, the aggregate benefits that the community has received are greater in amount than are the marketable benefits which he could have produced by the alternative use, and those marketable benefits determine the market value of the land. The requirement of compensation therefore imposes a test on the good faith of members of the community: do they really believe that the value of the land, when put to the public use, is greater than its private value? If they do, they gain by condemning it, even though they must pay. If they do not, they should not condemn it. Apart from the requirement of compensation, there is no limit on the extent to which a selfish majority in the community may appropriate for their own benefits the invested savings of fortuitously selected individuals.

There is still another reason why a community should proceed by way of condemnation. In any community not all lands will be developed simultaneously: first one parcel, then another is built upon, generally in the order in which the lands are best suited for development. When the point is reached at which development should stop, it makes eminently good sense that the parcels which happen to remain undeveloped be those selected to remain undeveloped indefinitely. Consider now a community in which the stopping point has not yet been reached. Consider the effect on incentives regarding development if all landholders in the community know that the rules of the game are to be that lands remaining undeveloped when the stopping point is reached will be taken without compensation. A very strong incentive for artificial development is created, an incentive to put the land to *some* commercial use, to assure that that parcel is not one of those whose private value is destroyed for the greater community good.

If the foothills are to be kept green, it is for the benefit of all of us who live here, and it is no more reasonable of us to expect to obtain those benefits without paying for the resources that confer them than it is for us to steal our food and clothing from the shelves of the local merchants.

Let me make one further observation—on the politics and income distribution effects of preserving undeveloped open spaces. The satisfactions that such lands provide are primarily aesthetic, and hence they must be seen as a kind of luxury good. If they are not in the same category as eight-year-old Scotch and European vacations, then certainly they fall near that end of the spectrum as opposed to basic food stuffs, clothing, and shelter. As is true of other luxury goods, the affluent, for perfectly sensible reasons, are prepared to devote not only more money but a much larger proportion of their disposable income to such goods, than are the poor. The decision to provide these satisfactions must be made politically—on something like a one-man, one-vote basis. Some quantity will be provided by government; that particular quantity will be available to all, and it will represent to each of us some particular fraction of his total of satisfactions. In terms of its social cost, although not in terms of the subjective satisfaction it yields, that quantity of environmental amenity will represent a much larger fraction of the total consumption of the poor than of the rich—precisely the opposite of the ratio which those income groups would choose to buy if the amenity was available on a free market. This much is inevitable; it is quite typical of political decisions with respect to resource use, that they are not susceptible to the degree of individuation that market decisions afford. The great advantage of free markets, which unfortunately will not work in this context, is that they afford each man the freedom to make his own choices on the basis of his own tastes. Not only the decision to provide *some* such satisfactions through undeveloped lands, but also the decision whether to provide somewhat more or somewhat less will be made politically; and the potential for conflict between different income groups is obvious. The rich will be disposed toward more of this luxury good and the poor toward less. Indeed, this conflict is already quite apparent in our political dialogues. Hardly a day passes that some black action group does not label the pursuit of environmental amenities a political cop-out designed to distract attention from their much more fundamental needs.

These facts have obvious implications for the kind of tax system by which the public acquisition of these amenities should be financed: it should be a distinctly progressive tax system, not only because payments will then be more nearly commensurate with benefits derived, but because such financing will diminish inter–income-group conflict and will diminish political resistance to the provision of such amenities and in the long run will enable us to have a larger, perhaps approximately optimum, amount of them.

Health Care

Individual decisions about health—about whether to undergo an operation, or to undergo chemotherapy, or even to exercise and lose weight—can have large impacts. Lives may be lengthened or shortened. The quality of those lives may change for better or for worse. Health is easy to take for granted, but its importance becomes obvious as soon as we get sick. Our health affects not only our current happiness but what we can reasonably expect from the future.

If individual decisions about health have great importance, collective decisions about the health care system have even greater significance. Improvements in the availability and quality of health care can benefit vast numbers of people. Declines in availability and quality can similarly harm vast numbers. Proposals for changes in health care—including proposals for universal health coverage, on which this section will focus—thus call out for utilitarian analysis. That is not to say that only utilitarian considerations matter—questions of dignity, needs, rights, and justice arise as well. But the costs and benefits of proposed changes are very large factors.

Many people are aware of the problems afflicting the current health care system in the United States. Many people are uninsured or underinsured; many people do not receive treatment for serious health problems. Costs are high and rising rapidly. And current ways of addressing these difficulties create further problems of inefficiency and unfairness. We must, many conclude, provide universal access to a reasonable level of health care for everyone.

The Health Security Act, popularly known as the Clinton plan, was proposed in 1993 and debated and ultimately rejected by Congress in 1994. The selections here explain the rationale and key features of the plan, designed to provide universal health care coverage through a system of regional alliances.

Fred Barnes maintains that discussions of health care reform typically confuse lack of health insurance with lack of health care. People who are uninsured, Barnes points out, do get care under current arrangements.

They may not get care as good or as efficient as the insured, but they do not lie bleeding in the streets. Barnes contends that the present U.S. health care system successfully meets the needs of the population, whether or not they are insured.

Norman Daniels and Daniel Callahan debate the issue on a more abstract level. Daniels argues that health care is a fundamental need that society ought to meet, guaranteeing everyone a fair equality of opportunity to health care. Callahan disagrees, maintaining that the line between needs and aspirations is blurred, and that trying to meet everyone's health care needs leads to endlessly spiraling costs.

Selections from the *Health Security Act*

Known as "the Clinton plan," the Health Security Act was debated and ultimately rejected by Congress in 1994.

QUESTIONS FOR REFLECTION

1. What are the chief purposes of the act?
2. What features of the Act are intended to reduce health care costs? Would they succeed, in your opinion? Do they have any disadvantages?
3. How would the act provide universal coverage? What alternatives might achieve the same goal?
4. How much choice would the act allow individual patients and doctors?
5. What effects might the act have on the quality of medical care?
6. Discuss the act's basic normative assumptions.

Sec. 2. Findings.

The Congress finds as follows:

(1) Under the current health care system in the United States—

(A) individuals risk losing their health care coverage when they move, when they lose or change jobs, when they become seriously ill, or when the coverage becomes unaffordable;

(B) continued escalation of health care costs threatens the economy of the United States, undermines the international competitiveness of the Nation, and strains Federal, State, and local budgets;

(C) an excessive burden of forms, paperwork, and bureaucratic procedures confuses consumers and overwhelms health care providers;

(D) fraud and abuse sap the strength of the health care system; and

(E) health care is a critical part of the economy of the United States and interstate commerce, consumes a significant percentage of public and private spending, and affects all industries and individuals in the United States.

(2) Under any reform of the health care system—

(A) health insurance and high quality health care should be secure, uninterrupted, and affordable for all individuals in the United States;

(B) comprehensive health care benefits that meet the full range of health needs, including primary, preventive, and specialized care, should be available to all individuals in the United States;

(C) the current high quality of health care in the United States should be maintained;

(D) individuals in the United States should be afforded a meaningful opportunity to choose among a range of health plans, health care providers, and treatments;

(E) regulatory and administrative burdens should be reduced;

(F) the rapidly escalating costs of health care should be contained without sacrificing high quality or impeding technological improvements;

(G) competition in the health care industry should ensure that health plans and health care providers are efficient and charge reasonable prices;

(H) a partnership between the Federal Government and each State should allow the State and its local communities to design an effective, high-quality system of care that serves the residents of the State;

(I) all individuals should have a responsibility to pay their fair share of the costs of health care coverage;

(J) a health care system should build on the strength of the employment-based coverage arrangements that now exist in the United States;

(K) the penalties for fraud and abuse should be swift and severe; and

(L) an individual's medical information should remain confidential and should be protected from unauthorized disclosure and use.

Sec. 3. Purposes.

The purposes of this Act are as follows:

(1) To guarantee comprehensive and secure health care coverage.

(2) To simplify the health care system for consumers and health care professionals.

(3) To control the cost of health care for employers, employees, and others who pay for health care coverage.

(4) To promote individual choice among health plans and health care providers.

(5) To ensure high quality health care.

(6) To encourage all individuals to take responsibility for their health care coverage.

TITLE I—HEALTH CARE SECURITY

Subtitle A—Universal Coverage and Individual Responsibility

Part 1—Universal Coverage

Sec. 1001. Entitlement to Health Benefits.

(a) IN GENERAL.—In accordance with this part, each eligible individual is entitled to the comprehensive benefit package under subtitle B through the applicable health plan in which the individual is enrolled consistent with this title.

(b) HEALTH SECURITY CARD.—Each eligible individual is entitled to a health security card to be issued by the alliance or other entity that offers the applicable health plan in which the individual is enrolled.

(c) ELIGIBLE INDIVIDUAL DEFINED.—In this Act, the term "eligible individual" means an individual who is residing in the United States and who is—

(1) a citizen or national of the United States;

(2) an alien permanently residing in the United States under color of law (as defined in section 1902(1)); or

(3) a long-term nonimmigrant (as defined in section 1902(19)).

(d) TREATMENT OF MEDICARE-ELIGIBLE INDIVIDUALS.—Subject to section 1012(a), a medicare-eligible individual is entitled to health benefits under the medicare program instead of the entitlement under subsection (a).

(e) TREATMENT OF PRISONERS.—A prisoner (as defined in section 1902(26)) is entitled to health care services provided by the authority responsible for the prisoner instead of the entitlement under subsection (a).

Sec. 1002. Individual Responsibilities.

(a) IN GENERAL.—In accordance with this Act, each eligible individual (other than a medicare-eligible individual)—

(1) must enroll in an applicable health plan for the individual, and

(2) must pay any premium required, consistent with this Act, with respect to such enrollment.

(b) LIMITATION ON DISENROLLMENT.—No eligible individual shall be disenrolled from an applicable health plan until the individual—

(1) is enrolled under another applicable health plan, or

(2) becomes a medicare-eligible individual.

Sec. 1003. Protection of Consumer Choice.

Nothing in this Act shall be construed as prohibiting the following:

(1) An individual from purchasing any health care services.

(2) An individual from purchasing supplemental insurance (offered consistent with this Act) to cover health care services not included within the comprehensive benefit package.

(3) An individual who is not an eligible individual from purchasing health insurance (other than through a regional alliance).

(4) Employers from providing coverage for benefits in addition to the comprehensive benefit package (subject to part 2 of subtitle E).

[. . .]

Part 4—Exclusions

Sec. 1141. Exclusions.

(a) MEDICAL NECESSITY.— The comprehensive benefit package does not include—

(1) an item or service (other than services referred to in paragraph (2)) that is not medically necessary or appropriate; or

(2) an item or service that the National Health Board may determine is not medically necessary or appropriate in a regulation promulgated under section 1154.

FRED BARNES

What Health Care Crisis?

Fred Barnes is a senior editor of The New Republic. *(Source: From* The American Spectator *[May 1993], pp. 20–23.*

QUESTIONS FOR REFLECTION

1. Barnes asserts that there is a big difference between having no health insurance and not having access to health care. Explain.
2. How does Barnes argue that U.S. health care is the world's best? Do you find his arguments persuasive?
3. How does Barnes criticize rival health care systems?
4. What, according to Barnes, are the real problems facing the U.S. health care system?

Bill and Hillary Clinton have contributed heavily to a national myth. Mrs. Clinton, as boss of the administration task force plotting to overhaul America's health-care system, refers routinely to "the health-care crisis." Her husband uses the same phrase ("Our government will never again be fully solvent until we tackle the health-care crisis," Clinton declared in his State of the Union address on February 17). And he goes one step further. "A lot of Americans don't have health insurance," he told a group of schoolkids February 20 during a nationally televised children's town meeting at the White House. "You know that, don't you? A lot of Americans don't have health care."

The press also trumpets the crisis theme. *Parade,* the popular Sunday supplement, emblazoned its February 28 cover with this headline: "THE GROWING CRISIS IN HEALTH CARE." The result is that the American people, despite their personal experience, now believe there actually is a health-care crisis. Most opinion polls show roughly three-quarters of Americans are satisfied with the availability and quality of the health care they receive. Yet, in most polls, 60 to 70 percent feel the health-care system is failing and needs significant, if not radical, reform.

There is no health-care crisis. It's a myth. If millions of seriously ill Americans were being denied medical care, that *would* be a crisis. But that's not happening. Everyone gets health care in this country—the poor, the uninsured, everyone. No, our health-care system isn't perfect. There isn't enough primary care—regular doctor's visits—for many Americans. Emergency rooms are often swamped. The way hospitals and doctors are financed is sometimes bizarre. Health care may (or may not) be too costly. But it's the best health care system in the world—not arguably the best, but the best. Its shortcomings can be remedied by tinkering, or at least by less-than-comprehensive changes. An overhaul of the sort Hillary Clinton envisions is not only unnecessary, it's certain to reduce, not expand, the amount of health care Americans receive (price controls always lead to less of the controlled commodity). Then we really will have a health-care crisis.

You don't have to take my word that there's no crisis now and that health care here is the world's best. There's solid evidence. Let's examine four key aspects of the health care debate: access, false measures of quality health care, true measures, and how America's system compares with those of other industrialized democracies (Canada, Germany, Japan, Great Britain).

Access

Will someone please tell Bill Clinton that having no health insurance is not the same as having no health care? The uninsured get health care, only less of it than the insured. Being uninsured means "one is more likely to use emergency-room care and less likely to use office, clinic, or regular inpatient care," said Richard Darman, President Bush's budget director, in congressional testimony in 1991. "This is not to suggest that this is desirable. It is not." But it *is* high-quality health care.

Doctors in emergency rooms are specialists. In fact, they have a professional organization, the American College of Emergency Physicians. Its motto is: "Our specialty is devoted to treating everyone in need, no questions asked." Turning away patients isn't an option. Federal law (section 9121 of the Consolidated Omnibus Budget Reconciliation Act of 1985) requires medical screening of everyone requesting care at a hospital emergency room. If treatment is needed, it must be provided. What this adds up to is "universal access" to health care in America, as one head of a hospital board told me.

It's no secret how much health care the uninsured get. The American Hospital Association estimated in 1991 that hospitals provide $10 billion in uncompensated care annually. Another study found that the 16.6 percent of the nonelderly population who are uninsured—36.3 million people—accounted for 11 percent of the nation's personal health-care expenditures in 1988. They had 37 percent fewer sessions with doctors and 69 percent fewer days in the hospital. There's a reason the uninsured get less health care, beyond the fact most work in low-paying jobs without health insurance. The uninsured tend to be young, thus healthy. According to a new poll by Frederick/Schneiders, 39 percent are 18–29 years of age and another 25 percent are 30–39. By the way, the elderly (65 and up), who require more medical care, are covered. Ninety-nine percent are eligible for Medicare.

To make sure we really have universal access, I checked on how victims of the most recent epidemic, AIDS, are treated. These are the folks doctors are supposed to be leery of dealing with.

What if a penniless AIDS patient shows up at, say, the Whitman-Walker Clinic in Washington, D.C.? That patient, even if indigent, gets treatment. When the time comes (T-cell count below 500), the patient is started on AZT, which costs about $5,000 a year. Later, the patient gets expensive, experimental drugs: DDI, DDC, D-4T. The drugs are paid for mostly by federal funds. There's also doctor care, painkillers, laboratory work. To prevent infections or complications, the patient is treated with prophylaxis.

A friend of mine volunteered to help an indigent, bedridden AIDS patient. He was amazed at the level of care. "It was an endless supply of extremely sophisticated drugs, an elaborate IV system [to feed the patient], and eventually a five-day-a-week home help nurse," my friend said. "Sometimes we had so much medicine, we had to throw it away. There was never a sense we'd be left in the lurch." The patient had no insurance. He lived with a boyfriend, but the boyfriend was not required to pay for any of the care. The federal and city governments—the taxpayers—footed the bill. The American Medical Association says "lifetime medical care" for a single AIDS patient costs $102,000.

False Tests

Judging by the two most common measures of health, life expectancy at birth and the infant mortality rate, health care in the United States is not the best or even among the best. In 1990, life expectancy in America was 72 years for males, 78.8 for women. This put the U.S. behind Canada, France, Germany, Italy, Japan, and Great Britain, among others. On infant mortality, the U.S. fared still worse, ranking nineteenth in 1989 with a rate of 9.7. (The infant mortality rate is the number of deaths of children under one year of age, divided by the number of births in a given year, multiplied by 1,000.) Finland, Spain, Ireland, East Germany, and Italy finished higher.

What's wrong with these measures? Just this: they're a reflection of health, not the health-care system. Life expectancy is determined by much more than the quality of a nation's health care. Social factors affect life expectancy, and this is where the U.S. runs into trouble. "Exacerbated social problems . . . adversely affect U.S. health outcomes," noted three Department of Health and Human Services officials in the fall 1992 issue of *Health Care Financing Review.* "The 20,000 annual U.S. homicides result in per capita homicide rates 10 times those of Great Britain and 4 times those of Canada. There are 100 assaults reported by U.S. emergency rooms for every homicide. About 25 percent of spinal cord injuries result from assaults." And so on. The incidence of AIDS is even more telling. Through June 1992, there were 230,179 reported AIDS cases here, two-thirds of whom have died. Japan, where life expectancy is four years longer for men than in the U.S. and three years longer for women, has had fewer than 300 AIDS cases. Once social factors have played out, the U.S. ranks at the top in life expectancy. At age 80, when most people are highly dependent on the health-care system, Americans have the longest life expectancy (7.1 years for men, 9.0 for women) in the world.

The infant mortality rate (IMR) is also "reflective of health and socioeconomic status and not just health care," wrote four Urban Institute scholars in the summer 1992 issue of *Health Care Financing Review.* And there are measurement problems. Many countries make no effort to save very-low-birth-weight infants. They aren't recorded as "live born" and aren't counted in infant mortality statistics. In contrast, American hospitals make heroic efforts in neonatal intensive care, saving some infants, losing others, and driving up the IMR. "The more resources a country's health-care system places on saving high-risk newborns, the more likely its registration will report a higher IMR," according to the Urban Institute scholars.

Social factors probably have a bigger impact. A poverty rate twice Canada's and Germany's, a rash of drug-exposed babies, a high incidence of unmarried teenage pregnancy—all lead to low-birth-weight infants and affect the IMR. "Infant mortality rates of babies born to unmarried mothers are about two times higher than the rates of babies born to married mothers," the scholars write. The point is not that America's high IMR is excusable, but that it's grown to abnormal levels in large part because of factors unrelated to the quality of health care.

Not only that. The entire medical system bears the brunt of social and behavioral problems that are far worse in the U.S. than in other industrialized democracies. "We have a large number of people who indulge in high-risk behavior," says Leroy L. Schwartz, M.D., of Health Policy International, a non-profit research group in Princeton, New Jersey. Behavioral problems become health problems: AIDS, drug abuse, assaults and violence, sexually transmitted diseases, etc. "The problem is not the health-care system," says Dr. Schwartz. "The problem is the people. Every year the pool of pathology in this country is getting bigger and bigger. We think we can take care of everything by calling it a health problem." But we can't.

Real Tests

While primary and preventive care are important, the best measure of a health-care system is how well it treats the seriously ill. What if you've got an enlarged prostate? Your chances of survival are better if you're treated here. The U.S. death rate from prostate trouble is one-seventh the rate in Sweden, one-fourth that in Great Britain, one-third that in Germany. Sweden, Great Britain, and Germany may have higher incidences of prostate illness, but not high enough to account for the wide disparity in death rates.

An ulcer of the stomach or intestine? The death rate per 100,000 persons is 2.7 in the U.S., compared to 2.8 in the Netherlands, 3.1 in Canada, 4.9 in Germany, 7.6 in Sweden, and 8 in Great Britain. A hernia or intestinal obstruction? The American death rate is 1.7. It's 2 in Canada, 2.7 in Germany, 3 in the Netherlands, 3.1 in Great Britain, and 3.2 in Sweden. Can these be attributed solely to varying incidences of ulcers and obstructions? Nope.

I could go on, and I will. The overall death rate from cancer is slightly higher in America than in Sweden or Germany, but lower than in Canada, the Netherlands, and Great Britain. But for specific cancers, the U.S. has the lowest death rate: stomach cancer, cervical cancer, uterine cancer. Only Sweden has a lower death rate from breast cancer. The U.S. also has the second lowest death rate from heart attack. No matter what the disease—epilepsy, hypertension, stroke, bronchitis—the U.S. compares well. For a country with a heterogeneous population and large pockets of pathology, this is remarkable. Life expectancy for American males at 65 is 14.7 years, only a tad less than Canada (15), Sweden (14.9), and Switzerland (14.9), more homogeneous countries with fewer social problems. (I'm grateful to Dr. Schwartz for all these figures.)

Another measure that's important is the proliferation of new technology. "Major medical technology has had a profound impact on modern medicine and promises even greater impact in the future," wrote Dale A. Rublee, an expert in cross-national health policy comparisons for the AMA's Center for Health Policy Research, in *Health Affairs*. He compared the availability of six technologies—open-heart surgery, cardiac catheterization, organ transplantation, radiation therapy, extracorporeal shock wave lithotripsy, and magnetic resonance imaging—in the U.S., Canada, and Germany in 1987. "Canada and Germany were selected because their overall health-care resources are fairly comparable to the United States," Rublee wrote. The U.S. came out ahead in every category, way ahead in several. In MRI's, the U.S. had 3.69 per one million people, Germany 0.94, Canada 0.46. For open-heart surgery, the U.S. had 3.26, Canada 1.23, Germany 0.74. For radiation therapy, the U.S. had 3.97, Germany 3.13, Canada 0.54. Small wonder that, as Rublee put it, "American physicians, with a universe of modern technology at their fingertips, are the envy of the world's physicians."

Rival Systems

Canadian politicians get special health care privileges, moving to the head of waiting lists or getting treatment at the elite National Defence Medical Centre. But that wasn't sufficient for Robert Bourassa, the premier of Quebec. He came to the National Cancer Institute in Bethesda, Maryland, for diagnosis, then returned to the U.S. for surgery, all at his own expense.

The Canadian health-care system has many nice attributes, but speedy treatment isn't one of them. Ian R. Munro, M.D., a Canadian doctor who emigrated to the U.S., wrote in *Reader's Digest* last September of a young boy in Canada who needed open-heart surgery to free the blood flow to his lungs. He was put on a waiting list. He got a surgery date only after news reports embarrassed health officials. After waiting two months, he died four hours before surgery. This was an extreme case, but waiting is common in the Canadian system, in which the government pays all costs, including set fees for private doctors. A study by the Fraser Institute in 1992 found that 250,000 people are awaiting medical care at any given time. "It is not uncommon for patients to wait months or even years for treatments such as cataract operations, hip replacements, tonsillectomies, gallbladder surgery, hysterectomies, heart operations, and major oral surgery," according to Edmund F. Haislmaier, the Heritage Foundation's health-care expert. Canada has other problems: health costs are rising faster than in the U.S., hospital beds and surgical rooms are dwindling, and doctors are fleeing (8,263 were practicing in the U.S. in 1990).

The Japanese model isn't any better. When Louis Sullivan, M.D., President Bush's secretary of health and human services, visited Japan, he was surprised to find medical care matched that of the U.S.—the U.S. of the 1950s. Japan has universal access and emphasizes primary care at clinics, financed mostly through quasi-public insurance companies. The problem is price controls. "Providers seek to maximize their revenue by seeing more patients," wrote Naoki Ikegami, professor of health at Keio University in Tokyo. "This dilutes the services provided."

Patients receive assembly-line treatment. "In outpatient care, a clinic physician sees an average of 49 patients per day [and] 13 percent see more than 100," Ikegami said. For the elderly, a survey found, the average number of doctor's visits for a six-month period was 17.3 (3.6 here) and the length of visits was 12 minutes (30 in the U.S.). Like Canada's queues, this is an extraordinarily inefficient way to dispense care. Patients return repeatedly to get the same care that in the U.S. is given in a single visit.

Japanese doctors also prescribe and sell drugs. Not surprisingly, they sell plenty. Thirty percent of the country's health expenditures are for drugs (7 percent in the U.S.). In Japan, wrote Ikegami, "no real incentives exist to maintain quality." The one exception is specialists at Japan's teaching hospitals. To avoid queues, patients pay bribes of $1,000 to $3,000 to be admitted to a private room and treated by a senior specialist.

Germany also has strict fees for doctors, with predictable results. Annual doctor's visits per capita are 11.5 (5.3 here), a figure exceeded only by Japan (12.9). In other words, price controls are as inefficient in Germany as in Japan. Hospitals face perverse incentives, too. The government pays a fixed rate per day, regardless of the patient's illness or length of stay. So hospitals pad their billings by keeping patients for unnecessarily long recuperations, which compensates for the losses they incur taking care of critically ill patients.

Then there's Great Britain, home of the National Health Service. Officials take great pride in having reduced the number of patients waiting more than two years for medical attention. In 1986, the number was 90,000; in 1991, 50,000. In April 1992, it was down to 1,600. Sounds great, but there's a catch. The number of patients waiting six months or less grew by 10 percent. The overall drop in waiting lists was only three percent. And this was achieved, a survey by the National Association of Health Authorities and Trusts found, chiefly because of a 13 percent hike in NHS spending in 1991, not increased efficiency. The good news in Great Britain is that private insurance is allowed and 6.6 million Brits have it. Insurance firms encourage beneficiaries to have an operation or other treatment in a private hospital. Sure, the company pays, but it knows that once a patient has experienced care in a private hospital, he'll never go back to the socialized medicine of NHS. And he'll keep buying health insurance. Private hospitals, anxious to fill empty beds, have their own come-on. At Christmas, they offer discount prices for operations.

In truth, the U.S. has little but painful lessons to learn from the health-care experience of other countries. There's practically nothing to emulate. On the contrary, foreign health officials, Germans especially, now look at the incentives in the American medical system as a way to remedy problems in their health care systems. Hillary Clinton and health policy wonks should stop apologizing for our system.

They won't. The existence of a few health care problems, chiefly the lack of proper primary care for several million Americans, allows them to declare a crisis and go on wartime footing. Liberals love this. Hillary's task force meets in private, keeps the names of its members secret, obsesses over leaks, spurns the advice of outsiders (doctors, Republicans). The program that emerges is sure to dwarf the problem. If enacted, it will make the problem worse. This is a common phenomenon in Washington. Some people never learn.

In 1991, an American official addressed Russian health experts in Moscow. He bemoaned that many Americans get care at emergency rooms and occasionally wait six or eight hours. To the American's shock, the Russians erupted in laughter. In Russia, with twice as many doctors per capita as the U.S., a wait of six to eight hours represented unusually fast service.

NORMAN DANIELS

from *Just Health Care*

Norman Daniels is Professor of Philosophy at Tufts University. (Source: Just Health Care, *Cambridge: Cambridge University Press, 1985. Notes have been omitted.*

QUESTIONS FOR REFLECTION

1. What requirements must a theory of health care needs fulfill?
2. How does Daniels distinguish needs that should be met by society from less urgent and fundamental needs?
3. Discuss Daniels's biomedical model of disease and health. Can you think of any problems that an advocate of the model must solve?
4. What does a fair equality of opportunity require of a health care system, in Daniels's view?

2 / HEALTH-CARE NEEDS

. . . A theory of health-care needs must come to grips with two widely held judgments: that there is something especially important about health care, and that some kinds of health care are more important than others. The philosophical task is to assess, explain, and justify or modify these distinctions we make about the importance of different wants, interests, or needs. Before turning to this task, it will be useful to consider one further objection to my strategy.

Can We Avoid Talk About Needs?

Many people view the notion of needs as vague and problematic and would prefer we avoid talk about them in favor of talk about preferences and strength of preferences. For example, the latter are the notions given prominence in welfare economics. Consider the following Argument From Fair Shares, which is intended to show that we can avoid talk about health care needs: Suppose we agreed to abide by a particular theory of distributive justice, and we knew that we each had a *fair income share* according to that theory. Suppose further that there was a *competitive medical market* in which a variety of insurance schemes could be bought, much as many US employees have a choice between enrolling in one of several pre-paid group plans (health maintenance organizations) or various traditional insurance schemes (Blue Cross/ Blue Shield, Aetna, etc.). Then we could protect ourselves against the risk of needing health care through voluntary purchase of insurance. We would each be responsible for buying insurance at a level of protection we desired. No one, except children or the congenitally handicapped, would have a *claim* on *social* resources to meet health-care needs. Each would be entitled—whatever his needs—only to what he was prudent enough to purchase from his fair income share, though charity might intervene to keep people from dying in the streets. In this market (so the argument assumes), demand, understood as our preferences for different insurance packages, will be *efficiently* matched to supply, understood as resources and services.

Such a system would provide protection against expensive but rare needs for health care, for which relatively inexpensive insurance could be bought. Similarly, common but inexpensive services could either be risk-shared through insurance or paid for out-of-pocket without great sacrifice, whichever might be preferred. But expensive and potentially common "needs"—for example, to be provided with artificial hearts or dialysis—would not become a drain on social resources. Individuals who want protection against facing these "needs" would have to buy expensive insurance out of their own fair shares. This way of meeting individual preferences for health services would not create a bottomless pit into which we are forced to drain all available social resources. No one could claim a right to have extravagant "needs" met—unless he had already bought appropriate insurance. Most importantly, in such a system we would need no general theory about which health-care needs we have social obligations to meet. The scheme allows individual preferences to resolve all resource allocation questions through a medical market.

This Argument From Fair Shares fails to show that we can do without a theory of health-care needs. Suppose we define a *reasonable* health-care insurance package as one which meets the health-care needs or risks it is rational for a prudent person to insure against. Though we know little else about "fair income shares," it seems plausible to insist that an income share is *fair only* if it is adequate to permit the purchase of a reasonable insurance package. If an income share is too small to cover the premium for a reasonable insurance package, then the share is inadequate: it is *unfair* that whoever has it cannot buy reasonable insurance. So, to know whether income shares are fair, we must know that they can buy reasonable coverage. But to know what coverage is reasonable, we need to know what health-care needs it is prudent to insure against. Thus we must talk about health-care needs after all! We cannot reduce the problem of just health care distribution to the problem of just income distribution, for the latter *presupposes income adequate to meet reasonable needs.*

My response to the Argument From Fair Shares is itself open to the following objection: There is no level of insurance which is "prudent" for all persons. What is prudent for an individual, so the objection goes, depends on his resources, needs, and preferences. The rich will not insure against all risks and the poor will prudently accept greater risks. So there is no sense to the notion of a "reasonable" health-care insurance package since there is no one package any prudent person would want to buy.

The kernel of truth to this objection is that prudent choices will vary with resource constraints, though not as drastically as is claimed. If the objection were the full story, then we would have to treat all cases of people excluded from certain markets—for food, clothing, shelter, and health care, for example—not as instances of "market failure" calling for income redistribution or aid-in-kind, but as instances of prudent choices made by the poor not to buy these goods. Our notion of prudence has a structure to it which reflects our concern for meeting certain basic needs, and we cannot use the notion in a way that ignores the difference between being able to participate in a market for those needs and being excluded from it. Indeed, we would probably be correct in saying that exclusion from the market for those needs denies people the chance to act prudently. For the purpose of my argument, then, we might acknowledge that the notion of a prudent person is hypothetical or abstract: not just any rational choice, given drastic resource limitations, counts as the choice a prudent person would make. My original conclusion still stands: The notion of a fair income share presupposes income adequate to meet reasonable health-care needs. . . .

Not All Preferences Are Created Equal

The conclusion of the preceding argument is that we must talk about health-care *needs* if we are to explain what is special about health care and thus be in a position to give an account of distributive justice for it. But the concept of needs has been in philosophical disrepute, and with good reason. The concept seems both too weak and too strong to get us very far toward a theory of distributive justice. Too many things become needs, and too few. And finding a middle ground seems to involve many of the issues of distributive justice one might hope to resolve by appeal to a clear notion of needs.

It is easy to see why too many things appear to be needs, for the concept is opportunistic. Without abuse of language, we refer to the means necessary to reach any of our goals as "needs." To reawaken memories of Miller's, the neighborhood delicatessen of my childhood, I need only the smell of sour pickles in a barrel. To stay at Cape Cod in August, I need a reservation. For emphasis, we often refer to things we simply desire or want as things we need: my son Noah insists he *needs* the latest space-fantasy action figure. Sometimes we invoke a distinction between noun and verb uses of "need," so that not everything we say we need counts as *a need.* But any conceptual distinction we might draw between noun and verb uses depends on our purposes and the context, and it would still require an explanation of the kind sought here. Since the concept of needs is so unabashedly expansive, the problem of the importance of needs seems to reduce to the problem of the importance or urgency of preferences or wants in general. (I leave aside the fact that not all the things we need are even expressed as preferences.)

Just as not all preferences are on a par—some are more important than others—so too not all the things we say we need are. It is possible to pick out various things we say we need, including needs for health care, which play a special role and are given special moral weight in a variety of moral contexts. If, in requesting $200, I appeal to my friend's duty to act beneficently, I will most likely get a quite different reaction if I tell him I need the money to get some root-canal work than if I tell him I need the money to go to the Brooklyn neighborhood of my childhood to smell pickles in a barrel. Indeed, it is not likely to matter in his assessment of *obligations* that I strongly *prefer* to go to Brooklyn. Nor is it likely to matter that I insist I feel a great *need* to reawaken memories of my childhood—I am overcome by nostalgia. Of course, he might give me the money for either purpose, but if he gives it so I can smell pickles, we would probably say he is not doing it out of any duty at all, that he feels no obligation, that it is just friendly generosity. Similarly, if my appeal was directed to some (even Utopian) social welfare agency rather than my friend, it would adopt criteria other than my mere preferences in assessing the importance of my request.

Part of what is going on here is that in certain contexts we use an *objective* rather than a *subjective* criterion in assessing well-being. . . . We need *some* such criterion to assess the importance of competing claims on resources in a variety of moral contexts. A *subjective* criterion uses the individual's own assessment of how well-off he is with and without the claimed benefit to determine the importance of his preference or claim. An *objective* criterion invokes a measure of importance independent of an individual's own assessment, i.e., independent of the individual's strength of preference for the benefit. In contexts of distributive justice and other moral contexts, we *in fact* appeal to some *objective* criteria of well-being. But it is important to see that it is not just a question of rejecting subjective criteria in favor of objective ones, say on the grounds that we can have better knowledge of them. The rejection is not epistemological. What counts is the *kind* of objective criteria we invoke. . . .

. . . Our philosophical task will be to characterize the relevant categories of needs in a way that *explains* two central properties they have. First, they are *objectively ascribable.* We can ascribe them to someone even if he does not realize he has them or even if he denies he does because his preferences run contrary to his needs. Second, and of greater interest to us, these needs are *objectively important:* we attach a special weight to claims based on them in a variety of moral contexts. Our task is to characterize the class of things we need which has these properties and to do so in a way that explains their importance.

Needs and Species-Typical Functioning

One plausible suggestion for distinguishing the relevant needs from all the things we can come to need is David Braybrooke's . . . distinction between "course-of-life needs" and "adventitious needs." *Course-of-life needs* are those needs which people "have all through their lives or at certain stages of life through which all must pass." *Adventitious needs* are the things we need because of the particular contingent projects, which may be long-term ones, on which we embark. Human course-of-life needs would include food, shelter, clothing, exercise, rest, companionship, a mate (in one's prime, says Braybrooke), and so on. Such needs are not themselves deficiencies, for example, when they are anticipated. But a deficiency with respect to them "endangers the normal functioning of the subject of need *considered as a member of a natural species*". . . A related suggestion can be found in J. H. McCloskey's discussion of the human and personal needs we appeal to in political argument. He argues that needs "relate to what it would be detrimental to us to lack, *where the detrimental is explained by reference to our natures as men and specific persons*" . . . Thus course-of-life needs are important when we abstract from many particular choices and preferences individuals might make or have.

Our hypothesis, then, is that the needs which interest us are necessary to achieve or maintain species-typical normal functioning. Do such needs have the two properties noted earlier? Clearly they are objectively ascribable, assuming we can come up with the appropriate notion of species-typical functioning. (So, incidentally, are adventitious needs, assuming we can determine the relevant goals by reference to which the adventitious needs become determinate.) Are these needs objectively important in the appropriate way? In a broad range of contexts we do treat them as such—a claim I shall not trouble to argue. What is of interest is to see *why* being in such a need category gives them their special importance.

A tempting first answer might be this: whatever our specific chosen goals or tasks, our ability to achieve them, and consequently our happiness, will be diminished if we fall short of normal species functioning. So whatever our specific goals, we need them whatever else we need. For example, it is sometimes said that whatever our chosen goals or tasks, we need our health, and so appropriate health care. But this claim is not, strictly speaking, true. For many of us, some of our goals, perhaps even those we feel are most important to us, are not necessarily undermined by failing health or disability. Moreover, we can often adjust our goals, and presumably our levels of satisfaction, to fit better with our dysfunction or disability. Coping in this way does not necessarily diminish happiness or satisfaction in life to a level below that achievable with normal functioning.

Though normal functioning is not in this way a necessary condition for satisfaction or happiness in life, meeting health-care needs may have a definite *tendency* to promote happiness. This tendency may be all the utilitarian needs to guide public policy, and it may give us an explanation of why health care is thought so special. I have no conclusive response to this position: it is a generalized version of the view that health care is special because it reduces pain and suffering, which much of it no doubt does. Of course, the advocate of this view must now be willing to weigh this reduction of pain and suffering against the satisfaction of all other kinds of preferences, if he takes as his goal the promotion of happiness. It is this empirical estimate of the strength of the tendency that makes health care special: the specialness disappears when the estimate changes. In what follows, I sketch an alternative to this account, one that I believe to be more plausible because it better explains the special importance or priority we seem to give to meeting health-care needs.

The alternative account turns on this basic fact: impairments of normal species functioning reduce the range of opportunity open to the individual in which he may construct his "plan of life" or "conception of the good." We may think of a life plan as a long-term plan in which an individual schedules activities so that he can harmoniously satisfy his desires. The good for an individual is defined by reference to this plan and the choice of goals, projects, and means for achieving them it contains. . . . We can consider a person happy when he is successful in carrying out his plan. The notion of a plan of life thus has some similarity to the utilitarian's notion of a utility function, but it directly implies a plan to satisfy desires over the long term.

Life plans for which we are otherwise suited and which we have a reasonable expectation of finding satisfying or happiness-producing are rendered unreasonable by impairments of normal functioning. Consequently, if persons have a fundamental interest in preserving the opportunity to revise their conceptions of the good through time, then they will have a pressing interest in maintaining normal species functioning (which will be defined more carefully in the next section) by establishing institutions, such as health-care systems, which do just that. So the kinds of needs picked out by reference to normal species functioning are objectively important because they meet this fundamental interest persons have in maintaining a normal range of opportunities. I shall try to refine this admittedly vague answer, but first I want to characterize health-care needs more specifically and show that they fit within this more general framework.

Disease and Health

To specify a notion of health-care needs, we need clear notions of health and disease. I shall begin with a narrow, if not uncontroversial, "biomedical" model: the basic idea is that health is the absence of disease, and diseases (I include deformities and disabilities that result from trauma) are *deviations from the natural functional organization of a typical member of a species.* The task of characterizing this natural functional organization falls to the biomedical sciences. These sciences must be thought of broadly. In some cases, for example, when a scientist makes claims about the natural function of certain features of an organism—when he makes "functional ascriptions"—he commits himself to other claims about the design of the species and its fitness to meeting biological goals. Thus we must include evolutionary theory among the relevant biomedical sciences. The concept of disease that results is not merely a statistical notion—deviation from the statistical norm. Rather, it draws on a theoretical account of the design of the organism.

The task of characterizing species-typical functional organization and departures from it is the same for man and beast with two complications. First, for humans we require an account of the species-typical functional organization that permits us to pursue biological goals as *social* animals. So there must be a way of characterizing the species-typical apparatus underlying such functions as the acquisition of knowledge, linguistic communication, and social cooperation in the broad and changing range of environments in which we live.

Second, adding mental disease and health into the picture, which we must do, complicates the issue further. We have a less well-developed theory of species-typical mental functions and functional organization. The biomedical model clearly presupposes we can eventually develop this missing account and that a reasonable part of what we now take to be psychopathology will show up as diseases within the model. . . . The difficulty of so extending the biomedical model to mental disease does not deter me from assuming such an extension here. To anticipate the result of this extension: psychopathology covers an important class of diseases which generate major health care needs, many of which are *unmet* in our health-care system.

The biomedical model has controversial features. First, some insist it too narrowly defines health as the absence of disease, a narrowness which encourages too much focus on acute care. In contrast, some—as in the definition codified by the World Health Organization—view health as an idealized level of well-being. But health is not happiness, and confusing the two over-medicalizes social philosophy. Nor does a "narrow" biomedical view of disease mean that we should ignore its social etiology. The bias of our health-care system toward acute care and its neglect of preventive and "holistic" care derives from many powerful economic and social forces, not an erroneous concept of disease.

Second, some insist that the concept of disease is not descriptive, as in the biomedical model, but strongly normative: a disease is a deviation from a *social norm* . . . , not merely a deviation from species-typical functional organization. But even if some conditions or behaviors historically have been *viewed* as diseases—for example, "drapetomania," the disease that made slaves run away, or masturbation—such views do not *make* them diseases. Whales were not fishes merely because people thought they were for centuries. Nor does the fact that many diseases are discovered and treated only when people complain about them make being an object of complaint a necessary feature of diseases. The biomedical model allows us, of course, to make normative judgments *about* diseases, for example, about which ones are undesirable and justify our entering into a "sick role." These normative judgments yield the normative notion of *illness,* not the theoretically more basic notion of *disease;* this distinction admittedly departs from looser ordinary usage.

Some pure forms of the biomedical model also involve a deeper claim, namely that species-normal functional organization can itself be characterized without invoking normative or value judgments. Here the debate turns on hard issues in the philosophy of biology. For example, we need an account of functional ascriptions in biology which does not depend on our making normative judgments. . . . More specifically, we need to be able to distinguish genetic variation from disease, and we must specify the range of environments taken as "natural" for the purpose of revealing dysfunction. The latter is critical to showing that the biomedical model is non-normative: for example, what range of social roles and environments is included in the natural range? If we allow too much of the social environment, then racially discriminatory environments might make being of the wrong race a disease; if we disallow all socially created environments, then we seem not to be able to call dyslexia a disease (remember I include certain disabilities).

Fortunately, these difficult issues need not detain us. My discussion does not turn on this deeper, strong claim about non-normativeness advanced by some advocates of the biomedical model. It is enough for my purposes that the line between disease and the absence of disease is, for the general run of cases, *uncontroversial* and *ascertainable through publicly acceptable methods,* such as those of the biomedical sciences. It will not matter if what counts as a disease category is relative to some features of social roles in a given society, and thus to some normative judgments, provided the core of the notion of species-normal functioning is left intact. The model would still, I presume, count infertility as a disease, even though some or many individuals might prefer to be infertile and seek medical treatment to render themselves so. Similarly, unwanted pregnancy is not a disease. Again, dysfunctional noses count as diseases, since noses have normal species functions and normal functional organization (or, simply, normal anatomy). If the dysfunction or deformity is serious, it might warrant treatment as an illness. But deviation of nasal anatomy from individual or social conceptions of beauty does not constitute disease. This is a distinction well-known to cosmetic plastic surgeons. Since most third-party payers will not reimburse for surgery that does not correct disease or deformity, some plastic surgeons conspire to commit fraud in order to obtain reimbursements for their patients by describing the surgery as corrective. In Massachusetts, Blue Cross/Blue Shield recently crossed this line in a different way: it suspended reimbursements for reconstructive plastic surgery following mastectomy. Public outcry reversed the policy, which made it clear that the public understood and wanted to preserve the distinction between restoration of anatomy to the normal range and mammoplasty undertaken for purely cosmetic reasons.

The biomedical model thus allows us to draw a fairly sharp line between uses of health-care services to prevent and treat diseases and uses which meet other social goals. The importance of such other goals may be different and may rest on other bases, for example, in the induced infertility or unwanted pregnancy cases. My intention is to show which principles of justice are relevant to distributing health-care services where we can take as fixed, primarily by nature, a generally uncontroversial baseline of species-normal functional organization. . . .

Though I have deliberately selected a rather narrow model of disease and health, at least by comparison to some fashionable views, *health-care needs* emerge as a broad and diverse set. Health care needs will be those things we need in order to maintain, restore, or provide functional equivalents (where possible) to normal species functioning. They can be divided into:

1. Adequate nutrition, shelter
2. Sanitary, safe, unpolluted living and working conditions
3. Exercise, rest, and some other features of lifestyle
4. Preventive, curative, and rehabilitative personal medical services
5. Non-medical personal and social support services

Of course, we do not tend to think of all these things as included among health-care needs, partly because we tend to think narrowly about personal medical services when we think about health care. But the list is not constructed to conform to our ordinary notion of health care, but to point out a functional relationship between quite diverse goods and services and the various institutions responsible for delivering them. . . .

Disease and Opportunity

. . . Among the kinds of preferences to which we tend to give special weight are those which meet certain *important* categories of need. I have argued that among the important needs are those necessary for maintaining normal functioning for individuals, viewed as members of a natural species. Health-care needs fit prominently into this characterization of important needs because they are things we need to prevent or cure diseases, which are deviations from normal functional organization.

But we now need to fill an important gap in this argument: What is so important about normal species functioning? Why give such moral importance to health-care needs and to the somewhat broader class of needs within which it falls, merely because they are necessary to preserve normal species functioning? To answer this question, I shall develop the remark made earlier about the relationship between species-typical functioning and opportunity, but this will require the notion of a normal opportunity range.

The *normal opportunity range* for a given society is the array of life plans reasonable persons in it are likely to construct for themselves. The normal range is thus dependent on key features of the society—its stage of historical development, its level of material wealth and technological development, and even important cultural facts about it. This is one way in which the notion of normal opportunity range is socially relative. Facts about social organization, including the conception of justice regulating its basic institutions, will also determine how that total normal range is distributed in the population. Nevertheless, that issue of distribution aside, normal species-typical functioning provides us with one clear parameter affecting the share of the normal range open to a given individual. It is this parameter which the distribution of health care affects.

The share of the normal range open to an individual is also *determined in a fundamental way by his talents and skills.* Fair equality of opportunity does not require opportunity to be equal for all persons. It requires only that it be equal for persons with similar skills and talents. Thus individual shares of the normal range will not in general be *equal,* even when they are *fair* to the individual. The general principle of fair equality of opportunity does not imply levelling individual differences. Within the general theory of justice, unequal chances of success which derive from unequal talents may be compensated for in other ways. For example, in Rawls's . . . theory, socioeconomic inequalities are allowed to work to the advantage of those with more marketable talents only if the inequalities also maximally benefit the worst-off individuals, who, we may suppose, have less marketable talents. I can now state a fact central to my approach: impairment of normal functioning through disease and disability restricts an individual's opportunity *relative to that portion of the normal range his skills and talents would have made available to him were he healthy.* If an individual's fair share of the normal range is the array of life plans he may reasonably choose, given his talents and skills, then disease and disability shrinks his share from what is fair.

Of course, we also know that skills and talents can be undeveloped or misdeveloped because of social conditions, e.g., family background or racist educational practices. So, if we are interested in having individuals enjoy a fair share of the normal opportunity range, we will want to correct for special disadvantages here too, say through compensatory educational or job-training programs. Still, restoring normal functioning through health care has a particular and *limited* effect on an individual's share of the normal range. It lets him enjoy that portion of the range to which his full array of skills and talents would give him access, assuming that these too are not impaired by special social disadvantages. Again, there is no presumption that we should eliminate or level individual differences: *these act as a baseline constraint on the degree to which individuals enjoy the normal range.* Only where differences in talents and skills are the results of disease and disability, not merely normal variation, is some effort required to correct for the effects of the "natural lottery." (There will be problem cases: Should we regard mental retardation as a disability? If so, why is it to be regarded as qualitatively different from lack of brilliance or mere dullness, which have their market value. These are matters I cannot pursue here.)

Two points about the normal opportunity range need emphasis. First, some diseases constitute more serious curtailments of opportunity than others relative to a given range. But, because normal ranges are defined by reference to particular societies, the same disease in two societies may impair opportunity differently and so have its importance assessed differently. For example, dyslexia may be less important to treat in an illiterate society than in a literate one (suppose we could cure it with brain surgery). Thus the social importance of particular diseases is a notion which we ought to view as socially relative.

Second, within a society the normal opportunity range abstracts from important individual differences in what I will call *effective opportunity.* From the perspective of an individual who has a particular plan of life and who has developed certain skills accordingly, the effective opportunity range will be only a part of his fair share of the normal range. Suppose a college teacher and a skilled laborer each finds his manual dexterity impaired by disease. The impairment of the effective opportunity range for the skilled laborer may be greater than for the college teacher, but if both originally had comparable dexterity, their shares of the normal range would be equally affected by the disease. By measuring the impact of disease on opportunity by reference to an individual's share of the normal range, and not by reference to its impairment of his effective range, I abstract from special effects that derive from an individual's conception of the "good" or plan of life. This way of proceeding seems plausible in light of judgments we are inclined to make about access to medical services: we do not want to be in the business, I believe, of deciding who gets what medical services on the basis of occupation or other results of prior individual choices of a similar sort. Thus the level of abstraction in my account seems appropriate given our search for a measure of the social importance, for claims of justice, of impairments of health.

My conclusion is that we should use impairment of the normal opportunity range as a fairly crude measure of the relative importance of health-care needs at the macro level. In general, it will be more important to prevent, cure, or compensate for those disease conditions which involve a greater curtailment of an individual's share of the normal opportunity range. Of course, impairment of normal species functioning has another distinct effect. It can diminish individual happiness or satisfaction, which depends on the individual's conception of the "good." Such effects are important at the micro level—for example, to individual decisions about utilizing health care. At this micro level, an individual is deciding which services to use from among those society is obliged to provide—if the society is just. Here individual choices about happiness will be the final determinant of what is done. But this appeal to individual happiness will not solve my central problem, which concerns what society is obliged to provide. . . .

Fair Equality of Opportunity

I have argued that we can explain the importance we attribute to meeting health-care needs once we observe the effect of disease on an individual's share of the normal opportunity range. But observing that individuals have an interest in protecting their shares of that range does not show that society *ought* to protect normal opportunity range, that there is any social obligation to do so. If we could show that justice required guaranteeing fair equality of opportunity, then we could complete our justification of the importance we attribute to meeting health-care needs. We would then be able to assert that the social obligation to meet health-care needs derives from the more general social obligation to guarantee fair equality of opportunity. As I noted earlier, I cannot offer that more general argument for a principle guaranteeing fair equality of opportunity without digressing too far into the general theory of justice. But I do want to suggest some widely held reasons for supporting such a principle.

Liberal political philosophy has relied on what is essentially a *procedural* notion, equality of opportunity, to justify a system in which unequal outcomes are thought morally acceptable. It is morally acceptable that there are winners and losers, even in races where the prize is a share of important social goods, provided the race is *fair* to all participants. Since major rewards in our society derive from jobs and offices, the competition for securing these positions must be fair. Specifically, certain *morally irrelevant* features of persons—race, religion, ethnic origin, sex—must not be the basis on which people are selected for positions. Rather, their talents and skills, at least those relevant to the positions being sought, should determine who is selected and ultimately rewarded. . . . In Rawls's theory of justice as fairness, for example, inequalities in shares of primary social goods are justified on the grounds that it would be irrational—even for the worst-off people—to rule out inequalities which work to their advantage. But a proviso is included: competition for positions must be fair, and a fair equality of opportunity principle is given high priority in Rawls's theory. Specifically, fair equality of opportunity cannot be traded away to provide material gains for individuals: fair equality of opportunity is given *lexical* or *lexicographical priority* over the principle which permits inequalities in other social goods. When a principle has lexical priority in a series of principles, it must be satisfied first, before we can move on to satisfy further principles.

Even this narrow notion of equal opportunity, concerned only with access to jobs and careers, is both problematic and controversial. It is conceptually problematic for several reasons. Thus, some claim equal opportunity is not well defined or is illusory. Irreducible differences in talents and skills between persons will always make opportunity greater for some in competitive situations. We cannot "level" people down to their "bare personhood," where all distinguishing traits of individuals—their talents, skills, and other accidental features which might confer advantages—are eliminated. We might try to avoid this complaint, by accepting some irreducible differences in talents and skills as a natural baseline, as I did earlier in defining normal opportunity range. . . . But this opens us to another difficulty. Any such baseline of talents and skills may seem to be morally arbitrary: we do not deserve the advantages or disadvantages the baseline confers. These talents and skills are largely the result of genetic accident or the social good fortune of having effective parents—neither of which we in any sense deserve. Rawls . . . tries to accommodate this point by arranging inequalities in other social goods, such as income and wealth, so that they work to make the worst-off individuals maximally well off, as well off as they could be under all alternative social arrangements with lesser inequalities. In this way, he treats talents and skills, in part at least, as a *social asset* which works to the advantage of the worst-off individuals, those with the least marketable talents and skills. This solution is challenged by many.

A different complaint is that equal opportunity is an unachievable goal. For example, there are ineliminable effects of family upbringing on the development of talents and skills. . . . This suggests that the goal of achieving equal opportunity completely is unrealizable unless we threaten liberty by interfering with parental autonomy in drastic ways. A somewhat pragmatic response would be to suggest that we achieve what equality we can without violating more basic liberties; we must then live with the fuzziness in the theory that results.

This conflict with liberty suggests another reason that equality of opportunity is a controversial notion. Some construe it as a *negative* constraint which requires only that society refrain from imposing certain barriers to equal opportunity, such as anti-black "Jim Crow" laws or racial or sexual quotas on hiring. This negative view gives us what Rawls . . . calls *formal* equality of opportunity. Others insist there is a *positive* obligation to correct for all the influences which interfere with equal opportunity. Where competitive disadvantage, such as the underdevelopment of talents and skills, results from racist or sexist practices or as effects of poor family background, then social programs to correct for the disadvantage are required. These might include compensatory education programs, like "Headstart" in the US, or "affirmative action" hiring procedures. This positive conception is called *fair* equality of opportunity. General distributive theories differ dramatically in their willingness to move from the negative to the positive conception, and resolving this dispute would take us far afield.

In this investigation we shall have to settle for less than a full justification of the principle of fair equality of opportunity. In particular, we shall settle for a weaker, conditional claim. Health-care institutions should be among those governed by a principle of fair equality of opportunity, provided two conditions obtain: (1) an acceptable general theory of justice includes a principle which requires basic institutions to guarantee fair equality of opportunity, and (2) the fair equality of opportunity principle acts as a constraint on permissible economic inequalities. A theory of just health care can go only this far. In the discussion that follows I will ignore these provisos—though I have not forgotten them. I urge the fair equality of opportunity principle as an appropriate principle to govern macro decisions about the design of our health-care system. Such a principle defines, from the perspective of justice, what the moral *function* of the health-care system must be—to help guarantee fair equality of opportunity. This is the fundamental insight underlying the approach developed here.

It is important to note that this conditional claim does not depend on the acceptability of any particular theory of justice, such as Rawls's contractarian theory. A utilitarian theory might suffice. For example, a principle of fair equality of opportunity might be part of a system of principles, an ideal moral code, general compliance with which produced at least as much utility as any alternative code. For example, the principle might be the most effective way to protect the society against the productivity lost when individuals are not given a fair opportunity to develop their skills and talents (although I have never seen a persuasive utilitarian argument of this sort). That utilitarian theory could then be extended to health care through the analysis provided here. It is far less likely that a libertarian theory would be compatible with any such fair equality of opportunity principle. . . .

Access and the Fair Equality of Opportunity Account

The fair equality of opportunity account of just health care . . . says that health care is special because meeting health-care needs has an important effect on the opportunity open to individuals to choose reasonable plans of life. Moreover, if there is a social obligation to protect fair equality of opportunity, construed in this broad way, then health-care institutions should be designed to meet that obligation. Consider the implications of this view for access to care.

First, the account is compatible with, though it *does not imply,* a multi-tiered health-care system. In contrast, the "market" approach *requires* at least a two-tier system—the lower tier provides the decent basic minimum, and upper tiers provide what the market will bear. Thus the fair equality of opportunity account shares with the market approach the view that health-care services have a variety of functions, only *some* of which may give rise to social obligations to provide them. As I noted earlier, the market approach does not explain the basis for obligations it recognizes, whereas my account is clear on that point. The basic tier on my account would include *health-care services that meet health-care needs, or at least important health-care needs—as judged by their impact on the normal opportunity range.* Other tiers, if they are allowed, might involve uses of health care services to meet less important health-care needs or to meet other needs and wants. My account leaves open the possibility that other tiers of the system might also be important enough to be given special precedence over other uses of social resources—but, if they were, it would be for reasons different from those which give such precedence to the basic tier. That is, there may be social obligations to provide access to services which fall in a tier above the basic one: this issue is not addressed by my account, incomplete as it is, though I return to it shortly.

Second, the fair equality of opportunity account provides a principled way of characterizing the health-care services that fall in the socially guaranteed tier. They are the services needed to maintain, restore, or compensate for the loss of normal species-typical functioning. In turn, normal functioning contributes substantially to defining the share of the normal opportunity range open to individuals. This "principled" way of characterizing the basic tier is, to be sure, abstract. It requires moral judgment in its application, as well as a considerable amount of information about health care and the resources available in the society. Still, it provides a basis for argument about what should be included in the basic tier, a basis which is lacking in the notion of a decent basic minimum or in glosses on the notion, such as Fried's . . . remark about "tolerable life prospects."

Third, however the upper tiers of the health-care system are to be financed, there should be no obstacles—financial, racial, geographical, and so on—to access to the basic tier. The importance of such equality of access to the basic tier follows from two main lines of argument. First, the basic tier is defined by reference to the impact of health-care services on opportunity, and inequalities of opportunity are not to be tolerated for the sorts of economic reasons that might make the preservation of these obstacles appealing. Second, the importance of equality of access follows I think from basic facts about the sociology and epistemology of the determination of health-care needs. The "felt needs" of patients are at best only initial indicators of the presence of real health-care needs. Structural and other process barriers to initial access, for example, to primary care, compel people to make their own determination of the importance of the symptoms they experience. Of course, every system requires some such assessment, but financial, geographical, and other process barriers (waiting time, for example) impose the burden for such assessment on particular groups of persons. Indeed, where it is felt that sociological and cultural barriers exist to people utilizing services, positive steps are needed (in the schools or through relevant community organizations) to make sure decisions are informed. . . .

DANIEL CALLAHAN

from *What Kind of Life?*

Daniel Callahan is President of the Institute for Social Ethics and the Life Sciences at the Hastings Center. (Source: What Kind of Life? *New York: Simon & Schuster, 1990. Notes have been omitted.*

QUESTIONS FOR REFLECTION

1. Why does Callahan doubt that we can distinguish needs from desires?
2. How does Daniels characterize needs that must be met by a just health care system? How does Callahan criticize Daniels's characterization? Do the criticisms succeed?
3. What happens to a health care system that tries to meet all medical needs, according to Callahan? Why?
4. How, in Callahan's view, might we determine an appropriate level of spending on health care?
5. Evaluate Callahan's recommended goals for health care policy.

ON THE RAGGED EDGE: NEEDS, ENDLESS NEEDS

Two powerful ideals have in recent decades dominated the provision of healthcare in the United States. The first is that of meeting individual health needs. The second is that of doing so in a way that is economically efficient. The emphasis upon individual need has long drawn from two sources, that of the moral traditions of medicine, directed toward individual patient welfare, and that of deep-seated American traditions, placing the good of the individual at the heart of national values. Efficiency as a value has somewhat shallower historical roots, but it has nonetheless long been part of American business and institutional beliefs that waste ought to be eliminated and maximum results obtained at the lowest possible cost. With the pressures of inflationary healthcare costs, the value of efficiency has become all the more pronounced. It is the driving force behind cost-containment efforts, and the spirit invoked in most recent proposals for universal health insurance. Taken together, meeting need and promoting efficiency generate a deep conviction: If the most efficacious medicine could be provided in the most efficient way, then the health needs of each and every individual could be met at an affordable price.

That is a wonderfully bracing, but mistaken, conviction. The ideal of meeting all individual need is neither possible as a reality nor plausible as a moral goal. No level of efficiency will overcome that impossibility. Medical progress has undone it as a feasible goal and competing social demands have undercut it as a meaningful goal. We will always have to live with unfinished medical progress, an always rough line dividing past success and present failure. Yet because of the persistence of an emphasis upon individual need, we have been left with an impossible task, that of solving the social problem of allocation—how we should distribute our collective resources—with ingredients that are private and individual. The evidence that it cannot be done is all around us and grows day by day. . . . The goal of efficiency and effective cost containment cannot be achieved unless the moral goal of meeting individual need is changed; they have become intimately related. The widespread belief that we can all get all we need if only we deliver healthcare efficiently is hopelessly wrong, a deep and fundamental illusion. We will never get all we think we need as individuals and will have to settle for something less. But it is possible that, if we can alter our understanding of individual need, and place it within a more meaningful societal context, we may actually be better served than we are at present. Quite apart from its impossibility as an actual achievement, the ideal of meeting individual need does not even promise to serve the human good, either that of individuals or that of society. It leads us to reckless aspirations, and to an inability to separate hopeful desire and genuine necessity.

The need for good health seems, at first glance, a basic and simple need, one that can be free of unchecked aspiration. We need good health in order that our body might function well, allowing us to do what we want or must do. The singularity of good health has always been its invisibility. When all goes well with our body, we do not notice it, but when it is sick we can notice nothing else. We do at that point feel the press of desire. We want, desperately so, to regain our good health, to restore it to invisibility in order that we can get on with our life. But beyond that obvious case, why should desire have any place at all in the quest for health? In devising public policy, moreover, why could we not use the meeting of individual health needs as the simple goal, carefully sorting out and putting to one side what is nothing more than unreasonable desire?

The plain answer to those questions is that we have all but lost our way. We cannot separate health needs from health desires in our own lives, and neither can we devise a public policy that can adequately separate them. I am not referring only to the common escalation of what we want into what we need, though that will be a potent force here as elsewhere. The fundamental problem stems from uncertainty about the limits of our health potential. How long a life can we live, ought we want to live, or do we need to live? How much pain and suffering can and should we be ready to endure? How much disability can we survive, and how much fitness do we need? How much unhappiness is compatible with mental health? How much psychological stability do we require? Those are questions about the place, and extent, of health in our lives, and about the human needs that underlie our unending quest for better health. The uncertainty that such questions generate is well exploited by a technological progress whose basic purpose is ostensibly to help us meet our needs, but which in fact systematically blurs the line between need and desire. We have lost our way because we have defined our unlimited hopes to transcend our mortality as our needs, and we have created a medical enterprise that engineers the transformation.

At the heart of the public demand for good health is the insistence that life not be burdened with illness and that death be held at bay. That understandable desire has been rendered plausible by medical advances. Disease causes illness and death, and disease we now know can be conquered. What can be done ought to be done, and what began as desire ends as need. That redefined need becomes open-ended and insatiable, admitting of no boundaries. This is the transformation of health goals that lies at the root of our present problems. We cannot hope to manage the healthcare system, or our own aspirations, unless we learn how to control this transformation and the dynamic behind it.

It is a dynamic that embodies a vision of human possibility, one whose scope and elements are widely familiar if not always coherently expressed as a whole. Let me try to articulate that reigning vision. It consists of three major ingredients: a broad, limitless definition of health; a highly subjective notion of individual need, one captivated by the diversity of personal goals and desires; and a strong view of human rights, in particular the right of individuals to have access to adequate healthcare. It is a vision that sees health as an unbounded good, that allows the individual considerable leeway in defining, or inventing, his or her own health needs, and that allows one to make in principle as much demand on the help of fellow citizens—in the name of his or her rights and their obligations—as is required to meet those needs. It is a wonderful vision, but it is seriously flawed. It is collapsing under its own weight, and it will no longer suffice to provide the foundations for a healthcare system.

. . . it is difficult to talk meaningfully of health solely as "the absence of disease or infirmity." What positive state of affairs are disease and infirmity an absence of? Against what are they being compared? The best we have historically been able to answer is to focus on the wholeness of the body, or its integrity. Those terms suggest that good health represents the proper functioning, the correct harmony of the parts of the body, just the kind of functioning which gives the healthy body the kind of invisibility noted earlier. But those classical ideas have always implied a positive state of some kind, not merely the absence of some harmful conditions. The full pursuit of that issue is beyond the scope of this book, but it is necessary to bring to a discussion of health resources some substantive notion of health. What is it that we want to protect or enhance in the individual and distribute through the healthcare system?

For the purpose of discussing allocation issues, we can usefully distinguish between health as a norm and health as an ideal. As a norm, it would be possible to speak in terms of deviation from some statistical standards, particularly if these standards were couched in terms not only of organic function but also of behavioral functioning. Thus someone can be called "healthy" if his heart, lungs, and kidneys function at a certain average level of efficiency and efficacy, if he can hear and see in a no less average way, if he is not suffering physical pain, and if his body is free of those pathological conditions that even if undetected or undetectable could impair organic function and eventually cause pain, illness, and death. When I go for a physical examination, my physician looks first for some deviation from accepted standards of average physical and biological functioning.

This way of thinking might be perfectly sufficient and satisfactory in a medically stagnant, or static, culture, and to a certain extent that is just the way we do think. The more subtle problem is that any notion of a statistical norm will be influenced by some kind of ideal of the self and its relationship to the body. Health presents itself as an ideal, a good, and not just a set of averages. Why should anyone care at all how his organs are functioning, much less how well they do so? Could it possibly be because certain departures from the statistical norm carry with them important implications for the self, for what the self considers good for it, an idea that transcends the medical state of the body? It would seem so. It is impossible, in fact, to draw any sharp distinction between conceptions of the human good—what benefits the self and its goals—and statistical norms of the body. . . .

Are we not then forced to say, to push the issue a step further, that if the complete absence of health represented by death means the complete absence of self, then any diminishment of health must represent, correspondingly, a diminishment of self? Not at all. As the experience of many people shows, a strong, active self is consistent with a heavy burden of disease and disability. The self and the body are not, it turns out, quite one and the same—even if a severe toothache can sometimes do what a fatal cancer does not always do: dominate our sense of self to the point of utter distraction and despair. We are left, then, with a profound puzzle, that of the relationship between health and individual human happiness. To be happy is not necessarily to be healthy, and to be healthy is not necessarily to be happy. . . .

Defining Our Needs

Nothing would seem more appropriate as a goal of healthcare than the meeting of individual health needs. We want to live and not to die, to be well rather than to be ill. We do not invent those goals. They seem part of our nature, basic and necessary conditions of our existing and flourishing as human beings. To call them "needs" is nothing more than to say that, without them, we can neither be nor be ourselves. Yet there is something oddly elusive about the idea of a "need," even if we look carefully at the individual. We call something a need because, unless it is met, we cannot achieve our other goals; yet that means we can say little about the significance of the needs unless we can define those goals. How much and what kind of health we want depends in part on what we want to do with our life. This is particularly true if it is a question of how long a life we would hope for, or how much physical vigor we think necessary, or how essential psychological stability might be. Before long we are forced to ask some broad and difficult questions about human nature and our own destinies. What goals ought we to have as human beings? What kind of life should we live? What do we want to do with the life that good health can give us?

The idea of need becomes all the more elusive in a liberal, pluralistic society that believes it wrong for the society even to try to determine what goals and ultimate ends are appropriate for individuals, to say just what it is that we should as persons seek in our lives. The idea that there is, or could be, a good common to all people, a part of their nature, is usually rejected. It is a notion that seems to fly in the face of a commitment to individual choice and self-determination, and in the face of a widespread belief that no unitary human good has or will be discovered. Technological progress plays into this cultural tendency by exploiting the desire for self-control and self-direction, and by the unwillingness and inability of the society to declare easily that the progress desired by some might pose a hazard, or burden, to others. But can we define "need" in some value-neutral way, and do so in a manner sufficiently solid to use it as the foundation for the allocation of healthcare?

To get at that question, it is first necessary to specify some meaning for individual "need" in the health context. Three fundamental human needs can be identified, and they lend themselves to a health explication. The first need is simply to be, by which I mean to exist, to live. That is the necessary foundation for all other human activities and that is why laws against murder are the most primary in any society. The next need is to think and to feel. We are rational, emotional, and social animals. An inability to think will mean that we have no chance to understand and manage our situation in the world or to know what sense there is to be made of things. An inability to feel cuts us off not only from the depths of our own self, but also from the richness of relationships with others; we are, as Aristotle long ago noted, social beings. While thinking and feeling can conceptually be separated, they are ordinarily joined in our actual lives. The third need is to act, to be an agent that can do something in the world. It is action that most visibly takes us out of ourselves, that extends ourselves to others and to the world around us, that changes the world in which we live or enables us to adapt our behavior to a world we cannot change.

These three needs may be spelled out in a health context as follows. We have what I will call *body needs,* corresponding to the need to be, to exist. The good health of our bodily organs is a necessary condition for our being alive at all. While the capacities of those organs can be compromised, and some even dispensed with altogether, there is a minimal level below which we cannot fall without the threat of death. The priority typically given to the saving of life in healthcare expresses the importance of our body needs. Our need to think and to feel I will call our *psychological needs.* A failure to have those needs met will mean our diminishment as human beings. We will be unable to live with ourselves or to enter into relationships with others. A mental impairment, as in Alzheimer's disease, or an emotional crisis, as in depression, will leave us crippled as a self. Our need to act I will call our *function needs,* encompassing within that term all those activities that enable us to do something, either to perceive the world (vision and hearing, for example) or to act in the world (walking and speaking, for instance). The capacity for action, mobility, and perception allows us to manage and respond actively to the world around us. . . .

Denial of the Limits of the Possible

Consider the need of the body to live. What can medicine bring to that need? It has already brought vaccines and antibiotics to deal with lethal infectious disease, respirators and dialysis units to cope with failing organ systems, transplants to provide new organs, surgery to remove tumors and repair lesions, and general biological knowledge to help us prevent potentially fatal disease. How far can all of this go? Who knows? There are no known theoretical limits. Mortality from heart disease has fallen in recent decades and continues to decline, and while cancer has yet to be conquered, there is no reason not to expect continuing progress. Organ transplantation becomes gradually more successful, and while there is a limit because of the availability of organs for transplant purposes, there is no necessary limit to the possibility of artificial organs. A gradual sharpening of the distinction between growing old (which cannot be helped) and becoming sick (which can be dealt with) does not make old age as such (in the eyes of some, at any rate) a necessarily fatal condition. Our need to live, then, admits of no discernible medical boundaries. There is no individual medical condition that does not, in principle, admit of the possibility of an eventual cure or significant amelioration. The most desperate class of patients, with the rarest of diseases, may eventually have their need to live met. It cannot be ruled out. Even now, available medical techniques can be used to gain a few hours, or days, even in the most desperate cases (which is one reason the termination of treatment has proved so difficult even with obviously dying patients).

To make these observations is to say more than that the standards of what counts as minimal or adequate will change over time. It is to say at least that much, but it is also to say that even at any given time it will not be possible to specify the necessary standards except in relatively arbitrary ways. There will be, for one thing, the claims of interest groups for resources to cope with the disease or condition of concern to them. Their aim is to *change* the existing standards, to declare them inadequate right now, to exploit research and clinical possibilities, and to expand our notions of the possible and desirable. There will, for another, be the claims of critically ill individual patients. It will be almost impossible in many cases to say that a patient could not, in some way, benefit from further efforts, or from a different method of treatment—his or her need might yet be met; something, however experimental, might already be available. Most important, one suggested and valuable standard, that of "normal species functioning," can readily be thrown into doubt. We know neither, at the upper end, just what we might aim for—how good our health might be, or how long our life might be—nor, at the lower end, what deprived level of functioning is (with technological assistance) minimally compatible with a satisfactory life.

The term "normal" comes to lose all meaning in the face of constant medical progress, whose very purpose, in its most ambitious moments, is to redefine "normal," to give us a new picture of human possibility. Our need to live, for instance, admits of no necessary boundary, either in our individual case or in the case of groups or classes of people afflicted with otherwise fatal illnesses. Why should we accept a now-normal average life expectancy of seventy-five years if medical science could give us something better? Is not the history of medical advancement one of running roughshod over supposedly immutable ideas of normalcy?

Or consider our psychological needs. The enormous expansion of demand for mental health services in recent years reflects a widespread belief that psychological needs can be as important as physical needs, and that therapy to meet psychological needs can be as helpful, even decisive, as therapy to meet physical needs. Both the research trend toward seeking a biological basis for the most serious pathologies (schizophrenia and depression, for instance) and the therapeutic trend toward short-term psychotherapies for lesser problems promise a growing ability to provide some help to most people, either now or at least in the future. The need for counseling and therapeutic help itself steadily expands, and the range of problems dealt with continues to widen, now encompassing substance abuse. This expansion is driven by a public perception of emotional and mental problems as now more socially acceptable than in the past, by the inclusion of therapy for them as part of standard packages of healthcare, and by the belief that such therapy can be efficacious. While there has been considerably less progress with the major and minor tranquilizers, as well as other psychoactive drugs, than was earlier thought possible, there remains a strong sense of optimism that the advances will eventually emerge. There is, then, no discernible boundary to what people will come to define as a psychological need and to what the various health sciences can do to respond to that need.

Last, consider the need to function. At one time, the fate of someone who had suffered a devastating accident and came out of it as a paraplegic or quadriplegic was grim. A short and cruel life was likely. Now rehabilitation has progressed. The infections that would have carried him off earlier can now be controlled, and skilled rehabilitation making use of technological devices can give him the possibility of some eventual mobility. Even more can be done for the elderly stroke victim. He or she can now be helped to regain speech and the use of paralyzed arms or legs, and can often enough be restored to normalcy. A gradual improvement in hearing aids deals with a less critical malady, but one that is important and widespread among the elderly. The severely handicapped newborn can be provided with shunts to drain excess fluid in the brain, artificial assistance for malfunctioning kidneys, surgery for a defective heart, and transplants for failed organs. Improved fetal surgery will eventually be able to correct some conditions prior to birth. The gradual rejection of the term "vegetable" applied to any human being reflects not simply repugnance at the use of a demeaning term. It also signals the growing optimism that hardly any human being, no matter how handicapped or disabled, is beyond some rehabilitation.

A denial of the limits of the possible in effecting cures is thus a central part of the ideology of scientific medicine. It is sustained in part by its actual success in overcoming earlier obstacles and curing illnesses once thought beyond reach, and in part as an act of faith that is at one with the general faith in science. But it is a most potent faith, reaffirmed again and again by actual advances.

Widening of the Distance Between Individual Needs—Creating Vertical Gaps

If it is a part of the reigning idea of medical progress that there are no fixed limits to the therapeutic possibility of cure or amelioration, and thus no boundaries to the meeting of individual needs, that same progress widens the gap among individuals in their potential demand on the healthcare system. One person, the most lucky, may only require a shot of penicillin at a cost of a few dollars to deal with a minor infection over the course of a lifetime—and the healthcare system can meet his individual need. Another person, not so lucky, may require a kidney transplant at a cost of over $200,000 to save his life, and still others may over the course of an extended illness require treatment costing as much as $1.5 million to $2 million; their needs, with more difficulty, might also be met. One newborn child may require a few extra days in the hospital for a few thousand dollars to clear up a minor problem while another may need months in a neonatal intensive care unit at a cost of over $400,000 (and perhaps additional years of extended rehabilitation once discharged); still another may require $800,000 worth of care. The possibilities of expensive rehabilitation for the teenage motorcycle victim or the elderly sufferer of a stroke—possibilities developed only recently—to mention other examples, are enormous. The chaos of state or county healthcare budgets devastated by highly expensive treatments needed by a handful of patients has become a not-uncommon story. A $2 million child welfare budget for an entire county consumed by only a few patients requiring extended neonatal care poses nearly impossible dilemmas for the officials who must manage such budgets. The only perfect escape is a constantly escalating budget, one designed to keep up with medical progress.

These commonplace instances point to what I would call the increasing *vertical gap* of care, that is, the widening cost of curative and life-saving care between the least and most expensive patients, both with the same and with different conditions. That vertical gap can take different forms. One is the gap between different patients with the same condition, a simple versus a complicated newborn case where both are, say, the result of a premature birth. Another is the gap between those with common, inexpensively treated conditions (pneumonia, for instance) and those with rare, expensively treated conditions (major organ failure). Still another is between those with common diseases for which cures (expensive or inexpensive) already exist and those with diseases that are both rare and as yet untreatable, but which might be treatable after more research. There may be what the economists call "marginal returns" in investments designed to equalize treatment for those who experience the gap, but it may just as well be that, if enough money is invested, the return for closing the gap could be a good one. But the cost of trying to do so may be enormously high.

The problem of the vertical gap is a direct consequence of attempting to meet individual needs. Those needs are diverse, but the progress of medicine in being able to do so with a widening range of patients means that there are also few boundaries here. Where death or illness would once quickly have taken the lives of those who suffered severe accidents or illnesses, they can now often be saved; but many can be saved only at great cost. Earlier, the costs would have clustered within a moderate range; now they can wildly vary. Yet if the accepted goal is the meeting of individual curative need—to give everyone a chance at, say, "normal species functioning"—then there is no logical choice but to accept the widening, and necessarily widening, vertical gap. By virtue of redefining what is "normal" and having more success at the margin, the possibilities of pursuing individual need become unlimited. It is just such situations, of course, that have occasioned a hope in cost-benefit analysis. But precisely because there is no way to quantify, or morally judge, the comparative benefits of meeting quite different individual needs, the technique must fail.

The possibilities have rarely been put better than they were by Enoch Powell, during his tenure as minister of health in Great Britain: "There is virtually no limit to the amount of medical care an individual is capable of absorbing. . . . Not only is the range of treatable conditions huge and rapidly growing, there is also a vast range of quality in the treatment of these conditions. . . . There is hardly a type of condition from the most trivial to the gravest which is not susceptible of alternative conditions affording a wide range of skill, care, comfort, privacy, efficiency, and so on. [Finally] there is the multiplier effect of successful medical treatment. Improvement in expectation of survival results in lives that demand further medical care. The poorer (medically speaking) the quality of the lives preserved by advancing medical science, the more intense are the demands they continue to make."

Blurring the Line Between Aspiration and Need

Medical progress has meant the near-banishment of fatalism. Given enough time, money, scientific research, and clinical ingenuity—it is widely believed—no disease, no disability, no stressful psychological state is beyond cure or amelioration. Our aspirations and hopes are at first made credible by medical progress; then, as they move closer to realization, they come to have the status, and the insistence, ordinarily accorded to need. This is the transformation of desire or aspiration into putative need. No one thought, a century ago, that a person suffering from heart disease "needed" a heart transplant; death was simply accepted. But the advent of heart transplants was stimulated first by hope, and that hope became concrete need as transplantation succeeded. People now "need" heart transplants. A whole new category of need has been created, a need originally thought to encompass only younger people but now coming to include older patients as well.

More and more people can be cured of their illnesses, and thus more aspirations turned into needs, those who cannot be cured can be better maintained or rehabilitated, and those who can only be maintained can be given an improved quality of life. That is the faith of modern medicine. When that deeply rooted faith is combined with the high value given individual choice and self-determination, then the meeting of individual need has still another dimension added to it. It will be left to the individual to decide what constitutes need and a decent "quality of life." That the idea of individual quality of life is notoriously subjective is one reason to leave it to individual choice. Still another is that, in a liberal society, it is taken as inappropriate to set societal standards about individual desires and needs. That would require a substantive and deep view of what is ultimately good for individuals, what they should find life worth living for, or be willing to live with. The irony, of course, is that by refusing to repudiate individualist conceptions of need, costs climb so damagingly high that the individual eventually loses. A paradoxical tyranny of egalitarianism also emerges. As we find more complex and expensive ways of meeting individual need, the demand rises that all should have access to such treatments; we then push on, creating still another crisis of equality with further medical progress. Yet we continue to bless the meeting of individual need.

The consequences of this widespread view can only be the blurring of the line between desire and need, particularly when combined with a belief in the indefinite possibility of medical progress. There is, above all, the problem of rising expectations, which opens the distance between aspiration for health and its actual achievement. . . .

. . . What does it mean to pursue a "right to healthcare" in the context of medical progress and its impact on the idea of individual need and, most specifically, to pursue the right to curative healthcare? My answer is direct: The quest becomes an impossible one, doomed to frustration. The claim that we have a right to healthcare is a claim that our neighbor (ordinarily through the instrumentality of government) has an obligation to provide that assistance necessary to meet our individual health needs. But medical progress, far from clarifying those needs, renders them all the more problematical. If those needs do not admit, in principle, of any limits or any clear specifications, then there are no boundaries to our claim for healthcare, certainly none intrinsic to the concept of individual need itself. Since we have, moreover, allowed the value of choice and freedom to overshadow other considerations, we have relinquished the possibility of meaningfully distinguishing morally among needs or attaching any fixed priorities to them. The claim of a right to healthcare becomes, therefore, hopelessly vague and open-ended. It cannot be used to deny on its intrinsic merits anything claimed by the individual in the name of health nor, in the face of a plethora of claims, does it have the ethical resources to set priorities among them.

Limits to claimed rights can of course be set, but that must be done externally; that is, by bringing in considerations foreign to the centrality given the individual in the traditions both of medicine and of individual rights. Overriding economic needs and other social and political priorities are of course prime instances of such foreign intrusions. But the rational foundation for doing so in any way other than through the arbitrary force of political decisions has been destroyed. The struggle within the political process determines the outcome, based on expressed preferences and not necessarily on deeply grounded need. There is no unitary set of values, or goals, that guides the process.

What is the result? By making individual needs open-ended, and embedding those needs within the values of a liberal and pluralistic society, the possibility of order, coherence, and meaningful purpose has been lost. Interest groups have a powerful sway in this setting. They can pursue their own ends unimpeded by any larger design of healthcare goals or priorities. They do not have either to take into consideration the needs of other groups or to propose limits on their own demands. Why should they? There is no incentive, much less reward, for doing so. Their needs are, simply as needs, as important as anyone else's. Since we would not ordinarily think of a claimed need, say, to discover a cure for cancer as narrowly or pejoratively "self-interested," we are not prone to object to such campaigns (unless they seem wasteful and inefficient—the only effective charge that can be entered against them). The net result of many competing health interest groups, however, is that victory tends to go to those with the most political power or the most potent emotional claims. Many other important social needs can thereby be neglected, and there is no reason to think that the general level of health will necessarily be improved.

There is an even more deleterious impact in tying together the idea of rights and individual health needs. Because medical progress renders individual need open-ended and subject to no intrinsic limiting principle, we are left bereft of any clear notion of what kind and scope of healthcare we actually owe each other as a society. We can give no clear meaning to terms such as "adequate care" or "minimal needs," and thus cannot establish policy in any sound way. It is not for nothing that the lesson of the dialysis experience has stuck in the craw of Congress. Established in 1973 as a universal entitlement for all who require dialysis to save their lives from kidney failure—as clear a body need as one could ask—the program grew wildly beyond all early projections and encompassed a wider and wider group of users, some 80,000 at present, including about 30 percent over the age of sixty-five (and the fastest-growing group on dialysis, increasing on average by 13 percent a year).

There has proved to be no feasible way to limit claims upon that program, however sick, old, or unpromising someone might be as a candidate for it. That is the direct and inevitable outcome of making individual need the criterion for access. Moreover, when surveyed, those on dialysis would prefer to continue dialysis even at the price of a great loss of quality of life; hence, medical efficacy itself is not necessarily the only measure of its acceptability to recipients. The widespread assumption that people would prefer to be dead than live a life of very low quality may be wrong. As the author of a study of kidney dialysis concluded, "We may no longer be able to take refuge in the belief that we are only prolonging misery. And if we conclude that the preference to live with an expensive, apparently debilitating chronic illness rather than die is reasonable, then we cannot, at the same time, expect to contain medical costs." If the patient or the patient's physician wants it, he or she will get it. The patient determines need, and the patient determines what counts as a decent quality of life on dialysis. A consequent result is a trend for older and sicker patients to be on dialysis. The fiscally terrifying prospect of similar results with all other illnesses by enacting additional unlimited entitlement programs, much less a comprehensive national health insurance program, has been a powerful obstacle to congressional action.

In that context, the slogan of a "right to healthcare" is one that rightly intimidates legislators. They know that such a claim, combined with intractable individual needs and constant medical innovation, could and probably must turn into an economic monster. The principle of a right to healthcare, lacking intrinsic limits, fails a most important contemporary legislative goal, that of developing principles of entitlement that contain within them some self-limiting boundaries. A principle that provides no way—as part of the principle itself—of setting priorities, no way of setting limits, and no way of setting shared societal goals cannot effectively be used for purposes of public policy. It is to write a blank check, to be filled in as each individual chooses and as medical progress conditions the individual to choose. . . .

Sexual Behavior

Teenagers and young adults often think of "morals" and "sexual morals" as equivalent expressions. Throughout life, our sexual identities and relationships remain central to our happiness and our conceptions of ourselves. The social roles implicit in being a husband, wife, lover, father, or mother remain among the most important we adopt. Our actions in the context of sexual relationships can thus affect other people more profoundly than almost anything else we do. We can make someone happy or break someone's heart. We can even call someone into existence. Sexual morality, for all these reasons, has special importance.

Vincent Punzo argues for traditional sexual morality. Sexual activity, he maintains, is permissible only in the context of long-term commitment—ordinarily, marriage. Our concepts of ourselves, like a proper concept of love, are historical. Only in the context of a long-term commitment, therefore, can people in a sexual relationship treat each other with full respect.

Thomas Mappes sees Kant's categorical imperative as providing the key, if not to all of morality, at least to sexual morality. Kant urged that we treat others as "ends in themselves," not as "means only." In other words, the categorical imperative insists that we not use people but, instead, treat them with the respect that we ourselves deserve as moral agents. Mappes contends, accordingly, that the cardinal principle of sexual behavior is "Don't use people." He discusses applications of the principle, pointing out that, while his theory is more permissive than traditional morality, it prohibits a variety of behaviors, from deception and harassment to rape.

Thomas Nagel discusses the concept of sexual perversion, using it to defend a liberal sexual morality. He develops a model of normal sexual interaction, and sees perversion as a disruption, or incomplete expression, of that model. Whether or not an act is perverted has some moral consequences, Nagel believes, but even perverted sex can be morally acceptable if no better options are available.

Andrea Dworkin takes the rather extreme view that sexual intercourse is always immoral. By its very nature, she contends, intercourse expresses contempt for women. Literally an occupation of a woman's body, it forces the woman into a subjugated role. Sexual equality, she maintains, would require new modes of sexual interaction.

Sidney Callahan, like Dworkin, is a feminist. But she thinks of equality very differently. Sexual equality, she insists, does not require abandoning sexual intercourse. Nor does it require adopting a "male," aggressive sexual attitude. Callahan examines traditionally feminine sex roles and identifies a number of virtues that protect women and the social structure at large. She rejects feminist demands for reproductive freedom as not, ultimately, in the best interests of women, men, or children.

Richard D. Mohr argues that homosexuals should be granted full legal equality with heterosexuals. Sexual identity, he points out, is fundamental to a person's self-concept. And civil rights are basic prerequisites for permitting people to pursue their own conceptions of the good.

Finally, the Ramsey Colloquium, a group of philosophers and theologians, distinguishes tolerance from acceptance. The group agrees with Mohr that homosexuals deserve tolerance. In general, society should not discriminate against people on the basis of sexual preference. The group sees gay rights activists, however, as favoring much more than this—as seeking acceptance of homosexuality as morally equal to heterosexuality. This, the group contends, homosexuals have no right to expect. The government and individual citizens should *tolerate* homosexuality but *prefer* heterosexuality, for the former ultimately threatens human dignity and the social order.

VINCENT C. PUNZO

Morality and Human Sexuality

Vincent C. Punzo is Professor of Philosophy at St. Louis University. (Source: Reflective Naturalism, *New York: Macmillan, 1969. Notes have been omitted. Copyright © 1969 by Vincent Punzo. Reprinted by permission.)*

QUESTIONS FOR REFLECTION

1. How do sexual relationships differ from other human relationships, according to Punzo? Do you agree?
2. What does Punzo mean when he says that the human self is historical? What role does this play in his argument?
3. What is *existential integrity*? How does it relate to Kant's concepts of respect, dignity, and treating a person as an end rather than as a means only?
4. What does existential integrity require of sexual relationships? Why, according to Punzo, does premarital sex lack that integrity? Do you agree?
5. What sort of commitment, in Punzo's view, should a sexual relationship involve? How does this commitment relate to marriage?

If one sees man's moral task as being simply that of not harming anyone, that is if one sees this task in purely negative terms, he will certainly not accept the argument to be presented in the following section. However, if one accepts the notion of the morality of aspiration, if one accepts the view that man's moral task involves the positive attempt to live up to what is best in man, to give reality to what he sees to be the perfection of himself as a human subject, the argument may be acceptable.

Sexuality and the Human Subject

[Prior discussion] has left us with the question as to whether sexual intercourse is a type of activity that is similar to choosing a dinner from a menu. This question is of utmost significance in that one's view of the morality of premarital intercourse seems to depend on the significance that one gives to the sexual encounter in human life. Those such as [John] Wilson and [Eustace] Chesser who see nothing immoral about the premarital character of sexual intercourse seem to see sexual intercourse as being no different from myriad of other purely aesthetic matters. This point is seen in Chesser's questioning of the reason for demanding permanence in the relationship of sexual partners when we do not see such permanence as being important to other human relationships. It is also seen in his asking why we raise a moral issue about premarital coition when two people may engage in it, with the resulting social and psychological consequences being no different than if they had gone to a movie.

Wilson most explicitly makes a case for the view that sexual intercourse does not differ significantly from other human activities. He holds that people think that there is a logical difference between the question "Will you engage in sexual intercourse with me?" and the question, "Will you play tennis with me?" only because they are influenced by the acquisitive character of contemporary society. Granted that the two questions may be identical from the purely formal perspective of logic, the ethician must move beyond this perspective to a consideration of their content. Men and women find themselves involved in many different relationships: for example, as buyer-seller, employer-employee, teacher-student, lawyer-client, and partners or competitors in certain games such as tennis or bridge. Is there any morally significant difference between these relationships and sexual intercourse? We cannot examine all the possible relationships into which a man and woman can enter, but we will consider the employer-employee relationship in order to get some perspective on the distinctive character of the sexual relationship.

A man pays a woman to act as his secretary. What rights does he have over her in such a situation? The woman agrees to work a certain number of hours during the day taking dictation, typing letters, filing reports, arranging appointments and flight schedules, and greeting clients and competitors. In short, we can say that the man has rights to certain of the woman's services or skills. The use of the word "services" may lead some to conclude that this relationship is not significantly different from the relationship between a prostitute and her client in that the prostitute also offers her "services."

It is true that we sometimes speak euphemistically of a prostitute offering her services to a man for a sum of money, but if we are serious about our quest for the difference between the sexual encounter and other types of human relationships, it is necessary to drop euphemisms and face the issue directly. The man and woman who engage in sexual intercourse are giving their bodies, the most intimate physical expression of themselves, over to the other. Unlike the man who plays tennis with a woman, the man who has sexual relations with her has literally entered her. A man and woman engaging in sexual intercourse have united themselves as intimately and as totally as is physically possible for two human beings. Their union is not simply a union of organs, but is as intimate and as total a physical union of two selves as is possible of achievement. Granted the character of this union, it seems strange to imply that there is no need for a man and a woman to give any more thought to the question of whether they should engage in sexual intercourse than to the question of whether they should play tennis.

In opposition to Wilson, I think that it is the acquisitive character of our society that has blinded us to the distinction between the two activities. Wilson's and Chesser's positions seem to imply that exactly the same moral considerations ought to apply to a situation in which a housewife is bartering with a butcher for a few pounds of pork chops and the situation in which two human beings are deciding whether sexual intercourse ought to be an ingredient of their relationship. So long as the butcher does not put his thumb on the scale in the weighing process, so long as he is truthful in stating that the meat is actually pork, so long as the woman pays the proper amount with the proper currency, the trade is perfectly moral. Reflecting on sexual intercourse from the same sort of economic perspective, one can say that so long as the sexual partners are truthful in reporting their freedom from contagious venereal diseases and so long as they are truthful in reporting that they are interested in the activity for the mere pleasure of it or to try out their sexual techniques, there is nothing immoral about such activity. That in the one case pork chops are being exchanged for money whereas in the other the decision concerns the most complete and intimate merging of one's self with another makes no difference to the moral evaluation of the respective cases.

It is not surprising that such a reductionistic outlook should pervade our thinking on sexual matters, since in our society sexuality is used to sell everything from shave cream to underarm deodorants, to soap, to mouthwash, to cigarettes, and to automobiles. Sexuality has come to play so large a role in our commercial lives that it is not surprising that our sexuality should itself come to be treated as a commodity governed by the same moral rules that govern any other economic transaction.

Once sexuality is taken out of this commercial framework, once the character of the sexual encounter is faced directly and squarely, we will come to see that Doctor Mary Calderone has brought out the type of questions that ought to be asked by those contemplating the introduction of sexual intercourse into their relationships: "How many times, and how casually, are you willing to invest a portion of your total self, and to be the custodian of a like investment from the other person, without the sureness of knowing that these investments are being made for keeps?" These questions come out of the recognition that the sexual encounter is a definitive experience, one in which the physical intimacy and merging involves also a merging of the nonphysical dimensions of the partners. With these questions, man moves beyond the negative concern with avoiding his or another's physical and psychological harm to the question of what he is making of himself and what he is contributing to the existential formation of his partner as a human subject.

If we are to make a start toward responding to Calderone's questions we must cease talking about human selfhood in abstraction. The human self is an historical as well as a physical being. He is a being who is capable of making at least a portion of his past an object of his consciousness and thus is able to make this past play a conscious role in his present and in his looking toward the future. He is also a being who looks to the future, who faces tomorrow with plans, ideals, hopes, and fears. The very being of a human self involves his past and his movement toward the future. Moreover, the human self is not completely shut off in his own past and future. Men and women are capable of consciously and purposively uniting themselves in a common career and venture. They can commit themselves to sharing the future with another, sharing it in all its aspects—in its fortunes and misfortunes, in its times of happiness and times of tragedy. Within the lives of those who have so committed themselves to each other, sexual intercourse is a way of asserting and confirming the fullness and totality of their mutual commitment.

Unlike those who have made such a commitment and who come together in the sexual act in the fullness of their selfhood, those who engage in premarital sexual unions and who have made no such commitment act as though they can amputate their bodily existence and the most intimate physical expression of their selfhood from their existence as historical beings. Granting that there may be honesty on the verbal level in that two people engaging in premarital intercourse openly state that they are interested only in the pleasure of the activity, the fact remains that such unions are morally deficient because they lack existential integrity in that there is a total merging and union on a physical level, on the one hand, and a conscious decision not to unite any other dimension of themselves, on the other hand. Their sexual union thus involves a "depersonalization" of their bodily existence, an attempt to cut off the most intimate physical expression of their respective selves from their very selfhood. The mutual agreement of premarital sex partners is an agreement to merge with the other not as a self, but as a body which one takes unto oneself, which one possesses in a most intimate and total fashion for one's own pleasure or designs, allowing the other to treat oneself in the same way. It may be true that no physical or psychological harm may result from such unions, but such partners have failed to existentially incorporate human sexuality, which is at the very least the most intimate physical expression of the human self, into the character of this selfhood.

In so far as premarital sexual unions separate the intimate and total physical union that is sexual intercourse from any commitment to the self in his historicity, human sexuality, and consequently the human body, have been fashioned into external things or objects to be handed over totally to someone else, whenever one feels that he can get possession of another's body, which he can use for his own purposes. The human body has thus been treated no differently from the pork chops spoken of previously or from any other object or commodity, which human beings exchange and haggle over in their day-to-day transactions. One hesitates to use the word that might be used to capture the moral value that has been sacrificed in premarital unions because in our day the word has taken on a completely negative meaning at best, and, at worst, it has become a word used by "sophisticates" to mock or deride certain attitudes toward human sexuality. However, because the word "chastity" has been thus abused is no reason to leave it in the hands of those who have misrepresented the human value to which it gives expression.

The chaste person has often been described as one intent on denying his sexuality. The value of chastity as conceived in this section is in direct opposition to this description. It is the unchaste person who is separating himself from his sexuality, who is willing to exchange human bodies as one would exchange money for tickets to a baseball game—honestly and with no commitment of self to self. Against this alienation of one's sexuality from one's self, an alienation that makes one's sexuality an object, which is to be given to another in exchange for his objectified sexuality, chastity affirms the integrity of the self in his bodily and historical existence. The sexuality of man is seen as an integral part of his subjectivity. Hence, the chaste man rejects depersonalized sexual relations as a reduction of man in his most intimate physical being to the status of an object or pure instrument for another. He asserts that man is a subject and end in himself, not in some trans-temporal, non-physical world, but in the historical-physical world in which he carries on his moral task and where he finds his fellow man. He will not freely make of himself in his bodily existence a thing to be handed over to another's possession, nor will he ask that another treat his own body in this way. The total physical intimacy of sexual intercourse will be an expression of total union with the other self on all levels of their beings. Seen from this perspective, chastity is one aspect of man's attempt to attain existential integrity, to accept his body as a dimension of his total personality.

In concluding this section, it should be noted that I have tried to make a case against the morality of premarital sexual intercourse even in those cases in which the partners are completely honest with each other. There is reason to question whether the complete honesty, to which those who see nothing immoral in such unions refer, is as a matter of fact actually found very often among premarital sex partners. We may well have been dealing with textbook cases which present these unions in their best light. One may be pardoned for wondering whether sexual intercourse often occurs under the following conditions: "Hello, my name is Josiah. I am interested in having a sexual experience with you. I can assure you that I am good at it and that I have no communicable disease. If it sounds good to you and if you have taken the proper contraceptive precautions, we might have a go at it. Of course, I want to make it clear to you that I am interested only in the sexual experience and that I have no intention of making any long-range commitment to you." If those, who defend the morality of premarital sexual unions so long as they are honestly entered into, think that I have misrepresented what they mean by honesty, then they must specify what they mean by an honest premarital union. . . .

Marriage as a Total Human Commitment

The preceding argument against the morality of premarital sexual unions was not based on the view that the moral character of marriage rests on a legal certificate or on a legal or religious ceremony. The argument was not directed against "preceremonial" intercourse, but against premarital intercourse. Morally speaking, a man and woman are married when they make the mutual and total commitment to share the problems and prospects of their historical existence in the world. . . .

. . . A total commitment to another means a commitment to him in his historical existence. Such a commitment is not simply a matter of words or of feelings, however strong. It involves a full existential sharing on the part of two beings of the burdens, opportunities, and challenges of their historical existence.

Granted the importance that the character of their commitment to each other plays in determining the moral quality of a couple's sexual encounter, it is clear that there may be nothing immoral in the behavior of couples who engage in sexual intercourse before participating in the marriage ceremony. For example, it is foolish to say that two people who are totally committed to each other and who have made all the arrangements to live this commitment are immoral if they engage in sexual intercourse the night before the marriage ceremony. Admittedly this position can be abused by those who have made a purely verbal commitment, a commitment, which will be carried out in some vague and ill-defined future. At some time or other, they will unite their two lives totally by setting up house together and by actually undertaking the task of meeting the economic, social, legal, medical responsibilities that are involved in living this commitment. Apart from the reference to a vague and amorphous future time when they will share the full responsibility for each other, their commitment presently realizes itself in going to dances, sharing a box of popcorn at Saturday night movies, and sharing their bodies whenever they can do so without taking too great a risk of having the girl become pregnant.

Having acknowledged that the position advanced in this section can be abused by those who would use the word "commitment" to rationalize what is an interest only in the body of the other person, it must be pointed out that neither the ethician nor any other human being can tell two people whether they actually have made the commitment that is marriage or are mistaking a "warm glow" for such a commitment. There comes a time when this issue falls out of the area of moral philosophy and into the area of practical wisdom. . . .

The characterization of marriage as a total commitment between two human beings may lead some to conclude that the marriage ceremony is a wholly superfluous affair. It must be admitted that people may be morally married without having engaged in a marriage ceremony. However, to conclude from this point that the ceremony is totally meaningless is to lose sight of the social character of human beings. The couple contemplating marriage do not exist in a vacuum, although there may be times when they think they do. Their existences reach out beyond their union to include other human beings. By making their commitment a matter of public record, by solemnly expressing it before the law and in the presence of their respective families and friends and, if they are religious people, in the presence of God and one of his ministers, they sink the roots of their commitment more deeply and extensively in the world in which they live, thus taking steps to provide for the future growth of their commitment to each other. The public expression of this commitment makes it more fully and more explicitly a part of a couple's lives and of the world in which they live. . . .

THOMAS A. MAPPES

Sexual Morality and the Concept of Using Another Person

Thomas A. Mappes is Professor of Philosophy at Frostburg State University, Maryland. (Source: From Thomas A. Mappes and Jane S. Zembaty (ed.), Social Ethics: Morality and Social Policy, *New York: McGraw-Hill, 1992. Notes have been omitted. Reprinted by permission of the author.)*

QUESTIONS FOR REFLECTION

1. How does Mappes interpret Kant's prohibition on using another person as a means only?
2. Can you think of cases where someone gives voluntary informed consent but is nevertheless in some sense used?
3. Conversely, can you think of cases in which someone is treated as an end without voluntary informed consent?
4. How does Mappes distinguish threats from offers? What, in his view, is the moral significance of the distinction? Do you agree?
5. What implications does Mappes's view have for sexual harassment?

The central tenet of *conventional* sexual morality is that nonmarital sex is immoral. A somewhat less restrictive sexual ethic holds that *sex without love* is immoral. If neither of these positions is philosophically defensible, and I would contend that neither is, it does not follow that there are no substantive moral restrictions on human sexual interaction. *Any* human interaction, including sexual interaction, may be judged morally objectionable to the extent that it transgresses a justified moral rule or principle. The way to construct a detailed account of sexual morality, it would seem, is simply to work out the implications of relevant moral rules or principles in the area of human sexual interaction.

As one important step in the direction of such an account, I will attempt to work out the implications of an especially relevant moral principle, the principle that it is wrong for one person to use another person. However ambiguous the expression "using another person" may seem to be, there is a determinate and clearly specificable sense according to which using another person is morally objectionable. Once this morally significant sense of "using another person" is identified and explicated, the concept of using another person can play an important role in the articulation of a defensible account of sexual morality.

I The Morally Significant Sense of "Using Another Person"

Historically, the concept of using another person is associated with the ethical system of Immanuel Kant. According to a fundamental Kantian principle, it is morally wrong for A to use B *merely as a means* (to achieve A's ends). Kant's principle does not rule out A using B as a means, only A using B *merely* as a means, that is, in a way incompatible with respect for B as a person. In the ordinary course of life, it is surely unavoidable (and morally unproblematic) that each of us in numerous ways uses others as a means to achieve our various ends. A college teacher uses students as a means to achieve his or her livelihood. A college student uses instructors as a means of gaining knowledge and skills. Such human interactions, presumably based on the voluntary participation of the respective parties, are quite compatible with the idea of respect for persons. But respect for persons entails that each of us recognize the rightful authority of other persons (as rational beings) to conduct their individual lives as they see fit. We may legitimately recruit others to participate in the satisfaction of our personal ends, but they are used merely as a means whenever we undermine the voluntary or informed character of their consent to interact with us in some desired way. A coerces B at knife point to hand over $200. A uses B merely as a means. If A had requested of B a gift of $200, leaving B free to determine whether or not to make the gift, A would have proceeded in a manner compatible with respect for B as a person. C deceptively rolls back the odometer of a car and thereby manipulates D's decision to buy the car. C uses D merely as a means.

On the basis of these considerations, I would suggest that the morally significant sense of "using another person" is best understood by reference to the notion of *voluntary informed consent.* More specifically, A immorally uses B if and only if A intentionally acts in a way that violates the requirement that B's involvement with A's ends be based on B's voluntary informed consent. If this account is correct, using another person (in the morally significant sense) can arise in at least two important ways: via *coercion,* which is antithetical to voluntary consent, and via *deception,* which undermines the informed character of voluntary consent. . . .

II Deception and Sexual Morality

. . . If we presume a state of affairs in which A desires some form of sexual interaction with B, we can say that this desired form of sexual interaction with B is A's end. Thus A sexually *uses* B if and only if A intentionally acts in a way that violates the requirement that B's sexual interaction with A be based on B's voluntary informed consent. It seems clear then that A may sexually use B in at least two distinctive ways, (1) via coercion and (2) via deception. However, before proceeding to discuss deception and then the more problematic case of coercion, one important point must be made. In emphasizing the centrality of coercion and deception as mechanisms for the sexual using of another person, I have in mind sexual interaction with a fully competent adult partner. We should also want to say, I think, that sexual interaction with a child inescapably involves the sexual using of another person. Even if a child "consents" to sexual interaction, he or she is, strictly speaking, incapable of *informed* consent. It's a matter of being *incompetent* to give consent. Similarly, to the extent that a mentally retarded person is rightly considered incompetent, sexual interaction with such a person amounts to the sexual using of that person, unless someone empowered to give "proxy consent" has done so. (In certain circumstances, sexual involvement might be in the best interests of a mentally retarded person.) We can also visualize the case of an otherwise fully competent adult temporarily disordered by drugs or alcohol. To the extent that such a person is rightly regarded as temporarily incompetent, winning his or her "consent" to sexual interaction could culminate in the sexual using of that person.

There are a host of clear cases in which one person sexually uses another precisely because the former employs deception in a way that undermines the informed character of the latter's consent to sexual interaction. Consider this example. One person, A, has decided, as a matter of personal prudence based on past experience, not to become sexually involved outside the confines of a loving relationship. Another person, B, strongly desires a sexual relationship with A but does not love A. B, aware of A's unwillingness to engage in sex without love, professes love for A, thereby hoping to win A's consent to a sexual relationship. B's ploy is successful; A consents. When the smoke clears and A becomes aware of B's deception, it would be both appropriate and natural for A to complain, "I've been used."

In the same vein, here are some other examples. (1) Mr. A is aware that Ms. B will consent to sexual involvement only on the understanding that in time the two will be married. Mr. A has no intention of marrying Ms. B but says that he will. (2) Ms. C has herpes and is well aware that Mr. D will never consent to sex if he knows of her condition. When asked by Mr. D, Ms. C denies that she has herpes. (3). Mr. E knows that Ms. F will not consent to sexual intercourse in the absence of responsible birth control measures. Mr. E tells Ms. F that he has had a vasectomy, which is not the case. (4) Ms. G knows that Mr. H. would not consent to sexual involvement with a married woman. Ms. G is married but tells Mr. H that she is single. (5) Ms. I is well aware that Ms. J is interested in a stable lesbian relationship and will not consent to become sexually involved with someone who is bisexual. Ms. I tells Ms. J that she is exclusively homosexual, whereas the truth is that she is bisexual.

If one person's consent to sex is predicated on false beliefs that have been intentionally and deceptively inculcated by one's sexual partner in an effort to win the former's consent, the resulting sexual interaction involves one person sexually using another. In each of the above cases, one person explicitly *lies* to another. False information is intentionally conveyed to win consent to sexual interaction, and the end result is the sexual using of another person.

As noted earlier, however, lying is not the only form of deception. Under certain circumstances, the simple withholding of information can be considered a form of deception. Accordingly, it is possible to sexually use another person not only by (deceptively) lying about relevant facts but also by (deceptively) not disclosing relevant facts. If A has good reason to believe that B would refuse to consent to sexual interaction should B become aware of certain factual information, and if A withholds disclosure of this information in order to enhance the possibility of gaining B's consent, then, if B does consent, A sexually uses B via deception. One example will suffice. Suppose that Mr. A meets Ms. B in a singles bar. Mr. A realizes immediately that Ms. B is the sister of Ms. C, a woman that Mr. A has been sexually involved with for a long time. Mr. A, knowing that it is very unlikely that Ms. B will consent to sexual interaction if she becomes aware of Mr. A's involvement with her sister, decides not to disclose this information. If Ms. B eventually consents to sexual interaction, since her consent is the product of Mr. A's deception, it is rightly thought that she has been sexually used by him.

III Coercion and Sexual Morality

We have considered the case of deception. The present task is to consider the more difficult case of coercion. Whereas deception functions to undermine the *informed* character of voluntary consent (to sexual interaction), coercion either obliterates consent entirely (the case of occurrent coercion) or undermines the voluntariness of consent (the case of dispositional coercion).

Forcible rape is the most conspicuous, and most brutal, way of sexually using another person via coercion. Forcible rape may involve either occurrent coercion or dispositional coercion. A man who rapes a woman by the employment of sheer physical force, by simply overpowering her, employs occurrent coercion. There is literally no sexual *interaction* in such a case; only the rapist performs an action. In no sense does the woman consent to or participate in sexual activity. She has no choice in what takes place, or rather, physical force results in her choice being simply beside the point. The employment of occurrent coercion for the purpose of rape "objectifies" the victim in the strongest sense of that term. She is treated like a physical object. One does not interact with physical objects; one acts upon them. In a perfectly ordinary (not the morally significant) sense of the term, we "use" physical objects. But when the victim of rape is treated as if she were a physical object, there we have one of the most vivid examples of the immoral using of another person.

Frequently, forcible rape involves not occurrent coercion (or not *only* occurrent coercion) but dispositional coercion. In dispositional coercion, the relevant factor is not physical force but the threat of harm. The rapist threatens his victim with immediate and serious bodily harm. For example, a man threatens to kill or beat a woman if she resists his sexual demands. She "consents," that is, she submits to his demands. He may demand only passive participation (simply not struggling against him) or he may demand some measure of active participation. Rape that employs dispositional coercion is surely just as wrong as rape that employs occurrent coercion, but there is a notable difference in the mechanism by which the rapist uses his victim in the two cases. With occurrent coercion, the victim's consent is entirely bypassed. With dispositional coercion, the victim's consent is not bypassed. It is coerced. Dispositional coercion undermines the *voluntariness* of consent. The rapist, by employing the threat of immediate and serious bodily harm, may succeed in bending the victim's will. He may gain the victim's "consent." But he uses another person precisely because consent is coerced.

The relevance of occurrent coercion is limited to the case of forcible rape. Dispositional coercion, a notion that also plays an indispensable role in an overall account of forcible rape, now becomes our central concern. Although the threat of immediate and serious bodily harm stands out as the most brutal way of coercing consent to sexual interaction, we must not neglect the employment of other kinds of threats to this same end. There are numerous ways in which one person can effectively harm, and thus effectively threaten, another. Accordingly, for example, consent to sexual interaction might be coerced by threatening to damage someone's reputation. If a person consents to sexual interaction to avoid a threatened harm, then that person has been sexually used (via dispositional coercion). In the face of a threat, of course, it remains possible that a person will refuse to comply with another's sexual demands. It is probably best to describe this sort of situation as a case not of coercion, which entails the *successful* use of threats to gain compliance, but of *attempted* coercion. Of course, the moral fault of an individual emerges with the *attempt* to coerce. A person who attempts murder is morally blameworthy even if the attempt fails. The same is true for someone who fails in an effort to coerce consent to sexual interaction.

Consider now each of the following cases:

Case 1 Mr. Supervisor makes a series of increasingly less subtle sexual overtures to Ms. Employee. These advances are consistently and firmly rejected by Ms. Employee. Eventually, Mr. Supervisor makes it clear that the granting of "sexual favors" is a condition of her continued employment.

Case 2 Ms. Debtor borrowed a substantial sum of money from Mr. Creditor, on the understanding that she would pay it back within one year. In the meantime, Ms. Debtor has become sexually attracted to Mr. Creditor, but he does not share her interest. At the end of the one-year period, Mr. Creditor asks Ms. Debtor to return the money. She says she will be happy to return the money so long as he consents to sexual interaction with her.

Case 3 Mr. Theatregoer has two tickets to the most talked-about play of the season. He is introduced to a woman whom he finds sexually attractive and who shares his interest in the theater. In the course of their conversation, she expresses disappointment that the play everyone is talking about is sold out; she would love to see it. At this point, Mr. Theatregoer suggests that she be his guest at the theater. "Oh, by the way," he says, "I always expect sex from my dates."

Case 4 Ms. Jetsetter is planning a trip to Europe. She has been trying for some time to develop a sexual relationship with a man who has shown little interest in her. She knows, however, that he has always wanted to go to Europe and that it is only lack of money that has deterred him. Ms. Jetsetter proposes that he come along as her traveling companion, all expenses paid, on the express understanding that sex is part of the arrangement.

Cases 1 and 2 involve attempts to sexually use another person whereas cases 3 and 4 do not. To see why this is so, it is essential to introduce a distinction between two kinds of proposals, viz., the distinction between *threats* and *offers*. The logical form of a threat differs from the logical form of an offer in the following way. Threat: "If you *do not* do what I am proposing you do, I will bring about an *undesirable consequence* for you." Offer: "If you *do* what I am proposing you do, I will bring about a *desirable consequence* for you." The person who makes a threat attempts to gain compliance by attaching an undesirable consequence to the alternative of noncompliance. This person attempts to *coerce* consent. The person who makes an offer attempts to gain compliance by attaching a desirable consequence to the alternative of compliance. This person attempts not to coerce but to *induce* consent.

Since threats are morally problematic in a way that offers are not, it is not uncommon for threats to be advanced in the language of offers. Threats are represented as if they were offers. An armed assailant might say, "I'm going to make you an *offer.* If you give me your money, I will allow you to go on living." Though this proposal on the surface has the logical form of an offer, it is in reality a threat. The underlying sense of the proposal is this: "If you do not give me your money, I will kill you." If, in a given case, it is initially unclear whether a certain proposal is to count as a threat or an offer, ask the following question. Does the proposal in question have the effect of making a person *worse off upon noncompliance?* The recipient of an offer, upon noncompliance, *is not worse off* than he or she was before the offer. In contrast, the recipient of a threat, upon noncompliance, *is worse off* than he or she was before the threat. Since the "offer" of our armed assailant has the effect, upon noncompliance, of rendering its recipient worse off (relative to the preproposal situation of the recipient), the recipient is faced with a threat, not an offer.

The most obvious way for a coercer to attach an undesirable consequence to the path of noncompliance is by threatening to render the victim of coercion materially worse off than he or she has heretofore been. Thus a person is threatened with loss of life, bodily injury, damage to property, damage to reputation, etc. It is important to realize, however, that a person can also be effectively coerced by being threatened with the withholding of something (in some cases, what we would call a "benefit") to which the person is entitled. Suppose that A is mired in quicksand and is slowly but surely approaching death. When B happens along, A cries out to B for assistance. All B need do is throw A a rope. B is quite willing to accommodate A, "provided you pay me $100,000 over the next ten years." Is B making A an offer? Hardly! B, we must presume, stands under a moral obligation to come to the aid of a person in serious distress, at least when such assistance entails no significant risk, sacrifice of time, etc. A is entitled to B's assistance. Thus, in reality, B attaches an undesirable consequence to A's noncompliance with the proposal that A pay B $100,000. A is undoubtedly better off that B has happened along, but A is not rendered better off *by B's proposal.* Before B's proposal, A legitimately expected assistance from B, "no strings attached." In attaching a very unwelcome string, B's proposal effectively renders A worse off. What B proposes, then, is not an offer of assistance. Rather, B threatens A with the withholding of something (assistance) that A is entitled to have from B.

Since threats have the effect of rendering a person worse off upon noncompliance, it is ordinarily the case that a person does not welcome (indeed, despises) them. Offers, on the other hand, are ordinarily welcome to a person. Since an offer provides no penalty for noncompliance with a proposal but only an inducement for compliance, there is *in principle* only potential advantage in being confronted with an offer. In real life, of course, there are numerous reasons why a person may be less than enthusiastic about being presented with an offer. Enduring the presentation of trivial offers does not warrant the necessary time and energy expenditures. Offers can be both annoying and offensive; certainly this is true of some sexual offers. A person might also be unsettled by an offer that confronts him or her with a difficult decision. All this, however, is compatible with the fact that an offer is fundamentally welcome to a rational person in the sense that the *content* of an offer necessarily widens the field of opportunity and thus provides, in principle, only potential advantage.

With the distinction between threats and offers clearly in view, it now becomes clear why cases 1 and 2 do indeed involve attempts to sexually use another person whereas cases 3 and 4 do not. Cases 1 and 2 embody threats, whereas cases 3 and 4 embody offers. In case 1, Mr. Supervisor proposes sexual interaction with Ms. Employee and, in an effort to gain compliance, threatens her with the loss of her job. Mr. Supervisor thereby attaches an undesirable consequence to one of Ms. Employee's alternatives, the path of noncompliance. Typical of the threat situation, Mr. Supervisor's proposal has the effect of rendering Ms. Employee worse off upon noncompliance. Mr. Supervisor is attempting via (dispositional) coercion to sexually use Ms. Employee. The situation in case 2 is similar. Ms. Debtor, as *she* might be inclined to say, "offers" to pay Mr. Creditor the money she owes him *if* he consents to sexual interaction with her. In reality, Ms. Debtor is threatening Mr. Creditor, attempting to coerce his consent to sexual interaction, attempting to sexually use him. Though Mr. Creditor is not now in possession of the money Ms. Debtor owes him, he is *entitled* to receive it from her at this time. She threatens to deprive him of something to which he is entitled. Clearly, her proposal has the effect of rendering him worse off upon noncompliance. Before her proposal, he had the legitimate expectation, "no strings attached," of receiving the money in question.

Cases 3 and 4 embody offers; neither involves an attempt to sexually use another person. Mr. Theatregoer simply provides an inducement for the woman he has just met to accept his proposal of sexual interaction. He offers her the opportunity to see the play that everyone is talking about. In attaching a desirable consequence to the alternative of compliance, Mr. Theatregoer in no way threatens or attempts to coerce his potential companion. Typical of the offer situation, his proposal does not have the effect of rendering her worse off upon noncompliance. She now has a new opportunity; if she chooses to forgo this opportunity, she is no worse off. The situation in case 4 is similar. Ms. Jetsetter provides an inducement for a man that she is interested in to accept her proposal of sexual involvement. She offers him the opportunity to see Europe, without expense, as her traveling companion. Before Ms. Jetsetter's proposal, he had no prospect of a European trip. If he chooses to reject her proposal, he is no worse off than he has heretofore been. Ms. Jetsetter's proposal embodies an offer, not a threat. She cannot be accused of attempting to sexually use her potential traveling companion.

Consider now two further cases, 5 and 6, each of which develops in the following way. Professor Highstatus, a man of high academic accomplishment, is sexually attracted to a student in one of his classes. He is very anxious to secure her consent to sexual interaction. Ms. Student, confused and unsettled by his sexual advances, has begun to practice "avoidance behavior." To the extent that it is possible, she goes out of her way to avoid him.

Case 5 Professor Highstatus tells Ms. Student that, though her work is such as to entitle her to a grade of B in the class, she will be assigned a D unless she consents to sexual interaction.

Case 6 Professor Highstatus tells Ms. Student that, though her work is such as to entitle her to a grade of B, she will be assigned an A if she consents to sexual interaction.

It is clear that case 5 involves an attempt to sexually use another person. Case 6, however, at least at face value, does not. In case 5, Professor Highstatus *threatens* to deprive Ms. Student of the grade she deserves. In case 6, he *offers* to assign her a grade that is higher than she deserves. In case 5, Ms. Student would be worse off upon noncompliance with Professor Highstatus' proposal. In case 6, she would not be worse off upon noncompliance with his proposal. In saying that case 6 does not involve an attempt to sexually use another person, it is not being asserted that Professor Highstatus is acting in a morally legitimate fashion. In offering a student a higher grade than she deserves, he is guilty of abusing his institutional authority. He is under an obligation to assign the grades that students earn, as defined by the relevant course standards. In case 6, Professor Highstatus is undoubtedly acting in a morally reprehensible way, but in contrast to case 5, where it is fair to say that he both abuses his institutional authority *and* attempts to sexually use another person, we can plausibly say that in case 6 his moral failure is limited to abuse of his institutional authority.

There remains, however, a suspicion that case 6 might after all embody an attempt to sexually use another person. There is no question that the literal content of what Professor Highstatus conveys to Ms. Student has the logical form of an offer and not a threat. Still, is it not the case that Ms. Student may very well feel threatened? Professor Highstatus, in an effort to secure consent to sexual interaction, has announced that he will assign Ms. Student a higher grade than she deserves. Can she really turn him down without substantial risk? Is he not likely to retaliate? If she spurns him, will he not lower her grade or otherwise make it harder for her to succeed in her academic program? He does, after all, have power over her. Will he use it to her detriment? Surely he is not above abusing his institutional authority to achieve his ends; this much is abundantly clear from his willingness to assign a grade higher than a student deserves.

Is Professor Highstatus naive to the threat that Ms. Student may find implicit in the situation? Perhaps. In such a case, if Ms. Student reluctantly consents to sexual interaction, we may be inclined to say that he has *unwittingly* used her. More likely, Professor Highstatus is well aware of the way in which Ms. Student will perceive his proposal. He knows that threats need not be verbally expressed. Indeed, it may even be the case that he consciously exploits his underground reputation. "Everyone knows what happens to the women who reject Professor Highstatus's little offers." To the extent, then, that Professor Highstatus intends to convey a threat in case 6, he is attempting via coercion to sexually use another person.

Many researchers "have pointed out the fact that the possibility of sanctions for noncooperation is implicit in all sexual advances across authority lines, as between teacher and student." I do not think that this consideration should lead us to the conclusion that a person with an academic appointment is obliged in all circumstances to refrain from attempting to initiate sexual involvement with one of his or her students. Still, since even "good faith" sexual advances may be ambiguous in the eyes of a student, it is an interesting question what precautions an instructor must take to avoid unwittingly coercing a student to consent to sexual interaction.

Much of what has been said about the professor/student relationship in an academic setting can be applied as well to the supervisor/subordinate relationship in an employment setting. A manager who functions within an organizational structure is required to evaluate fairly his or her subordinates according to relevant corporate or institutional standards. An unscrupulous manager, willing to abuse his or her institutional authority in an effort to win the consent of a subordinate to sexual interaction, can advance threats and/or offers related to the managerial task of employee evaluation. An employee whose job performance is entirely satisfactory can be threatened with an unsatisfactory performance rating, perhaps leading to termination. An employee whose job performance is excellent can be threatened with an unfair evaluation, designed to bar the employee from recognition, merit pay, consideration for promotion, etc. Such threats, when made in an effort to coerce employee consent to sexual interaction, clearly embody the attempt to sexually use another person. On the other hand, the manager who (abusing his or her institutional authority) offers to provide an employee with an inflated evaluation as an inducement for consent to sexual interaction does not, at face value, attempt to sexually use another person. Of course, all of the qualifications introduced in the discussion of case 6 above are applicable here as well.

THOMAS NAGEL

Sexual Perversion

Thomas Nagel is Professor of Philosophy at New York University. *(Source: From* Mortal Questions. *Notes have been omitted.*

QUESTIONS FOR REFLECTION

1. What is a perversion, in general? What conditions should any account of perversions meet?
2. Summarize Nagel's account of what sexual perversion is. What activities count as perversions, in his view? Do you agree?
3. What sexual activities, in Nagel's view, are not perversions? Do you agree?
4. What is the moral significance of sexual perversion?
5. Discuss Nagel's concept of sexual perversion from either a Kantian or a utilitarian point of view. Does it have any moral significance, from those perspectives?

4 / SEXUAL PERVERSION

There is something to be learned about sex from the fact that we possess a concept of sexual perversion. I wish to examine the idea, defending it against the charge of unintelligibility and trying to say exactly what about human sexuality qualifies it to admit of perversions. Let me begin with some general conditions that the concept must meet if it is to be viable at all. These can be accepted without assuming any particular analysis.

First, if there are any sexual perversions, they will have to be sexual desires or practices that are in some sense unnatural, though the explanation of this natural/unnatural distinction is of course the main problem. Second, certain practices will be perversions if anything is, such as shoe fetishism, bestiality, and sadism; other practices, such as unadorned sexual intercourse, will not be; about still others there is controversy. Third, if there are perversions, they will be unnatural sexual *inclinations* rather than just unnatural practices adopted not from inclination but for other reasons. Thus contraception, even if it is thought to be a deliberate perversion of the sexual and reproductive functions, cannot be significantly described as a *sexual* perversion. A sexual perversion must reveal itself in conduct that expresses an unnatural *sexual* preference. And although there might be a form of fetishism focused on the employment of contraceptive devices, that is not the usual explanation for their use.

The connection between sex and reproduction has no bearing on sexual perversion. The latter is a concept of psychological, not physiological, interest, and it is a concept that we do not apply to the lower animals, let alone to plants, all of which have reproductive functions that can go astray in various ways. (Think of seedless oranges.) Insofar as we are prepared to regard higher animals as perverted, it is because of their psychological, not their anatomical, similarity to humans. Furthermore, we do not regard as a perversion every deviation from the reproductive function of sex in humans: sterility, miscarriage, contraception, abortion.

Nor can the concept of sexual perversion be defined in terms of social disapprobation or custom. Consider all the societies that have frowned upon adultery and fornication. These have not been regarded as unnatural practices, but have been thought objectionable in other ways. What is regarded as unnatural admittedly varies from culture to culture, but the classification is not a pure expression of disapproval or distaste. In fact it is often regarded as a *ground* for disapproval, and that suggests that the classification has independent content.

I shall offer a psychological account of sexual perversion that depends on a theory of sexual desire and human sexual interactions. To approach this solution I shall first consider a contrary position that would justify skepticism about the existence of any sexual perversions at all, and perhaps even about the significance of the term. The skeptical argument runs as follows:

"Sexual desire is simply one of the appetites, like hunger and thirst. As such it may have various objects, some more common than others perhaps, but none in any sense 'natural.' An appetite is identified as sexual by means of the organs and erogenous zones in which its satisfaction can be to some extent localized, and the special sensory pleasures which form the core of that satisfaction. This enables us to recognize widely divergent goals, activities, and desires as sexual, since it is conceivable in principle that anything should produce sexual pleasure and that a nondeliberate, sexually charged desire for it should arise (as a result of conditioning, if nothing else). We may fail to empathize with some of these desires, and some of them, like sadism, may be objectionable on extraneous grounds, but once we have observed that they meet the criteria for being sexual, there is nothing more to be said on *that* score. Either they are sexual or they are not: sexuality does not admit of imperfection, or perversion, or any other such qualification—it is not that sort of affection."

This is probably the received radical position. It suggests that the cost of defending a psychological account may be to deny that sexual desire is an appetite. But insofar as that line of defense is plausible, it should make us suspicious of the simple picture of appetites on which the skepticism depends. Perhaps the standard appetites, like hunger, cannot be classed as pure appetites in that sense either, at least in their human versions.

Can we imagine anything that would qualify as a gastronomical perversion? Hunger and eating, like sex, serve a biological function and also play a significant role in our inner lives. Note that there is little temptation to describe as perverted an appetite for substances that are not nourishing: we should probably not consider someone's appetites *perverted* if he liked to eat paper, sand, wood, or cotton. Those are merely rather odd and very unhealthy tastes: they lack the psychological complexity that we expect of perversions. (Coprophilia, being already a sexual perversion, may be disregarded.) If on the other hand someone liked to eat cookbooks, or magazines with pictures of food in them, and preferred these to ordinary food—or if when hungry he sought satisfaction by fondling a napkin or ashtray from his favorite restaurant—then the concept of perversion might seem appropriate (it would be natural to call it gastronomical fetishism). It would be natural to describe as gastronomically perverted someone who could eat only by having food forced down his throat through a funnel, or only if the meal were a living animal. What helps is the peculiarity of the desire itself, rather than the inappropriateness of its object to the biological function that the desire serves. Even an appetite can have perversions if in addition to its biological function it has a significant psychological structure.

In the case of hunger, psychological complexity is provided by the activities that give it expression. Hunger is not merely a disturbing sensation that can be quelled by eating; it is an attitude toward edible portions of the external world, a desire to treat them in rather special ways. The method of ingestion: chewing, savoring, swallowing, appreciating the texture and smell, all are important components of the relation, as is the passivity and controllability of the food (the only animals we eat live are helpless mollusks). Our relation to food depends also on our size: we do not live upon it or burrow into it like aphids or worms. Some of these features are more central than others, but an adequate phenomenology of eating would have to treat it as a relation to the external world and a way of appropriating bits of that world, with characteristic affection. Displacements or serious restrictions of the desire to eat could then be described as perversions, if they undermined that direct relation between man and food which is the natural expression of hunger. This explains why it is easy to imagine gastronomical fetishism, voyeurism, exhibitionism, or even gastronomical sadism and Masochism. Some of these perversions are fairly common.

If we can imagine perversions of an appetite like hunger, it should be possible to make sense of the concept of sexual perversion. I do not wish to imply that sexual desire is an appetite—only that being an appetite is no bar to admitting of perversions. Like hunger, sexual desire has as its characteristic object a certain relation with something in the external world; only in this case it is usually a person rather than an omelet, and the relation is considerably more complicated. This added complication allows scope for correspondingly complicated perversions.

The fact that sexual desire is a feeling about other persons may encourage a pious view of its psychological content—that it is properly the expression of some other attitude, like love, and that when it occurs by itself it is incomplete or subhuman. (The extreme Platonic version of such a view is that sexual practices are all vain attempts to express something they cannot in principle achieve: this makes them all perversions, in a sense.) But sexual desire is complicated enough without having to be linked to anything else as a condition for phenomenological analysis. Sex may serve various functions—economic, social, altruistic—but it also has its own content as a relation between persons.

The object of sexual attraction is a particular individual, who transcends the properties that make him attractive. When different persons are attracted to a single person for different reasons—eyes, hair, figure, laugh, intelligence—we nevertheless feel that the object of their desire is the same. There is even an inclination to feel that this is so if the lovers have different sexual aims, if they include both men and women, for example. Different specific attractive characteristics seem to provide enabling conditions for the operation of a single basic feeling, and the different aims all provide expressions of it. We approach the sexual attitude toward the person through the features that we find attractive, but these features are not the objects of that attitude.

This is very different from the case of an omelet. Various people may desire it for different reasons, one for its fluffiness, another for its mushrooms, another for its unique combination of aroma and visual aspect; yet we do not enshrine the transcendental omelet as the true common object of their affections. Instead we might say that several desires have accidentally converged on the same object: any omelet with the crucial characteristics would do as well. It is not similarly true that any person with the same flesh distribution and way of smoking can be substituted as object for a particular sexual desire that has been elicited by those characteristics. It may be that they recur, but it will be a new sexual attraction with a new particular object, not merely a transfer of the old desire to someone else. (This is true even in cases where the new object is unconsciously identified with a former one.)

The importance of this point will emerge when we see how complex a psychological interchange constitutes the natural development of sexual attraction. This would be incomprehensible if its object were not a particular person, but rather a person of a certain *kind*. Attraction is only the beginning, and fulfillment does not consist merely of behavior and contact expressing this attraction, but involves much more. . . .

Sexual desire involves a kind of perception, but not merely a single perception of its object, for in the paradigm case of mutual desire there is a complex system of superimposed mutual perceptions—not only perceptions of the sexual object, but perceptions of oneself. Moreover, sexual awareness of another involves considerable self-awareness to begin with—more than is involved in ordinary sensory perception. The experience is felt as an assault on oneself by the view (or touch, or whatever) of the sexual object.

Let us consider a case in which the elements can be separated. For clarity we will restrict ourselves initially to the somewhat artificial case of desire at a distance. Suppose a man and a woman, whom we may call Romeo and Juliet, are at opposite ends of a cocktail lounge, with many mirrors on the walls which permit unobserved observation, and even mutual unobserved observation. Each of them is sipping a martini and studying other people in the mirrors. At some point Romeo notices Juliet. He is moved, somehow, by the softness of her hair and the diffidence with which she sips her martini, and this arouses him sexually. Let us say that *X senses Y* whenever *X* regards *Y* with sexual desire. (*Y* need not be a person, and *X*'s apprehension of *Y* can be visual, tactile, olfactory, etc., or purely imaginary; in the present example we shall concentrate on vision.) So Romeo senses Juliet, rather than merely noticing her. At this stage he is aroused by an unaroused object, so he is more in the sexual grip of his body than she of hers.

Let us suppose, however, that Juliet now senses Romeo in another mirror on the opposite wall, though neither of them yet knows that he is seen by the other (the mirror angles provide three-quarter views). Romeo then begins to notice in Juliet the subtle signs of sexual arousal, heavy-lidded stare, dilating pupils, faint flush, etc. This of course intensifies her bodily presence, and he not only notices but senses this as well. His arousal is nevertheless still solitary. But now, cleverly calculating the line of her stare without actually looking her in the eyes, he realizes that it is directed at him through the mirror on the opposite wall. That is, he notices, and moreover senses, Juliet sensing him. This is definitely a new development, for it gives him a sense of embodiment not only through his own reactions but through the eyes and reactions of another. Moreover, it is separable from the initial sensing of Juliet; for sexual arousal might begin with a person's sensing that he is sensed and being assailed by the perception of the other person's desire rather than merely by the perception of the person.

But there is a further step. Let us suppose that Juliet, who is a little slower than Romeo, now senses that he senses her. This puts Romeo in a position to notice, and be aroused by, her arousal at being sensed by him. He senses that she senses that he senses her. This is still another level of arousal, for he becomes conscious of his sexuality through his awareness of its effect on her and of her awareness that this effect is due to him. Once she takes the same step and senses that he senses her sensing him, it becomes difficult to state, let alone imagine, further iterations, though they may be logically distinct. If both are alone, they will presumably turn to look at each other directly, and the proceedings will continue on another plane. Physical contact and intercourse are natural extensions of this complicated visual exchange, and mutual touch can involve all the complexities of awareness present in the visual case, but with a far greater range of subtlety and acuteness.

Ordinarily, of course, things happen in a less orderly fashion—sometimes in a great rush—but I believe that some version of this overlapping system of distinct sexual perceptions and interactions is the basic framework of any full-fledged sexual relation and that relations involving only part of the complex are significantly incomplete. The account is only schematic, as it must be to achieve generality. Every real sexual act will be psychologically far more specific and detailed, in ways that depend not only on the physical techniques employed and on anatomical details, but also on countless features of the participants' conceptions of themselves and of each other, which become embodied in the act. (It is familiar enough fact, for example, that people often take their social roles and the social roles of their partners to bed with them.)

The general schema is important, however, and the proliferation of levels of mutual awareness it involves is an example of a type of complexity that typifies human interactions. Consider aggression, for example. If I am angry with someone, I want to make him feel it, either to produce self-reproach by getting him to see himself through the eyes of my anger, and to dislike what he sees—or else to produce reciprocal anger or fear, by getting him to perceive my anger as a threat or attack. What I want will depend on the details of my anger, but in either case it will involve a desire that the object of that anger be aroused. This accomplishment constitutes the fulfillment of my emotion, through domination of the object's feelings.

Another example of such reflexive mutual recognition is to be found in the phenomenon of meaning, which appears to involve an intention to produce a belief or other effect in another by bringing about his recognition of one's intention to produce that effect. . . . Sex has a related structure: it involves a desire that one's partner be aroused by the recognition of one's desire that he or she be aroused.

. . . Hunger leads to spontaneous interactions with food; sexual desire leads to spontaneous interactions with other persons, whose bodies are asserting their sovereignty in the same way, producing involuntary reactions and spontaneous impulses in *them*. These reactions are perceived, and the perception of them is perceived, and that perception is in turn perceived; at each step the domination of the person by his body is reinforced, and the sexual partner becomes more possessible by physical contact, penetration, and envelopment.

Desire is therefore not merely the perception of a pre-existing embodiment of the other, but ideally a contribution to his further embodiment which in turn enhances the original subject's sense of himself. This explains why it is important that the partner be aroused, and not merely aroused, but aroused by the awareness of one's desire. It also explains the sense in which desire has unity and possession as its object: physical possession must eventuate in creation of the sexual object in the image of one's desire, and not merely in the object's recognition of that desire, or in his or her own private arousal.

Even if this is a correct model of the adult sexual capacity, it is not plausible to describe as perverted every deviation from it. For example, if the partners in heterosexual intercourse indulge in private heterosexual fantasies, thus avoiding recognition of the real partner, that would, on this model, constitute a defective sexual relation. It is not, however, generally regarded as a perversion. Such examples suggest that a simple dichotomy between perverted and unperverted sex is too crude to organize the phenomena adequately.

Still, various familiar deviations constitute truncated or incomplete versions of the complete configuration, and may be regarded as perversions of the central impulse. If sexual desire is prevented from taking its full interpersonal form, it is likely to find a different one. The concept of perversion implies that a normal sexual development has been turned aside by distorting influences. I have little to say about this causal condition. But if perversions are in some sense unnatural, they must result from interference with the development of a capacity that is there potentially.

It is difficult to apply this condition, because environmental factors play a role in determining the precise form of anyone's sexual impulse. Early experiences in particular seem to determine the choice of a sexual object. To describe some causal influences as distorting and others as merely formative is to imply that certain general aspects of human sexuality realize a definite potential whereas many of the details in which people differ realize an indeterminate potential, so that they cannot be called more or less natural. What is included in the definite potential is therefore very important, although the distinction between definite and indeterminate potential is obscure. Obviously a creature incapable of developing the levels of interpersonal sexual awareness I have described could not be deviant in virtue of the failure to do so. (Though even a chicken might be called perverted in an extended sense if it had been conditioned to develop a fetishistic attachment to a telephone.) But if humans will tend to develop some version of reciprocal interpersonal sexual awareness unless prevented, then cases of blockage can be called unnatural or perverted.

Some familiar deviations can be described in this way. Narcissistic practices and intercourse with animals, infants, and inanimate objects seem to be stuck at some primitive version of the first stage of sexual feeling. If the object is not alive, the experience is reduced entirely to an awareness of one's own sexual embodiment. Small children and animals permit awareness of the embodiment of the other, but present obstacles to reciprocity, to the recognition by the sexual object of the subject's desire as the source of his (the object's) sexual self-awareness. Voyeurism and exhibitionism are also incomplete relations. The exhibitionist wishes to display his desire without needing to be desired in return; he may even fear the sexual attentions of others. A voyeur, on the other hand, need not require any recognition by his object at all: certainly not a recognition of the voyeur's arousal.

On the other hand, if we apply our model to the various forms that may be taken by two-party heterosexual intercourse, none of them seem clearly to qualify as perversions. Hardly anyone can be found these days to inveigh against oral–genital contact, and the merits of buggery are urged by such respectable figures as D. H. Lawrence and Norman Mailer. In general, it would appear that any bodily contact between a man and a woman that gives them sexual pleasure is a possible vehicle for the system of multi-level interpersonal awareness that I have claimed is the basic psychological content of sexual interaction. Thus a liberal platitude about sex is upheld.

The really difficult cases are sadism, masochism, and homosexuality. The first two are widely regarded as perversions and the last is controversial. In all three cases the issue depends partly on causal factors: do these dispositions result only when normal development has been prevented? Even the form in which this question has been posed is circular, because of the word "normal." We appear to need an independent criterion for a distorting influence, and we do not have one.

It may be possible to class sadism and masochism as perversions because they fall short of interpersonal reciprocity. Sadism concentrates on the evocation of passive self-awareness in others, but the sadist's engagement is itself active and requires a retention of deliberate control which may impede awareness of himself as a bodily subject of passion in the required sense. De Sade claimed that the object of sexual desire was to evoke involuntary responses from one's partner, especially audible ones. The infliction of pain is no doubt the most efficient way to accomplish this, but it requires a certain abrogation of one's own exposed spontaneity. A masochist on the other hand imposes the same disability on his partner as the sadist imposes on himself. The masochist cannot find a satisfactory embodiment as the object of another's sexual desire, but only as the object of his control. He is passive not in relation to his partner's passion but in relation to his nonpassive agency. In addition, the subjection to one's body characteristic of pain and physical restraint is of a very different kind from that of sexual excitement: pain causes people to contract rather than dissolve. These descriptions may not be generally accurate. But to the extent that they are, sadism and masochism would be disorders of the second stage of awareness—the awareness of oneself as an object of desire.

Homosexuality cannot similarly be classed as a perversion on phenomenological grounds. Nothing rules out the full range of interpersonal perceptions between persons of the same sex. The issue then depends on whether homosexuality is produced by distorting influences that block or displace a natural tendency to heterosexual development. And the influences must be more distorting than those which lead to a taste for large breasts or fair hair or dark eyes. These also are contingencies of sexual preference in which people differ, without being perverted.

The question is whether heterosexuality is the natural expression of male and female sexual dispositions that have not been distorted. It is an unclear question, and I do not know how to approach it. There is much support for an aggressive–passive distinction between male and female sexuality. In our culture the male's arousal tends to initiate the perceptual exchange, he usually makes the sexual approach, largely controls the course of the act, and of course penetrates whereas the woman receives. When two men or two women engage in intercourse they cannot both adhere to these sexual roles. But a good deal of deviation from them occurs in heterosexual intercourse. Women can be sexually aggressive and men passive, and temporary reversals of role are not uncommon in heterosexual exchanges of reasonable length. For these reasons it seems to be doubtful that homosexuality must be a perversion, though like heterosexuality it has perverted forms.

Let me close with some remarks about the relation of perversion to good, bad, and morality. The concept of perversion can hardly fail to be evaluative in some sense, for it appears to involve the notion of an ideal or at least adequate sexuality which the perversions in some way fail to achieve. So, if the concept is viable, the judgment that a person or practice or desire is perverted will constitute a sexual evaluation, implying that better sex, or a better specimen of sex, is possible. This in itself is a very weak claim, since the evaluation might be in a dimension that is of little interest to us. (Though, if my account is correct, that will not be true.)

Whether it is a moral evaluation, however, is another question entirely—one whose answer would require more understanding of both morality and perversion than can be deployed here. Moral evaluation of acts and of persons is a rather special and very complicated matter, and by no means all our evaluations of persons and their activities are moral evaluations. We make judgments about people's beauty or health or intelligence which are evaluative without being moral. Assessments of their sexuality may be similar in that respect.

Furthermore, moral issues aside, it is not clear that unperverted sex is necessarily *preferable* to the perversions. It may be that sex which receives the highest marks for perfection *as sex* is less enjoyable than certain perversions; and if enjoyment is considered very important, that might outweigh considerations of sexual perfection in determining rational preference.

That raises the question of the relation between the evaluative content of judgments of perversion and the rather common *general* distinction between good and bad sex. The latter distinction is usually confined to sexual acts, and it would seem, within limits, to cut across the other: even someone who believed, for example, that homosexuality was a perversion could admit a distinction between better and worse homosexual sex, and might even allow that good homosexual sex could be better *sex* than not very good unperverted sex. If this is correct, it supports the position that, if judgments of perversion are viable at all, they represent only one aspect of the possible evaluation of sex, even *qua sex*. Moreover it is not the only important aspect: sexual deficiencies that evidently do not constitute perversions can be the object of great concern.

Finally, even if perverted sex is to that extent not so good as it might be, bad sex is generally better than none at all. This should not be controversial: it seems to hold for other important matters, like food, music, literature, and society. In the end, one must choose from among the available alternatives, whether their availability depends on the environment or on one's own constitution. And the alternatives have to be fairly grim before it becomes rational to opt for nothing.

ANDREA DWORKIN

Occupation/Collaboration

Andrea Dworkin is a writer living in New York City. She is the author of Ice and Fire; Letters from a War Zone; Our Blood; Pornography; *and other works. (Source: From* Intercourse, *New York: Free Press, 1987. Notes have been omitted. Copyright © 1987 by Andrea Dworkin. Reprinted by permission.)*

QUESTIONS FOR REFLECTION

1. Dworkin argues that all sexual intercourse is morally objectionable. Why?
2. Why is intercourse, according to Dworkin, an attack on freedom rather than an exercise of freedom?
3. How, according to Dworkin, are women collaborators in male oppression?
4. Discuss Dworkin's views from a Kantian perspective. Do Dworkin and Kant have similar concepts of self-respect?
5. Could there be morally acceptable forms of sexual activity, in Dworkin's view? What would they be like?
6. Do you think Dworkin is right that intercourse is morally objectionable? Why, or why not?

This is nihilism; or this is truth. He has to push in past boundaries. There is the outline of a body, distinct, separate, its integrity an illusion, a tragic deception, because unseen there is a slit between the legs, and he has to push into it. There is never a real privacy of the body that can coexist with intercourse: with being entered. The vagina itself is muscled and the muscles have to be pushed apart. The thrusting is persistent invasion. She is opened up, split down the center. She is occupied—physically, internally, in her privacy.

A human being has a body that is inviolate; and when it is violated, it is abused. A woman has a body that is penetrated in intercourse: permeable, its corporeal solidness a lie. The discourse of male truth—literature, science, philosophy, pornography—calls that penetration *violation.* This it does with some consistency and some confidence. *Violation* is a synonym for intercourse. At the same time, the penetration is taken to be a use, not an abuse; a normal use; it is appropriate to enter her, to push into ("violate") the boundaries of her body. She is human, of course, but by a standard that does not include physical privacy. She is, in fact, human by a standard that precludes physical privacy, since to keep a man out altogether and for a lifetime is deviant in the extreme, a psychopathology, a repudiation of the way in which she is expected to manifest her humanity.

There is a deep recognition in culture and in experience that intercourse is both the normal use of a woman, her human potentiality affirmed by it, and a violative abuse, her privacy irredeemably compromised, her selfhood changed in a way that is irrevocable, unrecoverable. And it is recognized that the use and abuse are not distinct phenomena but somehow a synthesized reality: both are true at the same time as if they were one harmonious truth instead of mutually exclusive contradictions. Intercourse in reality is a use and an abuse simultaneously, experienced and described as such, the act parlayed into the illuminated heights of religious duty and the dark recesses of morbid and dirty brutality. She, a human being, is supposed to have a privacy that is absolute; except that she, a woman, has a hole between her legs that men can, must, do enter. This hole, her hole, is synonymous with entry. A man has an anus that can be entered, but his anus is not synonymous with entry. A woman has an anus that can be entered, but her anus is not synonymous with entry. The slit between her legs, so simple, so hidden—frankly, so innocent—for instance, to the child who looks with a mirror to see if it *could* be true—is there an entrance to her body down there? and something big comes into it? (how?) and something as big as a baby comes out of it? (how?) and doesn't that hurt?—that slit which means entry into her—intercourse—appears to be the key to women's lower human status. By definition, as the God who does not exist made her, she is intended to have a lesser privacy, a lesser integrity of the body, a lesser sense of self, since her body can be physically occupied and in the occupation taken over. By definition, as the God who does not exist made her, this lesser privacy, this lesser integrity, this lesser self, establishes her lesser significance: not just in the world of social policy but in the world of bare, true, real existence. She is defined by how she is made, that hole, which is synonymous with entry; and intercourse, the act fundamental to existence, has consequences to her being that may be intrinsic, not socially imposed.

There is no analogue anywhere among subordinated groups of people to this experience of being made for intercourse: for penetration, entry, occupation. There is no analogue in occupied countries or in dominated races or in imprisoned dissidents or in colonialized cultures or in the submission of children to adults or in the atrocities that have marked the twentieth century ranging from Auschwitz to the Gulag. There is nothing exactly the same, and this is not because the political invasion and significance of intercourse is banal up against these other hierarchies and brutalities. Intercourse is a particular reality for women as an inferior class; and it has in it, as part of it, violation of boundaries, taking over, occupation, destruction of privacy, all of which are construed to be normal and also fundamental to continuing human existence. There is nothing that happens to any other civilly inferior people that is the same in its meaning and in its effect even when those people are forced into sexual availability, heterosexual or homosexual; while subject people, for instance, may be forced to have intercourse with those who dominate them, the God who does not exist did not make human existence, broadly speaking, dependent on their compliance. The political meaning of intercourse for women is the fundamental question of feminism and freedom: can an occupied people—physically occupied inside, internally invaded—be free; can those with a metaphysically compromised privacy have self-determination; can those without a biologically based physical integrity have self-respect?

There are many explanations, of course, that try to be kind. Women are different but equal. Social policy is different from private sexual behavior. The staggering civil inequalities between men and women are simple, clear injustices unrelated to the natural, healthy act of intercourse. There is nothing implicit in intercourse that mandates male dominance in society. Each individual must be free to choose. . . . "The revolutionary," writes Octavio Paz paraphrasing Ortega y Gasset, "is always a radical, that is, he [*sic*] is trying to correct the uses themselves rather than the mere abuses . . ." With intercourse, the use is already imbued with the excitement, the derangement, of the abuse; and abuse is only recognized as such socially if the intercourse is performed so recklessly or so violently or so stupidly that the man himself has actually signed a confession through the manner in which he has committed the act. What intercourse *is* for women and what it *does* to women's identity, privacy, self-respect, self-determination, and integrity are forbidden questions; and yet how can a radical or any woman who wants freedom not ask precisely these questions? The quality of the sensation or the need for a man or the desire for love: these are not answers to questions of freedom; they are diversions into complicity and ignorance.

Some facts are known.

Most women do not experience orgasm from intercourse itself. When Shere Hite, in her groundbreaking study, asked women to report their own sexual experiences in detail and depth, she discovered that only three in ten women regularly experience orgasm from intercourse. The women's self-reports are not ideological. They want men, love, sex, intercourse; they want orgasm; but for most women, seven out of ten, intercourse does not *cause* orgasm. The women want, even strive for, orgasm from intercourse but are unable to achieve it. Hite, the strongest feminist and most honorable philosopher among sex researchers, emphasizes that women can and must take responsibility for authentic sexual pleasure: "the ability to orgasm when we want, to be in charge of our stimulation, represents owning our own bodies, being strong, free, and autonomous human beings."

Intercourse occurs in a context of a power relation that is pervasive and incontrovertible. The context in which the act takes place, whatever the meaning of the act in and of itself, is one in which men have social, economic, political, and physical power over women. Some men do not have all those kinds of power over all women; but all men have some kinds of power over all women; and most men have controlling power over what they call *their* women. . . . The power is predetermined by gender, by being male.

Intercourse as an act often expresses the power men have over women. Without being what the society recognizes as rape, it is what the society—when pushed to admit it—recognizes as dominance.

Intercourse often expresses hostility or anger as well as dominance.

Intercourse is frequently performed compulsively; and intercourse frequently requires as a precondition for male performance the objectification of the female partner. She has to look a certain way, be a certain type—even conform to preordained behaviors and scripts—for the man to want to have intercourse and also for the man to be able to have intercourse. The woman cannot exist before or during the act as a fully realized, existentially alive individual.

Despite all efforts to socialize women to want intercourse—e.g., women's magazines to pornography to *Dynasty;* incredible rewards and punishments to get women to conform and put out —women still want a more diffuse and tender sensuality that involves the whole body and a polymorphous tenderness.

There are efforts to reform the circumstances that surround intercourse, the circumstances that at least apparently contribute to its disreputable (in terms of rights and justice) legend and legacy. These reforms include: more deference to female sensuality prior to the act; less verbal assault as part of sexual expressiveness toward women; some lip service to female initiation of sex and female choice during lovemaking; less romanticizing of rape, at least as an articulated social goal. Those who are political activists working toward the equality of women have other contextual reforms they want to make: economic equity; women elected to political office; strong, self-respecting role models for girls; emphasis on physical strength and self-defense, athletic excellence and endurance; rape laws that work; strategies for decreasing violence against women. These contextual reforms would then provide for the possibility that intercourse could be experienced in a world of social equality for the sexes. These reforms do not in any way address the question of whether intercourse itself can be an expression of sexual equality.

Life can be better for women—economic and political conditions improved—and at the same time the status of women can remain resistant, indeed impervious, to change: so far in history this is precisely the paradigm for social change as it relates to the condition of women. Reforms are made, important ones; but the status of women relative to men does not change. Women are still less significant, have less privacy, less integrity, less self-determination. This means that women have less freedom. Freedom is not an abstraction, nor is a little of it enough. A little more of it is not enough either. Having less, being less, impoverished in freedom and rights, women then inevitably have less self-respect: less self-respect than men have and less self-respect than any human being needs to live a brave and honest life. Intercourse as domination battens on that awful absence of self-respect. It expands to fill the near-vacuum. The uses of women, now, in intercourse—not the abuses to the extent that they can be separated out—are absolutely permeated by the reality of male power over women. We are poorer than men in money and so we have to barter sex or sell it outright (which is why they keep us poorer in money). We are poorer than men in psychological well-being because for us self-esteem depends on the approval—frequently expressed through sexual desire—of those who have and exercise power over us. Male power may be arrogant or elegant; it can be churlish or refined: but we exist as persons to the extent that men in power recognize us. When they need some service or want some sensation, they recognize us somewhat, with a sliver of consciousness; and when it is over, we go back to ignominy, anonymous, generic womanhood. Because of their power over us, they are able to strike our hearts dead with contempt or condescension. We need their money; intercourse is frequently how we get it. We need their approval to be able to survive inside our own skins; intercourse is frequently how we get it. They force us to be compliant, turn us into parasites, then hate us for not letting go. . . .

It is not that there is no way out if, for instance, one were to establish or believe that intercourse itself determines women's lower status. New reproductive technologies have changed and will continue to change the nature of the world. Intercourse is not necessary to existence anymore. Existence does not depend on female compliance, nor on the violation of female boundaries, nor on lesser female privacy, nor on the physical occupation of the female body. But the hatred of women is a source of sexual pleasure for men in its own right. Intercourse appears to be the expression of that contempt in pure form, in the form of a sexed hierarchy; . . .

There has always been a peculiar irrationality to all the biological arguments that supposedly predetermine the inferior social status of women. Bulls mount cows and baboons do whatever; but human females do not have estrus or go into heat. The logical inference is not that we are *always* available for mounting but rather that we are never, strictly speaking, "available." Nor do animals have cultures; nor do they determine in so many things what they will do and how they will do them and what the meaning of their own behavior is. They do not decide what their lives will be. Only humans face the often complicated reality of having potential and having to make choices based on having potential. We are not driven by instinct, at least not much. We have possibilities, and we make up meanings as we go along. The meanings we create or learn do not exist only in our heads, in ineffable ideas. Our meanings also exist in our bodies—what we are, what we do, what we physically feel, what we physically know; and there is no personal psychology that is separate from what the body has learned about life. Yet when we look at the human condition, including the condition of women, we act as if we are driven by biology or some metaphysically absolute dogma. We refuse to recognize our possibilities because we refuse to honor the potential humans have, including human women, to make choices. Men too make choices. When will they choose not to despise us?

Being female in this world is having been robbed of the potential for human choice by men who love to hate us. One does not make choices in freedom. Instead, one conforms in body type and behavior and values to become an object of male sexual desire, which requires an abandonment of a wide-ranging capacity for choice. Objectification may well be the most singly destructive aspect of gender hierarchy, especially as it exists in relation to intercourse. The surrender occurs before the act that is supposed to accomplish the surrender takes place. She has given in; why conquer her? The body is violated before the act occurs that is commonly taken to be violation. The privacy of the person is lessened before the privacy of the woman is invaded: she has remade herself so as to prepare the way for the invasion of privacy that her preparation makes possible. The significance of the human ceases to exist as the value of the object increases: an expensive ornament, for instance, she is incapable of human freedom—taking it, knowing it, wanting it, being it. Being an object—living in the realm of male objectification—is abject submission, an abdication of the freedom and integrity of the body, its privacy, its uniqueness, its worth in and of itself because it is the human body of a human being. Can intercourse exist without objectification? Would intercourse be a different phenomenon if it could, if it did? . . .

There is the initial complicity, the acts of self-mutilation, self-diminishing, self-reconstruction, until there is no self, only the diminished, mutilated reconstruction. It is all superficial and unimportant, except what it costs the human in her to do it: except for the fact that it is submissive, conforming, giving up an individuality that would withstand object status or defy it. Something happens inside; a human forgets freedom; a human learns obedience; a human, this time a woman, learns how to goose-step the female way. Wilhelm Reich, that most optimistic of sexual liberationists, the only male one to abhor rape *really*, thought that a girl needed not only "a free genital sexuality" but also "an undisturbed room, proper contraceptives, a friend who is capable of love, that is, not a National Socialist . . ." All remain hard for women to attain; but especially the lover who is not a National Socialist. So the act goes beyond complicity to collaboration; but collaboration requires a preparing of the ground, an undermining of values and vision and dignity, a sense of alienation from the worth of other human beings—and this alienation is fundamental to females who are objectified because they do not experience themselves as human beings of worth except for their value on the market as objects. Knowing one's own human value is fundamental to being able to respect others: females are remade into objects, not human in any sense related to freedom or justice—and so what can females recognize in other females that is a human bond toward freedom? Is there anything in us to love if we do not love each other as the objects we have become? Who can love someone who is less than human unless love itself is domination per se? Alienation from human freedom is deep and destructive; it destroys whatever it is in us as humans that is creative, that causes us to want to find meaning in experiences, even hard experiences; it destroys in us that which wants freedom whatever the hardship of attaining it. In women, these great human capacities and dimensions are destroyed or mutilated; and so we find ourselves bewildered—who or what are these so-called persons in human form but even that not quite, not exactly, who cannot remember or manifest the physical reality of freedom, who do not seem to want or to value the individual experience of freedom? Being an object for a man means being alienated from other women—those like her in status, in inferiority, in sexual function. Collaboration by women with men to keep women civilly and sexually inferior has been one of the hallmarks of female subordination; we are ashamed when Freud notices it, but it is true. That collaboration, fully manifested when a woman values her lover, the National Socialist, above any woman, anyone of her own kind or class or status, may have simple beginnings: the first act of complicity that destroys self-respect, the capacity for self-determination and freedom. . . . The men have an answer: intercourse is freedom. Maybe it is second-class freedom for second-class humans.

. . . maybe we can only know this much for certain—that when intercourse exists and is experienced under conditions of force, fear, or inequality, it destroys in women the will to political freedom; it destroys the love of freedom itself. We become female: occupied; collaborators against each other, especially against those among us who resist male domination—the lone, crazy resisters, the organized resistance. The pleasure of submission does not and cannot change the fact, the cost, the indignity, of inferiority.

SIDNEY CALLAHAN

Abortion and the Sexual Agenda

Sidney Callahan is Professor of Psychology at Mercy College. (Source: From Commonweal *[April 25, 1986], pp. 232–238. Copyright © 1986 by* Commonweal, Inc.. *Reprinted by permission.)*

QUESTIONS FOR REFLECTION

1. How does Callahan distinguish masculine from feminine conceptions of sexuality?
2. How, according to Callahan, is the masculine conception of sexuality harmful for women and children? How is the feminine conception beneficial?
3. How, according to Callahan, should a feminist think of sexuality? Do you agree?
4. How does the abortion controversy relate to conceptions of sexuality, in Callahan's view?

. . . Pro-life feminists seek to expand and deepen the more communitarian, maternal elements of feminism—and move society from its male-dominated course. First and foremost women have to insist upon a different, woman-centered approach to sex and reproduction. While Margaret Mead stressed the "womb envy" of males in other societies, it has been more or less repressed in our own. In our male-dominated world, what men don't do, doesn't count. Pregnancy, childbirth, and nursing have been characterized as passive, debilitating, animal-like. The disease model of pregnancy and birth has been entrenched. This female disease or impairment, with its attendant "female troubles," naturally handicaps women in the "real" world of hunting, war, and the corporate fast track. Many pro-choice feminists, deliberately childless, adopt the male perspective when they cite the "basic injustice that women have to bear the babies," instead of seeing the injustice in the fact that men cannot. Women's biologically unique capacity and privilege has been denied, despised, and suppressed under male domination; unfortunately, many women have fallen for the phallic fallacy.

Childbirth often appears in pro-choice literature as a painful, traumatic, life-threatening experience. Yet giving birth is accurately seen as an arduous but normal exercise of lifegiving power, a violent and ecstatic peak experience, which men can never know. Ironically, some pro-choice men and women think and talk of pregnancy and childbirth with the same repugnance that ancient ascetics displayed toward orgasms and sexual intercourse. The similarity may not be accidental. The obstetrician Niles Newton, herself a mother, has written of the extended threefold sexuality of women, who can experience orgasm, birth, and nursing as passionate pleasure-giving experiences. All of these are involuntary processes of the female body. Only orgasm, which males share, has been glorified as an involuntary function that is nature's gift; the involuntary feminine processes of childbirth and nursing have been seen as bondage to biology.

Fully accepting our bodies as ourselves, what should women want? I think women will only flourish when there is a feminization of sexuality, very different from the current cultural trend toward masculinizing female sexuality. Women can never have the self-confidence and self-esteem they need to achieve feminist goals in society until a more holistic, feminine model of sexuality becomes the dominant cultural ethos. To say this affirms the view that men and women differ in the domain of sexual functioning, although they are more alike than different in other personality characteristics and competencies. For those of us committed to achieving sexual equality in the culture, it may be hard to accept the fact that sexual differences make it imperative to talk of distinct male and female models of sexuality. But if one wants to change sexual roles, one has to recognize preexisting conditions. A great deal of evidence is accumulating which points to biological pressures for different male and female sexual functioning.

Males always and everywhere have been more physically aggressive and more likely to fuse sexuality with aggression and dominance. Females may be more variable in their sexuality, but since Masters and Johnson, we know that women have a greater capacity than men for repeated orgasm and a more tenuous path to arousal and orgasmic release. Most obviously, women also have a far greater sociobiological investment in the act of human reproduction. On the whole, women as compared to men possess a sexuality which is more complex, more intense, more extended in time, involving higher investment, risks, and psychosocial involvement.

Considering the differences in sexual functioning, it is not surprising that men and women in the same culture have often constructed different sexual ideals. In Western culture, since the nineteenth century at least, most women have espoused a version of sexual functioning in which sex acts are embedded within deep emotional bonds and secure long-term commitments. Within these committed "pair bonds" males assume parental obligations. In the idealized Victorian version of the Christian sexual ethic, culturally endorsed and maintained by women, the double standard was not countenanced. Men and women did not need to marry to be whole persons, but if they did engage in sexual functioning, they were to be equally chaste, faithful, responsible, loving, and parentally concerned. Many of the most influential women in the nineteenth-century women's movement preached and lived this sexual ethic, often by the side of exemplary feminist men. While the ideal has never been universally obtained, a culturally dominant demand for monogamy, self-control, and emotionally bonded and committed sex works well for women in every stage of their sexual life cycles. When love, chastity, fidelity, and commitment for better or worse are the ascendant cultural prerequisites for sexual functioning, young girls and women expect protection from rape and seduction, adult women justifiably demand male support in childrearing, and older women are more protected from abandonment as their biological attractions wane.

Of course, these feminine sexual ideals always coexisted in competition with another view. A more male-oriented model of erotic or amative sexuality endorses sexual permissiveness without long-term commitment or reproductive focus. Erotic sexuality emphasizes pleasure, play, passion, individual self-expression, and romantic games of courtship and conquest. It is assumed that a variety of partners and sexual experiences are necessary to stimulate romantic passion. This erotic model of the sexual life has often worked satisfactorily for men, both heterosexual and gay, and for certain cultural elites. But for the average woman, it is quite destructive. Women can only play the erotic game successfully when like the "*Cosmopolitan* women," they are young, physically attractive, economically powerful, and fulfilled enough in a career to be willing to sacrifice family life. Abortion is also required. As our society increasingly endorses this male-oriented, permissive view of sexuality, it is all too ready to give women abortion on demand. Abortion helps a woman's body be more like a man's. It has been observed that *Roe* v. *Wade* removed the last defense women possessed against male sexual demands.

Unfortunately, the modern feminist movement made a mistaken move at a critical juncture. Rightly rebelling against patriarchy, unequal education, restricted work opportunities, and women's downtrodden political status, feminists also rejected the nineteenth-century feminine sexual ethic. Amative erotic, permissive sexuality (along with abortion rights) became symbolically identified with other struggles for social equality in education, work, and politics. This feminist mistake also turned off many potential recruits among women who could not deny the positive dimensions of their own traditional feminine roles, nor their allegiance to the older feminine sexual ethic of love and fidelity.

An ironic situation then arose in which many pro-choice feminists preach their own double standard. In the world of work and career, women are urged to grow up, to display mature self-discipline and self-control; they are told to persevere in long-term commitments, to cope with unexpected obstacles by learning to tough out the inevitable sufferings and setbacks entailed in life and work. But this mature ethic of commitment and self-discipline, recommended as the only way to progress in the world of work and personal achievement, is discounted in the domain of sexuality.

In pro-choice feminism, a permissive, erotic view of sexuality is assumed to be the only option. Sexual intercourse with a variety of partners is seen as "inevitable" from a young age and as a positive growth experience to be managed by access to contraception and abortion. Unfortunately, the pervasive cultural conviction that adolescents, or their elders, cannot exercise sexual self-control, undermines the responsible use of contraception. When a pregnancy occurs, the first abortion is viewed in some pro-choice circles as a *rite de passage.* Responsibly choosing an abortion supposedly ensures that a young woman will take charge of her own life, make her own decisions, and carefully practice contraception. But the social dynamics of a permissive, erotic model of sexuality, coupled with permissive laws, work toward repeat abortions. Instead of being empowered by their abortion choices, young women having abortions are confronting the debilitating reality of *not* bringing a baby into the world; *not* being able to count on a committed male partner; *not* accounting oneself strong enough, or the master of enough resources, to avoid killing the fetus. Young women are hardly going to develop the self-esteem, self-discipline, and self-confidence necessary to confront a male-dominated society through abortion.

The male-oriented sexual orientation has been harmful to women and children. It has helped bring us epidemics of venereal disease, infertility, pornography, sexual abuse, adolescent pregnancy, divorce, displaced older women, and abortion. Will these signals of something amiss stimulate pro-choice feminists to rethink what kind of sex ideal really serves women's best interests? While the erotic model cannot encompass commitment, the committed model can—happily—encompass and encourage romance, passion, and playfulness. In fact, within the security of long-term commitments, women may be more likely to experience sexual pleasure and fulfillment.

The pro-life feminist position is not a return to the old feminine mystique. That espousal of "the eternal feminine" erred by viewing sexuality as so sacred that it cannot be humanly shaped at all. Woman's *whole* nature was supposed to be opposite to man's, necessitating complementary and radically different social roles. Followed to its logical conclusion, such a view presumes that reproductive and sexual experience is necessary for human fulfillment. But as the early feminists insisted, no woman has to marry or engage in sexual intercourse to be fulfilled, nor does a woman have to give birth and raise children to be complete, nor must she stay home and function as an earth mother. But female sexuality does need to be deeply respected as a unique potential and trust. Since most contraceptives and sterilization procedures really do involve only the woman's body rather than destroying new life, they can be an acceptable and responsible moral option.

With sterilization available to accelerate the inevitable natural ending of fertility and childbearing, a woman confronts only a limited number of years in which she exercises her reproductive trust and may have to respond to an unplanned pregnancy. Responsible use of contraception can lower the probabilities even more. Yet abortion is not decreasing. The reason is the current permissive attitude embodied in the law, not the "hard cases" which constitute 3 percent of today's abortions. Since attitudes, the law, and behavior interact, pro-life feminists conclude that unless there is an enforced limitation of abortion, which currently confirms the sexual and social status quo, alternatives will never be developed. For women to get what they need in order to combine childbearing, education, and careers, society has to recognize that female bodies come with wombs. Women and their reproductive power, and the children women have, must be supported in new ways. Another and different round of feminist consciousness-raising is needed in which all of women's potential is accorded respect. This time, instead of humbly buying entrée by conforming to male lifestyles, women will demand that society accommodate to them.

New feminist efforts to rethink the meaning of sexuality, femininity, and reproduction are all the more vital as new techniques for artificial reproduction, surrogate motherhood, and the like present a whole new set of dilemmas. In the long run, the very long run, the abortion debate may be merely the opening round in a series of far-reaching struggles over the role of human sexuality and the ethics of reproduction. Significant changes in the culture, both positive and negative in outcome, may begin as local storms of controversy. We may be at one of those vaguely realized thresholds when we had best come to full attention. What kind of people are we going to be? Pro-life feminists pursue a vision for their sisters, daughters, and granddaughters. Will their great-granddaughters be grateful?

RICHARD D. MOHR

Civil Rights

Richard D. Mohr is Professor of Philosophy at the University of Illinois at Urbana. (Source: From A More Perfect Union: Why Straight America Must Stand Up for Gay Rights, *Boston: Beacon Press.*

QUESTIONS FOR REFLECTION

1. Why does Mohr consider it important to accord gays full civil rights?
2. How does Mohr link civil rights to civic rights? How does he use the connection to argue for civil rights for gays?
3. Mohr advocates allowing gays in the military. How might he respond to objections to that proposal?
4. Many people are reluctant to grant gays full equality with respect to the adoption of children and the legal status of marriage. How would Mohr argue against this reluctance? Do you find his arguments persuasive?

Current federal civil rights law bars private-sector discrimination in housing, employment, and public accommodations on the basis of race, national origin, ethnicity, gender, religion, age, and disability, but not sexual orientation. Where city councils and state legislatures have passed protections for gay men and lesbians, the protections have been under concerted and frequently successful attack through referendum initiatives. Thus in November 1992, Colorado adopted by referendum a state constitutional provision voiding existing city protections for gay men and lesbians and barring any future city or state protections for them. This chapter offers moral arguments for protecting lesbians and gay men from private-sector discrimination.

Even though civil rights legislation restricts somewhat the workings of free enterprise, it promotes other core American values that far outweigh this slight loss of entrepreneurial freedom. These values are self-respect, self-sufficiency, general prosperity, and individual flourishing.

No one in American society can have much self-respect or maintain a solid sense of self, if she is, in major ways affecting herself, subject to whimsical and arbitrary actions of others. Work, entertainment, and housing are major modes through which people identify themselves to themselves. Indeed in modern culture, work and housing rank just after personal relationships and perhaps (for some) religion, as the chief means by which people identify themselves to themselves. A large but largely unrecognized part of the misery of unemployment is not merely poverty and social embarrassment, but also a sense of loss of that by which one defined oneself, a loss which many people also experience upon retirement, even when their income and social esteem are left intact. People thrown out of work frequently compare this loss to the loss of a family member, especially to the loss of a child. Here the comparison is not simply to the intensity of the emotion caused by the loss, but to the nature of the loss: what was lost was a central means by which one constituted one's image of oneself.

Work is also the chief means by which people in America identify themselves to others. Indeed in America, one's job is tantamount to one's social identity. Socially one finds out who a person is by finding out what she or he does. At social gatherings, like parties, asking after a person's employment is typically the first substantive inquiry one makes of a person to whom one has been introduced. America is a nation of doers. When job discrimination is directed at lesbians and gay men, say, as a child care worker or museum director, it is a way of branding them as essentially un-American, as alien. It is a chief mode of expatriation from the national experience.

Discrimination in housing similarly affects one's social identity. The physical separation of a group and its concentration apart from the dominant social order are among the chief means by which a group is socially marked as worthy of less respect, unclean, and threatening. Housing discrimination against a despised group is apartheid writ small, but not small enough to be morally acceptable.

Discrimination in housing also affects one's self-perception. It perhaps goes without saying that the conversion of a house into a home is one of the main aspects of self-definition in America. Blocking or arbitrarily restricting the material basis of this conversion inhibits the development of self-respect and selectively disrupts the sanctities of private life. The common expression "keeping up with the Joneses," even in its mild censure or irony, attests to the role of housing in the way people identify themselves to themselves, in part, through the eyes of others. To be denied housing on the basis of some group status is another chief mode of social ostracism and exile.

In a nonsocialist, noncommunist society like America, there is a general expectation that each person is primarily responsible for meeting his or her own basic needs and that the government becomes an active provider only when all else fails. It is largely noncontroversial that people ought to have their basic needs met. For meeting basic needs is a necessary condition for anyone being able to carry out a life plan. If government aims at enhancing the conditions in which people are able to carry out their life plans, then enhancing the conditions in which basic needs are met will be a high government priority, all the more so if the means to this end themselves avoid greatly coercing people's life plans. . . .

Extending civil rights protection to gay men and lesbians is also justified as promoting general prosperity. Such legislation tends to increase the production of goods and services for society as a whole. It does so in three ways.

First, by eliminating extraneous factors in employment decisions, such legislation promotes an optimal fit between a worker's capacities and the tasks of her prospective work. Both the worker and her employer are advantaged because a worker is most productive when her talents and the requirements of her job mesh. Across the business community as a whole, such legislation further enhances the prospects that talent does not go wasting and that job vacancies are not filled by second bests.

In response to prospective discrimination, gays are prone to take jobs which only partially use their talents. Many gays take dead-end jobs; they do so in order to avoid reviews which might reveal their minority status and result in their dismissal. Many gay men and lesbians go into small business because big business will not have them. In turn, many small businesses or dead-end occupations, like being a florist, hairdresser, male nurse, female trucker or construction worker, have in society's mind become so closely associated with homosexuality that nongays who might otherwise go into these lines of employment do not do so out of fear that they will be socially branded as gay. In these circumstances, the talents of people—both gay and nongay—are simply wasted both to themselves and to society. Rights for gays are good for everyone.

Second, human resources are wasted if one's energies are constantly diverted and devoured by fear of arbitrary dismissal. The cost of life in the closet is not small, for the closet permeates and largely consumes the life of its occupant. In the absence of civil rights legislation for gays, society is simply wasting the human resources which are expended in the day-to-day anxiety—the web of lies, the constant worry—that attends leading a life of systematic disguise as a condition for continued employment.

Third, employment makes up a large part of what happiness is. To a large extent, happiness is job satisfaction. When one's employment is of a favorable sort, one finds a delight in its very execution—quite independently of any object which the job generates, whether product or wage. People whose work on its own is rich enough and interesting enough to count as a personal flourishing, people, for instance, employed in human services, academics, and other professionals, and people whose jobs entail a large element of craft, like editors and artisans, are indeed likely to view job satisfaction as a major constituent of happiness and rank it high both qualitatively and quantitatively among the sources of happiness. And even people who are forced by necessity or misfortune to take up employment which does not use their talents, or which is virtually mechanical, or positively dangerous, or which has other conditions that make the workplace hateful—even these people are likely to recognize that the workplace, if properly arranged, would be a locus of happiness, and this recognition of opportunity missed is part of the frustration which accompanies jobs which are necessarily unsatisfying to perform. Permitting discriminatory hiring practices reduces happiness generally by barring access to one of its main sources.

Civil rights legislation also promotes individual flourishing—not merely by enhancing the prospect that individuals' needs are met, but more so by expanding the ranges of individual choice. Government has a perceived obligation to enhance conditions which promote the flourishing of individual styles of living. Thus, for example, the general rationale for compulsory liberal education is that such compulsion ultimately issues in autonomous individuals capable of making decisions for themselves from a field of alternative opinions. Analogously, civil rights legislation, though a somewhat coercive force in the marketplace, promotes those conditions that enable people to draw up and carry out their life plans.

Such legislation withdraws the threat of punishment by social banishment, loss of employment, and the like from the arsenal of majoritarian coercion, so that individual lives need not be molded by social conventions and by the demands of conformity set by others. The result of such legislation is that the means by which one lives shall not be permitted to serve as instruments for the despotism of custom.

This justification for civil rights legislation has special import for gay men and lesbians. With the lessening of fear from threat of discovery, ordinary gays will begin to lead self-determining lives. Imagine the lives of those gays who systematically forgo the opportunity of sharing the common necessities of life and of sharing the emotional dimensions of intimacy as the price for the means by which they place bread on their table. Love and caring could cost you your job—if you're gay—while catch-as-catch-can sex and intimacy could cost you your life.

In the absence of civil rights legislation, lesbians and gay men are placed in the position of having to make zero-sum trade-offs between the components that go into making a full life, trade-offs, say, between a reasonable personal life and employment, trade-offs which the majority would not tolerate for themselves even for a minute.

As an invisible minority, gay men and lesbians also need civil rights protections in order for them to have reasonably guaranteed access to an array of fundamental rights which virtually everyone would agree are supposed to pertain equally to all persons.

By "invisible minority," I mean a minority whose members can be identified only through an act of will on someone's part, rather than merely through observation of the members' day-to-day actions in the public domain. Thus severely physically and mentally challenged people would rank along with racial classes, gender classes, and some ethnic and religious groups (like the Amish) as visible minorities, whereas diabetics, assimilated Jews, Lutherans, atheists, and released prisoners would rank along with gay men and lesbians as invisible minorities.

Let us presume the acceptability of a governmental system which is a constitutionally regulated representative democracy with a developed body of civic law. Such in broad outline is the government of the United States and its various states. Then, gay civil rights are a necessary precondition for the proper functioning of this system.

First, civil rights legislation for gay men and lesbians is warranted as being necessary for gays having equitable access to civic rights. By "civic rights," I mean rights to the impartial administration of civil and criminal law in defense of property and person. In the absence of such rights, there is no rule of law. An invisible minority historically subjected to widespread social discrimination has reasonably guaranteed access to these rights only when the minority is guaranteed nondiscrimination in employment, housing, and public services. . . .

Widespread social prejudice against lesbians and gay men also has the effect of eclipsing their political rights. In the absence of gay civil rights legislation, gays are—over the range of issues which most centrally affect their minority status—effectively denied access to the political rights of the First Amendment, that is, freedom of speech, freedom of press, freedom of assembly, and freedom to petition for the redress of grievances. In addition, they are especially denied the emergent constitutional right of association—an amalgam of the freedoms of speech and assembly—which establishes the right to join and be identified with other persons for common political goals.

Put concretely, does a gay person who has to laugh at and manufacture fag jokes in the workplace in order to deflect suspicion in an office which routinely fires gay employees have freedom to express his or her views on gay issues? Is it likely that such a person could reasonably risk appearing in public at a gay rights rally? Would such a person be able to participate in a march celebrating the Stonewall Riots and the start of gay activism? Would such a person be able to sign, let alone circulate, a petition protesting the firing of a gay worker? Would such a person likely try to persuade workmates to vote for a gay-positive city councilman? Would such a person sign a letter to the editor protesting abusive reportage of gay issues and events, or advocating the discussion of gay issues in schools? The answer to all these questions is "obviously not!" Such a person is usually so transfixed by fear that it is highly unlikely that he or she could even be persuaded to write out a check to a gay rights organization.

Further, it is hardly fair for gays as a statistical minority to be additionally encumbered in politics by having the majority of its members absent through social coercion from the public workings of the political process.

If First Amendment rights are not to be demoted to privileges to which only the dominant culture has access, then invisible minorities that are subject to widespread social discrimination will have to be guaranteed protection from those forces which maintain them in their position of invisibility. Civil rights protections take a very long step in that direction.

For at a minimum, all potentially effective political activity requires widely and pointedly disseminated political ideas. Only then is it possible for a minority political position on social policy to have a chance of becoming the majority opinion and so of becoming government policy and law. If the majority of people never have the occasion to change their opinions to those of a minority position, political rights would be pointless. Not surprisingly, then, all the actions protected by the First Amendment are public actions—speaking, publishing, petitioning, assembling, associating.

Now, a person who is a member of an invisible minority and who must remain invisible, hidden, and secreted in respect to her minority status as a condition for maintaining a livelihood is not free to be public about her minority status nor to incur suspicion by publicly associating with others who are open about their similar status. And so she is effectively denied all political power—except the right to vote. But voting aside, she will be denied the freedom to express her views in a public forum and to unite with or organize other like-minded individuals in an attempt to compete for votes which would elect persons who will support the policies advocated by her group. She is denied all effective use of legally available means of influencing public opinion prior to voting and all effective means of lobbying after elections are held. . . .

THE RAMSEY COLLOQUIUM

Morality and Homosexuality

The Ramsey Colloquium is a group of Christian and Jewish scholars sponsored by the Institute on Religion and Public Life. (Source: First Thing *[March 1994].*

QUESTIONS FOR REFLECTION

1. What presuppositions of the gay rights movement do the authors identify? Do you agree that they are presuppositions of the movement?
2. What do various aspects of the sexual revolution have in common, according to the authors? Do you agree?
3. How does homosexuality threaten society's heterosexual norms, in the authors' view? Evaluate their arguments.
4. On what particular issues are the authors most uncomfortable with the gay rights agenda? What is your view of those issues?

Homosexual behavior is a phenomenon with a long history, to which there have been various cultural and moral responses. But today in our public life there is something new that demands our attention and deserves a careful moral response.

The new thing is a gay and lesbian movement that variously presents itself as an appeal for compassion, an extension of civil rights to minorities and a cultural revolution. This movement aggressively proposes radical changes in social behavior, religion, morality and law.

As committed Christians and Jews, we share the uneasiness of most Americans with the proposals advanced by the gay and lesbian movement, and we seek to articulate some of the reasons for the largely intuitive and pre-articulate anxiety of most Americans regarding homosexuality.

Definition by Desire

While the gay and lesbian movement is indeed a new thing, its way was prepared by the so-called sexual revolution. That revolution is motored by presuppositions that ought to be challenged. Perhaps the key presupposition is that human health and flourishing require that sexual desire, understood as a "need," be acted upon and satisfied. Any discipline of denial or restraint has been popularly depicted as unhealthy and dehumanizing.

We insist, however, that it is dehumanizing to define ourselves by our desires alone. Nor does it seem plausible to suggest that what millennia of human experience have taught us to regard as self-command should now be dismissed as mere repression.

At the same time that the place of sex has been grotesquely exaggerated by the sexual revolution, it has also been trivialized. The mysteries of human sexuality are commonly reduced to matters of recreation or taste, not unlike one's preferences in diet, dress or sport. This peculiar mix of the exaggerated and the trivialized makes it possible for the gay and lesbian movement to demand, simultaneously, a respect for what is claimed to be most constitutively true of homosexuals and tolerance for what is, after all, simply a difference in "lifestyle."

It is important to recognize the linkages among the component parts of the sexual revolution. Permissive abortion, widespread adultery, easy divorce, radical feminism, and the gay and lesbian movement have not by accident appeared at the same historical moment. They have in common a declared desire for liberation from constraint—especially constraint associated with an allegedly oppressive culture and religious tradition. They also have in common the presupposition that the body is little more than an instrument for the fulfillment of desire, and that the fulfillment of desire is the essence of the self. Finally, they all rest on a doctrine of the autonomous self. We believe it is a false doctrine that leads neither to individual flourishing nor to social well-being.

Marriage and the family—husband, wife and children, joined by public recognition and legal bond—are the most effective institutions for the rearing of children, for the directing of sexual passion and for human flourishing in community. At the same time, it remains true that there are legitimate and honorable forms of love other than marriage. Indeed, one of the goods at stake in today's disputes is a long-honored tradition of friendship between men and men, women and women, women and men.

In the current climate, it becomes imperative to affirm the reality and beauty of sexually chaste relationships. We do not accept the notion that self-command is an unhealthy form of repression on the part of single people, whether their inclination is heterosexual or homosexual. Put differently, the choice is not limited to heterosexual marriage on the one hand and relationships involving extramarital or homogenital sex on the other.

We cannot settle the dispute about the roots—genetic or environmental—of homosexual orientation. Although some scientific evidence suggests a genetic predisposition, we must still ask whether such a predisposition should be acted on or whether it should be resisted.

In a fallen creation, many quite common attitudes and behaviors must be straightforwardly designated as sin. Although we are equal before God, we are not born equal in terms of our strengths and weaknesses, our tendencies and dispositions, our nature and nurture. We cannot utterly change the hand we have been dealt by inheritance and family circumstances, but we are responsible for how we play that hand.

Inclination and temptation are not sinful, although they surely result from humanity's fallen condition. Sin occurs in the joining of the will, freely and knowingly, to an act or way of life that is contrary to God's purpose. Religious communities in particular must lovingly support all the faithful in their struggle against temptation, while at the same time insisting, precisely for the sake of the faithful, on the sinfulness of the homogenital and extramarital heterosexual behavior to which some are drawn.

Since there are good reasons to support the heterosexual norm, since it has been developed with great difficulty, and since it can be maintained only if it is cared for and supported, we cannot be indifferent to attacks upon it. The social norms by which sexual behavior is inculcated and controlled are of urgent importance for families and for society as a whole.

Advocates of the gay and lesbian movement have the responsibility to set forth publicly their alternative proposals. This means more than calling for liberation from established standards. They must clarify for all of us how sexual mores are to be inculcated in the young, who are particularly vulnerable to seduction and solicitation. Public anxiety about homosexuality is pre-eminently a concern about the vulnerabilities of the young. This, we are persuaded, is a matter of legitimate and urgent public concern.

Gay and lesbian advocates sometimes claim that they are asking for no more than an end to discrimination, drawing an analogy with the early civil-rights movement. The analogy is unconvincing and misleading. Differences of race are in accord with—not contrary to—our nature, and such differences do not provide justification for behavior that is otherwise unacceptable.

Certain discriminations are in fact necessary within society; it is not too much to say that civilization itself depends on the making of such distinctions (between, finally, right and wrong). In our public life, some discrimination is in order—when, for example, in education and programs involving young people the intent is to prevent predatory behavior that can take place under the guise of supporting young people in their anxieties about their "sexual identity."

Support for Marriage

It is necessary to discriminate between relationships. Gay and lesbian "domestic partnerships," for example, should not be socially recognized as the moral equivalent of marriage. Marriage and the family are institutions necessary for our continued social well-being. In an individualistic society that tends to liberation from all constraint, they are fragile institutions in need of careful and continuing support.

To endure (tolerance), to pity (compassion), to embrace (affirmation): That is the sequence of change in attitude and judgment that has been advanced by the gay and lesbian movement with notable success. We expect that this success will encounter certain limits and that what is truly natural will reassert itself, but this may not happen before more damage is done to innumerable individuals and to our common life.

Hadley Arkes Amherst College

Matthew Berke First Things

Gerald Bradley Notre Dame Law School

Rabbi David Dalin University of Hartford

Ernest Fortin Boston College

Jorge Garcia Rutgers University

Rabbi Marc Gellman Hebrew Union College

Robert George Princeton University

The Rev. Hugh Haffenreffer Emanuel Lutheran Church (Hartford, Ct.)

John Hittinger College of Saint Francis

Russell Hittinger Catholic University of America

Robert Jenson St. Olaf College

Gilbert Meilaender Oberlin College

Jerry Muller Catholic University of America

Fr. Richard John Neuhaus Institute on Religion and Public Life

Rabbi David Novak University of Virginia

James Nuechterlein First Things

Max Stackhouse Princeton Theological Seminary

Philip Turner Berkeley Divinity School (Yale University)

George Weigel Ethics and Public Policy Center

Robert Wilken University of Virginia

PART III Rights and Responsibilities

We find it hard to talk for very long about ethics or politics without talking about rights. But talk of rights is young by philosophical standards. Rights first made their appearance in Western moral discourse about 340 years ago, in the writings of Thomas Hobbes. Hobbes and many later writers present rights in the context of a general theory of government. To understand their conceptions of rights, therefore, we must consider their overall political theories.

Hobbes revives an ancient idea: that a government is legitimate if people, given a choice, would voluntarily opt to be subject to its dominion. Facing this choice requires us to consider what life would be like without government, in what Hobbes calls the state of nature. Hobbes provides a brief but stunning glimpse of the state of nature where, in his view, life would be "solitary, poor, nasty, brutish, and short." Even the strongest and smartest would be vulnerable to the tricks and physical force of groups of others. No one would be safe; people would routinely fight each other to survive. To gain security, therefore, people would choose to form a government. They would be willing to sacrifice much of their freedom to gain relief from the brutality of the state of nature. The resulting compact among competing individuals underlies the legitimacy of government. Hobbes's account is thus a version of *social contract theory*.

Rights emerge at two levels of Hobbes's theory. First, people have some rights even in the state of nature. There are *natural* rights that do not depend on government. Second, people have rights bestowed by government, which they acquire through the social contract. These are *social,* or *civil,* rights. These kinds of rights rest on different foundations. Hobbes believes that natural rights must underlie civil rights, for civil rights are founded on a contract. That contract can bind the contracting parties only if they already recognize an obligation to keep promises and, correlatively, a right to have promises kept. This kind of right and obligation must be prior to civil rights, depending not on a social contract but on the nature of human beings.

In any version of social contract theory, we can ask two questions that determine much about the theory of government that results: (1) What do the parties hope to gain by entering into the social contract? (2) What are they willing to give up to achieve it? In Hobbes's theory, the parties hope to gain security, which, for them, is a matter of life and death. They are willing to give up much for the protection of government. As a result, in Hobbes's theory, there are few limitations on the government, which Hobbes calls by the name of a monster, *Leviathan*. People are willing to sacrifice even their natural rights in order to survive.

John Locke presents a very different social contract theory. He, too, considers government legitimate only if it would be chosen over the state of nature. But Locke's state of nature is far tamer than Hobbes's. Precisely because everyone is vulnerable to everyone else's revenge, few would commit crimes, and those few would meet severe punishment. In the state of nature, we would have natural rights of life, liberty, and property, which would give us the right to punish anyone who violated those rights. The chief danger Locke sees in this condition is that punishment, often at the hands of the people wronged or those closely associated with them, would tend to be harsh, indiscriminate, and unfair. Consequently, people would feel the need for an impartial judge who could enforce the law of nature. People would therefore contract to form a government to serve as impartial arbitrator of their disputes. What do they hope to gain? Impartiality. This is important, but not a matter of life and death, as in Hobbes, except in extreme cases. What, therefore, are people willing to give up? A limited amount, according to Locke. They would give up their right to enforce the laws of nature by themselves. But they would retain their natural rights to life, liberty, and property, as long as they did not violate the rights of others. And they would gain civil rights to impartial treatment as well. Stemming from Locke's conception of the social contract is a limited view of government, which has little role other than enforcement and arbitration.

Jean-Jacques Rousseau provides a third version of contract theory, in which people are willing to give up everything in order to regain everything. Rousseau sees the state of nature as inconvenient and difficult; people would band together, entering the social contract to overcome these difficulties through cooperation. Because cooperation is their major motivation, they would be willing to surrender everything they have to the community to help others, and also would expect the entire community to help them. For Rousseau, there are no natural rights; all rights—and all questions—arise from the social contract. All rights, for him, are civil rights. Government, according to Rousseau, has only one constraint: that it act in accord with the general will, that is, for the best of the whole community.

Rights are fundamental to our modern conception of ethics and political philosophy. But they give rise to a serious problem. Rights frequently seem to come into conflict. Abortion, capital punishment, and many other public problems can be seen as involving conflicts of rights. How are such conflicts to be resolved? Social contract theory, in itself, provides little help.

Some philosophers have maintained that conflicts cannot arise, because rights stem from a single, underlying moral principle: the categorical imperative, the principle of utility, or the law of nature, for example. But Edmund Burke maintains that there is no such principle. There are fundamentally different kinds of moral considerations, Burke contends; there is no theory that can take all into account and tell us, in every particular case, which considerations ought to take precedence. What is right or wrong depends on the circumstances, Burke says, and those may be extremely complex, involving many different kinds of values. The best we can do is to seek the right balance between those values. For that purpose, moral sensitivity and practical experience matter more than moral theories or talk of rights.

THOMAS HOBBES

from *Leviathan* (1651)

Thomas Hobbes (1588–1679) was born prematurely in Malmesbury, Wiltshire, England, when his mother heard of the approach of the Spanish Armada. "Fear and I were born twins," he later quipped. He was raised by an uncle after his father, a vicar, was involved in a fistfight outside the door of his church. Hobbes attended Magdalen Hall, Oxford, at fourteen, completing his degree five years later. He became tutor to an earl's son, a position that provided him a good library and the means to travel. He became a member of an intellectual circle in France that included Mersenne, Gassendi, and Descartes. In 1636, he met Galileo. In 1640, when King Charles I dissolved Parliament, Hobbes fled England for Paris.

Over the next decade, while in his fifties, Hobbes wrote a series of notable works: Human Nature, De Corpore Politico (On the Body Politic), De Cive (On the State), *and several works on optics. In 1646–1647, he tutored the future King Charles II in Paris. In 1651, Hobbes published* Leviathan, *probably his greatest work, in which he argued for absolute and undivided sovereignty in the state. Hobbes there gave the first modern defense of social contract theory, which, despite our contemporary distaste for monarchy, continues to be influential.*

When Charles II was restored to the throne in 1660, Hobbes returned to England. He was seventy-two, but still an avid tennis player. The king, in gratitude for Hobbes's tutoring and for his public defense of monarchy, granted him a government pension. In 1665, however, came the great plague; the great fire of London followed a year later. Parliament, taking these events as signs of divine displeasure, investigated anyone who was suspected of atheism. Hobbes's Leviathan *made him a target; he was forbidden to publish any further writings. Still vigorous, however, Hobbes continued to write, completing several major works while in his eighties. (Source: Reprinted from Thomas Hobbes,* Leviathan. *Oxford: Clarendon Press, 1909. Spelling and punctuation have been modernized for clarity.)*

QUESTIONS FOR REFLECTION

1. What is Hobbes's conception of the state of nature? Why would a person's life in that state be "solitary, poor, nasty, brutish, and short"?
2. What, for Hobbes, is liberty? What is a law of nature? How does Hobbes distinguish law from right?
3. What are the first three laws of nature, according to Hobbes? How does he derive them from the state of nature?
4. What motivates us, in the state of nature, to contract to form associations and governments? What are we willing to give up? What do we hope to gain?
5. Why, according to Hobbes, are we obliged to fulfill contracts, even when doing so is not in our best interest?
6. "Whatsoever is done to a man conformable to his own will, signified to the doer, is no injury to him." This is Hobbes's statement of a traditional principle: "To the willing no injustice is done." How does Hobbes argue for this? How does this principle relate to Mill's harm principle?

PART I, CHAPTER XIII / OF THE NATURAL CONDITION OF MANKIND AS CONCERNING THEIR FELICITY AND MISERY

Nature has made men so equal in the faculties of body and mind, as that though there be found one man sometimes manifestly stronger in body, or of quicker mind than another; yet when all is reckoned together, the difference between man and man is not so considerable, as that one man can thereupon claim to himself any benefit to which another may not pretend as well as he. For as to the strength of body, the weakest has strength enough to kill the strongest, either by secret machination or by confederacy with others, that are in the same danger with himself.

And as to the faculties of the mind (setting aside the arts grounded upon words, and especially that skill of proceeding upon general and infallible rules, called science; which very few have, and but in few things; as being not a native faculty, born with us; nor attained, [as prudence] while we look after somewhat else), I find yet a greater equality amongst men than that of strength. For prudence is but experience; which equal time equally bestows on all men in those things they equally apply themselves unto. That which may perhaps make such equality incredible is but a vain conceit of one's own wisdom which almost all men think they have in a greater degree than the vulgar; that is, than all men but themselves and a few others, whom by fame, or for concurring with themselves, they approve. For such is the nature of men, that howsoever they may acknowledge many others to be more witty, or more eloquent, or more learned; Yet they will hardly believe there be many so wise as themselves: For they see their own wit at hand, and other men's at a distance. But this proves rather that men are in that point equal, than unequal. For there is not ordinarily a greater sign of the equal distribution of anything, than that every man is contented with his share.

From this equality of ability, arises equality of hope in the attaining of our ends. And therefore if any two men desire the same thing, which nevertheless they cannot both enjoy, they become enemies; and in the way to their end (which is principally their own conservation, and sometimes their delectation only) endeavour to destroy or subdue one another. And from hence it comes to pass, that where an invader has no more to fear than another man's single power; if one plant, sow, build, or possess a convenient seat, others may probably be expected to come prepared with forces united to dispossess and deprive him not only of the fruit of his labour, but also of his life or liberty. And the invader again is in the like danger of another.

And from this diffidence of one another, there is no way for any man to secure himself, so reasonable, as anticipation; that is, by force or wiles to master the persons of all men he can, so long, till he see no other power great enough to endanger him: And this is no more than his own conservation requires and is generally allowed. Also because there be some, that taking pleasure in contemplating their own power in the acts of conquest, which they pursue farther than their security requires; if others, that otherwise would be glad to be at ease within modest bounds, should not by invasion increase their power, they would not be able, long time, by standing only on their defence, to subsist. And by consequence, such augmentation of dominion over men, being necessary to a man's conservation . . . ought to be allowed him.

Again, men have no pleasure (but on the contrary a great deal of grief) in keeping company where there is no power able to over-awe them all. For every man looks that his companion should value him at the same rate he sets upon himself: And upon all signs of contempt or undervaluing naturally endeavours, as far as he dares (which amongst them that have no common power to keep them in quite is far enough to make them destroy each other) to extort a greater value from his contemners, by dommage; and from others, by the example.

So that in the nature of man, we find three principal causes of quarrel. First, competition; secondly, diffidence; thirdly, glory.

The first makes men invade for gain; the second, for safety; and the third, for reputation. The first use violence to make themselves masters of other men's persons, wives, children, and cattle; the second, to defend them; the third, for trifles, as a word, a smile, a different opinion, and any other sign of undervalue, either direct in their persons, or by reflexion in their kindred, their friends, their nation, their profession, or their name.

Hereby it is manifest that during the time men live without a common power to keep them all in awe, they are in that condition which is called war; and such a war as is of every man against every man. For war consists not in battle only, or the act of fighting; but in a tract of time, wherein the will to contend by battle is sufficiently known: and therefore the notion of *time* is to be considered in the nature of war, as it is in the nature of weather. For as the nature of foul weather lies not in a shower or two of rain, but in an inclination thereto of many days together; So the nature of war consisteth not in actual fighting, but in the known disposition thereto during all the time there is no assurance to the contrary. All other time is peace.

Whatsoever therefore is consequent to a time of war, where every man is enemy to every man; the same is consequent to the time wherein men live without other security than what their own strength and their own invention shall furnish them withall. In such condition, there is no place for industry; because the fruit thereof is uncertain: and consequently no culture of the earth, no navigation, nor use of the commodities that may be imported by sea; no commodious building; no instruments of moving, and removing such things as require much force; no knowledge of the face of the earth; no account of time; no arts; no letters; no society; and which is worst of all, continual fear and danger of violent death; And the life of man, solitary, poor, nasty, brutish, and short.

It may seem strange to some man that has not well weighed these things that nature should thus dissociate and render man apt to invade and destroy one another: and he may therefore, not trusting to this inference made from the passions, desire perhaps to have the same confirmed by experience. Let him therefore consider with himself, when taking a journey, he arms himself and seeks to go well accompanied; when going to sleep, he locks his doors; when even in his house he locks his chests; and this when he knows there be laws and public officers armed to revenge all injuries shall be done him; what opinion he has of his fellow subjects, when he rides armed; of his fellow citizens, when he locks his doors; and of his children and servants when he locks his chests. Does he not there as much accuse mankind by his actions, as I do by my words? But neither of us accuse man's nature in it. The desires, and other passions of man, are in themselves no sin. No more are the actions, that proceed from those passions, till they know a law that forbids them: which till laws be made they cannot know: nor can any law be made, till they have agreed upon the person that shall make it.

It may peradventure be thought, there was never such a time, nor condition of war as this; and I believe it was never generally so, over all the world; but there are many places, where they live so now. For the savage people in many places of *America,* except the government of small families, that concord whereof depends on natural lust, have no government at all; and live at this day in that brutish manner, as I said before. Howsoever, it may be perceived what manner of life there would be where there were no common power to fear; by the manner of life, which men that have formerly lived under a peaceful government, use to degenerate into, in a civil war.

But though there had never been any time wherein particular men were in a condition of war one against another, yet in all times kings, and persons of sovereign authority, because of their Independence, are in continual jealousies and in the state and posture of gladiators, having their weapons pointing and their eyes fixed on one another; that is, their forts, garrisons, and guns, upon the frontiers of their kingdoms and continual spies upon their neighbours; which is a posture of war. But because they uphold thereby the industry of their subjects, there does not follow it that misery which accompanies the liberty of particular men.

To this war of every man against every man, this also is consequent; that nothing can be unjust. The notions of right and wrong, justice and injustice have no place. Where there is no common power, there is no law: where no law, no injustice. Force, and fraud are in war, and two cardinal virtues. Justice and injustice are none of the faculties neither of the body nor mind. If they were, they might be in a man that were alone in the world, as well as his senses and passions. They are qualities that relate to men in society, not in solitude. It is consequent also to the same condition, that there be no propriety, no dominion, no *mine* and *thine* distinct; but only that to be every man's, that he can get; and for so long as he can keep it. And thus much for the ill condition, which man by mere nature is actually placed in; though with a possibility to come out of it, consisting partly in the passions, partly in his reason.

The passions that incline men to peace are fear of death, desire of such things as are necessary to commodious living, and a hope by their industry to obtain them. And reason suggests convenient articles of peace, upon which men may be drawn to agreement. These articles are they, which otherwise are called the laws of nature, whereof I shall speak more particularly in the following chapters.

CHAPTER XIV / OF THE FIRST AND SECOND NATURAL LAWS AND OF CONTRACTS

The right of nature, which writers commonly call *jus naturale,* is the liberty each man has to use his own power, as he wills himself, for the preservation of his own nature; that is to say, of his own life; and consequently, of doing anything which in his own judgment and reasons he shall conceive to be the aptest means thereunto.

By liberty is understood, according to the proper signification of the word, the absence of external impediments: which impediments may oft take away part of a man's power to do what he would but cannot hinder him from using the power left him, according as his judgment and reason shall dictate to him.

A law of nature (*lex naturalis*) is a precept, or general rule, found out by reason, by which a man is forbidden to do that which is destructive of his life or takes away the means of preserving the same and to omit that by which he thinks it may be best preserved. For though they that speak of this subject used to confound *jus,* and *lex, right* and *law;* yet they ought to be distinguished, because right, consists in liberty to do or to forbear, whereas law determines and binds to one of them: so that law and right differ as much as obligation and liberty, which in one and the same matter are inconsistent.

And because the condition of man (as has been declared in the precedent chapter) is a condition of war of everyone against everyone, in which case everyone is governed by his own reason; and there is nothing he can make use of that may not be a help unto him in preserving his life against his enemies; it follows that in such a condition, every man has a right to everything; even to one another's body. And therefore, as long as this natural right of every man to every thing endures, there can be no security to any man (how strong or wise soever he be) of living out the time which nature ordinarily allows men to live. And consequently it is a precept or general rule of reason, *That every man ought to endeavour peace, as far as he has hope of obtaining it; and when he cannot obtain it, that he may seek, and use, all helps and advantages of war.* The first branch of which rule contains the first and fundamental law of nature; which is *to seek peace and follow it.* The second, the sum of the right of nature, which is by *all means we can, to defend ourselves.*

From this fundamental law of nature, by which men are commanded to endeavour peace, is derived this second law; *That a man be willing, when others are so too, as far-forth, as for peace and defence of himself he shall think it necessary to lay down this right to all things and be contented with so much liberty against other men as he would allow other men against himself.* For as long as every man holds this right of doing any thing he likes, so long are all men in the condition of war. But if other men will not lay down their right, as well as he, then there is no reason for anyone to devest himself of his: For that were to expose himself to prey (which no man is bound to) rather than to dispose himself to peace. This is that law of the gospel:

Whatsoever you require that others should do to you, that do ye to them. And that law of all men, *Quod tibi fieri non vis, alteri ne feceris.**

To *lay down* a man's *right* to any thing is to divest himself of the *liberty* of hindering another of the benefit of his own right to the same. For he that renounces or passes away his right gives not to any other man a right which he had not before; because there is nothing to which every man had not right by nature; but only stands out of his way, that he may enjoy his own original right without hindrance from him; not without hindrance from another. So that the effect which redounds to one man by another man's defect of right is but so much diminution of impediments to the use of his own right original.

Right is laid aside, either by simply renouncing it or by transferring it to another. By *simply* renouncing when he cares not to whom the benefit thereof redounds. By transferring when he intends the benefit thereof to some certain person or persons. And when a man has in either manner abandoned or granted away his right, then is he said to be obliged, or bound, not to hinder those to whom such right is granted or abandoned from the benefit of it; and that he *ought,* and it is his duty, not to make void that voluntary act of *his* own; and that such hindrance is injustice and injury, as being *sine jure,* the right being before renounced or transferred. So that *injury* or *injustice,* in the controversies of the world, is somewhat like to that which in the disputations of scholars is called *absurdity.* For as it is there called an absurdity to contradict what one maintained in the beginning: so in the world, it is called injustice and injury voluntarily to undo that which from the beginning he had voluntarily done. The way by which a man either simply renounces or transfers his right is a declaration or signification by some voluntary and sufficient sign or signs that he does so renounce or transfer, or has so renounced or transferred the same to him that accepts it. And these signs are either words only, or actions only, or (as it happens most often) both words and actions. And the same are the bonds by which men are bound and obliged: bonds that have their strength, not from their own nature (for nothing is more easily broken than a man's word), but from fear of some evil consequence upon the rupture.

* "What you do not want done to yourself, do not do to others." —ED.

Whensoever a man transfers his right or renounces it, it is either in consideration of some right reciprocally transferred to himself or for some other good he hopes for thereby. For it is a voluntary act: and of the voluntary acts of every man, the object is some *good to himself.* And therefore there be some rights which no man can be understood by any words, or other signs, to have abandoned or transferred. As first a man cannot lay down the right of resisting them, that assault him by force or take away his life, because he cannot be understood to aim thereby at any good to himself. The same may be said of wounds and chains and imprisonment, both because there is no benefit consequent to such patience, as there is to the patience of suffering another to be wounded or imprisoned, as also because a man cannot tell, when he sees men proceed against him by violence whether they intend his death or not. And lastly the motive, and end for which this renouncing and transferring of Right is introduced, is nothing else but the security of a man's person in his life and in the means of so preserving life as not to be weary of it. And therefore if a man by words, or other signs, seems to despoil himself of the End for which those signs were intended, he is not to be understood as if he meant it or that it was his will, but that he was ignorant of how such words and actions were to be interpreted.

The mutual transferring of right is that which men call contract.

There is difference between transferring of right to the thing and transferring, or tradition, that is, delivery of the thing itself. For the thing may be delivered together with the translation of the right, as in buying and selling with ready money or exchange of goods or lands, and it may be delivered some time after.

Again, one of the contractors may deliver the thing contracted for on his part and leave the other to perform his part at some determinate time after and in the meantime be trusted; and then the contract on his part, is called pact, or covenant: Or both parts may contract now to perform hereafter, in which cases he that is to perform in time to come, being trusted, his performance is called *keeping of promise,* or faith; and the failing of performance (if it be voluntary) *violation of faith.*

When the transferring of right is not mutual, but one of the parties transfers in hope to gain thereby friendship or service from another or from his friends; or in hope to gain the reputation of charity, or magnanimity; or to deliver his mind from the pain of compassion; or in hope of reward in heaven, this is not contract, but gift, free-gift, grace: which words signify one and the same thing.

Signs of contract are either *express* or by *inference.* Express are words spoken with understanding of what they signify: And such words are either of the time *present,* or *past*; as, *I give, I grant, I have given, I have granted, I will that this be yours:* Or of the future; as, *I will give, I will grant:* which words of the future, are called promise.

Signs by inference are sometimes the consequence of words; sometimes the consequence of silence; sometimes the consequence of actions; sometimes the consequence of forbearing an action: and generally a sign by inference, of any contract, is whatsoever sufficiently argues the will of the contractor. . . .

In contracts, the right passes not only where the words are of the time present or past, but also where they are of the future, because all contract is mutual translation, or change of right; and therefore he that promises only because he has already received the benefit for which he promises is to be understood as if he intended the right should pass: for unless he had been content to have his words so understood, the other would not have performed his part first. And for that cause, in buying, and selling, and other acts of contract, a promise is equivalent to a covenant; and therefore obligatory. . . .

If a covenant be made wherein neither of the parties perform presently but trust one another in the condition of mere nature (which is a condition of war of every man against every man) upon any reasonable suspicion, it is void: But if there be a common power set over them both, with right and force sufficient to compel performance, it is not void. For he that performs first has no assurance the other will perform after, because the bonds of words are too weak to bridle men's ambition, avarice, anger, and other passions without the fear of some coercive power; which in the condition of mere nature, where all men are equal and judges of the justness of their own fears, cannot possibly be supposed. And therefore he which performs first does but betray himself to his enemy; contrary to the right (he can never abandon) of defending his life, and means of living.

But in a civil estate, where there is a power set up to constrain those that would otherwise violate their faith, that fear is no more reasonable; and for that cause, he which by the covenant is to perform first is obliged so to do. . . .

Covenants entered into by fear, in the condition of mere nature, are obligatory. For example, if I covenant to pay a ransom or service for my life to an enemy, I am bound by it. For it is a contract, wherein one receives the benefit of life; the other is to receive money or service for it; and consequently, where no other law (as in the condition, of mere nature) forbids the performance, the covenant is valid. Therefore prisoners of war, if trusted with the payment of their ransom, are obliged to pay it: And if a weaker prince make a disadvantageous peace with a stronger for fear, he is bound to keep it, unless (as has been said before) there arises some new and just cause of fear to renew the war. And even in commonwealths, if I be forced to redeem myself from a thief by promising him money, I am bound to pay it till the civil law discharge me. For whatsoever I may lawfully do without obligation, the same I may lawfully covenant to do through fear: and what I lawfully covenant, I cannot lawfully break.

A former covenant makes void a later. For a man that has passed away his right to one man today has it not to pass tomorrow to another: and therefore the later promise passes no right, but is null.

A covenant not to defend myself from force, by force, is aways void. For (as I have shown before) no man can transfer or lay down his right to save himself from death, wounds, and imprisonment (the avoiding whereof is the only end of laying down any right) and therefore the promise of not resisting force in no covenant transfers any right nor is obliging. For though a man may covenant thus, *Unless I do so, or so, kill me;* he cannot covenant thus, *Unless I do so, or so, I will not resist you, when you come to kill me.* For man by nature chooses the lesser evil, which is danger of death in resisting; rather than the greater, which is certain and present death in not resisting. And this is granted to be true by all men, in that they lead criminals to execution and prison with armed men, notwithstanding that such criminals have consented to the law by which they are condemned.

A covenant to accuse oneself without assurance or pardon is likewise invalid. For in the condition of nature, where every man is judge, there is no place for accusation; and in the civil state, the accusation is followed with punishment, which, being Force, a man is not obliged not to resist. The same is also true of the accusation of those by whose condemnation a man falls into misery; as of a father, wife, or benefactor. For the testimony of such an accuser, if it be not willingly given, is presumed to be corrupted by nature and therefore not to be received: and where a man's testimony is not to be credited, he is not bound to give it. Also accusations upon torture are not to be reputed as testimonies. For torture is to be used but as means of conjecture, and light, in the further examination and search of truth; and what is in that case confessed tends to the ease of him that is tortured, not to the informing of the torturers, and therefore ought not to have the credit of a sufficient testimony; for whether he deliver himself by true or false accusation, he does it by the right of preserving his own life. . . .

JOHN LOCKE

from *Second Treatise of Government* (1690)

John Locke (1632–1704) was born in Wrington, Somerset, England. The son of an attorney, he was raised in a liberal Puritan family. At the age of fourteen, he entered Westminster School, where he studied the classics, Hebrew, and Arabic. At twenty, he entered Christ's Church, Oxford, where he earned a B.A. in 1656. After receiving an M.A., he was appointed censor of moral philosophy at Oxford.

When his father died in 1661, Locke received a small inheritance. He began studying for a medical degree, and in 1667 became personal physician to the earl of Shaftesbury. Locke received his medical degree in 1674; while completing his studies, he wrote the first two drafts of his Essay Concerning Human Understanding, *was appointed a fellow of the Royal Society, and was named secretary to the Council of Trade and Plantations.*

Locke spent several years in France, returning in 1679. Because of his ties to Shaftesbury, who had been implicated in a plot against the king, Locke was placed under surveillance; he fled to Holland in 1683. There he became an adviser to William of Orange, published a series of works, and wrote the third draft of the Essay. *The revolution of 1688 enabled him to return to England in the company of the future queen, Mary. In 1689 and 1690, Locke published the philosophical work that made him internationally famous: the* Essay *and the* Two Treatises of Government. *He became commissioner of the Board of Trade and Plantations, where he served with great distinction until failing health forced him to retire.*

Locke's Second Treatise *presents a classically liberal theory of government. People in the state of nature would choose to sacrifice a portion of their liberty for the impartial judgment the government can provide. The people nevertheless retain most of their natural rights, which place limits on the power of government. In addition, they receive social rights from the government itself. The government's purpose is the protection of life, liberty, and property; it can act only with the consent of the governed. (Source: Reprinted from John Locke,* Two Treatises of Government. *London: Printed for Awnsham Churchill, 1690. Spelling and punctuation have been modernized for clarity.)*

QUESTIONS FOR REFLECTION

1. In what sense is the state of nature a state of equality?
2. How does Locke distinguish liberty from license? Why is the state of nature characterized only by the former?
3. How does Locke argue for capital punishment?
4. What motivates us, in the state of nature, to contract to form a government? What are we willing to give up? What do we hope to gain?
5. Hobbes describes the state of nature as a "war of every man against every man." Locke, however, finds the state of nature different from a state of war. In what ways?
6. What, for Locke, is natural liberty? Liberty in society? Liberty under government?

CHAPTER II / OF THE STATE OF NATURE

§. 4. To understand political power right and derive it from its original, we must consider what state all men are naturally in, and that is a state of perfect freedom to order their actions and dispose of their possessions and persons, as they think fit, within the bounds of the law of nature, without asking leave or depending upon the will of any other man.

A state also of equality, wherein all the power and jurisdiction is reciprocal, no one having more than another; there being nothing more evident than that creatures of the same species and rank, promiscuously born to all the same advantages of nature and the use of the same faculties should also be equal one amongst another without subordination or subjection, unless the lord and master of them all should, by any manifest declaration of his will, set one above another and confer on him, by an evident and clear appointment, an undoubted right to dominion and sovereignty.

§. 5. This equality of men by nature the judicious Hooker* looks upon as so evident in itself and beyond all question that he makes it the foundation of that obligation to mutual love amongst men, on which he builds the duties they owe one another and from whence he derives the great maxims of justice and charity. His words are,

> The like natural inducement has brought men to know that it is no less their duty to love others than themselves; for seeing those things which are equal must needs all have one measure; if I cannot but wish to receive good, even as much at every man's hands as any man can wish unto his own soul, how should I look to have any part of my desire herein satisfied, unless myself be careful to satisfy the like desire, which is undoubtedly in other men, being of one and the same nature? To have anything offered them repugnant to this desire must needs in all respects grieve them as much as me; so that if I do harm, I must look to suffer, there being no reason that others should show greater measure of love to me than they have by me shown unto them: my desire therefore to be loved of my equals in nature, as much as possible may be, imposes upon me a natural duty of bearing to them fully the like affection; from which relation of equality between ourselves and them that are as ourselves, what several rules and canons natural reason has drawn for direction of life no man is ignorant, Eccl. Pol. Lib. 1.

§. 6. But though this be a state of liberty, yet it is not a state of licence: though man in that state have an uncontrollable liberty to dispose of his person or possessions, yet he has not liberty to destroy himself or so much as any creature in his possession, but where some nobler use than its bare preservation calls for it. The state of nature has a law of nature to govern it, which obliges every one: and reason, which is that law, teaches all mankind who will but consult it that being all equal and independent, no one ought to harm another in his life, health, liberty, or possessions: for men being all the workmanship of one omnipotent and infinitely wise maker, all the servants of one sovereign master, sent into the world by his order and about his business; they are his property, whose workmanship they are, made to last during his, not one another's pleasure: and being furnished with like faculties, sharing all in one community of nature, there cannot be supposed any such subordination among us that may authorize us to destroy one another, as if we were made for one another's uses, as the inferior ranks of creatures are for ours. Every one, as he is bound to preserve himself and not to quit his station wilfully, so by the like reason, when his own preservation comes not in competition, ought he as much as he can to preserve the rest of mankind and may not, unless it be to do justice on an offender, take away or impair the life or what tends to the preservation of the life, the liberty, health, limb, or goods of another.

§. 7. And that all men may be restrained from invading others' rights and from doing hurt to one another, and the law of nature be observed which wills the peace and preservation of all mankind, the execution of the law of nature is, in that state,

* Richard Hooker (1553–1600), English theologian and political philosopher, wrote *The Laws of Ecclesiastical Polity,* which focuses on reason and natural law as foundations of the state. —ED.

put into every man's hands, whereby everyone has a right to punish the transgressors of that law to such a degree as may hinder its violation: for the law of nature would, as all other laws that concern men in this world, be in vain if there were no body that in the state of nature had a power to execute that law and thereby preserve the innocent and restrain offenders. And if any one in the state of nature may punish another for any evil he has done, every one may do so: for in that state of perfect equality, where naturally there is no superiority or jurisdiction of one over another, what any may do in prosecution of that law everyone must needs have a right to do.

§. 8. And thus, in the state of nature, one man comes by a power over another; but yet no absolute or arbitrary power to use a criminal, when he has got him in his hands, according to the passionate heats, or boundless extravagancy of his own will; but only to retribute to him, so far as calm reason and conscience dictate, what is proportionate to his transgression, which is so much as may serve for reparation and restraint: for these two are the only reasons why one man may lawfully do harm to another, which is that we call punishment. In transgressing the law of nature, the offender declares himself to live by another rule than that of reason and common equity, which is that measure God has set to the actions of men for their mutual security; and so he becomes dangerous to mankind, the tie which is to secure them from injury and violence being slighted and broken by him. Which being a trespass against the whole species and the peace and safety of it provided for by the law of nature, every man upon this score, by the right he has to preserve mankind in general, may restrain or, where it is necessary, destroy things noxious to them and so may bring such evil on anyone who has transgressed that law, as may make him repent the doing of it and thereby deter him, and by his example others, from doing the like mischief. And in the case, and upon this ground, every man has a right to punish the offender and be executioner of the law of nature.

§. 9. I doubt not but this will seem a very strange doctrine to some men: but before they condemn it, I desire them to resolve me, by what right any prince or state can put to death or punish an alien for any crime he commits in their country. It is certain their laws, by virtue of any sanction they receive from the promulgated will of the legislative, reach not a stranger: they speak not to him, nor, if they did, is he bound to hearken to them. The legislative authority, by which they are in force over the subjects of that commonwealth, has no power over him. Those who have the supreme power of making laws in England, France or Holland are to an Indian but like the rest of the world, men without authority: and therefore, if by the law of nature every man has not a power to punish offences against it as he soberly judges the case to require, I see not how the magistrates of any community can punish an alien of another country; since, in reference to him, they can have no more power than what every man naturally may have over another.

§. 10. Besides the crime which consists in violating the law and varying from the right rule of reason, whereby a man so far becomes degenerate and declares himself to quit the principles of human nature and to be a noxious creature, there is commonly injury done to some person or other, and some other man receives damage by his transgression: in which case he who has received any damage has, besides the right of punishment common to him with other men, a particular right to seek reparation from him that has done it: and any other person who finds it just may also join with him that is injured and assist him in recovering from the offender so much as may make satisfaction for the harm he has suffered.

§. 11. From these two distinct rights, the one of punishing the crime for restraint and preventing the like offence, which right of punishing is in everybody; the other of taking reparation, which belongs only to the injured party, comes it to pass that the magistrate, who by being magistrate has the common right of punishing put into his hands, can often, where the public good demands not the execution of the law, remit the punishment of criminal offenses by his own authority, but yet cannot remit the satisfaction due to any private man for the damage he has received. That he who has suffered the damage has a right to demand in his own name, and he alone can remit: the damnified person has this power of appropriating to himself the goods or service of the offender by right of self-preservation, as every man has a power to punish the crime to prevent its being committed again, by the right he has of preserving all mankind and doing all reasonable things he can in order to that end: and thus it is that every man in the state of nature has a power to kill a murderer, both to deter others from doing the like injury, which no reparation can compensate, by the example of the punishment that attends it from everybody, and also to secure men from the attempts of a criminal, who having renounced reason, the common rule and measure God has given to mankind, has by the unjust violence and slaughter he has committed upon one, declared war against all mankind and therefore may be destroyed as a lion or a tiger, one of those wild savage beasts with whom men can have no society nor security: and upon this is grounded that great law of nature, *Whoso sheddeth man's blood, by man shall his blood be shed.* And Cain was so fully convinced that every one had a right to destroy such a criminal that after the murder of his brother, he cries out, *Every one that findeth me, shall slay me;* so plain was it writ in the hearts of all mankind.

§. 12. By the same reason may a man in the state of nature punish the lesser breaches of that law. It will perhaps be demanded, with death? I answer, each transgression may be punished to that degree and with so much severity as will suffice to make it an ill bargain to the offender, give him cause to repent, and terrify others from doing the like. Every offence that can be committed in the state of nature may in the state of nature be also punished equally, and as far forth as it may, in a commonwealth: for though it would be besides my present purpose to enter here into the particulars of the law of nature or its measures of punishment, yet, it is certain there is such a law, and that too as intelligible and plain to a rational creature and a studier of that law as the positive laws of commonwealths; nay, possibly plainer, as much as reason is easier to be understood than the fancies and intricate contrivances of men following contrary and hidden interests put into words; for so truly are a great part of the municipal laws of countries, which are only so far right as they are founded on the law of nature, by which they are to be regulated and interpreted.

§. 13. To this strange doctrine, *viz.* That in the state of nature every one has the executive power of the law of nature, I doubt not but it will be objected that it is unreasonable for men to be judges in their own cases, that self-love will make men partial to themselves and their friends, and, on the other side, that ill nature, passion and revenge will carry them too far in punishing others; and hence nothing but confusion and disorder will follow and that therefore God has certainly appointed government to restrain the partiality and violence of men. I easily grant that civil government is the proper remedy for the inconveniences of the state of nature, which must certainly be great where men may be judges in their own case, since it is easy to be imagined that he who was so unjust as to do his brother an injury will scarce be so just as to condemn himself for it: but I shall desire those who make this objection to remember that absolute monarchs are but men; and if government is to be the remedy of those evils which necessarily follow from men's being judges in their own cases and the state of nature is therefore not to be endured, I desire to know what kind of government that is and how much better it is than the state of nature, where one man commanding a multitude has the liberty to be judge in his own case and may do to all his subjects whatever he pleases, without the least liberty to anyone to question or control those who execute his pleasure? and in whatsoever he does, whether led by reason, mistake or passion, must be submitted to? Much better it is in the state of nature, where men are not bound to submit to the unjust will of another, and if he that judges judges amiss in his own or any other case, he is answerable for it to the rest of mankind.

§. 14. It is often asked as a mighty objection, where are, or ever were there, any men in such a state of nature? To which it may suffice as an answer at present that since all princes and rulers of independent governments all through the world are in a state of nature, it is plain the world never was, nor ever will be, without numbers of men in that state. I have named all governors of independent communities, whether they are or are not in league with others: for it is not every compact that puts an end to the state of nature between men, but only this one of agreeing together mutually to enter into the community and make one body politic; other promises and compacts men may make one with another and yet still be in the state of nature. The promises and bargains for truck, &c. between the two men in the desert island, mentioned by Garcilasso de la Vega in his history of Peru, or between a Swiss and an Indian in the woods of America are binding to them, though they are perfectly in a state of nature in reference to one another: for truth and keeping of faith belongs to men as men and not as members of society.

§. 15. To those that say there were never any men in the state of nature, I will not only oppose the authority of the judicious Hooker, *Eccl. Pol. lib.* i. *sect.* 10. where he says, *The laws which have been hitherto mentioned,* i.e. the laws of nature, *do bind men absolutely, even as they are men, although they have never any settled fellowship, never any solemn agreement amongst themselves what to do, or not to do: but forasmuch as we are not by ourselves sufficient to furnish ourselves with competent store of things, needful for such a life as our nature doth desire, a life fit for the dignity of man; therefore to supply those defects and imperfections which are in us, as living single and solely by ourselves, we are naturally induced to seek communion and fellowship with others: this was the cause of men's uniting themselves at first in politic societies.* But I moreover affirm that all men are naturally in that state and remain so until by their own consents they make themselves members of some politic society; and I doubt not in the sequel of this discourse, to make it very clear.

CHAPTER III / OF THE STATE OF WAR

§. 16. The state of war is a state of enmity and destruction: and therefore declaring by word or action, not a passionate and hasty, but a sedate settled design upon another man's life, puts him in a state of war with him against whom he has declared such an intention, and so has exposed his life to the other's power to be taken away by him or any one that joins with him in his defence and espouses his quarrel; it being reasonable and just, I should have a right to destroy that which threatens me with destruction: for by the fundamental law of nature, man being to be preserved as much as possible, when all cannot be preserved, the safety of the innocent is to be preferred: and one may destroy a man who makes war upon him or has discovered an enmity to his being, for the same reason that he may kill a wolf or a lion; because such men are not under the ties of the common law of reason, have no other rule but that of force and violence, and so may be treated as beasts of prey those dangerous and noxious creatures that will be sure to destroy him whenever he falls into their power.

§. 17. And hence it is that he who attempts to get another man into his absolute power does thereby put himself into a state of war with him, it being to be understood as a declaration of a design upon his life: for I have reason to conclude that he who would get me into his power without my consent would use me as he pleased when he had got me there and destroy me too when he had a fancy to it; for nobody can desire to have me in his absolute power, unless it be to compel me by force to that which is against the right of my freedom, i.e. make me a slave. To be free from such force is the only security of my preservation, and reason bids me look on him, as an enemy to my preservation, who would take away that freedom which is the fence to it; so that he who makes an attempt to enslave me thereby puts himself into a state of war with me. He that in the state of nature would take away the freedom that belongs to anyone in that state must necessarily be supposed to have a design to take away every thing else, that freedom being the foundation of all the rest; as he that in the state of society would take away the freedom belonging to those of that society or commonwealth must be supposed to design to take away from them everything else and so be looked on as in a state of war.

§. 18. This makes it lawful for a man to kill a thief who has not in the least hurt him nor declared any design upon his life any farther than by the use of force so to get him in his power, as to take away his money, or what he pleases, from him; because using force where he has no right to get me into his power, let his pretence be what it will, I have no reason to suppose that he who would take away my liberty would not, when he had me in his power, take away everything else. And therefore it is lawful for me to treat him as one who has put himself into a state of war with me, i.e. kill him if I can; for to that hazard does he justly expose himself, whoever introduces a state of war and is aggressor in it.

§. 19. And here we have the plain difference between the state of nature and the state of war, which however some men have confounded, are as far distant as a state of peace, good will, mutual assistance and preservation and a state of enmity, malice, violence and mutual destruction are one from another. Men living together according to reason, without a common superior on earth with authority to judge between them, is properly the state of nature. But force, or a declared design of force, upon the person of another, where there is no common superior on earth to appeal to for relief, is the state of war: and it is the want of such an appeal gives a man the right of war even against an aggressor, though he be in society and a fellow subject. Thus a thief, whom I cannot harm but by appeal to the law for having stolen all that I am worth, I may kill when he sets on me to rob me but of my horse or coat; because the law, which was made for my preservation where it cannot interpose to secure my life from present force, which, if lost, is capable of no reparation, permits me my own defence and the right of war, a liberty to kill the aggressor, because the aggressor allows not time to appeal to our common judge nor the decision of the law for remedy in a case where the mischief may be irreparable. Want of a common judge with authority puts all men in a state of nature: force without right upon a man's person makes a state of war, both where there is and is not a common judge.

§. 20. But when the actual force is over, the state of war ceases between those that are in society and are equally on both sides subjected to the fair determination of the law; because then there lies open the remedy of appeal for the past injury and to prevent future harm: but where no such appeal is, as in the state of nature, for want of positive laws and judges with authority to appeal to, the state of war once begun continues, with a right to the innocent party to destroy the other whenever he can until the aggressor offers peace and desires reconciliation on such terms as may repair any wrongs he has already done and secure the innocent for the future; nay, where an appeal to the law and constituted judges lies open, but the remedy is denied by a manifest perverting of justice and a barefaced wresting of the laws to protect or indemnify the violence or injuries of some men or party of men, there it is hard to imagine anything but a state of war: for wherever violence is used and injury done, though by hands appointed to administer justice, it is still violence and injury, however coloured with the name, pretences, or forms of law, the end whereof being to protect and redress the innocent by an unbiased application of it to all who are under it; wherever that is not *bona fide* done, war is made upon the sufferers, who, having no appeal on earth to right them, they are left to the only remedy in such cases, an appeal to heaven.

§. 21. To avoid this state of war (wherein there is no appeal but to heaven, and wherein every the least difference is apt to end where there is no authority to decide between the contenders) is one great reason of men's putting themselves into society and quitting the state of nature: for where there is an authority, a power on earth from which relief can be had by appeal there the continuance of the state of war is excluded, and the controversy is decided by that power. Had there been any such court, any superior jurisdiction on earth, to determine the right between Jephtha and the Ammonities, they had never come to a state of war: but we see he was forced to appeal to heaven. *The Lord the Judge* (says he) *be judge this day between the children of* Israel *and the children of* Ammon, *Judg.* xi. 27. and then prosecuting and relying on his appeal, he leads out his army to battle: and therefore in such controversies, where the question is put, *who shall be judge?* It cannot be meant, who shall decide the controversy; everyone knows what Jephtha here tells us, that the Lord the Judge shall judge. Where there is no judge on earth, the appeal lies to God in heaven. That question then cannot mean, who shall judge whether another has put himself in a state of war with me and whether I may, as Jephtha did, appeal to heaven in it? of that I myself can only be judge in my own conscience, as I will answer it, at the great day, to the supreme judge of all men.

CHAPTER IV / OF SLAVERY

§. 22. The natural liberty of man is to be free from any superior power on earth and not to be under the will or legislative authority of man, but to have only the law of nature for his rule. The liberty of man in society is to be under no other legislative power but that established by consent in the commonwealth, nor under the dominion of any will or restraint of any law but what that legislative shall enact according to the trust put in it. Freedom then is not what Sir Robert Filmer tells us, *Observations, A. 55. a liberty for every one to do what he lists, to live as he pleases, and not to be tied by any laws:* but *freedom of men under government* is to have a standing rule to live by, common to every one of that society and made by the legislative power erected in it; a liberty to follow my own will in all things, where the rule prescribes not; and not to be subject to the inconstant, uncertain, unknown, arbitrary will of another man: as freedom of nature is to be under no other restraint but the law of nature.

§. 23. This freedom from absolute, arbitrary power is so necessary to and closely joined with a man's preservation that he cannot part with it, but by what forfeits his preservation and life together: for a man, not having the power of his own life, cannot by compact or his own consent enslave himself to anyone nor put himself under the absolute, arbitrary power of another to take away his life when he pleases. Nobody can give more power than he has himself; and he that cannot take away his own life cannot give another power over it. Indeed, having by his fault forfeited his own life by some act that deserves death, he to whom he has forfeited it may (when he has him in his power) delay to take it and make use of him to his own service, and he does him no injury by it: for whenever he finds the hardship of his slavery outweigh the value of his life, it is in his power, by resisting the will of his master, to draw on himself the death he desires. . . .

JEAN-JACQUES ROUSSEAU

from *On the Social Contract* (1762)

Jean-Jacques Rousseau (1712–1778), philosopher, essayist, and novelist, was born in Geneva. His mother died a few days after he was born; he was raised by his somewhat unstable father and an aunt. Rousseau had little formal education. He studied for two years with a country minister. He became apprentice to a notary and then to an engraver, who treated him badly. Discouraged, Rousseau left Geneva at the age of sixteen. He went to France, where he met Madame de Warens, a convert to Roman Catholicism. They became friends; Rousseau too converted. He traveled with her and stayed at her estate in Chambéry. In 1740 he became a private tutor in Lyon.

At thirty-one, Rousseau became secretary to the French ambassador at Venice. He lost the post the next year after quarrelling with the ambassador. At thiry-three, he began an affair with Thérèse Le Vasseur, by whom he had five illegitimate children—all of whom he sent to an orphanage. Rousseau's intellectual career brought him in contact with the greatest minds of Europe, many of whom he met, befriended, and shortly thereafter, alienated.

In 1755, Rousseau published his Discourse on the Origin of Inequality, *which presented an idealized, romantic view of the state of nature, from which humanity fell by inventing the notion of property. In 1762,* On the Social Contract *appeared, which offers an account of the social contract and the power of government. According to that work, people band together to form a government by surrendering everything they have to the community. On balance, they gain from this arrangement, according to Rousseau, for each person receives in turn a share of the entire community and rights that arise from the community. The community has a general will, directed toward what is best for itself as a whole. Individual wills in conflict with the general will are in error. (Source: Reprinted from* The Social Contract and Discources, *translated by G. D. H. Cole, London: J. M. Dent & Sons Ltd., 1913.)*

QUESTIONS FOR REFLECTION

1. What, for Rousseau, is the foundation of all rights?
2. According to Rousseau, why does physical power have no moral force?
3. In Rousseau's view, why is slavery—even voluntary slavery—illegitimate?
4. Why, according to Rousseau, do people enter into a social compact? What do they give up? What do they hope to gain?
5. What is Rousseau's analysis of conflicts between an individual will and the general will?
6. Why does Rousseau approve of capital punishment?

CHAPTER I / SUBJECT OF THE FIRST BOOK

Man is born free; and everywhere he is in chains. One thinks himself the master of others, and still remains a greater slave than they. How did this change come about? I do not know. What can make it legitimate? That question I think I can answer.

If I took into account only force, and the effects derived from it, I should say: "As long as a people is compelled to obey, and obeys, it does well; as soon as it can shake off the yoke, and shakes it off, it does still better; for, regaining its liberty by the same right as took it away, either it is justified in resuming it, or there was no justification for those who took it away." But the social order is a sacred right which is the basis of all other rights. Nevertheless, this right does not come from nature, and must therefore be founded on conventions. Before coming to that, I have to prove what I have just asserted. . . .

CHAPTER III / THE RIGHT OF THE STRONGEST

The strongest is never strong enough to be always the master, unless he transforms strength into right, and obedience into duty. Hence the right of the strongest, which, though to all seeming meant ironically, is really laid down as a fundamental principle. But are we never to have an explanation of this phrase? Force is a physical power, and I fail to see what moral effect it can have. To yield to force is an act of necessity, not of will—at the most, an act of prudence. In what sense can it be a duty?

Suppose for a moment that this so-called "right" exists. I maintain that the sole result is a mass of inexplicable nonsense. For, if force creates right, the effect changes with the cause: every force that is greater than the first succeeds to its right. As soon as it is possible to disobey with impunity, disobedience is legitimate; and, the strongest being always in the right, the only thing that matters is to act so as to become the strongest. But what kind of right is that which perishes when force fails? If we must obey perforce, there is no need to obey because we ought; and if we are not forced to obey, we are under no obligation to do so. Clearly, the word "right" adds nothing to force: in this connection, it means absolutely nothing.

Obey the powers that be. If this means yield to force, it is a good precept, but superfluous: I can answer for its never being violated. All power comes from God, I admit; but so does all sickness: does that mean that we are forbidden to call in the doctor? A brigand surprises me at the edge of a wood: must I not merely surrender my purse on compulsion; but, even if I could withhold it, am I in conscience bound to give it up? For certainly the pistol he holds is also a power.

Let us then admit that force does not create right, and that we are obliged to obey only legitimate powers. In that case, my original question recurs.

CHAPTER IV / SLAVERY

Since no man has a natural authority over his fellow, and force creates no right, we must conclude that conventions form the basis of all legitimate authority among men.

If an individual, says Grotius, can alienate his liberty and make himself the slave of a master, why could not a whole people do the same and make itself subject to a king? There are in this passage plenty of ambiguous words which would need explaining; but let us confine ourselves to the word *alienate*. To alienate is to give or to sell. Now, a man who becomes the slave of another does not give himself; he sells himself, at the least for his subsistence: but for what does a people sell itself? A king is so far from furnishing his subjects with their subsistence that he gets his own only from them; and, according to Rabelais, kings do not live on nothing. Do subjects then give their persons on condition that the king takes their goods also? I fail to see what they have left to preserve.

It will be said that the despot assures his subjects civil tranquillity. Granted; but what do they gain, if the wars his ambition brings down upon them, his insatiable avidity, and the vexatious conduct of his ministers press harder on them than their own dissensions would have done? What do they gain, if the very tranquillity they enjoy is one of their miseries? Tranquillity is found also in dungeons; but is that enough to make them desirable places to live in? The Greeks imprisoned in the cave of the Cyclops lived there very tranquilly, while they were awaiting their turn to be devoured.

To say that a man gives himself gratuitously, is to say what is absurd and inconceivable; such an act is null and illegitimate, from the mere fact that he who does it is out of his mind. To say the same of a whole people is to suppose a people of madmen; and madness creates no right.

Even if each man could alienate himself, he could not alienate his children: they are born men and free; their liberty belongs to them, and no one but they has the right to dispose of it. Before they come to years of discretion, the father can, in their name, lay down conditions for their preservation and well-being, but he cannot give them irrevocably and without conditions: such a gift is contrary to the ends of nature, and exceeds the rights of paternity. It would therefore be necessary, in order to legitimise an arbitrary government, that in every generation the people should be in a position to accept or reject it; but, were this so, the government would be no longer arbitrary.

To renounce liberty is to renounce being a man, to surrender the rights of humanity and even its duties. For him who renounces everything no indemnity is possible. Such a renunciation is incompatible with man's nature; to remove all liberty from his will is to remove all morality from his acts. Finally, it is an empty and contradictory convention that sets up, on the one side, absolute authority, and, on the other, unlimited obedience. Is it not clear that we can be under no obligation to a person from whom we have the right to exact everything? Does not this condition alone, in the absence of equivalence or exchange, in itself involve the nullity of the act? For what right can my slave have against me, when all that he has belongs to me, and, his right being mine, this right of mine against myself is a phrase devoid of meaning?

Grotius and the rest find in war another origin for the so-called right of slavery. The victor having, as they hold, the right of killing the vanquished, the latter can buy back his life at the price of his liberty; and this convention is the more legitimate because it is to the advantage of both parties.

But it is clear that this supposed right to kill the conquered is by no means deducible from the state of war. Men, from the mere fact that, while they are living in their primitive independence, they have no mutual relations stable enough to constitute either the state of peace or the state of war, cannot be naturally enemies. War is constituted by a relation between things, and not between persons; and, as the state of war cannot arise out of simple personal relations, but only out of real relations, private war, or war of man with man, can exist neither in the state of nature, where there is no constant property, nor in the social state, where everything is under the authority of the laws.

Individual combats, duels and encounters, are acts which cannot constitute a state; while the private wars, authorised by the Establishments of Louis IX, King of France, and suspended by the Peace of God, are abuses of feudalism, in itself an absurd system if ever there was one, and contrary to the principles of natural right and to all good polity.

War then is a relation, not between man and man, but between State and State, and individuals are enemies only accidentally, not as men, nor even as citizens, but as soldiers; not as members of their country, but as its defenders. Finally, each State can have for enemies only other States, and not men; for between things disparate in nature there can be no real relation.

Furthermore, this principle is in conformity with the established rules of all times and the constant practice of all civilised peoples. Declarations of war are intimations less to powers than to their subjects. The foreigner, whether king, individual, or people, who robs, kills or detains the subjects, without declaring war on the prince, is not an enemy, but a brigand. Even in real war, a just prince, while laying hands, in the enemy's country, on all that belongs to the public, respects the lives and goods of individuals: he respects rights on which his own are founded. The object of the war being the destruction of the hostile State, the other side has a right to kill its defenders, while they are bearing arms; but as soon as they lay them down and surrender, they cease to be enemies or instruments of the enemy, and become once more merely men, whose life no one has any right to take. Sometimes it is possible to kill the State without killing a single one of its members; and war gives no right which is not necessary to the gaining of its object. These principles are not those of Grotius: they are not based on the authority of poets, but derived from the nature of reality and based on reason.

The right of conquest has no foundation other than the right of the strongest. If war does not give the conqueror the right to massacre the conquered peoples, the right to enslave them cannot be based upon a right which does not exist. No one has a right to kill an enemy except when he cannot make him a slave, and the right to enslave him cannot therefore be derived from the right to kill him. It is accordingly an unfair exchange to make him buy at the price of his liberty his life, over which the victor holds no right. Is it not clear that there is a vicious circle in founding the right of life and death on the right of slavery, and the right of slavery on the right of life and death?

Even if we assume this terrible right to kill everybody, I maintain that a slave made in war, or a conquered people, is under no obligation to a master, except to obey him as far as he is compelled to do so. By taking an equivalent for his life, the victor has not done him a favour; instead of killing him without profit, he has killed him usefully. So far then is he from acquiring over him any authority in addition to that of force, that the state of war continues to subsist between them: their mutual relation is the effect of it, and the usage of the right of war does not imply a treaty of peace. A convention has indeed been made; but this convention, so far from destroying the state of war, presupposes its continuance.

So, from whatever aspect we regard the question, the right of slavery is null and void, not only as being illegitimate, but also because it is absurd and meaningless. The words *slave* and *right* contradict each other, and are mutually exclusive. It will always be equally foolish for a man to say to a man or to a people: "I make with you a convention wholly at your expense and wholly to my advantage; I shall keep it as long as I like, and you will keep it as long as I like."

CHAPTER V / THAT WE MUST ALWAYS GO BACK TO A FIRST CONVENTION

Even if I granted all that I have been refuting, the friends of despotism would be no better off. There will always be a great difference between subduing a multitude and ruling a society. Even if scattered individuals were successively enslaved by one man, however numerous they might be, I still see no more than a master and his slaves, and certainly not a people and its ruler; I see what may be termed an aggregation, but not an association; there is as yet neither public good nor body politic. The man in question, even if he has enslaved half the world, is still only an individual; his interest, apart from that of others, is still a purely private interest. If this same man comes to die, his empire, after him, remains scattered and without unity, as an oak falls and dissolves into a heap of ashes when the fire has consumed it.

A people, says Grotius, can give itself to a king. Then, according to Grotius, a people is a people before it gives itself. The gift is itself a civil act, and implies public deliberation. It would be better, before examining the act by which a people gives itself to a king, to examine that by which it has become a people; for this act, being necessarily prior to the other, is the true foundation of society.

Indeed, if there were no prior convention, where, unless the election were unanimous, would be the obligation on the minority to submit to the choice of the majority? How have a hundred men who wish for a master the right to vote on behalf of ten who do not? The law of majority voting is itself something established by convention, and presupposes unanimity, on one occasion at least.

CHAPTER VI / THE SOCIAL COMPACT

I suppose men to have reached the point at which the obstacles in the way of their preservation in the state of nature show their power of resistance to be greater than the resources at the disposal of each individual for his maintenance in that state. That primitive condition can then subsist no longer; and the human race would perish unless it changed its manner of existence.

But, as men cannot engender new forces, but only unite and direct existing ones, they have no other means of preserving themselves than the formation, by aggregation, of a sum of forces great enough to overcome the resistance. These they have to bring into play by means of a single motive power, and cause to act in concert.

This sum of forces can arise only where several persons come together: but, as the force and liberty of each man are the chief instruments of his self-preservation, how can he pledge them without harming his own interests, and neglecting the care he owes to himself? This difficulty, in its bearing on my present subject, may be stated in the following terms—

"The problem is to find a form of association which will defend and protect with the whole common force the person and goods of each associate, and in which each, while uniting himself with all, may still obey himself alone, and remain as free as before." This is the fundamental problem of which the *Social Contract* provides the solution.

The clauses of this contract are so determined by the nature of the act that the slightest modification would make them vain and ineffective; so that, although they have perhaps never been formally set forth, they are everywhere the same and everywhere tacitly admitted and recognised, until, on the violation of the social compact, each regains his original rights and resumes his natural liberty, while losing the conventional liberty in favour of which he renounced it.

These clauses, properly understood, may be reduced to one—the total alienation of each associate, together with all his rights, to the whole community; for, in the first place, as each gives himself absolutely, the conditions are the same for all; and, this being so, no one has any interest in making them burdensome to others.

Moreover, the alienation being without reserve, the union is as perfect as it can be, and no associate has anything more to demand: for, if the individuals retained certain rights, as there would be no common superior to decide between them and the public, each, being on one point his own judge, would ask to be so on all; the state of nature would thus continue, and the association would necessarily become inoperative or tyrannical.

Finally, each man, in giving himself to all, gives himself to nobody; and as there is no associate over whom he does not acquire the same right as he yields others over himself, he gains an equivalent for everything he loses, and an increase of force for the preservation of what he has.

If then we discard from the social compact what is not of its essence, we shall find that it reduces itself to the following terms—

"Each of us puts his person and all his power in common under the supreme direction of the general will, and, in our corporate capacity, we receive each member as an indivisible part of the whole."

At once, in place of the individual personality of each contracting party, this act of association creates a moral and collective body, composed of as many members as the assembly contains votes, and receiving from this act its unity, its common identity, its life and its will. This public person, so formed by the union of all other persons, formerly took the name of *city,* and now takes that of *Republic* or *body politic;* it is called by its members *State* when passive, *Sovereign* when active, and *Power* when compared with others like itself. Those who are associated in it take collectively the name of *people,* and severally are called *citizens,* as sharing in the sovereign power, and *subjects,* as being under the laws of the State. But these terms are often confused and taken one for another: it is enough to know how to distinguish them when they are being used with precision.

CHAPTER VII / THE SOVEREIGN

This formula shows us that the act of association comprises a mutual undertaking between the public and the individuals, and that each individual, in making a contract, as we may say, with himself, is bound in a double capacity; as a member of the Sovereign he is bound to the individuals, and as a member of the State to the Sovereign. But the maxim of civil right, that no one is bound by undertakings made to himself, does not apply in this case; for there is a great difference between incurring an obligation to yourself and incurring one to a whole of which you form a part.

Attention must further be called to the fact that public deliberation, while competent to bind all the subjects to the Sovereign, because of the two different capacities in which each of them may be regarded, cannot, for the opposite reason, bind the Sovereign to itself; and that it is consequently against the nature of the body politic for the Sovereign to impose on itself a law which it cannot infringe. Being able to regard itself in only one capacity, it is in the position of an individual who makes a contract with himself; and this makes it clear that there neither is nor can be any kind of fundamental law binding on the body of the people—not even the social contract itself. This does not mean that the body politic cannot enter into undertakings with others, provided the contract is not infringed by them; for in relation to what is external to it, it becomes a simple being, an individual.

But the body politic or the Sovereign, drawing its being wholly from the sanctity of the contract, can never bind itself, even to an outsider, to do anything derogatory to the original act, for instance, to alienate any part of itself, or to submit to another Sovereign. Violation of the act by which it exists would be self-annihilation; and that which is itself nothing can create nothing.

As soon as this multitude is so united in one body, it is impossible to offend against one of the members without attacking the body, and still more to offend against the body without the members resenting it. Duty and interest therefore equally oblige the two contracting parties to give each other help; and the same men should seek to combine, in their double capacity, all the advantages dependent upon that capacity.

Again, the Sovereign, being formed wholly of the individuals who compose it, neither has nor can have any interest contrary to theirs; and consequently the sovereign power need give no guarantee to its subjects, because it is impossible for the body to wish to hurt all its members. We shall also see later on that it cannot hurt any in particular. The Sovereign, merely by virtue of what it is, is always what it should be.

This, however, is not the case with the relation of the subjects to the Sovereign, which, despite the common interest, would have no security that they would fulfil their undertakings, unless it found means to assure itself of their fidelity.

In fact, each individual, as a man, may have a particular will contrary or dissimilar to the general will which he has as a citizen. His particular interest may speak to him quite differently from the common interest: his absolute and naturally independent existence may make him look upon what he owes to the common cause as a gratuitous contribution, the loss of which will do less harm to others than the payment of it is burdensome to himself; and, regarding the moral person which constitutes the State as a *persona ficta,* because not a man, he may wish to enjoy the rights of citizenship without being ready to fulfil the duties of a subject. The continuance of such an injustice could not but prove the undoing of the body politic.

In order then that the social compact may not be an empty formula, it tacitly includes the undertaking, which alone can give force to the rest, that whoever refuses to obey the general will shall be compelled to do so by the whole body. This means nothing less than that he will be forced to be free; for this is the condition which, by giving each citizen to his country, secures him against all personal dependence. In this lies the key to the working of the political machine; this alone legitimises civil undertakings, which, without it, would be absurd, tyrannical, and liable to the most frightful abuses.

CHAPTER VIII / THE CIVIL STATE

The passage from the state of nature to the civil state produces a very remarkable change in man, by substituting justice for instinct in his conduct, and giving his actions the morality they had formerly lacked. Then only, when the voice of duty takes the place of physical impulses and right of appetite, does man, who so far had considered only himself, find that he is forced to act on different principles, and to consult his reason before listening to his inclinations. Although, in this state, he deprives himself of some advantages which he got from nature, he gains in return others so great, his faculties are so stimulated and developed, his ideas so extended, his feelings so ennobled, and his whole soul so uplifted, that, did not the abuses of this new condition often degrade him below that which he left, he would be bound to bless continually the happy moment which took him from it for ever, and, instead of a stupid and unimaginative animal, made him an intelligent being and a man.

Let us draw up the whole account in terms easily commensurable. What man loses by the social contract is his natural liberty and an unlimited right to everything he tries to get and succeeds in getting; what he gains is civil liberty and the proprietorship of all he possesses. If we are to avoid mistake in weighing one against the other, we must clearly distinguish natural liberty, which is bounded only by the strength of the individual, from civil liberty, which is limited by the general will; and possession, which is merely the effect of force or the right of the first occupier, from property, which can be founded only on a positive title.

We might, over and above all this, add, to what man acquires in the civil state, moral liberty, which alone makes him truly master of himself; for the mere impulse of appetite is slavery, while obedience to a law which we prescribe to ourselves is liberty. But I have already said too much on this head, and the philosophical meaning of the word liberty does not now concern us. . . .

CHAPTER V / THE RIGHT OF LIFE AND DEATH

The question is often asked how individuals, having no right to dispose of their own lives, can transfer to the Sovereign a right which they do not possess. The difficulty of answering this question seems to me to lie in its being wrongly stated. Every man has a right to risk his own life in order to preserve it. Has it ever been said that a man who throws himself out of the window to escape from a fire is guilty of suicide? Has such a crime ever been laid to the charge of him who perishes in a storm because, when he went on board, he knew of the danger?

The social treaty has for its end the preservation of the contracting parties. He who wills the end wills the means also, and the means must involve some risks, and even some losses. He who wishes to preserve his life at others' expense should also, when it is necessary, be ready to give it up for their sake. Furthermore, the citizen is no longer the judge of the dangers to which the law desires him to expose himself; and when the prince says to him: "It is expedient for the State that you should die," he ought to die, because it is only on that condition that he has been living in security up to the present, and because his life is no longer a mere bounty of nature, but a gift made conditionally by the State.

The death-penalty inflicted upon criminals may be looked on in much the same light: it is in order that we may not fall victims to an assassin that we consent to die if we ourselves turn assassins. In this treaty, so far from disposing of our own lives, we think only of securing them, and it is not to be assumed that any of the parties then expects to get hanged.

Again, every malefactor, by attacking social rights, becomes on forfeit a rebel and a traitor to his country; by violating its laws he ceases to be a member of it; he even makes war upon it. In such a case the preservation of the State is inconsistent with his own, and one or the other must perish; in putting the guilty to death, we slay not so much the citizen as an enemy. The trial and the judgment are the proofs that he has broken the social treaty, and is in consequence no longer a member of the State. Since, then, he has recognised himself to be such by living there, he must be removed by exile as a violator of the compact, or by death as a public enemy; for such an enemy is not a moral person, but merely a man; and in such a case the right of war is to kill the vanquished.

But, it will be said, the condemnation of a criminal is a particular act. I admit it: but such condemnation is not a function of the Sovereign; it is a right the Sovereign can confer without being able itself to exert it. All my ideas are consistent, but I cannot expound them all at once.

We may add that frequent punishments are always a sign of weakness or remissness on the part of the government. There is not a single ill-doer who could not be turned to some good. The State has no right to put to death, even for the sake of making an example, any one whom it can leave alive without danger.

The right of pardoning or exempting the guilty from a penalty imposed by the law and pronounced by the judge belongs only to the authority which is superior to both judge and law, *i.e.* the Sovereign; even its right in this matter is far from clear, and the cases for exercising it are extremely rare. In a well-governed State, there are few punishments, not because there are many pardons, but because criminals are rare; it is when a State is in decay that the multitude of crimes is a guarantee of impunity. Under the Roman Republic, neither the Senate nor the Consuls ever attempted to pardon; even the people never did so, though it sometimes revoked its own decision. Frequent pardons mean that crime will soon need them no longer, and no-one can help seeing whither that leads. But I feel my heart protesting and restraining my pen; let us leave these questions to the just man who has never offended, and would himself stand in no need of pardon.

CHAPTER VI / LAW

. . . Laws are, properly speaking, only the conditions of civil association. The people, being subject to the laws, ought to be their author: the conditions of the society ought to be regulated solely by those who come together to form it. But how are they to regulate them? Is it to be by common agreement, by a sudden inspiration? Has the body politic an organ to declare its will? Who can give it the foresight to formulate and announce its acts in advance? Or how is it to announce them in the hour of need? How can a blind multitude, which often does not know what it wills, because it rarely knows what is good for it, carry out for itself so great and difficult an enterprise as a system of legislation? Of itself the people wills always the good, but of itself it by no means always sees it. The general will is always in the right, but the judgment which guides it is not always enlightened. It must be got to see objects as they are, and sometimes as they ought to appear to it; it must be shown the good road it is in search of, secured from the seductive influences of individual wills, taught to see times and spaces as a series, and made to weigh the attractions of present and sensible advantages against the danger of distant and hidden evils. The individuals see the good they reject; the public wills the good it does not see. All stand equally in need of guidance. The former must be compelled to bring their wills into conformity with their reason; the latter must be taught to know what it wills. If that is done, public enlightenment leads to the union of understanding and will in the social body: the parts are made to work exactly together, and the whole is raised to its highest power. This makes a legislator necessary.

CHAPTER VII / THE LEGISLATOR

In order to discover the rules of society best suited to nations, a superior intelligence beholding all the passions of men without experiencing any of them would be needed. This intelligence would have to be wholly unrelated to our nature, while knowing it through and through; its happiness would have to be independent of us, and yet ready to occupy itself with ours; and lastly, it would have, in the march of time, to look forward to a distant glory, and, working in one century, to be able to enjoy in the next. It would take gods to give men laws.

What Caligula argued from the facts, Plato, in the dialogue called the *Politicus,* argued in defining the civil or kingly man, on the basis of right. But if great princes are rare, how much more so are great legislators? The former have only to follow the pattern which the latter have to lay down. The legislator is the engineer who invents the machine, the prince merely the mechanic who sets it up and makes it go. "At the birth of societies," says Montesquieu, "the rulers of Republics establish institutions, and afterwards the institutions mould the rulers."

He who dares to undertake the making of a people's institutions ought to feel himself capable, so to speak, of changing human nature, of transforming each individual, who is by himself a complete and solitary whole, into part of a greater whole from which he in a manner receives his life and being; of altering man's constitution for the purpose of strengthening it; and of substituting a partial and moral existence for the physical and independent existence nature has conferred on us all. He must, in a word, take away from man his own resources and give him instead new ones alien to him, and incapable of being made use of without the help of other men. The more completely these natural resources are annihilated, the greater and the more lasting are those which he acquires, and the more stable and perfect the new institutions; so that if each citizen is nothing and can do nothing without the rest, and the resources acquired by the whole are equal or superior to the aggregate of the resources of all the individuals, it may be said that legislation is at the highest possible point of perfection.

The legislator occupies in every respect an extraordinary position in the State. If he should do so by reason of his genius, he does so no less by reason of his office, which is neither magistracy, nor Sovereignty. This office, which sets up the Republic, nowhere enters into its constitution; it is an individual and superior function, which has nothing in common with human empire; for if he who holds command over men ought not to have command over the laws, he who has command over the laws ought not any more to have it over men; or else his laws would be the ministers of his passions and would often merely serve to perpetuate his injustices: his private aims would inevitably mar the sanctity of his work.

When Lycurgus gave laws to his country, he began by resigning the throne. It was the custom of most Greek towns to entrust the establishment of their laws to foreigners. The Republics of modern Italy in many cases followed this example; Geneva did the same and profited by it. Rome, when it was most prosperous, suffered a revival of all the crimes of tyranny, and was brought to the verge of destruction, because it put the legislative authority and the sovereign power into the same hands.

Nevertheless, the decemvirs* themselves never claimed the right to pass any law merely on their own authority. "Nothing we propose to you," they said to the people, "can pass into law without your consent. Romans, be yourselves the authors of the laws which are to make you happy."

He, therefore, who draws up the laws has, or should have, no right of legislation, and the people cannot, even if it wishes, deprive itself of this incommunicable right, because, according to the fundamental compact, only the general will can bind the individuals, and there can be no assurance that a particular will is in conformity with the general will, until it has been put to the free vote of the people. This I have said already; but it is worth while to repeat it.

Thus in the task of legislation we find together two things which appear to be incompatible: an enterprise too difficult for human powers, and, for its execution, an authority that is no authority. . . .

* The decimvirs: Roman magistrates constituting a body of ten men acting as a commission; especially, members of two such bodies who drew up the laws of the Twelve Tables and ruled Rome absolutely in 451 and 450 B.C.E.—ED.

EDMUND BURKE

from *Reflections on the Revolution in France* (1790)

(*Source: Reprinted from Edmund Burke,* Reflections on the Revolution in France. *London: Printed for J. Dodsley, 1790.*)

QUESTIONS FOR REFLECTION

1. How does Burke distinguish "real rights" from pretenders?
2. What real rights, in Burke's opinion, do people have? On what are these rights based?
3. What, according to Burke, is the purpose of government? Why does this lead Burke to claim that "the restraints on men, as well as their liberties, are to be reckoned among their rights"?
4. Why does reform require "infinite caution," in Burke's view? Why does Burke stress the importance of tradition?
5. What is the role of "natural feeling" and prejudice in Burke's theory?
6. How do we resolve conflicts between rights, according to Burke?

It is no wonder, therefore, that with these ideas of everything in their constitution and government at home, either in church or state, as illegitimate and usurped, or at best as a vain mockery, they look abroad with an eager and passionate enthusiasm. Whilst they are possessed by these notions, it is vain to talk to them of the practice of their ancestors, the fundamental laws of their country, the fixed form of a constitution whose merits are confirmed by the solid test of long experience and an increasing public strength and national prosperity. They despise experience as the wisdom of unlettered men; and as for the rest, they have wrought underground a mine that will blow up, at one grand explosion, all examples of antiquity, all precedents, charters, and acts of parliament. They have "the rights of men." Against these there can be no prescription, against these no agreement is binding; these admit no temperament and no compromise; anything withheld from their full demand is so much of fraud and injustice. Against these their rights of men let no government look for security in the length of its continuance, or in the justice and lenity of its administration. The objections of these speculatists, if its forms do not quadrate with their theories, are as valid against such an old and beneficent government as against the most violent tyranny or the greenest unsurpation. They are always at issue with governments, not on a question of abuse, but a question of competency and a question of title. I have nothing to say to the clumsy subtilty of their political metaphysics. Let them be their amusement in the schools.—*"Illa se jactet in aula Aeolus, et clauso ventorum carcere regnet"*.*—But let them not break prison to burst like a *Levanter,* to sweep the earth

* "Let Aeolus bluster [literally, "fling himself about"] in that hall, and reign in the closed prison of the winds" (Virgil, *Aeneid* I, 140–41). —Ed.

with their hurricane and to break up the fountains of the great deep to overwhelm us.

Far am I from denying in theory, full as far is my heart from withholding in practice (if I were of power to give or to withhold) the *real* rights of men. In denying their false claims of right, I do not mean to injure those which are real, and are such as their pretended rights would totally destroy. If civil society be made for the advantage of man, all the advantages for which it is made become his right. It is an institution of beneficence; and law itself is only beneficence acting by a rule. Men have a right to live by that rule; they have a right to do justice, as between their fellows, whether their fellows are in public function or in ordinary occupation. They have a right to the fruits of their industry and to the means of making their industry fruitful. They have a right to the acquisitions of their parents, to the nourishment and improvement of their offspring, to instruction in life, and to consolation in death. Whatever each man can separately do, without trespassing upon others, he has a right to do for himself; and he has a right to a fair portion of all which society, with all its combinations of skill and force, can do in his favor. In this partnership all men have equal rights, but not to equal things. He that has but five shillings in the partnership has as good a right to it as he that has five hundred pounds has to his larger proportion. But he has not a right to an equal dividend in the product of the joint stock; and as to the share of power, authority, and direction which each individual ought to have in the management of the state, that I must deny to be amongst the direct original rights of man in civil society; for I have in my contemplation the civil social man, and no other. It is a thing to be settled by convention.

If civil society be the offspring of convention, that convention must be its law. That convention must limit and modify all the descriptions of constitution which are formed under it. Every sort of legislative, judicial, or executory power are its creatures. They can have no being in any other state of things; *and how can any man claim under the conventions of civil rights which do not so much as suppose its existence—rights which are absolutely repugnant to it?* One of the first motives to civil society, and which becomes one of its fundamental rules, is *that no man should be judge in his own cause.* By this each person has at once divested himself of the first fundamental right of uncovenanted man, that is, to judge for himself and to assert his own cause. He abdicates all right to be his own governor. He inclusively, in a great measure, abandons the right of self-defense, the first law of nature. Men cannot enjoy the rights of an uncivil and of a civil state together. That he may obtain justice, he gives up his right of determining what it is in points the most essential to him. That he may secure some liberty, he makes a surrender in trust of the whole of it.

Government is not made in virtue of natural rights, which may and do exist in total independence of it, and exist in much greater clearness and in a much greater degree of abstract perfection; but their abstract perfection is their practical defect. By having a right to everything they want everything. Government is a contrivance of human wisdom to provide for human *wants.* Men have a right that these wants should be provided for by this wisdom. Among these wants is to be reckoned the want, out of civil society, of a sufficient restraint upon their passions. Society requires not only that the passions of individuals should be subjected, but that even in the mass and body, as well as in the individuals, the inclinations of men should frequently be thwarted, their will controlled, and their passions brought into subjection. This can only be done *by a power out of themselves,* and not, in the exercise of its function, subject to that will and to those passions which it is its office to bridle and subdue. In this sense the restraints on men, as well as their liberties, are to be reckoned among their rights. But as the liberties and the restrictions vary with times and circumstances and admit to infinite modifications, they cannot be settled upon any abstract rule; and nothing is so foolish as to discuss them upon that principle.

The moment you abate anything from the full rights of men, each to govern himself, and suffer any artificial, positive limitation upon those rights, from that moment the whole organization of government becomes a consideration of convenience. This it is which makes the constitution of a state and the due distribution of its powers a matter of the most delicate and complicated skill. It requires a deep knowledge of human nature and human necessities, and of the things which facilitate or obstruct the various ends which are to be pursued by the mechanism of civil institutions. The state is to have recruits to its strength, and remedies to its distempers. What is the use of discussing a man's abstract right to food or medicine? The question is upon the method of procuring and administering them. In that deliberation I shall always advise to call in the aid of the farmer and the physician rather than the professor of metaphysics.

The science of constructing a commonwealth, or renovating it, or reforming it, is, like every other experimental science, not to be taught *a priori*. Nor is it a short experience that can instruct us in that practical science, because the real effects of moral causes are not always immediate; but that which in the first instance is prejudicial may be excellent in its remoter operation, and its excellence may arise even from the ill effects it produces in the beginning. The reverse also happens: and very plausible schemes, with very pleasing commencements, have often shameful and lamentable conclusions. In states there are often some obscure and almost latent causes, things which appear at first view of little moment, on which a very great part of its prosperity or adversity may most essentially depend. The science of government being therefore so practical in itself and intended for such practical purposes—a matter which requires experience, and even more experience than any person can gain in his whole life, however sagacious and observing he may be—it is with infinite caution that any man ought to venture upon pulling down an edifice which has answered in any tolerable degree for ages the common purposes of society, or on building it up again without having models and patterns of approved utility before his eyes.

These metaphysic rights entering into common life, like rays of light which pierce into a dense medium, are by the laws of nature refracted from their straight line. Indeed, in the gross and complicated mass of human passions and concerns the primitive rights of men undergo such a variety of refractions and reflections that it becomes absurd to talk of them as if they continued in the simplicity of their original direction. The nature of man is intricate; the objects of society are of the greatest possible complexity; and, therefore, no simple disposition or direction of power can be suitable either to man's nature or to the quality of his affairs. When I hear the simplicity of contrivance aimed at and boasted of in any new political constitutions, I am at no loss to decide that the artificers are grossly ignorant of their trade or totally negligent of their duty. The simple governments are fundamentally defective, to say no worse of them. If you were to contemplate society in but one point of view, all these simple modes of polity are infinitely captivating. In effect each would answer its single end much more perfectly than the more complex is able to attain all its complex purposes. But it is better that the whole should be imperfectly and anomalously answered than that, while some parts are provided for with great exactness, others might be totally neglected or perhaps materially injured by the over-care of a favorite member.

The pretended rights of these theorists are all extremes; and in proportion as they are metaphysically true, they are morally and politically false. The rights of men are in a sort of *middle,* incapable of definition, but not impossible to be discerned. The rights of men in governments are their advantages; and these are often in balances between differences of good, in compromises sometimes between good and evil, and sometimes between evil and evil. Political reason is a computing principle: adding, subtracting, multiplying, and dividing, morally and not metaphysically or mathematically, true moral denominations.

By these theorists the right of the people is almost sophistically confounded with their power. The body of the community, whenever it can come to act, can meet with no effectual resistance; but till power and right are the same, the whole body of them has no right inconsistent with virtue, and the first of all virtues, prudence. Men have no right to what is not reasonable and to what is not for their benefit; for though a pleasant writer said, *liceat perire poetis,** when one of them, in cold blood, is said to have leaped into the flames of a volcanic revolution, *ardentem frigidus Aetnam insiluit,*† I consider such a frolic rather as an unjustifiable poetic license than as one of the franchises of Parnassus‡; and whether he was a poet, or divine, or politician that chose to exercise this kind of right, I think that more wise, because more charitable, thoughts would urge me rather to save the man than to preserve his brazen slippers as the monuments of his folly. . . .

. . . But the age of chivalry is gone. That of sophisters, economists, and calculators has succeeded, and the glory of Europe is extinguished forever. Never, never more shall we behold that generous loyalty to rank and sex, that proud submission, that dignified obedience, that subordination of the heart which kept alive, even in servitude itself, the spirit of an exalted freedom. The unbought grace of life, the cheap defense of nations, the nurse of manly sentiment and heroic enterprise, is gone! It is gone, that sensibility of principle, that chastity of honor which felt a stain like a wound, which inspired courage whilst it mitigated ferocity, which ennobled whatever it touched, and under which vice itself lost half its evil by losing all its grossness.

This mixed system of opinion and sentiment had its origin in the ancient chivalry; and the principle, though varied in its appearance by the varying state of human affairs, subsisted and influenced through a long succession of generations even to the time we live in. If it should ever be totally extinguished, the loss I fear will be great. It is this which has given its character to modern Europe. It is this which has distinguished it under all its forms of government, and distinguished it to its advantage, from the states of Asia and possibly from those states which flourished in the most brilliant periods of the antique world. It was this which, without confounding ranks, had produced a noble equality and handed it down through all the gradations of social life. It was this opinion which mitigated kings into companions and raised private men to be fellows with kings. Without force or opposition, it subdued the fierceness of pride and power, it obliged sovereigns to submit to the soft collar of social esteem, compelled stern authority to submit to elegance, and gave a domination, vanquisher of laws, to be subdued by manners.

But now all is to be changed. All the pleasing illusions which made power gentle and obedience liberal, which harmonized the different shades of life, and which, by a bland assimilation, incorporated into politics the sentiments which beautify and soften private society, are to be dissolved by this new conquering empire of light and reason. All the decent drapery of life is to be rudely torn off. All the superadded ideas, furnished from the wardrobe of a moral imagination, which the heart owns and the understanding ratifies as necessary to cover the defects of our naked, shivering nature, and to raise it to dignity in our own estimation, are to be exploded as a ridiculous, absurd, and antiquated fashion. . . .

On the scheme of this barbarous philosophy, which is the offspring of cold hearts and muddy understandings, and which is as void of solid wisdom as it is destitute of all taste and elegance, laws are to be supported only by their own terrors and by the concern which each individual may find in them from his own private speculations or can spare to them from his own private interests. In the groves of *their* academy, at the end of every vista, you see nothing but the gallows. Nothing is left which engages the affections on the part of the commonwealth. On the principles of this mechanic philosophy, our institutions can never be embodied, if I may use the expression, in persons, so as to create in us love, veneration, admiration, or attachment. But that sort of reason which banishes the affections is incapable of filling their place. These public affections, combined with manners, are required sometimes as supplements, sometimes as correctives, always as aids to law. The precept given by a wise man, as well as a great critic, for the construction of poems is equally true

* "Poets are permitted to perish." —ED.

† "In cold blood he jumped into burning Etna" (Horace, *Ars Poetica* 465–66). "He" refers to Empedocles. —ED.

‡ Parnassus: a mountain that in Greek mythology was sacred to Apollo and the Muses; later used as a symbol of poetry and literature in general. —ED.

as to states:—*Non satis est pulchra esse poemata, dulcia sunto.** There ought to be a system of manners in every nation which a well-informed mind would be disposed to relish. To make us love our country, our country ought to be lovely.

But power, of some kind or other, will survive the shock in which manners and opinions perish; and it will find other and worse means for its support. The usurpation which, in order to subvert ancient institutions, has destroyed ancient principles will hold power by arts similar to those by which it has acquired it. When the old feudal and chivalrous spirit of *fealty,* which, by freeing kings from fear, freed both kings and subjects from the precautions of tyranny, shall be extinct in the minds of men, plots and assassinations will be anticipated by preventive murder and preventive confiscation, and that long roll of grim and bloody maxims which form the political code of all power not standing on its own honor and the honor of those who are to obey it. Kings will be tyrants from policy when subjects are rebels from principle.

When ancient opinions and rules of life are taken away, the loss cannot possibly be estimated. From that moment we have no compass to govern us; nor can we know distinctly to what port we steer. . . .

Why do I feel so differently from the Reverend Dr. Price† and those of his lay flock who will choose to adopt the sentiments of his discourse?—For this plain reason: because it is *natural* I should; because we are so made as to be affected at such spectacles with melancholy sentiments upon the unstable condition of mortal prosperity and the tremendous uncertainty of human greatness; because in those natural feelings we learn great lessons; because in events like these our passions instruct our reason; because when kings are hurled from their thrones by the Supreme Director of this great drama and become the objects of insult to the base and of pity to the good, we behold such disasters in the moral as we should behold a miracle in the physical order of things. We are alarmed into reflection; our minds (as it has long since been observed) are purified by terror and pity, our weak, unthinking pride is humbled under the dispensations of a mysterious wisdom. . . .

. . . Thanks to our sullen resistance to innovation, thank to the cold sluggishness of our national character, we still bear the stamp of our forefathers. We have not (as I conceive) lost the generosity and dignity of thinking of the fourteenth century, nor as yet have we subtilized ourselves into savages. We are not the converts of Rousseau; we are not the disciples of Voltaire; Helvetius has made no progress amongst us. Atheists are not our preachers; madmen are not our lawgivers. We know that we have made no discoveries, and we think that no discoveries are to be made in morality, nor many in the great principles of government, nor in the ideas of liberty, which were understood long before we were born, altogether as well as they will be after the grace has heaped its mold upon our presumption and the silent tomb shall have imposed its law on our pert loquacity. In England we have not yet been completely embowelled of our natural entrails; we still feel within us, and we cherish and cultivate, those inbred sentiments which are the faithful guardians, the active monitors of our duty, the true supporters of all liberal and manly morals. We have not been drawn and trussed, in order that we may be filled, like stuffed birds in a museum, with chaff and rags and paltry blurred shreds of paper about the rights of men. We preserve the whole of our feelings still native and entire, unsophisticated by pedantry and infidelity. We have real hearts of flesh and blood beating in our bosoms. We fear God; we look up with awe to kings, with affection to parliaments, with duty to magistrates, with reverence to priests, and with respect to nobility. Why? Because when such ideas are brought before our minds, it is *natural* to be so affected; because all other feelings are false and spurious and tend to corrupt our minds, to vitiate our primary morals, to render us unfit for rational liberty, and, by teaching us a servile, licentious, and abandoned insolence, to be our low

* "It is not enough for poems to be beautiful; they must be delightful" (Horace, *Ars Poetica* 99). —ED.

† Richard Price (1723–1791) wrote *Observations on the Nature of Civil Liberty* in 1777 to defend the American Revolution and *A Discourse on the Love of Our Country*, a sermon to the Revolution Society, in 1789 to support the French Revolution. —ED.

sport for a few holidays, to make us perfectly fit for, and justly deserving of, slavery through the whole course of our lives.

You see, Sir, that in this enlightened age I am bold enough to confess that we are generally men of untaught feelings, that, instead of casting away all our old prejudices, we cherish them to a very considerable degree, and, to take more shame to ourselves, we cherish them because they are prejudices; and the longer they have lasted and the more generally they have prevailed, the more we cherish them. We are afraid to put men to live and trade each on his own private stock of reason, because we suspect that this stock in each man is small, and that the individuals would do better to avail themselves of the general bank and capital of nations and of ages. Many of our men of speculation, instead of exploding general prejudices, employ their sagacity to discover the latent wisdom which prevails in them. If they find what they seek, and they seldom fail, they think it more wise to continue the prejudice, with the reason involved, than to cast away the coat of prejudice and to leave nothing but the naked reason; because prejudice, with its reason, has a motive to give action to that reason, and an affection which will give it permanence. Prejudice is of ready application in the emergency; it previously engages the mind in a steady course of wisdom and virtue and does not leave the man hesitating in the moment of decision skeptical, puzzled, and unresolved. Prejudice renders a man's virtue his habit, and not a series of unconnected acts. Through just prejudice, his duty becomes a part of his nature. . . .

. . . Rage and frenzy will pull down more in half an hour than prudence, deliberation, and foresight can build up in a hundred years. The errors and defects of old establishments are visible and palpable. It calls for little ability to point them out; and where absolute power is given, it requires but a word wholly to abolish the vice and the establishment together. The same lazy but restless disposition which loves sloth and hates quiet directs the politicians when they come to work for supplying the place of what they have destroyed. To make everything the reverse of what they have seen is quite as easy as to destroy. No difficulties occur in what has never been tried. Criticism is almost baffled in discovering the defects of what has not existed; and eager enthusiasm and cheating hope have all the wide field of imagination in which they may expatiate with little or no opposition.

At once to preserve and to reform is quite another thing. When the useful parts of an old establishment are kept, and what is superadded is to be fitted to what is retained, a vigorous mind, steady, persevering attention, various powers of comparison and combination, and the resources of an understanding fruitful in expedients are to be exercised; they are to be exercised in a continued conflict with the combined force of opposite vices, with the obstinacy that rejects all improvement and the levity that is fatigued and disgusted with everything of which it is in possession. But you may object—"A process of this kind is slow. It is not fit for an assembly which glories in performing in a few months the work of ages. Such a mode of reforming, possibly, might take up many years." Without question it might; and it ought. It is one of the excellences of a method in which time is amongst the assistants, that its operation is slow and in some cases almost imperceptible. If circumspection and caution are a part of wisdom when we work only upon inanimate matter, surely they become a part of duty, too, when the subject of our demolition and construction is not brick and timber but sentient beings, by the sudden alteration of whose state, condition, and habits multitudes may be rendered miserable. But it seems as if it were the prevalent opinion in Paris that an unfeeling heart and an undoubting confidence are the sole qualifications for a perfect legislator. Far different are my ideas of that high office. The true lawgiver ought to have a heart full of sensibility. He ought to love and respect his kind, and to fear himself. It may be allowed to his temperament to catch his ultimate object with an intuitive glance, but his movements toward it ought to be deliberate. Political arrangement, as it is a work for social ends, is to be only wrought by social means. There mind must conspire with mind. Time is required to produce that union of minds which alone can produce all the good we aim at. Our patience will achieve more than our force. If I might venture to appeal to what is so much out of fashion in Paris, I mean to experience, I should tell you that in my course I have known and, according to my measure, have cooperated with great men; and I have never yet seen any plan which has not been mended by the observation of those who were much inferior in understanding to the person who took the lead in the business. By a slow but well-sustained progress the effect of each step is watched; the good or ill success of the first gives light to us in the second; and so, from light to light, we are conducted with safety through the whole series. We see that the parts of the system do not clash. The evils latent in the most promising contrivances are provided for as they arise. One advantage is as little as possible sacrificed to another. We compensate, we reconcile, we balance. We are enabled to unite into a consistent whole the various anomalies and contending principles that are found in the minds and affairs of men. From hence arises, not an excellence in simplicity, but one far superior, an excellence in composition. Where the great interests of mankind are concerned through a long succession of generations, that succession ought to be admitted into some share in the councils which are so deeply to affect them. If justice requires this, the work itself requires the aid of more minds than one age can furnish. It is from this view of things that the best legislators have been often satisfied with the establishment of some sure, solid, and ruling principle in government—a power like that which some of the philosophers have called a plastic nature; and having fixed the principle, they have left it afterwards to its own operation. . . .

Abortion

Abortion raises notoriously difficult ethical problems. At root, these problems seem to revolve around rights. Opponents of abortion speak of the right to life of the fetus; pro-choice advocates speak of a woman's right to choose. Obviously, these two putative rights come into conflict over abortion. One cannot respect both the right to life of the fetus and the woman's right to choose if the woman chooses to abort. Consequently, the abortion issue seems to call for some neutral or well-grounded way of deciding when some rights take precedence over others.

Of course, not everyone grants the rights in question. Some argue that the fetus is not a person and, indeed, is sufficiently unlike a person that it has no rights. Others argue that the woman may have obligations toward a fetus inside her even if it is there through no choice of her own. They deny that, at least in some cases, a woman has a right to choose abortion. The abortion problem thus raises two other very difficult issues: (1) What kinds of beings have rights? Fetuses, severely ill or injured people, and animals all share many basic human characteristics but lack others common to typical, healthy adults. Which characteristics, if any, are essential to having rights? In general, how do we decide the boundaries of our moral categories? (2) What kinds of obligations do we have toward others? Under what circumstances do other people have rights against us—rights to have us do certain things to help them and to refrain from doing things to harm them? To what extent do such obligations depend on our willingness to assume them? These questions are crucial to the abortion issue and, moreover, reach far beyond it.

Abortion had been illegal in most areas of the United States until 1973, when the Supreme Court decided, in *Roe* v. *Wade,* that the Constitution guarantees a right to privacy implying that the state may not restrict abortions in the first trimester (the first three months of pregnancy). The Court backed away from any decision about the ultimate moral status of the fetus; it treated fetuses as "potential people," having value if not rights. (Opponents of the decision contend that this failure to decide the status of the fetus is itself a decision, since the Court does not take the rights of fetuses into account.) Instead, the Court based its decision on the medical fact that first-trimester abortions are less risky than carrying a child to term, whereas later abortions are riskier. The government's interest in preserving the health and safety of the mother thus gives the government reason to restrict abortions, but only after the first trimester. The value of the fetus also gives the government reason to restrict abortions, but only after the fetus becomes "viable"—that is, able to survive outside the mother's body. Until then, the mother's right to privacy takes precedence. The Court's decision in *Roe* v. *Wade* raises profound constitutional questions and analogous moral questions: Is there a right to privacy? If so, what is it? How far does it extend? How does it relate to other rights? What obligations does it place on others?

Judith Jarvis Thomson contends that the unacceptability of abortion does not follow automatically from the right to life of the fetus. She grants, for the sake of argument, that the fetus has such a right. She then maintains that under many circumstances, a woman nevertheless has no obligation to carry a child to term. She distinguishes some important conceptions of our obligations to others and argues that only on a very (and, she thinks, unacceptably) strong conception does the woman generally have an obligation not to abort.

Jane English argues that both conservative and liberal positions on abortion are mistaken. She contends moreover that questions of personhood and rights are not as important to the moral issues surrounding abortion as many believe. Even if fetuses are persons with rights to life, she maintains, abortion is sometimes justifiable. And even if fetuses are not persons and have no rights, abortion is sometimes wrong. She concludes that we cannot resolve the abortion issue by reflecting on rights alone; we must reflect generally on our obligations to others.

Don Marquis contends that abortion is immoral for the same reason that murdering an adult human is immoral—it deprives something that would have had a human life of its future. Marquis does not argue, as many anti-abortionists have, that the fetus has a right to life or that abortion is murder; he argues instead that it is *like* murder in that it deprives something that would have gone on to experience a human life of that very opportunity.

JUSTICE HARRY BLACKMUN

majority opinion in *Roe* v. *Wade* (1973)

(Source: Roe v. Wade *410 U.S. 113 [1973]. Most legal references have been omitted.)*

QUESTIONS FOR REFLECTION

1. What, according to the majority, are the chief interests of the state in making a decision about abortion?
2. The majority bases its decision on the right of privacy. What is this right? How does the majority argue for it? What are its limitations?
3. The majority contends that the "compelling point" for balancing the rights and interests involved is viability. What is viability? Why does the majority settle on it as the compelling point? Do you find the argument convincing?

Mr. Justice Blackmun delivered the opinion of the Court. . . .

I

The Texas statutes that concern us here are Arts. 1191–1194 and 1196 of the State's Penal Code. These make it a crime to "procure an abortion," as therein defined, or to attempt one, except with respect to "an abortion procured or attempted by medical advice for the purpose of saving the life of the mother." Similar statutes are in existence in a majority of the States. . . .

II

Jane Roe, a single woman who was residing in Dallas County, Texas, instituted this federal action in March 1970 against the District Attorney of the county. She sought a declaratory judgment that the Texas criminal abortion statutes were unconstitutional on their face, and an injunction restraining the defendant from enforcing the statutes.

Roe alleged that she was unmarried and pregnant; that she wished to terminate her pregnancy by an abortion "performed by a competent, licensed physician, under safe, clinical conditions"; that she was unable to get a "legal" abortion in Texas because her life did not appear to be threatened by the continuation of her pregnancy; and that she could not afford to travel to another jurisdiction in order to secure a legal abortion under safe conditions. She claimed that the Texas statutes were unconstitutionally vague and that they abridged her right of personal privacy, protected by the First, Fourth, Fifth, Ninth, and Fourteenth Amendments. By an amendment to her complaint Roe purported to sue "on behalf of herself and all other women" similarly situated. . . .

VII

Three reasons have been advanced to explain historically the enactment of criminal abortion laws in the 19th century and to justify their continued existence.

It has been argued occasionally that these laws

were the product of a Victorian social concern to discourage illicit sexual conduct. Texas, however, does not advance this justification in the present case, and it appears that no court or commentator has taken the argument seriously. The appellants and *amici* contend, moreover, that this is not a proper state purpose at all and suggest that, if it were, the Texas statutes are overbroad in protecting it since the law fails to distinguish between married and unwed mothers.

A second reason is concerned with abortion as a medical procedure. When most criminal abortion laws were first enacted, the procedure was a hazardous one for the woman. This was particularly true prior to the development of antisepsis. Antiseptic techniques, of course, were based on discoveries by Lister, Pasteur, and others first announced in 1867, but were not generally accepted and employed until about the turn of the century. Abortion mortality was high. Even after 1900, and perhaps until as late as the development of antibiotics in the 1940's, standard modern techniques such as dilation and curettage were not nearly so safe as they are today. Thus, it has been argued that a State's real concern in enacting a criminal abortion law was to protect the pregnant woman, that is, to restrain her from submitting to a procedure that placed her life in serious jeopardy.

Modern medical techniques have altered this situation. Appellants and various *amici* refer to medical data indicating that abortion in early pregnancy, that is, prior to the end of the first trimester, although not without its risk, is now relatively safe. Mortality rates for women undergoing early abortions, where the procedure is legal, appear to be as low as or lower than the rates for normal childbirth. Consequently, any interest of the State in protecting the woman from an inherently hazardous procedure, except when it would be equally dangerous for her to forgo it, has largely disappeared. Of course, important state interests in the areas of health and medical standards do remain. The State has a legitimate interest in seeing to it that abortion, like any other medical procedure, is performed under circumstances that insure maximum safety for the patient. This interest obviously extends at least to the performing physician and his staff, to the facilities involved, to the availability of after-care, and to adequate provision for any complication or emergency that might arise. The prevalence of high mortality rates at illegal "abortion mills" strengthens, rather than weakens, the State's interest in regulating the conditions under which abortions are performed. Moreover, the risk to the woman increases as her pregnancy continues. Thus, the State retains a definite interest in protecting the woman's own health and safety when an abortion is proposed at a late stage of pregnancy.

The third reason is the State's interest—some phrase it in terms of duty—in protecting prenatal life. Some of the argument for this justification rests on the theory that a new human life is present from the moment of conception. The State's interest and general obligation to protect life then extends, it is argued, to prenatal life. Only when the life of the pregnant mother herself is at stake, balanced against the life she carries within her, should the interest of the embryo or fetus not prevail. Logically, of course, a legitimate state interest in this area need not stand or fall on acceptance of the belief that life begins at conception or at some other point prior to live birth. In assessing the State's interest, recognition may be given to the less rigid claim that as long as at least *potential* life is involved, the State may assert interests beyond the protection of the pregnant woman alone.

Parties challenging state abortion laws have sharply disputed in some courts the contention that a purpose of these laws, when enacted, was to protect prenatal life. Pointing to the absence of legislative history to support the contention, they claim that most state laws were designed solely to protect the woman. Because medical advances have lessened this concern, at least with respect to abortion in early pregnancy, they argue that with respect to such abortions the laws can no longer be justified by any state interest. There is some scholarly support for this view of original purpose. The few state courts called upon to interpret their laws in the late 19th and early 20th centuries did focus on the State's interest in protecting the woman's health rather than in preserving the embryo and fetus. Proponents of this view point out that in many States, including Texas, by statute or judicial interpretation, the pregnant woman herself could not be prosecuted for self-abortion or for cooperating in an abortion performed upon her by another. They claim that adoption of the "quickening" distinction through received common law and state statutes tacitly recognizes the greater health hazards inherent in late abortion and impliedly repudiates the theory that life begins at conception.

It is with these interests, and the weight to be attached to them, that this case is concerned.

VIII

The Constitution does not explicitly mention any right of privacy. In a line of decisions, however, going back perhaps as far as *Union Pacific R. Co.* v. *Botsford* (1891), the Court has recognized that a right of personal privacy, or a guarantee of certain areas or zones of privacy, does exist under the Constitution. . . . The decisions make it clear that only personal rights that can be deemed "fundamental" or "implicit in the concept of ordered liberty" are included in this guarantee of personal privacy. They also make it clear that the right has some extension to activities relating to marriage, procreation, contraception, family relationships, and child rearing and education.

This right of privacy, whether it be founded in the Fourteenth Amendment's concept of personal liberty and restrictions upon state action, as we feel it is, or, as the District Court determined, in the Ninth Amendment's reservation of rights to the people, is broad enough to encompass a woman's decision whether or not to terminate her pregnancy. The detriment that the State would impose upon the pregnant woman by denying this choice altogether is apparent. Specific and direct harm medically diagnosable even in early pregnancy may be involved. Maternity, or additional offspring, may force upon the woman a distressful life and future. Psychological harm may be imminent. Mental and physical health may be taxed by child care. There is also the distress, for all concerned, associated with the unwanted child, and there is the problem of bringing a child into a family already unable, psychologically and otherwise, to care for it. In other cases, as in this one, the additional difficulties and continuing stigma of unwed motherhood may be involved. All these are factors the woman and her responsible physician necessarily will consider in consultation.

On the basis of elements such as these, appellant and some *amici* argue that the woman's right is absolute and that she is entitled to terminate her pregnancy at whatever time, in whatever way, and for whatever reason she alone chooses. With this we do not agree. Appellant's arguments that Texas either has no valid interest at all in regulating the abortion decision, or no interest strong enough to support any limitation upon the woman's sole determination, are unpersuasive. The Court's decisions recognizing a right of privacy also acknowledge that some state regulation in areas protected by that right is appropriate. As noted above, a State may properly assert important interests in safeguarding health, in maintaining medical standards, and in protecting potential life. At some point in pregnancy, these respective interests become sufficiently compelling to sustain regulation of the factors that govern the abortion decision. The privacy right involved, therefore, cannot be said to be absolute. In fact, it is not clear to us that the claim asserted by some *amici* that one has an unlimited right to do with one's body as one pleases bears a close relationship to the right of privacy previously articulated in the Court's decisions. The Court has refused to recognize an unlimited right of this kind in the past.

We, therefore, conclude that the right of personal privacy includes the abortion decision, but that this right is not unqualified and must be considered against important state interests in regulation.

We note that those federal and state courts that have recently considered abortion law challenges have reached the same conclusion. A majority, in addition to the District Court in the present case, have held state laws unconstitutional, at least in part, because of vagueness or because of overbreadth and abridgment of rights.

Others have sustained state statutes.

Although the results are divided, most of these courts have agreed that the right of privacy, however based, is broad enough to cover the abortion decision; that the right, nonetheless, is not absolute and is subject to some limitations; and that at some point the state interests as to protection of health, medical standards, and prenatal life, become dominant. We agree with this approach.

Where certain "fundamental rights" are involved, the Court has held that regulation limiting these rights may be justified only by a "compelling state interest" and that legislative enactments must be narrowly drawn to express only the legitimate state interests at stake.

In . . . recent abortion cases . . . courts have recognized these principles. Those striking down state laws have generally scrutinized the State's interests in protecting health and potential life, and have concluded that neither interest justified broad limitations on the reasons for which a physician and his pregnant patient might decide that she should have an abortion in the early stages of pregnancy. Courts sustaining the state laws have held that the State's determinations to protect health or prenatal life are dominant and constitutionally justifiable.

IX

The District Court held that the appellee failed to meet his burden of demonstrating that the Texas statute's infringement upon Roe's rights was necessary to support a compelling state interest, and that, although the appellee presented "several compelling justifications for state presence in the area of abortions," the statutes outstripped these justifications and swept "far beyond any areas of compelling state interest." Appellant and appellee both contest that holding. Appellant, as has been indicated, claims an absolute right that bars any state imposition of criminal penalties in the area. Appellee argues that the State's determination to recognize and protect prenatal life from and after conception constitutes a compelling state interest. As noted above, we do not agree fully with either formulation.

A. The appellee and certain *amici* argue that the fetus is a "person" within the language and meaning of the Fourteenth Amendment. In support of this, they outline at length and in detail the well-known facts of fetal development. If this suggestion of personhood is established, the appellant's case, of course, collapses, for the fetus' right to life would then be guaranteed specifically by the Amendment. The appellant conceded as much on reargument. On the other hand, the appellee conceded on reargument that no case could be cited that holds that a fetus is a person within the meaning of the Fourteenth Amendment.

The Constitution does not define "person" in so many words. Section 1 of the Fourteenth Amendment contains three references to "person." The first, in defining "citizens," speaks of "persons born or naturalized in the United States." The word also appears both in the Due Process Clause and in the Equal Protection Clause. "Person" is used in other places in the Constitution. . . . But in nearly all these instances, the use of the word is such that it has application only postnatally. None indicates, with any assurance, that it has any possible prenatal application.

All this, together with our observation that throughout the major portion of the 19th century prevailing legal abortion practices were far freer than they are today, persuades us that the word "person," as used in the Fourteenth Amendment, does not include the unborn. This is in accord with the results reached in those few cases where the issue has been squarely presented. Indeed, our decision in *United States* v. *Vuitch* (1971), inferentially is to the same effect, for we there would not have indulged in statutory interpretation favorable to abortion in specified circumstances if the necessary consequence was the termination of life entitled to Fourteenth Amendment protection.

This conclusion, however, does not of itself fully answer the contentions raised by Texas, and we pass on to other considerations.

B. The pregnant woman cannot be isolated in

her privacy. She carries an embryo and, later, a fetus, if one accepts the medical definitions of the developing young in the human uterus. . . . The situation therefore is inherently different from marital intimacy, or bedroom possession of obscene material, or marriage, or procreation, or education, with which *Eisenstadt* and *Griswold, Stanley, Loving, Skinner,* and *Pierce* and *Meyer* were respectively concerned. As we have intimated above, it is reasonable and appropriate for a State to decide that at some point in time another interest, that of health of the mother or that of potential human life, becomes significantly involved. The woman's privacy is no longer sole and any right of privacy she possesses must be measured accordingly.

Texas urges that, apart from the Fourteenth Amendment, life begins at conception and is present throughout pregnancy, and that, therefore, the State has a compelling interest in protecting that life from and after conception. We need not resolve the difficult question of when life begins. When those trained in the respective disciplines of medicine, philosophy, and theology are unable to arrive at any consensus, the judiciary, at this point in the development of man's knowledge, is not in a position to speculate as to the answer.

It should be sufficient to note briefly the wide divergence of thinking on this most sensitive and difficult question. There has always been strong support for the view that life does not begin until live birth. This was the belief of the Stoics. It appears to be the predominant, though not the unanimous, attitude of the Jewish faith. It may be taken to represent also the position of a large segment of the Protestant community, insofar as that can be ascertained; organized groups that have taken a formal position on the abortion issue have generally regarded abortion as a matter for the conscience of the individual and her family. As we have noted, the common law found greater significance in quickening. Physicians and their scientific colleagues have regarded that event with less interest and have tended to focus either upon conception, upon live birth, or upon the interim point at which the fetus becomes "viable," that is, potentially able to live outside the mother's womb, albeit with artificial aid. Viability is usually placed at about seven months (28 weeks) but may occur earlier, even at 24 weeks. The Aristotelian theory of "mediate animation," that held sway throughout the Middle Ages and the Renaissance in Europe, continued to be official Roman Catholic dogma until the 19th century, despite opposition to this "ensoulment" theory from those in the Church who would recognize the existence of life from the moment of conception. The latter is now, of course, the official belief of the Catholic Church. As one brief *amicus* discloses, this is a view strongly held by many non-Catholics as well, and by many physicians. Substantial problems for precise definition of this view are posed, however, by new embryological data that purport to indicate that conception is a "process" over time, rather than an event, and by new medical techniques such as menstrual extraction, the "morning-after" pill, implantation of embryos, artificial insemination, and even artificial wombs.

In areas other than criminal abortion, the law has been reluctant to endorse any theory that life, as we recognize it, begins before live birth or to accord legal rights to the unborn except in narrowly defined situations and except when the rights are contingent upon live birth. For example, the traditional rule of tort law denied recovery for prenatal injuries even though the child was born alive. That rule has been changed in almost every jurisdiction. In most States, recovery is said to be permitted only if the fetus was viable, or at least quick, when the injuries were sustained, though few courts have squarely so held. In a recent development, generally opposed by the commentators, some States permit the parents of a stillborn child to maintain an action for wrongful death because of prenatal injuries. Such an action, however, would appear to be one to vindicate the parents' interest and is thus consistent with the view that the fetus, at most, represents only the potentiality of life. Similarly, unborn children have been recognized as acquiring rights or interests by way of inheritance or other devolution of property, and have been represented by guardians *ad litem*. Perfection of the interests involved, again, has generally been contingent upon live birth. In short, the unborn have never been recognized in the law as persons in the whole sense.

X

In view of all this, we do not agree that, by adopting one theory of life, Texas may override the rights of the pregnant woman that are at stake. We repeat, however, that the State does have an important and legitimate interest in preserving and protecting the health of the pregnant woman, whether she be a resident of the State or a nonresident who seeks medical consultation and treatment there, and that it has still *another* important and legitimate interest in protecting the potentiality of human life. These interests are separate and distinct. Each grows in substantiality as the woman approaches term and, at a point during pregnancy, each becomes "compelling."

With respect to the State's important and legitimate interest in the health of the mother, the "compelling" point, in the light of present medical knowledge, is at approximately the end of the first trimester. This is so because of the now-established medical fact . . . that until the end of the first trimester mortality in abortion may be less than mortality in normal childbirth. It follows that, from and after this point, a State may regulate the abortion procedure to the extent that the regulation reasonably relates to the preservation and protection of maternal health. Examples of permissible state regulation in this area are requirements as to the qualifications of the person who is to perform the abortion; as to the licensure of that person; as to the facility in which the procedure is to be performed, that is, whether it must be a hospital or may be a clinic or some other place of less-than-hospital status; as to the licensing of the facility; and the like.

This means, on the other hand, that, for the period of pregnancy prior to this "compelling" point, the attending physician, in consultation with his patient, is free to determine, without regulation by the State, that, in his medical judgment, the patient's pregnancy should be terminated. If that decision is reached, the judgment may be effectuated by an abortion free of interference by the State.

With respect to the State's important and legitimate interest in potential life, the "compelling" point is at viability. This is so because the fetus then presumably has the capability of meaningful life outside the mother's womb. State regulation protective of fetal life after viability thus has both logical and biological justifications. If the State is interested in protecting fetal life after viability, it may go so far as to proscribe abortion during that period, except when it is necessary to preserve the life or health of the mother.

Measured against these standards, Art. 1196 of the Texas Penal Code, in restricting legal abortions to those "procured or attempted by medical advice for the purpose of saving the life of the mother," sweeps too broadly. The statute makes no distinction between abortions performed early in pregnancy and those performed later, and it limits to a single reason, "saving" the mother's life, the legal justification for the procedure. The statute, therefore, cannot survive the constitutional attack made upon it here. . . .

XI

To summarize and to repeat:

1. A state criminal abortion statute of the current Texas type, that excepts from criminality only a *life-saving* procedure on behalf of the mother, without regard to pregnancy stage and without recognition of the other interests involved, is violative of the Due Process Clause of the Fourteenth Amendment.

   (a) For the stage prior to approximately the end of the first trimester, the abortion decision and its effectuation must be left to the medical judgment of the pregnant woman's attending physician.

(b) For the stage subsequent to approximately the end of the first trimester, the State, in promoting its interest in the health of the mother, may, if it chooses, regulate the abortion procedure in ways that are reasonably related to maternal health.

(c) wFor the stage subsequent to viability, the State in promoting its interest in the potentiality of human life may, if it chooses, regulate, and even proscribe, abortion except where it is necessary, in appropriate medical judgment, for the preservation of the life or health of the mother.

2. The State may define the term "physician," as it has been employed in the preceding paragraphs of this Part XI of this opinion, to mean only a physician currently licensed by the State, and may proscribe any abortion by a person who is not a physician as so defined. . . .

JUDITH JARVIS THOMSON

A Defense of Abortion

Judith Jarvis Thomson is Professor of Philosophy at the Massachusetts Institute of Technology. (Source: From Philosophy and Public Affairs, *Vol. I, No. 1 [Fall 1971], pp. 47–66.*

QUESTIONS FOR REFLECTION

1. What conclusions does Thomson draw from the violinist example? Do you agree with her interpretation of the example?
2. How does Thomson argue against what she calls "the extreme view"?
3. What is a right to life, for Thomson? Why does she reject other accounts of this right?
4. What is Good Samaritanism? Minimally Decent Samaritanism? Which, according to Thomson, is required of us? What does this imply for the morality of abortion?
5. Some philosophers have found Thomson's view on the violinist example inconsistent with her view that you do not have the right to torture someone, even to save your own life. Are these consistent? Explain.

Most opposition to abortion relies on the premise that the fetus is a human being, a person, from the moment of conception. The premise is argued for, but, as I think, not well. Take, for example, the most common argument. We are asked to notice that the development of a human being from conception through birth into childhood is continuous; then it is said that to draw a line, to choose a point in this development and say "before this point the thing is not a person, after this point it is a person" is to make an arbitrary choice, a choice for which in the nature of things no good reason can be given. It is concluded that the fetus is, or anyway that we had better say it is, a person from the moment of conception. But this conclusion does not follow. Similar things might be said about the development of an acorn into an oak tree, and it does not follow that acorns are oak trees, or that we had better say they are. Arguments of this form are sometimes called "slippery slope arguments"—the phrase is perhaps self-explanatory—and it is dismaying that opponents of abortion rely on them so heavily and uncritically.

I am inclined to agree, however, that the prospects for "drawing a line" in the development of the fetus look dim. I am inclined to think also that we shall probably have to agree that the fetus has already become a human person well before birth. Indeed, it comes as a surprise when one first learns how early in its life it begins to acquire human characteristics. By the tenth week, for example, it already has a face, arms and legs, fingers and toes; it has internal organs, and brain activity is detectable. On the other hand, I think that the premise is false, that the fetus is not a person from the moment of conception. A newly fertilized ovum, a newly implanted clump of cells, is no more a person than an acorn is an oak tree. But I shall not discuss any of this. For it seems to me to be of great interest to ask what happens if, for the sake of argument, we allow the premise. How, precisely, are we supposed to get from there to the conclusion that abortion is morally impermissible? Opponents of abortion commonly spend most of their time establishing that the fetus is a person, and hardly any time explaining the step from there to the impermissibility of abortion. Perhaps they think the step too simple and obvious to require much comment. Or perhaps instead they are simply being economical in argument. Many of those who defend abortion rely on the premise that the fetus is not a person, but only a bit of tissue that will become a person at birth; and why pay out more arguments than you have to? Whatever the explanation, I suggest that the step they take is neither easy nor obvious, that it calls for closer examination than it is commonly given, and that when we do give it this closer examination we shall feel inclined to reject it.

I propose, then, that we grant that the fetus is a person from the moment of conception. How does the argument go from here? Something like this, I take it. Every person has a right to life. So the fetus has a right to life. No doubt the mother has a right to decide what shall happen in and to her body; everyone would grant that. But surely a person's right to life is stronger and more stringent than the mother's right to decide what happens in and to her body, and so outweighs it. So the fetus may not be killed; an abortion may not be performed.

It sounds plausible. But now let me ask you to imagine this. You wake up in the morning and find yourself back to back in bed with an unconscious violinist. A famous unconscious violinist. He has been found to have a fatal kidney ailment, and the Society of Music Lovers has canvassed all the available medical records and found that you alone have the right blood type to help. They have therefore kidnapped you, and last night the violinist's circulatory system was plugged into yours, so that your kidneys can be used to extract poisons from his blood as well as your own. The director of the hospital now tells you, "Look, we're sorry the Society of Music Lovers did this to you—we would never have permitted it if we had known. But still, they did it, and the violinist now is plugged into you. To unplug you would be to kill him. But never mind, it's only for nine months. By then he will have recovered from his ailment, and can safely be unplugged from you." Is it morally incumbent on you to accede to this situation? No doubt it would be very nice of you if you did, a great kindness. But do you *have* to accede to it? What if it were not nine months, but nine years? Or longer still? What if the director of the hospital says, "Tough luck, I agree, but you've now got to stay in bed, with the violinist plugged into you, for the rest of your life. Because remember this. All persons have a right to life, and violinists are persons. Granted you have a right to decide what happens in and to your body, but a person's right to life outweighs your right to decide what happens in and to your body. So you cannot ever be unplugged from him." I imagine you would regard this as outrageous, which suggests that something really is wrong with that plausible-sounding argument I mentioned a moment ago.

In this case, of course, you were kidnapped; you didn't volunteer for the operation that plugged the violinist into your kidneys. Can those who oppose abortion on the ground I mentioned make an exception for a pregnancy due to rape? Certainly. They can say that persons have a right to life only if they didn't come into existence because of rape; or they can say that all persons have a right to life, but that some have less of a right to life than others, in particular, that those who came into existence because of rape have less. But these statements have a rather unpleasant sound. Surely the question of whether you have a right to life at all, or how much of it you have, shouldn't turn on the question of whether or not you are the product of a rape. And in fact the people who oppose abortion on the ground I mentioned do not make this distinction, and hence do not make an exception in case of rape.

Nor do they make an exception for a case in which the mother has to spend the nine months of her pregnancy in bed. They would agree that would be a great pity, and hard on the mother; but all the same, all persons have a right to life, the fetus is a person, and so on. I suspect, in fact, that they would not make an exception for a case in which, miraculously enough, the pregnancy went on for nine years, or even the rest of the mother's life.

Some won't even make an exception for a case in which continuation of the pregnancy is likely to shorten the mother's life; they regard abortion as impermissible even to save the mother's life. Such cases are nowadays very rare, and many opponents of abortion do not accept this extreme view. All the same, it is a good place to begin: a number of points of interest come out in respect to it.

1. Let us call the view that abortion is impermissible even to save the mother's life "the extreme view." I want to suggest first that it does not issue from the argument I mentioned earlier without the addition of some fairly powerful premises. Suppose a woman has become pregnant, and now learns that she has a cardiac condition such that she will die if she carries the baby to term. What may be done for her? The fetus, being a person, has a right to life, but as the mother is a person too, so has she a right to life. Presumably they have an equal right to life. How is it supposed to come out that an abortion may not be performed? If mother and child have an equal right to life, shouldn't we perhaps flip a coin? Or should we add to the mother's right to life her right to decide what happens in and to her body, which everybody seems to be ready to grant—the sum of her rights now outweighing the fetus' right to life?

The most familiar argument here is the following. We are told that performing the abortion would be directly killing the child, whereas doing nothing would not be killing the mother, but only letting her die. Moreover, in killing the child, one would be killing an innocent person, for the child has committed no crime, and is not aiming at his mother's death. And then there are a variety of ways in which this might be continued. (1) But as directly killing an innocent person is always and absolutely impermissible, an abortion may not be performed. Or, (2) as directly killing an innocent person is murder, and murder is always and absolutely impermissible, an abortion may not be performed. Or, (3) as one's duty to refrain from directly killing an innocent person is more stringent than one's duty to keep a person from dying, an abortion may not be performed. Or, (4) if one's only options are directly killing an innocent person or letting a person die, one must prefer letting the person die, and thus an abortion may not be performed.

Some people seem to have thought that these are not further premises which must be added if the conclusion is to be reached, but that they follow from the very fact that an innocent person has a right to life. But this seems to me to be a mistake, and perhaps the simplest way to show this is to bring out that while we must certainly grant that innocent persons have a right to life, the theses in (1) through (4) are all false. Take (2), for example. If directly killing an innocent person is murder, and thus is impermissible, then the mother's directly killing the innocent person inside her is murder, and thus is impermissible. But it cannot seriously be thought to be murder if the mother performs an abortion on herself to save her life. It cannot seriously be said that she *must* refrain, that she *must* sit passively by and wait for her death. Let us look again at the case of you and the violinist. There you are, in bed with the violinist, and the director of the hospital says to you, "It's all most distressing, and I deeply sympathize, but you see this is putting an additional strain on your kidneys, and you'll be dead within the month. But you *have* to stay where you are all the same. Because unplugging you would be directly killing an innocent violinist, and that's murder, and that's impermissible." If anything in the world is true, it is that you do not commit murder, you do not do what is impermissible, if you reach around to your back and unplug yourself from that violinist to save your life.

The main focus of attention in writings on abortion has been on what a third party may or may not do in answer to a request from a woman for an abortion. This is in a way understandable. Things being as they are, there isn't much a woman can safely do to abort herself. So the question asked is what a third party may do, and what the mother may do, if it is mentioned at all, is deduced, almost as an afterthought, from what it is concluded that third parties may do. But it seems to me that to treat the matter in this way is to refuse to grant to the mother that very status of person which is so firmly insisted on for the fetus. For we cannot simply read off what a person may do from what a third party may do. Suppose you find yourself trapped in a tiny house with a growing child. I mean a very tiny house, and a rapidly growing child—you are already up against the wall of the house and in a few minutes you'll be crushed to death. The child on the other hand won't be crushed to death; if nothing is done to stop him from growing he'll be hurt, but in the end he'll simply burst open the house and walk out a free man. Now I could well understand it if a bystander were to say, "There's nothing we can do for you. We cannot choose between your life and his, we cannot be the ones to decide who is to live, we cannot intervene." But it cannot be concluded that you too can do nothing, that you cannot attack it to save your life. However innocent the child may be, you do not have to wait passively while it crushes you to death. Perhaps a pregnant woman is vaguely felt to have the status of house, to which we don't allow the right of self-defense. But if the woman houses the child, it should be remembered that she is a person who houses it.

I should perhaps stop to say explicitly that I am not claiming that people have a right to do anything whatever to save their lives. I think, rather, that there are drastic limits to the right of self-defense. If someone threatens you with death unless you torture someone else to death, I think you have not the right, even to save your life, to do so. But the case under consideration here is very different. In our case there are only two people involved, one whose life is threatened, and one who threatens it. Both are innocent: the one who is threatened is not threatened because of any fault, the one who threatens does not threaten because of any fault. For this reason we may feel that we bystanders cannot intervene. But the person threatened can.

In sum, a woman surely can defend her life against the threat to it posed by the unborn child, even if doing so involves its death. And this shows not merely that the theses in (1) through (4) are false; it shows also that the extreme view of abortion is false, and so we need not canvass any other possible ways of arriving at it from the argument I mentioned at the outset.

2. The extreme view could of course be weakened to say that while abortion is permissible to save the mother's life, it may not be performed by the third party, but only by the mother herself. But this cannot be right either. For what we have to keep in mind is that the mother and the unborn child are not like two tenants in a small house which has, by an unfortunate mistake, been rented to both: the mother *owns* the house. The fact that she does adds to the offensiveness of deducing that the mother can do nothing from the supposition that third parties can do nothing. But it does more than this: it casts a bright light on the supposition that third parties can do nothing. Certainly it lets us see that a third party who says "I cannot choose between you" is fooling himself if he thinks this is impartiality. If Jones has found and fastened on a certain coat, which he needs to keep him from freezing, but which Smith also needs to keep him from freezing, then it is not impartiality that says "I cannot choose between you" when Smith owns the coat. Women have said again and again "This body is *my* body!" and they have reason to feel angry, reason to feel that it has been like shouting into the wind. Smith, after all, is hardly likely to bless us if we say to him, "Of course it's your coat, anybody would grant that it is. But no one may choose between you and Jones who is to have it."

We should really ask what it is that says "no one may choose" in the face of the fact that the body that houses the child is the mother's body. It may be simply a failure to appreciate this fact. But it may be something more interesting, namely the sense that one has a right to refuse to lay hands on people, even where it would be just and fair to do so, even where justice seems to require that somebody do so. Thus justice might call for somebody to get Smith's coat back from Jones, and yet you have a right to refuse to be the one to lay hands on Jones, a right to refuse to do physical violence to him. This, I think, must be granted. But then what should be said is not "no one may choose," but only "*I* cannot choose," and indeed not even this, but "*I* will not *act*," leaving it open that somebody else can or should, and in particular that anyone in a position of authority, with the job of securing people's rights, both can and should. So this is no difficulty. I have not been arguing that any given third party must accede to the mother's request that he perform an abortion to save her life, but only that he may.

I suppose that in some views of human life the mother's body is only on loan to her, the loan not being one which gives her any prior claim to it. One who held this view might well think it impartiality to say "I cannot choose." But I shall simply ignore this possibility. My own view is that if a human being has any just, prior claim to anything at all, he has a just, prior claim to his own body. And perhaps this needn't be argued for here anyway, since, as I mentioned, the arguments against abortion we are looking at do grant that the woman has a right to decide what happens in and to her body.

But although they do grant it, I have tried to show that they do not take seriously what is done in granting it. I suggest the same thing will reappear even more clearly when we turn away from cases in which the mother's life is at stake, and attend, as I propose we now do, to the vastly more common cases in which a woman wants an abortion for some less weighty reason than preserving her own life.

3. Where the mother's life is not at stake, the argument I mentioned at the outset seems to have a much stronger pull. "Everyone has a right to life, so the unborn person has a right to life." And isn't the child's right to life weightier than anything other than the mother's own right to life, which she might put forward as ground for an abortion?

This argument treats the right to life as if it were unproblematic. It is not, and this seems to me to be precisely the source of the mistake.

For we should now, at long last, ask what it comes to, to have a right to life. In some views having a right to life includes having a right to be given at least the bare minimum one needs for continued life. But suppose that what in fact *is* the bare minimum a man needs for continued life is something he has no right at all to be given? If I am sick unto death, and the only thing that will save my life is the touch of Henry Fonda's cool hand on my fevered brow, then all the same, I have no right to be given the touch of Henry Fonda's cool hand on my fevered brow. It would be frightfully nice of him to fly in from the West Coast to provide it. It would be less nice, though no doubt well meant, if my friends flew out to the West Coast and carried Henry Fonda back with them. But I have no right at all against anybody that he should do this for me. Or again, to return to the story I told earlier, the fact that for continued life that violinist needs the continued use of your kidneys does not establish that he has a right to be given the continued use of your kidneys. He certainly has no right against you that *you* should give him continued use of your kidneys. For nobody has any right to use your kidneys unless you give him such a right; and nobody has the right against you that you shall give him this right—if you do allow him to go on using your kidneys, this is kindness on your part, and not something he can claim from you as his due. Nor has he any right against anybody else that *they* should give him continued use of your kidneys. Certainly he had no right against the Society of Music Lovers that they should plug him into you in the first place. And if you now start to unplug yourself, having learned that you will otherwise have to spend nine years in bed with him, there is nobody in the world who must try to prevent you, in order to see to it that he is given something he has a right to be given.

Some people are rather stricter about the right to life. In their view, it does not include the right to be given anything, but amounts to, and only to, the right not to be killed by anybody. But here a related difficulty arises. If everybody is to refrain from killing that violinist, then everybody must refrain from doing a great many different sorts of things. Everybody must refrain from slitting his throat, everybody must refrain from shooting him—and everybody must refrain from unplugging you from him. But does he have a right against everybody that they shall refrain from unplugging you from him? To refrain from doing this is to allow him to continue to use your kidneys. It could be argued that he has a right against us that *we* should allow him to continue to use your kidneys. That is, while he had no right against us that we should give him the use of your kidneys, it might be argued that he anyway has a right against us that we shall not now intervene and deprive him of the use of your kidneys. I shall come back to third-party interventions later. But certainly the violinist has no right against you that *you* shall allow him to continue to use your kidneys. As I said, if you do allow him to use them, it is a kindness on your part, and not something you owe him.

The difficulty I point to here is not peculiar to the right to life. It reappears in connection with all the other natural rights; and it is something which an adequate account of rights must deal with. For present purposes it is enough just to draw attention to it. But I would stress that I am not arguing that people do not have a right to life—quite to the contrary, it seems to me that the primary control we must place on the acceptability of an account of rights is that it should turn out in that account to be a truth that all persons have a right to life. I am arguing only that having a right to life does not guarantee having either a right to be given the use of or a right to be allowed continued use of another person's body—even if one needs it for life itself. So the right to life will not serve the opponents of abortion in the very simple and clear way in which they seem to have thought it would.

4. There is another way to bring out the difficulty. In the most ordinary sort of case, to deprive someone of what he has a right to is to treat him unjustly. Suppose a boy and his small brother are jointly given a box of chocolates for Christmas. If the older boy takes the box and refuses to give his brother any of the chocolates, he is unjust to him, for the brother has been given a right to half of them. But suppose that, having learned that otherwise it means nine years in bed with that violinist, you unplug yourself from him. You surely are not being unjust to him, for you gave him no right to use your kidneys, and no one else can have given him any such right. But we have to notice that in unplugging yourself, you are killing him; and violinists, like everybody else, have a right to life, and thus in the view we were considering just now, the right not to be killed. So here you do what he supposedly has a right you shall not do, but you do not act unjustly to him in doing it.

The emendation which may be made at this point is this: the right to life consists not in the right not to be killed, but rather in the right not to be killed unjustly. This runs a risk of circularity, but never mind: it would enable us to square the fact that the violinist has a right to life with the fact that you do not act unjustly toward him in unplugging yourself, thereby killing him. For if you do not kill him unjustly, you do not violate his right to life, and so it is no wonder you do him no injustice.

But if this emendation is accepted, the gap in the argument against abortion stares us plainly in the face: it is by no means enough to show that the fetus is a person, and to remind us that all persons have a right to life—we need to be shown also that killing the fetus violates its right to life, i.e., that abortion is unjust killing. And is it?

I suppose we may take it as a datum that in a case of pregnancy due to rape the mother has not given the unborn person a right to the use of her body for food and shelter. Indeed, in what pregnancy could it be supposed that the mother has given the unborn person such a right? It is not as if there were unborn persons drifting about the world, to whom a woman who wants a child says "I invite you in."

But it might be argued that there are other ways one can have acquired a right to the use of another person's body than by having been invited to use it by that person. Suppose a woman voluntarily indulges in intercourse, knowing of the chance it will issue in pregnancy, and then she does become pregnant; is she not in part responsible for the presence, in fact the very existence, of the unborn person inside her? No doubt she did not invite it in. But doesn't her partial responsibility for its being there itself give it a right to the use of her body? If so, then her aborting it would be more like the boy's taking away the chocolates, and less like your unplugging yourself from the violinist—doing so would be depriving it of what it does have a right to, and thus would be doing it an injustice.

And then, too, it might be asked whether or not she can kill it even to save her own life: If she voluntarily called it into existence, how can she now kill it, even in self-defense?

The first thing to be said about this is that it is something new. Opponents of abortion have been so concerned to make out the independence of the fetus, in order to establish that it has a right to life, just as its mother does, that they have tended to overlook the possible support they might gain from making out that the fetus is *dependent* on the mother, in order to establish that she has a special kind of responsibility for it, a responsibility that gives it rights against her which are not possessed by any independent person—such as an ailing violinist who is a stranger to her.

On the other hand, this argument would give the unborn person a right to its mother's body only if her pregnancy resulted from a voluntary act, undertaken in full knowledge of the chance a pregnancy might result from it. It would leave out entirely the unborn person whose existence is due to rape. Pending the availability of some further argument, then, we would be left with the conclusion that unborn persons whose existence is due to rape have no right to the use of their mothers' bodies, and thus that aborting them is not depriving them of anything they have a right to and hence is not unjust killing.

And we should also notice that it is not at all plain that this argument really does go even as far as it purports to. For there are cases and cases, and the details make a difference. If the room is stuffy, and I therefore open a window to air it, and a burglar climbs in, it would be absurd to say, "Ah, now he can stay, she's given him a right to the use of her house—for she is partially responsible for his presence there, having voluntarily done what enabled him to get in, in full knowledge that there are such things as burglars, and that burglars burgle." It would be still more absurd to say this if I had had bars installed outside my windows, precisely to prevent burglars from getting in, and a burglar got in only because of a defect in the bars. It remains equally absurd if we imagine it is not a burglar who climbs in, but an innocent person who blunders or falls in. Again, suppose it were like this: people-seeds drift about in the air like pollen, and if you open your windows, one may drift in and take root in your carpets or upholstery. You don't want children, so you fix up your windows with fine mesh screens, the very best you can buy. As can happen, however, and on very, very rare occasions does happen, one of the screens is defective; and a seed drifts in and takes root. Does the person-plant who now develops have a right to the use of your house? Surely not—despite the fact that you voluntarily opened your windows, you knowingly kept carpets and upholstered furniture, and you knew that screens were sometimes defective. Someone may argue that you are responsible for its rooting, that it does have a right to your house, because after all you *could* have lived out your life with bare floors and furniture, or with sealed windows and doors. But this won't do—for by the same token anyone can avoid a pregnancy due to rape by having a hysterectomy, or anyway by never leaving home without a (reliable!) army.

It seems to me that the argument we are looking at can establish at most that there are *some* cases in which the unborn person has a right to the use of its mother's body, and therefore *some* cases in which abortion is unjust killing. There is room for much discussion and argument as to precisely which, if any. But I think we should sidestep this issue and leave it open, for at any rate the argument certainly does not establish that all abortion is unjust killing.

5. There is room for yet another argument here, however. We surely must all grant that there may be cases in which it would be morally indecent to detach a person from your body at the cost of his life. Suppose you learn that what the violinist needs is not nine years of your life, but only one hour: all you need do to save his life is to spend one hour in that bed with him. Suppose also that letting him use your kidneys for that one hour would not affect your health in the slightest. Admittedly you were kidnapped. Admittedly you did not give anyone permission to plug him into you. Nevertheless it seems to me plain you *ought* to allow him to use your kidneys for that hour—it would be indecent to refuse.

Again, suppose pregnancy lasted only an hour, and constituted no threat to life or health. And suppose that a woman becomes pregnant as a result of rape. Admittedly she did not voluntarily do anything to bring about the existence of a child. Admittedly she did nothing at all which would give the unborn person a right to the use of her body. All the same it might well be said, as in the newly emended violinist story, that she *ought* to allow it to remain for that hour—that it would be indecent in her to refuse.

Now some people are inclined to use the term "right" in such a way that it follows from the fact that you ought to allow a person to use your body for the hour he needs, that he has a right to use your body for the hour he needs, even though he has not been given that right by any person or act. They may say that it follows also that if you refuse, you act unjustly toward him. This use of the term is perhaps so common that it cannot be called wrong; nevertheless it seems to me to be an unfortunate loosening of what we would do better to keep a tight rein on. Suppose that box of chocolates I mentioned earlier had not been given to both boys jointly, but was given only to the older boy. There he sits, stolidly eating his way through the box, his small brother watching enviously. Here we are likely to say "You ought not to be so mean. You ought to give your brother some of those chocolates." My own view is that it just does not follow from the truth of this that the brother has any right to any of the chocolates. If the boy refuses to give his brother any, he is greedy, stingy, callous—but not unjust. I suppose that the people I have in mind will say it does follow that the brother has a right to some of the chocolates, and thus that the boy does act unjustly if he refuses to give his brother any. But the effect of saying this is to obscure what we should keep distinct, namely the difference between the boy's refusal in this case and the boy's refusal in the earlier case, in which the box was given to both boys jointly, and in which the small brother thus had what was from any point of view clear title to half.

A further objection to so using the term "right" that from the fact that A ought to do a thing for B, it follows that B has a right against A that A do it for him, is that it is going to make the question of whether or not a man has a right to a thing turn on how easy it is to provide him with it; and this seems not merely unfortunate, but morally unacceptable. Take the case of Henry Fonda again. I said earlier that I had no right to the touch of his cool hand on my fevered brow, even though I needed it to save my life. I said it would be frightfully nice of him to fly in from the West Coast to provide me with it, but that I had no right against him that he should do so. But suppose he isn't on the West Coast. Suppose he has only to walk across the room, place a hand briefly on my brow—and lo, my life is saved. Then surely he ought to do it, it would be indecent to refuse. Is it to be said "Ah, well, it follows that in this case she has a right to the touch of his hand on her brow, and so it would be an injustice in him to refuse"? So that I have a right to it when it is easy for him to provide it, though no right when it's hard? It's rather a shocking idea that anyone's rights should fade away and disappear as it gets harder and harder to accord them to him.

So my own view is that even though you ought to let the violinist use your kidneys for the one hour he needs, we should not conclude that he has a right to do so—we would say that if you refuse, you are, like the boy who owns all the chocolates and will give none away, self-centered and callous, indecent in fact, but not unjust. And similarly, that even supposing a case in which a woman pregnant due to rape ought to allow the unborn person to use her body for the hour he needs, we should not conclude that he has a right to do so; we should conclude that she is self-centered, callous, indecent, but not unjust, if she refuses. The complaints are no less grave; they are just different. However, there is no need to insist on this point. If anyone does wish to deduce "he has a right" from "you ought," then all the same he must surely grant that there are cases in which it is not morally required of you that you allow that violinist to use your kidneys, and in which he does not have a right to use them, and in which you do not do him an injustice if you refuse. And so also for mother and unborn child. Except in such cases as the unborn person has a right to demand it—and we were leaving open the possibility that there may be such cases—nobody is morally *required* to make large sacrifices, of health, of all other interests and concerns, of all other duties and commitments, for nine years, or even for nine months, in order to keep another person alive.

6. We have in fact to distinguish between two kinds of Samaritan: the Good Samaritan and what we might call the Minimally Decent Samaritan.

The story of the Good Samaritan, you will remember, goes like this:

> A certain man went down from Jerusalem to Jericho, and fell among thieves, which stripped him of his raiment, and wounded him, and departed, leaving him half dead.
>
> And by chance there came down a certain priest that way; and when he saw him, he passed by on the other side.
>
> And likewise a Levite, when he was at the place, came and looked on him, and passed by on the other side.
>
> But a certain Samaritan, as he journeyed, came where he was; and when he saw him he had compassion on him.
>
> And went to him, and bound up his wounds, pouring in oil and wine, and set him on his own beast, and brought him to an inn, and took care of him.
>
> And on the morrow, when he departed, he took out two pence, and gave them to the host, and said unto him, "Take care of him; and whatsoever thou spendest more, when I come again, I will repay thee."
>
> (Luke 10:30–35)

The Good Samaritan went out of his way, at some cost to himself, to help one in need of it. We are not told what the options were, that is, whether or not the priest and the Levite could have helped by doing less than the Good Samaritan did, but assuming they could have, then the fact they did nothing at all shows they were not even Minimally Decent Samaritans, not because they were not Samaritans, but because they were not even minimally decent.

These things are a matter of degree, of course, but there is a difference, and it comes out perhaps most clearly in the story of Kitty Genovese, who, as you will remember, was murdered while thirty-eight people watched or listened, and did nothing at all to help her. A Good Samaritan would have rushed out to give direct assistance against the murderer. Or perhaps we had better allow that it would have been a Splendid Samaritan who did this, on the ground that it would have involved a risk of death for himself. But the thirty-eight not only did not do this, they did not even trouble to pick up a phone to call the police. Minimally Decent Samaritanism would call for doing at least that, and their not having done it was monstrous.

After telling the story of the Good Samaritan, Jesus said "Go, and do thou likewise." Perhaps he meant that we are morally required to act as the Good Samaritan did. Perhaps he was urging people to do more than is morally required of them. At all events it seems plain that it was not morally required of any of the thirty-eight that he rush out to give direct assistance at the risk of his own life, and that it is not morally required of anyone that he give long stretches of his life—nine years or nine months—to sustaining the life of a person who has no special right (we were leaving open the possibility of this) to demand it.

Indeed, with one rather striking class of exceptions, no one in any country in the world is *legally* required to do anywhere near as much as this for anyone else. The class of exceptions is obvious. My main concern here is not the state of the law in respect to abortion, but it is worth drawing attention to the fact that in no state in this country is any man compelled by law to be even a Minimally Decent Samaritan to any person; there is no law under which charges could be brought against the thirty-eight who stood by while Kitty Genovese died. By contrast, in most states in this country women are compelled by law to be not merely Minimally Decent Samaritans, but Good Samaritans to unborn persons inside them. This doesn't by itself settle anything one way or the other, because it may well be argued that there should be laws in this country—as there are in many European countries—compelling at least Minimally Decent Samaritanism. But it does show that there is a gross injustice in the existing state of the law. And it shows also that the groups currently working against liberalization of abortion laws, in fact working toward having it declared unconstitutional for a state to permit abortion, had better start working for the adoption of Good Samaritan laws generally, or earn the charge that they are acting in bad faith.

I should think, myself, that Minimally Decent Samaritan laws would be one thing, Good Samaritan laws quite another, and in fact highly improper.

But we are not here concerned with the law. What we should ask is not whether anybody should be compelled by law to be a Good Samaritan, but whether we must accede to a situation in which somebody is being compelled—by nature, perhaps—to be a Good Samaritan. We have, in other words, to look now at third-party interventions. I have been arguing that no person is morally required to make large sacrifices to sustain the life of another who has no right to demand them, and this even where the sacrifices do not include life itself; we are not morally required to be Good Samaritans or anyway Very Good Samaritans to one another. But what if a man cannot extricate himself from such a situation? What if he appeals to us to extricate him? It seems to me plain that there are cases in which we can, cases in which a Good Samaritan would extricate him. There you are, you were kidnapped, and nine years in bed with that violinist lie ahead of you. You have your own life to lead. You are sorry, but you simply cannot see giving up so much of your life to the sustaining of his. You cannot extricate yourself, and ask us to do so. I should have thought that—in light of his having no right to the use of your body—it was obvious that we do not have to accede to your being forced to give up so much. We can do what you ask. There is no injustice to the violinist in our doing so.

7. Following the lead of the opponents of abortion, I have throughout been speaking of the fetus merely as a person, and what I have been asking is whether or not the argument we began with, which proceeds only from the fetus' being a person, really does establish its conclusion. I have argued that it does not.

But of course there are arguments and arguments, and it may be said that I have simply fastened on the wrong one. It may be said that what is important is not merely the fact that the fetus is a person, but that it is a person for whom the woman has a special kind of responsibility issuing from the fact that she is its mother. And it might be argued that all my analogies are therefore irrelevant—for you do not have that special kind of responsibility for that violinist, Henry Fonda does not have that special kind of responsibility for me. And our attention might be drawn to the fact that men and women both *are* compelled by law to provide support for their children.

I have in effect dealt (briefly) with this argument in section 4 above; but a (still briefer) recapitulation now may be in order. Surely we do not have any such "special responsibility" for a person unless we have assumed it, explicitly or implicitly. If a set of parents do not try to prevent pregnancy, do not obtain an abortion, and then at the time of birth of the child do not put it out for adoption, but rather take it home with them, then they have assumed responsibility for it, they have given it rights, and they cannot *now* withdraw support from it at the cost of its life because they now find it difficult to go on providing for it. But if they have taken all reasonable precautions against having a child, they do not simply by virtue of their biological relationship to the child who comes into existence have a special responsibility for it. They may wish to assume responsibility for it, or they may not wish to. And I am suggesting that if assuming responsibility for it would require large sacrifices, then they may refuse. A Good Samaritan would not refuse—or anyway, a Splendid Samaritan, if the sacrifices that had to be made were enormous. But then so would a Good Samaritan assume responsibility for that violinist; so would Henry Fonda, if he is a Good Samaritan, fly in from the West Coast and assume responsibility for me.

8. My argument will be found unsatisfactory on two counts by many of those who want to regard abortion as morally permissible. First, while I do argue that abortion is not impermissible, I do not argue that it is always permissible. There may well be cases in which carrying the child to term requires only Minimally Decent Samaritanism of the mother, and this is a standard we must not fall below. I am inclined to think it a merit of my account precisely that it does *not* give a general yes or a general no. It allows for and supports our sense that, for example, a sick and desperately frightened fourteen-year-old schoolgirl, pregnant due to rape, may *of course* choose abortion, and that any law which rules this out is an insane law. And it also allows for and supports our sense that in other cases resort to abortion is even positively

indecent. It would be indecent in the woman to request an abortion, and indecent in a doctor to perform it, if she is in her seventh month, and wants the abortion just to avoid the nuisance of postponing a trip abroad. The very fact that the arguments I have been drawing attention to treat all cases of abortion, or even all cases of abortion in which the mother's life is not at stake, as morally on a par ought to have made them suspect at the outset.

Secondly, while I am arguing for the permissibility of abortion in some cases, I am not arguing for the right to secure the death of the unborn child. It is easy to confuse these two things in that up to a certain point in the life of the fetus it is not able to survive outside the mother's body; hence removing it from her body guarantees its death. But they are importantly different. I have argued that you are not morally required to spend nine months in bed, sustaining the life of that violinist; but to say this is by no means to say that if, when you unplug yourself, there is a miracle and he survives, you then have a right to turn round and slit his throat. You may detach yourself even if this costs him his life; you have no right to be guaranteed his death, by some other means, if unplugging yourself does not kill him. There are some people who will feel dissatisfied by this feature of my argument. A woman may be utterly devastated by the thought of a child, a bit of herself, put out for adoption and never seen or heard of again. She may therefore want not merely that the child be detached from her, but more, that it die. Some opponents of abortion are inclined to regard this as beneath contempt—thereby showing insensitivity to what is surely a powerful source of despair. All the same, I agree that the desire for the child's death is not one which anybody may gratify, should it turn out to be possible to detach the child alive.

At this place, however, it should be remembered that we have only been pretending throughout that the fetus is a human being from the moment of conception. A very early abortion is surely not the killing of a person, and so is not dealt with by anything I have said here.

JANE ENGLISH

Abortion and the Concept of a Person

Jane English was Associate Professor of Philosophy at the University of North Carolina when she died in 1978. *(Source: Reprinted from* The Canadian Journal of Philosophy *5, 2 [October 1975], pp. 233–243.*

QUESTIONS FOR REFLECTION

1. English argues that "our concept of a person is not sharp or decisive enough" to resolve the abortion controversy. How does she reach this conclusion?
2. What is the point of English's arguments concerning self-defense? What do you think they show?
3. How does English distinguish abortion from infanticide?
4. Why, according to English, are some abortions impermissible?

The abortion debate rages on. Yet the two most popular positions seem to be clearly mistaken. Conservatives maintain that a human life begins at conception and that therefore abortion must be wrong because it is murder. But not all killings of humans are murders. Most notably, self defense may justify even the killing of an innocent person.

Liberals, on the other hand, are just as mistaken in their argument that since a fetus does not become a person until birth, a woman may do whatever she pleases in and to her own body. First, you cannot do as you please with your own body if it affects other people adversely. Second, if a fetus is not a person, that does not imply that you can do to it anything you wish. Animals, for example, are not persons, yet to kill or torture them for no reason at all is wrong.

At the center of the storm has been the issue of just when it is between ovulation and adulthood that a person appears on the scene. Conservatives draw the line at conception, liberals at birth. In this paper I first examine our concept of a person and conclude that no single criterion can capture the concept of a person and no sharp line can be drawn. Next I argue that if a fetus is a person, abortion is still justifiable in many cases; and if a fetus is not a person, killing it is still wrong in many cases. To a large extent, these two solutions are in agreement. I conclude that our concept of a person cannot and need not bear the weight that the abortion controversy has thrust upon it.

I

The several factions in the abortion argument have drawn battle lines around various proposed criteria for determining what is and what is not a person.

For example, Mary Anne Warren lists five features (capacities for reasoning, self-awareness, complex communication, etc.) as her criteria for personhood and argues for the permissibility of abortion because a fetus falls outside this concept. Baruch Brody uses brain waves. Michael Tooley picks having-a-concept-of-self as his criterion and concludes that infanticide and abortion are justifiable, while the killing of adult animals is not. On the other side, Paul Ramsey claims a certain gene structure is the defining characteristic. John Noonan prefers conceived-of-humans and presents counterexamples to various other candidate criteria. For instance, he argues against viability as the criterion because the newborn and infirm would then be non-persons, since they cannot live without the aid of others. He rejects any criterion that calls upon the sorts of sentiments a being can evoke in adults on the grounds that this would allow us to exclude other races as non-persons if we could just view them sufficiently unsentimentally.

These approaches are typical: foes of abortion propose sufficient conditions for personhood which fetuses satisfy, while friends of abortion counter with necessary conditions for personhood which fetuses lack. But these both presuppose that the concept of a person can be captured in a strait jacket of necessary and/or sufficient conditions. Rather, "person" is a cluster of features, of which rationality, having a self concept and being conceived of humans are only part.

What is typical of persons? Within our concept of a person we include, first, certain biological factors: descended from humans, having a certain genetic makeup, having a head, hands, arms, eyes, capable of locomotion, breathing, eating, sleeping. There are psychological factors: sentience, perception, having a concept of self and of one's own interests and desires, the ability to use tools, the ability to use language or symbol systems, the ability to joke, to be angry, to doubt. There are rationality factors: the ability to reason and draw conclusions, the ability to generalize and to learn from past experience, the ability to sacrifice present interests for greater gains in the future. There are social factors: the ability to work in groups and respond to peer pressures, the ability to recognize and consider as valuable the interests of others, seeing oneself as one among "other minds," the ability to sympathize, encourage, love, the ability to evoke from others the responses of sympathy, encouragement, love, the ability to work with others for mutual advantage. Then there are legal factors: being subject to the law and protected by it, having the ability to sue and enter contracts, being counted in the census, having a name and citizenship, the ability to own property, inherit, and so forth.

Now the point is not that this list is incomplete, or that you can find counterinstances to each of its points. People typically exhibit rationality, for instance, but someone who was irrational would not thereby fail to qualify as a person. On the other hand, something could exhibit the majority of these features and still fail to be a person, as an advanced robot might. There is no single core of necessary and sufficient features which we can draw upon with the assurance that they constitute what really makes a person; there are only features that are more or less typical.

This is not to say that no necessary or sufficient conditions can be given. Being alive is a necessary condition for being a person, and being a U.S. Senator is sufficient. But rather than falling inside a sufficient condition or outside a necessary one, a fetus lies in the penumbra region where our concept of a person is not so simple. For this reason I think a conclusive answer to the question whether a fetus is a person is unattainable.

Here we might note a family of simple fallacies that proceed by stating a necessary condition for personhood and showing that a fetus has that characteristic. This is a form of the fallacy of affirming the consequent. For example, some have mistakenly reasoned from the premise that a fetus is human (after all, it is a human fetus rather than, say, a canine fetus), to the conclusion that it is *a* human. Adding an equivocation on "being," we get the fallacious argument that since a fetus is something both living and human, it is a human being.

Nonetheless, it does seem clear that a fetus has very few of the above family of characteristics, whereas a newborn baby exhibits a much larger proportion of them—and a two-year-old has even more. Note that one traditional anti-abortion argument has centered on pointing out the many ways in which a fetus resembles a baby. They emphasize its development ("It already has ten fingers. . . . ") without mentioning its dissimilarities to adults (it still has gills and a tail). They also try to evoke the sort of sympathy on our part that we only feel toward other persons ("Never to laugh . . . or feel the sunshine?"). This all seems to be a relevant way to argue, since its purpose is to persuade us that a fetus satisfies so many of the important features on the list that it ought to be treated as a person. Also note that a fetus near the time of birth satisfies many more of these factors than a fetus in the early months of development. This could provide reason for making distinctions among the different stages of pregnancy, as the U.S. Supreme Court has done.

Historically, the time at which a person has been said to come into existence has varied widely. Muslims date personhood from fourteen days after conception. Some medievals followed Aristotle in placing ensoulment at forty days after conception for a male fetus and eighty days for a female fetus. In European common law since the Seventeenth Century, abortion was considered the killing of a person only after quickening, the time when a pregnant woman first feels the fetus move on its own. Nor is this variety of opinions surprising. Biologically, a human being develops gradually. We shouldn't expect there to be any specific time or sharp dividing point when a person appears on the scene.

For these reasons I believe our concept of a person is not sharp or decisive enough to bear the weight of a solution to the abortion controversy. To use it to solve that problem is to clarify *obscurum per obscurius*.

II

Next let us consider what follows if a fetus is a person after all. Judith Jarvis Thomson's landmark article, "A Defense of Abortion," correctly points out that some additional argumentation is needed at this point in the conservative argument to bridge the gap between the premise that a fetus is an innocent person and the conclusion that killing it is always wrong. To arrive at this conclusion, we would need the additional premise that killing an innocent person is always wrong. But killing an innocent person is sometimes permissible, most notably in self defense. Some examples may help draw out our intuitions or ordinary judgments about self defense.

Suppose a mad scientist, for instance, hypnotized innocent people to jump out of the bushes and attack innocent passers-by with knives. If you are so attacked, we agree you have a right to kill the attacker in self defense, if killing him is the only way to protect your life or to save yourself from serious injury. It does not seem to matter here that the attacker is not malicious but himself an innocent pawn, for your killing of him is not done in a spirit of retribution but only in self defense.

How severe an injury may you inflict in self defense? In part this depends upon the severity of the injury to be avoided: you may not shoot someone merely to avoid having your clothes torn. This might lead one to the mistaken conclusion that the defense may only equal the threatened injury in severity; that to avoid death you may kill, but to avoid a black eye you may only inflict a black eye or the equivalent. Rather, our laws and customs seem to say that you may create an injury somewhat, but not enormously, greater than the injury to be avoided. To fend off an attack whose outcome would be as serious as rape, a severe beating or the loss of a finger, you may shoot; to avoid having your clothes torn, you may blacken an eye.

Aside from this, the injury you may inflict should only be the minimum necessary to deter or incapacitate the attacker. Even if you know he intends to kill you, you are not justified in shooting him if you could equally well save yourself by the simple expedient of running away. Self defense is for the purpose of avoiding harms rather than equalizing harms.

Some cases of pregnancy present a parallel situation. Though the fetus is itself innocent, it may pose a threat to the pregnant woman's well-being, life prospects or health, mental or physical. If the pregnancy presents a slight threat to her interests, it seems self defense cannot justify abortion. But if the threat is on a par with a serious beating or the loss of a finger, she may kill the fetus that poses such a threat, even if it is an innocent person. If a lesser harm to the fetus could have the same defensive effect, killing it would not be justified. It is unfortunate that the only way to free the woman from the pregnancy entails the death of the fetus (except in very late stages of pregnancy). Thus a self defense model supports Thomson's point that the woman has a right only to be freed from the fetus, not a right to demand its death.

The self defense model is most helpful when we take the pregnant woman's point of view. In the pre-Thomson literature, abortion is often framed as a question for a third party: do you, a doctor, have a right to choose between the life of the woman and that of the fetus? Some have claimed that if you were a passer-by who witnessed a struggle between the innocent hypnotized attacker and his equally innocent victim, you would have no reason to kill either in defense of the other. They have concluded that the self defense model implies that a woman may attempt to abort herself, but that a doctor should not assist her. I think the position of the third party is somewhat more complex. We do feel some inclination to intervene on behalf of the victim rather than the attacker, other things equal. But if both parties are innocent, other factors come into consideration. You would rush to the aid of your husband whether he was attacker or attackee. If a hypnotized famous violinist were attacking a skid row bum, we would try to save the individual who is of more value to society. These considerations would tend to support abortion in some cases.

But suppose you are a frail senior citizen who wishes to avoid being knifed by one of these innocent hypnotics, so you have hired a bodyguard to accompany you. If you are attacked, it is clear we believe that the bodyguard, acting as your agent, has a right to kill the attacker to save you from a serious beating. Your rights of self defense are transferred to your agent. I suggest that we should similarly view the doctor as the pregnant woman's agent in carrying out a defense she is physically incapable of accomplishing herself.

Thanks to modern technology, the cases are rare in which pregnancy poses as clear a threat to a woman's bodily health as an attacker brandishing a switchblade. How does self defense fare when more subtle, complex and long-range harms are involved?

To consider a somewhat fanciful example, suppose you are a highly trained surgeon when you are kidnapped by the hypnotic attacker. He says he does not intend to harm you but to take you back to the mad scientist who, it turn out, plans to hypnotize you to have a permanent mental block against all your knowledge of medicine. This would automatically destroy your career which would in turn have a serious adverse impact on your family, your personal relationships and your happiness. It seems to me that if the only way you can avoid this outcome is to shoot the innocent attacker, you are justified in so doing. You are defending yourself from a drastic injury to your life prospects. I think it is no exaggeration to claim that unwanted pregnancies (most obviously among teenagers) often have such adverse life-long consequences as the surgeon's loss of livelihood.

Several parallels arise between various views on abortion and the self defense model. Let's suppose further that these hypnotized attackers only operate at night, so that it is well known that they can be avoided completely by the considerable inconvenience of never leaving your house after dark. One view is that since you could stay home at night, therefore if you go out and are selected by one of these hypnotized people, you have no right to defend yourself. This parallels the view that abstinence is the only acceptable way to avoid pregnancy. Others might hold that you ought to take along some defense such as Mace which will deter the hypnotized person without killing him, but that if this defense fails, you are obliged to submit to the resulting injury, no matter how severe it is. This parallels the view that contraception is all right but abortion is always wrong, even in cases of contraceptive failure.

A third view is that you may kill the hypnotized person only if he will actually kill you, but not if he will only injure you. This is like the position that abortion is permissible only if it is required to save a woman's life. Finally we have the view that it is all right to kill the attacker, even if only to avoid a very slight inconvenience to yourself and even if you knowingly walked down the very street where all these incidents have been taking place without taking along any Mace or protective escort. If we assume that a fetus is a person, this is the analogue of the view that abortion is always justifiable, "on demand."

The self defense model allows us to see an important difference that exists between abortion and infanticide, even if a fetus is a person from conception. Many have argued that the only way to justify abortion without justifying infanticide would be to find some characteristic of personhood that is acquired at birth. Michael Tooley, for one, claims infanticide is justifiable because the really significant characteristics of person are acquired some time after birth. But all such approaches look to characteristics of the developing human and ignore the relation between the fetus and the woman. What if, after birth, the presence of an infant or the need to support it posed a grave threat to the woman's sanity or life prospects? She could escape this threat by the simple expedient of running away. So a solution that does not entail the death of the infant is available. Before birth, such solutions are not available because of the biological dependence of the fetus on the woman. Birth is the crucial point not because of any characteristics the fetus gains, but because after birth the woman can defend herself by a means less drastic than killing the infant. Hence self defense can be used to justify abortion without necessarily thereby justifying infanticide.

III

On the other hand, supposing a fetus is not after all a person, would abortion always be morally permissible? Some opponents of abortion seem worried that if a fetus is not a full-fledged person, then we are justified in treating it in any way at all. However, this does not follow. Non-persons do get some consideration in our moral code, though of course they do not have the same rights as persons have (and in general they do not have moral responsibilities), and though their interests may be overridden by the interests of persons. Still, we cannot just treat them in any way at all.

Treatment of animals is a case in point. It is wrong to torture dogs for fun or to kill wild birds for no reason at all. It is wrong Period, even though dogs and birds do not have the same rights persons do. However, few people think it is wrong to use dogs as experimental animals, causing them considerable suffering in some cases, provided that the resulting research will probably bring discoveries of great benefit to people. And most of us think it all right to kill birds for food or to protect our crops. People's rights are different from the consideration we give to animals, then, for it is wrong to experiment on people, even if others might later benefit a great deal as a result of their suffering. You might volunteer to be a subject, but this would be supererogatory; you certainly have a right to refuse to be a medical guinea pig.

But how do we decide what you may or may not do to non-persons? This is a difficult problem, one for which I believe no adequate account exists. You do not want to say, for instance, that torturing dogs is all right whenever the sum of its effects on people is good—when it doesn't warp the sensibilities of the torturer so much that he mistreats people. If that were the case, it would be all right to torture dogs if you did it in private, or if the torturer lived on a desert island or died soon afterward, so that his actions had no effect on people. This is an inadequate account, because whatever moral consideration animals get, it has to be indefeasible, too. It will have to be a general proscription of certain actions, not merely a weighing of the impact on people on a case-by-case basis.

Rather, we need to distinguish two levels on which consequences of actions can be taken into account in moral reasoning. The traditional objections to Utilitarianism focus on the fact that it operates solely on the first level, taking all the consequences into account in particular cases only. Thus Utilitarianism is open to "desert island" and "lifeboat" counterexamples because these cases are rigged to make the consequences of actions severely limited.

Rawls' theory could be described as a teleological sort of theory, but with teleology operating on a higher level. In choosing the principles to regulate society from the original position, his hypothetical choosers make their decision on the basis of the total consequences of various systems. Furthermore, they are constrained to choose a general set of rules which people can readily learn and apply. An ethical theory must operate by generating a set of sympathies and attitudes toward others which reinforces the functioning of that set of moral principles. Our prohibition against killing people operates by means of certain moral sentiments including sympathy, compassion and guilt. But if these attitudes are to form a coherent set, they carry us further: we tend to perform supererogatory actions, and we tend to feel similar compassion toward person-like non-persons.

It is crucial that psychological facts play a role here. Our psychological constitution makes it the case that for our ethical theory to work, it must prohibit certain treatment of non-persons which are significantly person-like. If our moral rules allowed people to treat some person-like non-persons in ways we do not want people to be treated, this would undermine the system of sympathies and attitudes that makes the ethical system work. For this reason, we would choose in the original position to make mistreatment of some sorts of animals wrong in general (not just wrong in the cases with public impact), even though animals are not themselves parties in the original position. Thus it makes sense that it is those animals whose appearance and behavior are most like those of people that get the most consideration in our moral scheme.

It is because of "coherence of attitudes," I think, that the similarity of a fetus to a baby is very significant. A fetus one week before birth is so much like a newborn baby in our psychological space that we cannot allow any cavalier treatment of the former while expecting full sympathy and nurturative support for the latter. Thus, I think that anti-abortion forces are indeed giving their strongest arguments when they point to the similarities between a fetus and a baby, and when they try to evoke our emotional attachment to and sympathy for the fetus. An early horror story from New York about nurses who were expected to alternate between caring for six-week premature infants and disposing of viable 24-week aborted fetuses is just that—a horror story. These beings are so much alike that no one can be asked to draw a distinction and treat them so very differently.

Remember, however, that in the early weeks after conception, a fetus is very much unlike a person. It is hard to develop these feelings for a set of genes which doesn't yet have a head, hands, beating heart, response to touch or the ability to move by itself. Thus it seems to me that the alleged "slippery slope" between conception and birth is not so very slippery. In the early stages of pregnancy, abortion can hardly be compared to murder for psychological reasons, but in the latest stages it is psychologically akin to murder.

Another source of similarity is the bodily continuity between fetus and adult. Bodies play a surprisingly central role in our attitudes toward persons. One has only to think of the philosophical literature on how far physical identity suffices for personal identity or Wittgenstein's remark that the best picture of the human soul is the human body. Even after death, when all agree the body is no longer a person, we still observe elaborate customs of respect for the human body; like people who torture dogs, necrophiliacs are not to be trusted with people. So it is appropriate that we show respect to a fetus as the body continuous with the body of a person. This is a degree of resemblance to persons that animals cannot rival.

Michael Tooley also utilizes a parallel with animals. He claims that it is always permissible to drown newborn kittens and draws conclusions about infanticide. But it is only permissible to drown kittens when their survival would cause some hardship. Perhaps it would be a burden to feed and house six more cats or to find other homes for them. The alternative of letting them starve produces even more suffering than the drowning. Since the kittens get their rights secondhand, so to speak, *via* the need for coherence in our attitudes, their interests are often overridden by the interests of fullfledged persons. But if their survival would be no inconvenience to people at all, then it is wrong to drown them, *contra* Tooley.

Tooley's conclusions about abortion are wrong for the same reason. Even if a fetus is not a person, abortion is not always permissible, because of the resemblance of a fetus to a person. I agree with Thomson that it would be wrong for a woman who is seven months pregnant to have an abortion just to avoid having to postpone a trip to Europe. In the early months of pregnancy when the fetus hardly resembles a baby at all, then, abortion is permissible whenever it is in the interests of the pregnant woman or her family. The reasons would only need to outweigh the pain and inconvenience of the abortion itself. In the middle months, when the fetus comes to resemble a person, abortion would be justifiable only when the continuation of the pregnancy or the birth of the child would cause harms—physical, psychological, economic or social—to the woman. In the late months of pregnancy, even on our current assumption that a fetus is not a person, abortion seems to be wrong except to save a woman from significant injury or death.

The Supreme Court has recognized similar gradations in the alleged slippery slope stretching between conception and birth. To this point, the present paper has been a discussion of the moral status of abortion only, not its legal status. In view of the great physical, financial and sometimes psychological costs of abortion, perhaps the legal arrangement most compatible with the proposed moral solution would be the absence of restrictions, that is, so-called abortion "on demand."

So I conclude, first, that application of our concept of a person will not suffice to settle the abortion issue. After all, the biological development of a human being is gradual. Second, whether a fetus is a person or not, abortion is justifiable early in pregnancy to avoid modest harms and seldom justifiable late in pregnancy except to avoid significant injury or death.

DON MARQUIS

Why Abortion Is Immoral

Don Marquis is Associate Professor of Philosophy at the University of Kansas. (Source: Reprinted from The Journal of Philosophy *LXXXVI, 4 (April 1989): 183–202, with permission of the author and* The Journal of Philosophy.

QUESTIONS FOR REFLECTION

1. Marquis argues that usual anti-abortion and pro-choice arguments have symmetric problems and so are at a standoff. Review his reasoning. Do you agree?
2. Why, according to Marquis, is it wrong to kill an adult human being?
3. Marquis argues that it is wrong to kill a fetus for just the same reason that it is wrong to kill an adult. How does his argument go? Do you find it convincing?
4. Marquis compares his argument to one for the wrongness of the wanton infliction of pain on animals. Do you find the arguments analogous?
5. What are the discontinuation and desire accounts? Why does Marquis reject them?

The view that abortion is, with rare exceptions, seriously immoral has received little support in the recent philosophical literature. No doubt most philosophers affiliated with secular institutions of higher education believe that the anti-abortion position is either a symptom of irrational religious dogma or a conclusion generated by seriously confused philosophical argument. The purpose of this essay is to undermine this general belief. This essay sets out an argument that purports to show, as well as any argument in ethics can show, that abortion is, except possibly in rare cases, seriously immoral, that it is in the same moral category as killing an innocent adult human being.

The argument is based on a major assumption. Many of the most insightful and careful writers on the ethics of abortion—such as Joel Feinberg, Michael Tooley, Mary Anne Warren, H. Tristram Engelhardt, Jr., L. W. Sumner, John T. Noonan, Jr., and Philip Devine—believe that whether or not abortion is morally permissible stands or falls on whether or not a fetus is the sort of being whose life it is seriously wrong to end. The argument of this essay will assume, but not argue, that they are correct.

Also, this essay will neglect issues of great importance to a complete ethics of abortion. Some anti-abortionists will allow that certain abortions, such as abortion before implantation or abortion when the life of a woman is threatened by a pregnancy or abortion after rape, may be morally permissible. This essay will not explore the casuistry of these hard cases. The purpose of this essay is to develop a general argument for the claim that the overwhelming majority of deliberate abortions are seriously immoral.

I

A sketch of standard anti-abortion and pro-choice arguments exhibits how those arguments possess certain symmetries that explain why partisans of those positions are so convinced of the correctness of their own positions, why they are not successful in convincing their opponents, and why, to others, this issue seems to be unresolvable. An analysis of the nature of this standoff suggests a strategy for surmounting it.

Consider the way a typical anti-abortionist argues. She will argue or assert that life is present from the moment of conception or that fetuses look like babies or that fetuses possess a characteristic such as a genetic code that is both necessary and sufficient for being human. Anti-abortionists seem to believe that (1) the truth of all of these claims is quite obvious, and (2) establishing any of these claims is sufficient to show that abortion is morally akin to murder.

A standard pro-choice strategy exhibits similarities. The pro-choicer will argue or assert that fetuses are not persons or that fetuses are not rational agents or that fetuses are not social beings. Pro-choicers seem to believe that (1) the truth of any of these claims is quite obvious, and (2) establishing any of these claims is sufficient to show that an abortion is not a wrongful killing.

In fact, both the pro-choice and the anti-abortion claims do seem to be true, although the "it looks like a baby" claim is more difficult to establish the earlier the pregnancy. We seem to have a standoff. How can it be resolved?

As everyone who has taken a bit of logic knows, if any of these arguments concerning abortion is a good argument, it requires not only some claim characterizing fetuses, but also some general moral principle that ties a characteristic of fetuses to having or not having the right to life or to some other moral characteristic that will generate the obligation or the lack of obligation not to end the life of a fetus. Accordingly, the arguments of the anti-abortionist and the pro-choicer need a bit of filling in to be regarded as adequate.

Note what each partisan will say. The anti-abortionist will claim that her position is supported by such generally accepted moral principles as "It is always prima facie seriously wrong to take a human life" or "It is always prima facie seriously wrong to end the life of a baby." Since these are generally accepted moral principles, her position is certainly not obviously wrong. The pro-choicer will claim that her position is supported by such plausible moral principles as "Being a person is what gives an individual intrinsic moral worth" or "It is only seriously prima facie wrong to take the life of a member of the human community." Since these are generally accepted moral principles, the pro-choice position is certainly not obviously wrong. Unfortunately, we have again arrived at a standoff.

Now, how might one deal with this standoff? The standard approach is to try to show how the moral principles of one's opponent lose their plausibility under analysis. It is easy to see how this is possible. On the one hand, the anti-abortionist will defend a moral principle concerning the wrongness of killing which tends to be broad in scope in order that even fetuses at an early stage of pregnancy will fall under it. The problem with broad principles is that they often embrace too much. In this particular instance, the principle "It is always prima facie wrong to take a human life" seems to entail that it is wrong to end the existence of a living human cancer-cell culture, on the grounds that the culture is both living and human. Therefore, it seems that the anti-abortionist's favored principle is too broad.

On the other hand, the pro-choicer wants to find a moral principle concerning the wrongness of killing which tends to be narrow in scope in order that fetuses will *not* fall under it. The problem with narrow principles is that they often do not embrace enough. Hence, the needed principles such as "It is prima facie seriously wrong to kill only persons" or "It is prima facie wrong to kill only rational agents" do not explain why it is wrong to kill infants or young children or the severely retarded or even perhaps the severely mentally ill. Therefore, we seem again to have a standoff. The anti-abortionist charges, not unreasonably, that pro-choice principles concerning killing are too narrow to be acceptable; the pro-choicer charges, not unreasonably, that anti-abortionist principles concerning killing are too broad to be acceptable.

Attempts by both sides to patch up the difficulties in their positions run into further difficulties. The anti-abortionist will try to remove the problem in her position by reformulating her principle concerning killing in terms of human beings. Now we end up with: "It is always prima facie seriously wrong to end the life of a human being." This principle has the advantage of avoiding the problem of the human cancer-cell culture counterexample. But this advantage is purchased at a high price. For although it is clear that a fetus is both human and alive, it is not at all clear that a fetus is a human *being*. There is at least something to be said for the view that something becomes a human being only after a process of development, and that therefore first trimester fetuses and perhaps all fetuses are not yet human beings. Hence, the anti-abortionist, by this move, has merely exchanged one problem for another.

The pro-choicer fares no better. She may attempt to find reasons why killing infants, young children, and the severely retarded is wrong which are independent of her major principle that is supposed to explain the wrongness of taking human life, but which will not also make abortion immoral. This is no easy task. Appeals to social utility will seem satisfactory only to those who resolve not to think of the enormous difficulties with a utilitarian account of the wrongness of killing and the significant social costs of preserving the lives of the unproductive. A pro-choice strategy that extends the definition of "person" to infants or even to young children seems just as arbitrary as an anti-abortion strategy that extends the definition of "human being" to fetuses. Again, we find symmetries in the two positions and we arrive at a standoff.

There are even further problems that reflect symmetries in the two positions. In addition to counterexample problems, or the arbitrary application problems that can be exchanged for them, the standard anti-abortionist principle "It is prima facie seriously wrong to kill a human being," or one of its variants, can be objected to on the grounds of ambiguity. If "human being" is taken to be a *biological* category, then the anti-abortionist is left with the problem of explaining why a merely biological category should make a moral difference. Why, it is asked, is it any more reasonable to base a moral conclusion on the number of chromosomes in one's cells than on the color of one's skin? If "human being," on the other hand, is taken to be a *moral* category, then the claim that a fetus is a human being cannot be taken to be a premise in the anti-abortion argument, for it is precisely what needs to be established. Hence, either the anti-abortionist's main category is a morally irrelevant, merely biological category, or it is of no use to the anti-abortionist in establishing (noncircularly, of course) that abortion is wrong.

Although this problem with the anti-abortionist position is often noticed, it is less often noticed that the pro-choice position suffers from an analogous problem. The principle "Only persons have the right to life" also suffers from an ambiguity. The term "person" is typically defined in terms of psychological characteristics, although there will certainly be disagreement concerning which characteristics are most important. Supposing that this matter can be settled, the pro-choicer is left with the problem of explaining why *psychological* characteristics should make a *moral* difference. If the pro-choicer should attempt to deal with this problem by claiming that an explanation is not necessary, that in fact we do treat such a cluster of psychological properties as having moral significance, the sharp-witted anti-abortionist should have a ready response. We do treat being both living and human as having moral significance. If it is legitimate for the pro-choicer to demand that the anti-abortionist provide an explanation of the connection between the biological character of being a human being and the wrongness of being killed (even though people accept this connection), then it is legitimate for the anti-abortionist to demand that the pro-choicer provide an explanation of the connection between psychological criteria for being a person and the wrongness of being killed (even though that connection is accepted).

Feinberg has attempted to meet this objection (he calls psychological personhood "commonsense personhood"):

> The characteristics that confer commonsense personhood are not arbitrary bases for rights and duties, such as race, sex or species membership; rather they are traits that make sense out of rights and duties and without which those moral attributes would have no point or function. It is because people are conscious; have a sense of their personal identities; have plans, goals, and projects; experience emotions; are liable to pains, anxieties, and frustrations; can reason and bargain, and so on—it is because of these attributes that people have values and interests, desires and expectations of their own, including a stake in their own futures, and a personal well-being of a sort we cannot ascribe to unconscious or nonrational beings. Because of their developed capacities they can assume duties and responsibilities and can have and make claims on one another. Only because of their sense of self, their life plans, their value hierarchies, and their stakes in their own futures can they be ascribed fundamental rights. There is nothing arbitrary about these linkages.

The plausible aspects of this attempt should not be taken to obscure its implausible features. There is a great deal to be said for the view that being a psychological person under some description is a necessary condition for having duties. One cannot have a duty unless one is capable of behaving morally, and a being's capability of behaving morally will require having a certain psychology. It is far from obvious, however, that having rights entails consciousness or rationality, as Feinberg suggests. We speak of the rights of the severely retarded or the severely mentally ill, yet some of these persons are not rational. We speak of the rights of the temporarily unconscious. The New Jersey Supreme Court based their decision in the Quinlan case on Karen Ann Quinlan's right to privacy, and she was known to be permanently unconscious at that time. Hence, Feinberg's claim that having rights entails being conscious is, on its face, obviously false.

Of course, it might not make sense to attribute rights to a being that would never in its natural history have certain psychological traits. This modest connection between psychological personhood and moral personhood will create a place for Karen Ann Quinlan and the temporarily unconscious. But then it makes a place for fetuses also. Hence, it does not serve Feinberg's pro-choice purposes. Accordingly, it seems that the pro-choicer will have as much difficulty bridging the gap between psychological personhood and personhood in the moral sense as the anti-abortionist has bridging the gap between being a biological human being and being a human being in the moral sense.

Furthermore, the pro-choicer cannot any more escape her problem by making person a purely moral category than the anti-abortionist could escape by the analogous move. For if person is a moral category, then the pro-choicer is left without the resources for establishing (noncircularly, of course) the claim that a fetus is not a person, which is an essential premise in her argument. Again, we have both a symmetry and a standoff between pro-choice and anti-abortion views.

Passions in the abortion debate run high. There are both plausibilities and difficulties with the standard positions. Accordingly, it is hardly surprising that partisans of either side embrace with fervor the moral generalizations that support the conclusions they preanalytically favor, and reject with disdain the moral generalizations of their opponents as being subject to inescapable difficulties. It is easy to believe that the counterexamples to one's own moral principles are merely temporary difficulties that will dissolve in the wake of further philosophical research, and that the counterexamples to the principles of one's opponents are as straightforward as the contradiction between *A* and *O* propositions in traditional logic. This might suggest to an impartial observer (if there are any) that the abortion issue is unresolvable.

There is a way out of this apparent dialectical quandary. The moral generalizations of both sides are not quite correct. The generalizations hold for the most part, for the usual cases. This suggests that they are all *accidental* generalizations, that the moral claims made by those on both sides of the dispute do not touch on the *essence* of the matter.

This use of the distinction between essence and accident is not meant to invoke obscure metaphysical categories. Rather, it is intended to reflect the rather atheoretical nature of the abortion discussion. If the generalization a partisan in the abortion dispute adopts were derived from the reason why ending the life of a human being is wrong, then there could not be exceptions to that generalization unless some special case obtains in which there are even more powerful countervailing reasons. Such generalizations would not be merely accidental generalizations; they would point to, or be based upon, the essence of the wrongness of killing, what it is that makes killing wrong. All this suggests that a necessary condition of resolving the abortion controversy is a more theoretical account of the wrongness of killing. After all, if we merely believe, but do not understand, why killing adult human beings such as ourselves is wrong, how could we conceivably show that abortion is either immoral or permissible?

II

In order to develop such an account, we can start from the following unproblematic assumption concerning our own case: it is wrong to kill us. Why is it wrong? Some answers can be easily eliminated. It might be said that what makes killing us wrong is that a killing brutalizes the one who kills. But the brutalization consists of being inured to the performance of an act that is hideously immoral; hence, the brutalization does not explain the immorality. It might be said that what makes killing us wrong is the great loss others would experience due to our absence. Although such hubris is understandable, such an explanation does not account for the wrongness of killing hermits, or those whose lives are relatively independent and whose friends find it easy to make new friends.

A more obvious answer is better. What primarily makes killing wrong is neither its effect on the murderer nor its effect on the victim's friends and relatives, but its effect on the victim. The loss of one's life is one of the greatest losses one can suffer. The loss of one's life deprives one of all the experiences, activities, projects, and enjoyments that would otherwise have constituted one's future. Therefore, killing someone is wrong, primarily because the killing inflicts (one of) the greatest possible losses on the victim. To describe this as the loss of life can be misleading, however. The change in my biological state does not by itself make killing me wrong. The effect of the loss of my biological life is the loss to me of all those activities, projects, experiences, and enjoyments which would otherwise have constituted my future personal life. These activities, projects, experiences, and enjoyments are either valuable for their own sakes or are means to something else that is valuable for its own sake. Some parts of my future are not valued by me now, but will come to be valued by me as I grow older and as my values and capacities change. When I am killed, I am deprived both of what I now value which would have been part of my future personal life, but also what I would come to value. Therefore, when I die, I am deprived of all of the value of my future. Inflicting this loss on me is ultimately what makes killing me wrong. This being the case, it would seem that what makes killing *any* adult human being prima facie seriously wrong is the loss of his or her future.

How should this rudimentary theory of the wrongness of killing be evaluated? It cannot be faulted for deriving an "ought" from an "is," for it does not. The analysis assumes that killing me (or you, reader) is prima facie seriously wrong. The point of the analysis is to establish which natural property ultimately explains the wrongness of the killing, given that it is wrong. A natural property will ultimately explain the wrongness of killing, only if (1) the explanation fits with our intuitions about the matter and (2) there is no other natural property that provides the basis for a better explanation of the wrongness of killing. This analysis rests on the intuition that what makes killing a particular human or animal wrong is what it does to that particular human or animal. What makes killing wrong is some natural effect or other of the killing. Some would deny this. For instance, a divine-command theorist in ethics would deny it. Surely this denial is, however, one of those features of divine-command theory which renders it so implausible.

The claim that what makes killing wrong is the loss of the victim's future is directly supported by two considerations. In the first place, this theory explains why we regard killing as one of the worst of crimes. Killing is especially wrong, because it deprives the victim of more than perhaps any other crime. In the second place, people with AIDS or cancer who know they are dying believe, of course, that dying is a very bad thing for them. They believe that the loss of a future to them that they would otherwise have experienced is what makes their premature death a very bad thing for them. A better theory of the wrongness of killing would require a different natural property associated with killing which better fits with the attitudes of the dying. What could it be?

The view that what makes killing wrong is the loss to the victim of the value of the victim's future gains additional support when some of its implications are examined. In the first place, it is incompatible with the view that it is wrong to kill only beings who are biologically human. It is possible that there exists a different species from another planet whose members have a future like ours. Since having a future like that is what makes killing someone wrong, this theory entails that it would be wrong to kill members of such a species. Hence, this theory is opposed to the claim that only life that is biologically human has great moral worth, a claim which many anti-abortionists have seemed to adopt. This opposition, which this theory has in common with personhood theories, seems to be a merit of the theory.

In the second place, the claim that the loss of one's future is the wrong-making feature of one's being killed entails the possibility that the futures of some actual nonhuman mammals on our own planet are sufficiently like ours that it is seriously wrong to kill them also. Whether some animals do have the same right to life as human beings depends on adding to the account of the wrongness of killing some additional account of just what it is about my future or the futures of other adult human beings which makes it wrong to kill us. No such additional account will be offered in this essay. Undoubtedly, the provision of such an account would be a very difficult matter. Undoubtedly, any such account would be quite controversial. Hence, it surely should not reflect badly on this sketch of an elementary theory of the wrongness of killing that it is indeterminate with respect to some very difficult issues regarding animal rights.

In the third place, the claim that the loss of one's future is the wrong-making feature of one's being killed does not entail, as sanctity of human life theories do, that active euthanasia is wrong. Persons who are severely and incurably ill, who face a future of pain and despair, and who wish to die will not have suffered a loss if they are killed. It is, strictly speaking, the value of a human's future which makes killing wrong in this theory. This being so, killing does not necessarily wrong some persons who are sick and dying. Of course, there may be other reasons for a prohibition of active euthanasia, but that is another matter. Sanctity-of-human-life theories seem to hold that active euthanasia is seriously wrong even in an individual case where there seems to be good reason for it independently of public policy considerations. This consequence is most implausible, and it is a plus for the claim that the loss of a future of value is what makes killing wrong that it does not share this consequence.

In the fourth place, the account of the wrongness of killing defended in this essay does straightforwardly entail that it is prima facie seriously wrong to kill children and infants, for we do presume that they have futures of value. Since we do believe that it is wrong to kill defenseless little babies, it is important that a theory of the wrongness of killing easily account for this. Personhood theories of the wrongness of killing, on the other hand, cannot straightforwardly account for the wrongness of killing infants and young children. Hence, such theories must add special ad hoc accounts of the wrongness of killing the young. The plausibility of such ad hoc theories seems to be a function of how desperately one wants such theories to work. The claim that the primary wrong-making feature of a killing is the loss to the victim of the value of its future accounts for the wrongness of killing young children and infants directly; it makes the wrongness of such acts as obvious as we actually think it is. This is a further merit of this theory. Accordingly, it seems that this value of a future-like-ours theory of the wrongness of killing shares strengths of both sanctity-of-life and personhood accounts while avoiding weaknesses of both. In addition, it meshes with a central intuition concerning what makes killing wrong.

The claim that the primary wrong-making feature of a killing is the loss to the victim of the value of its future has obvious consequences for the ethics of abortion. The future of a standard fetus includes a set of experiences, projects, activities, and such which are identical with the futures of adult human beings and are identical with the futures of young children. Since the reason that is sufficient to explain why it is wrong to kill human beings after the time of birth is a reason that also applies to fetuses, it follows that abortion is prima facie seriously morally wrong.

This argument does not rely on the invalid inference that, since it is wrong to kill persons, it is wrong to kill potential persons also. The category that is morally central to this analysis is the category of having a valuable future like ours; it is not the category of personhood. The argument to the conclusion that abortion is prima facie seriously morally wrong proceeded independently of the notion of person or potential person or any equivalent. Someone may wish to start with this analysis in terms of the value of a human future, conclude that abortion is, except perhaps in rare circumstances, seriously morally wrong, infer that fetuses have the right to life, and then call fetuses "persons" as a result of their having the right to life. Clearly, in this case, the category of person is being used to state the *conclusion* of the analysis rather than to generate the *argument* of the analysis.

The structure of this anti-abortion argument can be both illuminated and defended by comparing it to what appears to be the best argument for the wrongness of the wanton infliction of pain on animals. This latter argument is based on the assumption that it is prima facie wrong to inflict pain on me (or you, reader). What is the natural property associated with the infliction of pain which makes such infliction wrong? The obvious answer seems to be that the infliction of pain causes suffering and that suffering is a misfortune. The suffering caused by the infliction of pain is what makes the wanton infliction of pain on me wrong. The wanton infliction of pain on other adult humans causes suffering. The wanton infliction of pain on animals causes suffering. Since causing suffering is what makes the wanton infliction of pain wrong and since the wanton infliction of pain on animals causes suffering, it follows that the wanton infliction of pain on animals is wrong.

This argument for the wrongness of the wanton infliction of pain on animals shares a number of structural features with the argument for the serious prima facie wrongness of abortion. Both arguments start with an obvious assumption concerning what it is wrong to do to me (or you, reader). Both then look for the characteristic or the consequence of the wrong action which makes the action wrong. Both recognize that the wrong-making feature of these immoral actions is a property of actions sometimes directed at individuals other than postnatal human beings. If the structure of the argument for the wrongness of the wanton infliction of pain on animals is sound, then the structure of the argument for the prima facie serious wrongness of abortion is also sound, for the structure of the two arguments is the same. The structure common to both is the key to the explanation of how the wrongness of abortion can be demonstrated without recourse to the category of person. In neither argument is that category crucial.

This defense of an argument for the wrongness of abortion in terms of a structurally similar argument for the wrongness of the wanton infliction of pain on animals succeeds only if the account regarding animals is the correct account. Is it? In the first place, it seems plausible. In the second place, its major competition is Kant's account. Kant believed that we do not have direct duties to animals at all, because they are not persons. Hence, Kant had to explain and justify the wrongness of inflicting pain on animals on the grounds that "he who is hard in his dealings with animals becomes hard also in his dealing with men." The problem with Kant's account is that there seems to be no reason for accepting this latter claim unless Kant's account is rejected. If the alternative to Kant's account is accepted, then it is easy to understand why someone who is indifferent to inflicting pain on animals is also indifferent to inflicting pain on humans, for one is indifferent to what makes inflicting pain wrong in both cases. But, if Kant's account is accepted, there is no intelligible reason why one who is hard in his dealings with animals (or crabgrass or stones) should also be hard in his dealings with men. After all, men are persons: animals are no more persons than crabgrass or stones. Persons are Kant's crucial moral category. Why, in short, should a Kantian accept the basic claim in Kant's argument?

Hence, Kant's argument for the wrongness of inflicting pain on animals rests on a claim that, in a world of Kantian moral agents, is demonstrably false. Therefore, the alternative analysis, being more plausible anyway, should be accepted. Since this alternative analysis has the same structure as the anti-abortion argument being defended here, we have further support for the argument for the immorality of abortion being defended in this essay.

Of course, this value of a future-like-ours argument, if sound, shows only that abortion is prima facie wrong, not that it is wrong in any and all circumstances. Since the loss of the future to a standard fetus, if killed, is, however, at least as great a loss as the loss of the future to a standard adult human being who is killed, abortion, like ordinary killing, could be justified only by the most compelling reasons. The loss of one's life is almost the greatest misfortune that can happen to one. Presumably abortion could be justified in some circumstances, only if the loss consequent on failing to abort would be at least as great. Accordingly, morally permissible abortions will be rare indeed unless, perhaps, they occur so early in pregnancy that a fetus is not yet definitely an individual. Hence, this argument should be taken as showing that abortion is presumptively very seriously wrong, where the presumption is very strong—as strong as the presumption that killing another adult human being is wrong.

III

How complete an account of the wrongness of killing does the value of a future-like-ours account have to be in order that the wrongness of abortion is a consequence? This account does not have to be an account of the necessary conditions for the wrongness of killing. Some persons in nursing homes may lack valuable human futures, yet it may be wrong to kill them for other reasons. Furthermore, this account does not obviously have to be the sole reason killing is wrong where the victim did have a valuable future. This analysis claims only that, for any killing where the victim did have a valuable future like ours, having that future by itself is sufficient to create the strong presumption that the killing is seriously wrong.

One way to overturn the value of a future-like-ours argument would be to find some account of the wrongness of killing which is at least as intelligible and which has different implications for the ethics of abortion. Two rival accounts possess at least some degree of plausibility. One account is based on the obvious fact that people value the experience of living and wish for that valuable experience to continue. Therefore, it might be said, what makes killing wrong is the discontinuation of that experience for the victim. Let us call this the *discontinuation account*. Another rival account is based upon the obvious fact that people strongly desire to continue to live. This suggests that what makes killing us so wrong is that it interferes with the fulfillment of a strong and fundamental desire, the fulfillment of which is necessary for the fulfillment of any other desires we might have. Let us call this the *desire account*.

Consider first the desire account as a rival account of the ethics of killing which would provide the basis for rejecting the anti-abortion position. Such an account will have to be stronger than the value of a future-like-ours account of the wrongness of abortion if it is to do the job expected of it. To entail the wrongness of abortion, the value of a future-like-ours account has only to provide a sufficient, but not a necessary, condition for the wrongness of killing. The desire account, on the other hand, must provide us also with a necessary condition for the wrongness of killing in order to generate a pro-choice conclusion on abortion. The reason for this is that presumably the argument from the desire account moves from the claim that what makes killing wrong is interference with a very strong desire to the claim that abortion is not wrong because the fetus lacks a strong desire to live. Obviously, this inference fails if someone's having the desire to live is not a necessary condition of its being wrong to kill that individual.

One problem with the desire account is that we do regard it as seriously wrong to kill persons who have little desire to live or who have no desire to live or, indeed, have a desire not to live. We believe it is seriously wrong to kill the unconscious, the sleeping, those who are tired of life, and those who are suicidal. The value-of-a-human-future account renders standard morality intelligible in these cases; these cases appear to be incompatible with the desire account.

The desire account is subject to a deeper difficulty. We desire life, because we value the goods of this life. The goodness of life is not secondary to our desire for it. If this were not so, the pain of one's own premature death could be done away with merely by an appropriate alteration in the configuration of one's desires. This is absurd. Hence, it would seem that it is the loss of the goods of one's future, not the interference with the fulfillment of a strong desire to live, which accounts ultimately for the wrongness of killing.

It is worth noting that, if the desire account is modified so that it does not provide a necessary, but only a sufficient, condition for the wrongness of killing, the desire account is compatible with the value of a future-like-ours account. The combined accounts will yield an anti-abortion ethic. This suggests that one can retain what is intuitively plausible about the desire account without a challenge to the basic argument of this paper.

It is also worth noting that, if future desires have moral force in a modified desire account of the wrongness of killing, one can find support for an anti-abortion ethic even in the absence of a value of a future-like-ours account. If one decides that a morally relevant property, the possession of which is sufficient to make it wrong to kill some individual, is the desire at some future time to live—one might decide to justify one's refusal to kill suicidal teenagers on these grounds, for example—then, since typical fetuses will have the desire in the future to live, it is wrong to kill typical fetuses. Accordingly, it does not seem that a desire account of the wrongness of killing can provide a justification of a pro-choice ethic of abortion which is nearly as adequate as the value of a human-future justification on an anti-abortion ethic.

The discontinuation account looks more promising as an account of the wrongness of killing. It seems just as intelligible as the value of a future-like-ours account, but it does not justify an anti-abortion position. Obviously, if it is the continuation of one's activities, experiences, and projects, the loss of which makes killing wrong, then it is not wrong to kill fetuses for that reason, for fetuses do not have experiences, activities, and projects to be continued or discontinued. Accordingly, the discontinuation account does not have the anti-abortion consequences that the value of a future-like-ours account has. Yet, it seems as intelligible as the value of a future-like-ours account, for when we think of what would be wrong with our being killed, it does seem as if it is the discontinuation of what makes our lives worthwhile which makes killing us wrong.

Is the discontinuation account just as good an account as the value of a future-like-ours account? The discontinuation account will not be adequate at all, if it does not refer to the *value* of the experience that may be discontinued. One does not want the discontinuation account to make it wrong to kill a patient who begs for death and who is in severe pain that cannot be relieved short of killing. (I leave open the question of whether it is wrong for other reasons.) Accordingly, the discontinuation account must be more than a bare discontinuation account. It must make some reference to the positive value of the patient's experiences. But, by the same token, the value of a future-like-ours account cannot be a bare future account either. Just having a future surely does not itself rule out killing the above patient. This account must make some reference to the value of the patient's future experiences and projects also. Hence, both accounts involve the value of experiences, projects, and activities. So far we still have symmetry between the accounts.

The symmetry fades, however, when we focus on the time period of the value of the experiences, etc., which has moral consequences. Although both accounts leave open the possibility that the patient in our example may be killed, this possibility is left open only in virtue of the utterly bleak future for the patient. It makes no difference whether the patient's immediate past contains intolerable pain, or consists in being in a coma (which we can imagine is a situation of indifference), or consists in a life of value. If the patient's future is a future of value, we want our account to make it wrong to kill the patient. If the patient's future is intolerable, whatever his or her immediate past, we want our account to allow killing the patient. Obviously, then, it is the value of that patient's future which is doing the work in rendering the morality of killing the patient intelligible.

This being the case, it seems clear that whether one has immediate past experiences or not does no work in the explanation of what makes killing wrong. The addition the discontinuation account makes to the value of a human future account is otiose. Its addition to the value-of-a-future account plays no role at all in rendering intelligible the wrongness of killing. Therefore, it can be discarded with the discontinuation account of which it is a part.

IV

The analysis of the previous section suggests that alternative general accounts of the wrongness of killing are either inadequate or unsuccessful in getting around the anti-abortion consequences of the value of a future-like-ours argument. A different strategy for avoiding these anti-abortion consequences involves limiting the scope of the value of a future argument. More precisely, the strategy involves arguing that fetuses lack a property that is essential for the value-of-a-future argument (or for any anti-abortion argument) to apply to them.

One move of this sort is based upon the claim that a necessary condition of one's future being valuable is that one values it. Value implies a valuer. Given this one might argue that, since fetuses cannot value their futures, their futures are not valuable to them. Hence, it does not seriously wrong them deliberately to end their lives.

This move fails, however, because of some ambiguities. Let us assume that something cannot be of value unless it is valued by someone. This does not entail that my life is of no value unless it is valued by me. I may think, in a period of despair, that my future is of no worth whatsoever, but I may be wrong because others rightly see value—even great value—in it. Furthermore, my future can be valuable to me even if I do not value it. This is the case when a young person attempts suicide, but is rescued and goes on to significant human achievements. Such young people's futures are ultimately valuable to them, even though such futures do not seem to be valuable to them at the moment of attempted suicide. A fetus's future can be valuable to it in the same way. Accordingly, this attempt to limit the anti-abortion argument fails.

Another similar attempt to reject the anti-abortion position is based on Tooley's claim that an entity cannot possess the right to life unless it has the capacity to desire its continued existence. It follows that, since fetuses lack the conceptual capacity to desire to continue to live, they lack the right to life. Accordingly, Tooley concludes that abortion cannot be seriously prima facie wrong. . . .

What could be the evidence for Tooley's basic claim? Tooley once argued that individuals have a prima facie right to what they desire and that the lack of the capacity to desire something undercuts the basis of one's right to it. . . . This argument plainly will not succeed in the context of the analysis of this essay, however, since the point here is to establish the fetus's right to life on other grounds. Tooley's argument assumes that the right to life cannot be established in general on some basis other than the desire for life. This position was considered and rejected in the preceding section of this paper.

One might attempt to defend Tooley's basic claim on the grounds that, because a fetus cannot apprehend continued life as a benefit, its continued life cannot be a benefit or cannot be something it has a right to or cannot be something that is in its interest. This might be defended in terms of the general proposition that, if an individual is literally incapable of caring about or taking an interest in some *X*, then one does not have a right to *X* or *X* is not a benefit or *X* is not something that is in one's interest.

Each member of this family of claims seems to be open to objections. As John C. Stevens has pointed out, one may have a right to be treated with a certain medical procedure (because of a health insurance policy one has purchased), even though one cannot conceive of the nature of the procedure. And, as Tooley himself has pointed out, persons who have been indoctrinated, or drugged, or rendered temporarily unconscious may be literally incapable of caring about or taking an interest in something that is in their interest or is something to which they have a right, or is something that benefits them. Hence, the Tooley claim that would restrict the scope of the value of a future-like-ours argument is undermined by counterexamples.

Finally, Paul Bassen has argued that, even though the prospects of an embryo might seem to be a basis for the wrongness of abortion, an embryo cannot be a victim and therefore cannot be wronged. An embryo cannot be a victim, he says, because it lacks sentience. His central argument for this seems to be that, even though plants and the permanently unconscious are alive, they clearly cannot be victims. What is the explanation of this? Bassen claims that the explanation is that their lives consist of mere metabolism and mere metabolism is not enough to ground victimizability. Mentation is required.

The problem with this attempt to establish the absence of victimizability is that both plants and the permanently unconscious clearly lack what Bassen calls "prospects" or what I have called "a future life like ours." Hence, it is surely open to one to argue that the real reason we believe plants and the permanently unconscious cannot be victims is that killing them cannot deprive them of a future life like ours; the real reason is not their absence of present mentation.

Bassen recognizes that his view is subject to this difficulty, and he recognizes that the case of children seems to support this difficulty, for "much of what we do for children is based on prospects." He argues, however, that, in the case of children and in other such cases, "potentiality comes into play only where victimizability has been secured on other grounds". . . .

Bassen's defense of his view is patently question-begging, since what is adequate to secure victimizability is exactly what is at issue. His examples do not support his own view against the thesis of this essay. Of course, embryos can be victims: when their lives are deliberately terminated, they are deprived of their futures of value, their prospects. This makes them victims, for it directly wrongs them.

The seeming plausibility of Bassen's view stems from the fact that paradigmatic cases of imagining someone as a victim involve empathy, and empathy requires mentation of the victim. The victims of flood, famine, rape, or child abuse are all persons with whom we can empathize. That empathy seems to be part of seeing them as victims.

In spite of the strength of these examples, the attractive intuition that a situation in which there is victimization requires the possibility of empathy is subject to counterexamples. Consider a case that Bassen himself offers: "Posthumous obliteration of an author's work constitutes a misfortune for him only if he had wished his work to endure". . . . The conditions Bassen wishes to impose upon the possibility of being victimized here seem far too strong. Perhaps this author, due to his unrealistic standards of excellence and his low self-esteem, regarded his work as unworthy of survival, even though it possessed genuine literary merit. Destruction of such work would surely victimize its author. In such a case, empathy with the victim concerning the loss is clearly impossible.

Of course, Bassen does not make the possibility of empathy a necessary condition of victimizability; he requires only mentation. Hence, on Bassen's actual view, this author, as I have described him, can be a victim. The problem is that the basic intuition that renders Bassen's view plausible is missing in the author's case. In order to attempt to avoid counterexamples, Bassen has made his thesis too weak to be supported by the intuitions that suggested it.

Even so, the mentation requirement on victimizability is still subject to counterexamples. Suppose a severe accident renders me totally unconscious for a month, after which I recover. Surely killing me while I am unconscious victimizes me, even though I am incapable of mentation during that time. It follows that Bassen's thesis fails. Apparently, attempts to restrict the value of a future-like-ours argument so that fetuses do not fall within its scope do not succeed.

V

In this essay, it has been argued that the correct ethic of the wrongness of killing can be extended to fetal life and used to show that there is a strong presumption that any abortion is morally impermissible. If the ethic of killing adopted here entails, however, that contraception is also seriously immoral, then there would appear to be a difficulty with the analysis of this essay.

But this analysis does not entail that contraception is wrong. Of course, contraception prevents the actualization of a possible future of value. Hence, it follows from the claim that futures of value should be maximized that contraception is prima facie immoral. This obligation to maximize does not exist, however; furthermore, nothing in the ethics of killing in this paper entails that it does. The ethics of killing in this essay would entail that contraception is wrong only if something were denied a human future of value by contraception. Nothing at all is denied such a future by contraception, however.

Candidates for a subject of harm by contraception fall into four categories: (1) some sperm or other, (2) some ovum or other, (3) a sperm and an ovum separately, and (4) a sperm and an ovum together. Assigning the harm to some sperm is utterly arbitrary, for no reason can be given for making a sperm the subject of harm rather than an ovum. Assigning the harm to some ovum is utterly arbitrary, for no reason can be given for making an ovum the subject of harm rather than a sperm. One might attempt to avoid these problems by insisting that contraception deprives both the sperm and the ovum separately of a valuable future like ours. On this alternative, too many futures are lost. Contraception was supposed to be wrong, because it deprived us of one future of value, not two. One might attempt to avoid this problem by holding that contraception deprives the combination of sperm and ovum of a valuable future like ours. But here the definite article misleads. At the time of contraception, there are hundreds of millions of sperm, one (released) ovum and millions of possible combinations of all of these. There is no actual combination at all. Is the subject of the loss to be a merely possible combination? Which one? This alternative does not yield an actual subject of harm either. Accordingly, the immorality of contraception is not entailed by the loss of a future-like-ours argument simply because there is no nonarbitrarily identifiable subject of the loss in the case of contraception.

VI

The purpose of this essay has been to set out an argument for the serious presumptive wrongness of abortion subject to the assumption that the moral permissibility of abortion stands or falls on the moral status of the fetus. Since a fetus possesses a property, the possession of which in adult human beings is sufficient to make killing an adult human being wrong, abortion is wrong. This way of dealing with the problem of abortion seems superior to other approaches to the ethics of abortion, because it rests on an ethics of killing which is close to self-evident, because the crucial morally relevent property clearly applies to fetuses, and because the argument avoids the usual equivocations on "human life," "human being," or "person." The argument rests neither on religious claims nor on Papal dogma. It is not subject to the objection of "speciesism." Its soundness is compatible with the moral permissibility of euthanasia and contraception. It deals with our intuitions concerning young children.

Finally, this analysis can be viewed as resolving a standard problem—indeed, *the* standard problem—concerning the ethics of abortion. Clearly, it is wrong to kill adult human beings. Clearly, it is not wrong to end the life of some arbitrarily chosen single human cell. Fetuses seem to be like arbitrarily chosen human cells in some respects and like adult humans in other respects. The problem of the ethics of abortion is the problem of determining the fetal property that settles this moral controversy. The thesis of this essay is that the problem of the ethics of abortion, so understood, is solvable.

Euthanasia

Euthanasia, or mercy killing, presents some very difficult and painful dilemmas for doctors, patients, family members, and moral philosophers. Sometimes a patient's condition is so poor and holds so little hope of future recovery that death seems better than life. Is it ever morally justifiable to allow such patients to die by withholding treatment that would otherwise be given? Is it ever justifiable to kill them?

Clearly, this topic concerns both rights and liberty. The patient has a right to life and perhaps a right to die. The patient may also have the liberty to make certain fundamental decisions about whether to continue treatment. Frequently, however, euthanasia becomes a serious issue only after the patient is comatose or otherwise incapable of making a competent decision. Moreover, many factors seem to be morally relevant to the decision between life and death. Is the patient conscious? Suffering? If so, how much? What are the prospects for improvement? Is the patient terminally ill? What kind of life can the patient hope to lead, and for how long? The course of action being contemplated may also matter: Cessation of "heroic" lifesaving efforts? Withdrawal of food and water? A lethal injection?

The Supreme Court of New Jersey, in a much-publicized case, decided in 1976 to allow the parents of Karen Ann Quinlan to remove her from a respirator. She was comatose and diagnosed as having no chance of regaining consciousness. The court decided that Quinlan's right of privacy gave her or her guardian the right to decide the course of her treatment, since a respirator, which might be deemed ordinary for a curable patient, should count as extraordinary for someone with her poor prognosis.

Eight years later, the Supreme Court of Missouri reached the opposite verdict in a related case. Nancy Cruzan, after an automobile accident, was "in a persistent vegetative state." She was nevertheless not terminally ill and not reliant on a respirator or other extraordinary machinery for support. However, she did require a feeding tube. Her guardians requested that fluids and nutrition be withdrawn. The court found no justification for granting that request, arguing that Cruzan's condition was significantly different from Quinlan's and that the relevant state interest is life, not the quality of life, as the *Quinlan* court seemed to suggest.

J. Gay-Williams argues that euthanasia is invariably wrong. It is, he contends, contrary to everyone's natural inclination to continue living. Moreover, it is extremely dangerous for several reasons. First, we can never know that death is really preferable to continued life. Second, people may choose death out of ignorance, a temporary feeling of hopelessness, or consideration for their families. Finally, euthanasia would lead to a lowered respect for life that could have serious consequences for medical care and society's treatment of the infirm.

James Rachels offers two arguments for the permissibility of euthanasia. First, he contends that mercy sometimes requires mercy killing. The pain involved in terminal illness may be so great that death is better than continued life. Second, he argues that the Golden Rule similarly indicates that euthanasia is sometimes acceptable, for we would be willing to be killed to escape extreme pain.

Carlos Gomez raises some doubts based on experience with euthanasia in the Netherlands. If euthanasia is to be permitted, it should surely be allowed only under certain circumstances—when the patient is terminal, suffers great pain, has no hope of recovery or even remission, gives consent, and so on—to prevent its abuse. Gomez finds that, in practice, the Dutch guidelines are rarely observed. Patients are euthanized, he finds, when they are severely injured but unconscious, or suffer birth defects, or are merely bored with living and tired of fighting disease. He suggests reasons why it is difficult to enforce any guidelines concerning mercy killing, even when they are philosophically justified and backed by the power of law.

Matter of Quinlan (1976)

(*Source:* Matter of Quinlan *70 N.J. 10, 355 A. 2d. 647 [1976]. Most legal references have been omitted.*)

QUESTIONS FOR REFLECTION

1. Which features of Karen Ann Quinlan's condition did the court find relevant to reaching a decision? Do you agree that these are all the relevant factors?
2. How did the court justify its decision? Do you find the justification persuasive?
3. In fact, when Karen Ann Quinlan was disconnected from life-support machinery after this decision, she did not die. If the court had known she would survive without the equipment, would the justification the court offered be weakened?

The Litigation

The central figure in this tragic case is Karen Ann Quinlan, a New Jersey resident. At the age of 22, she lies in a debilitated and allegedly moribund state at Saint Clare's Hospital in Denville, New Jersey. The litigation has to do, in final analysis, with her life—its continuance or cessation—and the responsibilities, rights and duties, with regard to any fateful decision concerning it, of her family, her guardian, her doctors, the hospital, the State through its law enforcement authorities, and finally the courts of justice.

Due to extensive physical damage fully described in the able opinion of the trial judge, Judge Muir, supporting that judgment, Karen allegedly was incompetent. Joseph Quinlan sought the adjudication of that incompetency. He wished to be appointed guardian of the person and property of his daughter. It was proposed by him that such letters of guardianship, if granted, should contain an express power to him as guardian to authorize the discontinuance of all extraordinary medical procedures now allegedly sustaining Karen's vital processes and hence her life, since these measures, he asserted, present no hope of her eventual recovery. A guardian *ad litem* was appointed by Judge Muir to represent the interest of the alleged incompetent.

The Factual Base

On the night of April 15, 1975, for reasons still unclear, Karen Quinlan ceased breathing for at least two 15 minute periods. She received some ineffectual mouth-to-mouth resuscitation from friends. She was taken by ambulance to Newton Memorial Hospital. There she had a temperature of 100 degrees, her pupils were unreactive and she was unresponsive even to deep pain. The history at the time of her admission to that hospital was essentially incomplete and uninformative.

Three days later, Dr. Morse examined Karen at the request of the Newton admitting physician, Dr. McGee. He found her comatose with evidence of decortication, a condition relating to derangement of the cortex of the brain causing a physical posture in which the upper extremities are flexed and the lower extremities are extended. She required a respirator to assist her breathing. Dr. Morse was unable to obtain an adequate account of the circumstances and events leading up to Karen's admission to the Newton Hospital. Such initial history or etiology is crucial in neurological diagnosis. Relying as he did upon the Newton Memorial records and his own examination, he concluded that prolonged lack of oxygen in the bloodstream, anoxia, was identified with her condition as he saw it upon first observation. When she was later transferred to Saint Clare's Hospital she was still unconscious, still on a respirator and a tracheotomy had been performed. On her arrival Dr. Morse conducted extensive and detailed examinations. An electroencephalogram (EEG) measuring electrical rhythm of the brain was performed and Dr. Morse characterized the result as "abnormal but it showed some activity and was consistent with her clinical state." Other significant neurological tests, including a brain scan, an angiogram, and a lumbar puncture were normal in result. Dr. Morse testified that Karen has been in a state of coma, lack of consciousness, since he began treating her. He explained that there are basically two types of coma, sleep-like unresponsiveness and awake unresponsiveness. Karen was originally in a sleep-like unresponsive condition but soon developed "sleep-wake" cycles, apparently a normal improvement for comatose patients occurring within three to four weeks. In the awake cycle she blinks, cries out and does things of that sort but is still totally unaware of anyone or anything around her.

Dr. Morse and other expert physicians who examined her characterized Karen as being in a "chronic persistent vegetative state." Dr. Fred Plum, one of such expert witnesses, defined this as a "subject who remains with the capacity to maintain the vegetative parts of neurological function but who . . . no longer has any cognitive function." . . .

It seemed to be the consensus not only of the treating physicians but also of the several qualified experts who testified in the case, that removal from the respirator would not conform to medical practices, standards and traditions.

The further medical consensus was that Karen in addition to being comatose is in a chronic and persistent "vegetative" state, having no awareness of anything or anyone around her and existing at a primitive reflex level. Although she does have some brain stem function (ineffective for respiration) and has other reactions one normally associates with being alive, such as moving, reacting to light, sound and noxious stimuli, blinking her eyes, and the like, the quality of her feeling impulses is unknown. She grimaces, makes stereotyped cries and sounds and has chewing motions. Her blood pressure is normal.

Karen is described as emaciated, having suffered a weight loss of at least 40 pounds, and undergoing a continuing deteriorative process. Her posture is described as fetal-like and grotesque; there is extreme flexion-rigidity of the arms, legs and related muscles and her joints are severely rigid and deformed.

From all of this evidence, and including the whole testimonial record, several basic findings in the physical area are mandated. Severe brain and associated damage, albeit of uncertain etiology, has left Karen in a chronic and persistent vegetative state. No form of treatment which can cure or improve that condition is known or available. As nearly as may be determined, considering the guarded area of remote uncertainties characteristic of most medical science predictions, she can *never* be restored to cognitive or sapient life. Even with regard to the vegetative level and improvement therein (if such it may be called) the prognosis is extremely poor and the extent unknown if it should in fact occur.

She is debilitated and moribund and although fairly stable at the time of argument before us (no new information having been filed in the meanwhile in expansion of the record), no physician risked the opinion that she could live more than a year and indeed she may die much earlier. Excellent medical and nursing care so far has been able to ward off the constant threat of infection, to which she is peculiarly susceptible because of the respirator, the tracheal tube and other incidents of care in her vulnerable condition. Her life accordingly is sustained by the respirator and tubal feeding, and removal from the respirator would cause her death soon, although the time cannot be stated with more precision.

It is from this factual base that the Court confronts and responds to three basic issues:

1. Was the trial court correct in denying the specific relief requested by plaintiff, i.e., authorization for termination of the life-supporting apparatus, on the case presented to him? Our determination on that question is in the affirmative.

2. Was the court correct in withholding letters of guardianship from the plaintiff and appointing in his stead a stranger? On that issue our determination is in the negative.

3. Should this Court, in the light of the foregoing conclusions, grant declaratory relief to the plaintiff? On that question our Court's determination is in the affirmative.

This brings us to a consideration of the constitutional and legal issues underlying the foregoing determinations.

Constitutional and Legal Issues

The Right of Privacy

It is the issue of the constitutional right of privacy that has given us most concern, in the exceptional circumstances of this case. Here a loving parent, *qua* parent and raising the rights of his incompetent and profoundly damaged daughter, probably irreversibly doomed to no more than a biologically vegetative remnant of life, is before the court. He seeks authorization to abandon specialized technological procedures which can only maintain for a time a body having no potential for resumption or continuance of other than a "vegetative" existence.

We have no doubt, in these unhappy circumstances, that if Karen were herself miraculously lucid for an interval (not altering the existing prognosis of the condition to which she would soon return) and perceptive of her irreversible condition, she could effectively decide upon discontinuance of the life-support apparatus, even if it meant the prospect of natural death. . . .

We have no hesitancy in deciding . . . that no external compelling interest of the State could compel Karen to endure the unendurable, only to vegetate a few measurable months with no realistic possibility of returning to any semblance of cognitive or sapient life. We perceive no thread of logic distinguishing between such a choice on Karen's part and a similar choice which, under the evidence in this case, could be made by a competent patient terminally ill, riddled by cancer and suffering great pain; such a patient would not be resuscitated or put on a respirator . . . and *a fortiori* would not be kept *against his will* on a respirator.

Although the Constitution does not explicitly mention a right of privacy, Supreme Court decisions have recognized that a right of personal privacy exists and that certain areas of privacy are guaranteed under the Constitution. . . .

The court in *Griswold* found the unwritten constitutional right of privacy to exist in the penumbra of specific guarantees of the Bill of Rights "formed by emanations from those guarantees that help give them life and substance." Presumably this right is broad enough to encompass a patient's decision to decline medical treatment under certain circumstances, in much the same way as it is broad enough to encompass a woman's decision to terminate pregnancy under certain conditions. . . .

The claimed interests of the State in this case are essentially the preservation and sanctity of human life and defense of the right of the physician to administer medical treatment according to his best judgment. In this case the doctors say that removing Karen from the respirator will conflict with their professional judgment. The plaintiff answers that Karen's present treatment serves only a maintenance function; that the respirator cannot cure or improve her condition but at best can only prolong her inevitable slow deterioration and death; and that the interests of the patient, as seen by her surrogate, the guardian, must be evaluated by the court as predominant, even in the face of an opinion *contra* by the present attending physicians. Plaintiff's distinction is significant. The nature of

Karen's care and the realistic chances of her recovery are quite unlike those of the patients discussed in many of the cases where treatments were ordered. In many of those cases the medical procedure required (usually a transfusion) constituted a minimal bodily invasion and the chances of recovery and return to functioning life were very good. We think that the State's interest *contra* weakens and the individual's right to privacy grows as the degree of bodily invasion increases and the prognosis dims. Ultimately there comes a point at which the individual's rights overcome the State interest. It is for that reason that we believe Karen's choice, if she were competent to make it, would be vindicated by the law. Her prognosis is extremely poor—she will never resume cognitive life. And the bodily invasion is very great—she requires 24 hour intensive nursing care, antibiotics, the assistance of a respirator, a catheter and feeding tube.

Our affirmation of Karen's independent right of choice, however, would ordinarily be based upon her competency to assert it. The sad truth, however, is that she is grossly incompetent and we cannot discern her supposed choice based on the testimony of her previous conversations with friends, where such testimony is without sufficient probative weight. . . . Nevertheless we have concluded that Karen's right of privacy may be asserted on her behalf by her guardian under the peculiar circumstances here present.

If a putative decision by Karen to permit this non-cognitive, vegetative existence to terminate by natural forces is regarded as a valuable incident of her right of privacy, as we believe it to be, then it should not be discarded solely on the basis that her condition prevents her conscious exercise of the choice. The only practical way to prevent destruction of the right is to permit the guardian and family of Karen to render their best judgment, subject to the qualifications hereinafter stated, as to whether she would exercise it in these circumstances. If their conclusion is in the affirmative this decision should be accepted by a society the overwhelming majority of whose members would, we think, in similar circumstances, exercise such a choice in the same way for themselves or for those closest to them. It is for this reason that we determine that Karen's right of privacy may be asserted in her behalf, in this respect, by her guardian and family under the particular circumstances presented by this record.

Regarding Mr. Quinlan's right of privacy, we agree with Judge Muir's conclusion that there is no parental constitutional right that would entitle him to a grant of relief *in propria persona*. . . . Insofar as a parental right of privacy has been recognized, it has been in the context of determining the rearing of infants and, as Judge Muir put it, involved "continuing life styles." . . . Karen Quinlan is a 22-year-old adult. Her right of privacy in respect of the matter before the court is to be vindicated by Mr. Quinlan as guardian, as hereinabove determined.

The Medical Factor

. . . We glean from the record here that physicians distinguish between curing the ill and comforting and easing the dying; that they refuse to treat the curable as if they were dying or ought to die, and that they have sometimes refused to treat the hopeless and dying as if they were curable. In this sense, as we were reminded by the testimony of Drs. Korein and Diamond, many of them have refused to inflict an undesired prolongation of the process of dying on a patient in irreversible condition when it is clear that such "therapy" offers neither human nor humane benefit. We think these attitudes represent a balanced implementation of a profoundly realistic perspective on the meaning of life and death and that they respect the whole Judeo-Christian tradition of regard for human life. No less would they seem consistent with the moral matrix of medicine, "to heal," very much in the sense of the endless mission of the law, "to do justice."

Yet this balance, we feel, is particularly difficult to perceive and apply in the context of the development by advanced technology of sophisticated and artificial life-sustaining devices. For those possibly curable, such devices are of great value, and, as ordinary medical procedures, are essential. Consequently, as pointed out by Dr. Diamond, they are necessary because of the ethic of medical practice. But in light of the situation in the present case (while the record here is somewhat hazy in distinguishing between "ordinary" and "extraordinary" measures), one would have to think that the use of the same respirator or life support could be considered "ordinary" in the context of the possibly curable patient but "extraordinary" in the context of the forced sustaining by cardiorespiratory processes of an irreversibly doomed patient. . . .

The evidence in this case convinces us that the focal point of decision should be the prognosis as to the reasonable possibility of return to cognitive and sapient life, as distinguished from the forced continuance of that biological vegetative existence to which Karen seems to be doomed.

In summary of the present Point of this opinion, we conclude that the state of the pertinent medical standards and practices which guided the attending physicians in this matter is not such as would justify this Court in deeming itself bound or controlled thereby in responding to the case for declaratory relief established by the parties on the record before us. . . .

Declaratory Relief

. . . [W]e herewith declare the following affirmative relief on behalf of the plaintiff. Upon the concurrence of the guardian and family of Karen, should the responsible attending physicians conclude that there is no reasonable possibility of Karen's ever emerging from her present comatose condition to a cognitive, sapient state and that the life-support apparatus now being administered to Karen should be discontinued, they shall consult with the hospital "Ethics Committee" or like body of the institution in which Karen is then hospitalized. If that consultative body agrees that there is no reasonable possibility of Karen's ever emerging from her present comatose condition to a cognitive, sapient state, the present life-support system may be withdrawn and said action shall be without any civil or criminal liability therefor on the part of any participant, whether guardian, physician, hospital or others. We herewith specifically so hold.

Cruzan v. *Harmon* (1984)

(Source: Cruzan v. Harmon *760 SW 2nd 408 [1984]. Most legal references have been omitted. This decision was upheld by the United States Supreme Court.)*

QUESTIONS FOR REFLECTION

1. Which features of Nancy Cruzan's condition did the court find relevant to reaching a decision? Do you agree that these are all the relevant factors?
2. How did the court justify its decision? Do you find the justification persuasive?
3. How does this case differ from that of Karen Ann Quinlan? Why does the court reject *Quinlan* as a guide?

. . . At 12:54 A.M., January 11, 1983, the Missouri Highway Patrol dispatched Trooper Dale Penn to the scene of a single car accident in Jasper County, Missouri. Penn arrived six minutes later to find Nancy Beth Cruzan lying face down in a ditch, approximately thirty-five feet from her overturned vehicle. The trooper examined Nancy and found her without detectable respiratory or cardiac function.

At 1:09 A.M., Paramedics Robert Williams and Rick Maynard arrived at the accident scene; they immediately initiated efforts to revive Nancy. By 1:12 A.M., cardiac function and spontaneous respiration had recommenced. The ambulance crew transported Nancy to the Freeman Hospital where exploratory surgery revealed a laceration of the liver. A CAT scan showed no significant abnormalities of her brain. The attending physician diagnosed a probable cerebral contusion compounded by significant anoxia (deprivation of oxygen) of unknown duration. The trial judge found that a deprivation of oxygen to the brain approaching six minutes would result in permanent brain damage; the best estimate of the period of Nancy's anoxia was twelve to fourteen minutes.

Nancy remained in a coma for approximately three weeks following the accident. Thereafter, she seemed to improve somewhat and was able to take nutrition orally. Rehabilitative efforts began. In order to assist her recovery and to ease the feeding process, a gastrostomy feeding tube was surgically implanted on February 7, 1983, with the consent of her (then) husband.

Over a substantial period of time, valiant efforts to rehabilitate Nancy took place, without success. She now lies in the Mount Vernon State Hospital. She receives the totality of her nutrition and hydration through the gastrostomy tube.

The trial court found that (1) her respiration and circulation are not artificially maintained and are within the normal limits of a thirty-year-old female; (2) she is "oblivious to her environment except for reflexive responses to sound and perhaps painful stimuli"; (3) she suffered anoxia of the brain resulting in a "massive enlargement of the ventricles filling with cerebrospinal fluid in the area where the brain has degenerated" and that "cerebral cortical atrophy is irreversible, permanent, progressive and ongoing"; (4) "her highest cognitive brain function is exhibited by her grimacing perhaps in recognition of ordinarily painful stimuli, indicating the experience of pain and apparent response to sound"; (5) she is a spastic quadriplegic; (6) her four extremities are contracted with irreversible muscular and tendon damage to all extremities; (7) "she has no cognitive or reflexive ability to swallow food or water to maintain her daily essential needs" and that "she will never recover her ability to swallow sufficient [sic] to satisfy her needs." In sum, Nancy is diagnosed as in a persistent vegetative state. She is not dead. She is not terminally ill. Medical experts testified that she could live another thirty years.

The trial court found that Nancy expressed, in "somewhat serious conversation" that if sick or injured she would not want to continue her life unless she could live "halfway normally." Based on this conversation, the trial court concluded that "she would not wish to continue with nutrition and hydration."

The court concluded that no state interest outweighed Nancy's "right to liberty" and that to deny Nancy's co-guardians authority to act under these circumstances would deprive Nancy of equal protection of the law. The court ordered state employees to "cause the request of the co-guardians to withdraw nutrition or hydration to be carried out."

As we said, this case presents a single issue for resolution: May a guardian order that food and water be withheld from an incompetent ward who is in a persistent vegetative state but who is otherwise alive . . . and not terminally ill? As the parties carefully pointed out in their thoughtful briefs, this issue is a broad one, invoking consideration of the authority of guardians of incompetent wards, the public policy of Missouri with regard to the termination of life-sustaining treatment and the amorphous mass of constitutional rights generally described as the "right to liberty," "the right to privacy," equal protection and due process.

This is also a case in which euphemisms readily find their way to the fore, perhaps to soften the reality of what is really at stake. But this is not a case in which we are asked to let someone die. Nancy is not dead. Nor is she terminally ill. This is a case in which we are asked to allow the medical profession to make Nancy die by starvation and dehydration. The debate here is thus not between life and death; it is between quality of life and death. We are asked to hold that the cost of maintaining Nancy's present life is too great when weighed against the benefit that life conveys both to Nancy and her loved ones and that she must die. . . .

The Right to Refuse Treatment

The common law recognizes the right of individual autonomy over decisions relating to one's health and welfare. From this root of autonomy, the common law developed the principle that a battery occurs when a physician performs a medical procedure without valid consent. . . . The doctrine of informed consent arose in recognition of the value society places on a person's autonomy and as the primary vehicle by which a person can protect the integrity of his body. If one can consent to treatment, one can also refuse it. Thus, as a necessary corollary to informed consent, the right to refuse treatment arose. "The patient's ability to control his bodily integrity . . . is significant only when one recognizes that this right also encompasses a right to informed refusal." . . .

A decision as to medical treatment must be informed.

> There are three basic prerequisites for informed consent: the patient must have the capacity to reason and make judgments, the decision must be made voluntarily and without coercion, and the patient must have a clear understanding of the risks and benefits of the proposed treatment alternatives or nontreatment, along with a full understanding of the nature of the disease and the prognosis.

. . . In the absence of these three elements, neither consent nor refusal can be informed. Thus, it is definitionally impossible for a person to make an informed decision—either to consent or to refuse—under hypothetical circumstances; under such circumstances, neither the benefits nor the risks of treatment can be properly weighed or fully appreciated.

The Right to Privacy

Quinlan, and cases which follow it, announce that a patient's right to refuse medical treatment also arises from a constitutional right of privacy. Although some courts find that right embedded in their state constitutions, the privacy argument is most often founded on decisions of the United States Supreme Court, primarily *Roe v. Wade,* . . . (1973). Unfortunately, the bare statement that the right of privacy extends to treatment decisions is seldom accompanied by any reasoned analysis as to the scope of that right or its application to the refusal of life-sustaining treatment.

. . . We . . . find no unfettered right of privacy under our constitution that would support the right of a person to refuse medical treatment in every circumstance.

If Nancy possesses such a right, it must be found to derive from the federal constitutional right to privacy announced by the United States Supreme Court. That Court "has recognized that a right of personal privacy, or a guarantee of certain areas or zones of privacy, does exist under the [United States] Constitution." . . . The Supreme Court has not, however, extended the right of privacy to permit a patient or her guardian to direct the withdrawal of food and water. We are left to determine for ourselves whether the penumbral right of privacy encompasses a right to refuse life-sustaining medical treatment.

Quinlan is the first case to apply a right of privacy to decisions regarding the termination of life-sustaining treatment. In deciding the applicability of the right to such determinations, *Quinlan* first cites *Griswold v. Connecticut,* . . . (1965), for the proposition that the right of privacy exists and, without further analysis states: "Presumably this right is broad enough to encompass a patient's decision to decline medical treatment under certain circumstances, in much the same way as it is broad enough to encompass a woman's decision to terminate a pregnancy under certain conditions."

. . . The presumption invoked by the New Jersey Supreme Court provides the precedent for the extension of this right of privacy by other courts whose decisions permitting the termination of life-sustaining treatment is founded on privacy.

Yet *Roe* itself counsels against such a broad reading.

> The privacy right involved, therefore, cannot be said to be absolute. In fact, it is not clear to us that the claim asserted by some amici that one has an unlimited right to do with one's body as one pleases bears a close relationship to the right of privacy previously articulated in the Court's decisions. The Court has refused to recognize an unlimited right of this kind in the past. . . .

The language in *Roe* is not an aberration. The Supreme Court's most recent privacy decision resisted expansion of the privacy right. In *Bowers v. Hardwick,* . . . (1986), the Supreme Court considered whether the right to privacy extended to the conduct of homosexuals. Noting that the prior right to privacy cases focused on a common theme of procreation and relationships within the bonds of marriage, the court refused to extend the right of privacy beyond those bounds, arguing that such an extension amounted to the discovery of a new right. . . .

Based on our analysis of the right to privacy decisions of the Supreme Court, we carry grave doubts as to the applicability of privacy rights to decisions to terminate the provision of food and water to an incompetent patient. As will be seen, however, even if we recognize such a broadly sweeping right of privacy, a decision by Nancy's co-guardians to withdraw food and water under these circumstances cannot be sustained. . . .

It is tempting to equate the state's interest in the preservation of life with some measure of quality of life. As the discussion which follows shows, some courts find quality of life a convenient focus when justifying the termination of treatment. But the state's interest is not in quality of life. The broad policy statements of the legislature make no such distinction; nor shall we. Were quality of life at issue, persons with all manner of handicaps might find the state seeking to terminate their lives. Instead, the state's interest is in life; that interest is unqualified.

Balancing the Patient's Rights and the State's Interest

1

In casting the balance between the patient's common law right to refuse treatment/constitutional right to privacy and the state's interest in life, we acknowledge that the great majority of courts allow the termination of life-sustaining treatment. In doing so, these courts invariably find that the patient's right to refuse treatment outweighs the state's interest in preserving life. In some cases, that result is the product of a hopeless medical prognosis; in others, the court allows concerns with quality of life to discount the state's interest in life. *Quinlan*, of course, is the source in each instance. . . .

Prior to *Quinlan*, the common law preferred to err on the side of life. Choices for incompetents were made to preserve life, not hasten death. *Quinlan* changed the calculus. Moving from the common law's prejudice in favor of life, *Quinlan* subtly recast the state's interest in life as an interest in the quality of life (cognitive and sapient), struck a balance between quality of life and Karen Quinlan's right to privacy and permitted the termination of a life-sustaining procedure. . . .

As we previously stated, however, the state's interest is not in quality of life. The state's interest is an unqualified interest in life. . . .

. . . Nancy's counsel argues that her treatment is invasive. The invasion took place when the gastrostomy tube was inserted with consent at a time when hope remained for recovery. Presently, the tube merely provides a conduit for the introduction of food and water. The *continuation* of feeding through the tube is not heroically invasive. . . .

The state's relevant interest is in life, both its preservation and its sanctity. Nancy is not dead. Her life expectancy is thirty years.

Nancy's care requirements, while total, are not burdensome to Nancy. The evidence at trial showed that the care provided did not cause Nancy pain. Nor is that care particularly burdensome for her, given that she does not respond to it.

Finally, there is no evidence that Nancy is terminally ill. The quality of her life is severely diminished to be sure. Yet if food and water are supplied, she will not die.

Given the fact that Nancy is alive and that the burdens of her treatment are not excessive for her, we do not believe her right to refuse treatment, whether that right proceeds from a constitutional right of privacy or a common law right to refuse treatment, outweighs the immense, clear fact of life in which the state maintains a vital interest. . . .

J. GAY-WILLIAMS

The Wrongfulness of Euthanasia

(*Source: Reprinted from Ronald Munson [ed.],* Intervention and Reflection: Basic Issues in Medical Ethics. *Copyright © 1979 by Wadsworth Publishing Company, Inc.)*

QUESTIONS FOR REFLECTION

1. Why does Gay-Williams object to the phrase "passive euthanasia"?
2. Gay-Williams argues that euthanasia is unnatural. In what way? How does this argument lead to the moral conclusion that euthanasia is wrong?
3. Can euthanasia ever be in a patient's self-interest, according to Gay-Williams? Do you agree?
4. What is Gay-Williams's "slippery slope" argument? How persuasive is it?

My impression is that euthanasia—the idea, if not the practice—is slowly gaining acceptance within our society. Cynics might attribute this to an increasing tendency to devalue human life, but I do not believe this is the major factor. The acceptance is much more likely to be the result of unthinking sympathy and benevolence. Well-publicized, tragic stories like that of Karen Quinlan elicit from us deep feelings of compassion. We think to ourselves, "She and her family would be better off if she were dead." It is an easy step from this very human response to the view that if someone (and others) would be better off dead, then it must be all right to kill that person. Although I respect the compassion that leads to this conclusion, I believe the conclusion is wrong. I want to show that euthanasia is wrong. It is inherently wrong, but it also wrong judged from the standpoints of self-interest and of practical effects.

Before presenting my arguments to support this claim, it would be well to define "euthanasia." An essential aspect of euthanasia is that it involves taking a human life, either one's own or that of another. Also, the person whose life is taken must be someone who is believed to be suffering from some disease or injury from which recovery cannot reasonably be expected. Finally, the action must be deliberate and intentional. Thus, euthanasia is intentionally taking the life of a presumably hopeless person. Whether the life is one's own or that of another, the taking of it is still euthanasia.

It is important to be clear about the deliberate and intentional aspect of the killing. If a hopeless person is given an injection of the wrong drug by mistake and this causes his death, this is wrongful killing but not euthanasia. The killing cannot be the result of accident. Furthermore, if the person is given an injection of a drug that is believed to be necessary to treat his disease or better his condition and the person dies as a result, then this is neither wrongful killing nor euthanasia. The intention was to make the patient well, not kill him. Similarily, when a patient's condition is such that it is not reasonable to hope that any medical procedures or treatments will save his life, a failure to implement the procedures or treatments is not euthanasia. If the person dies, this will be as a result of his injuries or disease and not because of his failure to receive treatment.

The failure to continue treatment after it has been realized that the patient has little chance of benefitting from it has been characterized by some as "passive euthanasia." This phrase is misleading and mistaken. In such cases, the person involved is not killed (the first essential aspect of euthanasia), nor is the death of the person intended by the withholding of additional treatment (the third essential aspect of euthanasia). The aim may be to spare the person additional and unjustifiable pain, to save him from the indignities of hopeless manipulations, and to avoid increasing the financial and emotional burden on his family. When I buy a pencil it is so that I can use it to write, not to contribute to an increase in the gross national product. This may be the unintended consequence of my action, but it is not the aim of my action. So it is with failing to continue the treatment of a dying person. I intend his death no more than I intend to reduce the GNP by not using medical supplies. His is an unintended dying, and so-called "passive euthanasia" is not euthanasia at all.

1 The Argument from Nature

Every human being has a natural inclination to continue living. Our reflexes and responses fit us to fight attackers, flee wild animals, and dodge out of the way of trucks. In our daily lives we exercise the caution and care necessary to protect ourselves. Our bodies are similarly structured for survival right down to the molecular level. When we are cut, our capillaries seal shut, our blood clots, and fibrogen is produced to start the process of healing the wound. When we are invaded by bacteria, antibodies are produced to fight against the alien organisms, and their remains are swept out of the body by special cells designed for clean-up work.

Euthanasia does violence to this natural goal of survival. It is literally acting against nature because all the processes of nature are bent towards the end of bodily survival. Euthanasia defeats these subtle mechanisms in a way that, in a particular case, disease and injury might not.

It is possible, but not necessary, to make an appeal to revealed religion in this connection. Man as trustee of his body acts against God, its rightful possessor, when he takes his own life. He also violates the commandment to hold life sacred and never to take it without just and compelling cause. But since this appeal will persuade only those who are prepared to accept that religion has access to revealed truths, I shall not employ this line of argument.

It is enough, I believe, to recognize that the organization of the human body and our patterns of behavioral responses make the continuation of life a natural goal. By reason alone, then, we can recognize that euthanasia sets us against our own nature. Furthermore, in doing so, euthanasia does violence to our dignity. Our dignity comes from seeking our ends. When one of our goals is survival, and actions are taken that eliminate that goal, then our natural dignity suffers. Unlike animals, we are conscious through reason of our nature and our ends. Euthanasia involves acting as if this dual nature—inclination towards survival and awareness of this as an end—did not exist. Thus, euthanasia denies our basic human character and requires that we regard ourselves or others as something less than fully human.

2 The Argument from Self-Interest

The above arguments are, I believe, sufficient to show that euthanasia is inherently wrong. But there are reasons for considering it wrong when judged by standards other than reason. Because death is final and irreversible, euthanasia contains within it the possibility that we will work against our own interest if we practice it or allow it to be practiced on us.

Contemporary medicine has high standards of excellence and a proven record of accomplishment, but it does not possess perfect and complete knowledge. A mistaken diagnosis is possible, and so is a mistaken prognosis. Consequently, we may believe that we are dying of a disease when, as a matter of fact, we may not be. We may think that we have no hope of recovery when, as a matter of fact, our chances are quite good. In such circumstances, if euthanasia were permitted, we would die needlessly. Death is final and the chance of error too great to approve the practice of euthanasia.

Also, there is always the possibility that an experimental procedure or a hitherto untried technique will pull us through. We should at least keep this option open, but euthanasia closes it off. Furthermore, spontaneous remission does occur in many cases. For no apparent reason, a patient simply recovers when those all around him, including his physicians, expected him to die. Euthanasia would just guarantee their expectations and leave no room for the "miraculous" recoveries that frequently occur.

Finally, knowing that we can take our life at any time (or ask another to take it) might well incline us to give up too easily. The will to live is strong in all of us, but it can be weakened by pain and suffering and feelings of hopelessness. If during a bad time we allow ourselves to be killed, we never have a chance to reconsider. Recovery from a serious illness requires that we fight for it, and anything that weakens our determination by suggesting that there is an easy way out is ultimately against our own interest. Also, we may be inclined towards euthanasia because of our concern for others. If we see our sickness and suffering as an emotional and financial burden on our family, we may feel that to leave our life is to make their lives easier. The very presence of the possibility of euthanasia may keep us from surviving when we might.

3 The Argument from Practical Effects

Doctors and nurses are, for the most part, totally committed to saving lives. A life lost is, for them, almost a personal failure, an insult to their skills and knowledge. Euthanasia as a practice might well alter this. It could have a corrupting influence so that in any case that is severe doctors and nurses might not try hard enough to save the patient. They might decide that the patient would simply be "better off dead" and take the steps necessary to make that come about. This attitude could then carry over to their dealings with patients less seriously ill. The result would be an overall decline in the quality of medical care.

Finally, euthanasia as a policy is a slippery slope. A person apparently hopelessly ill may be allowed to take his own life. Then he may be permitted to deputize others to do it for him should he no longer be able to act. The judgment of others then becomes the ruling factor. Already at this point euthanasia is not personal and voluntary, for others are acting "on behalf of" the patient as they see fit. This may well incline them to act on behalf of other patients who have not authorized them to exercise their judgment. It is only a short step, then, from voluntary euthanasia (self-inflicted or authorized), to directed euthanasia administered to a patient who has given no authorization, to involuntary euthanasia conducted as part of a social policy. Recently many psychiatrists and sociologists have argued that we define as "mental illness" those forms of behavior that we disapprove of. This gives us license then to lock up those who display the behavior. The category of the "hopelessly ill" provides the possibility of even worse abuse. Embedded in a social policy, it would give society or its representatives the authority to eliminate all those who might be considered too "ill" to function normally any longer. The dangers of euthanasia are too great to all to run the risk of approving it in any form. The first slippery step may well lead to a serious and harmful fall.

I hope that I have succeeded in showing why the benevolence that inclines us to give approval of euthanasia is misplaced. Euthanasia is inherently wrong because it violates the nature and dignity of human beings. But even those who are not convinced by this must be persuaded that the potential personal and social dangers inherent in euthanasia are sufficient to forbid our approving it either as a personal practice or as a public policy.

Suffering is surely a terrible thing, and we have a clear duty to comfort those in need and to ease their suffering when we can. But suffering is also a natural part of life with values for the individual and for others that we should not overlook. We may legitimately seek for others and for ourselves an easeful death. Euthanasia, however, is not just an easeful death. It is a wrongful death. Euthanasia is not just dying. It is killing.

JAMES RACHELS

The Morality of Euthanasia

James Rachels is Professor of Philosophy at the University of Alabama at Birmingham. (Source: From The End of Life: The Morality of Euthanasia, *Oxford: Oxford University Press. Copyright © 1986 by James Rachels. Reprinted by permission.)*

QUESTIONS FOR REFLECTION

1. Summarize and evaluate Rachels's utilitarian argument from mercy.
2. How does Rachels use the Golden Rule to argue for the permissibility of euthanasia? Do you think he succeeds?
3. Why does Rachels reject the argument from unexpected cures?
4. Does it make any difference, from the perspective of any of Rachels's arguments, whether a patient is sentient or comatose? Whether a patient consents or does not consent? Whether a patient is terminal or not? Whether the doctor withholds potentially life-prolonging treatment, assists the patient in committing suicide, or kills the patient outright? Should it make any difference?

An Absolute Rule?

The late Franz Ingelfinger, who was editor of the *New England Journal of Medicine,* observed that

> This is the heyday of the ethicist in medicine. He delineates the rights of patients, of experimental subjects, of fetuses, of mothers, of animals, and even of doctors. (And what a far cry it is from the days when medical "ethics" consisted of condemning economic improprieties such as fee splitting and advertising!) With impeccable logic—once certain basic assumptions are granted—and with graceful prose, the ethicist develops his arguments . . . Yet his precepts are essentially the products of armchair exercise and remain abstract and idealistic until they have been tested in the laboratory of experience.

One problem with such armchair exercises, he complained, is that in spite of the impeccable logic and the graceful prose, the result is often an absolutist ethic that is unsatisfactory when applied to particular cases, and that is therefore of little use to the practising physician. Unlike some absolutist philosophers (and theologians), "the practitioner appears to prefer the principles of individualism. As there are few atheists in fox holes, there tend to be few absolutists at the bedside."

Dr. Ingelfinger was right to be suspicious of absolute rules. However, despite his picture of the flexible physician, there are some rules that doctors do tend to regard as absolute. One such rule is the prohibition of mercy-killing. From the time of Hippocrates, whose oath has doctors pledge "not to give a deadly drug," they have held firm to this absolute "at the bedside" as well as in the seminar room. The "principles of individualism" have made little headway against it.

Are the doctors right? The arguments I have already presented, especially those concerning the sanctity of life and the two senses of "life," suggest that in fact euthanasia is morally acceptable, at least in some circumstances. As in the other matters, there is no need here to be an "absolutist at the bedside." But there are other arguments that demand attention before we can be confident of this conclusion.

. . . [W]e will examine some other arguments that are commonly advanced for and against euthanasia. We will be concerned with the morality of killing in what we might call the "standard case" of euthanasia—that is, the case of the suffering terminal patient who, while rational, requests to be killed as an alternative to a slow, lingering death. Moreover, we will be concerned with the morality of *individual acts* of killing in such cases: considered separately, are they morally wrong? This is slightly different from asking whether euthanasia ought to be illegal, in the way that questions of individual morality are often different from questions of social policy. . . .

The Argument from Mercy

The most common argument in support of euthanasia is one that we may call "the argument from mercy." It is an exceptionally simple argument, at least in its main idea, which makes one uncomplicated point. Terminal patients sometimes suffer pain so horrible that it can hardly be comprehended by those who have not actually experienced it. Their suffering can be so terrible that we do not like even to read about it or think about it; we recoil even from its description. The argument from mercy says: euthanasia is justified because it puts an end to *that.*

The great Irish satirist Jonathan Swift took eight years to die while, in the words of Joseph Fletcher, "His mind crumbled to pieces." At times the pain in his blinded eyes was so intense he had to be restrained from tearing them out. Knives and other potential instruments of suicide were kept from him. For the last three years of his life, he could do nothing but drool; and when he finally died it was only after convulsions that lasted thirty-six hours.

Swift died in 1745. Since then, doctors have learned how to eliminate much of the pain that accompanies terminal illness, but the victory has been far from complete. Here is a more recent example.

Stewart Alsop was a respected journalist who died in 1975 of a rare form of cancer. Before he died, he wrote movingly of his experiences as a terminal patient. Although he had not thought much about euthanasia before, he came to approve of it after sharing a room briefly with someone he called Jack:

> The third night that I roomed with Jack in our tiny double room in the solid-tumor ward of the cancer clinic of the National Institutes of Health in Bethesda, Md., a terrible thought occurred to me.
>
> Jack had a melanoma in his belly, a malignant solid tumor that the doctors guessed was about the size of a softball. The cancer had started a few months before with a small tumor in his left shoulder, and there had been several operations since. The doctors planned to remove the softball-sized tumor, but they knew Jack would soon die. The cancer had metastasized—it had spread beyond control.
>
> Jack was good-looking, about 28, and brave. He was in constant pain, and his doctor had prescribed an intravenous shot of a synthetic opiate—a pain-killer, or analgesic—every four hours. His wife spent many of the daylight hours with him, and she would sit or lie on his bed and pat him all over, as one pats a child, only more methodically, and this seemed to help control the pain. But at night, when his pretty wife had left (wives cannot stay overnight at the NIH clinic) and darkness fell, the pain would attack without pity.
>
> At the prescribed hour, a nurse would give Jack a shot of the synthetic analgesic, and this would control the pain for perhaps two hours or a bit more. Then he would begin to moan, or whimper, very low, as though he didn't want to wake me. Then he would begin to howl, like a dog.
>
> When this happened, either he or I would ring for a nurse, and ask for a pain-killer. She would give him some codeine or the like by mouth, but it never did any real good—it affected him no more than half an aspirin might affect a man who had just broken his arm. Always the nurse would explain as encouragingly as she could that there was not long to go before the next intravenous shot—"Only about 50 minutes now." And always poor Jack's whimpers and howls would become more loud and frequent until at last the blessed relief came.

> The third night of this routine, the terrible thought occurred to me. "If Jack were a dog," I thought, "what would be done with him?" The answer was obvious: the pound, and chloroform. No human being with a spark of pity could let a living thing suffer so, to no good end.

I have discussed this case with some physicians who were indignant that Jack was not given larger doses of the pain-killing drug more often. They suggest that modern medicine can deal better with this type of pain. But it is worth noting that the NIH clinic is one of the best-equipped modern facilities we have; it is not as though Jack's suffering was caused by neglect in some backward rural hospital. Few of us could expect better care, were we in Jack's position. Moreover, the moral issue regarding euthanasia is not affected by whether more could have been done for Jack. The moral issue is whether mercy-killing is permissible *if* it is the only alternative to this kind of torment. We may readily grant that in any particular case where suffering can be eliminated, the argument for euthanasia will be weaker. But we will still need to know what is morally permissible in those cases in which, for whatever reason, suffering cannot, or will not, be eliminated.

I have quoted Alsop at length not for the sake of indulging in gory details but to give a clear idea of the kind of suffering we are talking about. We should not gloss over these facts with euphemistic language, or squeamishly avert our eyes from them. For only by keeping them firmly and vividly in mind can we appreciate the full force of the argument from mercy: if a person prefers—and even begs for—death as an alternative to lingering on *in this kind of torment*, only to die anyway after a while, then surely it is not immoral to help this person die sooner. As Alsop put it, "No human being with a spark of pity could let a living thing suffer so, to no good end."

Utilitarianism

The basic idea of the argument from mercy is clear enough; but how is it to be developed into a rigorous argument? Among philosophers, the utilitarians attempted to do this. They held that actions should be judged right or wrong according to whether they cause happiness or misery; and they argued that when judged by this standard, euthanasia turns out to be morally acceptable. The classic utilitarian version of the argument may be elaborated like this:

1. Any action is morally right if it serves to increase the amount of happiness in the world or to decrease the amount of misery. Conversely, an action is morally wrong if it serves to decrease happiness or increase misery.
2. Killing a hopelessly ill patient, who is suffering great pain, at his own request, would decrease the amount of misery in the world.
3. Therefore, such an action would be morally right.

The first premise of this argument states the principle of utility, the basic utilitarian assumption. Today most philosophers think this principle is unacceptable, because they think the promotion of happiness and the avoidance of misery are not the *only* morally important things. To take one example: People *might* be happier if there were no freedom of religion; for, if everyone adhered to the same religious beliefs, there would be greater harmony among people. There would be no unhappiness caused by Jewish girls marrying Catholic boys; the religious element of conflicts such as in Northern Ireland would be removed; and so forth. Moreover, if people were brainwashed well enough, no one would mind not having freedom of choice. Thus happiness might be increased. But, the argument continues, even if happiness *could* be increased in this way, it would be wrong to do so, because people should be allowed to make their own choices. Therefore, the argument concludes, the principle of utility is unacceptable.

There is a related difficulty for utilitarianism, which connects more directly with euthanasia. Suppose a person is leading a miserable life—full of more unhappiness than happiness—but does not want to die. This person thinks a miserable life is better than none at all. Now I assume we would all agree that this person should not be killed; that would be plain, unjustifiable murder. Yet it *would* decrease the amount of misery in the world if we killed him—and so it is hard to see how, on strictly utilitarian grounds, it could be wrong. Again, the principle of utility seems to be an inadequate guide for determining right and wrong.

Such arguments have led many philosophers to reject this moral theory. Yet contemporary utilitarians have an easy answer. In the first place, in so far as euthanasia is concerned, the classical utilitarian argument retains considerable force, even if it is faulty. For even if the promotion of happiness and the avoidance of misery are not the *only* morally important things, they are still very important. So, when an action would decrease misery, that is *a* very strong reason in its favour. The utilitarian argument in favour of euthanasia might therefore be decisive, even if the general complaints about the principle of utility are sound.

Moreover, utilitarianism may also be defended against the general complaints. Classical utilitarianism, as set out by Bentham and Mill, is a combination of three ideas. The first is that actions are to be judged right or wrong entirely according to their *consequences*. Nothing else matters—actions are not good or bad "in themselves," and moral "rules" have no independent importance. Right actions are, simply, the ones that have the best results. The second idea is that good and evil are to be measured in terms of happiness and unhappiness—nothing else is ultimately valuable. Material goods, art and ideas, friendship, and so on, are good only *because* they contribute to happiness. Thus, right actions are said to be those that produce the most happiness, or prevent the most misery. Third, and finally, classical utilitarianism includes the idea of equality—each individual's happiness is counted as equally important.

The difficulties we noted for utilitarianism all may be traced to its narrow identification of good and evil with happiness and unhappiness. . . . All that is necessary to save it, therefore, is to adopt a broader conception of individual welfare. The basic idea of the theory is that actions are right or wrong as they increase or decrease welfare. So, suppose we substitute a better conception of welfare: rather than speaking of maximizing *happiness*, let us speak of maximizing *interests*—let the principle of utility say that actions are right if they satisfy as many interests as possible. Such a broader principle will still be "utilitarian" in that it still sees the rightness of actions as consisting in their effects on the welfare of the creatures affected by them. But the new principle avoids the problems that plagued the old one: if it is in a person's best interests to have freedom of choice in religion, or in choosing to remain alive, then the principle will not countenance taking away that freedom or that life. Armed with this better version of the principle of utility, we may then offer this improved argument concerning euthanasia:

1. If an action promotes the best interests of everyone concerned, then that action is morally acceptable.
2. In at least some cases, euthanasia promotes the best interests of everyone concerned.
3. Therefore, in at least some cases euthanasia is morally acceptable.

It would have been in everyone's best interests if euthanasia had been employed in the case of Stewart Alsop's room-mate Jack. First, and most important, it would have been in Jack's own interests, since it would have provided him with an easier death, without additional pain. Moreover, it would have been best for his wife. Her misery, helplessly watching him suffer, was second only to his. Third, the hospital staff's interests would have been served, since if Jack's dying had not been prolonged, they could have turned their attention to other patients whom they could have helped. Fourth, other patients would have benefited since medical resources would no longer have been used in the sad, pointless maintenance of Jack's physical existence. Finally, if Jack himself requested to be killed, the act would not have violated his rights. Considering all this, how can euthanasia be wrong?

Two additional comments are necessary before we leave the argument from mercy. First, I have discussed the utilitarians in connection with this argument, but one does not have to accept a general utilitarian theory of ethics to find it persuasive. There are other possible theories that one might prefer. However, no matter what ethical theory one accepts, the consequences of one's actions —whether they do or do not promote people's interests, or cause happiness or misery—must be among the matters considered important. An ethical theory that did *not* have an important place for this would have no credibility at all. And, to the extent that these matters *are* seen as important, the argument from mercy will be compelling.

Second, it should be noted that the argument does *not* imply that euthanasia is justified *whenever* a patient says he can no longer endure pain. Suppose the doctor, or the family, knows that the painful condition can be cured, and that the patient's request to die is only a temporary irrational reaction, which he will later repudiate. It is entirely reasonable for them to take this into account, and to refuse the irrational request. The argument from mercy does not say otherwise; in such circumstances euthanasia would not promote his best interests, and would hardly be "merciful" at all. This should not be taken to mean, however, that such requests are always irrational, or that pain always destroys a patient's ability to make sensible choices. Sadly, some requests to die, in circumstances such as those of Stewart Alsop's room-mate, are all too rational.

The Argument from the Golden Rule

"Do unto others as you would have them do unto you" is one of the oldest and most familiar moral maxims. Stated in just that way, it is not a very good maxim: suppose a sexual pervert, with fantasies of being raped, started treating others as he would like to be treated. We might not be happy with the results. Nevertheless, the idea behind the Golden Rule is a good one. Moral rules apply to everyone alike. You cannot say that you are justified in treating someone else in a certain way unless you are willing to admit that that person would be justified in treating *you* in that way if your positions were reversed.

Kant's moral philosophy is usually regarded as the major historical alternative to utilitarianism. Like the utilitarians, Kant sought to express all of morality in a single principle. Kant's principle may be viewed as a sophisticated version of the Golden Rule. He argued that we should act only on rules that we are willing to have applied universally; that is, we should behave as we would be willing to have *everyone* behave. Thus, the one supreme principle of morality, which he called the "Categorical Imperative," says:

> Act only according to that maxim which you can at the same time will to become a universal law.

What does this mean? When we are trying to decide whether to do a certain action, we must first ask what general rule we would be following if we did it. Then, we ask whether we would be willing for everyone to follow that rule, in similar circumstances. (This determines whether "the maxim of the act"—the rule we would be following—can be "willed" to be a "universal law.") If we would not be willing for the rule to be followed universally, then we should not follow it ourselves. Thus, if we are not willing for others to apply the rule to *us*, we ought not apply it to *them*.

In the eighteenth chapter of St. Matthew's gospel there is a story that perfectly illustrates this point. A man is owed money by another, who cannot pay, and so he has the debtor thrown into prison. But he himself owes money to the King and begs that *his* debt be forgiven. At first the King forgives the debt. However, when the King hears how this man has treated the one who owed him, he changes his mind and "delivers him unto the tormentors" until he can pay. The moral is clear: If you do not think that others should apply the rule "Don't forgive debts!" to *you*, then you should not apply it to others.

The application of this to the question of euthanasia is fairly obvious. Each of us is going to die some day, although most of us do not know when or how, and will probably have little choice in the matter. But suppose you were given a choice: suppose you were told that you would die in one of two ways, and were asked to choose between them. First, you could die quietly, and without pain, at the age of eighty, from a fatal injection. Or second, you could choose to die at the age of eighty-plus-a-few-days of an affliction so painful that for those few days before death you would be reduced to howling like a dog, with your family standing helplessly by. It is hard to believe that anyone would choose to have a rule applied that would force upon him or her the second option—if, that is, they were making a choice based upon *their own preferences*. And if we would not want such a rule, which excludes euthanasia, applied to us, then we should not apply such a rule to others.

The contemporary British philosopher R. M. Hare has made the same point in a slightly different way. Hare tells the following (true) story:

> The driver of a petrol lorry was caught in an accident in which his tanker overturned and immediately caught fire. He himself was trapped in the cab and could not be freed. He therefore besought the bystanders to kill him by hitting him on the head, so that he would not roast to death. I think that somebody did this, but I do not know what happened in the courts afterwards.
>
> Now will you please all ask yourselves, as I have many times asked myself, what you wish that men should do to you if you were in the situation of that driver. I cannot believe that anybody who considered the matter seriously, as if he himself were going to be in that situation and had now to give instructions as to what rule the bystanders should follow, would say that the rule should be one ruling out euthanasia absolutely.

There is a considerable irony here. Kant was personally opposed to mercy-killing; he thought it contrary to reason. Yet his own Categorical Imperative seems to sanction it. The larger irony, however, is for those in the Christian Church who have for centuries opposed euthanasia. The article written by Professor Hare, from which the story of the lorry driver is taken, has the title "Euthanasia: A Christian View." According to the New Testament accounts, Jesus himself promulgated the Golden Rule as the supreme moral principle—"This is the Law and the Prophets," he said. But, as Hare points out, if this is the supreme principle of morality, then how can euthanasia be absolutely wrong? This seems to be another one of those instances in which the historical Church has strayed from the principles laid down by its founder. . . .

The Possibility of Unexpected Cures

Euthanasia may also be opposed on the grounds that we cannot really tell when a patient's condition is hopeless. There are cases in which patients have recovered even after doctors have given up hope; if those patients had been killed, it would have been tragic, for they would have been deprived of many additional years of life. According to this argument, euthanasia is unacceptable because we never know for certain that a patient's situation is hopeless. *Any* so-called hopeless patient might defy the odds and recover.

The argument has two sources: first, it draws some plausibility from the fact that doctors have sometimes made mistakes; and second, it trades on a naive view of the possibilities of medical research.

It must be admitted, of course, that doctors have sometimes made mistakes in labelling cases "hopeless," and so we should be cautious in any given instance before saying there is no chance of recovery. But it does not follow from the fact that physicians have *sometimes* been mistaken that they can *never* know for sure that a case is hopeless. That would be like saying that since some people have confused a Rolls-Royce with a Mercedes, no one can ever be certain which is which. In fact, doctors do sometimes know for sure that a patient cannot recover. There may be spontaneous remissions of cancer, for example, at a relatively early stage of the disease. But after the cancer has spread throughout the body and reached an advanced stage of development, there may truly be no hope whatever. Although there may be some doubt about some cases—and where there is doubt, perhaps euthanasia should not be considered—no one with the slightest medical knowledge could have had any doubt about Jack. He was going to die of that cancer, and that is all there is to it. No one has ever recovered from *that* condition, and doctors can explain exactly why this is so.

The argument from the possibility of unexpected cures sometimes takes a slightly different form, and appeals to a naive view of medical research. According to this view, researchers are continually exploring new possibilities of treating disease; and we never know when a new "miracle cure" for a previously untreatable disease might be discovered. Thus, if we grant a dying patient's request for euthanasia, we run the risk that the next day a cure for his condition might be discovered—"If only we had waited, he could have been saved," it may be said.

This argument will have little appeal to those more familiar with the realities of medical research. Progress in treating disease comes, not with the sudden and unexpected discovery of magical remedies, but from slow and painstaking investigation. Whether it is reasonable to hope for a "cure" depends on the particular case in question. In the case of some diseases, investigators may have promising results from some lines of inquiry; here, it may be reasonable to hold out some hope for a dying patient, *if* death can be postponed long enough. In other cases, we may be dealing with a disease that is getting very little attention from researchers, or the researchers investigating it may obviously be very far from achieving any impressive results. Here, it may be simply dishonest to tell a patient with only a short time to live that there is hope. Or again, it may be that even if a cure is found, it will do a particular patient no good because in him the disease is so far advanced that the "cure" would not help *him* even if it were found.

What, then, are we to conclude? We may certainly conclude that extreme care should be taken so as to avoid declaring a patient "hopeless" when there really is a chance of recovery; and we may perhaps conclude that in any case where there is the slightest doubt, euthanasia should not be considered. However, we may *not* conclude that doctors *never* know that a case is hopeless. Nor may we always hold out the hope of a "miracle cure." Sadly, we know that in some cases there is no hope, and in those cases the possibility of an unexpected cure cannot be offered as an objection to euthanasia.

CARLOS GOMEZ

From Public Theory to Private Practice

(*Source:* *From* Regulating Death: Euthanasia and the Case of the Netherlands. *New York: Free Press, 1991. Copyright © 1991 by the Free Press. Notes have been omitted. Reprinted by permission.)*

QUESTIONS FOR REFLECTION

1. What criteria must be satisfied in the Netherlands for euthanasia to be permitted?
2. How are the phrases "unbearable suffering" and "intolerable situation" interpreted? Do you see morally relevant differences among cases in which these are invoked?
3. How is voluntariness defined and assessed in practice? What dangers does Gomez see in this assessment?
4. What are the chief problems Gomez sees as arising from the Dutch practice of euthanasia?
5. Can some of these problems be addressed? Or are they inherent in legalizing euthanasia?

Everybody in Holland is a Calvinist. The Protestants are Calvinists, but so are the Catholics. Even atheists like me are Calvinists. And the communists here, they're the worst Calvinists of all. What does this mean? We like many rules, but we don't like to be told what the rules mean.

—William Roose

The Evaluative Criteria

At first, attempting an evaluation of the practice of euthanasia in the Netherlands would seem an exercise in futility. By what criteria, for example, would one judge individual cases? There is no law directly addressing the practice, only court opinions in which it is suggested that the law will be overlooked if certain requirements are met. The government has tried, on three separate occasions, to bridge the chasm between written law and established practice, but each attempt has failed on the specifics of the legislation. Efforts to codify, for example, what is an extreme situation that compels euthanasia have failed to reconcile the opinions of those who choose to interpret the word *extreme* as implying the situation of a terminal patient in unbearable, unrelievable pain and those who believe that suffering is a matter too subjective—and therefore too private—to be dictated by public policy. . . .

What does seem a more appropriate response to the situation, however, would be to take the criteria—however loosely defined—upon which there is some consensus in the Netherlands and see how they play out in actual practice. There was no instance in which a person relating the clinical history professed ignorance of a particular guideline. Moreover, in instances in which the practice of euthanasia seemed to have gone beyond the generally assumed bounds, there was still an appeal to a more liberal interpretation of the criteria or an appeal to the exigencies of the particular case that, according to the narrator, excused him or her from following a particular guideline. Whatever the particularities of an individual patient's case, it seemed clear that the guidelines provided a backdrop against which the case evolved.

The guidelines, then, provide a generally accepted scheme within which the practice of euthanasia is to be confined. For the sake of this analysis, I restructure them according to the principles at which they aim, that is, four characteristics of a situation that, at a minimum, should be present before euthanasia can be said to have been properly administered.

The first is that a case of euthanasia be compelling: there should be unbearable suffering (either physical or psychological) on the part of the patient, and there should be no alternative measure the patient would accept that might relieve that suffering. Thus, euthanasia is to be accepted as the *ultimum refugium* only after all other options have been tried or offered, and it should occur (to use the KNMG's phrase) only when the patient and physician have "their backs to the wall."

Secondly, it needs to be established that the request for euthanasia is completely voluntary. The patient must not be acting under duress or coercion, nor under false assumptions or inadequate information; as a corollary, it is the physician's duty to assure himself or herself that this situation obtains and that the patient is exercising the right to autonomy prudently. This, at least, is how I interpret the stipulation that a patient must have a "reasonable understanding" of alternatives, a criterion that can be met only with the physician's cooperation.

This interpretation of the guidelines, moreover, points to a third characteristic of permissible euthanasia: it should engage professional judgment and discretion. In other words, euthanasia is a medical act. The task of performing euthanasia may not be delegated to a nonphysician, and the physician may not act unilaterally. Permissible euthanasia is to be evaluated (and executed) solely as a tool of the medical profession. Moreover, the gravity and finality of such an act dictate that the physician test his or her assessment of the situation with at least one other person. Some have chosen to interpret this latter stipulation more strictly than others, using ethics committees or terminal-care teams, for example, to evaluate a situation. Others follow a looser version of the consultation criterion, meeting only the formal requirement that one other person be involved in the decision.

However these criteria are met, they should be recorded and given some public airing. That is, the doctors need to account for their actions, at some level, in a more public forum. This fourth and final stipulation, given the data published, for example, by the Ministry of Justice, is routinely ignored in most (though not all) cases of euthanasia performed in the Netherlands and certainly in the ones I document. Nevertheless, it seems fair to include this as one evaluative element of the case analyses. The Dutch have not yet legalized the practice, and at least at a formal, juridical level, the practice is tolerated only if it can be shown that a physician's actions were careful and reasonable. Such tolerance rests, however, on the documentation and review of the particularities of a case and assumes (however disingenuously) that cases of euthanasia receive careful outside scrutiny. . . .

Euthanasia as a Last Resort

One test of a practice's exceptional quality would be to study its prevalence, a piece of information that is clearly beyond the reach of this book, or for that matter, beyond the bounds of present knowledge. Were euthanasia a routine occurrence—were it to account, as some have alleged, for a tenth of all deaths in Holland—it would suggest that the practice had achieved rather pedestrian status, that it had become simply one more among other options available to dying patients. That euthanasia is *not* to be considered routine and ordinary care, however, is made clear by the language of the guidelines. Moreover, even if we knew the frequency of the practice, we would still be left to ponder what about these cases made them exceptional—that is, why they were excepted from the general prohibitions against killing. It has been pointed out that the reluctance of the courts or the medical profession to specify what constitutes a compelling circumstance for performing euthanasia derives, in part, from a sense that "unbearable suffering" is a uniquely personal, subjective description of one's state. It describes not only what a person feels but also how the person evaluates those sensations in relation to other aspects of his or her life and to prospects for the future. The pain or disability of young people may seem tolerable to them in light of their aspirations for the future, for example, or the loves and affections they have for the people around them, while a similar situation may be intolerable to those who see no prospects for relief and who have lost (through death, for example) the human supports that might have made such afflictions bearable. The reluctance of the guidelines to restrict euthanasia to cases of terminally ill people is in part an acknowledgment of the futility of codifying in public policy what is essentially a private judgment: once one has decided that unbearable suffering may provide grounds for justifiable euthanasia, one has all but closed the door on further qualifications.

But the latitude granted by the courts on this matter is, depending on one's perspective, either the great strength or weakness of the guidelines. The range of what "unbearable suffering" means, in practice, finds wide expression in the clinical histories, and it highlights the problem of setting public limits on what is essentially private judgment. The notion of a "matter of last resort" becomes an elastic concept, stretched in various directions by circumstance.

For example, in some instances, it is an expression of the pain brought on by the lesion inflicted by the disease or in consort with the treatment for the disease. The patient in Case 1, for example, who suffered from metastatic cancer, complained not only of a persistent, cramping pain in his abdomen but also of the effects of the chemotherapy, which caused, among other things, nausea. Both the disease and the treatment for the disease caused the man's suffering. Similarly, the 72-year-old widow, who is the subject of Case 4, had already undergone surgical treatment and chemotherapy for her lung cancer, but the widening tumor made control of her symptoms difficult. She had discontinued the chemotherapy (precisely, she said, because of the treatment's harsh side effects) and was admitted for her final hospital stay because of dyspnea (difficulty breathing—a decidedly unpleasant and alarming sensation) and pain, which the drugs her family physician was using could not contain.

Physical pain from disease, or from the abrasive effects of therapies used to control disease, was a prominent feature of almost all the case histories. It was especially notable in cases involving cancer (nine out of the twenty-six), but also figured heavily in others. The woman with amyotrophic lateral sclerosis (Case 2), for example, experienced horror at her continual hunger for air and her dependence on a respirator, and expressly asked her physician not to continue the treatments ("she asked not to suffer"). Similarly, in the cases of the two men with AIDS (Cases 12 and 18), both of whom were suffering from pneumonia on their final admissions, the constricting, painful sensation of a spreading infection in the lungs, making each breath an effort, was perceived as intolerable. Even after partial remission and relief (as in Case 12), the patient's memory of the event was harsh enough for him to insist that the therapy not be repeated a second time.

These latter cases point to another prominent interpretation of the criterion of unbearable suffering, namely, that it may also include an element of weariness, of a fatigue with either the disease or the therapies that can stave off death temporarily but not cure the underlying lesion. Thus, the 86-year-old woman in Case 3, with chronic obstructive pulmonary disease and recurring bouts of pneumonia that left her successively weaker each time, was said by her doctor "to be tired" of her illness. She had said "no more of this," which at first was taken as refusal of further treatment but which she made even more specific by explicitly requesting euthanasia. Similarly, the young woman in Case 14, with leukemia, who had been in remission for one year, opted for euthanasia over further treatment or palliation. Moreover, as the story is recounted, she had made this decision in a moment of relative good health and in consultation with her husband, preferring the certain quickness of death by a lethal drug over the slower course of a natural death (and certainly over further curative interventions).

The weariness that comes from fighting a disease, moreover, can become unbearable in light of other circumstances. One could plausibly suggest that the absence of family or friends, for example, plays a role in some patients' request for euthanasia. The man in Case 1 was divorced and had no children. In six other cases, the people narrating the histories made note of the death of a spouse, the absence of children, or a situation of virtual social isolation. The 81-year-old woman in Case 26, for example, was almost blind and living alone. Although the narrative is not precise on this point, the woman's phrase that she wanted "no family, no friends" involved suggests, at the very least, some distance or estrangement in her social relations. Similarly, the narrative of the 89-year-old woman described in Case 7, alludes to a frail person disengaged from most social contacts. The efforts of her physician to relieve her burden (by enlisting the aid of a visiting nurse and part-time helper, for example) failed to mollify her desire to die. Even the physician's attempt to engage her son in the deliberations was futile. The only social contact mentioned in the narrative was a neighbor, who went with the patient to plead the sincerity of the patient's desire to die.

Under current interpretations of the guidelines, moreover, a compelling case for euthanasia can be derived from more subtle criteria. A fear of indefinite dependence—either on a machine or on other people—was a factor in several patients' stories. In the case of the 59-year-old man with the brain tumor (Case 15), whose relative related the history, one senses that the normal life of the extended family had been completely disrupted: "Like giving everyone in the family a disease of depression," the relative says. The youngest child interrupted university studies to be with the father; another child quit a job to move back home. To be sure, there is no overt hint of coercion on the family's part in this matter; on the contrary, the story, and the manner in which it was told, bespeaks a sincere devotion to the patient. However, a sense of the extent to which one's illness impinges on and disrupts the rhythm of loved ones' lives cannot but help to contribute to a sense of "unbearable suffering."

Similarly, the loss of personal autonomy, the inability to advance or articulate one's own interests, is another facet of this issue of dependency that comes to light in other histories. The lawyer in Case 19, for example, anticipated the end that he feared the most. For him, what would have been intolerable was the indefinite twilight of an unconscious or semiconscious existence. So great, it seems, was this fear, that he prepared an advance directive in anticipation of just such a possibility. When he in fact suffered a massive cerebrovascular accident, his physicians waited a short while (to look for possible signs of recovery), then consented to his prior request. Case 25, involving an 81-year-old man in rapidly declining health, further illustrates this notion of someone anticipating what for him or her would be an intolerable existence. Although the physician notes that the patient made a quick recovery from a "small stroke," the event was disturbing enough to the patient that he preferred death under known circumstances to what he saw as the grim uncertainty of the future: "He understood exactly what the future was for him, and this was no longer tolerable. He was afraid that [after] the next [stroke], he would not be able to speak his wishes anymore, and preferred death." This same issue comes to the fore in Case 21, involving the woman with Alzheimer's disease who went into congestive heart failure. Although the issue of consent in this instance is much murkier (as I suggest in the next section), the physician justifies the actions taken by an appeal to the patient's prior sense of what an intolerable situation would be for her.

It is worth noting here again that the Dutch have also interpreted an intolerable situation as one involving "disfigurement of the personality," a phrase that they encapsulate in their word *ontluisteren,* a rough equivalent to our own phrase *loss of dignity.* The AIDS patients, for example, whose sense of self-worth began to deteriorate in tandem with the progress of their disease; or the man in Case 11, who said in anticipation of a devastating stroke that "this was no way for a man to live," manifest the different shadings that this word can take. Loss of self-esteem, physical deterioration, loss of dignity, or in the literal translation of the word, "a condition of not being heard"—all become compelling circumstances under which euthanasia is permitted.

Finally, I note two cases where the notion of "unbearable suffering" takes on a completely different meaning. In the narrative of the 56-year-old man with massive trauma (Case 22), the physician appeals, implicitly, to relieving the suffering of the family, not the patient. It is clear that to this physician, the patient was essentially dead. Moreover, if there "would soon be no [brain] signals for a neurologist to see," the patient would be unlikely to experience pain (or any other subjective sensation of suffering). The physician calls this a "terrible situation"; that is, it is terrible for the family to have to wait for what the physician sees as sure death. So the physician dispatches the patient out of consideration for the family.

The case of the child born with Down's syndrome and duodenal atresia (Case 20) falls even further beyond the bounds of "unbearable suffering" within which euthanasia is to be constrained. The child's inevitable mental retardation had no medical cure (though many of the children born with this syndrome do respond well to other nonmedical interventions); his intestinal malformation, however, did have a known, well-tested, and efficacious surgical solution. Without surgical intervention, the child would surely have died, but only after dehydration and starvation, a particularly gruesome way for a sentient human to approach death. How the alternatives of this case were presented to the parents is not clear to me, even after pressing the narrator for more details. The ethicist who presented this history notes, "I said that they did not have to approve surgery; there [were] already two problems here, and who is to know how many more would come."

Whether the possibility of euthanasia was discussed in connection with the refusal of surgical intervention remains uncertain; the ethicist adds by way of justification that "once there was a decision [not to treat], it becomes a very cruel thing to starve a baby. The mother wanted no suffering [for the child], and this I told her we could do." This phrasing of the issue at least suggests the possibility that the availability of euthanasia made a painful decision by the parents less painful. Alternatively, it could be suggested that once the parents made a decision not to treat, the ethicist's response was to try to assure the parents that the child would not suffer. The latter possibility places the locus of suffering on the patient, and thus it finds justification for euthanasia in what would otherwise be the child's lingering and disturbing passage into death through starvation.

The former possibility, however, raises the issue of whether the existence of euthanasia changes the context in which medical decisions are made. Much as it is suggested that the desire to die must emanate solely from a patient—that the experience of unbearable suffering be uniquely the patient's—the clinical histories of these patients suggest that unbearable suffering is a contingent experience. The data from the case histories suggest the different shadings of meaning that "unbearable suffering" can take on. The context in which one suffers, one's history, one's sense of the future, all shape the prism through which one filters an experience and finds it intolerable. However, if the experience of suffering is contingent, and if it is a prior and necessary condition that must exist before euthanasia is permitted, then one's decision to choose euthanasia, too, must contain at least some element of contingency. At the very least, physicians deciding whether or not to honor a request for euthanasia must satisfy themselves that patients' requests for euthanasia are not wholly contingent, that they do not arise solely out of temporary or remediable conditions. How this criterion is established is a problem to which the next section gives fuller treatment.

Euthanasia as Voluntary

Broadly conceived, the issue of voluntariness in euthanasia addresses two related dangers of the practice. One, clearly, is a fear that patients' requests for euthanasia do not reflect their own true wishes but the wishes of others. Patients acting under coercion—either tacit or explicit—from unsympathetic or overburdened family members, for example, are vulnerable to having their sentiments distorted or misrepresented. Two, voluntariness is also a function of knowledge and understanding: patients who choose euthanasia must be aware of the facts of their case, and must comprehend alternative solutions to their condition. Although not quite the same as coercion, choosing euthanasia out of ignorance or misunderstanding of one's situation undermines the concept of voluntariness. But voluntariness, like the earlier notion of euthanasia as *ultimum refugium,* takes on various meanings in the clinical cases.

The guidelines say specifically that a legitimate request for euthanasia may come only from the patient, but they are silent on precisely what means the physician is to use in determining that fact. In this sense, the determination of voluntariness rests with a judgment on the part of the physician or medical staff that patients' requests for euthanasia actually reflect their true sentiments. The lack of further instructions in this area finds expression in the varying ways that physicians or medical institutions determine voluntariness.

For instance, some institutions that allow physicians to practice euthanasia insist that a patient making such a request be approached alone, away from family, in the hopes of eliminating outside influences. Others, however, make no such stipulation, and some, in fact, insist on family involvement with the decision. Still others are as unclear on this point as are the guidelines. . . .

. . . [T]he presence of institutional mechanisms to determine voluntariness seems to have little impact on the final determination of the sincerity and stability of a patient's request for euthanasia. In the cases from Source H, for example, which occurred in a hospital, no standards of consent are referred to other than the physician's own judgment (though admittedly there was a committee that sometimes considered "the more difficult situations"). The case of the man brought in to the hospital following a car accident (Case 22), permits no determination of the man's wishes. The narrative suggests that the man would never again be able to express his desires; it is equally obvious, however, that the physician did not want to wait for the family to see if, alternatively, there had been some prior discussions on the subject or if the man had executed an advance directive or had left some other instrument that might have documented his wishes.

In this physician's eyes such wishes would only have postponed what was an imminent death. The physician chose to avoid the subject altogether (and makes an implicit appeal here to compassion—the desire to spare the family any further anguish). The physician also makes a claim that this is not really euthanasia, preferring to reserve that term for patients for whom medical intervention could, conceivably, extend their lives or alter the trajectory of their illness. Thus, in Case 23, the physician attempts to document the prior wishes of the patient by speaking to the family and to the patient's family doctor (requesting, at one point, a letter from the general practitioner) but says that the request for euthanasia cannot come from the patient because it was clear that the patient "was not going to be awake." The physician notes the avowed claims of the family and the family's doctor that the mother had previously requested euthanasia, makes a determination of the hopelessness of the case, and performs euthanasia. . . .

Other cases collected in this study are even more troubling and point, I think, to the difficulty of assuring that a patient chooses euthanasia with a clear understanding of the facts of the case and of other options for treatment. The young woman with leukemia (Case 14), for example, chooses euthanasia after she relapses following her first induction. She in fact had made this decision during the period of her initial remission. However, relapses after a first round of chemotherapy are the norm in leukemia, not the exception. That she relapsed so soon after the initial remission (the history says within a year) bodes a poor long-term prognosis but does not necessarily doom the patient's chances for a second remission. The details of this case are insufficient to judge the exact course of this patient's leukemia; neither do they speak to whatever difficulty and pain she experienced during the initial phase of the illness and its treatment. Nevertheless, without trivializing this patient's suffering—and without judging *post hoc* her decision—one should question why the decision to ask for euthanasia, in one so young, came relatively early in the disease and what the physician's role was in this decision. Were other, less toxic, palliative regimens offered, for example? The therapies available to patients such as this are not limited to a choice between full-scale, cytotoxic regimens (with all their miserable side effects) and euthanasia. A middle ground, with corticosteroids and narcotics, for example, is available. It does not cure, but palliates and slows the progression of the disease. Whether or not the patient was offered this choice, or other alternative choices, is not clear. What is clear, however, is that even given the existence of alternatives, the patient was euthanized.

Similarly, the clinical history of the 79-year-old woman in Case 10 raises again the issue of a well-informed decision. The narrative says that the patient had made her wishes known that she was not to be resuscitated in the event of a cardiac arrest; moreover, she let it be known that if she became comatose, she wanted euthanasia. Neither of these events occurred, but she enters the hospital a few months later, short of breath and coughing. Diagnosed as being in congestive heart failure, she is given appropriate therapy, and her symptoms abate. Yet she begins to press her case for euthanasia, even in this period of relative stability. What alternatives were available to this woman is, again, unspecified in the narrative. Yet it is noted that the symptoms that brought her into the hospital resolved. Whether or not her condition could have found better medical management in the future is uncertain. Given her prior history and compromised health, this resolution may well have represented little more than a temporary respite, but it does suggest that her symptoms were not beyond the reach of medicine's palliative power. Whether or not this case was made to her, and whether or not it would have made a difference in her decision, are unclear from the details of the history. As in the case above of the young woman with leukemia, however, it suggests that a patient's desire for euthanasia is influenced by his or her understanding of the medical facts of the case, an understanding that is influenced to a greater or lesser degree by the physician's skill, experience, and ability to convey this information.

In neither of these last two cases could one say with certainty that a more attractive presentation of alternatives to euthanasia would have made a difference in the patient's wishes. Nevertheless, it is troubling that readily available alternatives were not chosen by the patients and that, in the face of these alternatives, the physicians acquiesced to a request for euthanasia. It raises, at least in my mind, the question of whether euthanasia as a possibility does not, in some way, already influence clinical decisions. As an example, I return to the case of the child with Down's syndrome and duodenal atresia (Case 20). Whether or not the availability of euthanasia affected the parents' decision to decline treatment in this case is unclear from the narrative. As the narrator relates the story, the parents declined treatment first, then the issue of euthanasia arose. However, the short length of time within which the decision occurred (the child was 2 days old) should give one pause.

How the clinician presented the alternatives to the parents appears nowhere in the narrative. It is the ethicist called in to consult on the case who tells the story here. The ethicist is loathe to call this a case of euthanasia, and the treatment the clinician chose in the case (large doses of benzodiazepines to make the child "more comfortable") suggests at least some ambivalence, if not in intent, then, in the resolution and rationalization of the case. Benzodiazepines are relatively safe drugs; curare is not. The ethicist, however, did agree that the drug was given in sufficient doses so that whatever agony the child felt would be palliated first, then ended, by toxic levels of the drug. The choice of medications points again to the role of clinical judgment in these cases. It points, too, to the enormous influence a physician can have in these matters. . . .

Euthanasia as a Regulated Practice

To note that euthanasia seems to be aired, broadly speaking, among members of the medical profession is not the same as suggesting that it is a well-regulated practice. Rigter, Borst-Eilers, and Leenen, who publicly claim as much, have to contend with the fact that most cases of euthanasia receive no external scrutiny. Even if one takes their lowest estimate of 3,300 cases of euthanasia per year, the number of cases reviewed by the Ministry of Justice suggests that around 6% of cases of euthanasia are reported to the public prosecutor. Taking Rigter, Borst-Eilers, and Leenen's own higher estimates (5,000 to 10,000 cases per year) places the number of cases under external review at from 2% to 4%. In the cases I sampled, the prosecutor was notified less than 2% of the time.

What was most noteworthy, however, was the prime reason people gave for not contacting the prosecutor: every source mentioned saving the family embarrassment or additional grief. Notifying a prosecutor almost invariably involves some sort of interview with the family. To most of the people giving these clinical narratives, this was an unseemly and public intrusion on what should be a strictly private matter. The fear of personal liability—of prosecution—did not come up. In each of these instances, those relating the narrative felt that the guidelines had been well followed and that euthanasia was justified.

Dr. van der Meer, for example, suggested that to *exclude* the prosecutor from such cases was a matter of clinical judgment:

> What does it do to such a family to have the police come to the home, or to be having to answer such questions before a prosecutor? You must remember that after a patient is dead, the family is still a patient. And [although] the family knows death [comes] truly [with certainty], there is still sadness, grief. Then is not the time for such questions.

Admiraal disagrees and notes that he contacts the prosecutor with regularity in such cases. To do otherwise, he says, leaves the door open to abuses. I asked Dr. van der Meer about this possibility—specifically, whether the medical profession was able to police itself adequately. Did he believe that the lack of formal oversight that currently exists is a fertile field for abuse?

> But do you know such doctors? Do you know this [for a fact]? Because if there exist such doctors, they should not be in medicine . . . they are bad not only here [that is, in regards to euthanasia], but bad in other places too. People here [in the hospital] see euthanasia, and it would soon be known of such bad cases. No, I do not think this problem exists here. Perhaps in your country.

Dr. van der Meer also notes, however, that in his decades of practice, he thought that euthanasia was acceptable in "only a few cases." He thought it more instructive to tell of cases in which he had refused euthanasia:

> An old woman, very old, comes to the hospital many times. She says "now kill me," but I do not. She has pulmonia [pneumonia], and I treat this. She becomes better, then does not want to die. The family thought she should die, but the [right] to die is not to be given over [to another person]; if they cannot speak, they cannot die. But other times, perhaps I should have. A psychiatrist who was a friend has cancer. I cannot help him with medicines. He says he wants death, but I refuse: euthanasia is not an acute thing. But he leaves the hospital, and the next [day], the wife calls. He has died. I go to the home, and she says, "He died soon." A suicide? Perhaps, but whatever I did, it was not good medicine.

If it seems to one that Dr. van der Meer's faith in the ability of Dutch medicine to regulate itself seems overly optimistic, it should nevertheless be noted that his perspective is shared by many in the Netherlands and abroad. Those who practice euthanasia invariably thought that it was being well policed by the profession itself. Moreover, many of those who do not practice euthanasia (for a variety of reasons) also seemed to think that it was not currently being abused, though they were less certain about prospects for the future.

Dr. Richard Fenigsen, whose opposition to this practice I have already noted, strongly dissents on all counts: "If people say to you that we would know about 'bad' cases of euthanasia, then ask how this could be so. Do dead people now talk? Do doctors anywhere [inform] on their colleagues? Where are the prosecutors who would see such things?" Fenigsen's point of view is supported by others, though they represent a vocal minority in the Netherlands. Dr. van der Sluis, a physician involved in organizing a hospice movement in the Netherlands, agrees with Fenigsen that the practice is being abused and that what passes for voluntary euthanasia contains elements of professional and societal coercion. Others have conducted surveys in the Netherlands suggesting that elderly people generally oppose euthanasia (which, the authors add, expresses a fear of being involuntarily euthanized), and an alternative patients' rights movement, called Sanctuary, provides its members with advance directives stipulating that euthanasia not be performed on them under any circumstances. Even Admiraal pointed out to me that some nursing homes now advertise publicly that they do not perform euthanasia, and one of the nursing homes I visited gave me a document that they hand out to the families of newly arrived residents, which declares that the facility does not practice euthanasia.

What is one to make of this? My own sample of cases suggests that the guidelines are variously interpreted, though most fall within the broadest limits of permissible euthanasia stipulated by the KNMG. Some, clearly, did not meet the criteria. But the greatest curiosity to me was the unwillingness of most of the people with whom I spoke to criticize what seemed to be violations of one or more of the guidelines. In the abstract, everyone who practiced euthanasia could agree on the generalities: "Of course euthanasia may only be voluntary," said one physician. "How could it be otherwise? This is murder." But the specifics of the cases made people more timid in their assessments. I mentioned the case of the child with Down's syndrome to another physician (who said he practiced euthanasia under the "most strict interpretation"). He said the case was "difficult," but he could not say that euthanizing the child was "totally in error." Perhaps, he said, he would not have done the euthanasia, but other people have different beliefs. Even the case of the physician who killed the trauma victim with potassium chloride did not elicit a protest from this physician, who said again that such cases are "difficult." To another ethicist at another university hospital, to whom I brought this same case, the response was less ambiguous, "If you want rules, you should not do medical ethics. Society has limits, but people who live in those limits must still make decisions."

If there seems to be such disagreement as to what the guidelines mean—or a reluctance to criticize other people's interpretation of the guidelines—what is the point of guidelines or, what is more, of enforcing the guidelines? William Roose's comment at the outset of this chapter ("We're all Calvinists") plays out well in the case histories. Broadly speaking, the Dutch do seem to like rules on this subject. No fewer than seven governmental or professional organizations have issued guidelines on euthanasia since 1981. At the same time, they cannot agree on precisely what the rules mean. To give one an idea of the flexibility of the situation, a widely discussed case of euthanasia in the Netherlands is illustrative.

In 1984, a physician was suspected of having involuntarily euthanized several patients at a nursing home in the Hague called Der Terp. The physician was indicted on seven counts; three were brought to trial. The case was eventually thrown out of court because the evidence gathered was deemed inadmissible (the police had taken medical charts out of the nursing home without executing a proper search warrant). What is particularly perplexing about this case was the role of the KNMG, which entered the trial on the side of the physician, claiming that this was a matter for the medical disciplinary courts to handle, not the civil courts. The physician escaped civil punishment but was censured by the profession and lost the license to practice for one year.

Some have pointed to this case to demonstrate that involuntary euthanasia does not go unnoticed (though the physician went unpunished, it was due to a procedural technicality). Others call the case an embarrassment and say that it does not represent the status of euthanasia in the Netherlands. Opponents of the practice, however, use the case to bolster their contention that, at the very least, the current practice of euthanasia merits further regulation (though they believe that any regulatory policy will fall short of what the situation would require). . . .

How Public a Public Policy?

. . . One is left, then, with this odd situation. Euthanasia has no formal legal sanction in the Netherlands, yet it finds tolerance to the extent that one can make a *public* case for extenuating circumstances. Official protestations aside, however, public regulation of euthanasia devolves, as a matter of practice, onto a particular segment of society—the physicians. Neither the courts nor the other branches of the Dutch government seem to play as active a role in managing and restricting euthanasia as the guidelines would imply, nor as defenders of the practice in the Netherlands have suggested. The role of both participant and regulator has fallen to the medical practitioners, with what seems to be the tacit consent of most of the rest of Dutch society.

I find this a deeply troubling state of affairs. If, as I have tried to demonstrate, restraint and regulation in the matter of euthanasia rests, to a large extent, on the individual practitioners, it bespeaks a remarkable trust in the medical profession in the Netherlands or an almost cavalier attitude toward those—however many or few their numbers—who cannot challenge a decision to have euthanasia performed on them. Public policy regarding euthanasia in the Netherlands operates under the assumption that the responsible parties—physicians and patients—will exercise this enormous autonomy with wisdom and caution. To the extent that public policy fails to protect those who can be neither responsible nor truly autonomous from those who are neither wise nor cautious, it fails altogether. . . .

Capital Punishment

Ordinarily, we think that people have a right to life and that governments, if they have any obligations at all, are obliged to protect that right. But many people believe that the government is nevertheless justified in putting certain kinds of criminals to death. Generally, they believe that the government needs to deprive some people of the right to life in order to protect that right for others—indeed, for the vast majority of its citizens. From this belief arises the issue of capital punishment: Can the government be justified in putting someone to death?

The death penalty raises important questions about the origin, status, and extent of the right to life. Most people believe that they have the right to defend themselves against an assailant. They believe, in particular, that they have the right to kill an attacker if their own lives are in danger. Some philosophers have extended this reasoning to the state as a whole. The murderer, for example, can be seen as attacking society; society is justified in using lethal force to defend itself. Of course, once apprehended, the murderer no longer threatens society in quite the same way. But if murderers are likely to murder again, the self-protection argument may apply. This strategy argues that the right to life is limited so that those who threaten death to others lose their own right to life or, at least, deserve to have it overridden by the rights of others.

Other philosophers have argued in favor of a right to revenge. Society, having suffered a serious harm, has the right to take retribution by punishing the offender. Moreover, the punishment that seems appropriate for causing death is suffering death. They have thus maintained that justice sometimes requires the death penalty.

Still others have stressed deterrence as a justification for capital punishment. Putting a criminal to death, on this view, deters others from committing similar crimes. Enforcing the death penalty thus promotes the good of society; it may save more lives than it costs. Statistical studies of the effects of capital punishment tend to be inconclusive; it is not clear whether the death penalty actually has this effect. But some studies report that each execution saves several lives by deterring prospective murderers.

These arguments raise large issues beyond those involving the right to life itself. What rights does society have to defend itself against criminal activity? What is the moral justification for punishment? When can the interests of a larger group justify violating the rights of an individual? Under what circumstances does a person lose or surrender rights? In each case, arguments for and against capital punishment take or presuppose controversial stands.

In *Furman* v. *Georgia,* in 1972, the Supreme Court held that a Georgia capital punishment law was unconstitutional. The Court found that the death penalty, under the circumstances of its application there, was incompatible with human dignity and violated the Eighth Amendment prohibiting "cruel and unusual" punishment. Some members of the Court argued that the death penalty was in itself objectionable. The majority, however, concluded simply that its application was too haphazard, unprincipled, and unjust to count as constitutional.

In *Gregg* v. *Georgia,* four years later, the Court upheld Georgia's revision of its capital punishment law. Under that revision, the jury receives detailed instructions about the appropriateness of the death penalty. Certain kinds of circumstances are aggravating, tending to justify the death penalty; others are mitigating, tending to justify an alternative sentence. The Court decided that the death penalty, administered in this way, is constitutionally acceptable.

Strictly speaking, these decisions rest on legal rather than moral grounds. They are not, however, morally irrelevant. Cruel and unusual punishments are ethically as well as legally objectionable. Consequently, the legal arguments of the justices in these cases parallel moral arguments about the permissibility of capital punishment.

Ernest van den Haag goes beyond typical defenses of capital punishment in at least two ways. First, he argues that deterrence provides an argument for the death penalty, even if we cannot determine whether it succeeds in deterring or not. If there is a chance that it does, he contends, then we place innocent lives at risk by failing to carry it out. Second, he argues that certain special cases justify capital punishment, even if it is unacceptable in most cases. Thus, we may be justified in executing war criminals and criminals who murder in prison while already serving life terms, even if we are not justified in executing most murderers.

JUSTICE WILLIAM BRENNAN

concurring opinion in *Furman* v. *Georgia* (1972)

William Brennan was Justice of the United States Supreme Court from 1956 to 1990. (Source: Furman v. Georgia *408 U.S. 238 [1972]. Most legal references have been omitted.)*

QUESTIONS FOR REFLECTION

1. Justice Brennan offers four principles for determining whether a punishment "comports with human dignity." Explain them.
2. Why, in Justice Brennan's view, is capital punishment incompatible with human dignity?
3. How is human dignity connected to the "right to have rights," in Justice Brennan's view?
4. What is the moral significance of the rare application and seeming arbitrariness of the death penalty?
5. Capital punishment was legal in most states in 1972, and remains legal in most states today. Texas and California each have almost 400 prisoners waiting on death row. Polls show that a majority of Americans support capital punishment. Does this contradict Justice Brennan's claim that contemporary society rejects the death penalty? Why, or why not?

. . . Mr. Justice Brennan, concurring.

The question presented in these cases is whether death is today a punishment for crime that is "cruel and unusual" and consequently, by virtue of the Eighth and Fourteenth Amendments, beyond the power of the State to inflict. . . .

[I . . .]

II

Ours would indeed be a simple task were we required merely to measure a challenged punishment against those that history has long condemned. That narrow and unwarranted view of the Clause, however, was left behind with the 19th century. Our task today is more complex. We know "that the words of the [Clause] are not precise, and that their scope is not static." We know, therefore, that the Clause "must draw its meaning from the evolving standards of decency that mark the progress of a maturing society." That knowledge, of course, is but the beginning of the inquiry.

In *Trop* v. *Dulles*, it was said that "[t]he question is whether [a] penalty subjects the individual to a fate forbidden by the principle of civilized treatment guaranteed by the [Clause]." It was also said that a challenged punishment must be examined "in light of the basic prohibition against inhuman treatment" embodied in the Clause. It was said, finally, that:

> "The basic concept underlying the [Clause] is nothing less than the dignity of man. While the State has the power to punish, the [Clause] stands to assure

that this power be exercised within the limits of civilized standards."

At bottom, then, the Cruel and Unusual Punishments Clause prohibits the infliction of uncivilized and inhuman punishments. The State, even as it punishes, must treat its members with respect for their intrinsic worth as human beings. A punishment is "cruel and unusual," therefore, if it does not comport with human dignity.

This formulation, of course, does not of itself yield principles for assessing the constitutional validity of particular punishments. Nevertheless, even though "[t]his Court has had little occasion to give precise content to the [Clause]," there are principles recognized in our cases and inherent in the Clause sufficient to permit a judicial determination whether a challenged punishment comports with human dignity.

The primary principle is that a punishment must not be so severe as to be degrading to the dignity of human beings. Pain, certainly, may be a factor in the judgment. The infliction of an extremely severe punishment will often entail physical suffering. Yet the Framers also knew "that there could be exercises of cruelty by laws other than those which inflicted bodily pain or mutilation." Even though "[t]here may be involved no physical mistreatment, no primitive torture," *Trop* v. *Dulles,* severe mental pain may be inherent in the infliction of a particular punishment. That, indeed, was one of the conclusions underlying the holding of the plurality in *Trop* v. *Dulles* that the punishment of expatriation violates the Clause. And the physical and mental suffering inherent in the punishment of *cadena temporal** was an obvious basis for the Court's decision in *Weems* v. *United States* that the punishment was "cruel and unusual."

More than the presence of pain, however, is comprehended in the judgment that the extreme severity of a punishment makes it degrading to the dignity of human beings. The barbaric punishments condemned by history, "punishments which inflict torture, such as the rack, the thumbscrew, the iron boot, the stretching of limbs and the like," are, of course, "attended with acute pain and suffering." When we consider why they have been condemned, however, we realize that the pain involved is not the only reason. The true significance of these punishments is that they treat members of the human race as nonhumans, as objects to be toyed with and discarded. They are thus inconsistent with the fundamental premise of the Clause that even the vilest criminal remains a human being possessed of common human dignity.

The infliction of an extremely severe punishment, then, like the one before the Court in *Weems* v. *United States,* from which "[n]o circumstance of degradation [was] omitted," may reflect the attitude that the person punished is not entitled to recognition as a fellow human being. That attitude may be apparent apart from the severity of the punishment itself. In *Louisiana ex rel. Francis* v. *Resweber* (1947), for example, the unsuccessful electrocution, although it caused "mental anguish and physical pain," was the result of "an unforeseeable accident." Had the failure been intentional, however, the punishment would have been, like torture, so degrading and indecent as to amount to a refusal to accord the criminal human status. Indeed, a punishment may be degrading to human dignity solely because it is a punishment. A State may not punish a person for being "mentally ill, or a leper, or . . . afflicted with a venereal disease," or for being addicted to narcotics. To inflict punishment for having a disease is to treat the individual as a diseased thing rather than as a sick human being. That the punishment is not severe, "in the abstract," is irrelevant; "[e]ven one day in prison would be a cruel and unusual punishment for the 'crime' of having a common cold." Finally, of course, a punishment may be degrading simply by reason of its enormity. A prime example is expatriation, a "punishment more primitive than torture," for it necessarily involves a denial by society of the individual's existence as a member of the human community.

In determining whether a punishment comports with human dignity, we are aided also by a second principle inherent in the Clause—that the

* *Cadena temporal:* a punishment requiring a period of hard and painful labor in chains, followed by perpetual probation. In *Weems* v. *United States,* the period of hard and painful labor was twelve years. —ED.

State must not arbitrarily inflict a severe punishment. This principle derives from the notion that the State does not respect human dignity when, without reason, it inflicts upon some people a severe punishment that it does not inflict upon others. Indeed, the very words "cruel and unusual punishments" imply condemnation of the arbitrary infliction of severe punishments. And, as we now know, the English history of the Clause reveals a particular concern with the establishment of a safeguard against arbitrary punishments. . . .

A third principle inherent in the Clause is that a severe punishment must not be unacceptable to contemporary society. Rejection by society, of course, is a strong indication that a severe punishment does not comport with human dignity. In applying this principle, however, we must make certain that the judicial determination is as objective as possible. Thus, for example, *Weems* v. *United States* and *Trop* v. *Dulles* suggest that one factor that may be considered is the existence of the punishment in jurisdictions other than those before the Court. *Wilkerson* v. *Utah* suggests that another factor to be considered is the historic usage of the punishment. *Trop* v. *Dulles* combined present acceptance with past usage by observing that "the death penalty has been employed throughout our history, and, in a day when it is still widely accepted, it cannot be said to violate the constitutional concept of cruelty." In *Robinson* v. *California*, which involved the infliction of punishment for narcotics addiction, the Court went a step further, concluding simply that "in the light of contemporary human knowledge, a law which made a criminal offense of such a disease would doubtless be universally thought to be an infliction of cruel and unusual punishment."

The question under this principle, then, is whether there are objective indicators from which a court can conclude that contemporary society considers a severe punishment unacceptable. Accordingly, the judicial task is to review the history of a challenged punishment and to examine society's present practices with respect to its use. Legislative authorization, of course, does not establish acceptance. The acceptability of a severe punishment is measured, not by its availability, for it might become so offensive to society as never to be inflicted, but by its use.

The final principle inherent in the Clause is that a severe punishment must not be excessive. A punishment is excessive under this principle if it is unnecessary: The infliction of a severe punishment by the State cannot comport with human dignity when it is nothing more than the pointless infliction of suffering. If there is a significantly less severe punishment adequate to achieve the purposes for which the punishment is inflicted, the punishment inflicted is unnecessary and therefore excessive. . . .

There are, then, four principles by which we may determine whether a particular punishment is "cruel and unusual." The primary principle, which I believe supplies the essential predicate for the application of the others, is that a punishment must not by its severity be degrading to human dignity. The paradigm violation of this principle would be the infliction of a torturous punishment of the type that the Clause has always prohibited. Yet "[i]t is unlikely that any State at this moment in history" would pass a law providing for the infliction of such a punishment. Indeed, no such punishment has ever been before this Court. The same may be said of the other principles. It is unlikely that this Court will confront a severe punishment that is obviously inflicted in wholly arbitrary fashion; no State would engage in a reign of blind terror. Nor is it likely that this Court will be called upon to review a severe punishment that is clearly and totally rejected throughout society; no legislature would be able even to authorize the infliction of such a punishment. Nor, finally, is it likely that this Court will have to consider a severe punishment that is patently unnecessary; no State today would inflict a severe punishment knowing that there was no reason whatever for doing so. In short, we are unlikely to have occasion to determine that a punishment is fatally offensive under any one principle.

Since the Bill of Rights was adopted, this Court has adjudged only three punishments to be within the prohibition of the Clause. See *Weems* v. *United States* (1910) (12 years in chains at hard and painful labor); *Trop* v. *Dulles* (1958) (expatriation);

Robinson v. *California* (1962) (imprisonment for narcotics addiction). Each punishment, of course, was degrading to human dignity, but of none could it be said conclusively that it was fatally offensive under one or the other of the principles. Rather, these "cruel and unusual punishments" seriously implicated several of the priniciples, and it was the application of the principles in combination that supported the judgment. That, indeed, is not surprising. The function of these principles, after all, is simply to provide means by which a court can determine whether a challenged punishment comports with human dignity. They are, therefore, interrelated, and in most cases it will be their convergence that will justify the conclusion that a punishment is "cruel and unusual." The test, then, will ordinarily be a cumulative one: If a punishment is unusually severe, if there is a strong probability that it is inflicted arbitrarily, if it is substantially rejected by contemporary society, and if there is no reason to believe that it serves any penal purpose more effectively than some less severe punishment, then the continued infliction of that punishment violates the command of the Clause that the State may not inflict inhuman and uncivilized punishments upon those convicted of crimes.

III

. . . The question, then, is whether the deliberate infliction of death is today consistent with the command of the Clause that the State may not inflict punishments that do not comport with human dignity. I will analyze the punishment of death in terms of the principles set out above and the cumulative test to which they lead: It is a denial of human dignity for the State arbitrarily to subject a person to an unusually severe punishment that society has indicated it does not regard as acceptable, and that cannot be shown to serve any penal purpose more effectively than a significantly less drastic punishment. Under these principles and this test, death is today a "cruel and unusual" punishment.

Death is a unique punishment in the United States. In a society that so strongly affirms the sanctity of life, not surprisingly the common view is that death is the ultimate sanction. This natural human feeling appears all about us. There has been no national debate about punishment, in general or by imprisonment, comparable to the debate about the punishment of death. No other punishment has been so continuously restricted, nor has any State yet abolished prisons, as some have abolished this punishment. And those States that still inflict death reserve it for the most heinous crimes. Juries, of course, have always treated death cases differently, as have governors exercising their commutation powers. Criminal defendants are of the same view. "As all practicing lawyers know, who have defended persons charged with capital offenses, often the only goal possible is to avoid the death penalty." Some legislatures have required particular procedures, such as two-stage trials and automatic appeals, applicable only in death cases. "It is the universal experience in the administration of criminal justice that those charged with capital offenses are granted special considerations." This Court, too, almost always treats death cases as a class apart. And the unfortunate effect of this punishment upon the functioning of the judicial process is well known; no other punishment has a similar effect.

The only explanation for the uniqueness of death is its extreme severity. Death is today an unusually severe punishment, unusual in its pain, in its finality, and in its enormity. No other existing punishment is comparable to death in terms of physical and mental suffering. Although our information is not conclusive, it appears that there is no method available that guarantees an immediate and painless death. Since the discontinuance of flogging as a constitutionally permissible punishment, death remains as the only punishment that may involve the conscious infliction of physical pain. In addition, we know that mental pain is an inseparable part of our practice of punishing criminals by death, for the prospect of pending execution exacts a frightful toll during the inevitable long wait between the imposition of sentence and the actual infliction of death. As the California Supreme Court pointed out, "the process of carrying out a verdict of death is often so degrading and brutalizing to the human spirit as to constitute psychological torture." Indeed, as Mr. Justice Frankfurter noted, "the onset of insanity while awaiting execution of a death sentence is not a rare phenomenon." The "fate of ever-increasing fear and distress" to which the expatriate is subjected can only exist to a greater degree for a person confined in prison awaiting death.

The unusual severity of death is manifested most clearly in its finality and enormity. Death, in these respects, is in a class by itself. Expatriation, for example, is a punishment that "destroys for the individual the political existence that was centuries in the development," that "strips the citizen of his status in the national and international political community," and that puts "[h]is very existence" in jeopardy. Expatriation thus inherently entails "the total destruction of the individual's status in organized society." "In short, the expatriate has lost the right to have rights." Yet, demonstrably, expatriation is not "a fate worse than death." Although death, like expatriation, destroys the individual's "political existence" and his "status in organized society," it does more, for, unlike expatriation, death also destroys "[h]is very existence." There is, too, at least the possibility that the expatriate will in the future regain "the right to have rights." Death forecloses even that possibility.

Death is truly an awesome punishment. The calculated killing of a human being by the State involves, by its very nature, a denial of the executed person's humanity. The contrast with the plight of a person punished by imprisonment is evident. An individual in prison does not lose "the right to have rights." A prisoner retains, for example, the constitutional rights to the free exercise of religion, to be free of cruel and unusual punishments, and to treatment as a "person" for purposes of due process of law and the equal protection of the laws. A prisoner remains a member of the human family. Moreover, he retains the right of access to the courts. His punishment is not irrevocable. Apart from the common charge, grounded upon the recognition of human fallibility, that the punishment of death must inevitably be inflicted upon innocent men, we know that death has been the lot of men whose convictions were unconstitutionally secured in view of later, retroactively applied, holdings of this Court. The punishment itself may have been unconstitutionally inflicted, yet the finality of death precludes relief. An executed person has indeed "lost the right to have rights." As one 19th century proponent of punishing criminals by death declared, "When a man is hung, there is an end of our relations with him. His execution is a way of saying, 'You are not fit for this world, take your chance elsewhere.'"

In comparison to all other punishments today, then, the deliberate extinguishment of human life by the State is uniquely degrading to human dignity. I would not hesitate to hold, on that ground alone, that death is today a "cruel and unusual" punishment, were it not that death is a punishment of longstanding usage and acceptance in this country. I therefore turn to the second principle—that the State may not arbitrarily inflict an unusually severe punishment.

The outstanding characteristic of our present practice of punishing criminals by death is the infrequency with which we resort to it. The evidence is conclusive that death is not the ordinary punishment for any crime.

There has been a steady decline in the infliction of this punishment in every decade since the 1930's, the earliest period for which accurate statistics are available. In the 1930's, executions averaged 167 per year; in the 1940's, the average was 128; in the 1950's, it was 72; and in the years 1960–1962, it was 48. There have been a total of 46 executions since then, 36 of them in 1963–1964. Yet our population and the number of capital crimes committed have increased greatly over the past four decades. The contemporary rarity of the infliction of this punishment is thus the end result of a long-continued decline. That rarity is plainly revealed by an examination of the years 1961–1970, the last 10-year period for which statistics are available. During that time, an average of 106 death sentences was imposed each year. Not nearly that number, however, could be carried out, for many were precluded by commutations to life or a term of years, transfers to mental institutions because of insanity, resentences to life or a term of years, grants of new trials and orders for resentencing, dismissals of indictments and reversals of convictions, and deaths by suicide and natural causes. On January 1, 1961, the death row population was 219; on December 31, 1970, it was 608; during that span, there were 135 executions. Consequently, had the 389 additions to death row also been executed, the annual average would have been 52. In short, the country might, at most, have executed one criminal each week. In fact, of course, far fewer were executed. Even before the moratorium on executions began in 1967, executions totaled only 42 in 1961 and 47 in 1962, an average of less than one per week; the number dwindled to 21 in 1963, to 15 in 1964, and to seven in 1965; in 1966, there was one execution, and in 1967, there were two.

When a country of over 200 million people inflicts an unusually severe punishment no more than 50 times a year, the inference is strong that the punishment is not being regularly and fairly applied. To dispel it would indeed require a clear showing of nonarbitrary infliction.

Although there are not exact figures available, we know that thousands of murders and rapes are committed annually in States where death is an authorized punishment for those crimes. However the rate of infliction is characterized—as "freakishly" or "spectacularly" rare, or simply as rare—it would take the purest sophistry to deny that death is inflicted in only a minute fraction of these cases. How much rarer, after all, could the infliction of death be?

When the punishment of death is inflicted in a trivial number of the cases in which it is legally available, the conclusion is virtually inescapable that it is being inflicted arbitrarily. Indeed, it smacks of little more than a lottery system. The States claim, however, that this rarity is evidence not of arbitrariness, but of informed selectivity: Death is inflicted, they say, only in "extreme" cases.

Informed selectivity, of course, is a value not to be denigrated. Yet presumably the States could make precisely the same claim if there were 10 executions per year, or five, or even if there were but one. That there may be as many as 50 per year does not strengthen the claim. When the rate of infliction is at this low level, it is highly implausible that only the worst criminals or the criminals who commit the worst crimes are selected for this punishment. No one has yet suggested a rational basis that could differentiate in those terms the few who die from the many who go to prison. Crimes and criminals simply do not admit of a distinction that can be drawn so finely as to explain, on that ground, the execution of such a tiny sample of those eligible. Certainly the laws that provide for this punishment do not attempt to draw that distinction; all cases to which the laws apply are necessarily "extreme." Nor is the distinction credible in fact. If, for example, petitioner Furman or his crime illustrates the "extreme," then nearly all murderers and their murders are also "extreme."* Furthermore, our procedures in death cases, rather than resulting in the selection of "extreme" cases for this punishment, actually sanction an arbitrary selection. For this Court has held that juries may, as they do, make the decision whether to impose a death sentence wholly unguided by standards governing that decision. In other words, our proce-

* The victim surprised Furman in the act of burglarizing the victim's home in the middle of the night. While escaping, Furman killed the victim with one pistol shot fired through the closed kitchen door from the outside. At the trial, Furman gave his version of the killing:

"They got me charged with murder and I admit, I admit going to these folks' home and they did caught me in there and I was coming back out, backing up and there was a wire down there on the floor. I was coming out backwards and fell back and I didn't intend to kill nobody. I didn't know they was behind the door. The gun went off and I didn't know nothing about no murder until they arrested me, and when the gun went off I was down on the floor and I got up and ran. That's all to it."

The Georgia Supreme Court accepted that version:

"The admission in open court by the accused . . . that during the period in which he was involved in the commission of a criminal act at the home of the deceased, he accidentally tripped over a wire in leaving the premises causing the gun to go off, together with other facts and circumstances surrounding the death of the deceased by violent means, was sufficient to support the verdict of guilty of murder. . . . "

About Furman himself, the jury knew only that he was black and that, according to his statement at trial, he was 26 years old and worked at "Superior Upholstery." It took the jury one hour and 35 minutes to return a verdict of guilt and a sentence of death.

dures are not constructed to guard against the totally capricious selection of criminals for the punishment of death.

Although it is difficult to imagine what further facts would be necessary in order to prove that death is, as my Brother Stewart puts it, "wantonly and . . . freakishly" inflicted, I need not conclude that arbitrary infliction is patently obvious. I am not considering this punishment by the isolated light of one principle. The probability of arbitrariness is sufficiently substantial that it can be relied upon, in combination with the other principles, in reaching a judgment on the constitutionality of this punishment.

When there is a strong probability that an unusually severe and degrading punishment is being inflicted arbitrarily, we may well expect that society will disapprove of its infliction. I turn, therefore, to the third principle. An examination of the history and present operation of the American practice of punishing criminals by death reveals that this punishment has been almost totally rejected by contemporary society.

I cannot add to my Brother Marshall's comprehensive treatment of the English and American history of this punishment. I emphasize, however, one significant conclusion that emerges from that history. From the beginning of our Nation, the punishment of death has stirred acute public controversy. Although pragmatic arguments for and against the punishment have been frequently advanced, this longstanding and heated controversy cannot be explained solely as the result of differences over the practical wisdom of a particular government policy. At bottom, the battle has been waged on moral grounds. The country has debated whether a society for which the dignity of the individual is the supreme value can, without a fundamental inconsistency, follow the practice of deliberately putting some of its members to death. In the United States, as in other nations of the western world, "the struggle about this punishment has been one between ancient and deeply rooted beliefs in retribution, atonement or vengeance on the one hand, and, on the other, beliefs in the personal value and dignity of the common man that were born of the democratic movement of the eighteenth century, as well as beliefs in the scientific approach to an understanding of the motive forces of human conduct, which are the result of the growth of the sciences of behavior during the nineteenth and twentieth centuries." It is this essentially moral conflict that forms the backdrop for the past changes in and the present operation of our system of imposing death as a punishment for crime.

Our practice of punishing criminals by death has changed greatly over the years. One significant change has been in our methods of inflicting death. Although this country never embraced the more violent and repulsive methods employed in England, we did for a long time rely almost exclusively upon the gallows and the firing squad. Since the development of the supposedly more humane methods of electrocution late in the 19th century and lethal gas in the 20th, however, hanging and shooting have virtually ceased. Our concern for decency and human dignity, moreover, has compelled changes in the circumstances surrounding the execution itself. No longer does our society countenance the spectacle of public executions, once thought desirable as a deterrent to criminal behavior by others. Today we reject public executions as debasing and brutalizing to us all.

Also significant is the drastic decrease in the crimes for which the punishment of death is actually inflicted. While esoteric capital crimes remain on the books, since 1930 murder and rape have accounted for nearly 99% of the total executions, and murder alone for about 87%. In addition, the crime of capital murder has itself been limited. As the Court noted in *McGautha* v. *California*, there was in this country a "rebellion against the common-law rule imposing a mandatory death sentence on all convicted murderers." Initially, that rebellion resulted in legislative definitions that distinguished between degrees of murder, retaining the mandatory death sentence only for murder in the first degree. Yet "[t]his new legislative criterion for isolating crimes appropriately by death soon proved as unsuccessful as the concept of 'malice aforethought,'" the common-law means of separating murder from manslaughter. Not only was the distinction between degrees of murder confusing and uncertain in practice, but even in clear cases of first-degree murder juries continued to take the law into their own hands: if they felt that death was an inappropriate punishment, "they simply refused to convict of the capital offense." The phenomenon of jury nullification thus remained to counteract the rigors of mandatory death sentences. Bowing to reality, "legislatures did not try, as before, to refine further the definition of capital homicides. Instead they adopted the method of forthrightly granting juries the discretion which they had been exercising in fact." In consequence, virtually all death sentences today are discretionarily imposed. Finally, it is significant that nine States no longer inflict the punishment of death under any circumstances, and five others have restricted it to extremely rare crimes.

Thus, although "the death penalty has been employed throughout our history," in fact the history of this punishment is one of successive restriction. What was once a common punishment has become, in the context of a continuing moral debate, increasingly rare. The evolution of this punishment evidences, not that it is an inevitable part of the American scene, but that it has proved progressively more troublesome to the national conscience. The result of this movement is our current system of administering the punishment, under which death sentences are rarely imposed and death is even more rarely inflicted. It is, of course, "We, the People" who are responsible for the rarity both of the imposition and the carrying out of this punishment. Juries, "express[ing] the conscience of the community on the ultimate question of life or death," *Witherspoon* v. *Illinois*, have been able to bring themselves to vote for death in a mere 100 or so cases among the thousands tried each year where the punishment is available. Governors, elected by and acting for us, have regularly commuted a substantial number of those sentences. And it is our society that insists upon due process of law to the end that no person will be unjustly put to death, thus ensuring that many more of those sentences will not be carried out. In sum, we have made death a rare punishment today.

The progressive decline in, and the current rarity of, the infliction of death demonstrate that our society seriously questions the appropriateness of this punishment today. The States point out that many legislatures authorize death as the punishment for certain crimes and that substantial segments of the public, as reflected in opinion polls and referendum votes, continue to support it. Yet the availability of this punishment through statutory authorization, as well as the polls and referenda, which amount simply to approval of that authorization, simply underscores the extent to which our society has in fact rejected this punishment. When an unusually severe punishment is authorized for wide-scale application but not, because of society's refusal, inflicted save in a few instances, the inference is compelling that there is a deep-seated reluctance to inflict it. Indeed, the likelihood is great that the punishment is tolerated only because of its disuse. The objective indicator of society's view of an unusually severe punishment is what society does with it, and today society will inflict death upon only a small sample of the eligible criminals. Rejection could hardly be more complete without becoming absolute. At the very least, I must conclude that contemporary society views this punishment with substantial doubt.

The final principle to be considered is that an unusually severe and degrading punishment may not be excessive in view of the purposes for which it is inflicted. This principle, too, is related to the others. When there is a strong probability that the State is arbitrarily inflicting an unusually severe punishment that is subject to grave societal doubts, it is likely also that the punishment cannot be shown to be serving any penal purpose that could not be served equally well by some less severe punishment.

The States' primary claim is that death is a necessary punishment because it prevents the commission of capital crimes more effectively than any less severe punishment. The first part of this claim is that the infliction of death is necessary to stop the individuals executed from committing further crimes. The sufficient answer to this is that if a criminal convicted of a capital crime poses a danger to society, effective administration of the

State's pardon and parole laws can delay or deny his release from prison, and techniques of isolation can eliminate or minimize the danger while he remains confined.

The more significant argument is that the threat of death prevents the commission of capital crimes because it deters potential criminals who would not be deterred by the threat of imprisonment. The argument is not based upon evidence that the threat of death is a superior deterrent. Indeed, as my Brother Marshall establishes, the available evidence uniformly indicates, although it does not conclusively prove, that the threat of death has no greater deterrent effect than the threat of imprisonment. The States argue, however, that they are entitled to rely upon common human experience, and that experience, they say, supports the conclusion that death must be a more effective deterrent than any less severe punishment. Because people fear death the most, the argument runs, the threat of death must be the greatest deterrent.

It is important to focus upon the precise import of this argument. It is not denied that many, and probably most, capital crimes cannot be deterred by the threat of punishment. Thus the argument can apply only to those who think rationally about the commission of capital crimes. Particularly is that true when the potential criminal, under this argument, must not only consider the risk of punishment, but also distinguish between two possible punishments. The concern, then, is with a particular type of potential criminal, the rational person who will commit a capital crime knowing that the punishment is long-term imprisonment, which may well be for the rest of his life, but will not commit the crime knowing that the punishment is death. On the face of it, the assumption that such persons exist is implausible.

In any event, this argument cannot be appraised in the abstract. We are not presented with the theoretical question whether under any imaginable circumstances the threat of death might be a greater deterrent to the commission of capital crimes than the threat of imprisonment. We are concerned with the practice of punishing criminals by death as it exists in the United States today. Proponents of this argument necessarily admit that its validity depends upon the existence of a system in which the punishment of death is invariably and swiftly imposed. Our system, of course, satisfies neither condition. A rational person contemplating a murder or rape is confronted, not with the certainty of a speedy death, but with the slightest possibility that he will be executed in the distant future. The risk of death is remote and improbable; in contrast, the risk of long-term imprisonment is near and great. In short, whatever the speculative validity of the assumption that the threat of death is a superior deterrent, there is no reason to believe that as currently administered the punishment of death is necessary to deter the commission of capital crimes. Whatever might be the case were all or substantially all eligible criminals quickly put to death, unverifiable possibilities are an insufficient basis upon which to conclude that the threat of death today has any greater deterrent efficacy than the threat of imprisonment.*

There is, however, another aspect to the argument that the punishment of death is necessary for the protection of society. The infliction of death, the States urge, serves to manifest the community's outrage at the commission of the crime. It is, they say, a concrete public expression of moral indignation that inculcates respect for the law and helps assure a more peaceful community. Moreover, we are told, not only does the punishment of death exert this widespread moralizing influence upon community values, it also satisfies the popular demand for grievous condemnation of abhorrent crimes and thus prevents disorder, lynching, and

* There is also the more limited argument that death is a necessary punishment when criminals are already serving or subject to a sentence of life imprisonment. If the only punishment available is further imprisonment, it is said, those criminals will have nothing to lose by committing further crimes, and accordingly the threat of death is the sole deterrent. But "life" imprisonment is a misnomer today. Rarely, if ever, do crimes carry a mandatory life sentence without possibility of parole. That possibility ensures that criminals do not reach the point where further crimes are free of consequences. Moreover, if this argument is simply an assertion that the threat of death is a more effective deterrent than the threat of increased imprisonment by denial of release on parole, then, as noted above, there is simply no evidence to support it.

attempts by private citizens to take the law into their own hands.

The question, however, is not whether death serves these supposed purposes of punishment, but whether death serves them more effectively than imprisonment. There is no evidence whatever that utilization of imprisonment rather than death encourages private blood feuds and other disorders. Surely if there were such a danger, the execution of a handful of criminals each year would not prevent it. The assertion that death alone is a sufficiently emphatic denunciation for capital crimes suffers from the same defect. If capital crimes require the punishment of death in order to provide moral reinforcement for the basic values of the community, those values can only be undermined when death is so rarely inflicted upon the criminals who commit the crimes. Furthermore, it is certainly doubtful that the infliction of death by the State does in fact strengthen the community's moral code; if the deliberate extinguishment of human life has any effect at all, it more likely tends to lower our respect for life and brutalize our values. That, after all, is why we no longer carry out public executions. In any event, this claim simply means that one purpose of punishment is to indicate social disapproval of crime. To serve that purpose our laws distribute punishments according to the gravity of crimes and punish more severely the crimes society regards as more serious. That purpose cannot justify any particular punishment as the upper limit of severity.

There is, then, no substantial reason to believe that the punishment of death, as currently administered, is necessary for the protection of society. The only other purpose suggested, one that is independent of protection for society, is retribution. Shortly stated, retribution in this context means that criminals are put to death because they deserve it.

Although it is difficult to believe that any State today wishes to proclaim adherence to "naked vengeance," the States claim, in reliance upon its statutory authorization, that death is the only fit punishment for capital crimes and that this retributive purpose justifies its infliction. In the past, judged by its statutory authorization, death was considered the only fit punishment for the crime of forgery, for the first federal criminal statute provided a mandatory death penalty for that crime. Obviously, concepts of justice change; no immutable moral order requires death for murderers and rapists. The claim that death is a just punishment necessarily refers to the existence of certain public beliefs. The claim must be that for capital crimes death alone comports with society's notion of proper punishment. As administered today, however, the punishment of death cannot be justified as a necessary means of exacting retribution from criminals. When the overwhelming number of criminals who commit capital crimes go to prison, it cannot be concluded that death serves the purpose of retribution more effectively than imprisonment. The asserted public belief that murderers and rapists deserve to die is flatly inconsistent with the execution of a random few. As the history of the punishment of death in this country shows, our society wishes to prevent crime; we have no desire to kill criminals simply to get even with them.

In sum, the punishment of death is inconsistent with all four principles: Death is an unusually severe and degrading punishment; there is a strong probability that it is inflicted arbitrarily; its rejection by contemporary society is virtually total; and there is no reason to believe that it serves any penal purpose more effectively than the less severe punishment of imprisonment. The function of these principles is to enable a court to determine whether a punishment comports with human dignity. Death, quite simply, does not. . . .

JUSTICE THURGOOD MARSHALL

concurring opinion in *Furman* v. *Georgia* (1972)

Justice Thurgood Marshall argued the famous school desegregation case, Brown v. Board of Education of the City of Topeka, *in 1954 and served as Justice of the United States Supreme Court from 1967 to 1991.*

QUESTIONS FOR REFLECTION

1. Why does Justice Marshall reject retribution as a rationale for the death penalty? Do you agree?
2. Justice Marshall argues that the death penalty does not deter criminals. Why? Do you find his arguments persuasive?
3. Some argue that the death penalty is needed for particularly dangerous criminals. Justice Marshall rejects that argument. Why? Do you agree?

Mr. Justice Marshall, concurring. . . .

V

In order to assess whether or not death is an excessive or unnecessary penalty, it is necessary to consider the reasons why a legislature might select it as punishment for one or more offenses, and examine whether less severe penalties would satisfy the legitimate legislative wants as well as capital punishment. If they would, then the death penalty is unnecessary cruelty, and, therefore, unconstitutional.

There are six purposes conceivably served by capital punishment: retribution, deterrence, prevention of repetitive criminal acts, encouragement of guilty pleas and confessions, eugenics, and economy. These are considered *seriatim* below.

A. The concept of retribution is one of the most misunderstood in all of our criminal jurisprudence. The principal source of confusion derives from the fact that, in dealing with the concept, most people confuse the question "why do men in fact punish?" with the question "what justifies men in punishing?" Men may punish for any number of reasons, but the one reason that punishment is morally good or morally justifiable is that someone has broken the law. Thus, it can correctly be said that breaking the law is the *sine qua non* of punishment, or, in other words, that we only tolerate punishment as it is imposed on one who deviates from the norm established by the criminal law.

The fact that the State may seek retribution against those who have broken its laws does not mean that retribution may then become the State's sole end in punishing. Our jurisprudence has always accepted deterrence in general, deterrence of individual recidivism, isolation of dangerous persons, and rehabilitation as proper goals of punishment. Retaliation, vengeance, and retribution have been roundly condemned as intolerable aspirations for a government in a free society.

Punishment as retribution has been condemned by scholars for centuries, and the Eighth Amendment itself was adopted to prevent punishment from becoming synonymous with vengeance. . . .

B. The most hotly contested issue regarding capital punishment is whether it is better than life imprisonment as a deterrent to crime.

While the contrary position has been argued, it is my firm opinion that the death penalty is a more severe sanction than life imprisonment. Admittedly, there are some persons who would rather die than languish in prison for a lifetime. But, whether or not they should be able to choose death as an alternative is a far different question from that presented here—*i. e.*, whether the State can impose death as a punishment. Death is irrevocable; life imprisonment is not. Death, of course, makes rehabilitation impossible; life imprisonment does not. In short, death has always been viewed as the ultimate sanction, and it seems perfectly reasonable to continue to view it as such.

It must be kept in mind, then, that the question to be considered is not simply whether capital punishment is a deterrent, but whether it is a better deterrent than life imprisonment.

There is no more complex problem than determining the deterrent efficacy of the death penalty. "Capital punishment has obviously failed as a deterrent when a murder is committed. We can number its failures. But we cannot number its successes. No one can ever know how many people have refrained from murder because of the fear of being hanged." This is the nub of the problem and it is exacerbated by the paucity of useful data. The United States is more fortunate than most countries, however, in that it has what are generally considered to be the world's most reliable statistics.

The two strongest arguments in favor of capital punishment as a deterrent are both logical hypotheses devoid of evidentiary support, but persuasive nonetheless. The first proposition was best stated by Sir James Stephen in 1864:

> "No other punishment deters men so effectually from committing crimes as the punishment of death. This is one of those propositions which it is difficult to prove, simply because they are in themselves more obvious than any proof can make them. It is possible to display ingenuity in arguing against it, but that is all. The whole experience of mankind is in the other direction. The threat of instant death is the one to which resort has always been made when there was an absolute necessity for producing some result. . . . No one goes to certain inevitable death except by compulsion. Put the matter the other way. Was there ever yet a criminal who, when sentenced to death and brought out to die, would refuse the offer of a commutation of his sentence for the severest secondary punishment? Surely not. Why is this? It can only be because 'All that a man has will he give for his life.' In any secondary punishment, however terrible, there is hope; but death is death; its terrors cannot be described more forcibly."

This hypothesis relates to the use of capital punishment as a deterrent for any crime. The second proposition is that "if life imprisonment is the maximum penalty for a crime such as murder, an offender who is serving a life sentence cannot then be deterred from murdering a fellow inmate or a prison officer." This hypothesis advocates a limited deterrent effect under particular circumstances.

Abolitionists attempt to disprove these hypotheses by amassing statistical evidence to demonstrate that there is no correlation between criminal activity and the existence or nonexistence of a capital sanction. Almost all of the evidence involves the crime of murder, since murder is punishable by death in more jurisdictions than are other offenses, and almost 90% of all executions since 1930 have been pursuant to murder convictions.

Thorsten Sellin, one of the leading authorities on capital punishment, has urged that if the death penalty deters prospective murderers, the following hypotheses should be true:

"(a) Murders should be less frequent in states that have the death penalty than in those that have abolished it, other factors being equal. Comparisons of this nature must be made among states that are as alike as possible in all other respects—character of population, social and economic condition, etc.—in order not to introduce factors known to influence murder rates in a serious manner but present in only one of these states.

"(b)Murders should increase when the death penalty is abolished and should decline when it is restored.

"(c) The deterrent effect should be greatest and

should therefore affect murder rates most powerfully in those communities where the crime occurred and its consequences are most strongly brought home to the population.

"(d) Law enforcement officers would be safer from murderous attacks in states that have the death penalty than in those without it."

Sellin's evidence indicates that not one of these propositions is true. This evidence has its problems, however. One is that there are no accurate figures for capital murders; there are only figures on homicides and they, of course, include noncapital killings. A second problem is that certain murders undoubtedly are misinterpreted as accidental deaths or suicides, and there is no way of estimating the number of such undetected crimes. A third problem is that not all homicides are reported. Despite these difficulties, most authorities have assumed that the proportion of capital murders in a State's or nation's homicide statistics remains reasonably constant, and that the homicide statistics are therefore useful.

Sellin's statistics demonstrate that there is no correlation between the murder rate and the presence or absence of the capital sanction. He compares States that have similar characteristics and finds that irrespective of their position on capital punishment, they have similar murder rates. In the New England States, for example, there is no correlation between executions and homicide rates. The same is true for Midwestern States, and for all others studied. Both the United Nations and Great Britain have acknowledged the validity of Sellin's statistics.

Sellin also concludes that abolition and/or reintroduction of the death penalty had no effect on the homicide rates of the various States involved. This conclusion is borne out by others who have made similar inquiries and by the experience of other countries. Despite problems with the statistics, Sellin's evidence has been relied upon in international studies of capital punishment.

Statistics also show that the deterrant effect of capital punishment is no greater in those communities where executions take place than in other communities. In fact, there is some evidence that imposition of capital punishment may actually encourage crime, rather than deter it. And, while police and law enforcement officers are the strongest advocates of capital punishment, the evidence is overwhelming that police are no safer in communities that retain the sanction than in those that have abolished it.

There is also a substantial body of data showing that the existence of the death penalty has virtually no effect on the homicide rate in prisons. Most of the persons sentenced to death are murderers, and murderers tend to be model prisoners. . . .

C. Much of what must be said about the death penalty as a device to prevent recidivism is obvious—if a murderer is executed, he cannot possibly commit another offense. The fact is, however, that murderers are extremely unlikely to commit other crimes either in prison or upon their release. For the most part, they are first offenders, and when released from prison they are known to become model citizens. Furthermore, most persons who commit capital crimes are not executed. With respect to those who are sentenced to die, it is critical to note that the jury is never asked to determine whether they are likely to be recidivists. In light of these facts, if capital punishment were justified purely on the basis of preventing recidivism, it would have to be considered to be excessive; no general need to obliterate all capital offenders could have been demonstrated, nor any specific need in individual cases.

D. The three final purposes which may underlie utilization of a capital sanction—encouraging guilty pleas and confessions, eugenics, and reducing state expenditures—may be dealt with quickly. If the death penalty is used to encourage guilty pleas and thus to deter suspects from exercising their rights under the Sixth Amendment to jury trials, it is unconstitutional. Its elimination would do little to impair the State's bargaining position in criminal cases, since life imprisonment remains a severe sanction which can be used as leverage for bargaining for pleas or confessions in exchange either for charges of lesser offenses or recommendations of leniency.

Moreover, to the extent that capital punishment is used to encourage confessions and guilty pleas, it is not being used for punishment purposes. A State that justifies capital punishment on its utility as part of the conviction process could not profess to rely on capital punishment as a deterrent. Such a State's system would be structured with twin goals only: obtaining guilty pleas and confessions and imposing *imprisonment* as the maximum sanction. Since life imprisonment is sufficient for bargaining purposes, the death penalty is excessive if used for the same purposes.

In light of the previous discussion on deterrence, any suggestions concerning the eugenic benefits of capital punishment are obviously meritless. As I pointed out above, there is not even any attempt made to discover which capital offenders are likely to be recidivists, let alone which are positively incurable. No test or procedure presently exists by which incurables can be screened from those who would benefit from treatment. On the one hand, due process would seem to require that we have some procedure to demonstrate incurability before execution; and, on the other hand, equal protection would then seemingly require that all incurables be executed. In addition, the "cruel and unusual" language would require that life imprisonment, treatment, and sterilization be inadequate for eugenic purposes. More importantly, this Nation has never formally professed eugenic goals, and the history of the world does not look kindly on them. If eugenics is one of our purposes, then the legislatures should say so forthrightly and design procedures to serve this goal. Until such time, I can only conclude, as has virtually everyone else who has looked at the problem, that capital punishment cannot be defended on the basis of any eugenic purposes.

As for the argument that it is cheaper to execute a capital offender than to imprison him for life, even assuming that such an argument, if true, would support a capital sanction, it is simply incorrect. A disproportionate amount of money spent on prisons is attributable to death row. Condemned men are not productive members of the prison community, although they could be, and executions are expensive. Appeals are often automatic, and courts admittedly spend more time with death cases.

At trial, the selection of jurors is likely to become a costly, time-consuming problem in a capital case, and defense counsel will reasonably exhaust every possible means to save his client from execution, no matter how long the trial takes.

During the period between conviction and execution, there are an inordinate number of collateral attacks on the conviction and attempts to obtain executive clemency, all of which exhaust the time, money, and effort of the State. There are also continual assertions that the condemned prisoner has gone insane. Because there is a formally established policy of not executing insane persons, great sums of money may be spent on detecting and curing mental illness in order to perform the execution. Since no one wants the responsibility for the execution, the condemned man is likely to be passed back and forth from doctors to custodial officials to courts like a ping-pong ball. The entire process is very costly.

When all is said and done, there can be no doubt that it costs more to execute a man than to keep him in prison for life.

E. There is but one conclusion that can be drawn from all of this—*i. e.,* the death penalty is an excessive and unnecessary punishment that violates the Eighth Amendment. The statistical evidence is not convincing beyond all doubt, but it is persuasive. It is not improper at this point to take judicial notice of the fact that for more than 200 years men have labored to demonstrate that capital punishment serves no purpose that life imprisonment could not serve equally well. And they have done so with great success. Little, if any, evidence has been adduced to prove the contrary. The point has now been reached at which deference to the legislatures is tantamount to abdication of our judicial roles as factfinders, judges, and ultimate arbiters of the Constitution. We know that at some point the presumption of constitutionality accorded legislative acts gives way to a realistic assessment of those acts. This point comes when there is sufficient evidence available so that judges can determine, not whether the legislature acted wisely, but whether it had any rational basis whatsoever for acting. We have this evidence before us now. There is no rational basis for concluding that capital punishment is not excessive. It therefore violates the Eighth Amendment. . . .

JUSTICES STEWART, POWELL, AND STEVENS

majority opinion in *Gregg* v. *Georgia* (1976)

(Source: Gregg v. Georgia *428 U.S. 153 [1976]. Most legal references have been omitted.)*

QUESTIONS FOR REFLECTION

1. The majority argues that the death penalty is sometimes justified. What are the majority's chief arguments?
2. In *Furman* v. *Georgia*, Justice Brennan outlined four principles for determining the acceptability of a punishment. Does the majority in *Gregg* v. *Georgia* accept those principles? Does it present arguments that the death penalty can satisfy them?

Judgment of the Court, and opinion of Mr. Justice Stewart, Mr. Justice Powell, and Mr. Justice Stevens, announced by Mr. Justice Stewart. . . .

III

. . . The Court on a number of occasions has both assumed and asserted the constitutionality of capital punishment. In several cases that assumption provided a necessary foundation for the decision, as the Court was asked to decide whether a particular method of carrying out a capital sentence would be allowed to stand under the Eighth Amendment. But until *Furman* v. *Georgia,* the Court never confronted squarely the fundamental claim that the punishment of death always, regardless of the enormity of the offense or the procedure followed in imposing the sentence, is cruel and unusual punishment in violation of the Constitution. Although this issue was presented and addressed in *Furman,* it was not resolved by the Court. Four Justices would have held that capital punishment is not unconstitutional *per se;* two Justices would have reached the opposite conclusion; and three Justices, while agreeing that the statutes then before the Court were invalid as applied, left open the question whether such punishment may ever be imposed. We now hold that the punishment of death does not invariably violate the Constitution.

A

The history of the prohibition of "cruel and unusual" punishment already has been reviewed at length. The phrase first appeared in the English Bill of Rights of 1689, which was drafted by Parliament at the accession of William and Mary. The English version appears to have been directed against punishments unauthorized by statute and beyond the jurisdiction of the sentencing court, as well as those disproportionate to the offense involved. The American draftsmen, who adopted the English phrasing in drafting the Eighth Amendment, were primarily concerned, however, with proscribing "tortures" and other "barbarous" methods of punishment. . . .

. . . A penalty also must accord with "the dignity of man," which is the "basic concept underlying the Eighth Amendment." This means, at least, that the punishment not be "excessive." When a form of punishment in the abstract (in this case, whether capital punishment may ever be imposed as a sanction for murder) rather than in the particular (the propriety of death as a penalty to be applied to a specific defendant for a specific crime) is under consideration, the inquiry into "excessiveness" has two aspects. First, the punishment must not involve the unnecessary and wanton infliction of pain. Second, the punishment must not be grossly out of proportion to the severity of the crime.

B

Of course, the requirement of the Eighth Amendment must be applied with an awareness of the limited role to be played by the courts. This does not mean that judges have no role to play, for the Eighth Amendment is a restraint upon the exercise of legislative power. . . .

But, while we have an obligation to insure that constitutional bounds are not overreached, we may not act as judges as we might as legislators.

> "Courts are not representative bodies. They are not designed to be a good reflex of a democratic society. Their judgment is best informed, and therefore most dependable, within narrow limits. Their essential quality is detachment, founded on independence. History teaches that the independence of the judiciary is jeopardized when courts become embroiled in the passions of the day and assume primary responsibility in choosing between competing political, economic and social pressures."

Therefore, in assessing a punishment selected by a democratically elected legislature against the constitutional measure, we presume its validity. We may not require the legislature to select the least severe penalty possible so long as the penalty selected is not cruelly inhumane or disproportionate to the crime involved. And a heavy burden rests on those who would attack the judgment of the representatives of the people.

This is true in part because the constitutional test is intertwined with an assessment of contemporary standards and the legislative judgment weighs heavily in ascertaining such standards. "[I]n a democratic society legislatures, not courts, are constituted to respond to the will and consequently the moral values of the people." The deference we owe to the decisions of the state legislatures under our federal system is enhanced where the specification of punishments is concerned, for "these are peculiarly questions of legislative policy." Caution is necessary lest this Court become, "under the aegis of the Cruel and Unusual Punishment Clause, the ultimate arbiter of the standards of criminal responsibility . . . throughout the country." A decision that a given punishment is impermissible under the Eighth Amendment cannot be reversed short of a constitutional amendment. The ability of the people to express their preference through the normal democratic processes, as well as through ballot referenda, is shut off. Revisions cannot be made in the light of further experience.

C

In the discussion to this point we have sought to identify the principles and considerations that guide a court in addressing an Eighth Amendment claim. We now consider specifically whether the sentence of death for the crime of murder is a *per se* violation of the Eighth and Fourteenth Amendments to the Constitution. We note first that history and precedent strongly support a negative answer to this question.

The imposition of the death penalty for the crime of murder has a long history of acceptance both in the United States and in England. The common-law rule imposed a mandatory death sentence on all convicted murderers. And the penalty continued to be used into the 20th century by most American States, although the breadth of the common-law rule was diminished, initially by narrowing the class of murders to be punished by death and subsequently by widespread adoption of laws expressly granting juries the discretion to recommend mercy.

It is apparent from the text of the Constitution itself that the existence of capital punishment was accepted by the Framers. At the time the Eighth Amendment was ratified, capital punishment was a common sanction in every State. Indeed, the First Congress of the United States enacted legislation providing death as the penalty for specified crimes. The Fifth Amendment, adopted at the same time as the Eighth, contemplated the continued existence of the capital sanction by imposing certain limits on the prosecution of capital cases:

> "No person shall be held to answer for a capital, or otherwise infamous crime, unless on a presentment or indictment of a Grand Jury . . . ; nor shall any person be subject for the same offense to be twice put in jeopardy of life or limb; . . . nor be deprived of life, liberty, or property, without due process of law. . . . "

And the Fourteenth Amendment, adopted over three-quarters of a century later, similarly contemplates the existence of the capital sanction in providing that no State shall deprive any person of "life, liberty, or property" without due process of law.

For nearly two centuries, this Court, repeatedly and often expressly, has recognized that capital punishment is not invalid *per se*. . . .

Four years ago, the petitioners in *Furman* and its companion cases predicated their argument primarily upon the asserted proposition that standards of decency had evolved to the point where capital punishment no longer could be tolerated. The petitioners in those cases said, in effect, that the evolutionary process had come to an end, and that standards of decency required that the Eighth Amendment be construed finally as prohibiting capital punishment for any crime regardless of its depravity and impact on society. This view was accepted by two Justices. Three other Justices were unwilling to go so far; focusing on the procedures by which convicted defendants were selected for the death penalty rather than on the actual punishment inflicted, they joined in the conclusion that the statutes before the Court were constitutionally invalid.

The petitioners in the capital cases before the Court today renew the "standards of decency" argument, but developments during the four years since *Furman* have undercut substantially the assumptions upon which their argument rested. Despite the continuing debate, dating back to the 19th century, over the morality and utility of capital punishment, it is now evident that a large proportion of American society continues to regard it as an appropriate and necessary criminal sanction.

The most marked indication of society's endorsement of the death penalty for murder is the legislative response to *Furman*. The legislatures of at least 35 States have enacted new statutes that provide for the death penalty for at least some crimes that result in the death of another person. And the Congress of the United States, in 1974, enacted a statute providing the death penalty for aircraft piracy that results in death. These recently adopted statutes have attempted to address the concerns expressed by the Court in *Furman* primarily (i) by specifying the factors to be weighed and the procedures to be followed in deciding when to impose a capital sentence, or (ii) by making the death penalty mandatory for specified crimes. But all of the post-*Furman* statutes make clear that capital punishment itself has not been rejected by the elected representatives of the people.

In the only statewide referendum occurring since *Furman* and brought to our attention, the people of California adopted a constitutional amendment that authorized capital punishment, in effect negating a prior ruling by the Supreme Court of California in *People* v. *Anderson* (1972) that the death penalty violated the California Constitution.

The jury also is a significant and reliable objective index of contemporary values because it is so directly involved. The Court has said that "one of the most important functions any jury can perform in making . . . a selection [between life imprisonment and death for a defendant convicted in a capital case] is to maintain a link between contemporary community values and the penal system." It may be true that evolving standards have influenced juries in recent decades to be more discriminating in imposing the sentence of death. But the relative infrequency of jury verdicts imposing the death sentence does not indicate rejection of capital punishment *per se*. Rather, the reluctance of juries in many cases to impose the sentence may well reflect the humane feeling that this most irrevocable of sanctions should be reserved for a small number of extreme cases. Indeed, the actions of juries in many States since *Furman* are fully compatible with the legislative judgments, reflected in the new statutes, as to the continued utility and necessity of capital punishment in approriate cases. At the close of 1974 at least 254 persons had been sentenced to death since *Furman*, and by the end of March 1976, more than 460 persons were subject to death sentences.

As we have seen, however, the Eighth Amendment demands more than that a challenged punishment be acceptable to contemporary society. The Court also must ask whether it comports with the basic concept of human dignity at the core of the Amendment. Although we cannot "invalidate a category of penalties because we deem less severe penalties adequate to serve the ends of penology," the sanction imposed cannot be so totally without penological justification that it results in the gratuitous infliction of suffering.

The death penalty is said to serve two principal social purposes: retribution and deterrence of capital crimes by prospective offenders.

In part, capital punishment is an expression of society's moral outrage at particularly offensive conduct. This function may be unappealing to many, but it is essential in an ordered society that asks its citizens to rely on legal processes rather than self-help to vindicate their wrongs.

> "The instinct for retribution is part of the nature of man, and channeling that instinct in the administration of criminal justice serves an important purpose in promoting the stability of a society governed by law. When people begin to believe that organized society is unwilling or unable to impose upon criminal offenders the punishment they 'deserve,' then there are sown the seeds of anarchy—of self-help, vigilante justice, and lynch law." *Furman v. Georgia* (Stewart, J., concurring).

"Retribution is no longer the dominant objective of the criminal law," but neither is it a forbidden objective nor one inconsistent with our respect for the dignity of men. Indeed, the decision that capital punishment may be the appropriate sanction in extreme cases is an expression of the community's belief that certain crimes are themselves so grievous an affront to humanity that the only adequate response may be the penalty of death.

Statistical attempts to evaluate the worth of the death penalty as a deterrent to crimes by potential offenders have occasioned a great deal of debate. The results simply have been inconclusive. As one opponent of capital punishment has said:

> "[A]fter all possible inquiry, including the probing of all possible methods of inquiry, we do not know, and for systematic and easily visible reasons cannot know, what the truth about this 'deterrent' effect may be. . . .
>
> "The inescapable flaw is . . . that social conditions in any state are not constant through time, and that social conditions are not the same in any two states. If an effect were observed (and the observed effects, one way or another, are not large) then one could not at all tell whether any of this effect is attributable to the presence or absence of capital punishment. A 'scientific'—that is to say, a soundly based—conclusion is simply impossible, and no methodological path out of this tangle suggests itself."

Although some of the studies suggest that the death penalty may not function as a significantly greater deterrent than lesser penalties, there is no convincing empirical evidence either supporting or refuting this view. We may nevertheless assume safely that there are murderers, such as those who act in passion, for whom the threat of death has little or no deterrent effect. But for many others, the death penalty undoubtedly is a significant deterrent. There are carefully contemplated murders, such as murder for hire, where the possible penalty of death may well enter into the cold calculus that precedes the decision to act. And there are some categories of murder, such as murder by a life prisoner, where other sanctions may not be adequate.

The value of capital punishment as a deterrent of crime is a complex factual issue the resolution of which properly rests with the legislatures, which can evaluate the results of statistical studies in terms of their own local conditions and with a flexibility of approach that is not available to the courts. Indeed, many of the post-*Furman* statutes reflect just such a responsible effort to define those crimes and those criminals for which capital punishment is most probably an effective deterrent.

In sum, we cannot say that the judgment of the Georgia Legislature that capital punishment may be necessary in some cases is clearly wrong. Considerations of federalism, as well as respect for the ability of a legislature to evaluate, in terms of its particular State, the moral consensus concerning the death penalty and its social utility as a sanction, require us to conclude, in the absence of more convincing evidence, that the infliction of death as a punishment for murder is not without justification and thus is not unconstitutionally severe.

Finally, we must consider whether the punishment of death is disproportionate in relation to the crime for which it is imposed. There is no question that death as a punishment is unique in its severity and irrevocability. When a defendant's life is at stake, the Court has been particularly sensitive to insure that every safeguard is observed. But we are concerned here only with the imposition of capital punishment for the crime of murder, and when a life has been taken deliberately by the offender, we cannot say that the punishment is invariably disproportionate to the crime. It is an extreme sanction, suitable to the most extreme of crimes.

We hold that the death penalty is not a form of punishment that may never be imposed, regardless of the circumstances of the offense, regardless of the character of the offender, and regardless of the procedure followed in reaching the decision to impose it.

IV

[A . . .]

B

We now turn to consideration of the constitutionality of Georgia's capital-sentencing procedures. In the wake of *Furman,* Georgia amended its capital punishment statute, but chose not to narrow the scope of its murder provisions. Thus, now as before *Furman,* in Georgia "[a] person commits murder when he unlawfully and with malice aforethought, either express or implied, causes the death of another human being." All persons convicted of murder "shall be punished by death or by imprisonment for life."

Georgia did act, however, to narrow the class of murderers subject to capital punishment by specifying 10 statutory aggravating circumstances, one of which must be found by the jury to exist beyond a reasonable doubt before a death sentence can ever be imposed. In addition, the jury is authorized to consider any other appropriate aggravating or mitigating circumstances. The jury is not required to find any mitigating circumstances in order to make a recommendation of mercy that is binding on the trial court, but it must find a *statutory* aggravating circumstance before recommending a sentence of death.

These procedures require the jury to consider the circumstances of the crime and the criminal before it recommends sentence. No longer can a Georgia jury do as Furman's jury did: reach a finding of the defendant's guilt and then, without guidance or direction, decide whether he should live or die. Instead, the jury's attention is directed to the specific circumstances of the crime: Was it committed in the course of another capital felony? Was it committed for money? Was it committed upon a peace officer or judicial officer? Was it committed in a particularly heinous way or in a manner that endangered the lives of many persons? In addition, the jury's attention is focused on the characteristics of the person who committed the crime: Does he have a record of prior convictions for capital offenses? Are there any special facts about this defendant that mitigate against imposing capital punishment (*e. g.*, his youth, the extent of his cooperation with the police, his emotional state at the time of the crime). As a result, while some jury discretion still exists, "the discretion to be exercised is controlled by clear and objective standards so as to produce non-discriminatory application."

As an important additional safeguard against arbitrariness and caprice, the Georgia statutory scheme provides for automatic appeal of all death sentences to the State's Supreme Court. That court is required by statute to review each sentence of death and determine whether it was imposed under the influence of passion or prejudice, whether the evidence supports the jury's finding of a statutory aggravating circumstance, and whether the sentence is disproportionate compared to those sentences imposed in similar cases.

In short, Georgia's new sentencing procedures require as a prerequisite to the imposition of the death penalty, specific jury findings as to the circumstances of the crime or the character of the defendant. Moreover, to guard further against a situation comparable to that presented in *Furman*, the Supreme Court of Georgia compares each death sentence with the sentences imposed on similarly situated defendants to ensure that the sentence of death in a particular case is not disproportionate. On their face these procedures seem to satisfy the concerns of *Furman*. No longer should there be "no meaningful basis for distinguishing the few cases in which [the death penalty] is imposed from the many cases in which it is not." . . .

V

The basic concern of *Furman* centered on those defendants who were being condemned to death capriciously and arbitrarily. Under the procedures before the Court in that case, sentencing authorities were not directed to give attention to the nature or circumstances of the crime committed or to the character or record of the defendant. Left unguided, juries imposed the death sentence in a way that could only be called freakish. The new Georgia sentencing procedures, by contrast, focus the jury's attention on the particularized nature of the crime and the particularized characteristics of the individual defendant. While the jury is permitted to consider any aggravating or mitigating circumstances, it must find and identify at least one statutory aggravating factor before it may impose a penalty of death. In this way the jury's discretion is channeled. No longer can a jury wantonly and freakishly impose the death sentence; it is always circumscribed by the legislative guidelines. In addition, the review function of the Supreme Court of Georgia affords additional assurance that the concerns that prompted our decision in *Furman* are not present to any significant degree in the Georgia procedure applied here.

For the reasons expressed in this opinion, we hold that the statutory system under which Gregg was sentenced to death does not violate the Constitution. Accordingly, the judgment of the Georgia Supreme Court is affirmed. . . .

ERNEST VAN DEN HAAG

from *The Death Penalty: A Debate*

Ernest van den Haag is Professor of Jurisprudence and Public Policy at Fordham University. (Source: Excerpts from Ernest van den Haag and Joseph P. Conrad, The Death Penalty: A Debate, *Plenum Press, 1983.*

QUESTIONS FOR REFLECTION

1. Van den Haag argues that we should accept the deterrent value of the death penalty, despite the inconclusive results of most statistical studies. What are his arguments?
2. In what special circumstances, according to van den Haag, is capital punishment justified, even if it is unacceptable in most cases? Do you agree?
3. Why, in van den Haag's view, is the death penalty compatible with human dignity?

CHAPTER 4 / MORE ON THE DETERRENT EFFECT OF THE DEATH PENALTY

If it is difficult, perhaps impossible, to prove statistically—and just as hard to disprove—that the death penalty deters more from capital crimes than available alternative punishments do (such as life imprisonment), why do so many people believe so firmly that the death penalty is a more effective deterrent?

Some are persuaded by irrelevant arguments. They insist that the death penalty at least makes sure that the person who suffered it will not commit other crimes. True. Yet this confuses incapacitation with a specific way to bring it about: death. Death is the surest way to bring about the most total incapacitation, and it is irrevocable. But does incapacitation need to be that total? And is irrevocability necessarily an advantage? Obviously it makes correcting mistakes and rehabilitation impossible. What is the advantage of execution, then, over alternative ways of achieving the desired incapacitation?

More important, the argument for incapacitation confuses the elimination of one murderer (or of any number of murderers) with a reduction in the homicide rate. But the elimination of any specific number of actual or even of potential murderers—and there is some doubt that the actual murderers of the past are the most likely future (potential) murderers—will not affect the homicide rate, except through deterrence. There are enough potential murderers around to replace all those incapacitated. Deterrence may prevent the potential from becoming actual murderers. But incapacitation of some or all actual murderers is not likely to have much effect by itself. Let us then return to the question: Does capital punishment deter more than life imprisonment?

Science, logic, or statistics often have been unable to prove what common sense tells us to be true. Thus, the Greek philosopher Zeno some

2000 years ago found that he could not show that motion is possible; indeed, his famous paradoxes appear to show that motion is impossible. Though nobody believed them to be true, nobody succeeded in showing the fallacy of these paradoxes until the rise of mathematical logic less than a hundred years ago. But meanwhile, the world did not stand still. Indeed, nobody argued that motion should stop because it had not been shown to be logically possible. There is no more reason to abolish the death penalty than there was to abolish motion simply because the death penalty has not been, and perhaps cannot be, shown statistically to be a deterrent over and above other penalties. Indeed, there are two quite satisfactory, if nonstatistical, indications of the marginal deterrent effect of the death penalty.

In the first place, our experience shows that the greater the threatened penalty, the more it deters. *Ceteris paribus,* the threat of 50 lashes, deters more than the threat of 5; a $1000 fine deters more than a $10 fine; 10 years in prison deter more than 1 year in prison—just as, conversely, the promise of a $1000 reward is a greater incentive than the promise of a $10 reward, etc. There may be diminishing returns. Once a reward exceeds, say, $1 million, the additional attraction may diminish. Once a punishment exceeds, say, 10 years in prison (net of parole), there may be little additional deterrence in threatening additional years. We know hardly anything about diminishing returns of penalties. It would still seem likely, however, that the threat of life in prison deters more than any other term of imprisonment.

The threat of death may deter still more. For it is a mistake to regard the death penalty as though it were of the same kind as other penalties. If it is not, then diminishing returns are unlikely to apply. And death differs significantly, in kind, from any other penalty. Life in prison is still life, however unpleasant. In contrast, the death penalty does not just threaten to make life unpleasant—it threatens to take life altogether. This difference is perceived by those affected. We find that when they have the choice between life in prison and execution, 99% of all prisoners under sentence of death prefer life in prison. By means of appeals, pleas for commutation, indeed by all means at their disposal, they indicate that they prefer life in prison to execution.

From this unquestioned fact a reasonable conclusion can be drawn in favor of the superior deterrent effect of the death penalty. Those who have the choice in practice, those whose choice has actual and immediate effects on their life and death, fear death more than they fear life in prison or any other available penalty. If they do, it follows that the threat of the death penalty, all other things equal, is likely to deter more than the threat of life in prison. One is most deterred by what one fears most. From which it follows that whatever statistics fail, or do not fail, to show, the death penalty is likely to be more deterrent than any other.

Suppose now one is not fully convinced of the superior deterrent effect of the death penalty. I believe I can show that even if one is genuinely uncertain as to whether the death penalty adds to deterrence, one should still favor it, from a purely deterrent viewpoint. For if we are not sure, we must choose either to (1) trade the certain death, by execution, of a convicted murderer for the probable survival of an indefinite number of murder victims whose future murder is less likely (whose survival is more likely)—if the convicted murderer's execution deters prospective murderers, as it might, or to (2) trade the certain survival of the convicted murderer for the probable loss of the lives of future murder victims more likely to be murdered because the convicted murderer's nonexecution might not deter prospective murderers, who could have been deterred by executing the convicted murderer.

To restate the matter: If we were quite ignorant about the marginal deterrent effects of execution, we would have to choose—like it or not—between the certainty of the convicted murderer's death by execution and the likelihood of the survival of future victims of other murderers on the one hand, and on the other his certain survival and the likelihood of the death of new victims. I'd rather execute a man convicted of having murdered others than to put the lives of innocents at risk. I find it hard to understand the opposite choice.

However, I doubt that those who insist that the death penalty has not been demonstrated to be more deterrent than other penalties really believe that it is not. Or that it matters. I am fairly certain that the deterrent effect of the death penalty, or its absence, is not actually important to them. Rather, I think, they use the lack of statistical demonstration of a marginal deterrent effect to rationalize an opposition to the death penalty that has nonrational sources yet to be examined. In fact, although they use the alleged inconclusiveness of statistical demonstrations of deterrence as an argument to dissuade others from the death penalty, it can be shown that most abolitionists are not quite serious about the relevance of their own argument from insufficient deterrence.

In numerous discussions I have asked those who oppose capital punishment because, in their opinion, it will not deter capital crimes enough, whether they would favor the death penalty if it could be shown to deter more than life imprisonment does. My question usually led to some embarrassment and to attempts to dodge it by saying that additional deterrence has not been shown. However, when I persisted, conceding as much but asking abolitionists to give a hypothetical answer to a hypothetical question, they would admit that they would continue to oppose the death penalty—even if it were shown to deter more than life imprisonment. Which is to say that the argument based on the alleged lack of superior deterrence is factitious.

At times I have pursued the question. I would ask: "Suppose it were shown that every time we execute a person convicted of murder, ten fewer homicides are committed annually than were otherwise expected—would you still favor abolition?" The answer has been "yes" in all cases I can recall. I would persist: "Suppose every time we execute a convicted murderer, 500 fewer persons are murdered than otherwise would be expected to be murdered; suppose that, by executing the convicted murderer, we so much more deter others, who are not deterred by the threat of life imprisonment, that 500 victims will be spared?" After some hesitation, such staunch abolitionists as Professor Hugo Adam Bedau (Tufts University); Ramsey Clark, attorney general of the United States under President Johnson; Professor Charles Black (Yale); and Mr. Henry Schwarzchild, capital punishment project director of the American Civil Liberties Union, admitted that if they had the choice, they would rather see 500 innocents murdered than execute one convict found guilty of murder. This leads me to doubt the sincerity of abolitionist arguments based on the alleged lack of significant additional deterrent effect of capital punishment.

I also wonder why anyone would hold more precious the life of a convicted murderer than that of 500 innocents, if by executing him he could save them. . . .

CHAPTER 10 / SPECIAL CASES

There are some special cases—special because the threat of the death penalty is the only threat that may deter the crime. We do not know that it will. We do know that in these cases no other threat can.

Unless threatened with the death penalty, prisoners serving life sentences without parole can murder fellow prisoners or guards with impunity. Without the death penalty we give effective immunity, we promise impunity, to just those persons who are most likely to need deterrent threats if they are to be restrained. From a moral viewpoint one may add that if a prisoner already convicted of a crime sufficient to send him to prison for life commits a murder, the death penalty seems likely to be well deserved. At any rate, without the death penalty his fellow prisoners and the correctional officers can and will be victimized with impunity should he decide to murder them. To avoid threatening the convict with the only punishment available to restrain him, their lives are put at risk. This seems hard to justify.

The matter is all too well illustrated by the following:

> Two hard-case inmates apparently wangled their way into the warden's offices and stabbed the warden and his deputy to death with sharpened mess-hall knives.
>
> . . . investigators said that the death mission had been specifically ordered the night before at a meeting of Muslim inmates because Fromhold had resisted

their demands "once too often." Fromhold was stabbed thirteen times in the back and chest; Warden Patrick Curran, 47, who dashed into his deputy's first-floor office, was stabbed three times in the back.

Neither inmate had much to lose. Burton was doing life in the cold-blooded execution of a Philadelphia police sergeant, and Bowen was awaiting trial in another cop-killing and the shooting of an elderly couple.*

I can think of no reason for giving permanent immunity to homicidal life prisoners, thereby victimizing guards and other prisoners.

Outside prison, too, the threat of the death penalty is the only threat that is likely to restrain some criminals. Without the death penalty an offender having committed a crime that leads to imprisonment for life has nothing to lose if he murders the arresting officer. By murdering the officer or, for that matter, witnesses to their crimes, such criminals increase their chances of escape, without increasing the severity of the punishment they will suffer if caught. This is the case for all criminals likely to be given life imprisonment if caught who commit an additional crime such as murdering the arresting officer. Only the death penalty could rationally restrain them.

In some states the death penalty is threatened to those who murder a police officer in the performance of his duties. Thus, special protection is extended to police officers, who, after all, are specially exposed. They deserve that extra protection. But it seems to me that everyone deserves the protection against murder that the death penalty can provide.

There are still other cases in which the death penalty alone is likely to be perceived as the threat that may deter from the crime. Thus, there is little point in imprisoning a spy in wartime: He expects his side to win, to be liberated by it, and to become a hero. On the other hand, if he had to fear immediate execution, the victory of his side would help the spy little. This may deter some people from becoming spies. It may not deter the man who does not mind becoming a patriotic martyr, but it may deter a man who does his spying for money.

A deserter, too, afraid of the risk of death on the battlefield, afraid enough to desert, is not going to be restrained by the threat of a prison sentence. But he may be afraid of certain death by firing squad. So may be anyone who deserts for any reason whatsoever.

Even the death penalty cannot restrain certain crimes. Once a man has committed a first murder for which, if convicted, he would be punished by execution, he can commit additional murders without fear of additional punishment. The range of punishments is limited. The range of crimes is not. The death penalty is the most severe punishment we can impose. It is reserved for the most serious crimes. But we can add nothing for still more serious crimes such as multiple murders or torture murders.

Unlike death, which we will all experience, torture is repulsive to us. Thus, we will not apply it even to those who richly deserve it. It is, moreover, most unlikely that anyone not deterred by death would be deterred by torture or that death with torture would be more deterrent than death without. Thus, there is little point in trying to extend the range of punishment upward, beyond death.

Unfortunately, criminals can and sometimes do torture victims. They also can and sometimes do murder more than one person. The law cannot threaten more than death. But at least it should not threaten less. Although the threat of the death penalty may not restrain the second murder, it may restrain the first. . . .

CHAPTER 16 / THE ADVOCATE ADVOCATES

There are two basic arguments for the death penalty; they are independent of, yet consistent with, one another.

The first argument is moral: The death penalty is just; it is deserved for certain crimes. One can explain why one feels that certain crimes deserve

* *Newsweek*, 11 June 1973.

the death penalty. But as usual with moral arguments, one cannot show this conviction to be *factually* correct (or, for that matter, incorrect) since moral arguments rest not on facts but on our evaluation of them. My evaluation leads me to believe that, e.g., premeditated murder or treason (a fact) is so grave and horrible a crime (an evaluation) as to deserve nothing less than the death penalty, that only the death penalty (a fact) is proportionate to the gravity of the crime (an evaluation).

My widely shared view is opposed by abolitionists, who claim that the death penalty is unjust for any crime, and inconsistent with human dignity. . . . Since most abolitionists believe, as I do, that punishments should be proportionate to the perceived gravity of crimes, the abolitionist claim seems to me logically precarious. It implies either that murder is not so horrible after all—not horrible enough, at any rate, to deserve death—or that the death penalty is too harsh a punishment for it, and indeed for any conceivable crime. I find it hard to believe that one can hold either view seriously, let alone both. . . .

I must confess that I have never understood the assorted arguments claiming that the death penalty is inconsistent with human dignity or that, somehow, society has no right to impose it. One might as well claim that death generally, or at least death from illness, is inconsistent with human dignity, or that birth is, or any suffering or any undesirable social condition. Most of these are unavoidable. At least death by execution can be avoided by not killing someone else, by not committing murder. One can preserve one's dignity in this respect if one values it. Incidentally, execution may be physically less humiliating and painful than death in a hospital. It is, however, morally more humiliating and meant to be: It indicates the extreme blame we attach to the crime of murder by deliberately expelling the murderer from among the living.

As for the dignity of society, it seems to me that by executing murderers it tries to keep its promise to secure the lives of innocents, to vindicate the law, and to impose retribution on those who so horribly violate it. To do anything less would be inconsistent with the dignity of society.

I see no evidence for society somehow not having "the right" to execute murderers. It has always done so. Traditional laws and Scriptures have always supported the death penalty. I know of no reasoning, even in a religious (theocratic) state, that denies the right of secular courts to impose it. We in America have a secular republic, of course, and therefore, the suggestion that the right to punish belongs only to God, or that the right to impose capital punishment does, is clearly out of place. It is not a religious but a secular task to put murderers to death. Our Constitution does provide for it (Amendments V and XIV). However much we believe in divine justice, it is to occur after, not in, this life. As for justice here and now, it is done by the courts, which are authorized in certain cases to impose the death penalty. A secular state cannot leave it to God. And incidentally, no theocratic state ever has. If they make mistakes, one can hope that God will correct the courts hereafter—but this is no ground for depriving courts of their duty to impose the penalties provided by law where required, nor is it a ground for depriving the law of the ability to prescribe the punishments felt to be just, including the death penalty.

The second argument in favor of capital punishment is material, grounded on empirical facts. They are contested, as readers of this book know, but no one would deny that what is contested are facts. The factual question is: Does the death penalty deter murder more than life imprisonment, or does it make no difference? . . .

Statistics have their place. But here I think they scarcely are needed. Harsher penalties are more deterrent than milder ones. Not only does our whole criminal justice system accept this view; we all do to the extent to which deterrence is aimed at in our everyday life. All other things equal, we penalize our children, our friends, or our business partners the more harshly the more we feel we must deter them and others in the future from a wrong they have done. Social life would not be possible if we did not believe that we can attract people to actions we desire by giving them incentives, and deter them from actions we do not desire by disincentives. The incentives and disincentives are usually proportionate to the felt desirability or undesirability of what we want to attract to or deter from. Why should murder be an exception? Why should we not believe that the greatest disincentive—the threat of death—is most likely to be the greatest deterrent?

Where there is life there is hope. This certainly is one major argument in favor of the death penalty. The murderer who premeditates his crime—and crimes of passion are not subject to capital punishment—if he contemplates the risk of life imprisonment is not likely to believe that, if convicted, he will remain in prison for life. He knows, however inchoately, about parole, pardons, commutations—he believes above all that he, a smart and superior fellow, will find a way to escape. Few prisoners actually do escape. But practically all "lifers" believe that they will, at least when they start their sentence. So believing, they do not greatly fear a sentence of life imprisonment and are not deterred by it. This is why the rate of stranger-murders—murders in which victim and murderer do not know one another and to which the threat of the death penalty should apply—as a proportion of all murders has steadily climbed in the last twenty years. The murderers knew that in practice they would get away with life imprisonment, from which they would be paroled after a few years. Or they hoped they would escape. After all, we executed all of five prisoners in 1981, only one of whom was executed against his wishes. (All of them were white, to the great disappointment of the civil liberties lobby.) At this rate no murderer can foresee execution or be deterred by it.

I find it hard to believe . . . that most men are incapable of murder. . . . I am optimistic, however, in my own way, which seems more realistic to me: I believe that most men can be deterred from murder by the threat of the death penalty.

Even if . . . only a few men would ever become murderers in the absence of the threat of punishment, I should continue to advocate the death penalty to deter these few men. And even if only some of these men need the threat of capital punishment to be deterred, while others would be deterred by the threat of life imprisonment, I should advocate the death penalty to deter the very few who . . . do, or even just may, require it to be deterred. The lives of the innocents that will or may be spared because of the death penalty are more valuable to me, and to any civilized society, than the lives of murderers. I do not want to risk their lives for the sake of the lives of murderers.

The reader will have to decide for himself on which side he wants to be.

PART IV Justice

Aristotle distinguishes several different senses of justice. He identifies one sense of justice with virtue as a whole, but specifically in relation to other people. Another sense of justice pertains to rectification—setting right previous wrongs. This section concerns distributive justice: the problem of distributing goods and obligations among the members of a society.

Aristotle holds a simple but extremely powerful theory of distributive justice. He believes that both goods and obligations ought to be distributed according to merit. He considers a group of people who have somehow obtained a flute. Who in the group should get the flute? The best flute player, Aristotle answers. Similarly, goods ought to go to those who deserve them—that is, those who can make the best use of them. This answer has very strong intuitive appeal. How should a professor assign grades? The top grades should go to those with the most merit, those who have performed best. Who should receive a Grammy award? Those who have produced the best music. Who should receive political power? Those who have the most political virtue, Aristotle answers—the people with the greatest ability to bring about good government.

Aristotle's theory is a *patterned* theory of justice. It says that people should receive goods of a certain kind to the extent that they have merit of that kind. Thus, it answers the question of distributive justice in terms of who has what other characteristics now or at some other definite time. Jean-Jacques Rousseau, Karl Marx, Friedrich Engels, and John Rawls all propose very different theories of justice, but all are similarly patterned; all specify who should get what in terms of who has what now or at some other time.

Rousseau's analysis of distributive justice is somewhat vague. He makes clear that no one should have too much and no one too little. Within the bounds this principle establishes, however, the general will rules. Recall that according to Rousseau's conception of the social contract, we would agree to form a government because we hope to gain from the cooperation it makes possible. We are willing to commit everything we have in the interests of cooperation and expect to receive in return our share of everything that anyone else has. Distribution, then, is in the hands of the community as a whole. Rousseau treats the community as a body with its own interests. He characterizes limits on the community's behavior in terms of the general will. Roughly, the community can legitimately do only what accords with the general will—that is, with the community's own self-interest. This seems to imply that a just distribution is one that accords with the interests of the community as a whole. What this distribution is, of course, is an empirical matter. But Rousseau feels confident enough to say that the multitude should not lack necessities and that the fortunate should not be able to pursue luxuries.

Marx and Engels take Rousseau's position to a more definite conclusion. They analyze social structures in terms of class struggle. They see moral language as little more than a tool in class struggle; consequently, they are reluctant to offer a general theory of justice. But Marx does provide a slogan that embodies such a theory: "From each according to his abilities, to each according to his needs!" This, too, is a patterned theory. It determines who should receive what by considering who has what abilities and needs. Note that Marx's theory has something in common with Aristotle's; both agree that responsibilities are functions of ability. Aristotle, however, believes that rewards should also be proportionate to ability; Marx believes that they should go to those in need, regardless of merit or contribution.

John Rawls offers another development of Rousseau's approach. Imagine being in the state of nature, choosing whether or not to submit to a government. To determine principles of justice, Rawls says, we must imagine that we make the choice based not on any contingent features of our own characters, but on the basis of what we share with all other human beings. Rawls thus imagines us making the choice from behind the veil of ignorance, in which we know everything we need to know about economics, political science, sociology, and so on, but know nothing about our own position in the social structure. What principles, Rawls asks, would we choose from behind the veil of ignorance? What institutions would be rational choices? He concludes that we would choose to minimize risk and so opt for a system that would make the least well-off in society as well-off as possible; that is, we would choose to maximize the welfare of the least advantaged. We would not choose to maximize good overall, as a utilitarian would, for we would fear coming out a loser in the social order. We would not choose absolute equality, for we have no reason to object to inequality as long as it does not disadvantage us, no matter where we might end up in the resulting society. Rawls thus advocates two principles of justice. The first is a principle of liberty, that each person should have the most liberty compatible with an equal liberty for all. The second has two parts: (*a*) inequalities should be to everyone's advantage (that is, those who receive less would be even worse off if others weren't receiving more) and (*b*) the positions to which benefits attach should be open to everyone. Part (*a*) is often called the *difference principle*; part (*b*) is a principle of equal opportunity. The difference principle, by far, has stirred the most controversy concerning Rawls's theory.

Rawls's approach to distributive justice is also a patterned theory. We determine whether a set of institutions is just by looking at the distribution they produce—not now, perhaps, but at some point in the future when the distribution stabilizes. John Locke and Robert Nozick offer a very different theory of justice. How do we determine whether people hold their possessions justly? Locke and Nozick deny that any sort of structural account can provide an answer. Do you, for example, possess this book justly? To answer that question, in their view, we need to ask, not about your abilities or your needs or your total wealth or whether your possession of the book benefits everyone, but about how you obtained it. Did you steal it? Did you buy it from someone who had the right to sell it? Locke takes property as a fundamental natural and civil right. The purpose of government, Locke insists, is to preserve property. Consequently, government cannot consider every good in society its own and reflect abstractly on how to distribute it. People acquire goods justly from nature. They buy and sell them justly. When an injustice occurs, they try to compensate for it. To determine whether a distribution is just, according to Locke and Nozick, we must see how it came about. Were the initial acquisitions just? Were subsequent transfers just? Were any injustices sufficiently rectified? If we can answer yes to these questions, then, Locke and Nozick believe, the distribution is just. Their theories are thus *historical* theories: whether a distribution is just depends on how it came about.

ARISTOTLE

from *Nicomachean Ethics* and *Politics*

(Source: Reprinted from Aristotle's Nichomachean Ethics, *translated by W. D. Ross [1925], by permission of Oxford University Press.* Politics *selections from* The Works of Aristotle, *Vol. X, Oxford: Clarendon Press, 1921. Translated by Benjamin Jowett. Notes have been omitted, and punctuation has been modernized for clarity.)*

QUESTIONS FOR REFLECTION

1. What does Aristotle mean by his assertion that the unjust are "grasping"?
2. How does justice in the broadest sense relate to virtue?
3. What particular kinds of justice does Aristotle discuss? Explain each.
4. According to Aristotle's theory of distributive justice, the just is the proportional. What does this mean? What should be proportional to what?

from *Nicomachean Ethics*

Book V

1

. . . Now "justice" and "injustice" seem to be ambiguous, but because their different meanings approach near to one another the ambiguity escapes notice and is not obvious as it is, comparatively, when the meanings are far apart, e. g. (for here the difference in outward form is great) as the ambiguity in the use of *kleis* for the collar-bone of an animal and for that with which we lock a door. Let us take as a starting-point, then, the various meanings of "an unjust man." Both the lawless man and the grasping and unfair man are thought to be unjust, so that evidently both the law-abiding and the fair man will be just. The just, then, is the lawful and the fair, the unjust the unlawful and the unfair.

Since the unjust man is grasping, he must be concerned with goods—not all goods, but those with which prosperity and adversity have to do, which taken absolutely are always good, but for a particular person are not always good. Now men pray for and pursue these things; but they should not, but should pray that the things that are good absolutely may also be good for them, and should choose the things that *are* good for them. The unjust man does not always choose the greater, but also the less—in the case of things bad absolutely; but because the lesser evil is itself thought to be in a sense good, and graspingness is directed at the good, therefore he is thought to be grasping. And he is unfair; for this contains and is common to both.

Since the lawless man was seen to be unjust and the law-abiding man just, evidently all lawful acts are in a sense just acts; for the acts laid down by the legislative art are lawful, and each of these, we say, is just. Now the laws in their enactments on all subjects aim at the common advantage either of all or of the best or of those who hold power, or something of the sort; so that in one sense we call those acts just that tend to produce and preserve happiness and its components for the political society. And the law bids us do both the acts of a brave man (e. g. not to desert our post nor take to flight nor throw away our arms), and those of a temperate man (e. g. not to commit adultery nor to gratify one's lust), and those of a good-tempered man (e.g. not to strike another nor to speak evil), and similarly with regard to the other virtues and forms of wickedness, commanding some acts and forbidding others; and the rightly-framed law does this rightly, and the hastily conceived one less well.

This form of justice, then, is complete virtue, but not absolutely, but in relation to our neighbour. And therefore justice is often thought to be the greatest of virtues, and "neither evening nor morning star" is so wonderful; and proverbially "in justice is every virtue comprehended." And it is complete virtue in its fullest sense, because it is the actual exercise of complete virtue. It is complete because he who possesses it can exercise his virtue not only in himself but towards his neighbour also; for many men can exercise virtue in their own affairs, but not in their relations to their neighbour. This is why the saying of Bias is thought to be true, that "rule will show the man"; for a ruler is necessarily in relation to other men and a member of a society. For this same reason justice, alone of the virtues, is thought to be "another's good," because it is related to our neighbour; for it does what is advantageous to another, either a ruler or a copartner. Now the worst man is he who exercises his wickedness both towards himself and towards his friends, and the best man is not he who exercises his virtue towards himself but he who exercises it towards another; for this is a difficult task. Justice in this sense, then, is not part of virtue but virtue entire, nor is the contrary injustice a part of vice but vice entire. What the difference is between virtue and justice in this sense is plain from what we have said; they are the same but their essence is not the same; what, as a relation to one's neighbour, is justice is, as a certain kind of state without qualification, virtue.

2

But at all events what we are investigating is the justice which is a *part* of virtue; for there is a justice of this kind, as we maintain. Similarly it is with injustice in the particular sense that we are concerned.

That there is such a thing is indicated by the fact that while the man who exhibits in action the other forms of wickedness acts wrongly indeed, but not graspingly (e. g. the man who throws away his shield through cowardice or speaks harshly through bad temper or fails to help a friend with money through meanness), when a man acts graspingly he often exhibits none of these vices—no, nor all together, but certainly wickedness of some kind (for we blame him) and injustice. There is, then, another kind of injustice which is a part of injustice in the wide sense, and a use of the word "unjust" which answers to a part of what is unjust in the wide sense of "contrary to the law." Again, if one man commits adultery for the sake of gain and makes money by it, while another does so at the bidding of appetite though he loses money and is penalized for it, the latter would be held to be self-indulgent rather than grasping, but the former is unjust, but not self-indulgent; evidently, therefore, he is unjust by reason of his making gain by his act. Again, all other unjust acts are ascribed invariably to some particular kind of wickedness, e. g. adultery to self-indulgence, the desertion of a comrade in battle to cowardice, physical violence to anger; but if a man makes gain, his action is ascribed to no form of wickedness but injustice. Evidently, therefore, there is apart from injustice in the wide sense another, "particular," injustice which shares the name and nature of the first, because its definition falls within the same genus; for the significance of both consists in a relation to one's neighbour, but the one is concerned with honour or money or safety—or that which includes all these, if we had a single name for it—and its motive is the pleasure that arises from gain; while the other is concerned with all the objects with which the good man is concerned.

It is clear, then, that there is more than one kind of justice, and that there is one which is distinct from virtue entire; we must try to grasp its genus and differentia.

The unjust has been divided into the unlawful and the unfair, and the just into the lawful and the fair. To the unlawful answers the afore-mentioned sense of injustice. But since the unfair and the unlawful are not the same, but are different as a part is from its whole (for all that is unfair is unlawful, but not all that is unlawful is unfair), the unjust and injustice in the sense of the unfair are not the same as but different from the former kind, as part from whole; for injustice in this sense is a part of injustice in the wide sense, and similarly justice in the one sense of justice in the other. Therefore we must speak also about particular justice and particular injustice, and similarly about the just and the unjust. The justice, then, which answers to the whole of virtue, and the corresponding injustice, one being the exercise of virtue as a whole, and the other that of vice as a whole, towards one's neighbour, we may leave on one side. And how the meanings of "just" and "unjust" which answer to these are to be distinguished is evident; for practically the majority of the acts commanded by the law are those which are prescribed from the point of view of virtue taken as a whole; for the law bids us practise every virtue and forbids us to practise any vice. And the things that tend to produce virtue taken as a whole are those of the acts prescribed by the law which have been prescribed with a view to education for the common good. But with regard to the education of the individual as such, which makes him without qualification a good *man,* we must determine later whether this is the function of the political art or of another; for perhaps it is not the same to be a good man and a good citizen of any state taken at random.

Of particular justice and that which is just in the corresponding sense, (A) one kind is that which is manifested in distributions of honour or money or the other things that fall to be divided among those who have a share in the constitution (for in these it is possible for one man to have a share either unequal or equal to that of another), and (B) one is that which plays a rectifying part in transactions between man and man. Of this there are two divisions; of transactions (1) some are voluntary and (2) others involuntary—voluntary such transactions as sale, purchase, loan for consumption, pledging, loan for use, depositing, letting (they are called voluntary because the origin of these transactions is voluntary), while of the involuntary (*a*) some are clandestine, such as theft, adultery, poisoning, procuring, enticement of slaves, assassination, false witness, and (*b*) others are violent, such as assault, imprisonment, murder, robbery with violence, mutilation, abuse, insult.

3

(A) We have shown that both the unjust man and the unjust act are unfair or unequal; now it is clear that there is also an intermediate between the two unequals involved in either case. And this is the equal; for in any kind of action in which there is a more and a less there is also what is equal. If, then, the unjust is unequal, the just is equal, as all men suppose it to be, even apart from argument. And since the equal is intermediate, the just will be an intermediate. Now equality implies at least two things. The just, then, must be both intermediate and equal and relative (i. e. for certain persons). And *qua* intermediate it must be between certain things (which are respectively greater and less); *qua* equal, it involves *two* things; *qua* just, it is for certain people. The just, therefore, involves at least four terms; for the persons for whom it is in fact just are two, and the things in which it is manifested, the objects distributed, are two. And the same equality will exist between the persons and between the things concerned; for as the latter—the things concerned—are related, so are the former; if they are not equal, they will not have what is equal, but this is the origin of quarrels and complaints—when either equals have and are awarded unequal shares, or unequals equal shares. Further, this is plain from the fact that awards should be "according to merit"; for all men agree that what is just in distribution must be according to merit in some sense, though they do not all specify the same sort of merit, but democrats identify it with the status of freeman, supporters of oligarchy with wealth (or with noble birth), and supporters of aristocracy with excellence.

The just, then, is a species of the proportionate (proportion being not a property only of the kind of number which consists of abstract units, but of number in general). For proportion is equality of ratios, and involves four terms at least (that discrete proportion involves four terms is plain, but so does continuous proportion, for it uses one term as two and mentions it twice; e. g. "as the line A is to the line B, so is the line B to the line C"; the line B, then, has been mentioned twice, so that if the line B be assumed twice, the proportional terms will be four); and the just, too, involves at least four terms, and the ratio between one pair is the same as that between the other pair; for there is a similar distinction between the persons and between the things. As the term A, then, is to B, so will C be to D, and therefore, *alternando,* as A is to C, B will be to D. Therefore also the whole is in the same ratio to the whole; and this coupling the distribution effects, and, if the terms are so combined, effects justly. The conjunction, then, of the term A with C and of B with D is what is just in distribution, and this species of the just is intermediate, and the unjust is what violates the proportion; for the proportional is intermediate, and the just is proportional. (Mathematicians call this kind of proportion geometrical; for it is in geometrical proportion that it follows that the whole is to the whole as either part is to the corresponding part.)

This proportion is not continuous; for we cannot get a single term standing for a person and a thing.

This, then, is what the just is—the proportional; the unjust is what violates the proportion. Hence one term becomes too great, the other too small, as indeed happens in practice; for the man who acts unjustly has too much, and the man who is unjustly treated too little, of what is good. In the case of evil the reverse is true; for the lesser evil is reckoned a good in comparison with the greater evil, since the lesser evil is rather to be chosen than the greater, and what is worthy of choice is good, and what is worthier of choice a greater good. . . .

from *Politics*

Book III

Section 12

In all sciences and arts the end is a good, and the greatest good and in the highest degree a good in the most authoritative of all—this is the political science of which the good is justice, in other words, the common interest. All men think justice to be a sort of equality; and to a certain extent they agree in the philosophical distinctions which have been laid down by us about Ethics. For they admit that justice is a thing and has a relation to persons, and that equals ought to have equality. But there still remains a question: equality or inequality of what? here is a difficulty which calls for political speculation. For very likely some persons will say that offices of state ought to be unequally distributed according to superior excellence, in whatever respect, of the citizen, although there is no other difference between him and the rest of the community; for that those who differ in any one respect have different rights and claims. But, surely, if this is true, the complexion or height of a man, or any other advantage, will be a reason for his obtaining a greater share of political rights. The error here lies upon the surface, and may be illustrated from the other arts and sciences. When a number of flute-players are equal in their art, there is no reason why those of them who are better born should have better flutes given to them; for they will not play any better on the flute, and the superior instrument should be reserved for him who is the superior artist. If what I am saying is still obscure, it will be made clearer as we proceed. For if there were a superior flute-player who was far inferior in birth and beauty, although either of these may be a greater good than the art of flute-playing, and may excel flute-playing in a greater ratio than he excels the others in his art, still he ought to have the best flutes given to him, unless the advantages of wealth and birth contribute to excellence in flute-playing, which they do not. Moreover, upon this principle any good may be compared with any other. For if a given height may be measured against wealth and against freedom, height in general may be so measured. Thus if A excels in height more than B in virtue, even if virtue in general excels height still more, all goods will be commensurable; for if a certain amount is better than some other, it is clear that some other will be equal. But since no such comparison can be made, it is evident that there is good reason why in politics men do not ground their claim to office on every sort of inequality any more than in the arts. For if some be slow, and others swift, that is no reason why the one should have little and the others much; it is in gymnastic contests that such excellence is rewarded. Whereas the rival claims of candidates for office can only be based on the possession of elements which enter into the composition of a state. And therefore the noble, or free-born, or rich, may with good reason claim office; for holders of offices must be freemen and tax-payers: a state can be no more composed entirely of poor men than entirely of slaves. But if wealth and freedom are necessary elements, justice and valour are equally so; for without the former qualities a state cannot exist at all, without the latter not well. . . .

JOHN LOCKE

from *Second Treatise of Government* (1690)

(Source: Reprinted from John Locke, Two Treatises of Government. *London: Printed for Awnsham Churchill, 1690. Spelling and punctuation have been modernized for clarity.)*

QUESTIONS FOR REFLECTION

1. Locke takes the right to property as natural. Why? What allows me to appropriate things I find in nature? Are there limits to my right of appropriation?
2. What, for Locke, justifies allowing a person to appropriate more than he or she needs?
3. How does money affect principles of property, in Locke's view?
4. What, for Locke, is the chief end of government? How does it limit government action?
5. Why, according to Locke, is the minority bound to follow the majority's decision?

CHAPTER V / OF PROPERTY

§. 25. Whether we consider natural reason, which tells us that men, being once born, have a right to their preservation and consequently to meat and drink and such other things as nature affords for their subsistence, or revelation, which gives us an account of those grants God made of the world to Adam and to Noah and his sons, it is very clear that God, as king David says, Psal. cxv. 16. has given the earth to the children of men: given it to mankind in common. But this being supposed, it seems to some a very great difficulty how anyone should ever come to have a property in any thing: I will not content myself to answer that if it be difficult to make out property upon a supposition that God gave the world to Adam and his posterity in common, it is impossible that any man, but one universal monarch, should have any property upon a supposition that God gave the world to Adam and his heirs in succession, exclusive of all the rest of his posterity. But I shall endeavour to show how men might come to have a property in several parts of that which God gave to mankind in common, and that without any express compact of all the commoners.

§. 26. God, who has given the world to men in common, has also given them reason to make use of it to the best advantage of life and convenience. The earth and all that is therein is given to men for the support and comfort of their being. And though all the fruits it naturally produces and beasts it feeds belong to mankind in common, as they are produced by the spontaneous hand of nature, and nobody has originally a private dominion exclusive of the rest of mankind, in any of them, as they are thus in their natural state; yet being given for the use of men, there must of necessity be a means to appropriate them some way or other before they can be of any use or at all beneficial to any particular man. The fruit or venison which nourishes the wild Indian, who knows no inclosure and is still a tenant in common, must be his, and so his, *i.e.* a part of him, that another can no longer have any right to it before it can do him any good for the support of his life.

§. 27. Though the earth and all inferior creatures be common to all men, yet every man has a property in his own person: this no body has any right to but himself. The labour of his body and the work of his hands, we may say, are properly his. Whatsoever then he removes out of the state that nature has provided, and left in it, he has mixed his labour with and joined to it something that is his own and thereby makes it his property. It being by him removed from the common state nature has placed it in, it has by this labour something annexed to it that excludes the common right of other men: for this labour being the unquestionable property of the labourer, no man but he can have a right to what that is once joined to, at least where there is enough, and as good, left in common for others.

§. 28. He that is nourished by the acorns he picked up under an oak or the apples he gathered from the trees in the wood has certainly appropriated them to himself. Nobody can deny but the nourishment is his. I ask then, when did they begin to be his? when he digested? or when he ate? or when he boiled? or when he brought them home? or when he picked them up? and it is plain, if the first gathering made them not his, nothing else could. That labour put a distinction between them and common: that added something to them more than nature, the common mother of all, had done; and so they became his private right. And will anyone say he had no right to those acorns or apples he thus appropriated, because he had not the consent of all mankind to make them his? Was it a robbery thus to assume to himself what belonged to all in common? If such a consent as that was necessary, man had starved, notwithstanding the plenty God had given him. We see in commons, which remain so by compact, that it is the taking any part of what is common and removing it out of the state nature leaves it in, which begins the property, without which the common is of no use. And the taking of this or that part does not depend on the express consent of all the commoners. Thus the grass my horse has bit, the turfs my servant has cut, and the ore I have digged in any place where I have a right to them in common with others became my property, without the assignation or consent of any body. The labour that was mine, removing them out of that common state they were in, has fixed my property to them.

§. 29. By making an explicit consent of every commoner necessary to anyone's appropriating to himself any part of what is given in common, children or servants could not cut the meat which their father or master had provided for them in common without assigning to every one his peculiar part. Though the water running in the fountain be everyone's, yet who can doubt but that in the pitcher is his only who drew it out? His labour has taken it out of the hands of nature, where it was common and belonged equally to all her children, and has thereby appropriated it to himself.

§. 30. Thus this law of reason makes the deer that Indian's who has killed it; it is allowed to be his goods, who has bestowed his labour upon it, though before it was the common right of everyone. And amongst those who are counted the civilized part of mankind, who have made and multiplied positive laws to determine property, this original law of nature, for the beginning of property, in what was before common, still takes place; and by virtue thereof, what fish anyone catches in the ocean, that great and still remaining common of mankind, or what ambergris anyone takes up here, is by the labour that removes it out of that common state nature left it in made his property, who takes that pains about it. And even amongst us, the hare that anyone is hunting is thought his who pursues her during the chase: for being a beast that is still looked upon as common and no man's private possession, whoever has employed so much labour about any of that kind as to find and pursue her has thereby removed her from the state of nature, wherein she was common, and has begun a property.

§. 31. It will perhaps be objected to this, that if gathering the acorns, or other fruits of the earth, &c. makes a right to them, then any one may ingross as much as he will. To which I answer, Not so. The same law of nature that does by this means give us property does also bound that property too. *God has given us all things richly,* 1 Tim. vi. 12. is the voice of reason confirmed by inspiration. But how far has he given it us? To enjoy. As much as anyone can make use of to any advantage of life before it spoils, so much he may by his labour fix a property in: whatever is beyond this is more than his share and belongs to others. Nothing was made by God for man to spoil or destroy. And thus, considering the plenty of natural provisions there was a long time in the world and the few spenders and to how small a part of that provision the industry of one man could extend itself and ingross it to the prejudice of others, especially keeping within the bounds, set by reason, of what might serve for his use, there could be then little room for quarrels or contentions about property so established.

§. 32. But the chief matter of property being now not the fruits of the earth and the beasts that subsist on it, but the earth itself, as that which takes in and carries with it all the rest; I think it is plain that property in that too is acquired as the former. As much land as a man tills, plants, improves, cultivates, and can use the product of, so much is his property. He by his labour does, as it were, enclose it from the common. Nor will it invalidate his right to say everybody else has an equal title to it and therefore he cannot appropriate, he cannot enclose, without the consent of all his fellow-commoners, all mankind. God, when he gave the world in common to all mankind, commanded man also to labour, and the penury of his condition required it of him. God and his reason commanded him to subdue the earth, *i.e.* improve it for the benefit of life, and therein lay out something upon it that was his own, his labour. He that in obedience to this command of God, subdued, tilled and sowed any part of it thereby annexed to it something that was his property, which another had no title to nor could without injury take from him.

§. 33. Nor was this appropriation of any parcel of land, by improving it, any prejudice to any other man, since there was still enough and as good left; and more than the yet unprovided could use. So that, in effect, there was never the less left for others because of his enclosure for himself: for he that leaves as much as another can make use of does as good as take nothing at all. Nobody could think himself injured by the drinking of another man, though he took a good draught, who had a whole river of the same water left him to quench his thirst; and the case of land and water, where there is enough of both, is perfectly the same.

§. 34. God gave the world to men in common, but since he gave it them for their benefit and the greatest conveniencies of life they were capable to draw from it, it cannot be supposed he meant it should always remain common and uncultivated. He gave it to the use of the industrious and rational (and labour was to be his title to it), not to the fancy or covetousness of the quarrelsome and contentious. He that had as good left for his improvement as was already taken up needed not complain, ought not meddle with what was already improved by another's labour; if he did, it is plain he desired the benefit of another's pains, which he had no right to, and not the ground which God had given him in common with others to labour on and whereof there was as good left as that already possessed, and more than he knew what to do with or his industry could reach to. . . .

§. 37. This is certain, that in the beginning, before the desire of having more than man needed had altered the intrinsic value of things, which depends only on their usefulness to the life of man or had agreed that a little piece of yellow metal which would keep without wasting or decay should be worth a great piece of flesh or a whole heap of corn; though men had a right to appropriate by their labour each one of himself as much of the things of nature as he could use, yet this could not be much, nor to the prejudice of others, where the same plenty was still left to those who would use the same industry. To which let me add, that he who appropriates land to himself by his labour does not lessen, but increases the common stock of mankind; for the provisions serving to the support of human life produced by one acre of enclosed and cultivated land are (to speak much within compass) ten times more than those which are yielded by an acre of land of an equal richness lying waste in common. And therefore he that encloses land and has a greater plenty of the conveniencies of life from ten acres than he could have from an hundred left to nature may truly be said to give ninety acres to mankind: for his labour now supplies him with provisions out of ten acres which were but the product of an hundred lying in common. I have here rated the improved land very low in making its product but as ten to one, when it is much nearer a hundred to one; for I ask whether in the wild woods and uncultivated waste of America, left to nature, without any improvement, tillage or husbandry, a thousand acres yield the needy and wretched inhabitants as many conveniencies of life as ten acres of equally fertile land do in Devonshire, where they are well cultivated?

Before the appropriation of land, he who gathered as much of the wild fruit, killed, caught, or tamed as many of the beasts as he could; he that so employed his pains about any of the spontaneous products of nature as any way to alter them from the state which nature put them in, by placing any of his labour on them, did thereby acquire a propriety in them: but if they perished in his possession, without their due use; if the fruits rotted or the venison putrified before he could spend it, he offended against the common law of nature and was liable to be punished; he invaded his neighbour's share, for he had no right farther than his use called for any of them, and they might serve to afford him conveniencies of life. . . .

§. 44. From all which it is evident that though the things of nature are given in common, yet man, by being master of himself, and proprietor of his own person and the actions or labour of it had still in himself the great foundation of property; and that which made up the great part of what he applied to the support or comfort of his being, when invention and arts had improved the conveniencies of life, was perfectly his own and did not belong in common to others.

§. 45. Thus labour, in the beginning, gave a right of property wherever anyone was pleased to employ it upon what was common, which remained a long while the far greater part and is yet more than mankind makes use of. Men, at first, for the most part, contented themselves with what unassisted nature offered to their necessities; and though afterwards, in some parts of the world (where the increase of people and stock, with the use of money, had made land scarce and so of some value), the several communities settled the bounds of their distinct territories, and by laws within themselves regulated the properties of the private men of their society, and so, by compact and agreement, settled the property which labour and industry began; and the leagues that have been made between several states and kingdoms, either expressly or tacitly disowning all claim and right to the land in the others' possession, have, by common consent, given up their pretences to their natural common right, which originally they had to those countries, and so have, by positive agreement, settled a property amongst themselves in distinct parts and parcels of the earth; yet there are still great tracts of ground to be found, which (the inhabitants thereof not having joined with the rest of mankind in the consent of the use of their common money) lie waste and are more than the people who dwell on it do or can make use of and so still lie in common; though this can scarce happen amongst that part of mankind that have consented to the use of money.

§. 46. The greatest part of things really useful to the life of man, and such as the necessity of subsisting made the first commoners of the world look after, as it does the Americans now, are generally things of short duration such as, if they are not consumed by use, will decay and perish of themselves; gold, silver and diamonds are things that fancy or agreement has put the value on, more than real use and the necessary support of life. Now of those good things which nature has provided in common, everyone had a right (as has been said) to as much as he could use, and property in all that he could effect with his labour; all that his industry could extend to, to alter from the state nature had put in it, was his. He that gathered a hundred bushels of acorns or apples had thereby a property in them; they were his goods as soon as gathered. He was only to look that he used them before they spoiled, else he took more than his share and robbed others. And indeed it was a foolish thing, as well as dishonest, to hoard up more than he could make use of. If he gave away a part to any body else, so that it perished not uselessly in his possession, these he also made use of. And if he also bartered away plums that would have rotted in a week for nuts that would last good for his eating a whole year, he did no injury; he wasted not the common stock, destroyed no part of the portion of goods that belonged to others, so long as nothing perished uselessly in his hands. Again, if he would give his nuts for a piece of metal, pleased with its colour; or exchange his sheep for shells, or wool for a sparkling pebble or a diamond, and keep those by him all his life, he invaded not the right of others; he might heap up as much of these durable things as he pleased, the exceeding of the bounds of his just property not lying in the largeness of his possession, but the perishing of any thing uselessly in it.

§. 47. And thus came in the use of money, some lasting thing that men might keep without spoiling and that by mutual consent men would take in exchange for the truly useful but perishable supports of life.

§. 48. And as different degrees of industry were apt to give men possessions in different proportions, so this invention of money gave them the opportunity to continue and enlarge them: for supposing an island, separate from all possible commerce with the rest of the world, wherein there were but a hundred families, but there were sheep, horses and cows, with other useful animals, wholesome fruits, and land enough for corn for a hundred thousand times as many, but nothing in the island, either because of its commonness or perishableness fit to supply the place of money; what reason could any one have there to enlarge his possessions beyond the use of his family and a plentiful supply to its consumption, either in what their own industry produced or they could barter for like perishable, useful commodities with others? Where there is not something both lasting and scarce and so valuable to be hoarded up, there men will not be apt to enlarge their possessions of land, were it never so rich, never so free for them to take: for I ask, what would a man value ten thousand or a hundred thousand acres of excellent land, ready cultivated and well stocked too with cattle, in the middle of the inland parts of America, where he had no hopes of commerce with other parts of the world, to draw money to him by the sale of the product? It would not be worth the enclosing, and we should see him give up again to the wild common of nature whatever was more than would supply the conveniencies of life to be had there for him and his family.

§. 49. Thus in the beginning all the world was America, and more so than that is now; for no such thing as money was any where known. Find out something that has the use and value of money amongst his neighbours; you shall see the same man will begin presently to enlarge his possessions.

§. 50. But since gold and silver, being little useful to the life of man in proportion to food, raiment, and carriage, has its value only from the consent of men, whereof labour yet makes in great part the measure, it is plain that men have agreed to a disproportionate and unequal possession of the earth, they having by a tacit and voluntary consent found out a way how a man may fairly possess more land than he himself can use the product of, by receiving in exchange for the overplus gold and silver which may be hoarded up without injury to anyone, these metals not spoiling or decaying in the hands of the possessor. This partage of things in an inequality of private possessions, men have made practicable out of the bounds of society, and without compact, only by putting a value on gold and silver and tacitly agreeing in the use of money; for in governments, the laws regulate the right of property, and the possession of land is determined by positive constitutions.

§. 51. And thus, I think, it is very easy to conceive, without any difficulty, how labour could at first begin a title of property in the common things of nature and how the spending it upon our uses bounded it. So that there could then be no reason of quarrelling about title nor any doubt about the largeness of possession it gave. Right and convenience went together; for as a man had a right to all he could employ his labour upon, so he had no temptation to labour for more than he could make use of. This left no room for controversy about the title, nor for encroachment on the right of others; what portion a man carved to himself was easily seen; and it was useless, as well as dishonest, to carve himself too much or take more than he needed.

CHAPTER VIII / OF THE BEGINNING OF POLITICAL SOCIETIES

§. 95. Men being, as has been said, by nature all free, equal, and independent, no one can be put out of this estate and subjected to the political power of another without his own consent. The only way whereby any one divests himself of his natural liberty and puts on the bonds of civil society is by agreeing with other men to join and unite into a community for their comfortable, safe, and peaceable living one amongst another, in a secure enjoyment of their properties and a greater security against any that are not of it. This any number of men may do, because it injures not the freedom of the rest; they are left as they were in the liberty of the state of nature. When any number of men have so consented to make one community or government, they are thereby presently encorporated and make one body politic, wherein the majority have a right to act and conclude the rest.

§. 96. For when any number of men have, by the consent of every individual, made a community, they have thereby made that community one body, with a power to act as one body, which is only by the will and determination of the majority: for that which acts any community, being only the consent of the individuals of it, and it being necessary to that which is one body to move one way, it is necessary the body should move that way whither the greater force carries it, which is the consent of the majority; or else it is impossible it should act or continue one body, one community, which the consent of every individual that united into it agreed that it should; and so everyone is bound by that consent to be concluded by the majority. And therefore we see that in assemblies empowered to act by positive laws, where no number is set by that positive law which impowers them, the act of the majority passes for the act of the whole and of course determines as having, by the law of nature and reason, the power of the whole.

§. 97. And thus every man, by consenting with others to make one body politic under one government, puts himself under an obligation to everyone of that society to submit to the determination of the majority and to be concluded by it; or else this original compact, whereby he with others incorporated into one society, would signify nothing and be no compact if he be left free and under no other ties than he was in before in the state of nature. For what appearance would there be of any compact? what new engagement if he were no farther tied by any decrees of the society than he himself thought fit and did actually consent to? This would be still as great a liberty as he himself had before his compact, or anyone else in the state of nature has, who may submit himself and consent to any acts of it if he thinks fit.

§. 98. For if the consent of the majority shall not, in reason, be received as the act of the whole and conclude every individual, nothing but the consent of every individual can make anything to be the act of the whole: but such a consent is next to impossible ever to be had, if we consider the infirmities of health and avocations of business, which in a number, though much less than that of a commonwealth, will necessarily keep many away from the public assembly. To which if we add the variety of opinions and contrariety of interest which unavoidably happen in all collections of men, the coming into society upon such terms would be only like Cato's coming into the theatre only to go out again. Such a constitution as this would make the mighty Leviathan of a shorter duration than the feeblest creatures and not let it outlast the day it was born in, which cannot be supposed until we can think that rational creatures should desire and constitute societies only to be dissolved, for where the majority cannot conclude the rest, there they cannot act as one body and consequently will be immediately dissolved again.

§. 99. Whosoever therefore out of a state of nature unite into a community must be understood to give up all the power necessary to the ends for which they unite into society to the majority of the community, unless they expressly agreed in any number greater than the majority. And this is done by barely agreeing to unite into one political society, which is all the compact that is, or needs be, between the individuals that enter into or make up a commonwealth. And thus that which begins and actually constitutes any political society is nothing but the consent of any number of freemen capable of a majority to unite and incorporate into such a society. And this is that, and that only, which did or could give beginning to any lawful government in the world. . . .

CHAPTER IX / OF THE ENDS OF POLITICAL SOCIETY AND GOVERNMENT

§. 123. If man in the state of nature be so free, as has been said; if he be absolute lord of his own person and possessions, equal to the greatest and subject to nobody, why will he part with his freedom? why will he give up this empire and subject himself to the dominion and control of any other power? To which it is obvious to answer that though in the state of nature he hath such a right, yet the enjoyment of it is very uncertain and constantly exposed to the invasion of others; for all being kings as much as he, every man his equal, and the greater part no strict observers of equity and justice, the enjoyment of the property he has in this state is very unsafe, very unsecure. This makes him willing to quit a condition which, however free, is full of fears and continual dangers; and it is not without reason that he seeks out and is willing to join in society with others who are already united, or have a mind to unite, for the mutual preservation of their lives, liberties and estates, which I call by the general name *property.*

§. 124. The great and chief end, therefore, of men's uniting into commonwealths, and putting themselves under government is the preservation of their property. To which in the state of nature there are many things wanting.

First, there wants an established, settled, known law, received and allowed by common consent to be the standard of right and wrong, and the common measure to decide all controversies between them; for though the law of nature be plain and intelligible to all rational creatures, yet men being biased by their interest, as well as ignorant for want of study of it, are not apt to allow of it as a law binding to them in the application of it to their particular cases.

§. 125. *Secondly,* in the state of nature there wants a known and indifferent judge with authority to determine all differences according to the established law; for everyone in that state being both judge and executioner of the law of nature, men being partial to themselves, passion and revenge is very apt to carry them too far and with too much heat in their own cases, as well as negligence and unconcernedness to make them too remiss in other men's.

§. 126. *Thirdly,* in the state of nature there often wants power to back and support the sentence when right and to give it due execution. They who by any injustice offended will seldom fail where they are able by force to make good their injustice; such resistance many times makes the punishment dangerous and frequently destructive to those who attempt it.

§. 127. Thus mankind, notwithstanding all the privileges of the state of nature, being but in an ill condition while they remain in it, are quickly driven into society. Hence it comes to pass that we seldom find any number of men live any time together in this state. The inconveniences that they are therein exposed to by the irregular and uncertain exercise of the power every man has of punishing the transgressions of others make them take sanctuary under the established laws of government and therein seek the preservation of their property. It is this makes them so willingly give up every one his single power of punishing, to be exercised by such alone as shall be appointed to it amongst them and by such rules as the community, or those authorized by them to that purpose, shall agree on. And in this we have the original right and rise of both the legislative and executive power, as well as of the governments and societies themselves.

§. 128. For in the state of nature, to omit the liberty he has of innocent delights, a man has two powers.

The first is to do whatsoever he thinks fit for the preservation of himself and others within the permission of the law of nature, by which law, common to them all, he and all the rest of mankind are one community, make up one society, distinct from all other creatures. And were it not for the corrruption and vitiousness of degenerate men, there would be no need of any other, no necessity that men should separate from this great and natural community and by positive agreements combine into smaller and divided associations.

The other power a man has in the state of nature is the power to punish the crimes committed against that law. Both these he gives up when he joins in a private, if I may so call it, or particular politic society and encorporates into any commonwealth separate from the rest of mankind.

§. 129. The first power, *viz.* of doing whatsoever he thought for the preservation of himself and the rest of mankind, he gives up to be regulated by laws made by the society, so far forth as the preservation of himself and the rest of that society shall require; which laws of the society in many things confine the liberty he had by the law of nature.

§. 130. Secondly, the power of punishing he wholly gives up and engages his natural force (which he might before employ in the execution of the law of nature, by his own single authority, as he thought fit) to assist the executive power of the society, as the law thereof shall require; for being now in a new state, wherein he is to enjoy many conveniencies from the labour, assistance, and society of others in the same community, as well as protection from its whole strength, he is to part also with as much of his natural liberty in providing for himself as the good, prosperity, and safety of the society shall require; which is not only necessary, but just, since the other members of the society do the like.

§. 131. But though men, when they enter into society, give up the equality, liberty, and executive power they had in the state of nature, into the hands of the society to be so far disposed of by the legislative as the good of the society shall require, yet, it being only with an intention in everyone the better to preserve himself, his liberty and property (for no rational creature can be supposed to change his condition with an intention to be worse), the power of the society, or legislative constituted by them, can never be supposed to extend farther than the common good but is obliged to secure everyone's property by providing against those three defects above mentioned that made the state of nature so unsafe and uneasy. And so whoever has the legislative or supreme power of any commonwealth is bound to govern by established standing laws promulgated and known to the people, and not by extemporary decrees; by indifferent and upright judges, who are to decide controversies by those laws and to employ the force of the community at home only in the execution of such laws or abroad to prevent or redress foreign injuries and secure the community from inroads and invasion. And all this to be directed to no other end but the peace, safety, and public good of the people.

CHAPTER XI / OF THE EXTENT OF THE LEGISLATIVE POWER

§. 134. The great end of men's entering into society, being the enjoyment of their properties in peace and safety, and the great instrument and means of that being the laws established in that society, the first and fundamental positive law of all commonwealths is the establishing of the legislative power; as the first and fundamental natural law, which is to govern even the legislative itself, is the preservation of the society and (as far as will consist with the public good) of every person in it. This legislative is not only the supreme power of the commonwealth, but sacred and unalterable in the hands where the community have once placed it; nor can any edict of anybody else, in what form soever conceived or by what power soever backed, have the force and obligation of a law which has not its sanction from that legislative which the public has chosen and appointed; for without this the law could not have that which is absolutely necessary to its being a law, the consent of the society, over whom no body can have a power to make laws but by their own consent and by authority received from them; and therefore all the obedience, which by the most solemn ties any one can be obliged to pay, ultimately terminates in this supreme power and is directed by those laws which it enacts; nor can any oaths to any foreign power whatsoever or any domestic subordinate power discharge any member of the society from his obedience to the legislative acting pursuant to their trust, nor oblige him to any obedience contrary to the laws so enacted or farther than they do allow, it being ridiculous to imagine one can be tied ultimately to obey any power in the society which is not the supreme.

§. 135. Though the legislative, whether placed in one or more, whether it be always in being or only by intervals, though it be the supreme power in every commonwealth; yet,

First, it is not nor can possibly be absolutely arbitrary over the lives and fortunes of the people; for it being but the joint power of every member of the society given up to that person, or assembly which is legislator, it can be no more than those persons had in a state of nature before they entered into society and gave up to the community; for nobody can transfer to another more power than he has in himself, and nobody has an absolute arbitrary power over himself or over any other to destroy his own life or take away the life or property of another. A man, as has been proved, cannot subject himself to the arbitrary power of another; and having in the state of nature no arbitrary power over the life, liberty, or possession of another, but only so much as the law of nature gave him for the preservation of himself and the rest of mankind, this is all he does, or can give up to the commonwealth, and by it to the legislative power, so that the legislative can have no more than this. Their power, in the utmost bounds of it, is limited to the public good of the society. It is a power that has no other end but preservation and therefore can never have a right to destroy, enslave, or designedly to impoverish the subjects. The obligations of the law of nature cease not in society, but only in many cases are drawn closer and have by human laws known penalties annexed to them to enforce their observation. Thus the law of nature stands as an eternal rule to all men, legislators as well as others. The rules that they make for other men's actions, must, as well as their own and other men's actions, be conformable to the law of nature, *i.e.* to the will of God, of which that is a declaration, and the fundamental law of nature being the preservation of mankind, no human sanction can be good or valid against it.

§. 136. *Secondly,* the legislative, or supreme authority, cannot assume to itself a power to rule by extemporary arbitrary decrees, but is bound to dispense justice and decide the rights of the subject by promulgated standing laws and known authorized judges; for the law of nature being unwritten and so nowhere to be found but in the minds of men, they who through passion or interest shall miscite or misapply it cannot so easily be convinced of their mistake where there is no established judge; and so it serves not, as it ought, to determine the rights and fence the properties of those that live under it, especially where everyone is judge, interpreter, and executioner of it too, and that in his own case; and he that has right on his side, having ordinarily but his own single strength, has not force enough to defend himself from injuries or to punish delinquents. To avoid these inconveniences, which disorder men's properties in the state of nature, men unite into societies that they may have the united strength of the whole society to secure and defend their properties and may have standing rules to bound it, by which everyone may know what is his. To this end it is that men give up all their natural power to the society which they enter into, and the community put the legislative power into such hands as they think fit, with this trust, that they shall be governed by declared laws, or else their peace, quiet, and property will still be at the same uncertainty as it was in the state of nature.

§. 137. Absolute arbitrary power, or governing without settled standing laws, can neither of them consist with the ends of society and government, which men would not quit the freedom of the state of nature for, and tie themselves up under, were it not to preserve their lives, liberties and fortunes, and by stated rules of right and property to secure their peace and quiet. It cannot be supposed that they should intend, had they a power so to do, to give to anyone, or more, an absolute arbitrary power over their persons and estates and put a force into the magistrate's hand to execute his unlimited will arbitrarily upon them. This were to put themselves into a worse condition than the state of nature, wherein they had a liberty to defend their right against the injuries of others and were upon equal terms of force to maintain it, whether invaded by a single man or many in combination. Whereas by supposing they have given up themselves to the absolute arbitrary power and will of a legislator, they have disarmed themselves and armed him to make a prey of them when he pleases; he being in a much worse condition, who is exposed to the arbitrary power of one man who has the command of 100,000, then he that is exposed to the arbitrary power of 100,000 single men; nobody being secure, that his will, who has such a command, is better than that of other men, though his force be 100,000 times stronger. And therefore, whatever form the commonwealth is under, the ruling power ought to govern by declared and received laws, and not by extemporary dictates and undetermined resolutions: for then mankind will be in a far worse conditon than in the state of nature, if they shall have armed one, or a few men with the joint power of a multitude, to force them to obey at pleasure the exorbitant and unlimited decrees of their sudden thoughts or unrestrained, and until that moment unkown wills, without having any measures set down which may guide and justify their actions; for all the power the government has, being only for the good of the society, as it ought not to be arbitrary and at pleasure, so it ought to be exercised by established and promulgated laws that both the people may know their duty and be safe and secure within the limits of the law and the rulers too kept within their bounds and not be tempted by the power they have in their hands to employ it to such purposes and by such measures as they would not have known and own not willingly.

§. 138. *Thirdly,* the supreme power cannot take from any man any part of his property without his own consent; for the preservation of property being the end of government and that for which men enter into society, it necessarily supposes and requires that the people should have property, without which they must be supposed to lose that, by entering into society, which was the end for which they entered into it; too gross an absurdity for any man to own. Men therefore in society having property, they have such a right to the goods which by the law of the community are theirs, that nobody has a right to take their substance or any part of it from them without their own consent: without this they have no property at all; for I have truly no property in that which another can by right take from me when he pleases against my consent. Hence it is a mistake to think that the supreme or legislative power of any commonwealth can do what it will and dispose of the estates of the subject arbitrarily or take any part of them at pleasure. This is not much to be feared in governments where the legislative consists, wholly or in part, in assemblies which are variable, whose members upon the dissolution of the assembly are subjects under the common laws of their country equally with the rest. But in governments, where the legislative is in one lasting assembly always in being, or in one man, as in absolute monarchies, there is danger still that they will think themselves to have a distinct interest from the rest of the community and so will be apt to increase their own riches and power by taking what they think fit from the people; for a man's property is not at all secure, though there be good and equitable laws to set the bounds of it between him and his fellow subjects, if he who commands those subjects have power to take from any private man what part he pleases of his property and use and dispose of it as he thinks good.

§. 139. But government, into whatsoever hands it is put, being, as I have before shown, entrusted with this condition and for this end, that men might have and secure their properties, the prince or senate, however it may have power to make laws for the regulating of property between the subjects one amongst another, yet can never have a power to take to themselves the whole or any part of the subjects property without their own consent: for this would be in effect to leave them no property at all. And to let us see that even absolute power, where it is necessary, is not arbitrary by being absolute but is still limited by that reason and confined to those ends which required it in some cases to be absolute, we need look no farther than the common practice of martial discipline: for the preservation of the army, and in it of the whole commonwealth, requires an absolute obedience to the command of every superior officer, and it is justly death to disobey or dispute the most dangerous or unreasonable of them; but yet we see that neither the sergeant that could command a soldier to march up to the mouth of a cannon or stand in a breach where he is almost sure to perish can command that soldier to give him one penny of his money; nor the general that can condemn him to death for deserting his post or for not obeying the most desperate orders can yet, with all his absolute power of life and death, dispose of one farthing of that soldier's estate or seize one jot of his goods, whom yet he can command anything, and hang for the least disobedience; because such a blind obedience is necessary to that end for which the commander has his power, *viz.* the preservation of the rest, but the disposing of his goods has nothing to do with it.

§. 140. It is true, governments cannot be supported without great charge, and it is fit everyone who enjoys his share of the protection should pay out of his estate his proportion for the maintenance of it. But still it must be with his own consent, *i.e.* the consent of the majority, giving it either by themselves or their representatives chosen by them; for if any one shall claim a power to lay and levy taxes on the people by his own authority and without such consent of the people, he thereby invades the fundamental law of property and subverts the end of government: for what property have I in that which another may be right take when he pleases to himself?

§. 141. *Fourthly,* the legislative cannot transfer the power of making laws to any other hands, for it being but a delegated power from the people, they who have it cannot pass it over to others. The people alone can appoint the form of the commonwealth, which is by constituting the legislative and appointing in whose hands that shall be. And when the people have said, We will submit to rules and be governed by laws made by such men and in such forms, nobody else can say other men shall make laws for them; nor can the people be bound by any laws but such as are enacted by those whom they have chosen and authorized to make laws for them. The power of the legislative, being derived from the people by a positive voluntary grant and institution, can be no other than what that positive grant conveyed, which being only to make laws and not to make legislators, the legislative can have no power to transfer their authority to making laws and place it in other hands.

§. 142. These are the bounds which the trust that is put in them by the society and the law of God and nature have set to the legislative power of every commonwealth, in all forms of government.

First, they are to govern by promulgated established laws, not to be varied in particular cases, but to have one rule for rich and poor, for the favourite at court, and the country man at plough.

Secondly, these laws also ought to be designed for no other end ultimately but the good of the people.

Thirdly, they must not raise taxes on the property of the people without the consent of the people, given by themselves or their deputies. And this properly concerns only such governments where the legislative is always in being, or at least where the people have not reserved any part of the legislative to deputies, to be from time to time chosen by themselves.

Fourthly, the legislative neither must nor can transfer the power of making laws to any body else or place it anywhere but where the people have.

JEAN-JACQUES ROUSSEAU

from *Discourse on the Origin of Inequality* (1755) and *On the Social Contract* (1762)

(Source: Reprinted from The Social Contract and Discources, *translated by G. D. H. Cole. London: J. M. Dent & Sons, Ltd., 1913.)*

QUESTIONS FOR REFLECTION

1. What is Rousseau's conception of the state of nature in the *Discourse on the Origin of Inequality*? Does it differ from that of *On the Social Contract*?
2. Why, in Rousseau's view, does property give rise to deception?
3. How does Rousseau criticize the right to property?
4. What stages of inequality does Rousseau discuss? What is the final stage?
5. What principles of distributive justice does Rousseau advocate? Are they compatible with one another?
6. According to Rousseau, are there any limits on government power? If so, what are they?

from *Discourse on the Origin of Inequality*

The Second Part

The first man who, having enclosed a piece of ground, bethought himself of saying *This is mine,* and found people simple enough to believe him, was the real founder of civil society. From how many crimes, wars and murders, from how many horrors and misfortunes might not any one have saved mankind, by pulling up the stakes, or filling up the ditch, and crying to his fellows, "Beware of listening to this impostor; you are undone if you once forget that the fruits of the earth belong to us all, and the earth itself to nobody." But there is great probability that things had then already come to such a pitch, that they could no longer continue as they were; for the idea of property depends on many prior ideas, which could only be acquired successively, and cannot have been formed all at once in the human mind. Mankind must have made very considerable progress, and acquired considerable knowledge and industry which they must also have transmitted and increased from age to age, before they arrived at this last point of the state of nature. Let us then go farther back, and endeavour to unify under a single point of view that slow succession of events and discoveries in the most natural order.

Man's first feeling was that of his own existence, and his first care that of self-preservation. The produce of the earth furnished him with all he needed, and instinct told him how to use it. Hunger and other appetites made him at various times experience various modes of existence; and among these was one which urged him to propagate his species—a blind propensity that, having nothing to do with the heart, produced a merely animal act. The want once gratified, the two sexes knew each other no more; and even the offspring was nothing to its mother, as soon as it could do without her. . . .

Other men, it is true, were not then to him what they now are to us, and he had no greater intercourse with them than with other animals; yet they were not neglected in his observations. The conformities, which he would in time discover between them, and between himself and his female, led him to judge of others which were not then perceptible; and finding that they all behaved as he himself would have done in like circumstances, he naturally inferred that their manner of thinking and acting was altogether in conformity with his own. This important truth, once deeply impressed on his mind, must have induced him, from an intuitive feeling more certain and much more rapid than any kind of reasoning, to pursue the rules of conduct, which he had best observe towards them, for his own security and advantage.

Taught by experience that the love of well-being is the sole motive of human actions, he found himself in a position to distinguish the few cases, in which mutual interest might justify him in relying upon the assistance of his fellows; and also the still fewer cases in which a conflict of interests might give cause to suspect them. In the former case, he joined in the same herd with them, or at most in some kind of loose association, that laid no restraint on its members, and lasted no longer than the transitory occasion that formed it. In the latter case, every one sought his own private advantage, either by open force, if he thought himself strong enough, or by address and cunning, if he felt himself the weaker. . . .

As ideas and feelings succeeded one another, and heart and head were brought into play, men continued to lay aside their original wildness; their private connections became every day more intimate as their limits extended. They accustomed themselves to assemble before their huts round a large tree; singing and dancing, the true offspring of love and leisure, became the amusement, or rather the occupation, of men and women thus assembled together with nothing else to do. Each one began to consider the rest, and to wish to be considered in turn; and thus a value came to be attached to public esteem. Whoever sang or danced best, whoever was the handsomest, the strongest, the most dexterous, or the most eloquent, came to be of most consideration; and this was the first step towards inequality, and at the same time towards vice. From these first distinctions arose on the one side vanity and contempt and on the other shame and envy: and the fermentation caused by these new leavens ended by producing combinations fatal to innocence and happiness.

As soon as men began to value one another, and the idea of consideration had got a footing in the mind, every one put in his claim to it, and it became impossible to refuse it to any with impunity. Hence arose the first obligations of civility even among savages; and every intended injury became an affront; because, besides the hurt which might result from it, the party injured was certain to find in it a contempt for his person, which was often more insupportable than the hurt itself.

Thus, as every man punished the contempt shown him by others, in proportion to his opinion of himself, revenge became terrible, and men bloody and cruel. This is precisely the state reached by most of the savage nations known to us: and it is for want of having made a proper distinction in our ideas, and seen how very far they already are from the state of nature, that so many writers have hastily concluded that man is naturally cruel, and requires civil institutions to make him more mild; whereas nothing is more gentle than man in his primitive state, as he is placed by nature at an equal distance from the stupidity of brutes, and the fatal ingenuity of civilised man. Equally confined by instinct and reason to the sole care of guarding himself against the mischiefs which threaten him, he is restrained by natural compassion from doing any injury to others, and is not led to do such a thing even in return for injuries received. For, according to the axiom of the wise Locke, *There can be no injury, where there is no property.*

But it must be remarked that the society thus formed, and the relations thus established among men, required of them qualities different from those which they possessed from their primitive constitution. Morality began to appear in human actions, and every one, before the institution of law, was the only judge and avenger of the injuries done him, so that the goodness which was suitable in the pure state of nature was no longer proper in the new-born state of society. Punishments had to be made more severe, as opportunities of offending became more frequent, and the dread of vengeance had to take the place of the rigour of the law. Thus, though men had become less patient, and their natural compassion had already suffered some diminution, this period of expansion of the human faculties, keeping a just mean between the indolence of the primitive state and the petulant activity of our egoism, must have been the happiest and most stable of epochs. The more we reflect on it, the more we shall find that this state was the least subject to revolutions, and altogether the very best man could experience; so that he can have departed from it only through some fatal accident, which, for the public good, should never have happened. The example of savages, most of whom have been found in this state, seems to prove that men were meant to remain in it, that it is the real youth of the world, and that all subsequent advances have been apparently so many steps towards the perfection of the individual, but in reality towards the decrepitude of the species.

So long as men remained content with their rustic huts, so long as they were satisfied with clothes made of the skins of animals and sewn together with thorns and fishbones, adorned themselves only with feathers and shells, and continued to paint their bodies different colours, to improve and beautify their bows and arrows and to make with sharp-edged stones fishing boats or clumsy musical instruments; in a word, so long as they undertook only what a single person could accomplish, and confined themselves to such arts as did not require the joint labour of several hands, they lived free, healthy, honest and happy lives, so long as their nature allowed, and as they continued to enjoy the pleasures of mutual and independent intercourse. But from the moment one man began to stand in need of the help of another; from the moment it appeared advantageous to any one man to have enough provisions for two, equality disappeared, property was introduced, work became indispensable, and vast forests became smiling fields, which man had to water with the sweat of his brow, and where slavery and misery were soon seen to germinate and grow up with the crops.

Metallurgy and agriculture were the two arts which produced this great revolution. The poets tell us it was gold and silver, but, for the philosophers, it was iron and corn, which first civilised men, and ruined humanity. Thus both were unknown to the savages of America, who for that reason are still savage: the other nations also seem to have continued in a state of barbarism while they practised only one of these arts. One of the best reasons, perhaps, why Europe has been, if not longer, at least more constantly and highly civilised than the rest of the world, is that it is at once the most abundant in iron and the most fertile in corn. . . .

The cultivation of the earth necessarily brought about its distribution; and property, once recognised, gave rise to the first rules of justice; for, to secure each man his own, it had to be possible for each to have something. Besides, as men began to look forward to the future, and all had something to lose, every one had reason to apprehend that reprisals would follow any injury he might do to another. This origin is so much the more natural, as it is impossible to conceive how property can come from anything but manual labour: for what else can a man add to things which he does not originally create, so as to make them his own property? It is the husbandman's labour alone that, giving him a title to the produce of the ground he has tilled, gives him a claim also to the land itself, at least till harvest; and so, from year to year, a constant possession which is easily transformed into property. When the ancients, says Grotius, gave to Ceres* the title of Legislatrix, and to a festival celebrated in her honour the name of Thesmophoria, they meant by that that the distribution of lands had produced a new kind of right: that is to say, the right of property, which is different from the right deducible from the law of nature.

In this state of affairs, equality might have been sustained, had the talents of individuals been equal, and had, for example, the use of iron and the consumption of commodities always exactly balanced each other; but, as there was nothing to preserve this balance, it was soon disturbed; the strongest did most work; the most skilful turned his labour to best account; the most ingenious devised methods of diminishing his labour: the husbandman wanted more iron, or the smith more corn, and, while both laboured equally, the one gained a great deal by his work, while the other could hardly support himself. Thus natural inequality unfolds itself insensibly with that of combination, and the difference between men, developed by their different circumstances, becomes more sensible and permanent in its effects, and begins to have an influence, in the same proportion, over the lot of individuals.

Matters once at this pitch, it is easy to imagine the rest. I shall not detain the reader with a description of the successive invention of other arts, the development of language, the trial and utilisation of talents, the inequality of fortunes, the use and abuse of riches, and all the details connected with them which the reader can easily supply for himself. I shall confine myself to a glance at mankind in this new situation.

Behold then all human faculties developed, memory and imagination in full play, egoism interested, reason active, and the mind almost at the highest point of its perfection. Behold all the natural qualities in action, the rank and condition of every man assigned him; not merely his share of property and his power to serve or injure others, but also his wit, beauty, strength or skill, merit or talents: and these being the only qualities capable

* Ceres was the goddess of agriculture.—Ed.

of commanding respect, it soon became necessary to possess or to affect them.

It now became the interest of men to appear what they really were not. To be and to seem became two totally different things; and from this distinction sprang insolent pomp and cheating trickery, with all the numerous vices that go in their train. On the other hand, free and independent as men were before, they were now, in consequence of a multiplicity of new wants, brought into subjection, as it were, to all nature, and particularly to one another; and each became in some degree a slave even in becoming the master of other men: if rich, they stood in need of the services of others; if poor, of their assistance; and even a middle condition did not enable them to do without one another. Man must now, therefore, have been perpetually employed in getting others to interest themselves in his lot, and in making them, apparently at least, if not really, find their advantage in promoting his own. Thus he must have been sly and artful in his behaviour to some, and imperious and cruel to others; being under a kind of necessity to ill-use all the persons of whom he stood in need, when he could not frighten them into compliance, and did not judge it his interest to be useful to them. Insatiable ambition, the thirst of raising their respective fortunes, not so much from real want as from the desire to surpass others, inspired all men with a vile propensity to injure one another, and with a secret jealousy, which is the more dangerous, as it puts on the mask of benevolence, to carry its point with greater security. In a word, there arose rivalry and competition on the one hand, and conflicting interests on the other, together with a secret desire on both of profiting at the expense of others. All these evils were the first effects of property, and the inseparable attendants of growing inequality.

Before the invention of signs to represent riches, wealth could hardly consist in anything but lands and cattle, the only real possessions men can have. But, when inheritances so increased in number and extent as to occupy the whole of the land, and to border on one another, one man could aggrandise himself only at the expense of another; at the same time the supernumeraries, who had been too weak or too indolent to make such acquisitions, and had grown poor without sustaining any loss, because, while they saw everything change around them, they remained still the same, were obliged to receive their subsistence, or steal it, from the rich; and this soon bred, according to their different characters, dominion and slavery, or violence and rapine. The wealthy, on their part, had no sooner begun to taste the pleasure of command, than they disdained all others, and, using their old slaves to acquire new, thought of nothing but subduing and enslaving their neighbours; like ravenous wolves, which, having once tasted human flesh, despise every other food and thenceforth seek only men to devour.

Thus, as the most powerful or the most miserable considered their might or misery as a kind of right to the possessions of others, equivalent, in their opinion, to that of property, the destruction of equality was attended by the most terrible disorders. Usurpations by the rich, robbery by the poor, and the unbridled passions of both, suppressed the cries of natural compassion and the still feeble voice of justice, and filled men with avarice, ambition and vice. Between the title of the strongest and that of the first occupier, there arose perpetual conflicts, which never ended but in battles and bloodshed. The new-born state of society thus gave rise to a horrible state of war; men thus harassed and depraved were no longer capable of retracing their steps or renouncing the fatal acquisitions they had made, but, labouring by the abuse of the faculties which do them honour, merely to their own confusion, brought themselves to the brink of ruin.

Attonitus novitate mali, divesque miserque,
*Effugere optat opes; et quæ modo voverat odit.**

It is impossible that men should not at length have reflected on so wretched a situation, and on the calamities that overwhelmed them. The rich, in particular, must have felt how much they suffered

* [Ovid, Metamorphoses xi, 127.
Both rich and poor, shocked at their new-found ills,
Would fly from wealth, and lose what they had sought.]

by a constant state of war, of which they bore all the expense; and in which, though all risked their lives, they alone risked their property. Besides, however speciously they might disguise their usurpations, they knew that they were founded on precarious and false titles; so that, if others took from them by force what they themselves had gained by force, they would have no reason to complain. Even those who had been enriched by their own industry, could hardly base their proprietorship on better claims. It was in vain to repeat, "I built this well; I gained this spot by my industry." Who gave you your standing, it might be answered, and what right have you to demand payment of us for doing what we never asked you to do? Do you not know that numbers of your fellow-creatures are starving, for want of what you have too much of? You ought to have had the express and universal consent of mankind, before appropriating more of the common subsistence than you needed for your own maintenance. Destitute of valid reasons to justify and sufficient strength to defend himself, able to crush individuals with ease, but easily crushed himself by a troop of bandits, one against all, and incapable, on account of mutual jealousy, of joining with his equals against numerous enemies united by the common hope of plunder, the rich man, thus urged by necessity, conceived at length the profoundest plan that ever entered the mind of man: this was to employ in his favour the forces of those who attacked him, to make allies of his adversaries, to inspire them with different maxims, and to give them other institutions as favourable to himself as the law of nature was unfavourable.

With this view, after having represented to his neighbours the horror of a situation which armed every man against the rest, and made their possessions as burdensome to them as their wants, and in which no safety could be expected either in riches or in poverty, he readily devised plausible arguments to make them close with his design. "Let us join," said he, "to guard the weak from oppression, to restrain the ambitious, and secure to every man the possession of what belongs to him: let us institute rules of justice and peace, to which all without exception may be obliged to conform; rules that may in some measure make amends for the caprices of fortune, by subjecting equally the powerful and the weak to the observance of reciprocal obligations. Let us, in a word, instead of turning our forces against ourselves, collect them in a supreme power which may govern us by wise laws, protect and defend all the members of the association, repulse their common enemies, and maintain eternal harmony among us."

Far fewer words to this purpose would have been enough to impose on men so barbarous and easily seduced; especially as they had too many disputes among themselves to do without arbitrators, and too much ambition and avarice to go long without masters. All ran headlong to their chains, in hopes of securing their liberty; for they had just wit enough to perceive the advantages of political institutions, without experience enough to enable them to foresee the dangers. The most capable of foreseeing the dangers were the very persons who expected to benefit by them; and even the most prudent judged it not inexpedient to sacrifice one part of their freedom to ensure the rest; as a wounded man has his arm cut off to save the rest of his body.

Such was, or may well have been, the origin of society and law, which bound new fetters on the poor, and gave new powers to the rich; which irretrievably destroyed natural liberty, eternally fixed the law of property and inequality, converted clever usurpation into unalterable right, and, for the advantage of a few ambitious individuals, subjected all mankind to perpetual labour, slavery and wretchedness. It is easy to see how the establishment of one community made that of all the rest necessary, and how, in order to make head against united forces, the rest of mankind had to unite in turn. Societies soon multiplied and spread over the face of the earth, till hardly a corner of the world was left in which a man could escape the yoke, and withdraw his head from beneath the sword which he saw perpetually hanging over him by a thread. Civil right having thus become the common rule among the members of each community, the law of nature maintained its place only between different communities, where, under the name of the right of nations, it was qualified by certain tacit conventions, in order to make commerce practicable, and serve as a substitute for natural compassion, which lost, when applied to societies, almost all the influence it had over individuals, and survived no longer except in some great cosmopolitan spirits, who, breaking down the imaginary barriers that separate different peoples, follow the example of our Sovereign Creator, and include the whole human race in their benevolence.

But bodies politic, remaining thus in a state of nature among themselves, presently experienced the inconveniences which had obliged individuals to forsake it; for this state became still more fatal to these great bodies than it had been to the individuals of whom they were composed. Hence arose national wars, battles, murders, and reprisals, which shock nature and outrage reason; together with all those horrible prejudices which class among the virtues the honour of shedding human blood. The most distinguished men hence learned to consider cutting each other's throats a duty; at length men massacred their fellow-creatures by thousands without so much as knowing why, and committed more murders in a single day's fighting, and more violent outrages in the sack of a single town, than were committed in the state of nature during whole ages over the whole earth. Such were the first effects which we can see to have followed the division of mankind into different communities. . . .

If we follow the progress of inequality in these various revolutions, we shall find that the establishment of laws and of the right of property was its first term, the institution of magistracy the second, and the conversion of legitimate into arbitrary power the third and last; so that the condition of rich and poor was authorised by the first period; that of powerful and weak by the second; and only by the third that of master and slave, which is the last degree of inequality, and the term at which all the rest remain, when they have got so far, till the government is either entirely dissolved by new revolutions, or brought back again to legitimacy.

To understand this progress as necessary we must consider not so much the motives for the establishment of the body politic, as the forms it assumes in actuality, and the faults that necessarily attend it: for the flaws which make social institutions necessary are the same as make the abuse of them unavoidable. . . .

This is the last term of inequality, the extreme point that closes the circle, and meets that from which we set out. Here all private persons return to their first equality, because they are nothing; and, subjects having no law but the will of their master, and their master no restraint but his passions, all notions of good and all principles of equity again vanish. There is here a complete return to the law of the strongest, and so to a new state of nature, differing from that we set out from; for the one was a state of nature in its first purity, while this is the consequence of excessive corruption. There is so little difference between the two states in other respects, and the contract of government is so completely dissolved by despotism, that the despot is master only so long as he remains the strongest; as soon as he can be expelled, he has no right to complain of violence. The popular insurrection that ends in the death or deposition of a Sultan is as lawful an act as those by which he disposed, the day before, of the lives and fortunes of his subjects. As he was maintained by force alone, it is force alone that overthrows him. Thus everything takes place according to the natural order; and, whatever may be the result of such frequent and precipitate revolutions, no one man has reason to complain of the injustice of another, but only of his own ill-fortune or indiscretion.

If the reader thus discovers and retraces the lost and forgotten road, by which man must have passed from the state of nature to the state of society; if he carefully restores, along with the intermediate situations which I have just described, those which want of time has compelled me to suppress, or my imagination has failed to suggest, he cannot fail to be struck by the vast distance which separates the two states. It is in tracing this slow succession that he will find the solution of a number of problems of politics and morals, which philosophers cannot settle. He will feel that, men being different in different ages, the reason why Diogenes could not find a man was that he sought among his contemporaries a man of an earlier period. He will see that Cato died with Rome and liberty, because he did not fit the age in which he lived; the greatest of men served only to astonish a world which he would certainly have ruled, had he lived five hundred years sooner. In a word, he will explain how the soul and the passions of men insensibly change their very nature; why our wants and pleasures in the end seek new objects; and why, the original man having vanished by degrees, society offers to us only an assembly of artificial men and factitious passions, which are the work of all these new relations, and without any real foundation in nature. We are taught nothing on this subject, by reflection, that is not entirely confirmed by observation. The savage and the civilised man differ so much in the bottom of their hearts and in their inclinations, that what constitutes the supreme happiness of one would reduce the other to despair. The former breathes only peace and liberty; he desires only to live and be free from labour; even the *ataraxia* of the Stoic falls far short of his profound indifference to every other object. Civilised man, on the other hand, is always moving, sweating, toiling and racking his brains to find still more laborious occupations: he goes on in drudgery to his last moment, and even seeks death to put himself in a position to live, or renounces life to acquire immortality. He pays his court to men in power, whom he hates, and to the wealthy, whom he despises; he stops at nothing to have the honour of serving them; he is not ashamed to value himself on his own meanness and their protection; and, proud of his slavery, he speaks with disdain of those, who have not the honour of sharing it. What a sight would the perplexing and envied labours of a European minister of State present to the eyes of a Caribean! How many cruel deaths would not this indolent savage prefer to the horrors of such a life, which is seldom even sweetened by the pleasure of doing good! But, for him to see into the motives of all this solicitude, the words *power* and *reputation*, would have to bear some meaning in his mind; he would have to know that there are men who set a value on the opinion of the rest of the world; who can be made happy and satisfied with themselves rather on the testimony of other people than on their own. In reality, the source of all these differences is, that the savage lives within himself, while social man lives constantly outside himself, and only knows how to live in the opinion of others, so that he seems to receive the consciousness of his own existence merely from the judgment of others concerning him. It is not to my present purpose to insist on the indifference to good and evil which arises from this disposition, in spite of our many fine works on morality, or to show how, everything being reduced to appearances, there is but art and mummery in even honour, friendship, virtue, and often vice itself, of which we at length learn the secret of boasting; to show, in short, how, always asking others what we are, and never daring to ask ourselves, in the midst of so much philosophy, humanity and civilisation, and of such sublime codes of morality, we have nothing to show for ourselves but a frivolous and deceitful appearance, honour without virtue, reason without wisdom, and pleasure without happiness. It is sufficient that I have proved that this is not by any means the original state of man, but that it is merely the spirit of society, and the inequality which society produces, that thus transform and alter all our natural inclinations.

I have endeavoured to trace the origin and progress of inequality, and the institution and abuse of political societies, as far as these are capable of being deduced from the nature of man merely by the light of reason, and independently of those sacred dogmas which give the sanction of divine right to sovereign authority. It follows from this survey that, as there is hardly any inequality in the state of nature, all the inequality which now prevails owes its strength and growth to the development of our faculties and the advance of the human mind, and becomes at last permanent and legitimate by the establishment of property and laws. Secondly, it follows that moral inequality, authorised by positive right alone, clashes with natural right, whenever it is not proportionate to physical inequality; a distinction which sufficiently determines what we ought to think of that species of inequality which prevails in all civilised countries; since it is plainly contrary to the law of nature, however defined, that children should command old men, fools wise men, and that the privileged few should gorge themselves with superfluities, while the starving multitude are in want of the bare necessities of life.

from *On the Social Contract*

Book I

CHAPTER IX / REAL PROPERTY

Each member of the community gives himself to it, at the moment of its foundation, just as he is, with all the resources at his command, including the goods he possesses. This act does not make possession, in changing hands, change its nature, and become property in the hands of the Sovereign; but, as the forces of the city are incomparably greater than those of an individual, public possession is also, in fact, stronger and more irrevocable, without being any more legitimate, at any rate from the point of view of foreigners. For the State, in relation to its members, is master of all their goods by the social contract, which, within the State, is the basis of all rights; but, in relation to other powers, it is so only by the right of the first occupier, which it holds from its members.

The right of the first occupier, though more real than the right of the strongest, becomes a real right only when the right of property has already been established. Every man has naturally a right to everything he needs; but the positive act which makes him proprietor of one thing excludes him from everything else. Having his share, he ought to keep to it, and can have no further right against the community. This is why the right of the first occupier, which in the state of nature is so weak, claims the respect of every man in civil society. In this right we are respecting not so much what belongs to another as what does not belong to ourselves.

In general, to establish the right of the first occupier over a plot of ground, the following conditions are necessary: first, the land must not yet be inhabited; secondly, a man must occupy only the amount he needs for his subsistence; and, in the third place, possession must be taken, not by an empty ceremony, but by labour and cultivation, the only sign of proprietorship that should be respected by others, in default of a legal title.

In granting the right of first occupancy to necessity and labour, are we not really stretching it as far as it can go? Is it possible to leave such a right unlimited? Is it to be enough to set foot on a plot of common ground, in order to be able to call yourself at once the master of it? Is it to be enough that a man has the strength to expel others for a moment, in order to establish his right to prevent them from ever returning? How can a man or a people seize an immense territory and keep it from the rest of the world except by a punishable usurpation, since all others are being robbed, by such an act, of the place of habitation and the means of subsistence which nature gave them in common? When Nuñez Balbao, standing on the sea-shore, took possession of the South Seas and the whole of South America in the name of the crown of Castille, was that enough to dispossess all their actual inhabitants, and to shut out from them all the princes of the world? On such a showing, these ceremonies are idly multiplied, and the Catholic King need only take possession all at once, from his apartment, of the whole universe, merely making a subsequent reservation about what was already in the possession of other princes.

We can imagine how the lands of individuals, where they were contiguous and came to be united, became the public territory, and how the right of Sovereignty, extending from the subjects over the lands they held, became at once real and personal. The possessors were thus made more dependent, and the forces at their command used to guarantee their fidelity. The advantage of this does not seem to have been felt by ancient monarchs, who called themselves King of the Persians, Scythians, or Macedonians, and seemed to regard themselves more as rulers of men than as masters of a country. Those of the present day more cleverly call themselves Kings of France, Spain, England, etc.: thus holding the land, they are quite confident of holding the inhabitants.

The peculiar fact about this alienation is that, in taking over the goods of individuals, the community, so far from despoiling them, only assures them legitimate possession, and changes usurpation into a true right and enjoyment into proprietorship. Thus the possessors, being regarded as depositories of the public good, and having their rights respected by all the members of the State and maintained against foreign aggression by all its forces, have, by a cession which benefits both the public and still more themselves, acquired, so to speak, all that they gave up. This paradox may easily be explained by the distinction between the rights which the Sovereign and the proprietor have over the same estate, as we shall see later on.

It may also happen that men begin to unite one with another before they possess anything, and that, subsequently occupying a tract of country which is enough for all, they enjoy it in common, or share it out among themselves, either equally or according to a scale fixed by the Sovereign. However the acquisition be made, the right which each individual has to his own estate is always subordinate to the right which the community has over all: without this, there would be neither stability in the social tie, nor real force in the exercise of Sovereignty.

I shall end this chapter and this book by remarking on a fact on which the whole social system should rest: *i.e.* that, instead of destroying natural inequality, the fundamental compact substitutes, for such physical inequality as nature may have set up between men, an equality that is moral and legitimate, and that men, who may be unequal in strength or intelligence, become every one equal by convention and legal right.[1]

Book II

CHAPTER III / WHETHER THE GENERAL WILL IS FALLIBLE

It follows from what has gone before that the general will is always right and tends to the public advantage; but it does not follow that the deliberations of the people are always equally correct. Our will is always for our own good, but we do not always see what that is; the people is never corrupted, but it is often deceived, and on such occasions only does it seem to will what is bad.

There is often a great deal of difference between the will of all and the general will; the latter considers only the common interest, while the former takes private interest into account, and is no more than a sum of particular wills: but take away from these same wills the pluses and minuses that cancel one another, and the general will remains as the sum of the differences.

If, when the people, being furnished with adequate information, held its deliberations, the citizens had no communication one with another, the grand total of the small differences would always give the general will, and the decision would always be good. But when factions arise, and partial associations are formed at the expense of the great association, the will of each of these associations becomes general in relation to its members, while it remains particular in relation to the State:

[1] Under bad governments, this equality is only apparent and illusory: it serves only to keep the pauper in his poverty and the rich man in the position he has usurped. In fact, laws are always of use to those who possess and harmful to those who have nothing: from which it follows that the social state is advantageous to men only when all have something and none too much.

it may then be said that there are no longer as many votes as there are men, but only as many as there are associations. The differences become less numerous and give a less general result. Lastly, when one of these associations is so great as to prevail over all the rest, the result is no longer a sum of small differences, but a single difference; in this case there is no longer a general will, and the opinion which prevails is purely particular.

It is therefore essential, if the general will is to be able to express itself, that there should be no partial society within the State, and that each citizen should think only his own thoughts: which was indeed the sublime and unique system established by the great Lycurgus. But if there are partial societies, it is best to have as many as possible and to prevent them from being unequal, as was done by Solon, Numa* and Servius. These precautions are the only ones that can guarantee that the general will shall be always enlightened, and that the people shall in no way deceive itself.

CHAPTER IV / THE LIMITS OF THE SOVEREIGN POWER

If the State is a moral person whose life is in the union of its members, and if the most important of its cares is the care for its own preservation, it must have a universal and compelling force, in order to move and dispose each part as may be most advantageous to the whole. As nature gives each man absolute power over all his members, the social compact gives the body politic absolute power over all its members also; and it is this power which, under the direction of the general will, bears, as I have said, the name of Sovereignty.

But, besides the public person, we have to consider the private persons composing it, whose life and liberty are naturally independent of it. We are bound then to distinguish clearly between the respective rights of the citizens and the Sovereign,[1] and between the duties the former have to fulfil as subjects, and the natural rights they should enjoy as men.

Each man alienates, I admit, by the social compact, only such part of his powers, goods and liberty as it is important for the community to control; but it must also be granted that the Sovereign is sole judge of what is important.

Every service a citizen can render the State he ought to render as soon as the Sovereign demands it; but the Sovereign, for its part, cannot impose upon its subjects any fetters that are useless to the community, nor can it even wish to do so; for no more by the law of reason than by the law of nature can anything occur without a cause.

The undertakings which bind us to the social body are obligatory only because they are mutual; and their nature is such that in fulfilling them we cannot work for others without working for ourselves. Why is it that the general will is always in the right, and that all continually will the happiness of each one, unless it is because there is not a man who does not think of "each" as meaning him, and consider himself in voting for all? This proves that equality of rights and the idea of justice which such equality creates originate in the preference each man gives to himself, and accordingly in the very nature of man. It proves that the general will, to be really such, must be general in its object as well as its essence; that it must both come from all and apply to all; and that it loses its natural rectitude when it is directed to some particular and determinate object, because in such a case we are judging of something foreign to us, and have no true principle of equity to guide us.

Indeed, as soon as a question of particular fact or right arises on a point not previously regulated by a general convention, the matter becomes contentious. It is a case in which the individuals concerned are one party, and the public the other, but in which I can see neither the law that ought to be

* Lycurgus was a legendary Spartan lawgiver of about the ninth century B.C.E. Solon was an Athenian lawgiver, and Numa was Rome's second king.—ED.

[1] Attentive readers, do not, I pray, be in a hurry to charge me with contradicting myself. The terminology made it unavoidable, considering the poverty of the language; but wait and see.

followed nor the judge who ought to give the decision. In such a case, it would be absurd to propose to refer the question to an express decision of the general will, which can be only the conclusion reached by one of the parties and in consequence will be, for the other party, merely an external and particular will, inclined on this occasion to injustice and subject to error. Thus, just as a particular will cannot stand for the general will, the general will, in turn, changes its nature, when its object is particular, and, as general, cannot pronounce on a man or a fact. When, for instance, the people of Athens nominated or displaced its rulers, decreed honours to one, and imposed penalties on another, and, by a multitude of particular decrees, exercised all the functions of government indiscriminately, it had in such cases no longer a general will in the strict sense; it was acting no longer as Sovereign, but as magistrate. This will seem contrary to current views; but I must be given time to expound my own.

It should be seen from the foregoing that what makes the will general is less the number of voters than the common interest uniting them; for, under this system, each necessarily submits to the conditions he imposes on others: and this admirable agreement between interest and justice gives to the common deliberations an equitable character which at once vanishes when any particular question is discussed, in the absence of a common interest to unite and identify the ruling of the judge with that of the party.

From whatever side we approach our principle, we reach the same conclusion, that the social compact sets up among the citizens an equality of such a kind, that they all bind themselves to observe the same conditions and should therefore all enjoy the same rights. Thus, from the very nature of the compact, every act of Sovereignty, *i.e.* every authentic act of the general will, binds or favours all the citizens equally; so that the Sovereign recognises only the body of the nation, and draws no distinctions between those of whom it is made up. What, then, strictly speaking, is an act of Sovereignty? It is not a convention between a superior and an inferior, but a convention between the body and each of its members. It is legitimate, because based on the social contract, and equitable, because common to all; useful, because it can have no other object than the general good, and stable, because guaranteed by the public force and the supreme power. So long as the subjects have to submit only to conventions of this sort, they obey no-one but their own will; and to ask how far the respective rights of the Sovereign and the citizens extend, is to ask up to what point the latter can enter into undertakings with themselves, each with all, and all with each.

We can see from this that the sovereign power, absolute, sacred and inviolable as it is, does not and cannot exceed the limits of general conventions, and that every man may dispose at will of such goods and liberty as these conventions leave him; so that the Sovereign never has a right to lay more charges on one subject than on another, because, in that case, the question becomes particular, and ceases to be within its competency.

When these distinctions have once been admitted, it is seen to be so untrue that there is, in the social contract, any real renunciation on the part of the individuals, that the position in which they find themselves as a result of the contract is really preferable to that in which they were before. Instead of a renunciation, they have made an advantageous exchange: instead of an uncertain and precarious way of living they have got one that is better and more secure; instead of natural independence they have got liberty, instead of the power to harm others security for themselves, and instead of their strength, which others might overcome, a right which social union makes invincible. Their very life, which they have devoted to the State, is by it constantly protected; and when they risk it in the State's defence, what more are they doing than giving back what they have received from it? What are they doing that they would not do more often and with greater danger in the state of nature, in which they would inevitably have to fight battles at the peril of their lives in defence of that which is the means of their preservation? All have indeed to fight when their country needs them; but then no one has ever to fight for himself. Do we not gain something by running, on behalf of what gives us our security, only some of the risks we should have to run for ourselves, as soon as we lost it? . . .

CHAPTER XI / THE VARIOUS SYSTEMS OF LEGISLATION

If we ask in what precisely consists the greatest good of all, which should be the end of every system of legislation, we shall find it reduce itself to two main objects, liberty and equality—liberty, because all particular dependence means so much force taken from the body of the State, and equality, because liberty cannot exist without it.

I have already defined civil liberty; by equality, we should understand, not that the degrees of power and riches are to be absolutely identical for everybody; but that power shall never be great enough for violence, and shall always be exercised by virtue of rank and law; and that, in respect of riches, no citizen shall ever be wealthy enough to buy another, and none poor enough to be forced to sell himself:* which implies, on the part of the great, moderation in goods and position, and, on the side of the common sort, moderation in avarice and covetousness.

Such equality, we are told, is an unpractical ideal that cannot actually exist. But if its abuse is inevitable, does it follow that we should not at least make regulations concerning it? It is precisely because the force of circumstances tends continually to destroy equality that the force of legislation should always tend to its maintenance. . . .

* If the object is to give the State consistency, bring the two extremes as near to each other as possible; allow neither rich men nor beggars. These two estates, which are naturally inseparable, are equally fatal to the common good; from the one come the friends of tyranny, and from the other tyrants. It is always between them that public liberty is put up to auction: the one buys, and the other sells.

KARL MARX AND FRIEDRICH ENGELS

from *Manifesto of the Communist Party* (1848)

and

KARL MARX

from *Critique of the Gotha Program* (1872)

Karl Marx (1818–1883) was born in Treves, in the German Rhineland, to a Jewish family that had converted to Lutheranism. After studying law in Bonn and philosophy and history in Berlin, he earned his doctorate at Jena in 1841 with a dissertation on the ancient Greek philosophers Epicurus and Democritus. He became editor of a liberal Cologne newspaper, which was suppressed in 1843. He fled to Paris; two years later he was expelled from France and fled to Brussels.

Friedrich Engels (1820–1895), born in Barmen, also in the Rhineland, was the son of a textile manufacturer. He worked for his father in a cotton mill in Manchester, England, as a clerk, manager, and part owner. He met Marx in Cologne in 1842 and again in Paris in 1844. In 1848, they collaborated to write The Communist Manifesto. *Engels returned to England. Marx also ended up there a year later, after being expelled from Belgium, France, and Germany. He lived for the rest of his life in London, supported by Engels.*

Though a vision of justice lies behind much of their work, Marx and Engels wrote little about it. The Communist Manifesto *and the* Critique of the Gotha Program *contain some of their most explicit comments about distributive justice. The former work details the theory of class struggle; the latter presents Marx's famous slogan, "From each according to his abilities, to each according to his needs!" which summarizes his conception of just distribution. (Source: Reprinted from Karl Marx and Friedrich Engels,* Manifesto of the Communist Party, *New York: International Publishers, 1932, and Karl Marx,* Critique of the Gotha Program, *New York, International Publishers, 1933.)*

QUESTIONS FOR REFLECTION

1. What is the bourgeoisie? What is the proletariat?
2. Why, according to Marx and Engels, are the bourgeoisie and the proletariat in conflict?
3. What is communism?
4. What arguments do Marx and Engels advance for the abolition of private property? What objections might be raised against that program?
5. What practical measures do Marx and Engels advocate? How do they relate to the primary aim of communism?
6. What is Marx's conception of distributive justice?

from *Manifesto of the Communist Party*

I. Bourgeois and Proletarians*

The history of all hitherto existing society is the history of class struggles.

Freeman and slave, patrician and plebeian, lord and serf, guild-master and journeyman, in a word, oppressor and oppressed, stood in constant opposition to one another, carried on an uninterrupted, now hidden, now open fight, a fight that each time ended, either in a revolutionary re-constitution of society at large, or in the common ruin of the contending classes.

In the earlier epochs of history, we find almost everywhere a complicated arrangement of society into various orders, a manifold gradation of social rank. In ancient Rome we have patricians, knights, plebeians, slaves; in the Middle Ages, feudal lords, vassals, guild-masters, journeymen, apprentices, serfs; in almost all of these classes, again, subordinate gradations.

The modern bourgeois society that has sprouted from the ruins of feudal society has not done away with class antagonisms. It has but established new classes, new conditions of oppression, new forms of struggle in place of the old ones.

Our epoch, the epoch of the bourgeoisie, possesses, however, this distinctive feature: it has simplified the class antagonisms: Society as a whole is more and more splitting up into two great hostile camps, into two great classes directly facing each other: Bourgeoisie and Proletariat. . . .

* By bourgeoisie is meant the class of modern Capitalists, owners of the means of social production and employers of wage-labour. By proletariat, the class of modern wage-labourers who, having no means of production of their own, are reduced to selling their labour-power in order to live.

The bourgeoisie, historically, has played a most revolutionary part.

The bourgeoisie, wherever it has got the upper hand, has put an end to all feudal, patriarchal, idyllic relations. It has pitilessly torn asunder the motley feudal ties that bound man to his "natural superiors," and has left remaining no other nexus between man and man than naked self-interest, than callous "cash payment." It has drowned the most heavenly ecstasies of religious fervour, of chivalrous enthusiasm, of philistine sentimentalism, in the icy water of egotistical calculation. It has resolved personal worth into exchange value, and in place of the numberless indefeasible chartered freedoms, has set up that single, unconscionable freedom—Free Trade. In one word, for exploitation, veiled by religious and political illusions, it has substituted naked, shameless, direct, brutal exploitation.

The bourgeoisie has stripped of its halo every occupation hitherto honoured and looked up to with reverent awe. It has converted the physician, the lawyer, the priest, the poet, the man of science, into its paid wage-labourers.

The bourgeoisie has torn away from the family its sentimental veil, and has reduced the family relation to a mere money relation.

The bourgeoisie has disclosed how it came to pass that the brutal display of vigour in the Middle Ages, which Reactionists so much admire, found its fitting complement in the most slothful indolence. It has been the first to show what man's activity can bring about. It has accomplished wonders far surpassing Egyptian pyramids, Roman aqueducts, and Gothic cathedrals; it has conducted expeditions that put in the shade all former Exoduses of nations and crusades.

The bourgeoisie cannot exist without constantly revolutionising the instruments of production, and thereby the relations of production, and with them the whole relations of society. Conservation of the old modes of production in unaltered form, was, on the contrary, the first condition of existence for all earlier industrial classes. Constant revolutionising of production, uninterrupted disturbance of all social conditions, everlasting uncertainty and agitation distinguish the bourgeois epoch from all earlier ones. All fixed, fast-frozen relations, with their train of ancient and venerable prejudices and opinions, are swept away, all new-formed ones become antiquated before they can ossify. All that is solid melts into air, all that is holy is profaned, and man is at last compelled to face with sober senses, his real conditions of life, and his relations with his kind.

The need of a constantly expanding market for its products chases the bourgeoisie over the whole surface of the globe. It must nestle everywhere, settle everywhere, establish connexions everywhere.

The bourgeoisie has through its exploitation of the world-market given a cosmopolitan character to production and consumption in every country. To the great chagrin of Reactionists, it has drawn from under the feet of industry the national ground on which it stood. All old-established national industries have been destroyed or are daily being destroyed. They are dislodged by new industries, whose introduction becomes a life and death question for all civilised nations, by industries that no longer work up indigenous raw material, but raw material drawn from the remotest zones; industries whose products are consumed, not only at home, but in every quarter of the globe. In place of the old wants, satisfied by the productions of the country, we find new wants, requiring for their satisfaction the products of distant lands and climes. In place of the old local and national seclusion and self-sufficiency, we have intercourse in every direction, universal interdependence of nations. And as in material, so also in intellectual production. The intellectual creations of individual nations become common property. National one-sidedness and narrow-mindedness become more and more impossible, and from the numerous national and local literatures, there arises a world literature.

The bourgeoisie, by the rapid improvement of all instruments of production, by the immensely facilitated means of communication, draws all, even the most barbarian, nations into civilisation. The cheap prices of its commodities are the heavy artillery with which it batters down all Chinese walls, with which it forces the barbarians' intensely obstinate hatred of foreigners to capitulate. It compels all nations, on pain of extinction, to adopt the bourgeois mode of production; it compels them to introduce what it calls civilisation into their midst, *i.e.*, to become bourgeois themselves. In one word, it creates a world after its own image.

The bourgeoisie has subjected the country to the rule of the towns. It has created enormous cities, has greatly increased the urban population as compared with the rural, and has thus rescued a considerable part of the population from the idiocy of rural life. Just as it has made the country dependent on the towns, so it has made barbarian and semi-barbarian countries dependent on the civilised ones, nations of peasants on nations of bourgeois, the East on the West.

The bourgeoisie keeps more and more doing away with the scattered state of the population, of the means of production, and of property. It has agglomerated population, centralised means of production, and has concentrated property in a few hands. The necessary consequence of this was political centralisation. Independent, or but loosely connected provinces, with separate interests, laws, government and systems of taxation, became lumped together into one nation, with one government, one code of laws, one national class-interest, one frontier and one customs-tariff. . . .

. . . Modern bourgeois society with its relations of production, of exchange and of property, a society that has conjured up such gigantic means of production and of exchange, is like the sorcerer, who is no longer able to control the powers of the nether world whom he has called up by his spells. For many a decade past the history of industry and commerce is but the history of the revolt of modern productive forces against modern conditions of production, against the property relations that are the conditions for the existence of the bourgeoisie and of its rule. It is enough to mention the commercial crises that by their periodical return put on its trial, each time more threateningly, the existence of the entire bourgeois society. In these crises a great part not only of the existing products, but also of the previously created productive forces, are periodically destroyed. In these crises there breaks out an epidemic that, in all earlier epochs, would have seemed an absurdity—the epidemic of over-production. Society suddenly finds itself put back into a state of momentary barbarism; it appears as if a famine, a universal war of devastation had cut off the supply of every means of subsistence; industry and commerce seem to be destroyed; and why? Because there is too much civilisation, too much means of subsistence, too much industry, too much commerce. The productive forces at the disposal of society no longer tend to further the development of the conditions of bourgeois property; on the contrary, they have become too powerful for these conditions, by which they are fettered, and so soon as they overcome these fetters, they bring disorder into the whole of bourgeois society, endanger the existence of bourgeois property. The conditions of bourgeois society are too narrow to comprise the wealth created by them. And how does the bourgeoisie get over these crises? On the one hand by enforced destruction of a mass of productive forces; on the other, by the conquest of new markets, and by the more thorough exploitation of the old ones. That is to say, by paving the way for more extensive and more destructive crises, and by diminishing the means whereby crises are prevented.

The weapons with which the bourgeoisie felled fuedalism to the ground are now turned against the bourgeoisie itself.

But not only has the bourgeoisie forged the weapons that bring death to itself; it has also called into existence the men who are to wield those weapons—the modern working class—the proletarians.

In proportion as the bourgeoisie, *i.e.*, capital, is developed, in the same proportion is the proletariat, the modern working class, developed—a class of labourers, who live only so long as they find work, and who find work only so long as their labour increases capital. These labourers, who must sell themselves piece-meal, are a commodity, like every other article of commerce, and are consequently exposed to all the vicissitudes of competition, to all the fluctuations of the market.

Owing to the extensive use of machinery and to division of labour, the work of the proletarians has lost all individual character, and consequently, all charm for the workman. He becomes an appendage of the machine, and it is only the most simple, most monotonous, and most easily acquired knack, that is required of him. Hence, the cost of production of a workman is restricted, almost entirely, to the means of subsistence that he requires for his maintenance, and for the propagation of his race. But the price of a commodity, and therefore also of labour, is equal to its cost of production. In proportion, therefore, as the repulsiveness of the work increases, the wage decreases. Nay more, in proportion as the use of machinery and division of labour increases, in the same proportion the burden of toil also increases, whether by prolongation of the working hours, by increase of the work exacted in a given time or by increased speed of the machinery, *etc.*

Modern industry has converted the little workshop of the patriarchal master into the great factory of the industrial capitalist. Masses of labourers, crowded into the factory, are organised like soldiers. As privates of the industrial army they are placed under the command of a perfect hierarchy of officers and sergeants. Not only are they slaves of the bourgeois class, and of the bourgeois State; they are daily and hourly enslaved by the machine, by the over-looker, and, above all, by the individual bourgeois manufacturer himself. The more openly this despotism proclaims gain to be its end and aim, the more petty, the more hateful and the more embittering it is.

The less the skill and exertion of strength implied in manual labour, in other words, the more modern industry becomes developed, the more is the labour of men superseded by that of women. Differences of age and sex have no longer any distinctive social validity for the working class. All are instruments of labour, more or less expensive to use, according to their age and sex. . . .

Now and then the workers are victorious, but only for a time. The real fruit of their battles lies, not in the immediate result, but in the ever-expanding union of the workers. This union is helped on by the improved means of communication that are created by modern industry and that place the workers of different localities in contact with one another. It was just this contact that was needed to centralise the numerous local struggles, all of the same character, into one national struggle between classes. But every class struggle is a political struggle. And that union, to attain which the burghers of the Middle Ages, with their miserable highways, required centuries, the modern proletarians, thanks to railways, achieve in a few years.

This organisation of the proletarians into a class, and consequently into a political party, is continually being upset again by the competition between the workers themselves. But it ever rises up again, stronger, firmer, mightier. It compels legislative recognition of particular interests of the workers, by taking advantage of the divisions among the bourgeoisie itself. Thus the ten-hours' bill in England was carried.

Altogether collisions between the classes of the old society further, in many ways, the course of development of the proletariat. The bourgeoisie finds itself involved in a constant battle. At first with the aristocracy; later on, with those portions of the bourgeoisie itself, whose interests have become antagonistic to the progress of industry; at all times, with the bourgeoisie of foreign countries. In all these battles it sees itself compelled to appeal to the proletariat, to ask for its help, and thus, to drag it into the political arena. The bourgeoisie itself, therefore, supplies the proletariat with its own elements of political and general education, in other words, it furnishes the proletariat with weapons for fighting the bourgeoisie.

Further, as we have already seen, entire sections of the ruling classes are, by the advance of industry, precipitated into the proletariat, or are at least threatened in their conditions of existence. These also supply the proletariat with fresh elements of enlightenment and progress.

Finally, in times when the class struggle nears the decisive hour, the process of dissolution going on within the ruling class, in fact within the whole range of society, assumes such a violent, glaring character, that a small section of the ruling class cuts itself adrift, and joins the revolutionary class, the class that holds the future in its hands. Just as, therefore, at an earlier period, a section of the nobility went over to the bourgeoisie, so now a portion of the bourgeoisie goes over to the proletariat, and in particular, a portion of the bourgeois ideologists, who have raised themselves to the level of comprehending theoretically the historical movement as a whole.

Of all the classes that stand face to face with the bourgeoisie today, the proletariat alone is a really revolutionary class. The other classes decay and finally disappear in the face of Modern Industry; the proletariat is its special and essential product. . . .

Hitherto, every form of society has been based, as we have already seen, on the antagonism of oppressing and oppressed classes. But in order to oppress a class, certain conditions must be assured to it under which it can, at least, continue its slavish existence. The serf, in the period of serfdom, raised himself to membership in the commune, just as the petty bourgeois, under the yoke of feudal absolutism, managed to develop into a bourgeois. The modern labourer, on the contrary, instead of rising with the progress of industry, sinks deeper and deeper below the conditions of existence of his own class. He becomes a pauper, and pauperism develops more rapidly than population and wealth. And here it becomes evident, that the bourgeoisie is unfit any longer to be the ruling class in society, and to impose its conditions of existence upon society as an over-riding law. It is unfit to rule because it is incompetent to assure an existence to its slave within his slavery, because it cannot help letting him sink into such a state, that it has to feed him, instead of being fed by him. Society can no longer live under this bourgeoisie, in other words, its existence is no longer compatible with society.

The essential condition for the existence, and

for the sway of the bourgeois class, is the formation and augmentation of capital; the condition for capital is wage-labour. Wage-labour rests exclusively on competition between the labourers. The advance of industry, whose involuntary promoter is the bourgeoisie, replaces the isolation of the labourers, due to competition, by their revolutionary combination, due to association. The development of Modern Industry, therefore, cuts from under its feet the very foundation on which the bourgeoisie produces and appropriates products. What the bourgeoisie, therefore, produces, above all, is its own grave-diggers. Its fall and the victory of the proletariat are equally inevitable.

II. Proletarians and Communists

In what relation do the Communists stand to the proletarians as a whole?

The Communists do not form a separate party opposed to other working-class parties.

They have no interests separate and apart from those of the proletariat as a whole.

They do not set up any sectarian principles of their own, by which to shape and mould the proletarian movement.

The Communists are distinguished from the other working-class parties by this only: (1) In the national stuggles of the proletarians of the different countries, they point out and bring to the front the common interests of the entire proletariat, independently of all nationality. (2) In the various stages of development which the struggle of the working class against the bourgeoisie has to pass through, they always and everywhere represent the interests of the movement as a whole.

The Communists, therefore, are on the one hand, practically, the most advanced and resolute section of the working-class parties of every country, that section which pushes forward all others; on the other hand, theoretically, they have over the great mass of the proletariat the advantage of clearly understanding the line of march, the conditions, and the ultimate general results of the proletarian movement.

The immediate aim of the Communists is the same as that of all the other proletarian parties: formation of the proletariat into a class, overthrow of the bourgeois supremacy, conquest of political power by the proletariat.

The theoretical conclusions of the Communists are in no way based on ideas or principles that have been invented, or discovered, by this or that would-be universal reformer.

They merely express, in general terms, actual relations springing from an existing class struggle, from a historical movement going on under our very eyes. The abolition of existing property relations is not at all a distinctive feature of Communism.

All property relations in the past have continually been subject to historical change consequent upon the change in historical conditions.

The French Revolution, for example, abolished feudal property in favour of bourgeois property.

The distinguishing feature of Communism is not the abolition of property generally, but the abolition of bourgeois property. But modern bourgeois private property is the final and most complete expression of the system of producing and appropriating products, that is based on class antagonisms, on the exploitation of the many by the few.

In this sense, the theory of the Communists may be summed up in the single sentence: Abolition of private property. . . .

You are horrified at our intending to do away with private property. But in your existing society, private property is already done away with for nine-tenths of the population; its existence for the few is solely due to its non-existence in the hands of those nine-tenths. You reproach us, therefore, with intending to do away with a form of property, the necessary condition for whose existence is the non-existence of any property for the immense majority of society.

In one word, you reproach us with intending to do away with your property. Precisely so; that is just what we intend.

From the moment when labour can no longer be converted into capital, money, or rent, into a social power capable of being monopolised, *i.e.*, from the moment when individual property can no longer be transformed into bourgeois property, into capital, from that moment, you say, individuality vanishes.

You must, therefore, confess that by "individual" you mean no other person than the bourgeois, than the middle-class owner of property. This person must, indeed, be swept out of the way, and made impossible.

Communism deprives no man of the power to appropriate the products of society; all that it does is to deprive him of the power to subjugate the labour of others by means of such appropriation.

It has been objected that upon the abolition of private property all work will cease, and universal laziness will overtake us.

According to this, bourgeois society ought long ago to have gone to the dogs through sheer idleness; for those of its members who work, acquire nothing, and those who acquire anything, do not work. The whole of this objection is but another expression of the tautology: that there can no longer be any wage-labour when there is no longer any capital.

All objections urged against the Communistic mode of producing and appropriating material products, have, in the same way, been urged against the Communistic modes of producing and appropriating intellectual products. Just as, to the bourgeois, the disappearance of class property is the disappearance of production itself, so the disappearance of class culture is to him identical with the dissappearance of all culture.

That culture, the loss of which he laments, is, for the enormous majority, a mere training to act as a machine.

But don't wrangle with us so long as you apply, to our intended abolition of bourgeois property, the standard of your bourgeois notions of freedom, culture, law, &c. Your very ideas are but the outgrowth of the conditions of your bourgeois production and bourgeois property, just as your jurisprudence is but the will of your class made into a law for all, a will, whose essential character and direction are determined by the economical conditions of existence of your class. . . .

Does it require deep intuition to comprehend that man's ideas, views and conceptions, in one word, man's consciousness, changes with every change in the conditions of his material existence, in his social relations and in his social life?

What else does the history of ideas prove, than that intellectual production changes its character in proportion as material production is changed? The ruling ideas of each age have ever been the ideas of its ruling class. . . .

We have seen above, that the first step in the revolution by the working class, is to raise the proletariat to the position of ruling class, to win the battle of democracy.

The proletariat will use its political supremacy to wrest, by degrees, all capital from the bourgeoisie, to centralise all instruments of production in the hands of the State, *i.e.*, of the proletariat organised as the ruling class; and to increase the total of productive forces as rapidly as possible.

Of course, in the beginning, this cannot be effected except by means of despotic inroads on the rights of property, and on the conditions of bourgeois production; by means of measures, therefore, which appear economically insufficient and untenable, but which, in the course of the movement, outstrip themselves, necessitate further inroads upon the old social order, and are unavoidable as a means of entirely revolutionising the mode of production.

These measures will of course be different in different countries.

Nevertheless in the most advanced countries, the following will be pretty generally applicable.

1. Abolition of property in land and application of all rents of land to public purposes.

2. A heavy progressive or graduated income tax.

3. Abolition of all right of inheritance.

4. Confiscation of the property of all emigrants and rebels.

5. Centralisation of credit in the hands of the State, by means of a national bank with State capital and an exclusive monopoly.

6. Centralisation of the means of communication and transport in the hands of the State.

7. Extention of factories and instruments of production owned by the State; the bringing into

cultivation of waste-lands, and the improvement of the soil generally in accordance with a common plan.

8. Equal liability of all to labour. Establishment of industrial armies, especially for agriculture.

9. Combination of agriculture with manufacturing industries; gradual abolition of the distinction between town and country, by a more equable distribution of the population over the country.

10. Free education for all children in public schools. Abolition of children's factory labour in its present form. Combination of education with industrial production, &c., &c.

When, in the course of development, class distinctions have disappeared, and all production has been concentrated in the hands of a vast association of the whole nation, the public power will lose its political character. Political power, properly so called, is merely the organised power of one class for oppressing another. If the proletariat during its contest with the bourgeoisie is compelled, by the force of circumstances, to organise itself as a class, if, by means of a revolution, it makes itself the ruling class, and, as such, sweeps away by force the old conditions of production, then it will, along with these conditions, have swept away the conditions for the existence of class antagonisms and of classes generally, and will thereby have abolished its own supremacy as a class.

In place of the old bourgeois society, with its classes and class antagonisms, we shall have an association, in which the free development of each is the condition for the free development of all.

IV. Position of the Communists in Relation to the Various Existing Opposition Parties

. . . In short, the Communists everywhere support every revolutionary movement against the existing social and political order of things.

In all these movements they bring to the front, as the leading question in each, the property question, no matter what its degree of development at the time.

Finally, they labour everywhere for the union and agreement of the democratic parties of all countries.

The Communists disdain to conceal their views and aims. They openly declare that their ends can be attained only by the forcible overthrow of all existing social conditions. Let the ruling classes tremble at a Communistic revolution. The proletarians have nothing to lose but their chains. They have a world to win.

WORKING MEN OF ALL COUNTRIES, UNITE!

from *Critique of the Gotha Program*

... What is "a fair distribution"?

Do not the bourgeois assert that the present-day distribution is "fair"? And is it not, in fact, the only "fair" distribution on the basis of the present-day mode of production? Are economic relations regulated by legal conceptions or do not, on the contrary, legal relations arise from economic ones? Have not also the socialist sectarians the most varied notions about "fair" distribution?

To understand what is implied in this connection by the phrase "fair distribution," we must take the first paragraph and this one together. The latter presupposes a society wherein "the instruments of labour are common property and the total labour is cooperatively regulated," and from the first paragraph we learn that "the proceeds of labour belong undiminished with equal right to all members of society."

"To all members of society"? To those who do not work as well? What remains then of the "undiminished proceeds of labour"? Only to those members of society who work? What remains then of the "equal right" of all members of society?

But "all members of society" and "equal right" are obviously mere phrases. The kernel consists in this, that in this communist society every worker must receive the "undiminished" Lassallean* "proceeds of labour."

Let us take first of all the words "proceeds of labour" in the sense of the product of labour; then the co-operative proceeds of labour are the *total social product.*

From this must now be deducted:

First, cover for replacement of the means of production used up.

Secondly, additional portion for expansion of production.

Thirdly, reserve or insurance funds to provide against accidents, dislocations caused by natural calamities, etc.

These deductions from the "undiminished proceeds of labour" are an economic necessity and their magnitude is to be determined according to available means and forces, and partly by computation of probabilities, but they are in no way calculable by equity.

There remains the other part of the total product, intended to serve as means of consumption.

Before this is divided among the individuals, there has to be deducted again, from it:

First, the general costs of administration not belonging to production.

This part will, from the outset, be very considerably restricted in comparison with present-day society and it diminishes in proportion as the new society develops.

Secondly, that which is intended for the common satisfaction of needs, such as schools, health services, etc.

From the outset this part grows considerably in comparison with present-day society and it grows in proportion as the new society develops.

Thirdly, funds for those unable to work, etc., in short, for what is included under so-called official poor relief today.

Only now do we come to the "distribution" which the programme, under Lassallean influence, alone has in view in its narrow fashion, namely, to that part of the means of consumption which is divided among the individual producers of the co-operative society.

* Ferdinand Lassalle (1825–1864), German socialist and correspondent of Marx, founded the first political party for German workers in 1863. It is the ancestor of today's German Social Democratic Party. —Ed.

The "undiminished proceeds of labour" have already unnoticeably become converted into the "diminished" proceeds, although what the producer is deprived of in his capacity as a private individual benefits him directly or indirectly in his capacity as a member of society.

Just as the phrase of the "undiminished proceeds of labour" has disappeared, so now does the phrase of the "proceeds of labour" disappear altogether.

Within the co-operative society based on common ownership of the means of production, the producers do not exchange their products; just as little does the labour employed on the products appear here *as the value* of these products, as a material quality possessed by them, since now, in contrast to capitalist society, individual labour no longer exists in an indirect fashion but directly as a component part of the total labour. The phrase "proceeds of labour," objectionable also today on account of its ambiguity, thus loses all meaning.

What we have to deal with here is a communist society, not as it has *developed* on its own foundations, but, on the contrary, just as it *emerges* from capitalist society; which is thus in every respect, economically, morally and intellectually, still stamped with the birth marks of the old society from whose womb it emerges. Accordingly, the individual producer receives back from society—after the deductions have been made—exactly what he gives to it. What he has given to it is his individual quantum of labour. For example, the social working day consists of the sum of the individual hours of work; the individual labour time of the individual producer is the part of the social working day contributed by him, his share in it. He receives a certificate from society that he has furnished such and such an amount of labour (after deducting his labour for the common funds), and with this certificate he draws from the social stock of means of consumption as much as costs the same amount of labour. The same amount of labour which he has given to society in one form he receives back in another.

Here obviously the same principle prevails as that which regulates the exchange of commodities, as far as this is exchange of equal values. Content and form are changed, because under the altered circumstances no one can give anything except his labour, and because, on the other hand, nothing can pass to the ownership of individuals except individual means of consumption. But, as far as the distribution of the latter among the individual producers is concerned, the same principle prevails as in the exchange of commodity equivalents: a given amount of labour in one form is exchanged for an equal amount of labour in another form.

Hence, *equal right* here is still in principle—*bourgeois right,* although principle and practice are no longer at loggerheads, while the exchange of equivalents in commodity exchange only exists *on the average* and not in the individual case.

In spite of this advance, this *equal right* is still constantly stigmatised by a bourgeois limitation. The right of the producers is *proportional* to the labour they supply; the equality consists in the fact that measurement is made with an *equal standard,* labour.

But one man is superior to another physically or mentally and so supplies more labour in the same time, or can labour for a longer time; and labour, to serve as a measure, must be defined by its duration or intensity, otherwise it ceases to be a standard of measurement. This *equal* right is an unequal right for unequal labour. It recognises no class differences, because everyone is only a worker like everyone else; but it tacitly recognises unequal individual endowment and thus productive capacity as natural privileges. *It is, therefore, a right of inequality, in its content, like every right.* Right by its very nature can consist only in the application of an equal standard; but unequal individuals (and they would not be different individuals if they were not unequal) are measurable only by an equal standard in so far as they are brought under an equal point of view, are taken from one *definite* side only, for instance, in the present case, are regarded *only as workers* and nothing more is seen in them, everything else being ignored. Further, one worker is married, another not; one has more children than another, and so on and so forth. Thus, with an equal performance of labour, and hence an equal share in the social consumption fund, one will in fact receive more than another, one will be richer than another, and so on. To avoid all these defects, right instead of being equal would have to be unequal.

But these defects are inevitable in the first phase of communist society as it is when it has just emerged after prolonged birth pangs from capitalist society. Right can never be higher than the economic structure of society and its cultural development conditioned thereby.

In a higher phase of communist society, after the enslaving subordination of the individual to the division of labour, and therewith also the antithesis between mental and physical labour, has vanished; after labour has become not only a means of life but life's prime want; after the productive forces have also increased with the all-round development of the individual, and all the springs of co-operative wealth flow more abundantly—only then can the narrow horizon of bourgeois right be crossed in its entirety and society inscribe on its banner: From each according to his ability, to each according to his needs!

I have dealt more at length with the "undiminished proceeds of labour," on the one hand, and with "equal right" and "fair distribution," on the other, in order to show what a crime it is to attempt, on the one hand, to force on our Party again, as dogmas, ideas which in a certain period had some meaning but have now become obsolete verbal rubbish, while again perverting, on the other, the realistic outlook, which it cost so much effort to instil into the Party but which has now taken root in it, by means of ideological nonsense about right and other trash so common among the democrats and French Socialists.

Quite apart from the analysis so far given, it was in general a mistake to make a fuss about so-called *distribution* and put the principal stress on it.

Any distribution whatever of the means of consumption is only a consequence of the distribution of the conditions of production themselves. The latter distribution, however, is a feature of the mode of production itself. The capitalist mode of production, for example, rests on the fact that the material conditions of production are in the hands of non-workers in the form of property in capital and land, while the masses are only owners of the personal condition of production, of labour power. If the elements of production are so distributed, then the present-day distribution of the means of consumption results automatically. If the material conditions of production are the co-operative property of the workers themselves, then there likewise results a distribution of the means of consumption different from the present one. Vulgar socialism (and from it in turn a section of the democracy) has taken over from the bourgeois economists the consideration and treatment of distribution as independent of the mode of production and hence the presentation of socialism as turning principally on distribution. After the real relation has long been made clear, why retrogress again? . . .

JOHN RAWLS

from *A Theory of Justice* (1970)

John Rawls is Professor of Philosophy at Harvard University. (Source: Reprinted by permission of the publishers from A Theory of Justice *by John Rawls, Cambridge, Mass.: Harvard University Press. Copyright © 1971 by the President and Fellows of Harvard College.)*

QUESTIONS FOR REFLECTION

1. What is a well-ordered society?
2. What is the original position? What is the role of the veil of ignorance?
3. What is reflective equilibrium? What is its significance for moral theory?
4. What are Rawls's two principles of justice? Can they come into conflict? If so, how can the conflict be resolved?

CHAPTER I / JUSTICE AS FAIRNESS

1. The Role of Justice

Justice is the first virtue of social institutions, as truth is of systems of thought. A theory however elegant and economical must be rejected or revised if it is untrue; likewise laws and institutions no matter how efficient and well-arranged must be reformed or abolished if they are unjust. Each person possesses an inviolability founded on justice that even the welfare of society as a whole cannot override. For this reason justice denies that the loss of freedom for some is made right by a greater good shared by others. It does not allow that the sacrifices imposed on a few are outweighed by the larger sum of advantages enjoyed by many. Therefore in a just society the liberties of equal citizenship are taken as settled; the rights secured by justice are not subject to political bargaining or to the calculus of social interests. The only thing that permits us to acquiesce in an erroneous theory is the lack of a better one; analogously, an injustice is tolerable only when it is necessary to avoid an even greater injustice. Being first virtues of human activities, truth and justice are uncompromising.

These propositions seem to express our intuitive conviction of the primacy of justice. No doubt they are expressed too strongly. In any event I wish to inquire whether these contentions or others similar to them are sound, and if so how they can be accounted for. To this end it is necessary to work out a theory of justice in the light of which these assertions can be interpreted and assessed. I shall begin by considering the role of the principles of justice. Let us assume, to fix ideas, that a society is a more or less self-sufficient association of persons who in their relations to one another recognize certain rules of conduct as binding and who for the most part act in accordance with them. Suppose further that these rules specify a system of cooperation designed to advance the good of those taking part in it. Then, although a society is a cooperative venture for mutual advantage, it is typically marked by a conflict as well as by an identity of interests. There is an identity of interests since social cooperation makes possible a better life for all than any would have if each were to live solely by his own efforts. There is a conflict of interests since persons are not indifferent as to how the greater benefits produced by their collaboration are distributed, for in order to pursue their ends they each prefer a larger to a lesser share. A set of principles is required for choosing among the various social arrangements which determine this division of advantages and for underwriting an agreement on the proper distributive shares. These principles are the principles of social justice: they provide a way of assigning rights and duties in the basic institutions of society and they define the appropriate distribution of the benefits and burdens of social cooperation.

Now let us say that a society is well-ordered when it is not only designed to advance the good of its members but when it is also effectively regulated by a public conception of justice. That is, it is a society in which (1) everyone accepts and knows that the others accept the same principles of justice, and (2) the basic social institutions generally satisfy and are generally known to satisfy these principles. In this case while men may put forth excessive demands on one another, they nevertheless acknowledge a common point of view from which their claims may be adjudicated. If men's inclination to self-interest makes their vigilance against one another necessary, their public sense of justice makes their secure association together possible. Among individuals with disparate aims and purposes a shared conception of justice establishes the bonds of civic friendship; the general desire for justice limits the pursuit of other ends. One may think of a public conception of justice as constituting the fundamental charter of a well-ordered human association.

Existing societies are of course seldom well-ordered in this sense, for what is just and unjust is usually in dispute. Men disagree about which principles should define the basic terms of their association. Yet we may still say, despite this disagreement, that they each have a conception of justice. That is, they understand the need for, and they are prepared to affirm, a characteristic set of principles for assigning basic rights and duties and for determining what they take to be the proper distribution of the benefits and burdens of social cooperation. Thus it seems natural to think of the concept of justice as distinct from the various conceptions of justice and as being specified by the role which these different sets of principles, these different conceptions, have in common. Those who hold different conceptions of justice can, then, still agree that institutions are just when no arbitrary distinctions are made between persons in the assigning of basic rights and duties and when the rules determine a proper balance between competing claims to the advantages of social life. Men can agree to this description of just institutions since the notions of an arbitrary distinction and of a proper balance, which are included in the concept of justice, are left open for each to interpret according to the principles of justice that he accepts. These principles single out which similarities and differences among persons are relevant in determining rights and duties and they specify which division of advantages is appropriate. Clearly this distinction between the concept and the various conceptions of justice settles no important questions. It simply helps to identify the role of the principles of social justice.

Some measure of agreement in conceptions of justice is, however, not the only prerequisite for a viable human community. There are other fundamental social problems, in particular those of coordination, efficiency, and stability. Thus the plans of individuals need to be fitted together so that their activities are compatible with one another and they can all be carried through without anyone's legitimate expectations being severely disappointed. Moreover, the execution of these plans should lead to the achievement of social ends in ways that are efficient and consistent with justice. And finally, the scheme of social cooperation must be stable: it must be more or less regularly complied with and its basic rules willingly acted upon; and when infractions occur, stabilizing forces should exist that prevent further violations and tend to restore the arrangement. Now it is evident that these three problems are connected with that of justice. In the absence of a certain measure of agreement on what is just and unjust, it is clearly more difficult for individuals to coordinate their plans efficiently in order to insure that mutually beneficial arrangements are maintained. Distrust and resentment corrode the ties of civility, and suspicion and hostility tempt men to act in ways they would otherwise avoid. So while the distinctive role of conceptions of justice is to specify basic rights and duties and to determine the appropriate distributive shares, the way in which a conception does this is bound to affect the problems of efficiency, coordination, and stability. We cannot, in general, assess a conception of justice by its distributive role alone, however useful this role may be in identifying the concept of justice. We must take into account its wider connections; for even though justice has a certain priority, being the most important virtue of institutions, it is still true that, other things equal, one conception of justice is preferable to another when its broader consequences are more desirable. . . .

3. The Main Idea of the Theory of Justice

My aim is to present a conception of justice which generalizes and carries to a higher level of abstraction the familiar theory of the social contract as found, say, in Locke, Rousseau, and Kant. In order to do this we are not to think of the original contract as one to enter a particular society or to set up a particular form of government. Rather, the guiding idea is that the principles of justice for the basic structure of society are the object of the original agreement. They are the principles that free and rational persons concerned to further their own interests would accept in an initial position of equality as defining the fundamental terms of their association. These principles are to regulate all further agreements; they specify the kinds of social cooperation that can be entered into and the forms of government that can be established. This way of regarding the principles of justice I shall call justice as fairness.

Thus we are to imagine that those who engage in social cooperation choose together, in one joint act, the principles which are to assign basic rights and duties and to determine the division of social benefits. Men are to decide in advance how they are to regulate their claims against one another and what is to be the foundation charter of their society. Just as each person must decide by rational reflection what constitutes his good, that is, the system of ends which it is rational for him to pursue, so a group of persons must decide once and for all what is to count among them as just and unjust. The choice which rational men would make in this hypothetical situation of equal liberty, assuming for the present that this choice problem has a solution, determines the principles of justice.

In justice as fairness the original position of equality corresponds to the state of nature in the traditional theory of the social contract. This original position is not, of course, thought of as an actual historical state of affairs, much less as a primitive condition of culture. It is understood as a purely hypothetical situation characterized so as to lead to a certain conception of justice. Among the essential features of this situation is that no one knows his place in society, his class position or social status, nor does any one know his fortune in the distribution of natural assets and abilities, his intelligence, strength, and the like. I shall even assume that the parties do not know their conceptions of the good or their special psychological propensities. The principles of justice are chosen behind a veil of ignorance. This ensures that no one is advantaged or disadvantaged in the choice of principles by the outcome of natural chance or the contingency of social circumstances. Since all are similarly situated and no one is able to design principles to favor his particular condition, the principles of justice are the result of a fair agreement or bargain. For given the circumstances of the original position, the symmetry of everyone's relations to each other, this initial situation is fair between individuals as moral persons, that is, as rational beings with their own ends and capable, I shall assume, of a sense of justice. The original position is, one might say, the appropriate initial status quo, and thus the fundamental agreements reached in it are fair. This explains the propriety of the name "justice as fairness": it conveys the idea that the principles of justice are agreed to in an initial situation that is fair. The name does not mean that the concepts of justice and fairness are the same, any more than the phrase "poetry as metaphor" means that the concepts of poetry and metaphor are the same.

Justice as fairness begins, as I have said, with one of the most general of all choices which persons might make together, namely, with the choice of the first principles of a conception of justice which is to regulate all subsequent criticism and reform of institutions. Then, having chosen a conception of justice, we can suppose that they are to choose a constitution and a legislature to enact laws, and so on, all in accordance with the principles of justice initially agreed upon. Our social situation is just if it is such that by this sequence of hypothetical agreements we would have contracted into the general system of rules which defines it. Moreover, assuming that the original position does determine a set of principles (that is, that a particular conception of justice would be chosen), it will then be true that whenever social institutions satisfy these principles those engaged in them can say to one another that they are cooperating on terms to which they would agree if they were free and equal persons whose relations with respect to one another were fair. They could all view their arrangements as meeting the stipulations which they would acknowledge in an initial situation that embodies widely accepted and reasonable constraints on the choice of principles. The general recognition of this fact would provide the basis for a public acceptance of the corresponding principles of justice. No society can, of course, be a scheme of cooperation which men enter voluntarily in a literal sense; each person finds himself placed at birth in some particular position in some particular society, and the nature of this position materially affects his life prospects. Yet a society satisfying the principles of justice as fairness comes as close as a society can to being a voluntary scheme, for it meets the principles which free and equal persons would assent to under circumstances that are fair. In this sense its members are autonomous and the obligations they recognize self-imposed.

One feature of justice as fairness is to think of the parties in the initial situation as rational and mutually disinterested. This does not mean that the parties are egoists, that is, individuals with only certain kinds of interests, say in wealth, prestige, and domination. But they are conceived as not taking an interest in one another's interests. They are to presume that even their spiritual aims may be opposed, in the way that the aims of those of different religions may be opposed. Moreover, the concept of rationality must be interpreted as far as possible in the narrow sense, standard in economic theory, of taking the most effective means to given ends. I shall modify this concept to some extent, . . . but one must try to avoid introducing into it any controversial ethical elements. The initial situation must be characterized by stipulations that are widely accepted.

In working out the conception of justice as fairness one main task clearly is to determine which principles of justice would be chosen in the original position. To do this we must describe this situation in some detail and formulate with care the problem of choice which it presents. . . . It may be observed, however, that once the principles of justice are thought of as arising from an original agreement in a situation of equality, it is an open question whether the principle of utility would be acknowledged. Offhand it hardly seems likely that persons who view themselves as equals, entitled to press their claims upon one another, would agree to a principle which may require lesser life prospects for some simply for the sake of a greater sum of advantages enjoyed by others. Since each desires to protect his interests, his capacity to advance his conception of the good, no one has a reason to acquiesce in an enduring loss for himself in order to bring about a greater net balance of satisfaction. In the absence of strong and lasting benevolent impulses, a rational man would not accept a basic structure merely because it maximized the algebraic sum of advantages irrespective of its permanent effects on his own basic rights and interests. Thus it seems that the principle of utility is incompatible with the conception of social cooperation among equals for mutual advantage. It appears to be inconsistent with the idea of reciprocity implicit in the notion of a well-ordered society. Or, at any rate, so I shall argue.

I shall maintain instead that the persons in the initial situation would choose two rather different principles: the first requires equality in the assignment of basic rights and duties, while the second holds that social and economic inequalities, for example inequalities of wealth and authority, are just only if they result in compensating benefits for everyone, and in particular for the least advantaged members of society. These principles rule out justifying institutions on the grounds that the hardships of some are offset by a greater good in the aggregate. It may be expedient but it is not just that some should have less in order that others may prosper. But there is no injustice in the greater benefits earned by a few provided that the situation of persons not so fortunate is thereby improved. The intuitive idea is that since everyone's well-being depends upon a scheme of cooperation without which no one could have a satisfactory life, the division of advantages should be such as to draw forth the willing cooperation of everyone taking part in it, including those less well situated. Yet this can be expected only if reasonable terms are proposed. The two principles mentioned seem to be a fair agreement on the basis of which those better endowed, or more fortunate in their social position, neither of which we can be said to deserve, could expect the willing cooperation of others when some workable scheme is a necessary condition of the welfare of all. Once we decide to look for a conception of justice that nullifies the accidents of natural endowment and the contingencies of social circumstance as counters in quest for political and economic advantage, we are led to these principles. They express the result of leaving aside those aspects of the social world that seem arbitrary from a moral point of view.

The problem of the choice of principles, however, is extremely difficult. I do not expect the answer I shall suggest to be convincing to everyone. It is, therefore, worth noting from the outset that justice as fairness, like other contract views, consists of two parts: (1) an interpretation of the initial situation and of the problem of choice posed there, and (2) a set of principles which, it is argued, would be agreed to. One may accept the first part of the theory (or some variant thereof), but not the other, and conversely. The concept of the initial contractual situation may seem reasonable although the particular principles proposed are rejected. . . .

4. The Original Position and Justification

I have said that the original position is the appropriate initial status quo which insures that the fundamental agreements reached in it are fair. This fact yields the name "justice as fairness." It is clear, then, that I want to say that one conception of justice is more reasonable than another, or justifiable with respect to it, if rational persons in the initial situation would choose its principles over those of the other for the role of justice. Conceptions of justice are to be ranked by their acceptability to persons so circumstanced. Understood in this way the question of justification is settled by working out a problem of deliberation: we have to ascertain which principles it would be rational to adopt given the contractual situation. This connects the theory of justice with the theory of rational choice.

If this view of the problem of justification is to succeed, we must, of course, describe in some detail the nature of this choice problem. A problem of rational decision has a definite answer only if we know the beliefs and interests of the parties, their relations with respect to one another, the alternatives between which they are to choose, the procedure whereby they make up their minds, and so on. As the circumstances are presented in different ways, correspondingly different principles are accepted. The concept of the original position, as I shall refer to it, is that the most philosophically favored interpretation of this initial choice situation for the purposes of a theory of justice.

But how are we to decide what is the most favored interpretation? I assume, for one thing, that there is a broad measure of agreement that principles of justice should be chosen under certain conditions. To justify a particular description of the initial situation one shows that it incorporates these commonly shared presumptions. One argues from widely accepted but weak premises to more specific conclusions. Each of the presumptions should by itself be natural and plausible; some of them may seem innocuous or even trivial. The aim of the contract approach is to establish that taken together they impose significant bounds on acceptable principles of justice. The ideal outcome would be that these conditions determine a unique set of principles; but I shall be satisfied if they suffice to rank the main traditional conceptions of social justice.

One should not be misled, then, by the somewhat unusual conditions which characterize the original position. The idea here is simply to make vivid to ourselves the restrictions that it seems reasonable to impose on arguments for principles of justice, and therefore on these principles themselves. Thus it seems reasonable and generally acceptable that no one should be advantaged or disadvantaged by natural fortune or social circumstances in the choice of principles. It also seems widely agreed that it should be impossible to tailor principles to the circumstances of one's own case. We should insure further that particular inclinations and aspirations, and persons' conceptions of their good do not affect the principles adopted. The aim is to rule out those principles that it would be rational to propose for acceptance, however little the chance of success, only if one knew certain things that are irrelevant from the standpoint of justice. For example, if a man knew that he was wealthy, he might find it rational to advance the principle that various taxes for welfare measures be counted unjust; if he knew that he was poor, he would most likely propose the contrary principle. To represent the desired restrictions one imagines a situation in which everyone is deprived of this sort of information. One excludes the knowledge of those contingencies which sets men at odds and allows them to be guided by their prejudices. In this manner the veil of ignorance is arrived at in a natural way. This concept should cause no difficulty if we keep in mind the constraints on arguments that it is meant to express. At any time we can enter the original position, so to speak, simply by following a certain procedure, namely, by arguing for principles of justice in accordance with these restrictions.

It seems reasonable to suppose that the parties in the original position are equal. That is, all have the same rights in the procedure for choosing principles; each can make proposals, submit reasons for their acceptance, and so on. Obviously the purpose of these conditions is to represent equality between human beings as moral persons, as creatures having a conception of their good and capable of a sense of justice. The basis of equality is taken to be similarity in these two respects. Systems of ends are not ranked in value; and each man is presumed to have the requisite ability to understand and to act upon whatever principles are adopted. Together with the veil of ignorance, these conditions define the principles of justice as those which rational persons concerned to advance their interests would consent to as equals when none are known to be advantaged or disadvantaged by social and natural contingencies.

There is, however, another side to justifying a particular description of the original position. This is to see if the principles which would be chosen match our considered convictions of justice or extend them in an acceptable way. We can note whether applying these principles would lead us to make the same judgments about the basic structure of society which we now make intuitively and in which we have the greatest confidence; or whether, in cases where our present judgments are in doubt and given with hesitation, these principles offer a resolution which we can affirm on reflection. There are questions which we feel sure must be answered in a certain way. For example, we are confident that religious intolerance and racial discrimination are unjust. We think that we have examined these things with care and have reached what we believe is an impartial judgment not likely to be distorted by an excessive attention to our own interests. These convictions are provisional fixed points which we presume any conception of justice must fit. But we have much less assurance as to what is the correct distribution of wealth and authority. Here we may be looking for a way to remove our doubts. We can check an interpretation of the initial situation, then, by the capacity of its principles to accommodate our firmest convictions and to provide guidance where guidance is needed.

In searching for the most favored description of this situation we work from both ends. We begin by describing it so that it represents generally shared and preferably weak conditions. We then see if these conditions are strong enough to yield a significant set of principles. If not, we look for further premises equally reasonable. But if so, and these principles match our considered convictions of justice, then so far well and good. But presumably there will be discrepancies. In this case we have a choice. We can either modify the account of the initial situation or we can revise our existing judgments, for even the judgments we take provisionally as fixed points are liable to revision. By going back and forth, sometimes altering the conditions of the contractual circumstances, at others withdrawing our judgments and conforming them to principle, I assume that eventually we shall find a description of the initial situation that both expresses reasonable conditions and yields principles which match our considered judgments duly pruned and adjusted. This state of affairs I refer to as reflective equilibrium. It is an equilibrium because at last our principles and judgments coincide; and it is reflective since we know to what principles our judgments conform and the premises of their derivation. At the moment everything is in order. But this equilibrium is not necessarily stable. It is liable to be upset by further examination of the conditions which should be imposed on the contractual situation and by particular cases which may lead us to revise our judgments. Yet for the time being we have done what we can to render coherent and to justify our convictions of social justice. We have reached a conception of the original position.

I shall not, of course, actually work through this process. Still, we may think of the interpretation of the original position that I shall present as the result of such a hypothetical course of reflection. It represents the attempt to accommodate within one scheme both reasonable philosophical conditions on principles as well as our considered judgments of justice. In arriving at the favored interpretation of the initial situation there is no point at which an appeal is made to self-evidence in the traditional sense either of general conceptions or particular convictions. I do not claim for the principles of justice proposed that they are necessary truths or derivable from such truths. A conception of justice cannot be deduced from self-evident premises or conditions on principles; instead, its justification is a matter of the mutual support of many considerations, of everything fitting together into one coherent view.

A final comment. We shall want to say that certain principles of justice are justified because they would be agreed to in an initial situation of equality. I have emphasized that this original position is purely hypothetical. It is natural to ask why, if this agreement is never actually entered into, we should take any interest in these principles, moral or otherwise. The answer is that the conditions embodied in the description of the original position are ones that we do in fact accept. Or if we do not, then perhaps we can be persuaded to do so by philosophical reflection. Each aspect of the contractual situation can be given supporting grounds. Thus what we shall do is to collect together into one conception a number of conditions on principles that we are ready upon due consideration to recognize as reasonable. These constraints express what we are prepared to regard as limits on fair terms of social cooperation. One way to look at the idea of the original position, therefore, is to see it as an expository device which sums up the meaning of these conditions and helps us to extract their consequences. On the other hand, this conception is also an intuitive notion that suggests its own elaboration, so that led on by it we are drawn to define more clearly the standpoint from which we can best interpret moral relationships. We need a conception that enables us to envision our objective from afar: the intuitive notion of the original position is to do this for us. . . .

11. Two Principles of Justice

I shall now state in a provisional form the two principles of justice that I believe would be chosen in the original position. In this section I wish to make only the most general comments, and therefore the first formulation of these principles is tentative. . . .

The first statement of the two principles reads as follows.

First: each person is to have an equal right to the most extensive basic liberty compatible with a similar liberty for others.

Second: social and economic inequalities are to be arranged so that they are both (a) reasonably expected to be to everyone's advantage, and (b) attached to positions and offices open to all. . . .

By way of general comment, these principles primarily apply, as I have said, to the basic structure of society. They are to govern the assignment of rights and duties and to regulate the distribution of social and economic advantages. As their formulation suggests, these principles presuppose that the social structure can be divided into two more or less distinct parts, the first principle applying to the one, the second to the other. They distinguish between those aspects of the social system that define and secure the equal liberties of citizenship and those that specify and establish social and economic inequalities. The basic liberties of citizens are, roughly speaking, political liberty (the right to vote and to be eligible for public office) together with freedom of speech and assembly; liberty of conscience and freedom of thought; freedom of the person along with the right to hold (personal) property; and freedom from arbitrary arrest and seizure as defined by the concept of the rule of law. These liberties are all required to be equal by the first principle, since citizens of a just society are to have the same basic rights.

The second principle applies, in the first approximation, to the distribution of income and wealth and to the design of organizations that make use of differences in authority and responsibility, or chains of command. While the distribution of wealth and income need not be equal, it must be to everyone's advantage, and at the same time, positions of authority and offices of command must be accessible to all. One applies the second principle by holding positions open, and then, subject to this constraint, arranges social and economic inequalities so that everyone benefits.

These principles are to be arranged in a serial order with the first principle prior to the second. This ordering means that a departure from the institutions of equal liberty required by the first principle cannot be justified by, or compensated for, by greater social and economic advantages. The distribution of wealth and income, and the hierarchies of authority, must be consistent with both the liberties of equal citizenship and equality of opportunity.

It is clear that these principles are rather specific in their content, and their acceptance rests on certain assumptions that I must eventually try to explain and justify. A theory of justice depends upon a theory of society in ways that will become evident as we proceed. For the present, it should be observed that the two principles (and this holds for all formulations) are a special case of a more general conception of justice that can be expressed as follows.

All social values—liberty and opportunity, income and wealth, and the bases of self-respect—are to be distributed equally unless an unequal distribution of any, or all, of these values is to everyone's advantage.

Injustice, then, is simply inequalities that are not to the benefit of all. Of course, this conception is extremely vague and requires interpretation.

As a first step, suppose that the basic structure of society distributes certain primary goods, that is, things that every rational man is presumed to want. These goods normally have a use whatever a person's rational plan of life. For simplicity, assume that the chief primary goods at the disposition of society are rights and liberties, powers and opportunities, income and wealth. . . . These are the social primary goods. Other primary goods such as health and vigor, intelligence and imagination, are natural goods; although their possession is influenced by the basic structure, they are not so directly under its control. Imagine, then, a hypothetical initial arrangement in which all the social primary goods are equally distributed: everyone has similar rights and duties, and income and wealth are evenly shared. This state of affairs provides a benchmark for judging improvements. If certain inequalities of wealth and organizational powers would make everyone better off than in this hypothetical starting situation, then they accord with the general conception. . . .

ROBERT NOZICK

from *Anarchy, State, and Utopia* (1974)

Robert Nozick is Professor of Philosophy at Harvard University. (Source: From Anarchy, State, and Utopia *by Robert Nozick.*

QUESTIONS FOR REFLECTION

1. Outline Nozick's entitlement theory. What principles would be required, if the world were perfect? What principle is needed because it is not?
2. How do historical principles differ from end-result principles?
3. What is a patterned theory of justice? Is Nozick's theory patterned? Can a theory be both patterned and historical?
4. Why, according to Nozick, are patterned theories of justice incompatible with liberty?

CHAPTER 7 / DISTRIBUTIVE JUSTICE

The minimal state is the most extensive state that can be justified. Any state more extensive violates people's rights. Yet many persons have put forth reasons purporting to justify a more extensive state. . . . In this chapter we consider the claim that a more extensive state is justified, because necessary (or the best instrument) to achieve distributive justice.

The term "distributive justice" is not a neutral one. Hearing the term "distribution," most people presume that some thing or mechanism uses some principle or criterion to give out a supply of things. Into this process of distributing shares some error may have crept. So it is an open question, at least, whether *re*distribution should take place; whether we should do again what has already been done once, though poorly. However, we are not in the position of children who have been given portions of pie by someone who now makes last minute adjustments to rectify careless cutting. There is no *central* distribution, no person or group entitled to control all the resources, jointly deciding how they are to be doled out. What each person gets, he gets from others who give to him in exchange for something, or as a gift. In a free society, diverse persons control different resources, and new holdings arise out of the voluntary exchanges and actions of persons. There is no more a distributing or distribution of shares than there is a distributing of mates in a society in which persons choose whom they shall marry. The total result is the product of many individual decisions which the different individuals involved are entitled to make. Some uses of the term "distribution," it is true, do not imply a previous distributing appropriately judged by some criterion (for example, "probability distribution"); nevertheless, despite the title of this chapter, it would be best to use a terminology that clearly is neutral. We shall speak of people's holdings; a principle of justice in holdings describes (part of) what justice tells us (requires) about holdings. I shall state first what I take to be the correct view about justice in holdings, and then turn to the discussion of alternate views.

Section I

The Entitlement Theory

The subject of justice in holdings consists of three major topics. The first is the *original acquisition of holdings*, the appropriation of unheld things. This includes the issues of how unheld things may come to be held, the process, or processes, by which unheld things may come to be held, the things that may come to be held by these processes, the extent of what comes to be held by a particular process, and so on. We shall refer to the complicated truth about this topic, which we shall not formulate here, as the principle of justice in acquisition. The second topic concerns the *transfer of holdings* from one person to another. By what processes may a person transfer holdings to another? How may a person acquire a holding from another who holds it? Under this topic come general descriptions of voluntary exchange, and gift and (on the other hand) fraud, as well as reference to particular conventional details fixed upon in a given society. The complicated truth about this subject (with placeholders for conventional details) we shall call the principle of justice in transfer. (And we shall suppose it also includes principles governing how a person may divest himself of a holding, passing it into an unheld state.)

If the world were wholly just, the following inductive definition would exhaustively cover the subject of justice in holdings.

1. A person who acquires a holding in accordance with the principle of justice in acquisition is entitled to that holding.
2. A person who acquires a holding in accordance with the principle of justice in transfer, from someone else entitled to the holding, is entitled to the holding.
3. No one is entitled to a holding except by (repeated) applications of 1 and 2.

The complete principle of distributive justice would say simply that a distribution is just if everyone is entitled to the holdings they possess under the distribution.

A distribution is just if it arises from another just distribution by legitimate means. The legitimate means of moving from one distribution to another are specified by the principle of justice in transfer. The legitimate first "moves" are specified by the principle of justice in acquisition. Whatever arises from a just situation by just steps is itself just. The means of change specified by the principle of justice in transfer preserve justice. As correct rules of inference are truth-preserving, and any conclusion deduced via repeated application of such rules from only true premisses is itself true, so the means of transition from one situation to another specified by the principle of justice in transfer are justice-preserving, and any situation actually arising from repeated transitions in accordance with the principle from a just situation is itself just. The parallel between justice-preserving transformations and truth-preserving transformations illuminates where it fails as well as where it holds. That a conclusion could have been deduced by truth-preserving means from premisses that are true suffices to show its truth. That from a just situation a situation *could* have arisen via justice-preserving means does not suffice to show its justice. The fact that a thief's victims voluntarily *could* have presented him with gifts does not entitle the thief to his ill-gotten gains. Justice in holdings is historical; it depends upon what actually has happened. We shall return to this point later.

Not all actual situations are generated in accordance with the two principles of justice in holdings: the principle of justice in acquisition and the principle of justice in transfer. Some people steal from others, or defraud them, or enslave them, seizing their product and preventing them from living as they choose, or forcibly exclude others from competing in exchanges. None of these are permissible modes of transition from one situation to another. And some persons acquire holdings by means not sanctioned by the principle of justice in acquisition. The existence of past injustice (previous violations of the first two principles of justice in holdings) raises the third major topic under justice in holdings: the rectification of injustice in holdings. If past injustice has shaped present holdings in various ways, some identifiable and some not, what now, if anything, ought to be done to rectify these injustices? What obligations do the performers of injustice have toward those whose position is worse than it would have been had the injustice not been done? Or, than it would have been had compensation been paid promptly? How, if at all, do things change if the beneficiaries and those made worse off are not the direct parties in the act of injustice, but, for example, their descendants? Is an injustice done to someone whose holding was itself based upon an unrectified injustice? How far back must one go in wiping clean the historical slate of injustices? What may victims of injustice permissibly do in order to rectify the injustices being done to them, including the many injustices done by persons acting through their government? I do not know of a thorough or theoretically sophisticated treatment of such issues. Idealizing greatly, let us suppose theoretical investigation will produce a principle of rectification. This principle uses historical information about previous situations and injustices done in them (as defined by the first two principles of justice and rights against interference), and information about the actual course of events that flowed from these injustices, until the present, and it yields a description (or descriptions) of holdings in the society. The principle of rectification presumably will make use of its best estimate of subjunctive information about what would have occurred (or a probability distribution over what might have occurred, using the expected value) if the injustice had not taken place. If the actual description of holdings turns out not to be one of the descriptions yielded by the principle, then one of the descriptions yielded must be realized.

The general outlines of the theory of justice in holdings are that the holdings of a person are just if he is entitled to them by the principles of justice in acquisition and transfer, or by the principle of rectification of injustice (as specified by the first two principles). If each person's holdings are just, then the total set (distribution) of holdings is just. To turn these general outlines into a specific theory we would have to specify the details of each of the three principles of justice in holdings: the principle of acquisition of holdings, the principle of transfer of holdings, and the principle of rectification of violations of the first two principles. I shall not attempt that task here. (Locke's principle of justice in acquisition is discussed below.)

Historical Principles and End-Result Principles

The general outlines of the entitlement theory illuminate the nature and defects of other conceptions of distributive justice. The entitlement theory of justice in distribution is *historical;* whether a distribution is just depends upon how it came about. In contrast, *current time-slice principles* of justice hold that the justice of a distribution is determined by how things are distributed (who has what) as judged by some *structural* principle(s) of just distribution. A utilitarian who judges between any two distributions by seeing which has the greater sum of utility and, if the sums tie, applies some fixed equality criterion to choose the more equal distribution, would hold a current time-slice principle of justice. As would someone who had a fixed schedule of trade-offs between the sum of happiness and equality. According to a current time-slice principle, all that needs to be looked at, in judging the justice of a distribution, is who ends up with what; in comparing any two distributions one need look only at the matrix presenting the distributions. No further information need be fed into a principle of justice. It is a consequence of such principles of justice that any two structurally identical distributions are equally just. (Two distributions are structurally identical if they present the same profile, but perhaps have different persons occupying the particular slots. My having ten and your having five, and my having five and your having ten are structurally identical distributions.) Welfare economics is the theory of current time-slice principles of justice. The subject is conceived as operating on matrices representing only current information about distribution. This, as well as some of the usual conditions (for example, the choice of distribution is invariant under relabeling of columns), guarantees that welfare economics will be a current time-slice theory, with all of its inadequacies.

Most persons do not accept current time-slice principles as constituting the whole story about distributive shares. They think it relevant in assessing the justice of a situation to consider not only the distribution it embodies, but also how that distribution came about. If some persons are in prisons for murder or war crimes, we do not say that to assess the justice of the distribution in the society we must look only at what this person has, and that person has, and that person has, . . . at the current time. We think it relevant to ask whether someone did something so that he *deserved* to be punished, deserved to have a lower share. Most will agree to the relevance of further information with regard to punishments and penalties. Consider also desired things. One traditional socialist view is that workers are entitled to the produce and full fruits of their labor; they have earned it; a distribution is unjust if it does not give the workers what they are entitled to. Such entitlements are based upon some past history. No socialist holding this view would find it comforting to be told that because the actual distribution *A* happens to coincide structurally with the one he desires *D*, *A* therefore is no less just than *D*; it differs only in that the "parasitic" owners of capital receive under *A* what the workers are entitled to under *D*, and the workers receive under *A* what the owners are entitled to under *D*, namely very little. This socialist rightly, in my view, holds onto the notions of earning, producing, entitlement, desert, and so forth, and he rejects current time-slice principles that look only to the structure of the resulting set of holdings. (The set of holdings resulting from what? Isn't it implausible that how holdings are produced and come to exist has no effect at all on who should hold what?) His mistake lies in his view of what entitlements arise out of what sorts of productive processes.

We construe the position we discuss too narrowly by speaking of *current* time-slice principles. Nothing is changed if structural principles operate upon a time sequence of current time-slice profiles and, for example, give someone more now to counterbalance the less he has had earlier. A utilitarian or an egalitarian or any mixture of the two over time will inherit the difficulties of his more myopic comrades. He is not helped by the fact that *some* of the information others consider relevant in assessing a distribution is reflected, unrecoverably, in past matrices. Henceforth, we shall refer to such unhistorical principles of distributive justice, including the current time-slice principles, as *end-result principles* or *end-state principles.*

In contrast to end-result principles of justice, *historical principles* of justice hold that past circumstances or actions of people can create differential entitlements or differential deserts to things. An injustice can be worked by moving from one distribution to another structurally identical one, for the second, in profile the same, may violate people's entitlements or deserts; it may not fit the actual history.

Patterning

The entitlement principles of justice in holdings that we have sketched are historical principles of justice. To better understand their precise character, we shall distinguish them from another subclass of the historical principles. Consider, as an example, the principle of distribution according to moral merit. This principle requires that total distributive shares vary directly with moral merit; no person should have a greater share than anyone whose moral merit is greater. (If moral merit could be not merely ordered but measured on an interval or ratio scale, stronger principles could be formulated.) Or consider the principle that results by substituting "usefulness to society" for "moral merit" in the previous principle. Or instead of "distribute according to moral merit," or "distribute according to usefulness to society," we might consider "distribute according to the weighted sum of moral merit, usefulness to society, and need," with the weights of the different dimensions equal. Let us call a principle of distribution *patterned* if it specifies that a distribution is to vary along with some natural dimension, weighted sum of natural dimensions, or lexicographic ordering of natural dimensions. And let us say a distribution is patterned if it accords with some patterned principle. (I speak of natural dimensions, admittedly without a general criterion for them, because for any set of holdings some artificial dimensions can be gimmicked up to vary along with the distribution of the set.) The principle of distribution in accordance with moral merit is a patterned historical principle, which specifies a patterned distribution. "Distribute according to I.Q." is a patterned principle that looks to information not contained in distributional matrices. It is not historical, however, in that it does not look to any past actions creating differential entitlements to evaluate a distribution; it requires only distributional matrices whose columns are labeled by I.Q. scores. The distribution in a society, however, may be composed of such simple patterned distributions, without itself being simply patterned. Different sectors may operate different patterns, or some combination of patterns may operate in different proportions across a society. A distribution composed in this manner, from a small number of patterned distributions, we also shall term "patterned." And we extend the use of "pattern" to include the overall designs put forth by combinations of end-state principles.

Almost every suggested principle of distributive justice is patterned: to each according to his moral merit, or needs, or marginal product, or how hard he tries, or the weighted sum of the foregoing, and so on. The principle of entitlement we have sketched is *not* patterned. There is no one natural dimension or weighted sum or combination of a small number of natural dimensions that yields the distributions generated in accordance with the principle of entitlement. The set of holdings that results when some persons receive their marginal products, others win at gambling, others receive a share of their mate's income, others receive gifts from foundations, others receive interest on loans, others receive gifts from admirers, others receive returns on investment, others make for themselves much of what they have, others find things, and so on, will not be patterned. Heavy strands of patterns will run through it; significant portions of the variance in holdings will be accounted for by pattern-variables. If most people most of the time choose to transfer some of their entitlements to others only in exchange for something from them, then a large part of what many people hold will vary with what they held that others wanted. More details are provided by the theory of marginal productivity. But gifts to relatives, charitable donations, bequests to children, and the like, are not best conceived, in the first instance, in this manner. Ignoring the strands of pattern, let us suppose for the moment that a distribution actually arrived at by the operation of the principle of entitlement is random with respect to any pattern. Though the resulting set of holdings will be unpatterned, it will not be incomprehensible, for it can be seen as arising from the operation of a small number of principles. These principles specify how an initial distribution may arise (the principle of acquisition of holdings) and how distributions may be transformed into others (the principle of transfer of holdings). The process whereby the set of holdings is generated will be intelligible, though the set of holdings itself that results from this process will be unpatterned.

The writings of F. A. Hayek focus less than is usually done upon what patterning distributive justice requires. Hayek argues that we cannot know enough about each person's situation to distribute to each according to his moral merit (but would justice demand we do so if we did have this knowledge?); and he goes on to say, "our objection is against all attempts to impress upon society a deliberately chosen pattern of distribution, whether it be an order of equality or of inequality." However, Hayek concludes that in a free society there will be distribution in accordance with value rather than moral merit; that is, in accordance with the perceived value of a person's actions and services to others. Despite his rejection of a patterned conception of distributive justice, Hayek himself suggests a pattern he thinks justifiable: distribution in accordance with the perceived benefits given to others, leaving room for the complaint that a free society does not realize exactly this pattern. Stating this patterned strand of a free capitalist society more precisely, we get "To each according to how much he benefits others who have the resources for benefiting those who benefit them." This will seem arbitrary unless some acceptable initial set of holdings is specified, or unless it is held that the operation of the system over time washes out any significant effects from the initial set of holdings. As an example of the latter, if almost anyone would have bought a car from Henry Ford, the supposition that it was an arbitrary matter who held the money then (and so bought) would not place Henry Ford's earnings under a cloud. In any event, *his* coming to hold it is not arbitrary. Distribution according to benefits to others *is* a major patterned strand in a free capitalist society, as Hayek correctly points out, but it is only a strand and does not constitute the whole pattern of a system of entitlements (namely, inheritance, gifts for arbitrary reasons, charity, and so on) or a standard that one should insist a society fit. Will people tolerate for long a system yielding distributions that they believe are unpatterned? No doubt people will not long accept a distribution they believe is *unjust*. People want their society to be and to look just. But must the look of justice reside in a resulting pattern rather than in the underlying generating principles? We are in no position to conclude that the inhabitants of a society embodying an entitlement conception of justice in holdings will find it unacceptable. Still, it must be granted that were people's reasons for transferring some of their holdings to others always irrational or arbitrary, we would find this disturbing. (Suppose people always determined what holdings they would transfer, and to whom, by using a random device.) We feel more comfortable upholding the justice of an entitlement system if most of the transfers under it are done for reasons. This does not mean necessarily that all deserve what holdings they receive. It means only that there is a purpose or point to someone's transferring a holding to one person rather than to another; that usually we can see what the transferrer thinks he's gaining, what cause he thinks he's serving, what goals he thinks he's helping to achieve, and so forth. Since in a capitalist society people often transfer holdings to others in accordance with how much they perceive these others benefiting them, the fabric constituted by the individual transactions and transfers is largely reasonable and intelligible. (Gifts to loved ones, bequests to children, charity to the needy also are nonarbitrary components of the fabric.) In stressing the large strand of distribution in accordance with benefit to others, Hayek shows the point of many transfers, and so shows that the system of transfer of entitlements is not just spinning its gears aimlessly. The system of entitlements is defensible when constituted by the individual aims of individual transactions. No overarching aim is needed, no distributional pattern is required.

To think that the task of a theory of distributive justice is to fill in the blank in "to each according to his ___________" is to be predisposed to search for a pattern; and the separate treatment of "from each according to his ___________" treats production and distribution as two separate and independent issues. On an entitlement view these are *not* two separate questions. Whoever makes something, having bought or contracted for all other held resources used in the process (transferring some of his holdings for these cooperating factors), is entitled to it. The situation is *not* one of something's getting made, and there being an open question of who is to get it. Things come into the world already attached to people having entitlements over them. From the point of view of the historical entitlement conception of justice in holdings, those who start afresh to complete "to each according to his ___________" treat objects as if they appeared from nowhere, out of nothing. A complete theory of justice might cover this limit case as well; perhaps here is a use for the usual conceptions of distributive justice.

So entrenched are maxims of the usual form that perhaps we should present the entitlement conception as a competitor. Ignoring acquisition and rectification, we might say:

> From each according to what he chooses to do, to each according to what he makes for himself (perhaps with the contracted aid of others) and what others choose to do for him and choose to give him of what they've been given previously (under this maxim) and haven't yet expended or transferred.

This, the discerning reader will have noticed, has its defects as a slogan. So as a summary and great simplification (and not as a maxim with any independent meaning) we have:

From each as they choose, to each as they are chosen.

How Liberty Upsets Patterns

It is not clear how those holding alternative conceptions of distributive justice can reject the entitlement conception of justice in holdings. For suppose a distribution favored by one of these nonentitlement conceptions is realized. Let us suppose it is your favorite one and let us call this distribution D_1; perhaps everyone has an equal share, perhaps shares vary in accordance with some dimension you treasure. Now suppose that Wilt Chamberlain is greatly in demand by basketball teams, being a great gate attraction. (Also suppose contracts run only for a year, with players being free agents.) He signs the following sort of contract with a team: In each home game, twenty-five cents from the price of each ticket of admission goes to him. (We ignore the question of whether he is "gouging" the owners, letting them look out for themselves.) The season starts, and people cheerfully attend his team's games; they buy their tickets, each time dropping a separate twenty-five cents of their admission price into a special box with Chamberlain's name on it. They are excited about seeing him play; it is worth the total admission price to them. Let us suppose that in one season one million persons attend his home games, and Wilt Chamberlain winds up with $250,000, a much larger sum than the average income and larger even than anyone else has. Is he entitled to this income? Is this new distribution D_2, unjust? If so, why? There is *no* question about whether each of the people was entitled to the control over the resources they held in D_1; because that was the distribution (your favorite) that (for the purposes of argument) we assumed was acceptable. Each of these persons *chose* to give twenty-five cents of their money to Chamberlain. They could have spent it on going to the movies, or on candy bars, or on copies of *Dissent* magazine, or of *Monthly Review*. But they all, at least one million of them, converged on giving it to Wilt Chamberlain in exchange for watching him play basketball. If D_1 was a just distribution, and people voluntarily moved from it to D_2, transferring parts of their shares they were given under D_1 (what was it for if not to do something with?), isn't D_2 also just? If the people were entitled to dispose of the resources to which they were entitled (under D_1), didn't this include their being entitled to give it to, or exchange it with, Wilt Chamberlain? Can anyone else complain on grounds of justice? Each other person already has his legitimate share under D_1, Under D_1, there is nothing that anyone has that anyone else has a claim of justice against. After someone transfers something to Wilt Chamberlain, third parties *still* have their legitimate shares; *their* shares are not changed. By what process could such a transfer among two persons give rise to a legitimate claim of distributive justice on a portion of what was transferred, by a third party who had no claim of justice on any holding of the others *before* the transfer? To cut off objections irrelevant here, we might imagine the exchanges occurring in a socialist society, after hours. After playing whatever basketball he does in his daily work, or doing whatever other daily work he does, Wilt Chamberlain decides to put in *overtime* to earn additional money. (First his work quota is set; he works time over that.) Or imagine it is a skilled juggler people like to see, who puts on shows after hours.

Why might someone work overtime in a society in which it is assumed their needs are satisfied? Perhaps because they care about things other than needs. I like to write in books that I read, and to have easy access to books for browsing at odd hours. It would be very pleasant and convenient to have the resources of Widener Library in my back yard. No society, I assume, will provide such resources close to each person who would like them as part of his regular allotment (under D_1). Thus, persons either must do without some extra things that they want, or be allowed to do something extra to get some of these things. On what basis could the inequalities that would eventuate be forbidden? Notice also that small factories would spring up in a socialist society, unless forbidden. I melt down some of my personal possessions (under D_1) and build a machine out of the material. I offer you, and others, a philosophy lecture once a week in exchange for your cranking the handle on my machine, whose products I exchange for yet other things, and so on. (The raw materials used by the machine are given to me by others who possess them under D_1, in exchange for hearing lectures.) Each person might participate to gain things over and above their allotment under D_1. Some persons even might want to leave their job in socialist industry and work full time in this private sector. . . . Here I wish merely to note how private property even in means of production would occur in a socialist society that did not forbid people to use as they wished some of the resources they are given under the socialist distribution D_1. The socialist society would have to forbid capitalist acts between consenting adults.

The general point illustrated by the Wilt Chamberlain example and the example of the entrepreneur in a socialist society is that no end-state principle or distributional patterned principle of justice can be continuously realized without continuous interference with people's lives. Any favored pattern would be transformed into one unfavored by the principle, by people choosing to act in various ways; for example, by people exchanging goods and services with other people, or giving things to other people, things the transferrers are entitled to under the favored distributional pattern. To maintain a pattern one must either continually interfere to stop people from transferring resources as they wish to, or continually (or periodically) interfere to take from some persons resources that others for some reason chose to transfer to them. (But if some time limit is to be set on how long people may keep resources others voluntarily transfer to them, why let them keep these resources for *any* period of time? Why not have immediate confiscation?) It might be objected that all persons voluntarily will choose to refrain from actions which would upset the pattern. This presupposes unrealistically (1) that all will most want to maintain the pattern (are those who don't, to be "reeducated" or forced to undergo "self-criticism"?), (2) that each can gather enough information about his own actions and the ongoing activities of others to discover which of his actions will upset the pattern, and (3) that diverse and far-flung persons can coordinate their actions to dovetail into the pattern. Compare the manner in which the market is neutral among persons' desires, as it reflects and transmits widely scattered information via prices, and coordinates persons' activities.

It puts things perhaps a bit too strongly to say that every patterned (or end-state) principle is liable to be thwarted by the voluntary actions of the individual parties transferring some of their shares they receive under the principle. For perhaps some *very* weak patterns are not so thwarted. Any distributional pattern with any egalitarian component is overturnable by the voluntary actions of individual persons over time; as is every patterned condition with sufficient content so as actually to have been proposed as presenting the central core of distributive justice. Still, given the possibility that some weak conditions or patterns may not be unstable in this way, it would be better to formulate an explicit description of the kind of interesting and contentful patterns under discussion, and to prove a theorem about their instability. Since the weaker the patterning, the more likely it is that the entitlement system itself satisfies it, a plausible conjecture is that any patterning either is unstable or is satisfied by the entitlement system. . . .

World Hunger

The central problem of distributive justice is how goods should be allotted to members of society. Ordinarily, this is a problem within a given society. Methods of allotment may leave some with very little, while others possess much. Some may not have enough to eat. Some may have inadequate housing or no housing at all. Some may lack basic medical care or education. The problem of distributive justice, from this perspective, is to determine which methods of allocating a society's goods to its members are just, or, to put it another way, respect the members' rights.

The same points arise, however, in contemplating global allocations of goods. Some societies are wealthy while others are poor. Some nations enjoy high living standards while others face starvation, malnutrition, and disease. The problem of distributive justice in a global setting is, in practical terms, to determine the extent to which richer societies have obligations to help less fortunate societies.

Garrett Hardin takes a global and pessimistic view of problems of poverty. He compares the world to a sea, with about one-third of the population in a lifeboat and the other two-thirds trying to avoid drowning and hoping to climb aboard. The lifeboat, he argues, has a limited capacity and cannot admit many more members. We have no obligation to admit anyone—and certainly no obligation to surrender our place. Hardin asserts further that aid to the poor does not help them; on the contrary, it damages the environment, leading to a "tragedy of the commons," and harms future generations.

Peter Singer, too, treats the problem on a global scale. People in wealthy countries enjoy a comfortable life, whereas many in poor countries suffer and starve. This, he contends, is not just unfair; it is tantamount to homicide. Inhabitants of wealthy countries could prevent the hungry from dying without large sacrifices. He rejects the theory of distributive justice proposed by Locke and Nozick, arguing that we have very serious moral obligations to help those in danger of starvation. He also contends that Hardin's lifeboat analogy is inappropriate.

Frances Moore Lappé and Joseph Collins investigate the causes of hunger, insisting that the problem is not a shortage of food. Even in the poorest countries, there is usually enough food to go around. Why, then, do people go hungry? Sometimes, natural disasters such as droughts and earthquakes are responsible. Sometimes, governments are themselves responsible, by seeking to starve political enemies or simply by distributing food foolishly and unfairly. Sometimes, poverty is responsible. Frequently, Lappé and Collins find, there is enough food, but people do not have the money to buy it. They argue for market reforms that give economic power to the people.

Finally, Kim R. Holmes describes a paradox of foreign aid. A society's wealth correlates with the degree of economic freedom it allows. Poor societies, then, are typically not very free. They suffer from extensive government control of the economy, which keeps their citizens poor and their rulers rich. The rulers of such countries tend to subvert aid, redirecting it from its intended uses to their own pockets. The more a country needs our help, Holmes concludes, the less likely aid is to reach those we seek to help.

GARRETT HARDIN

The Case Against Helping the Poor

Garrett Hardin is Professor of Biology at the University of California at Santa Barbara. (Source: Reprinted with permission from Psychology Today Magazine, *Copyright © 1974, Sussex Publishers, Inc.)*

QUESTIONS FOR REFLECTION

1. Explain Hardin's lifeboat analogy.
2. What role does population play in Hardin's argument? What are his factual premises about population? Do you find them plausible?
3. What is "the tragedy of the commons"?
4. What, in Hardin's view, would be the consequences of establishing a world food bank?

Environmentalists use the metaphor of the earth as a "spaceship" in trying to persuade countries, industries and people to stop wasting and polluting our natural resources. Since we all share life on this planet, they argue, no single person or institution has the right to destroy, waste, or use more than a fair share of its resources.

But does everyone on earth have an equal right to an equal share of its resources? The spaceship metaphor can be dangerous when used by misguided idealists to justify suicidal policies for sharing our resources through uncontrolled immigration and foreign aid. In their enthusiastic but unrealistic generosity, they confuse the ethics of a spaceship with those of a lifeboat.

A true spaceship would have to be under the control of a captain, since no ship could possibly survive if its course were determined by committee. Spaceship Earth certainly has no captain; the United Nations is merely a toothless tiger, with little power to enforce any policy upon its bickering members.

If we divide the world crudely into rich nations and poor nations, two thirds of them are desperately poor, and only one third comparatively rich, with the United States the wealthiest of all. Metaphorically each rich nation can be seen as a lifeboat full of comparatively rich people. In the ocean outside each lifeboat swim the poor of the world, who would like to get in, or at least to share some of the wealth. What should the lifeboat passengers do?

First, we must recognize the limited capacity of any lifeboat. For example, a nation's land has a limited capacity to support a population and as the current energy crisis has shown us, in some ways we have already exceeded the carrying capacity of our land.

Adrift in a Moral Sea

So here we sit, say fifty people in our lifeboat. To be generous, let us assume it has room for ten more, making a total capacity of sixty. Suppose the fifty of us in the lifeboat see 100 others swimming in the water outside, begging for admission to our boat or for handouts. We have several options: we may be tempted to try to live by the Christian ideal of being "our brother's keeper," or by the Marxist ideal of "to each according to his needs." Since the needs of all in the water are the same, and since they can all be seen as "our brothers," we could take them all into our boat, making a total of 150 in a boat designed for sixty. The boat swamps, everyone drowns. Complete justice, complete catastrophe.

Since the boat has an unused excess capacity of ten more passengers, we could admit just ten more to it. But which ten do we let in? How do we choose? Do we pick the best ten, the neediest ten, "first come, first served"? And what do we say to the ninety we exclude? If we do let an extra ten into our lifeboat, we will have lost our "safety factor," an engineering principle of critical importance. For example, if we don't leave room for excess capacity as a safety factor in our country's agriculture, a new plant disease or a bad change in the weather could have disastrous consequences.

Suppose we decide to preserve our small safety factor and admit no more to the lifeboat. Our survival is then possible, although we shall have to be constantly on guard against boarding parties.

While this last solution clearly offers the only means of our survival, it is morally abhorrent to many people. Some say they feel guilty about their good luck. My reply is simple: "Get out and yield your place to others." This may solve the problem of the guilt-ridden person's conscience, but it does not change the ethics of the lifeboat. The needy person to whom the guilt-ridden person yields his place will not himself feel guilty about his good luck. If he did, he would not climb aboard. The net result of conscience-striken people giving up their unjustly held seats is the elimination of that sort of conscience from the lifeboat.

This is the basic metaphor within which we must work out our solutions. Let us now enrich the image, step by step, with substantive additions from the real world, a world that must solve real and pressing problems of overpopulation and hunger.

The harsh ethics of the lifeboat become even harsher when we consider the reproductive differences between the rich nations and the poor nations. The people inside the lifeboats are doubling in numbers every eighty-seven years; those swimming around outside are doubling, on the average, every thirty-five years, more than twice as fast as the rich. And since the world's resources are dwindling, the difference in prosperity between the rich and the poor can only increase.

As of 1973, the U.S. had a population of 210 million people, who were increasing by 0.8 percent per year. Outside our lifeboat, let us imagine another 210 million people, (say the combined populations of Colombia, Ecuador, Venezuela, Morocco, Pakistan, Thailand, and the Philippines) who are increasing at a rate of 3.3 percent per year. Put differently, the doubling time for this aggregate population is twenty-one years, compared to eighty-seven years for the U.S.

Multiplying the Rich and the Poor

Now suppose the U.S. agreed to pool its resources with those seven countries, with everyone receiving an equal share. Initially the ratio of Americans to non-Americans in this model would be one-to-one. But consider what the ratio would be after eighty-seven years, by which time the Americans would have doubled to a population of 420 million. By then, doubling every twenty-one years, the other group would have swollen to 354 billion. Each American would have to share the available resources with more than eight people.

But, one could argue, this discussion assumes that current population trends will continue, and they may not. Quite so. Most likely the rate of population increase will decline much faster in the U.S. than it will in the other countries, and there does not seem to be much we can do about it. In sharing with "each according to his needs," we must recognize that needs are determined by population size, which is determined by the rate of reproduction, which at present is regarded as a sovereign right of every nation, poor or not. This being so, the philanthropic load created by the sharing ethic of the spaceship can only increase.

The Tragedy of the Commons

The fundamental error of spaceship ethics, and the sharing it requires, is that it leads to what I call "the tragedy of the commons." Under a system of private property, the men who own property recognize their responsibility to care for it, for if they don't they will eventually suffer. A farmer, for instance, will allow no more cattle in a pasture than its carrying capacity justifies. If he overloads it, erosion sets in, weeds take over, and he loses the use of the pasture.

If a pasture becomes a commons open to all, the right of each to use it may not be matched by a corresponding responsibility to protect it. Asking everyone to use it with discretion will hardly do, for the considerate herdsman who refrains from overloading the commons suffers more than a selfish one who says his needs are greater. If everyone would restrain himself, all would be well; but it takes only one less than everyone to ruin a system of voluntary restraint. In a crowded world of less than perfect human beings, mutual ruin is inevitable if there are no controls. This is the tragedy of the commons.

One of the major tasks of education today should be the creation of such an acute awareness of the dangers of the commons that people will recognize its many varieties. For example, the air and water have become polluted because they are treated as commons. Further growth in the population or per-capita conversion of natural resources into pollutants will only make the problem worse. The same holds true for the fish of the oceans. Fishing fleets have nearly disappeared in many parts of the world, technological improvements in the art of fishing are hastening the day of complete ruin. Only the replacement of the system of the commons with a responsible system of control will save the land, air, water and oceanic fisheries.

The World Food Bank

In recent years there has been a push to create a new commons called a World Food Bank, an international depository of food reserves to which nations would contribute according to their abilities and from which they would draw according to their needs. This humanitarian proposal has received support from many liberal international groups, and from such prominent citizens as Margaret Mead, U.N. Secretary General Kurt Waldheim, and Senators Edward Kennedy and George McGovern.

A world food bank appeals powerfully to our humanitarian impulses. But before we rush ahead with such a plan, let us recognize where the greatest political push comes from, lest we be disillusioned later. Our experience with the "Food for Peace program," or Public Law 480, gives us the answer. This program moved billions of dollars worth of U.S. surplus grain to food-short, population-long countries during the past two decades. But when P.L. 480 first became law, a headline in the business magazine *Forbes* revealed the real power behind it: "Feeding the World's Hungry Millions: How It Will Mean Billions for U.S. Business."

And indeed it did. In the years 1960 to 1970, U.S. taxpayers spent a total of $7.9 billion on the Food for Peace program. Between 1948 and 1970, they also paid an additional $50 billion for other economic-aid programs, some of which went for food and food-producing machinery and technology. Though all U.S. taxpayers were forced to contribute to the cost of P.L. 480, certain special interest groups gained handsomely under the program. Farmers did not have to contribute the grain; the Government, or rather the taxpayers, bought it from them at full market prices. The increased demand raised prices of farm products generally. The manufacturers of farm machinery, fertilizers and pesticides benefited by the farmers' extra efforts to grow more food. Grain elevators profited from storing the surplus until it could be shipped. Railroads made money hauling it to ports, and shipping lines profited from carrying it overseas. The implementation of P.L. 480 required the creation of a vast Government bureaucracy, which then acquired its own vested interest in continuing the program regardless of its merits.

Extracting Dollars

Those who proposed and defended the Food for Peace program in public rarely mentioned its importance to any of these special interests. The public emphasis was always on its humanitarian effects. The combination of silent selfish interests and highly vocal humanitarian apologists made a powerful and successful lobby for extracting money from taxpayers. We can expect the same lobby to push now for the creation of a World Food Bank.

However great the potential benefit to selfish interests, it should not be a decisive argument against a truly humanitarian program. We must ask if such a program would actually do more good than harm, not only momentarily but also in the long run. Those who propose the food bank usually refer to a current "emergency" or "crisis" in terms of world food supply. But what is an emergency? Although they may be infrequent and sudden, everyone knows that emergencies will occur from time to time. A well-run family, company, organization or country prepares for the likelihood of accidents and emergencies. It expects them, it budgets for them, it saves for them.

Learning the Hard Way

What happens if some organizations or countries budget for accidents and others do not? If each country is solely responsible for its own well-being, poorly managed ones will suffer. But they can learn from experience. They may mend their ways, and learn to budget for infrequent but certain emergencies. For example, the weather varies from year to year, and periodic crop failures are certain. A wise and competent government saves out of the production of the good years in anticipation of bad years to come. Joseph taught this policy to Pharaoh in Egypt more than 2,000 years ago. Yet the great majority of the governments in the world today do not follow such a policy. They lack either the wisdom or the competence, or both. Should those nations that do manage to put something aside be forced to come to the rescue each time an emergency occurs among the poor nations?

"But it isn't their fault!" some kindhearted liberals argue. "How can we blame the poor people who are caught in an emergency? Why must they suffer for the sins of their governments?" The concept of blame is simply not relevant here. The real question is, what are the operational consequences of establishing a world food bank? If it is open to every country every time a need develops, slovenly rulers will not be motivated to take Joseph's advice. Someone will always come to their aid. Some countries will deposit food in the world food bank, and others will withdraw it. There will be almost no overlap. As a result of such solutions to food shortage emergencies, the poor countries will not learn to mend their ways, and will suffer progressively greater emergencies as their populations grow.

Population Control the Crude Way

On the average, poor countries undergo a 2.5 percent increase in population each year; rich countries, about 0.8 percent. Only rich countries have anything in the way of food reserves set aside, and even they do not have as much as they should. Poor countries have none. If poor countries received no food from the outside, the rate of their population growth would be periodically checked by crop failures and famines. But if they can always draw on a world food bank in time of need, their population can continue to grow unchecked, and so will their "need" for aid. In the short run, a world food bank may diminish that need, but in the long run it actually increases the need without limit.

Without some system of worldwide food sharing, the proportion of people in the rich and poor nations might eventually stabilize. The overpopulated poor countries would decrease in numbers, while the rich countries that had room for more people would increase. But with a well-meaning system of sharing, such as a world food bank, the growth differential between the rich and the poor countries will not only persist, it will increase.

Because of the higher rate of population growth in the poor countries of the world, 88 percent of today's children are born poor, and only 12 percent rich. Year by year the ratio becomes worse, as the fast-reproducing poor outnumber the slow-reproducing rich.

A world food bank is thus a commons in disguise. People will have more motivation to draw from it than to add to any common store. The less provident and less able will multiply at the expense of the abler and more provident, bringing eventual ruin upon all who share in the commons. Besides, any system of "sharing" that amounts to foreign aid from the rich nations to the poor nations will carry the taint of charity, which will contribute little to the world peace so devoutly desired by those who support the idea of a world food bank.

As past U.S. foreign-aid programs have amply and depressingly demonstrated, international charity frequently inspires mistrust and antagonism rather than gratitude on the part of the recipient nation.

Chinese Fish and Miracle Rice

The modern approach to foreign aid stresses the export of technology and advice, rather than money and food. As an ancient Chinese proverb goes: "Give a man a fish and he will eat for a day; teach him how to fish and he will eat for the rest of his days." Acting on this advice, the Rockefeller and Ford Foundations have financed a number of programs for improving agriculture in the hungry nations. Known as the "Green Revolution," these programs have led to the development of "miracle rice" and "miracle wheat," new strains that offer bigger harvests and greater resistance to crop damage. Norman Borlaug, the Nobel Prize winning agronomist who, supported by the Rockefeller Foundation, developed "miracle wheat," is one of the most prominent advocates of a world food bank.

Whether or not the Green Revolution can increase food production as much as its champions claim is a debatable but possibly irrelevant point. Those who support this well-intended humanitarian effort should first consider some of the fundamentals of human ecology. Ironically, one man who did was the late Alan Gregg, a vice president of the Rockefeller Foundation. Two decades ago he expressed strong doubts about the wisdom of such attempts to increase food production. He likened the growth and spread of humanity over the surface of the earth to the spread of cancer in the human body, remarking that "cancerous growths demand food; but, as far as I know, they have never been cured by getting it."

Overloading the Environment

Every human born constitutes a draft on all aspects of the environment: food, air, water, forests, beaches, wildlife, scenery and solitude. Food can, perhaps, be significantly increased to meet a growing demand. But what about clean beaches, unspoiled forests, and solitude? If we satisfy a growing population's need for food, we necessarily decrease its per capita supply of the other resources needed by men.

India, for example, now has a population of 600 million, which increases by 15 million each year. This population already puts a huge load on a relatively impoverished environment. The country's forests are now only a small fraction of what they were three centuries ago, and floods and erosion continually destroy the insufficient farmland that remains. Every one of the 15 million new lives added to India's population puts an additional burden on the environment, and increases the economic and social costs of crowding. However humanitarian our intent, every Indian life saved through medical or nutritional assistance from abroad diminishes the quality of life for those who remain, and for subsequent generations. If rich countries make it possible, through foreign aid, for 600 million Indians to swell to 1.2 billion in a mere twenty-eight years, as their current growth rate threatens, will future generations of Indians thank us for hastening the destruction of their environment? Will our good intentions be sufficient excuse for the consequences of our actions?

My final example of a commons in action is one for which the public has the least desire for rational discussion—immigration. Anyone who publicly questions the wisdom of current U.S. immigration policy is promptly charged with bigotry, prejudice, ethnocentrism, chauvinism, isolationism or selfishness. Rather than encounter such accusations, one would rather talk about other matters, leaving immigration policy to wallow in the crosscurrents of special interests that take no account of the good of the whole, or the interests of posterity.

Perhaps we still feel guilty about things we said in the past. Two generations ago the popular press frequently referred to Dagos, Wops, Polacks, Chinks and Krauts, in articles about how America was being "overrun" by foreigners of supposedly inferior genetic stock. But because the implied inferiority of foreigners was used then as justification for keeping them out, people now assume that restrictive policies could only be based on such misguided notions. There are other grounds.

A Nation of Immigrants

Just consider the numbers involved. Our Government acknowledges a net inflow of 400,000 immigrants a year. While we have no hard data on the extent of illegal entries, educated guesses put the figure at about 600,000 a year. Since the natural increase (excess of births over deaths) of the resident population now runs about 1.7 million per year, the yearly gain from immigration amounts to at least 19 percent of the total annual increase, and may be as much as 37 percent if we include the estimate for illegal immigrants. Considering the growing use of birth-control devices, the potential effect of educational campaigns by such organizations as Planned Parenthood Federation of America and Zero Population Growth, and the influence of inflation and the housing shortage, the fertility rate of American women may decline so much that immigration could account for all the yearly increase in population. Should we not at least ask if that is what we want?

For the sake of those who worry about whether the "quality" of the average immigrant compares favorably with the quality of the average resident, let us assume that immigrants and nativeborn citizens are of exactly equal quality, however one defines that term. We will focus here only on quantity; and since our conclusions will depend on nothing else, all charges of bigotry and chauvinism become irrelevant.

Immigration vs. Food Supply

World food banks *move food to the people,* hastening the exhaustion of the environment of the poor countries. Unrestricted immigration, on the other hand, *moves people to the food,* thus speeding up the destruction of the environment of the rich countries. We can easily understand why poor people should want to make this latter transfer, but why should rich hosts encourage it?

As in the case of foreign-aid programs, immigration receives support from selfish interests and humanitarian impulses. The primary selfish interest in unimpeded immigration is the desire of employers for cheap labor, particularly in industries and trades that offer degrading work. In the past, one wave of foreigners after another was brought into the U.S. to work at wretched jobs for wretched wages. In recent years the Cubans, Puerto Ricans and Mexicans have had this dubious honor. The interests of the employers of cheap labor mesh well with the guilty silence of the country's liberal intelligentsia. White Anglo-Saxon Protestants are particularly reluctant to call for a closing of the doors to immigration for fear of being called bigots.

But not all countries have such reluctant leadership. Most educated Hawaiians, for example, are keenly aware of the limits of their environment, particularly in terms of population growth. There is only so much room on the islands, and the islanders know it. To Hawaiians, immigrants from the other forty-nine states present as great a threat as those from other nations. At a recent meeting of Hawaiian government officials in Honolulu, I had the ironic delight of hearing a speaker, who like most of his audience was of Japanese ancestry, ask how the country might practically and constitutionally close its doors to further immigration. One member of the audience countered: "How can we shut the doors now? We have many friends and relatives in Japan that we'd like to bring here some day so that they can enjoy Hawaii too." The Japanese-American speaker smiled sympathetically and answered: "Yes, but we have children now, and someday we'll have grandchildren too. We can bring more people here from Japan only by giving away some of the land that we hope to pass on to our grandchildren some day. What right do we have to do that?"

At this point, I can hear U.S. liberals asking: "How can you justify slamming the door once you're inside? You say that immigrants should be kept out. But aren't we all immigrants, or the descendants of immigrants? If we insist on staying, must we not admit all others?" Our craving for intellectual order leads us to seek and prefer symmetrical rules and morals: a single rule for me and everybody else; the same rule yesterday, today, and tomorrow. Justice, we feel, should not change with time and place.

We Americans of non-Indian ancestry can look upon ourselves as the descendants of thieves who are guilty morally, if not legally, of stealing this land from its Indian owners. Should we then give back the land to the now living American descendants of those Indians? However morally or logically sound this proposal may be, I, for one, am unwilling to live by it and I know no one else who is. Besides, the logical consequence would be absurd. Suppose that intoxicated with a sense of pure justice, we should decide to turn our land over to the Indians. Since all our wealth has also been derived from the land, wouldn't we be morally obliged to give that back to the Indians too?

Pure Justice vs. Reality

Clearly, the concept of pure justice produces an infinite regression to absurdity. Centuries ago, wise men invented statutes of limitations to justify the rejection of such pure justice, in the interest of preventing continual disorder. The law zealously defends property rights, but only relatively recent property rights. Drawing a line after an arbitrary time has elapsed may be unjust, but the alternatives are worse.

We are all the descendants of thieves, and the world's resources are inequitably distributed. But we must begin the journey to tomorrow from the point where we are today. We cannot remake the past. We cannot safely divide the wealth equitably among all peoples so long as people reproduce at different rates. To do so would guarantee that our grandchildren, and everyone else's grandchildren, would have only a ruined world to inhabit.

To be generous with one's own possessions is quite different from being generous with those of posterity. We should call this point to the attention of those who, from a commendable love of justice and equality, would institute a system of the commons, either in the form of a world food bank, or of unrestricted immigration. We must convince them if we wish to save at least some parts of the world from environmental ruin.

Without a true world government to control reproduction and the use of available resources, the sharing ethic of the spaceship is impossible. For the foreseeable future, our survival demands that we govern our actions by the ethics of a lifeboat, harsh though they may be. Posterity will be satisfied with nothing less.

Addendum 1989

Can anyone watch children starve on television without wanting to help? Naturally sympathetic, a normal human being thinks that he can imagine what it is like to be starving. We all want to do unto others as we would have them do unto us.

But wanting is not doing. Forty years of activity by the U.S. Agency for International Development, as well as episodic nongovernmental attempts to feed the world's starving, have produced mixed results. Before we respond to the next appeal we should ask, "Does what we call 'aid' really help?"

Some of the shortcomings of food aid can be dealt with briefly. Waste is unavoidable: Because most poor countries have wretched transportation systems, food may sit on a dock until it rots. Then there are the corrupt politicians who take donated food away from the poor and give it to their political supporters. In Somalia in the 1980s, fully 70 percent of the donated food went to the army.

We can school ourselves to accept such losses. Panicky projects are always inefficient: Waste and corruption are par for the course. But there is another kind of loss that we cannot—in fact, we should not—accept, and that is the loss caused by the boomerang effects of philanthropy. Before we jump onto the next "feed-the-starving" bandwagon we need to understand how well-intentioned efforts can be counterproductive.

Briefly put, it is a mistake to focus only on starving people while ignoring their surroundings. Where there is great starvation there is usually an impoverished environment: poor soil, scarce water and wildly fluctuating weather. As a result, the "carrying capacity" of the environment is low. The territory simply cannot support the population that is trying to live on it. Yet if the population were much smaller, and if it would stay smaller, the people would not need to starve.

Let us look at a particular example. Nigeria, like all the central African countries, has increased greatly in population in the last quarter-century. Over many generations, Nigerians learned that their farmlands would be most productive if crop-growing alternated with "fallow years"—years in which the land was left untilled to recover its fertility.

When modern medicine reduced the death rate, the population began to grow. More food was demanded from the same land. Responding to that need, Nigerians shortened the fallow periods. The result was counterproductive. In one carefully studied village, the average fallow period was shortened from 5.3 to 1.4 years. As a result, the yearly production (averaged over both fallow and crop years) fell by 30 percent.

Are Nigerian farmers stupid? Not at all! They know perfectly well what they are doing. But a farmer whose family has grown too large for his farm has to take care of next year's need before he can provide for the future. To fallow or not to fallow translates into this choice: zero production in a fallow year or a 30 percent shortfall over the long run. Starvation cannot wait. Long-term policies have to give way to short-term ones. So the farmer plows up his overstressed fields, thus diminishing long-term productivity.

PETER SINGER

from *Practical Ethics*

Peter Singer is Professor of Philosophy and Director of the Center for Human Bioethics at Monash University, Australia. (Source: Reprinted from Peter Singer, Practical Ethics*. Copyright ©1979 by Cambridge University Press. Reprinted with the permission of Cambridge University Press.)*

QUESTIONS FOR REFLECTION

1. What is absolute poverty?
2. Can the world support its people, according to Singer? Why or why not?
3. Why, according to Singer, do some people go hungry?
4. Singer questions our intuitive moral sense that living affluently is different from murdering people. What are his arguments? Do you find them persuasive?
5. How does Singer criticize Locke's and Nozick's theories of rights?
6. Evaluate Singer's argument for our obligation to assist the absolutely poor.
7. How does Singer respond to Hardin's lifeboat argument?

Some Facts

Consider these facts: by the most cautious estimates, 400 million people lack the calories, protein, vitamins and minerals needed for a normally healthy life. Millions are constantly hungry; others suffer from deficiency diseases and from infections they would be able to resist on a better diet. Children are worst affected. According to one estimate, 15 million children under five die every year from the combined effects of malnutrition and infection. In some areas, half the children born can be expected to die before their fifth birthday.

Nor is lack of food the only hardship of the poor. To give a broader picture, Robert McNamara, President of the World Bank, has suggested the term "absolute poverty." The poverty we are familiar with in industrialized nations is relative poverty—meaning that some citizens are poor, relative to the wealth enjoyed by their neighbours. People living in relative poverty in Australia might be quite comfortably off by comparison with old-age pensioners in Britain, and British old-age pensioners are not poor in comparison with the poverty that exists in Mali or Ethiopia. Absolute poverty, on the other hand, is poverty by any standard. In McNamara's words:

> Poverty at the absolute level . . . is life at the very margin of existence.
>
> The absolute poor are severely deprived human beings struggling to survive in a set of squalid and degraded circumstances almost beyond the power of our sophisticated imaginations and privileged circumstances to conceive.
>
> Compared to those fortunate enough to live in developed countries individuals in the poorest nations have
>
> An infant mortality rate eight times higher
> A life expectancy one-third lower

> An adult literacy rate 60% less
>
> A nutritional level, for one out of every two in the population, below acceptable standards; and for millions of infants, less protein than is sufficient to permit optimum development of the brain.

And McNamara has summed up absolute poverty as:

> a condition of life so characterized by malnutrition, illiteracy, disease, squalid surroundings, high infant mortality and low life expectancy as to be beneath any reasonable definition of human decency.

Absolute poverty is, as McNamara has said, responsible for the loss of countless lives, especially among infants and young children. When absolute poverty does not cause death it still causes misery of a kind not often seen in the affluent nations. Malnutrition in young children stunts both physical and mental development. It has been estimated that the health, growth and learning capacity of nearly half the young children in developing countries are affected by malnutrition. Millions of people on poor diets suffer from deficiency diseases, like goitre, or blindness caused by a lack of vitamin A. The food value of what the poor eat is further reduced by parasites such as hookworm and ringworm, which are endemic in conditions of poor sanitation and health education.

Death and disease apart, absolute poverty remains a miserable condition of life, with inadequate food, shelter, clothing, sanitation, health services and education. According to World Bank estimates which define absolute poverty in terms of income levels insufficient to provide adequate nutrition, something like 800 million people—almost 40% of the people of developing countries—live in absolute poverty. Absolute poverty is probably the principal cause of human misery today.

This is the background situation, the situation that prevails on our planet all the time. It does not make headlines. People died from malnutrition and related diseases yesterday, and more will die tomorrow. The occasional droughts, cyclones, earthquakes and floods that take the lives of tens of thousands in one place and at one time are more newsworthy. They add greatly to the total amount of human suffering; but it is wrong to assume that when there are no major calamities reported, all is well.

The problem is not that the world cannot produce enough to feed and shelter its people. People in the poor countries consume, on average, 400 lbs. of grain a year, while North Americans average more than 2000 lbs. The difference is caused by the fact that in the rich countries we feed most of our grain to animals, converting it into meat, milk and eggs. Because this is an inefficient process, wasting up to 95% of the food value of the animal feed, people in rich countries are responsible for the consumption of far more food than those in poor countries who eat few animal products. If we stopped feeding animals on grains, soybeans and fishmeal the amount of food saved would—if distributed to those who need it—be more than enough to end hunger throughout the world.

These facts about animal food do not mean that we can easily solve the world food problem by cutting down on animal products, but they show that the problem is essentially one of distribution rather than production. The world does produce enough food. Moreover the poorer nations themselves could produce far more if they made more use of improved agricultural techniques.

So why are people hungry? Poor people cannot afford to buy grain grown by American farmers. Poor farmers cannot afford to buy improved seeds, or fertilizers, or the machinery needed for drilling wells and pumping water. Only by transferring some of the wealth of the developed nations to the poor of the underdeveloped nations can the situation be changed.

That this wealth exists is clear. Against the picture of absolute poverty that McNamara has painted, one might pose a picture of "absolute affluence." Those who are absolutely affluent are not necessarily affluent by comparison with their neighbours, but they are affluent by any reasonable definition of human needs. This means that they have more income than they need to provide themselves adequately with all the basic necessities of life. After buying food, shelter, clothing, necessary health services and education, the absolutely affluent are still able to spend money on luxuries. The absolutely affluent choose their food for the pleasures of the palate, not to stop hunger; they buy new clothes to look fashionable, not to keep warm; they move house to be in a better neighbourhood or have a play room for the children, not to keep out the rain; and after all this there is still money to spend on books and records, colour television, and overseas holidays.

At this stage I am making no ethical judgments about absolute affluence, merely pointing out that it exists. Its defining characteristic is a significant amount of income above the level necessary to provide for the basic human needs of oneself and one's dependents. By this standard Western Europe, North America, Japan, Australia, New Zealand and the oil-rich Middle Eastern states are all absolutely affluent, and so are many, if not all, of their citizens. The USSR and Eastern Europe might also be included on this list. To quote McNamara once more:

> The average citizen of a developed country enjoys wealth beyond the wildest dreams of the one billion people in countries with per capita incomes under $200. . . .

These, therefore, are the countries—and individuals—who have wealth which they could, without threatening their own basic welfare, transfer to the absolutely poor.

At present, very little is being transferred. Members of the Organization of Petroleum Exporting Countries lead the way, giving an average of 2.1% of their Gross National Product. Apart from them, only Sweden, The Netherlands and Norway have reached the modest UN target of 0.7% of GNP. Britain gives 0.38% of its GNP in official development assistance and a small additional amount in unofficial aid from voluntary organizations. The total comes to less than £1 per month per person, and compares with 5.5% of GNP spent on alcohol, and 3% on tobacco. Other, even wealthier nations, give still less: Germany gives 0.27%, the United States 0.22% and Japan 0.21%.

The Moral Equivalent of Murder?

If these are the facts, we cannot avoid concluding that by not giving more than we do, people in rich countries are allowing those in poor countries to suffer from absolute poverty, with consequent malnutrition, ill health and death. This is not a conclusion which applies only to governments. It applies to each absolutely affluent individual, for each of us has the opportunity to do something about the situation; for instance, to give our time or money to voluntary organizations like Oxfam, War on Want, Freedom From Hunger, and so on. If, then, allowing someone to die is not intrinisically different from killing someone, it would seem that we are all murderers.

Is this verdict too harsh? Many will reject it as self-evidently absurd. They would sooner take it as showing that allowing to die cannot be equivalent to killing than as showing that living in an affluent style without contributing to Oxfam is ethically equivalent to going over to India and shooting a few peasants. And no doubt, put as bluntly as that, the verdict *is* too harsh.

There are several significant differences between spending money on luxuries instead of using it to save lives, and deliberately shooting people.

First, the motivation will normally be different. Those who deliberately shoot others go out of their way to kill; they presumably want their victims dead, from malice, sadism, or some equally unpleasant motive. A person who buys a colour television set presumably wants to watch television in colour—not in itself a terrible thing. At worst, spending money on luxuries instead of giving it away indicates selfishness and indifference to the sufferings of others, characteristics which may be understandable but are not comparable with actual malice or similar motives.

Second, it is not difficult for most of us to act in accordance with a rule against killing people: it is, on the other hand, very difficult to obey a rule which commands us to save all the lives we can. To live a comfortable, or even luxurious life it is not necessary to kill anyone; but it is necessary to allow some to die whom we might have saved, for the money that we need to live comfortably could have been given away. Thus the duty to avoid killing is much easier to discharge completely than the duty to save. Saving every life we could would mean cutting our standard of living down to the bare essentials needed to keep us alive.* To discharge this duty completely would require a degree of moral heroism utterly different from what is required by mere avoidance of killing.

A third difference is the greater certainty of the outcome of shooting when compared with not giving aid. If I point a loaded gun at someone and pull the trigger, it is virtually certain that the person will be injured, if not killed; whereas the money that I could give might be spent on a project than turns out to be unsuccessful and helps no one.

Fourth, when people are shot there are identifiable individuals who have been harmed. We can point to them and to their grieving families. When I buy my colour television, I cannot know who my money would have saved if I had given it away. In a time of famine I may see dead bodies and grieving families on my new television, and I might not doubt that my money would have saved some of them; even then it is impossible to point to a body and say that had I not bought the set, that person would have survived.

Fifth, it might be said that the plight of the hungry is not my doing, and so I cannot be held responsible for it. The starving would have been starving if I had never existed. If I kill, however, I am responsible for my victims' deaths, for those people would not have died if I had not killed them. . . .

Do the five differences not only explain, but also justify, our attitudes? Let us consider them one by one:

1. Take the lack of an identifiable victim first. Suppose that I am a travelling salesman, selling tinned food, and I learn that a batch of tins contains a contaminant, the known effect of which when consumed is to double the risk that the consumer will died from stomach cancer. Suppose I continue to sell the tins. My decision may have no identifiable victims. Some of those who eat the food will die from cancer. The proportion of consumers dying in this way will be twice that of the community at large, but which among the consumers died because they ate what I sold, and which would have contracted the disease anyway? It is impossible to tell; but surely this impossibility makes my decision no less reprehensible than it would have been had the contaminant had more readily detectable, though equally fatal, effects.

2. The lack of certainty that by giving money I could save a life does reduce the wrongness of not giving, by comparison with deliberate killing; but it is insufficient to show that not giving is acceptable conduct. The motorist who speeds through pedestrian crossings, heedless of anyone who might be on them, is not a murderer. She may never actually hit a pedestrian; yet what she does is very wrong indeed.

3. The notion of responsibility for acts rather than omissions is more puzzling. On the one hand we feel ourselves to be under a greater obligation to help those whose misfortunes we have caused. (It is for this reason that advocates of overseas aid often argue that Western nations have created the poverty of Third World nations, through forms of economic exploitation which go back to the colonial system.) On the other hand any consequentialist would insist that we are responsible for all the consequences of our actions, and if a consequence of my spending money on a luxury item is that someone dies, I am responsible for that death. It is true that the person would have died even if I had never existed, but what is the relevance of that? The fact is that I do exist, and the consequen-

* Strictly, we would need to cut down to the minimum level compatible with earning the income which, after providing for our needs, left us most to give away. Thus if my present position earns me, say, £10,000 a year, but requires me to spend £1,000 a year on dressing respectably and maintaining a car, I cannot save more people by giving away the car and clothes if that will mean taking a job which, although it does not involve me in these expenses, earns me only £5,000.

tialist will say that our responsibilities derive from the world as it is, not as it might have been.

One way of making sense of the nonconsequentialist view of responsibility is by basing it on a theory of rights of the kind proposed by John Locke or, more recently, Robert Nozick. If everyone has a right to life, and this right is a right *against* others who might threaten my life, but not a right *to* assistance from others when my life is in danger, then we can understand the feeling that we are responsible for acting to kill but not for omitting to save. The former violates the rights of others, the latter does not.

Should we accept such a theory of rights? If we build up our theory of rights by imagining, as Locke and Nozick do, individuals living independently from each other in a "state of nature," it may seem natural to adopt a conception of rights in which as long as each leaves the other alone, no rights are violated. I might, on this view, quite properly have maintained my independent existence if I had wished to do so. So if I do not make you any worse off than you would have been if I had had nothing at all to do with you, how can I have violated your rights? But why start from such an unhistorical, abstract and ultimately inexplicable idea as an independent individual? We now know that our ancestors were social beings long before they were human beings, and could not have developed the abilities and capacities of human beings if they had not been social beings first. In any case we are not, now, isolated individuals. If we consider people living together in a community, it is less easy to assume that rights must be restricted to rights against interference. We might, instead, adopt the view that taking rights to life seriously is incompatible with standing by and watching people die when one could easily save them.

4. What of the difference in motivation? That a person does not positively wish for the death of another lessens the severity of the blame she deserves; but not by as much as our present attitudes to giving aid suggest. The behaviour of the speeding motorist is again comparable, for such motorists usually have no desire at all to kill anyone. They merely enjoy speeding and are indifferent to the consequences. Despite their lack of malice, those who kill with cars deserve not only blame but also severe punishment.

5. Finally, the fact that to avoid killing people is normally not difficult, whereas to save all one possibly could save is heroic, must make an important difference to our attitude to failure to do what the respective principles demand. Not to kill is a minimum standard of acceptable conduct we can require of everyone; to save all one possibly could is not something that can realistically be required, especially not in societies accustomed to giving as little as ours do. Given the generally accepted standards, people who give, say, £100 a year to Oxfam are more aptly praised for above average generosity than blamed for giving less than they might. The appropriateness of praise and blame is, however, a separate issue from the rightness or wrongness of actions. The former evaluates the agent: the latter evaluates the action. Perhaps people who give £100 really ought to give at least £1,000, but to blame them for not giving more could be counterproductive. It might make them feel that what is required is too demanding, and if one is going to be blamed anyway, one might as well not give anything at all.

(That an ethic which put saving all one possibly can on the same footing as not killing would be an ethic for saints or heroes should not lead us to assume that the alternative must be an ethic which makes it obligatory not to kill, but puts us under no obligation to save anyone. There are positions in between these extremes, as we shall soon see.)

To summarize our discussion of the five differences which normally exist between killing and allowing to die, in the context of absolute poverty and overseas aid. The lack of an identifiable victim is of no moral significance, though it may play an important role in explaining our attitudes. The idea that we are directly responsible for those we kill, but not for those we do not help, depends on a questionable notion of responsibility, and may need to be based on a controversial theory of rights. Differences in certainty and motivation are ethically significant, and show that not aiding the poor is not to be condemned as murdering them; it could, however, be on a par with killing someone as a result of reckless driving, which is serious enough. Finally the difficulty of completely discharging the duty of saving all one possibly can makes it inappropriate to blame those who fall short of this target as we blame those who kill; but this does not show that the act itself is less serious. Nor does it indicate anything about those who, far from saving all they possibly can, make no effort to save anyone.

These conclusions suggest a new approach. Instead of attempting to deal with the contrast between affluence and poverty by comparing not saving with deliberate killing, let us consider afresh whether we have an obligation to assist those whose lives are in danger, and if so, how this obligation applies to the present world situation.

The Obligation to Assist

The Argument for an Obligation to Assist

The path from the library at my university to the Humanities lecture theatre passes a shallow ornamental pond. Suppose that on my way to give a lecture I notice that a small child has fallen in and is in danger of drowning. Would anyone deny that I ought to wade in and pull the child out? This will mean getting my clothes muddy, and either cancelling my lecture or delaying it until I can find something dry to change into; but compared with the avoidable death of a child this is insignificant.

A plausible principle that would support the judgment that I ought to pull the child out is this: if it is in our power to prevent something very bad happening, without thereby sacrificing anything of comparable moral significance, we ought to do it. This principle seems uncontroversial. It will obviously win the assent of consequentialists; but non-consequentialists should accept it too, because the injunction to prevent what is bad applies only when nothing comparably significant is at stake. Thus the principle cannot lead to the kinds of actions of which non-consequentialists strongly disapprove—serious violations of individual rights, injustice, broken promises, and so on. If a non-consequentialist regards any of these as comparable in moral significance to the bad thing that is to be prevented, he will automatically regard the principle as not applying in those cases in which the bad thing can only be prevented by violating rights, doing injustice, breaking promises, or whatever else is at stake. Most non-consequentialists hold that we ought to prevent what is bad and promote what is good. Their dispute with consequentialists lies in their insistence that this is not the sole ultimate ethical principle; that it is *an* ethical principle is not denied by any plausible ethical theory.

Nevertheless the uncontroversial appearance of the principle that we ought to prevent what is bad when we can do so without sacrificing anything of comparable moral significance is deceptive. If it were taken seriously and acted upon, our lives and our world would be fundamentally changed. For the principle applies, not just to rare situations in which one can save a child from a pond, but to the everyday situation in which we can assist those living in absolute poverty. In saying this I assume that absolute poverty, with its hunger and malnutrition, lack of shelter, illiteracy, disease, high infant mortality and low life expectancy, is a bad thing. And I assume that it is within the power of the affluent to reduce absolute poverty, without sacrificing anything of comparable moral significance. If these two assumptions and the principle we have been discussing are correct, we have an obligation to help those in absolute poverty which is no less strong than our obligation to rescue a drowning child from a pond. Not to help would be wrong, whether or not it is intrinsically equivalent to killing. Helping is not, as conventionally thought, a charitable act which it is praiseworthy to do, but not wrong to omit; it is something that everyone ought to do.

This is the argument for an obligation to assist. Set out more formally, it would look like this.

First premise: If we can prevent something bad without sacrificing anything of comparable significance, we ought to do it.

Second premise:	Absolute poverty is bad.
Third premise:	There is some absolute poverty we can prevent without sacrificing anything of comparable moral significance.
Conclusion:	We ought to prevent some absolute poverty.

The first premise is the substantive moral premise on which the argument rests, and I have tried to show that it can be accepted by people who hold a variety of ethical positions.

The second premise is unlikely to be challenged. Absolute poverty is, as McNamara put it, "beneath any reasonable definition of human decency" and it would be hard to find a plausible ethical view which did not regard it as a bad thing.

The third premise is more controversial, even though it is cautiously framed. It claims only that some absolute poverty can be prevented without the sacrifice of anything of comparable moral significance. It thus avoids the objection that any aid I can give is just "drops in the ocean" for the point is not whether my personal contribution will make any noticeable impression on world poverty as a whole (of course it won't) but whether it will prevent some poverty. This is all the argument needs to sustain its conclusion, since the second premise says that any absolute poverty is bad, and not merely the total amount of absolute poverty. If without sacrificing anything of comparable moral significance we can provide just one family with the means to raise itself out of absolute poverty, the third premise is vindicated. I have left the notion of moral significance unexamined in order to show that the argument does not depend on any specific values or ethical principles. I think the third premise is true for most people living in industrialized nations, on any defensible view of what is morally significant. Our affluence means that we have income we can dispose of without giving up the basic necessities of life, and we can use this income to reduce absolute poverty. Just how much we will think ourselves obliged to give up will depend on what we consider to be of comparable moral significance to the poverty we could prevent: colour television, stylish clothes, expensive dinners, a sophisticated stereo system, overseas holidays, a (second?) car, a larger house, private schools for our childen. . . . For a utilitarian, none of these is likely to be of comparable significance to the reduction of absolute poverty; and those who are not utilitarians surely must, if they subscribe to the principle of universalizability, accept that at least *some* of these things are of far less moral significance than the absolute poverty that could be prevented by the money they cost. . . .

Objections to the Argument

Property Rights

Do people have a right to private property, a right which contradicts the view that they are under an obligation to give some of their wealth away to those in absolute poverty? According to some theories of rights (for instance, Robert Nozick's) provided one has acquired one's property without the use of unjust means like force and fraud, one may be entitled to enormous wealth while others starve. This individualistic conception of rights is in contrast to other views, like the early Christian doctrine to be found in the works of Thomas Aquinas, which holds that since property exists for the satisfaction of human needs, "whatever a man has in superabundance is owed, of natural right, to the poor for their sustenance." A socialist would also, of course, see wealth as belonging to the community rather than the individual, while utilitarians, whether socialist or not, would be prepared to override property rights to prevent great evils.

Does the argument for an obligation to assist others therefore presuppose one of these other theories of property rights, and not an individualistic theory like Nozick's? Not necessarily. A theory of property rights can insist on our *right* to retain wealth without pronouncing on whether the rich *ought* to give to the poor. Nozick, for example, rejects the use of compulsory means like taxation to redistribute income, but suggests that we can achieve the ends we deem morally desirable by voluntary means. So Nozick would reject the claim that rich people have an "obligation" to give to the poor, in so far as this implies that the poor have a right to our aid, but might accept that giving is something we ought to do and failing to give, though within one's rights, is wrong—for rights is not all there is to ethics.

The argument for an obligation to assist can survive, with only minor modifications, even if we accept an individualistic theory of property rights. In any case, however, I do not think we should accept such a theory. It leaves too much to chance to be an acceptable ethical view. For instance, those whose forefathers happened to inhabit some sandy wastes around the Persian Gulf are now fabulously wealthy, because oil lay under those sands; while those whose forefathers settled on better land south of the Sahara live in absolute poverty, because of drought and bad harvests. Can this distribution be acceptable from an impartial point of view? If we imagine ourselves about to begin life as a citizen of either Kuwait or Chad—but we do not know which—would we accept the principle that citizens of Kuwait are under no obligation to assist people living in Chad?

Population and the Ethics of Triage

Perhaps the most serious objection to the argument that we have an obligation to assist is that since the major cause of absolute poverty is over-population, helping those now in poverty will only ensure that yet more people are born to live in poverty in the future.

In its most extreme form, this objection is taken to show that we should adopt a policy of "triage." The term comes from medical policies adopted in wartime. With too few doctors to cope with all the casualties, the wounded were divided into three categories: those who would probably survive without medical assistance, those who might survive if they received assistance, but otherwise probably would not, and those who even with medical assistance probably would not survive. Only those in the middle category were given medical assistance. The idea, of course, was to use limited medical resources as effectively as possible. For those in the first category, medical treatment was not strictly necessary; for those in the third category, it was likely to be useless. It has been suggested that we should apply the same policies to countries, according to their prospects of becoming self-sustaining. We would not aid countries which even without our help will soon be able to feed their populations. We would not aid countries which, even with our help, will not be able to limit their population to a level they can feed. We would aid those countries where our help might make the difference between success and failure in bringing food and population into balance.

Advocates of this theory are understandably reluctant to give a complete list of the countries they would place into the "hopeless" category; but Bangladesh is often cited as an example. Adopting the policy of triage would, then, mean cutting off assistance to Bangladesh and allowing famine, disease and natural disasters to reduce the population of that country (now around 80 million) to the level at which it can provide adequately for all.

In support of this view Garrett Hardin has offered a metaphor: we in the rich nations are like the occupants of a crowded lifeboat adrift in a sea full of drowning people. If we try to save the drowning by bringing them aboard our boat will be overloaded and we shall all drown. Since it is better that some survive than none, we should leave the others to drown. In the world today, according to Hardin, "lifeboat ethics" apply. The rich should leave the poor to starve, for otherwise the poor will drag the rich down with them.

Against this view, some writers have argued that over-population is a myth. The world produces ample food to feed its population, and could, according to some estimates, feed ten times as many. People are hungry not because there are too many but because of inequitable land distribution, the manipulation of Third World economies by the developed nations, wastage of food in the West, and so on.

Putting aside the controversial issue of the extent to which food production might one day be increased, it is true, as we have already seen, that the world now produces enough to feed its inhabitants—the amount lost by being fed to animals itself being enough to meet existing grain shortages. Nevertheless population growth cannot be ignored. Bangladesh could, with land reform and using better techniques, feed its present population of 80 million; but by the year 2000, according to World Bank estimates, its population will be 146 million. The enormous effort that will have to go into feeding an extra 66 million people, all added to the population within a quarter of a century, means that Bangladesh must develop at full speed to stay where she is. Other low income countries are in similar situations. By the end of the century, Ethiopia's population is expected to rise from 29 to 54 million; Somalia's from 3 to 7 million, India's from 620 to 958 million, Zaire's from 25 to 47 million. What will happen then? Population cannot grow indefinitely. It will be checked by a decline in birth rates or a rise in death rates. Those who advocate triage are proposing that we allow the population growth of some countries to be checked by a rise in death rates—that is, by increased malnutrition, and related diseases; by widespread famines; by increased infant mortality; and by epidemics of infectious diseases.

The consequences of triage on this scale are so horrible that we are inclined to reject it without further argument. How could we sit by our television sets, watching millions starve while we do nothing? Would not that be the end of all notions of human equality and respect for human life? Don't people have a right to our assistance, irrespective of the consequences?

Anyone whose initial reaction to triage was not one of repugnance would be an unpleasant sort of person. Yet initial reactions based on strong feelings are not always reliable guides. Advocates of triage are rightly concerned with the long-term consequences of our actions. They say that helping the poor and starving now merely ensures more poor and starving in the future. When our capacity to help is finally unable to cope—as one day it must be—the suffering will be greater than it would be if we stopped helping now. If this is correct, there is nothing we can do to prevent absolute starvation and poverty, in the long run, and so we have no obligation to assist. Nor does it seem reasonable to hold that under these circumstances people have a right to our assistance. If we do accept such a right, irrespective of the consequences, we are saying that, in Hardin's metaphor, we would continue to haul the drowning into our lifeboat until the boat sank and we all drowned.

If triage is to be rejected it must be tackled on its own ground, within the framework of consequentialist ethics. Here it is vulnerable. Any consequentialist ethics must take probability of outcome into account. A course of action that will certainly produce some benefit is to be preferred to an alternative course that may lead to a slightly larger benefit, but is equally likely to result in no benefit at all. Only if the greater magnitude of the uncertain benefit outweighs its uncertainty should we choose it. Better one certain unit of benefit than a 10% chance of 5 units; but better a 50% chance of 3 units than a single certain unit. The same principle applies when we are trying to avoid evils.

The policy of triage involves a certain, very great evil: population control by famine and disease. Tens of millions would die slowly. Hundreds of millions would continue to live in absolute poverty, at the very margin of existence. Against this prospect, advocates of the policy place a possible evil which is greater still: the same process of famine and disease, taking place in, say, fifty years time, when the world's population may be three times its present level, and the number who will die from famine, or struggle on in absolute poverty, will be that much greater. The question is: how probable is this forecast that continued assistance now will lead to greater disasters in the future?

Forecasts of population growth are notoriously fallible, and theories about the factors which affect it remain speculative. One theory, at least as plausible as any other, is that countries pass through a "demographic transition" as their standard of living rises. When people are very poor and have no access to modern medicine their fertility is high, but population is kept in check by high death rates. The introduction of sanitation, modern medical techniques and other improvements reduces the death rate, but initially has little effect on the birth rate. Then population grows rapidly. Most poor countries are now in this phase. If standards of living continue to rise, however, couples begin to realize that to have the same number of children surviving to maturity as in the past, they do not need to give birth to as many children as their parents did. The need for children to provide economic support in old age diminishes. Improved education and the emancipation and employment of women also reduce the birthrate, and so population growth begins to level off. Most rich nations have reached this stage, and their populations are growing only very slowly.

If this theory is right, there is an alternative to the disasters accepted as inevitable by supporters of triage. We can assist poor countries to raise the living standards of the poorest members of their population. We can encourage the governments of these countries to enact land reform measures, improve education, and liberate women from a purely childbearing role. We can also help other countries to make contraception and sterilization widely available. There is a fair chance that these measures will hasten the onset of the demographic transition and bring population growth down to a manageable level. Success cannot be guaranteed; but the evidence that improved economic security and education reduce population growth is strong enough to make triage ethically unacceptable. We cannot allow millions to die from starvation and disease when there is a reasonable probability that population can be brought under control without such horrors.

Population growth is therefore not a reason against giving overseas aid, although it should make us think about the kind of aid to give. Instead of food handouts, it may be better to give aid that hastens the demographic transition. This may mean agricultural assistance for the rural poor, or assistance with education, or the provision of contraceptive services. Whatever kind of aid proves most effective in specific circumstances, the obligation to assist is not reduced.

One awkward question remains. What should we do about a poor and already overpopulated country which, for religious or nationalistic reasons, restricts the use of contraceptives and refuses to slow its population growth? Should we nevertheless offer development assistance? Or should we make our offer conditional on effective steps being taken to reduce the birthrate? To the latter course, some would object that putting conditions on aid is an attempt to impose our own ideas on independent sovereign nations. So it is—but is this imposition unjustifiable? If the argument for an obligation to assist is sound, we have an obligation to reduce absolute poverty: but we have no obligation to make sacrifices that, to the best of our knowledge, have no prospect of reducing poverty in the long run. Hence we have no obligation to assist countries whose governments have policies which will make our aid ineffective. This could be very harsh on poor citizens of these countries—for they may have no say in the government's policies—but we will help more people in the long run by using our resources where they are most effective. (The same principles may apply, incidentally, to countries that refuse to take other steps that could make assistance effective—like refusing to reform systems of land holding that impose intolerable burdens on poor tenant farmers.) . . .

Too High a Standard?

The final objection to the argument for an obligation to assist is that it sets a standard so high that none but a saint could attain it. How many people can we really expect to give away everything not comparable in moral significance to the poverty their donation could relieve? For most of us, with commonsense views about what is of moral significance, this would mean a life of real austerity. Might it not be counterproductive to demand so much? Might not people say: "As I can't do what is morally required anyway, I won't bother to give at all." If, however, we were to set a more realistic standard, people might make a genuine effort to reach it. Thus setting a lower standard might actually result in more aid being given.

It is important to get the status of this objection clear. Its accuracy as a prediction of human behaviour is quite compatible with the argument that we are obliged to give to the point at which by giving more we sacrifice something of comparable moral significance. What would follow from the objection is that public advocacy of this standard of giving is undesirable. It would mean that in order to do the maximum to reduce absolute poverty, we should advocate a standard lower than the amount we think people really ought to give. Of course we ourselves—those of us who accept the original argument, with its higher standard—would know that we ought to do more than we publicly propose people ought to do, and we might actually give more than we urge others to give. There is no inconsistency here, since in both our private and our public behaviour we are trying to do what will most reduce absolute poverty.

For a consequentialist, this apparent conflict between public and private morality is always a possibility, and not in itself an indication that the underlying principle is wrong. The consequences of a principle are one thing, the consequences of publicly advocating it another.

Is it true that the standard set by our argument is so high as to be counterproductive? There is not much evidence to go by, but discussions of the argument, with students and others have led me to think it might be. On the other hand the conventionally accepted standard—a few coins in a collection tin when one is waved under your nose—is obviously far too low. What level should we advocate? Any figure will be arbitrary, but there may be something to be said for a round percentage of one's income like, say, 10%—more than a token donation, yet not so high as to be beyond all but saints. (This figure has the additional advantage of being reminiscent of the ancient tithe, or tenth, which was traditionally given to the church, whose responsibilities included care of the poor in one's local community. Perhaps the idea can be revived and applied to the global community.) Some families, of course, will find 10% a considerable strain on their finances. Others may be able to give more without difficulty. No figure should be advocated as a rigid minimum or maximum; but it seems safe to advocate that those earning average or above average incomes in affluent societies, unless they have an unusually large number of dependents or other special needs, ought to give a tenth of their income to reducing absolute poverty. By any reasonable ethical standards this is the minimum we ought to do, and we do wrong if we do less.

FRANCES MOORE LAPPE AND JOSEPH COLLINS

from *World Hunger: Twelve Myths*

Frances Moore Lappé cofounded the Institute for Food and Development Policy in San Francisco, and is cofounder and codirector of the Center for Living Democracy in Brattleboro, Vermont. Joseph Collins is author of, among other works, Food First: Beyond the Myth of Scarcity, No Free Lunch, *and* What Difference Could a Revolution Make? *(Source: From* World Hunger: Twelve Myths. *The Institute for Food and Development Policy. Notes have been omitted. Copyright © 1986 by Frances Moore Lappé and Joseph Collins. Reprinted by permission of Grove/Atlantic, Inc.)*

QUESTIONS FOR REFLECTION

1. Summarize the authors' arguments that world hunger problems do not result from a shortage of food.
2. What is responsible for world hunger, in the authors' view? Do you find their analysis convincing?
3. Lappé and Collins argue that food should be considered a basic right. Why? What does that mean? What follows from a basic right to eat?
4. What are the problems with the free market? Why, according to Lappé and Collins, can it not solve hunger problems on its own? Do you agree?
5. What role do Lappé and Collins advocate for government? Assess their recommendations for government intervention.

CHAPTER ONE / MYTH 1: THERE'S SIMPLY NOT ENOUGH FOOD

MYTH: With food-producing resources in so much of the world stretched to the limit, there's simply not enough food to go around. Unfortunately, some people have to go hungry.

OUR RESPONSE: The world today produces enough grain alone to provide every human being on the planet with 3,600 calories a day. That's enough to make most people fat! And this estimate does not even count the many other commonly eaten foods—vegetables, beans, nuts, root crops, fruits, grass-fed meats, and fish.

Abundance, not scarcity, best describes the supply of food in the world today. Rarely has the world seen such a glut of food looking for buyers. Increases in food production during the past 25 years have outstripped the world's unprecedented population growth by about 16 percent. Indeed, mountains of unsold grain on world markets have pushed prices downward over the past three decades.

All well and good for the global picture, you might be thinking, but doesn't such a broad stroke tell us little? Aren't people starving because of food shortages where most hungry people live—in Africa, Asia, and Latin America?

Hunger in the face of ample food is all the more shocking in the third world. In every region except Africa, gains in food production since 1950 have kept ahead of population growth. During the 1970s, only 12 percent of the world's population lived in countries where food production per person was falling.

One hypothetical question best highlights how misleading it is to think of food shortages in the third world as the root cause of hunger: how much of the food now available within third world countries would it take to make up for the total food lacking in the diets of each country's chronically hungry people?

According to the World Bank, the answer is but a tiny percentage. In India, home of over a third of the world's hungry people, the reallocation of a mere 5.6 percent of current food production would wipe out hunger, making an active life possible for everyone. For Indonesia, with the second greatest number of undernourished people in the world, only 2 percent of the country's food supply would make the difference. And in Africa, 7.8 percent of the food supply of Tanzania and 2.5 percent of that of both Senegal and Sudan could meet the needs of the hungry.

This is, we underline, a hypothetical exercise. As the World Bank itself cautions, even though enough food exists, the poor are not able to purchase it.

Thus, even most "hungry countries" have enough food for all their people right now. This finding turns out to be true using official statistics even though experts warn us that newly modernizing societies invariably underestimate farm production—just as a century ago at least a third of the U.S. wheat crop went uncounted. Moreover, many nations can't realize their full food production potential because of the gross inefficiencies caused by inequitable ownership of resources. . . .

Finally, many of the countries in which hunger is rampant export much more in agricultural goods than they import. It is the industrial countries, not the third world countries, that import more than two-thirds of all food and farm commodities in world trade. Imports by the 30 lowest-income countries, on the other hand, account for only 6 percent of all international commerce in food and farm commodities.

Looking more closely at some of the world's hunger-ravaged countries and regions confirms that scarcity is clearly not the cause of hunger.

India. India ranks near the top among third world agricultural exporters. While as many as 300 million Indians go hungry, the country exports everything from wheat to beef and government officials agonize over how to get rid of mounting "surpluses" of wheat and rice—24 million tons in 1985, more than double the entire world's annual food aid shipments in a typical year.

Bangladesh. Beginning with its famine of the early 1970s, Bangladesh came to symbolize the frightening consequences of people overrunning food resources. Yet Bangladesh's official yearly rice output alone—which some experts say is seriously underreported—could provide each person with more than a pound of grain per day, or 2,064 calories. Adding to that small amounts of vegetables, fruits, and legumes could prevent hunger for everyone. Yet the poorest third of the people in Bangladesh eat at most only 1,500 calories a day, dangerously below what is needed for a healthy life.

With about 100 million people living in an area the size of Wisconsin, Bangladesh may be judged overcrowded by any number of standards, but its population density is not a viable excuse for its widespread hunger. Bangladesh is blessed with exceptional agricultural endowments, yet its current rice yields fall significantly below the all-Asia average. The extraordinary potential of Bangladesh's rich alluvial soils and plentiful water has hardly been fully used. If the country's irrigation potential were realized, experts predict its rice yields could double or even triple.

Brazil. While Brazil has become the world's second-largest food exporter (after only the United States), 86 million Brazilians do not have enough to eat.

Africa. Bombarded by images of barren landscapes in Sub-Saharan Africa, many of us are surprised to learn that the region is a net exporter of agricultural commodities.

Despite widening hunger, food exports from the Horn of Africa—Ethiopia, Kenya, Somalia, the Sudan, Tanzania, and Uganda—were worth nearly $1 billion more in 1983 than the food imported. When all agricultural commodities are counted in, the difference rises to $1.5 billion.

The Sahelian countries of West Africa are known for recurrent famines, but in most years they export more agricultural products than they import. Even during the drought years 1970 to 1974, the value of the region's agricultural exports —$1.25 billion—was three times greater than the value of grain imported, and such figures don't take into account unreported exports. Reports from two of the Sahelian countries, Niger and Burkina Faso (formerly Upper Volta), estimate that traders smuggle out as much as half the grain produced to sell elsewhere to customers able to pay more.

While television coverage has awakened the world to hunger in the Horn of Africa and the Sahel, some of Africa's worst hunger is rarely covered. In South Africa, some 50,000 black children starve to death every year; 136 die every day. Yet South Africa is a net exporter of agricultural products, even exporting corn, the basic staple of black families.

Despite the productive capacity suggested by Africa's agricultural exports, by the mid-1980s food production per person had been declining for more than a decade and as much as a quarter of the continent's grain consumption was reportedly coming from imports. With so much of Africa's food production undercounted—especially the food poor women grow for their own families—a truly accurate assessment of the problem is impossible. But repeated reports about Africa's failing agriculture and growing dependence on imports have led many to assume that simply too many people are pressing against too meager resources. Africa's food crisis is real—but how true is this assumption?

Many longtime observers of Africa's agricultural development tell us that the real reasons for Africa's food problems are no mystery. Africa's food potential has been distorted and thwarted.

Colonizers and, subsequently, national and international agencies, have discredited peasant producers' often sophisticated knowledge of ecologically appropriate farming systems. Promoting "modern," often imported, and ecologically destructive technologies, they have cut Africa's food producers out from economic decisions most affecting their very survival.

Public resources, including research and agricultural credit, have been channeled to export crops to the virtual exclusion of peasant-produced food crops such as millet, sorghum, and root crops. In the 1980s, pressure to export to pay interest on foreign debt only reinforced this imbalance.

While Africa's principal food producers are women, decisions over land use and credit have been made the domain of men.

Governments beholden to urban classes demanding cheap food have paid peasants so poorly for their crops that they have often had little incentive to produce for the market.

Aid policies unaccountable to African peasant producers and pastoralists have generally bypassed their needs in favor of expensive, large-scale projects. Africa receives less aid for agriculture than any other continent, and of the $14 billion pouring into the eight Sahelian nations in the decade ending 1984, less than 5 percent went to rainfed agriculture, although it accounts for 95 percent of grain production. What funds did go to farming went overwhelmingly to the irrigated systems of the richer farmers.

African governments—like most in the third world—allocate, on average, less than 10 percent of their budgets to agriculture, in contrast to a much larger share going to the military and police.

Many governments have also overvalued their currencies, making imported food artificially cheap and undercutting local producers of millet, sorghum, and cassava. Urban tastes then increasingly shift to imported grain, particularly wheat, which few countries in Africa can grow economically. Twenty years ago, only a small minority of urban dwellers in Sub-Saharan Africa ate wheat. Today bread is a staple for many urbanites, and wheat products account for over a third of all the region's grain imports. U.S. food aid and advertising by multinational corporations ("He'll be smart. He'll go far. He'll eat bread.") have played their part in molding African tastes to what the industrial countries have to sell.

Thus beneath the "scarcity diagnosis" of Africa's

food situation lie many human-made and therefore reversible causes. Even Africa's high birth rates are not independent variables but are determined by social realities that shape people's reproductive choices. . . .

CHAPTER SEVEN / MYTH 7: THE FREE MARKET CAN END HUNGER

MYTH: If governments just got out of the way, the free market could work to alleviate hunger.

OUR RESPONSE: Unfortunately, such a market-is-good-government-is-bad formula can never help address the causes of hunger. Such thinking misleads us into believing that a society can opt for one or the other, when in fact every economy on earth combines the market and government in allocating resources and distributing goods.

Even the division between so-called capitalist and socialist societies is hardly clear-cut. In West Germany's "capitalist" economy, government expenditures are a significantly bigger share of the gross national product than in Spain's more "socialist" one. Nicaragua's economy relies as much on the market as does Mexico's. South Korea and Taiwan, the favorites of free-market purists like Milton Friedman, owe much of their striking growth records to numerous government interventions, not the least of which have been government-imposed land reforms and support for key industries.

Worst of all, such black-and-white thinking blocks us from identifying the truly critical questions we must ask to learn how *either* the market *or* government can alleviate hunger.

Defenders of the market have a lot of evidence on their side—certainly any society that has tried to do away with the market has faced serious headaches. The problem comes when a useful device gets raised to the level of dogma. We lose sight of what it can and cannot do. For all the market's virtues, three of its shortcomings contribute directly to the causes of hunger.

We recently had the opportunity of publicly responding to perhaps the market's greatest advocate, Nobel laureate Milton Friedman. Friedman insists that the most salient virtue of the free market is that it responds to individual preferences. In our response we said we thought that the preference of most individuals is to eat when they're hungry—yet more than half a billion people living in market economies are *not* eating.

The lesson is unmistakable: the first shortcoming of the market is that it does not respond to individual preferences—or even needs. It responds to money.

Let's look at the hunger consequences of this simple lesson. From the beginning of our book, we've described the increasing concentration of decision-making power over all that it takes to grow and distribute food—fewer and fewer people owning more and more land, controlling credit, water, marketing channels, and so forth. As the poor in ever greater numbers are pushed from the land, they are less and less able to make their demand for food register in the market.

In parallel urban development, a small elite often controls banking, industry, and commercial institutions. In Chile, for example, after only six years of the Pinochet military regime's free-market economics, the country's five largest financial clans had taken control of two-thirds of the country's 250 largest firms. In the Philippines, the Marcos family and their rich friends came to control a huge share of that nation's corporate assets. With such concentrated power, the wealthy are free to indulge in investments that employ relatively few workers and to resist workers' demands for a living wage.

Under these conditions, what does the market do? The only thing it can: it responds to the tastes of those who can pay, the privileged minority. They alone have the income to make what economists call effective demand. Production inevitably shifts to items desired by the better off, such as meat, fresh fruits and vegetables, imported VCRs, and Chivas Regal. . . . we spoke of an invisible food revolution in which basic foods for the majority are increasingly displaced by luxury crops for the minority. In international commerce, food flows from the hungry to the well-fed. . . .

Here in the United States, we witness the same affront to logic and our sensitivities. While soup lines lengthened in the early 1980s, the food industry spawned a record number of new-fangled food items—2,000 in 1982 alone—including Pac Man cereal and a juice treat for dogs.

Left to its own devices, the market simply mirrors inequalities in wealth and income and should be seen for what it is: a useful device and nothing more. We must not delude ourselves into thinking that it registers the needs and wishes of all people.

A second drawback of the market is that it is blind—blind to the social and resource costs of the production engine it is supposed to drive.

An example from the United States will make this clear. During the 1970s, U.S. agricultural exports boomed, rising sixfold in value in only a decade. At their peak in 1981, our agricultural exports brought in over $44 billion in foreign exchange. What a bonanza! the market told us. All that grain could pay for imported oil.

But the market failed to tell us that producing all that grain required an energy expenditure equivalent to at least a third of the money generated, that topsoil was eroding from prime farmland at an accelerated and alarming rate, and that the push to export was pumping groundwater out of the earth much faster than nature could replenish it.

The market also failed to tell us about the social costs of farmers being made more vulnerable to the vagaries of the international market. Hundreds of thousands of livelihoods wiped out, increased rural landlessness, the decline of whole rural communities, and the shocking sight of farmers on food stamps—to all of this destruction the market is blind.

Finally, left to its own devices, the market has another drawback that undermines some of our most deeply held values. It leads to the concentration of economic power. Those with greater economic power undercut and gobble up those with less. The 1980s "merger mania" involving some of the largest corporations in the United States is only the most recent manifestation of this tendency. In 1984 alone, $122 billion went into over 2,500 mergers that even *Business Week* doubts were economically justified.

The resulting concentration of economic power directly contributes to hunger and seriously compromises political democracy. . . . This is relatively easy to see when we look at the third world. The connection between hunger in El Salvador and the fact that six families control as much land as 300,000 peasants is obvious. Can we see such a connection between the accelerating concentration of economic power and needless human suffering here at home?

Let's take the example of U.S. agriculture again. At the mercy of international markets, U.S. farmers in the 1970s experienced an incredible concentration of reward. By the early 1980s, a mere 1 percent captured 60 percent of net farm income. . . . Market theory alone doesn't explain such a dramatic transformation. In theory, the market rewards hard work; in reality, it *requires* hard work and production, but only *rewards* those who have considerable equity in their land—those who have wealth. They have easier access to credit and can therefore better withstand the market's inevitable swings, and only the wealthy can expand to make up in volume what all are losing in profits per acre, as a production push leads inevitably to price-depressing gluts.

Once made aware of the market's drawbacks, it might be tempting to throw out the market altogether in favor of government control. But to get at the root of hunger, we must take a more thoughtful, studied approach.

How Can the Market Work to End Hunger?

For those who believe in the usefulness of the market and who also want to end world hunger, the urgent question is, under what conditions can the market respond to human needs and preferences?

Since, by definition, the market responds to economic power and not to need, the answer in our view is fairly straightforward. *The more widely dispersed is purchasing power, the more the market will respond to actual human preferences and needs and the more power the market will have to end hunger.*

In other words, what must be promoted is not the market but the customers! For where there are customers, there will be entrepreneurs—and voilà! The market booms. In China, to the extent that the greater use of the market works to serve broad-based development goals, it is because purchasing power is relatively widely distributed, the fruit of making access to work and productive resources more equitable.

For those who believe in the utility of the market, the challenge is to promote policies that counter the concentration of buying power and ensure its wider dispersion. But this prescription raises a final question. Focused on the market, we have yet to take up the equally challenging issue: under what conditions can government serve genuine development?

Ending Hunger: Is There a Role for Government?

Those who see government, by definition, as the obstacle to development fail to appreciate the role that government has played in our own society's development. Without public support for infrastructure, including not only roads, bridges, railroads, and the like but also public education and public health, where would our nation be?

Government is clearly essential to development. But having acknowledged that, the temptation is to debate *how much* government versus *how much* market will best contribute to development. This simple tradeoff helps us little. It fails to probe the nature of government's contribution. For example:

- Is a government's public health budget spent largely on big hospitals in urban centers using expensive imported technology, as in the Philippines? Or is that same amount of money spread throughout the countryside, as in the Indian state of Kerala, to support primary health clinics serving the majority?
- Is the government's agricultural budget going to costly state farms, while ignoring the needs of the majority of rural producers, as in Ethiopia? Or is priority given to small farmers through cheaper credit and appropriate technical assistance?
- Is the government using its foreign exchange earnings to import late-model combines and computers for the country's wealthiest farmers, as in South Africa, or does a greater share of the earnings go to import tools and fertilizers to help small farmers who grow staple foods?

These and many similar questions are the really meaningful ones to ask about the nature of a government's role in development. They will be answered according to whom a government sees itself as accountable. A government beholden to a wealthy elite will use its resources for that group's disproportionate gain. A government that knows its survival depends on the support of the majority will work to respond to that majority's needs.

In addition to vital human and material infrastructure, many societies recognize two other critical roles for government. We feel they are just as important in determining whether it can help alleviate hunger.

Government as Protector of the Market

As we emphasized above, the market left to its own devices will concentrate wealth and purchasing power and therefore undermine its usefulness in meeting human needs. But a government responsible to majority interests can make rules and allocate resources to counteract the tendency toward concentration. These two instruments of economic life need not be in competition. Here's where the government can *help* the market!

Specifically related to hunger, such a mandate requires genuine land reform—including enforcing rules to keep ownership from becoming reconcentrated. It means tax and credit policies that benefit poor farmers. And it requires that all public policies—credit, tax, land, social welfare, or workplace reforms—actively disperse buying power. Perhaps most critical to such wide dispersion is making sure that anyone who wants a job can get one.

This isn't interference with the market. Policies that disperse purchasing power actually help the market do what it is supposed to do—respond to human needs and preferences.

Do We Have a Right to Eat?

Finally, government's role is to protect rights. Indeed, government uniquely has the power to do so, for nothing is an effective right until government protects citizens' enjoyment of it. We have a meaningful right to free speech, for example, only to the degree that the courts will stop anyone who tries to prevent us from speaking.

A few societies have decided that among basic human rights should be the right to life itself—that indeed this right should be of primary concern. For . . . how can we enjoy any other right without it?

Not all democratic societies protect the right to life. Many protect life only when threatened by physical assault, not by physical deprivation. Some, like our own, assume that while government should organize fire departments and police forces for the physical safety of its citizens, those citizens should fend for themselves when it comes to getting a decent job, enough to eat, or affordable medical care.

Only when the concept of basic rights is enlarged to include life itself, is government obligated to ensure that each citizen has access to employment, a healthy diet, and adequate health services. *This does not mean necessarily that government itself provides these goods; it means only that government ensures no one goes without them.* A variety of approaches can be discovered in a wide spectrum of societies.

Consider the experience of the Indian state of Kerala, which we highlighted in our discussion of population in chapter 3. Within India, Kerala has considerably less hunger than the rest of the country, as suggested by an infant death rate half the all-India average and a much longer life expectancy. Kerala still tolerates extreme concentrations of landownership but has mitigated the effects by turning poor renters of farmland into owners. And it no longer treats food grain and certain other basic goods as mere market commodities to be sold to the highest bidder. Fair-price shops keep food prices low.

In the industrial world, the Scandinavian countries illustrate a positive role for government in protecting family-farm agriculture. Take Sweden, for example. Although wealth is still tightly concentrated in Swedish society, Swedes some time ago decided that farming and food were too important to be left to the market alone. So in Sweden, only working farmers can own farmland, and sales of farmland are closely monitored by county boards to ensure that prices paid are not so high as to eliminate family farmers from the competition. Moreover, wholesale food prices are not allowed to fluctuate with the market, wreaking havoc on the family farm. Instead they are periodically set when farm representatives, government, agribusiness, and consumer food cooperatives sit down at the negotiating table.

These far-flung illustrations suggest a growing willingness to acknowledge the failure of the market alone to alleviate hunger. To the degree that hunger in urban Mexico was eased for some during the 1970s, for example, it was not the result of greater output but increased government price subsidies for consumers. Even the World Bank in its previously mentioned study *Poverty and Hunger* concluded that growth alone could not alleviate chronic hunger in an acceptable period of time—direct intervention in the market is necessary to enhance the ability of the hungry to acquire food.

In such a brief book, we cannot hope to provide answers to the critical controversy over the proper role of the market and government as instruments of development and promoters of human freedom. More modestly, we hope to show that hunger will never be eliminated if our vision is blocked by rigid dogma, detached from real life experience. The government-*or*-market tradeoff fails to help us grasp the truly urgent questions we must address in order to end hunger.

Under what conditions can both the market and government serve to alleviate hunger? Clearly the answer to such a question cannot be found in economic theory alone, but rests on the relationship of citizens to decision-making power. For neither the market nor government can end hunger as long as control over economic resources is in the hands of a few and political authority responds largely to the booming voice of wealth. . . .

KIM R. HOLMES

In Search of Free Markets

Kim R. Holmes is Vice President and Director of Foreign Policy Studies at the Heritage Foundation in Washington, D.C. *(Source: From* The Wall Street Journal, *December 12, 1994.*

QUESTIONS FOR REFLECTION

1. What is the paradox of foreign aid? What does it mean for foreign aid in general?
2. Are there ways of directing foreign aid to avoid the paradox?
3. Why does freedom correlate so strongly with wealth? What does this imply about the role of government in solving problems of hunger?

Much has been made of the collapse of state socialism and the post-Cold War march toward free markets. In reality, progress has been slow. Even today, only a relative handful of countries are blessed with free economies.

While U.S. and global policy makers and opinion-leaders over the years have rightly focused on political freedom, economic freedom has received scant attention, as if it barely matters. But it does matter: If a country has a free economy, it can lift itself—and its people—out of poverty. We see this today in Asia, Latin America, and even in parts of the former Soviet empire. We also see that economic freedom is a breeding ground for political freedom.

Vivid Proof

Taiwan, South Korea, Chile, Mexico and many other emerging-market countries have provided vivid proof that economic prosperity depends on a free economy, not on U.S. aid, the heavy hand of government planning, or even advanced infrastructure and abundant natural resources. Freedom is what counts most. Indeed, the data show clearly that the wealthiest countries in the world are the most economically free, while the poorest countries are the most unfree.

Thus, economic freedom is a critical factor in the relative wealth of nations. The more government interferes in the market, the more it impedes economic growth and lowers the standard of living of its citizens.

Unfortunately, most countries still do not have free economies. Of the 101 countries examined in The Heritage Foundation's "Index of Economic Freedom," just 43 were found to have free or "mostly free" economies, while 50 have economies that are "mostly unfree" and eight have repressive economies.

The "Index," the first comparative analysis of its kind, measures the degree of economic freedom each country allows in 10 key areas: trade policy; taxation policy; government consumption of economic output; monetary policy; capital flows and foreign investment; banking policy; wage and price controls; property rights; regulations; and the

Index of Economic Freedom

Here are the rankings of all the countries graded in order from most economically free to least economically free*

FREE

1 Hong Kong
2 Singapore
3 Bahrain
4 U.S.
5 Japan
6 Taiwan
7 U.K.

MOSTLY FREE

8 Canada
9 Germany
10 Austria
11 Bahamas
12 Czech Rep.
13 S. Korea
14 Malaysia
15 Australia
16 Ireland
17 Estonia
18 France
19 Thailand
20 Chile
21 Italy
22 Spain
23 El Salvador
24 Oman
25 Sweden
26 Belize
27 Columbia
28 Panama
29 Paraguay
30 Slovakia
31 Greece
32 Hungary
33 Jamaica
34 Portugal
35 Sri Lanka
36 Argentina
37 Tunisia
38 Costa Rica
39 Jordan
40 Morocco
41 Swaziland
42 Uruguay
43 Uganda

MOSTLY UNFREE

44 S. Africa
45 Turkey
46 Venezuela
47 Botswana
48 Gabon
49 Guatemala
50 Kenya
51 Mexico
52 Zambia
53 Israel
54 Algeria
55 Honduras
56 Nigeria
57 Pakistan
58 Bolivia
59 Ecuador
60 Ivory Coast
61 Malta
62 Poland
63 Brazil
64 Fiji
65 Ghana
66 Philippines
67 Mongolia
68 Guinea
69 Indonesia
70 DominicanR.
71 Malawi
72 Peru
73 Russia
74 Bulgaria
75 Cameroon
76 Egypt
77 Madagascar
78 Mali
79 Tanzania
80 Zimbabwe
81 Albania
82 Romania
83 Belarus
84 Yemen
85 Guyana
86 India
87 China
88 Ethiopia
89 Bangladesh
90 Congo
91 Nicaragua
92 Ukraine
93 Sierra Leone

REPRESSED

94 Moldova
95 Haiti
96 Sudan
97 Angola
98 Mozambique
99 Vietnam
100 Cuba
101 N. Korea

*In case of a tie, the countries were ranked aphabetically.

Freedom and Wealth

A comparison of economic freedom and wealth

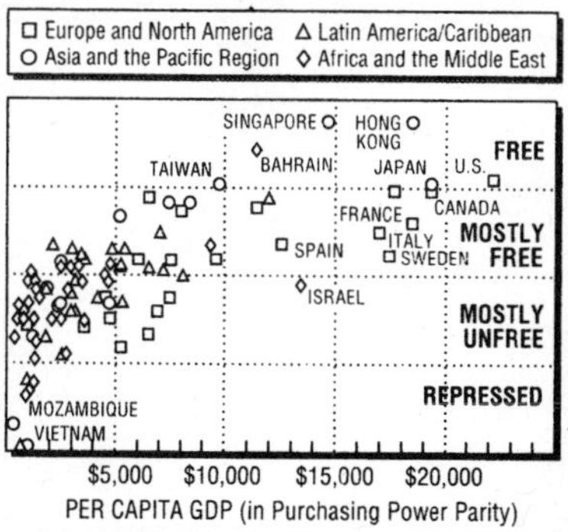

Source: Heritage Foundation

black market. Each country's performance in these areas was given a numerical "score." For example, in the area of corporate taxes, a nation earns a "1" if it has limited or no taxes imposed on corporate profits. A flat corporate tax of less than 25% or a progressive top tax of less than 25% earns it a "2"; a top rate between 26% and 35% earns it a "3"; a rate between 36% and 45% earns a "4"; and top rates above 46% earn a "5." Obviously, the lower the score the better. We didn't attempt to examine all economic factors; our task was to find accurate data for the most important factors, and then to provide the most comprehensive and accurate comparison possible.

In order to avoid paralyzing academic debates, authors Bryan Johnson and Thomas Sheehy focused on what is known. The result, we believe, is the most accurate snapshot possible of how the countries of the world measure up to the standards of economic freedom.

There will be a variety of uses for the "Index." While many countries are encouraging foreign investment through privatization and other means, and have more open economies than in the past, the "Index" shows that a country's economic fundamentals—such as tax rates, the stability of the currency, trade policy and private property rights—can be more important to successful investing than the strengths or weaknesses of particular companies or business sectors.

For this reason, the "Index" should be a first stop for any investor who wishes to explore economic opportunities in a given country or region. While investment decisions always require in-depth, hands-on research, the "Index" can be used as a starting point to discern economic trends and regional comparisons.

Policy makers also will find it useful. The new Republican leaders of Congress have already made it clear that they intend to take a serious second look at U.S. foreign-aid policy. The "Index" illustrates clearly that the main cause of poverty around the world is not the failure of rich countries to spread the wealth through foreign-aid programs, but the misguided economic policies of developing countries themselves.

This presents a paradox: The countries that appear to most need U.S. aid are the ones that least deserve it because their government-controlled economies will misuse the money. By the same token, the countries that are least likely to squander U.S. aid—because they have free economies—are the countries that least need it.

Indeed, of the 15 countries examined in the "Index" that received the largest amounts of U.S. development assistance last year, 12 are rated as "mostly unfree," one has a "repressed" economy, and two earned "mostly free" ratings. Overall, of the 58 countries whose economies were classified as mostly unfree or repressive, more than 40 received U.S. development aid.

The "Index of Economic Freedom" demonstrates unequivocally that countries with the highest level of economic freedom also have the highest living standards. Likewise, countries with the least amount of economic freedom have the lowest living standards.

Ineffectual Foreign Aid

The data also show that developing countries that pursue rapid economic liberalization quickly become the richest in the world. Conversely, developing countries that drag their feet on economic liberalization remain poor—no matter how much foreign aid they receive. Hong Kong and Singapore, for example, have the most-free economies in the world. Between 1980 and 1991, Hong Kong's gross national product grew at an average annual rate of 5.6%, while Singapore's economy grew at an average rate of 5.3%. By contrast, countries such as Angola, Bangladesh and Haiti have the least-free economies and have experienced the least amount of economic growth.

Above all, the "Index of Economic Freedom" disproves the notion that economic growth and prosperity can be bought by huge transfers of wealth from the industrialized economies of the West to the less-developed economies. People in Angola, Haiti, Mozambique and Ukraine are not poor because wealthy people in the West haven't been generous toward them. They are poor because their governments pursue destructive economic policies that depress free enterprise. In today's world, poverty is not the natural state of mankind, but the result of misguided economic policies.

Welfare

The central problem of distributive justice is how goods should be allotted to members of a society. In many societies, the prevailing methods of allotment leave some with very little. Some may not have enough to eat; some may have inadequate housing or no housing at all. Some may lack basic medical care. Some may receive no, or very poor, education. How should society respond to these problems?

Clearly, this question raises two major issues. One is philosophical: What are the proper principles of distribution? What, in other words, is the correct theory of distributive justice? The other is practical: Given a set of principles of distribution, how can we devise policies to bring about distributions in accord with them? Answering the first question defines our obligations to help others; answering the second defines a way of fulfilling them in practice. The first question is prior. Only if we know what we are trying to accomplish can we judge how well various policies accomplish it.

These questions go to the root of our conception of political and economic organization. A society that alters its laws about capital punishment, abortion, or pornography, for example, may bring about significant changes by doing so, but it does not fundamentally change the way it is organized. Changing one's conception of distribution, however, can change social organization. Socialism, capitalism, communism, and other forms of economic organization aim at satisfying different principles of distribution. Within each system arise important questions about policies for satisfying them.

Kai Nielsen defends egalitarianism—the view that everyone is entitled to equality. Almost all moral philosophers agree that people ought to be treated equally in some respects. The formal principle of justice, which requires that similar cases receive similar treatment, commands nearly universal assent. Nielsen argues for a more substantive entitlement to equality, one which, he argues, requires fundamental changes in social organization.

Ronald Dworkin defends liberalism. He argues that liberals do not merely assign a greater weight to equality, and a smaller weight to liberty, than conservatives. Instead, liberals share the belief that government ought to be neutral on the question of what the good is. Neutrality leads the government to protect liberty in the sphere of civil rights but to promote equal opportunity in economic matters. That, he maintains, provides a justification for welfare programs.

J. Donald Moon also seeks to defend a liberal, democratic welfare state in a different way. He begins with "Hegel's dilemma"—that market economies create great inequalities, yet state interventions usually undermine the self-respect of those they try to help. Moon finds Dworkin's liberalism inadequate, both as a general theory of justice and as a solution to Hegel's dilemma. He argues for a welfare state that would help the poor without injuring their self-respect.

Philosopher John Hospers argues in favor of libertarianism, the view that the government may act only to prevent harm to others. Taking Mill's harm principle and applying it broadly, Hospers finds little justification for any government action concerning distribution. The government may of course enforce laws against stealing, for example, because that involves direct harm to others. But nothing justifies government action to take from A and give to B simply because B has less than A. Hospers argues that all other conceptions of government and of distributive justice give people rights over the lives of others—rights that, in his view, they do not have.

Social worker and theorist Charles Murray addresses the practical problem of welfare. He assumes that government is justified in attempting to eliminate poverty, homelessness, and other social problems, but asks how it can do so. Murray draws several laws about social programs, which imply that such programs inevitably do more harm than good. Murray concludes that a society without any welfare programs at all would be better off than one in which government expends a great deal of energy and money trying to redistribute income and other goods. If Murray is right, there is a sense in which the practical problem of welfare policy may be prior to the question of distributive justice: perhaps no policies can achieve anything worth achieving—on any plausible conception of justice—without doing even greater harm. If so, then what conception of justice is correct makes no difference for social policy, for no combination of welfare programs could bring about a just distribution.

KAI NIELSEN

Egalitarian Justice: Equality as a Goal and Equality as a Right

Kai Nielsen is Professor of Philosophy at the University of Calgary. (Source: From Equality and Liberty, *Totowa, New Jersey: Rowman & Allenheld. Notes have been omitted.*

QUESTIONS FOR REFLECTION

1. What is the formal principle of justice? What implications does it have for equality?
2. What is the difference between treating equality as a goal and treating it as a right, in Nielsen's view?
3. What is the difference between positive and negative rights?
4. Why does Nielsen advocate a right to conditions of equality? Do you find the argument convincing?

I

The argument in this chapter will attempt to show that justice should be linked closely to equality and that, so construed, it is not, as conservatives and even some liberals think, the mortal enemy of liberty. I shall also argue that equality, in an important reading, should be regarded as a goal—indeed as a fundamental human good. Moreover, it is something which is both instrumentally and intrinsically good. There is also a reading—a compatible but distinct reading from the reading mentioned above—in which equality is a right. I shall elucidate and also argue for that reading but I shall principally be concerned with arguing for equality as a fundamental goal, a goal essential for justice, which a perfectly just society would realize. In our class societies, and indeed in our dark times, such justice is not in the immediate offing. It is not the sort of thing we are going to achieve in the next decade or so. But such a conception of justice should remain a heuristic ideal in our emancipatory struggles. . . .

II

Richards starts out his "Justice and Equality" by remarking that repeatedly in social and political thought "justice has been supposed to involve or implicate the idea of equality." There have been shifts in our beliefs about what equality is or should be, but in reflections about justice it has remained a central issue. Richards is concerned with how the idea of equality should be interpreted and with its role in common-sense reflections about justice and in theories of justice.

He first sorts out a conception of formal justice,

namely the idea of treating like cases alike. But this formal conception, though philosophically uncontroversial, is compatible with very very different moral theories and substantive principles of justice, including radically inegalitarian ones. Indeed, even moral sceptics could readily accept that formal conception of justice. They could believe that justice is indeed treating like cases alike, while continuing to believe that "each person's opinion of what makes cases alike as good as any other's."

The formal conception of justice does, however, rest on an idea of equality, for cases are judged to be alike relative to some standard which specifies that the cases are alike. What the underlying task is (or so at least it seems) is to *specify what that standard is.* What we should be looking for is an adequate formulation of a substantive theory of equality in terms of which issues of justice can be properly adjudicated.

In many serious, relatively non-philosophical discussions of justice, the criteria appealed to for ascertaining when like cases are alike are *rights, desert,* or *needs.* But people differ radically about which of these conceptions to appeal to, the interpretation to give to these criteria and the weight to place on them. Herbert Spencer, for example, focuses on desert and repudiates any appeal to needs, while Peter Kropotkin (to take someone at the other end of the spectrum) takes needs to be the only sound grounds for the making of judgments of distributive justice and rejects any appeal to desert as immoral. And apart from the import attached to the different criteria, the various criteria themselves get different readings. Conservatives run a tight ship as to what will count as a right, while left-leaning liberals will have a more expansive conception of rights. They might think, for example, that there is something like a right to work or a right to health care, while conservatives would regard this as a dangerous expansion of rights-talk. Desert will similarly get different readings. Some will only count effort in judgments of desert. Others will count, as well, talent, contribution, and even good fortune. Still others . . . will simply count contribution. And what will go on lists of needs, let alone what a need should be taken to be, will again be rather various. The short of it is that there is no general consensus among reflective people about these matters. We are sometimes told that formal justice, understood as treating like cases alike or even as giving each its due, can be interpreted in "terms of common-sense criteria of likeness or oneness (rights or desert or needs), but we find, on examination, that these criteria are extremely controversial, both in the interpretation and the relative weighting of each of them."

[III . . .]

[IV . . .]

V

In putting it in this way, we should come back to our question of whether equality is a right or a goal or both. Let us assume, for a moment, that egalitarians have successfully specified the equalities they think it is desirable to attain. Then we need to ask, are these desirable things—also things people have a *right* to—or are they simply things that egalitarians, perhaps quite correctly, take it to be desirable that all people, as far as possible, have? Some egalitarians will not defend equality—or at least all the egalitarian conditions it is desirable to attain—as something people have a right to but simply judge it as desirable (morally preferable) that human beings be treated as being equal in certain respects, beyond what is strictly required to treat them as moral equals. These respects might be that people share equally, as far as is reasonably possible, the benefits and burdens of their society or have equal opportunities for self-development or all equally have the institutional bases for having their basic needs satisfied. (It is also debatable whether justice can be so nonglobal. Its scope, arguably, should be the whole world and not just a particular society.)

It is important to see that to take equality as a matter of a set of rights that people have and to take equality as a goal could be importantly different. If we stick to negative rights (rights not to be interfered with), a system of equal rights will predictably lead to very unequal distributions of wealth, power and well-being. If we admit, as genuine rights, positive rights as well, then, depending on what positive rights we admit, there may not be much of a practical difference between the two conceptions.

VI

I want now to consider equality as a goal, though this is not to say that some equalities are not rights, though how this can be needs, of course, to be elucidated. As a goal, as an ideal state of affairs to be obtained, an egalitarian is committed to trying to provide the social basis for an equality of *condition* for all human beings. The ideal, putting it minimally as a first step, is to provide the social basis for an equality of life prospects such that there cannot be anything like the vast disparities in whole life prospects that exist now.

Suppose we ask, "Why should this be thought to be desirable?" We are, I believe, so close to bedrock here that it is difficult to know what to say. That such a condition is desirable gives expression, to speak autobiographically for a moment, to a root pre-analytical (pre-theoretical) conception of a central element in a good society and to my pre-analytic (pre-theoretical) conception of what fairness between persons comes to. Vis-à-vis fairness/unfairness, I have in mind the sense of unfairness which goes with the acceptance, where something non-catastrophic could be done about it, of the existence of very different life prospects of equally talented, equally energetic children from very different social backgrounds: say the children of a successful businessman and a dishwasher. Their whole life prospects are very unequal indeed and, given the manifest quality of that difference, that this should be so seems to me very unfair. It conflicts sharply with my sense of justice.

My egalitarian ideal is a generalization of that. I can understand someone saying that the existence of such disparities is unfortunate, that life itself in that respect is not fair, but to try to do something about it would be still worse for it would entail an onslaught on the family, the undermining of liberty, the violation of individual rights and the like. That being so, we must just live with these disparities in life prospects. Here we have something we can reason about in a common universe of discourse. But what I do not see, what indeed seems both incredible and morally monstrous, is someone who would honestly think that if none of these consequences obtained, with regard to the family, liberty, rights, and so on, they would *still* not see that there is any unfairness in a society, particularly an abundant society, so structured. There is nothing wrong, they seem at least to think, with such people having such radically unequal life prospects even when something could be done about it without violating anyone's rights or causing a social catastrophe. If someone sees no unfairness here, nothing that, other things being equal, should be corrected in the direction of equality, then I do not know where to turn. It is almost like a situation in which someone says that he sees nothing wrong with racial bigotry, religious intolerance or torturing people to get them to confess to petty crimes. It seems that there are very basic considered judgments (moral intuitions, if you will) being appealed to here and that there is little likelihood of getting back of them to something more fundamental or evident. It seems to me to be an intrinsic good that fair relations obtain between people and that it is intrinsically desirable that at least between equally deserving people there obtain, if that is reasonably possible, an equality of life conditions. Equality seems to me to be an intrinsic good, though surely not the sole intrinsic good.

VII

However, and perhaps more importantly, equality is also a very important instrumental good. Where there are extensive differences in life prospects between people, at least within a single society, where their condition is markedly unequal, where there are extensive income differentials, the better off people in this respect tend to gain a predominance of power and control in society. It is as evident as anything can be that there is a close correlation between wealth and power. If we are reasonably clear-headed, and if we prize liberty and autonomy, and if we prize democracy, we will also be egalitarians. With those inequalities of power and control, liberty and democracy must suffer. Equality, liberty, autonomy, democracy and justice, I shall argue, come as a packaged deal. To have any of them in any secure or extensive manner we must have all of them.

VIII

I also want to argue that a certain kind of equality is a right. That everyone, where this is reasonably possible, is to have his or her needs equally met is an egalitarian *goal;* that people be treated as equals, that in the design of our institutions people have an equal right to respect, that none be treated as a means only, are natural *rights.* That kind of equality is something we have by right. (By a "natural right" I mean nothing more arcane than rights which need not be legal rights or rights which must be conventionally acknowledged.) It is not that I am saying that a right is a goal. What I am saying is that *a certain condition of equality* is a goal that we should strive toward and that, quite independently of its attainment, there are certain rights that we all have, the covering formula for which is the claim that we all are to be treated as moral equals. This is something that could obtain now, though it is certainly not observed, and it is something that we could and should claim as a right, while the egalitarian goal I speak of is something for the future when the productive forces are more developed and when the productive relations and parallel political and legal formations have been transformed.

The link between such rights-talk and such goals-talk is this: if we believe that we human beings have an equal right to respect and that our institutions should be designed so as to achieve and sustain this, we are also very likely, when we think about what this comes to, to say that all human beings also have an equal right to concern on the part of society. By this we mean that our social institutions should be impartially concerned with all human beings under their jurisdiction. We cannot allow any playing of favorites here. If we get this far, it is a very short step, or so at least we are going to be naturally inclined to believe, to the belief that we must not construct our lives together in such a way that the needs of any human being are simply ignored. Beyond that we will also be inclined to believe that there must be an equal concern on the part of society for the satisfaction of the needs of all human beings. (I am, of course, talking about situations of plenty where this is possible.) No one in such a circumstance can be treated as being simply expendable. Rather, all needs and all interests must, as far as that is possible, be equally considered. What starts as a goal—what in some historical circumstances is little more than a heuristic ideal—turns into a right when the goal can realistically be achieved. And a just social order, if such is ever to come into existence, must have these egalitarian commitments.

It is not likely that a condition of moral equality between human beings can be stably sustained where there is not something approaching a rough equality of condition. Where people do not stand in that condition, one person is very likely to have, in various ways, some subtle and some not so subtle, greater power than another. Because of this, it will be the case that in some ways at least some will gain control over others or at least will be in a position to exercise control or partial control, and that in turn limits the autonomy of some and works to undermine their self-respect. If we want a world of moral equals, we also need a world in which people stand to each other in a rough equality of condition. To have a world in which a condition of equal respect and concern obtain, we need, where a person's whole lifetime is the measure, a rough equality of resources. If equality as a right is to be secure; that is, if that is a right that people actually can securely exercise, we must attain the goal of equality of condition. That, of course, is something we are not within a country mile of attaining. To think about justice seriously is to think about what must be done to be on our way to attaining it. . . .

RONALD DWORKIN

Liberalism

Ronald Dworkin is Professor of Jurisprudence at Oxford University, Professor of Law at New York University, and Professor-at-Large at Cornell University. (Source: From A Matter of Principle, *Cambridge: Harvard University Press, 1985. Notes have been omitted.*

QUESTIONS FOR REFLECTION

1. What is liberalism, according to Dworkin?
2. Why, in Dworkin's view, can we not think of liberalism and conservatism as assigning different weights to equality and liberty as competing values? Do you agree?
3. Why would a liberal choose a market economy, according to Dworkin? What would be a proper role for government in the economy?
4. Because most conservatives would also choose a market economy, where would they disagree with Dworkin's liberals about the role of government in economic matters?
5. What does liberalism imply about the goals of welfare policies, in Dworkin's view, and in your view?

. . . Is there a thread of principle that runs through the core liberal positions, and that distinguishes these from the corresponding conservative positions? There is a familiar answer to this question that is mistaken, but mistaken in an illuminating way. The politics of democracies, according to this answer, recognizes several independent constitutive political ideals, the most important of which are the ideals of liberty and equality. Unfortunately, liberty and equality often conflict: sometimes the only effective means to promote equality require some limitation of liberty, and sometimes the consequences of promoting liberty are detrimental to equality. In these cases, good government consists in the best compromise between the competing ideals, but different politicians and citizens will make that compromise differently. Liberals tend relatively to favor equality more and liberty less than conservatives do, and the core set of liberal positions I described is the result of striking the balance that way.

This account offers a theory about what liberalism is. Liberalism shares the same constitutive principles with many other political theories, including conservatism, but is distinguished from these by attaching different relative importance to different principles. The theory therefore leaves room, on the spectrum it describes, for the radical who cares even more for equality and less for liberty than the liberal, and therefore stands even farther away from the extreme conservative. The liberal becomes the man in the middle, which explains why liberalism is so often now considered wishy-washy, an untenable compromise between two more forthright positions.

No doubt this description of American politics could be made more sophisticated. It might make room for other independent constitutive ideals shared by liberalism and its opponents, like stability or security, so that the compromises involved in particular decisions are made out to be more complex. But if the nerve of the theory remains the competition between liberty and equality as constitutive ideals, then the theory cannot succeed. . . . It seems to apply, at best, to only a limited number of the political controversies it tries to explain. It is designed for economic controversies, but is either irrelevant or misleading in the case of censorship and pornography, and indeed, in the criminal law generally.

But there is a much more important defect in this explanation. It assumes that liberty is measurable so that, if two political decisions each invades the liberty of a citizen, we can sensibly say that one decision takes more liberty away from him than the other. That assumption is necessary, because otherwise the postulate, that liberty is a constitutive ideal of both the liberal and conservative political structures, cannot be maintained. Even firm conservatives are content that their liberty to drive as they wish (for example, to drive uptown on Lexington Avenue) may be invaded for the sake, not of some important competing political ideal, but only for marginal gains in convenience or orderly traffic patterns. But since traffic regulation plainly involves some loss of liberty, the conservative cannot be said to value liberty as such unless he is able to show that, for some reason, less liberty is lost by traffic regulation than by restrictions on, for example, free speech, or the liberty to sell for prices others are willing to pay, or whatever other liberty he takes to be fundamental.

That is precisely what he cannot show, because we do not have a concept of liberty that is quantifiable in the way that demonstration would require. He cannot say, for example, that traffic regulations interfere less with what most men and women want to do than would a law forbidding them to speak out in favor of Communism, or a law requiring them not to fix their prices as they think best. Most people care more about driving than speaking for Communism, and have no occasion to fix prices even if they want to. I do not mean that we can make no sense of the idea of fundamental liberties, like freedom of speech. But we cannot argue in their favor by showing that they protect more liberty, taken to be an even roughly measurable commodity, than does the right to drive as we wish; the fundamental liberties are important because we value something else that they protect. But if that is so, then we cannot explain the difference between liberal and conservative political positions by supposing that the latter protect the commodity of liberty, valued for its own sake, more effectively than the former.

It might now be said, however, that the other half of the liberty–equality explanation may be salvaged. Even if we cannot say that conservatives value liberty, as such, more than liberals, we can still say that they value equality less, and that the different political positions may be explained in that way. Conservatives tend to discount the importance of equality when set beside other goals, like general prosperity or even security; while liberals value equality relatively more, and radicals more still. Once again, it is apparent that this explanation is tailored to the economic controversies, and fits poorly with the noneconomic controversies. Once again, however, its defects are more general and more important. We must identify more clearly the sense in which equality could be a constitutive ideal for either liberals or conservatives. Once we do so, we shall see that it is misleading to say that the conservative values equality, in that sense, less than the liberal. We shall want to say, instead, that he has a different conception of what equality requires.

We must distinguish between two different principles that take equality to be a political ideal. The first requires that the government treat all those in its charge *as equals,* that is, as entitled to its equal concern and respect. That is not an empty requirement: most of us do not suppose that we must, as individuals, treat our neighbor's children with the same concern as our own, or treat everyone we meet with the same respect. It is nevertheless plausible to think that any government should treat all its citizens as equals in that way. The second principle requires that the government treat all those in its charge *equally* in the distribution of some resource of opportunity, or at least work to secure the state of affairs in which they all are equal or more nearly equal in that respect. It is conceded by everyone that the government cannot make everyone equal in every respect, but people do disagree about how far government should try to secure equality in some particular resource, for example, in monetary wealth.

If we look only at the economic–political controversies, then we might well be justified in saying that liberals want more equality in the sense of the second principle than conservatives do. But it would be a mistake to conclude that they value equality in the sense of the first and more fundamental principle any more highly. I say that the first principle is more fundamental because I assume that, for both liberals and conservatives, the first is constitutive and the second derivative. Sometimes treating people equally is the only way to treat them as equals; but sometimes not. Suppose a limited amount of emergency relief is available for two equally populous areas injured by floods; treating the citizens of both areas as equals requires giving more aid to the more seriously devastated area rather than splitting the available funds equally. The conservative believes that in many other, less apparent, cases treating citizens equally amounts to not treating them as equals. He might concede, for example, that positive discrimination in university admissions will work to make the two races more nearly equal in wealth, but nevertheless maintain that such programs do not treat black and white university applicants as equals. If he is a utilitarian, he will have a similar, though much more general, argument against any redistribution of wealth that reduces economic efficiency. He will say that the only way to treat people as equals is to maximize the average welfare of all members of community, counting gains and losses to all in the same scales, and that a free market is the only, or best, instrument for achieving that goal. This is not (I think) a good argument, but if the conservative who makes it is sincere, he cannot be said to have discounted the importance of treating all citizens as equals.

So we must reject the simple idea that liberalism consists in a distinctive weighting between constitutive principles of equality and liberty. But our discussion of the idea of equality suggests a more fruitful line. I assume (as I said) that there is broad agreement within modern politics that the government must treat all its citizens with equal concern and respect. I do not mean to deny the great power of prejudice in, for example, American politics. But few citizens, and even fewer politicians, would now admit to political convictions that contradict the abstract principle of equal concern and respect. Different people hold, however, as our discussion made plain, very different conceptions of what that abstract principle requires in particular cases.

What does it mean for the government to treat its citizens as equals? That is, I think, the same question as the question of what it means for the government to treat all its citizens as free, or as independent, or with equal dignity. In any case, it is a question that has been central to political theory at least since Kant.

It may be answered in two fundamentally different ways. The first supposes that government must be neutral on what might be called the question of the good life. The second supposes that government cannot be neutral on that question, because it cannot treat its citizens as equal human beings without a theory of what human beings ought to be. I must explain that distinction further. Each person follows a more-or-less articulate conception of what gives value to life. The scholar who values a life of contemplation has such a conception; so does the television-watching, beer-drinking citizen who is fond of saying "This is the life," though he has thought less about the issue and is less able to describe or defend his conception.

The first theory of equality supposes that political decisions must be, so far as is possible, independent of any particular conception of the good life, or of what gives value to life. Since the citizens of a society differ in their conceptions, the government does not treat them as equals if it prefers one conception to another, either because the officials believe that one is intrinsically superior, or because one is held by the more numerous or more powerful group. The second theory argues, on the contrary, that the content of equal treatment cannot be independent of some theory about the good for man or the good of life, because treating a person as an equal means treating him the way the good or truly wise person would wish to be treated. Good government consists in fostering or at least recognizing good lives; treatment as an equal consists in treating each person as if he were desirous of leading the life that is in fact good, at least so far as this is possible.

This distinction is very abstract, but it is also very important. I shall now argue that liberalism takes, as its constitutive political morality, the first conception of equality. I shall try to support that claim in this way. In the next section of this essay I shall show how it is plausible, and even likely, that a thoughtful person who accepted the first conception of equality would, given the economic and political circumstances of the United States in the last several decades, reach the positions I identified as the familiar core of liberal positions. . . . it is plausible and even likely that someone who held a particular version of the second theory of equality would reach what are normally regarded as the core of American conservative positions. I say "a particular version of" because American conservatism does not follow automatically from rejecting the liberal theory of equality. The second (or nonliberal) theory of equality holds merely that the treatment government owes citizens is at least partly determined by some conception of the good life. Many political theories share that thesis, including theories as far apart as, for example, American conservatism and various forms of socialism or Marxism, though these differ in the conception of the good life they adopt, and hence in the political institutions and decisions they endorse. In this respect, liberalism is decidedly not some compromise or halfway house between more forceful positions, but stands on one side of an important line that distinguishes it from all competitors taken as a group. . . .

I now define a liberal as someone who holds the first, or liberal, theory of what equality requires. Suppose that a liberal is asked to found a new state. He is required to dictate its constitution and fundamental institutions. He must propose a general theory of political distribution, that is, a theory of how whatever the community has to assign, by way of goods or resources or opportunities, should be assigned. He will arrive initially at something like this principle of rough equality: resources and opportunities should be distributed, so far as possible, equally, so that roughly the same share of whatever is available is devoted to satisfying the ambitions of each. Any other general aim of distribution will assume either that the fate of some people should be of greater concern than that of others, or that the ambitions or talents of some are more worthy, and should be supported more generously on that account.

Someone may object that this principle of rough equality is unfair because it ignores the fact that people have different tastes, and that some of these are more expensive to satisfy than others, so that, for example, the man who prefers champagne will need more funds if he is not to be frustrated than the man satisfied with beer. But the liberal may reply that tastes as to which people differ are, by and large, not afflictions, like diseases, but are rather cultivated, in accordance with each person's theory of what his life should be like. The most effective neutrality, therefore, requires that the same share be devoted to each, so that the choice between expensive and less expensive tastes can be made by each person for himself, with no sense that his overall share will be enlarged by choosing a more expensive life, or that, whatever he chooses, his choice will subsidize those who have chosen more expensively.

But what does the principle of rough equality of distribution require in practice? If all resources were distributed directly by the government through grants of food, housing, and so forth; if every opportunity citizens have were provided directly by the government through the provisions of civil and criminal law; if every citizen had exactly the same talents; if every citizen started his life with no more than what any other citizen had at the start; and if every citizen had exactly the same theory of the good life and hence exactly the same scheme of preferences as every other citizen, including preferences between productive activity of different forms and leisure, then the principle of rough equality of treatment could be satisfied simply by equal distributions of everything to be distributed and by civil and criminal laws of universal application. Government would arrange for production that maximized the mix of goods, including jobs and leisure, that everyone favored, distributing the product equally.

Of course, none of these conditions of similarity holds. But the moral relevance of different sorts of diversity are very different, as may be shown by the following exercise. Suppose all the conditions of similarity I mentioned did hold except the last: citizens have different theories of the good and hence different preferences. They therefore disagree about what product the raw materials and labor and savings of the community should be used to produce, and about which activities should be prohibited or regulated so as to make others possible or easier. The liberal, as lawgiver, now needs mechanisms to satisfy the principles of equal treatment in spite of these disagreements. He will decide that there are no better mechanisms available, as general political institutions, than the two main institutions of our own political economy: the economic market, for decisions about what goods shall be produced and how they shall be distributed, and representative democracy, for collective decisions about what conduct shall be prohibited or regulated so that other conduct might be made possible or convenient. Each of these familiar institutions may be expected to provide a more egalitarian division than any other general arrangement. The market, if it can be made to function efficiently, will determine for each product a price that reflects the cost in resources of material, labor, and capital that might have been applied to produce something different that someone else wants. That cost determines, for anyone who consumes that product, how much his account should be charged in computing the egalitarian division of social resources. It provides a measure of how much more his account should be charged for a house than a book, and for one book rather than another. The market will also provide, for the laborer, a measure of how much should be credited to his account for his choice of productive activity over leisure, and for one activity rather than another. It will tell us, through the price it puts on his labor, how much he should gain or lose by his decision to pursue one career rather than another. These measurements make a citizen's own distribution a function of the personal preferences of others as well as of his own, and it is the sum of these personal preferences that fixes the true cost to the community of meeting his own preferences for goods and activities. The egalitarian distribution, which requires that the cost of satisfying one person's preferences should as far as is possible be equal to the cost of satisfying another's, cannot be enforced unless those measurements are made.

We are familiar with the anti-egalitarian consequences of free enterprise in practice; it may therefore seem paradoxical that the liberal as lawgiver should choose a market economy for reasons of equality rather than efficiency. But, under the special condition that people differ only in preferences for goods and activities, the market is more egalitarian than any alternative of comparable generality. The most plausible alternative would be to allow decisions of production, investment, price, and wage to be made by elected officials in a socialist economy. But what principles should officials use in making those decisions? The liberal might tell them to mimic the decisions that a market would make if it was working efficiently under proper competition and full knowledge. This mimicry would be, in practice, much less efficient than an actual market would be. In any case, unless the liberal had reason to think it would be much more efficient, he would have good reason to reject it. Any minimally efficient mimicking of a hypothetical market would require invasions of privacy to determine what decisions individuals would make if forced actually to pay for their investment, consumption, and employment decisions at market rates, and this information gathering would be, in many other ways, much more expensive than an actual market. Inevitably, moreover, the assumptions officials make about how people would behave in a hypothetical market reflect the officials' own beliefs about how people should behave. So there would be, for the liberal, little to gain and much to lose in a socialist economy in which officials were asked to mimic a hypothetical market.

But any other instructions would be a direct violation of the liberal theory of what equality requires, because if a decision is made to produce and sell goods at a price below the price a market would fix, then those who prefer those goods are, *pro tanto,* receiving more than an equal share of the resources of the community at the expense of those who would prefer some other use of the resources. Suppose the limited demand for books, matched against the demand for competing uses for wood pulp, would fix the price of books at a point higher than the socialist managers of the economy will charge; those who want books are having less charged to their account than the egalitarian principle would require. It might be said that in a socialist economy books are simply valued more, because they are inherently more worthy uses of social resources, quite apart from the popular demand for books. But the liberal theory of equality rules out that appeal to the inherent value of one theory of what is good in life.

In a society in which people differed only in preferences, then, a market would be favored for its egalitarian consequences. Inequality of monetary wealth would be the consequence only of the fact that some preferences are more expensive than others, including the preference for leisure time rather than the most lucrative productive activity. But we must now return to the real world. In the actual society for which the liberal must construct political institutions, there are all the other differences. Talents are not distributed equally, so the decision of one person to work in a factory rather than a law firm, or not to work at all, will be governed in large part by his abilities rather than his preferences for work or between work and leisure. The institutions of wealth, which allow people to dispose of what they receive by gift, means that children of the successful will start with more wealth than the children of the unsuccessful. Some people have special needs, because they are handicapped; their handicap will not only disable them from the most productive and lucrative employment, but will incapacitate them from using the proceeds of whatever employment they find as efficiently, so that they will need more than those who are not handicapped to satisfy identical ambitions.

These inequalities will have great, often catastrophic, effects on the distribution that a market economy will provide. But, unlike differences in preferences, the differences these inequalities make are indefensible according to the liberal conception of equality. It is obviously obnoxious to the liberal conception, for example, that someone should have more of what the community as a whole has to distribute because he or his father had superior skill or luck. The liberal lawgiver therefore faces a difficult task. His conception of equality requires an economic system that produces certain inequalities (those that reflect the true differential costs of goods and opportunities) but not others (those that follow from differences in ability, inheritance, and so on). The market produces both the required and the forbidden inequalities, and there is no alternative system that can be relied upon to produce the former without the latter.

The liberal must be tempted, therefore, to a reform of the market through a scheme of redistribution that leaves its pricing system relatively intact but sharply limits, at least, the inequalities in welfare that his initial principle prohibits. No solution will seem perfect. The liberal may find the best answer in a scheme of welfare rights financed through redistributive income and inheritance taxes of the conventional sort, which redistributes just to the Rawlsian point, that is, to the point at which the worst-off group would be harmed rather than benefited by further transfers. In that case, he will remain a reluctant capitalist, believing that a market economy so reformed is superior, from the standpoint of his conception of equality, to any practical socialist alternative. Or he may believe that the redistribution that is possible in a capitalist economy will be so inadequate, or will be purchased at the cost of such inefficiency, that it is better to proceed in a more radical way, by substituting socialist for market decisions over a large part of the economy, and then relying on the political process to insure that prices are set in a manner at least roughly consistent with his conception of equality. In that case he will be a reluctant socialist, who acknowledges the egalitarian defects of socialism but counts them as less severe than the practical alternatives. In either case, he chooses a mixed economic system—either redistributive capitalism or limited socialism—not in order to compromise antagonistic ideals of efficiency and equality, but to achieve the best practical realization of the demands of equality itself.

Let us assume that in this manner the liberal either refines or partially retracts his original selection of a market economy. He must now consider the second of the two familiar institutions he first selected, which is representative democracy. Democracy is justified because it enforces the right of each person to respect and concern as an individual; but in practice the decisions of a democratic majority may often violate that right, according to the liberal theory of what the right requires. Suppose a legislature elected by a majority decides to make criminal some act (like speaking in favor of an unpopular political position, or participating in eccentric sexual practices), not because the act deprives others of opportunities they want, but because the majority disapproves of those views or that sexual morality. The political decision, in other words, reflects not just some accommodation of the *personal* preferences of everyone, in such a way as to make the opportunities of all as nearly equal as may be, but the domination of one set of *external* preferences, that is, preferences people have about what others shall do or have. The decision invades rather than enforces the right of citizens to be treated as equals.

How can the liberal protect citizens against that sort of violation of their fundamental right? It will not do for the liberal simply to instruct legislators, in some constitutional exhortation, to disregard the external preferences of their constituents. Citizens will vote these preferences in electing their representatives, and a legislator who chooses to ignore them will not survive. In any case, it is sometimes impossible to distinguish, even by introspection, the external and personal components of a political position: this is the case, for example, with associational preferences, which are the preferences some people have for opportunities, like the opportunity to attend public schools —but only with others of the same "background."

The liberal, therefore, needs a scheme of civil rights whose effect will be to determine those political decisions that are antecedently likely to reflect strong external preferences and to remove those decisions from majoritarian political institutions altogether. The scheme of rights necessary to do this will depend on general facts about the prejudices and other external preferences of the majority at any given time, and different liberals will disagree about what is needed at any particular time. But the rights encoded in the Bill of Rights of the United States Constitution, as interpreted (on the whole) by the Supreme Court, are those that a substantial number of liberals would think reasonably well suited to what the United States now requires (though most would think that the protection of the individual in certain important areas, including sexual publication and practice, are much too weak).

The main parts of the criminal law, however, present a special problem not easily met by a scheme of civil rights that disable the legislature from taking certain political decisions. The liberal knows that many of the most important decisions required by an effective criminal law are not made by legislators at all, but by prosecutors deciding whom to prosecute for what crime, and by juries and judges deciding whom to convict and what sentences to impose. He also knows that these decisions are antecedently very likely to be corrupted by the external preferences of those who make these decisions because those they judge, typically, have attitudes and ways of life very different from their own. The liberal does not have available, as protection against these decisions, any strategy comparable to the strategy of civil rights that merely remove a decision from an institution. Decisions to prosecute, convict, and sentence must be made by someone. But he has available, in the notion of procedural rights, a different device to protect equality in a different way. He will insist that criminal procedure be structured to achieve a margin of safety in decisions, so that the process is biased strongly against the conviction of the innocent. It would be a mistake to suppose that the liberal thinks that these procedural rights will improve the *accuracy* of the criminal process, that is, the probability that any particular decision about guilt or innocence will be the right one. Procedural rights intervene in the process, even at the cost of inaccuracy, to compensate in a rough way for the antecedent risk that a criminal process, especially if it is largely administered by one class against another, will be corrupted by the impact of external preferences that cannot be eliminated directly. This is only the briefest sketch of how various substantive and procedural civil rights follow from the liberal's initial conception of equality; it is meant to suggest, rather than demonstrate, the more precise argument that would be available for more particular rights.

So the liberal, drawn to the economic market and to political democracy for distinctly egalitarian reasons, finds that these institutions will produce inegalitarian results unless he adds to his scheme different sorts of individual rights. These rights will function as trump cards held by individuals; they will enable individuals to resist particular decisions in spite of the fact that these decisions are or would be reached through the normal workings of general institutions that are not themselves challenged. The ultimate justification for these rights is that they are necessary to protect equal concern and respect; but they are not to be understood as representing equality in contrast to some other goal or principle served by democracy or the economic market. The familiar idea, for example, that rights of redistribution are justified by an ideal of equality that overrides the efficiency ideals of the market in certain cases, has no place in liberal theory. For the liberal, rights are justified, not by some principle in competition with an independent justification of the political and economic institutions they qualify, but in order to make more perfect the only justification on which these other institutions may themselves rely. If the liberal arguments for a particular right are sound, then the right is an unqualified improvement in political morality, not a necessary but regrettable compromise of some other independent goal, like economic efficiency.

[. . .]

. . . This form of liberalism insists that government must treat people as equals in the following sense. It must impose no sacrifice or constraint on any citizen in virtue of an argument that the citizen could not accept without abandoning his sense of his equal worth. This abstract principle requires liberals to oppose the moralism of the New Right, because no self-respecting person who believes that a particular way to live is most valuable for him can accept that this way of life is base or degrading. No self-respecting atheist can agree that a community in which religion is mandatory is for that reason finer, and no one who is homosexual that the eradication of homosexuality makes the community purer.

So liberalism as based on equality justifies the traditional liberal principle that government should not enforce private morality of this sort. But it has an economic as well as a social dimension. It insists on an economic system in which no citizen has less than an equal share of the community's resources just in order that others may have more of what he lacks. I do not mean that liberalism insists on what is often called "equality of result," that is, that citizens must each have the same wealth at every moment of their lives. A government bent on the latter ideal must constantly redistribute wealth, eliminating whatever inequalities in wealth are produced by market transactions. But this would be to devote *unequal* resources to different lives. Suppose that two people have very different bank accounts, in the middle of their careers, because one decided not to work, or not to work at the most lucrative job he could have found, while the other single-mindedly worked for gain. Or because one was willing to assume especially demanding or responsible work, for example, which the other declined. Or because one took larger risks which might have been disastrous but which were in fact successful, while the other invested conservatively. The principle that people must be treated as equals provides no good reason for redistribution in these circumstances; on the contrary, it provides a good reason *against* it.

For treating people as equals requires that each be permitted to use, for the projects to which he devotes his life, no more than an equal share of the resources available for all, and we cannot compute how much any person has consumed, on balance, without taking into account the resources he has contributed as well as those he has taken from the economy. The choices people make about work and leisure and investment have an impact on the resources of the community as a whole, and this impact must be reflected in the calculation equality demands. If one person chooses work that contributes less to other people's lives than different work he might have chosen, then, although this might well have been the right choice for him, given his personal goals, he has nevertheless added less to the resources available for others, and this must be taken into account in the egalitarian calculation. If one person chooses to invest in a productive enterprise rather than spend his funds at once, and if his investment is successful because it increases the stock of goods or services other people actually want, without coercing anyone, his choice has added more to social resources than the choice of someone who did not invest, and this, too, must be reflected in any calculation of whether he has, on balance, taken more than his share.

This explains, I think, why liberals have in the past been drawn to the idea of a market as a method of allocating resources. An efficient market for investment, labor, and goods works as a kind of auction in which the cost to someone of what he consumes, by way of goods and leisure, and the value of what he adds, through his productive labor or decisions, is fixed by the amount his use of some resource costs others, or his contributions benefit them, in each case measured by their willingness to pay for it. Indeed, if the world were very different from what it is, a liberal could accept the results of an efficient market as *defining* equal shares of community resources. If people start with equal amounts of wealth, and have roughly equal levels of raw skill, then a market allocation would ensure that no one could properly complain that he had less than others, over his whole life. He could have had the same as they if he had made the decisions to consume, save, or work that they did.

But in the real world people do not start their lives on equal terms; some begin with marked advantages of family wealth or of formal and informal education. Others suffer because their race is despised. Luck plays a further and sometimes devastating part in deciding who gains or keeps jobs everyone wants. Quite apart from these plain inequities, people are not equal in raw skill or intelligence or other native capacities; on the contrary, they differ greatly, through no choice of their own, in the various capacities that the market tends to reward. So some people who are perfectly willing, even anxious, to make exactly the choices about work and consumption and savings that other people make end up with fewer resources, and no plausible theory of equality can accept this as fair. This is the defect of the ideal fraudulently called "equality of opportunity": fraudulent because in a market economy people do not have equal opportunity who are less able to produce what others want.

So a liberal cannot, after all, accept the market results as defining equal shares. His theory of economic justice must be complex, because he accepts two principles which are difficult to hold in the administration of a dynamic economy. The first requires that people have, at any point in their lives, different amounts of wealth insofar as the genuine choices they have made have been more or less expensive or beneficial to the community, measured by what other people want for their lives. The market seems indispensable to this principle. The second requires that people not have different amounts of wealth just because they have different inherent capacities to produce what others want, or are differently favored by chance. This means that market allocations must be corrected in order to bring some people closer to the share of resources they would have had but for these various differences of initial advantage, luck, and inherent capacity.

Obviously any practical program claiming to respect both these principles will work imperfectly and will inevitably involve speculation, compromise, and arbitrary lines in the face of ignorance. For it is impossible to discover, even in principle, exactly which aspects of any person's economic position flow from his choices and which from advantages or disadvantages that were not matters of choice; and even if we could make this determination for particular people, one by one, it would be impossible to develop a tax system for the nation as a whole that would leave the first in place and repair only the second. There is therefore no such thing as the perfectly just program of redistribution. We must be content to choose whatever programs we believe bring us closer to the complex and unattainable ideal of equality, all things considered, than the available alternatives, and be ready constantly to reexamine that conclusion when new evidence or new programs are proposed.

Nevertheless, in spite of the complexity of that ideal, it may sometimes be apparent that a society falls far short of any plausible interpretation of its requirements. It is, I think, apparent that the United States falls far short now. A substantial minority of Americans are chronically unemployed or earn wages below any realistic "poverty line" or are handicapped in various ways or burdened with special needs; and most of these people would do the work necessary to earn a decent living if they had the opportunity and capacity. Equality of resources would require more rather than less redistribution than we now offer.

This does not mean, of course, that we should continue past liberal programs, however inefficient these have proved to be, or even that we should insist on "targeted" programs of the sort some liberals have favored—that is, programs that aim to provide a particular opportunity or resource, like education or medicine, to those who need it. Perhaps a more general form of transfer, like a negative income tax, would prove on balance more efficient and fairer, in spite of the difficulties in such schemes. And whatever devices are chosen for bringing distribution closer to equality of resources, some aid undoubtedly goes to those who have avoided rather than sought jobs. This is to be regretted, because it offends one of the two principles that together make up equality of resources. But we come closer to that ideal by tolerating this inequity than by denying aid to the far greater number who would work if they could. If equality of resources were our only goal, therefore, we could hardly justify the present retreat from redistributive welfare programs.

[. . .]

. . . If people are asked to sacrifice for their community, they must be offered some reason why the community which benefits from that sacrifice is their community; there must be some reason why, for example, the unemployed blacks of Detroit should take more interest in either the public virtue or the future generations of Michigan than they do in those of Mali.

We must ask in what circumstances someone with the proper sense of his own independence and equal worth can take pride in a community as being his community, and two conditions, at least, seem necessary to this. He can take pride in its present attractiveness—in the richness of its culture, the justice of its institutions, the imagination of its education—only if his life is one that in some way draws on and contributes to these public virtues. He can identify himself with the future of the community and accept present deprivation as sacrifice rather than tyranny, only if he has some power to help determine the shape of that future, and only if the promised prosperity will provide at least equal benefit to the smaller, more immediate communities for which he feels special responsibilities, for example, his family, his descendants, and, if the society is one that has made this important to him, his race.

These seem minimal conditions, but they are nevertheless exigent. Together they impose serious restraints on any policy that denies any group of citizens, however small or politically negligible, the equal resources that equal concern would otherwise grant them. Of course no feasible program can provide every citizen with a life valuable in his own eyes. But these constraints set a limit to what a government that respects equality may deliberately choose when other choices are available. People must not be condemned, unless this is unavoidable, to lives in which they are effectively denied any active part in the political, economic, and cultural life of the community. So if economic policy contemplates an increase in unemployment, it must also contemplate generous public provision for retraining or public employment. The children of the poor must not be stinted of education or otherwise locked into positions at the bottom of society. Otherwise their parents' loyalty to them acts not as a bridge but as a bar to any identification with the future these parents are meant to cherish.

If this is right, then it suggests an order of priorities which any retrenchment in welfare programs should follow. Programs like food stamps, Aid to Families with Dependent Children, and those using federal funds to make higher education available for the poor are the last programs that should be curtailed, or (what amounts to the same thing) remitted to the states through some "new federalism." If "targeted" programs like these are thought to be too expensive, or too inefficient, then government must show how alternative plans or programs will restore the promise of participation in the future that these programs offered. In any case, cutbacks in the overall level of welfare provided to the poor should be accompanied by efforts to improve the social integration and political participation of blacks and other minorities who suffer most, in order to assure them a more prominent role in the community for which they sacrifice. Reductions in welfare should not be joined to any general retreat from affirmative action and other civil rights programs, or to any effort to repeal or resist improvements in the Voting Rights Act. . . .

. . . If government pushes people below the level at which they can help shape the community and draw value from it for their own lives, or if it holds out a bright future in which their own children are promised only second-class lives, then it forfeits the only premise on which its conduct might be justified. . . .

J. DONALD MOON

The Moral Basis of the Democratic Welfare State

J. Donald Moon is Professor of Government at Wesleyan University. (Source: From Amy Gutmann [ed.], Democracy and the Welfare State. *Most notes have been omitted.*

QUESTIONS FOR REFLECTION

1. What is Hegel's dilemma? What is Hegel's solution? Why, in Moon's opinion, will it fail?
2. How does Moon criticize rights to welfare and theories based on them? Do you find his criticisms persuasive?
3. Why does Moon reject Dworkin's justification for welfare?
4. How does Moon propose solving Hegel's dilemma? Are there problems with his solution?

. . . Even the friends of the welfare state seem perplexed by its complexity, and offer accounts of its fundamental aims that ignore some of its most characteristic practices and institutions. . . . Although welfare rights are an important aspect of the welfare state, accounts centering on them cannot explain why so many social services are provided through some kind of "insurance" scheme that includes identifiable contributions on the part of recipients. On the other hand, it is implausible to view equality as the principal objective of the welfare state, for one of the characteristic features of welfare-state programs is universality of coverage or participation. In most welfare states, unemployment benefits, pensions, education, and medical care are provided to everyone, the prosperous as well as the poor. This significantly limits the redistributive potential of these programs.

What is missing from these accounts, it seems to me, is sufficient attention to the "self-understandings" of the citizens of welfare states—to the ways in which social and political practices appear to participants in them, and the ways in which these practices express ideals and principles that give point and meaning to their lives. In particular, both neglect the value of self-respect and ignore the norms that specify what one has to be and to do to attain self-respect. Other accounts suffer similar weaknesses.

In contrast to approaches that focus on rights or equality, I will argue that we can best begin to understand the democratic welfare state as an attempt to solve a serious moral dilemma that necessarily results from the central role of markets in modern society. Because Hegel was one of the first to perceive and to diagnose this dilemma, I will begin by reviewing his formulation of it, and the failure of his proposed solutions.

The Moral Dilemma of the Market: Hegel's View

In *The Philosophy of Right* (1821), Hegel observed that the organization of economic life through the market appears necessarily to produce great poverty alongside great wealth. This poverty is a threat to the modern state—both materially in that it breeds discontent that can cause instability, and morally in that the institutions of civil society bring about undeserved and unjustifiable suffering. In Hegel's words,

> The poor still have the needs common to civil society, and yet since society has withdrawn from them the natural means of acquisition . . . and broken the bonds of the family . . . , their poverty leaves them more or less deprived of all the advantages of society, of the opportunity of acquiring skill or education of any kind, as well as of the administration of justice, the public health services, and often even of the consolations of religion.

It is important to see that Hegel's dilemma involves a deep, moral contradiction, and not merely a practical problem. The justification for organizing economic life through the market is based upon a conception of the individual as an agent, capable of choice and deliberation, and entitled to certain rights and to be treated with respect. The individual must therefore be independent in the minimal sense that no private person may use the powers of another without the other's consent. More positively, there must be a fairly extensive sphere within which individuals are free to direct their energies and to use their powers to realize purposes they have set for themselves. But this justification of the market is weakened if the normal operation of the market deprives some people—through no fault of their own—of the very means of survival, not to mention the possibility of maintaining their well-being and dignity. The significance of poverty, then, is not just the suffering it involves, though that is obviously important, but the fact that it represents an undeserved exile from society. It is the failure of libertarian arguments to recognize and come to terms with this fact that ultimately destroys their moral viability. There is something deeply and undeniably unjust about a social order that necessarily frustrates fulfillment of the promises it makes.

Unfortunately, as Hegel perceptively notes, the obvious remedy for this suffering—simply redistributing income or wealth to the poor—is not adequate. Hegel argues that since the principles of a market society are freedom and the exchange of equivalents, membership in civil society requires that one support oneself by selling one's labor power, or other assets one owns, in exchange for what one needs. Were the poor to receive support without giving anything in exchange, they would fail to observe the basic principles of civil society. Merely giving them money, therefore, would undermine their status or membership in civil society, and with that their dignity and self-respect.

As Avinieri has pointed out, Hegel never solved the problem he posed. Considering Hegel's rather remarkable ability to find formulas that "reconcile" apparent contradictions, or to find "meaning" in the most arbitrary and pointless practices, it is striking that he left this problem unresolved, offering only a few remarks about the need for the state to step in and regulate the market in such a way as to prevent the problem from getting out of hand. But his suggestions, though they have frequently been acted upon, are hardly adequate. He proposes, for example, that the state should regulate the prices of essential commodities, which would make it possible for the poor to purchase them. Such a policy is viable when temporary shortages occur, perhaps as a result of a war or natural calamity, at least for those states that have reasonably honest and competent administrations and whose citizens display a reasonable level of civic virtue. But it is not a solution for the fundamental dilemma of civil society. The policy of regulating some prices causes distortions in the market that will eventually undermine either the state or the market system, or (perhaps most commonly) both. Either the state will be forced to allocate directly more and more goods and services, thereby replacing the market, or black markets and other forms of evasion will develop, corrupting both the administration and the citizenry.

Hegel also suggested a system of "corporations," consisting of producer organizations in each industry or trade linking the state and civil society. The idea that many of the problems of capitalism can be solved through a system of mixed or quasi-public and private groups has had great appeal. Durkheim's vision of a just capitalist and democratic order is based upon an elaborate system of corporate groups; corporatist policies and practices are pervasive in Western Europe and, to a lesser extent, North America as well. But corporatist structures have not proven adequate to solve the problem of poverty, even when they have been given direct responsibilities for welfare. In Hegel's vision, corporations would maintain funds contributed by their members and would use them to support members in distress. Individuals who needed assistance could turn to their corporation. And they could do so without a loss of dignity because, having contributed to the fund, their receiving its benefits would not be a violation of reciprocity.

But this system would work only if everyone were at least initially a member of some corporation, and if the burdens on any particular producer organization did not grow too large. In a dynamic economy, however—where some industries are in secular decline and where workers move from area to area and industry to industry—these assumptions do not hold, as Hegel himself realized. Even under ideal circumstances, too many people needing help would find (and have found) the system of corporate groups inadequate to meet their needs. Since these needs cannot be met through private or quasi-public organizations, the state must take on the task of relieving the distress occasioned by the operation of the market. But we are still left with the question of how it can do so, consistent with the moral requirements of civil society itself. Is a morally coherent welfare state possible?

Rights as the Moral Basis of the Welfare State: Plant's View

On the face of it, one of the most promising ways to think about the welfare state is to see it as based on an extension of the classical list of human rights to include "social" or "welfare" rights. From this perspective, we can see the welfare state as an essentially internal development of the idea of human rights that is basic to the liberal tradition. Just as Locke asserted that a limited, constitutional state is necessary to protect our rights to life, liberty, health, and possessions, proponents of this view argue that the welfare state is required to guarantee a wider set of rights, including the "social" rights to employment, economic security, health care, and education.

This way of understanding the welfare state has been advocated not only because it provides a convenient link to a well-established tradition of political thought, but also because it is said to solve Hegel's problem. For if one has a right to certain services and benefits, then receiving those benefits should not, according to this view, be demeaning. . . .

. . . But the idea of a right to welfare is not sufficient to account for the moral basis of the welfare state.

The entire approach of analyzing the welfare state simply in terms of a human right to welfare is mistaken. Even if it could be shown that we have such rights, this approach would not solve the problem that Hegel diagnosed, because providing relief to those in need, even when they have a right to it, may nevertheless still cause them to lose status and self-respect. What is demeaning about receiving welfare is in part the invidious distinction that the receipt of welfare itself makes between those who receive it and those who do not. Even if one has a right to receive a benefit, if the need to exercise that right is a sign of failure, it will be stigmatizing to do so.

This is not to say that anyone who receives benefits will necessarily experience a loss of self-esteem. "Self-esteem" is a very broad concept; as used by social-psychologists, it means a "generally favorable or unfavorable, positive or negative, pro or con feeling toward [oneself] as a whole." In this general sense, there are many bases on which one may come to consider oneself "a person of worth," including the favorable appraisals one receives from family and friends, comparisons of self with others, and attainments in areas one considers important. Since we have at least some freedom in selecting those against whom we might compare ourselves, and in selecting those values which we deem important, it is possible for some individuals to have high self-esteem, even if most people in the society hold them in little regard. For example, delinquents or criminals may take pride in qualities and activities which others condemn.

This very general concept of self-esteem is important, and has considerable relevance to an evaluation of the justice or desirability of a social and political order. But because it is so general, and because it can be affected in particular cases by so many idiosyncratic factors, it is necessary to focus on a more specific concept. Although the notion of self-respect is often used synonymously with self-esteem, in this paper I will use it in a narrower sense to refer to one's belief that one lives up to certain standards that define what it is to be a person of worth, a person entitled to respect. It is thus, for most people, a crucial component of self-esteem, but it expresses a specifically moral judgment of the self.

In using the concept of self-respect in this way, I am following Walzer, who has argued that self-respect is dependent upon one's measuring up to a standard. It is a concept that is essentially tied to notions of worth and honor: to have self-respect is to have "proper regard for the dignity of one's person or one's position," where dignity is "the quality of being worthy or honourable." Because self-respect requires that one hold and live up to standards, the concept invokes ideals of excellence and is expressed in the language of duties, rather than the language of rights. Thus, self-respect is an achievement, earned by living in a way that is worthy or honorable, not a good that one can have simply by virtue of being a person. As something to be achieved, self-respect cannot be guaranteed; it is always possible for a person to fail to measure up, and so to lose his or her self-respect. . . .

There are, it goes without saying, many standards or norms to which people must measure up if they are to achieve self-respect. Among these standards in American society is "independence," which requires at least able, working-age men to provide for their own needs and those of their family. That Americans have this expectation is a legacy of their past; it is not by any means a necessary feature of social organization as such. It is greatly affected by other institutions of American society, in particular, the family (and associated gender roles), and by the centrality of markets in economic life. This conception of independence both expresses and reflects social understandings of work, vocation, and other values. And the meaning of this standard changes with the changing context of practices and concepts in which it is embedded.

The expectation of independence is grounded in our understanding of ourselves as morally equal, autonomous agents, whose relationships are governed in part by a norm of reciprocity. In the context of civil society, dependence of one person on another violates the ideal of reciprocity. Often such dependence involves relationships of moral inequality, premised on the subordination of one person to another. But even when subordination is absent, the dependent person receives something without offering anything in return. As Hegel put it, for people to receive their subsistence from the state "directly, not by means of their work, . . . would violate the principle of civil society and the feeling of individual independence and self-respect in its individual members." That is why the need to exercise one's right to welfare is, in American society, a sign of failure. It is certainly true that the way welfare is administered can worsen the stigma associated with receiving it; but as long as people are expected to support themselves, that stigma is inevitable. . . .

It is important not to misunderstand the role of equal respect and equal rights. Equal rights and equal respect have become necessary conditions of self-respect, but they are not sufficient. Self-respect is not a matter of having a certain status or enjoying particular rights. Rather, it requires that one perform certain duties or, better, live up to some ideal. One cannot achieve self-respect simply by having one's rightful claims recognized. Indeed, the opposite may be more nearly true: to be able to assert one's rights depends upon one's having self-respect, that is to say, feeling oneself to be worthy of exercising those rights. And that depends upon one's living up to the standards one holds. To have self-respect, we must be accorded the rights of citizens; to gain self-respect, we must perform the duties of citizens.

This poses a serious dilemma for a polity that aspires to be a welfare state. For if people hold the norm that they should be independent (in the sense of self-supporting), then how can the state provide them with the means of subsistence without violating their self-respect? Walzer describes the welfare state as an effort "to guarantee effective membership" in society, thus helping to make self-respect possible. But if self-respect requires that one satisfy one's own needs, and the needs of one's family, then how can the state meet these needs in a way that will not be degrading to the people for whom it provides benefits?

If the strategy of basing the welfare state on a general theory of human rights to welfare is inadequate, it at least points to an important truth: that the moral basis of the welfare state cannot be charity or altruism on the part of those more fortunate individuals whose taxes pay for its services. Of course, to the extent that people are altruistic, or believe themselves to have a duty of benevolence to advance the well-being of others, they will be motivated to contribute their resources to meet the needs of the disadvantaged. But, as David Miller has argued, the state may be an inappropriate instrumentality for the expression of altruism. State provision is compulsory, and compulsion suggests a form of obligation that is incompatible with the idea of charity. Making charitable donations expresses one's altruistic sentiments, but paying taxes does not.

It is arguable that altruism can be squared with compulsion by viewing the problem of welfare as somehow involving public goods or, perhaps, high transaction costs, for voluntary efforts would then be insufficient to provide an adequate level of welfare provision. But a more serious objection to seeing altruism as the basis of the welfare state is that it is difficult if not impossible to reconcile the self-respect of beneficiaries with the receipt of charity in a democratic society. In a hierarchical society, people who occupy lower-status positions might be able to receive charity from their "betters" without a loss of dignity. Their sense of self-respect depends upon their living up to the demands of their (inferior) station. The acknowledgment of inferiority need not, at least in principle, threaten one's self-respect, so long as there is no expectation of equality. But in a democracy, one may receive something gratuitously only in intimate relationships or relationships that involve a reciprocal exchange of gifts or services.

At best, then, altruism may help to explain the willingness of (some of) the advantaged to support welfare programs, but it cannot be the basis of the welfare state. . . .

Equality as the Moral Basis of the Welfare State: Dworkin's View

. . . This theory requires that we allow (possibly quite significant) inequalities among people based upon their choices regarding leisure, risk, and the unpleasantness of different tasks, but that we eliminate all inequalities based upon differences in genetic luck. To do this Dworkin proposes a progressive income tax coupled with redistribution in the form of transfer payments to those with low incomes. The actual rates of taxation and redistribution would be set by means of a simulated insurance scheme, designed to model the choices people would make if they did not know what their own talents would enable them to earn, and wished to insure against falling below a certain level of income. Although this scheme would not, of course, equalize people's talents, its aim would be "to put [the less talented] in the position they would have been in had the risk of their fate been subjectively equally shared." The less talented would receive transfer payments that would bring their income up to the level that the average member of the society would not wish his or her income to fall below. And everyone would be willing to insure against that possibility by offering some part of his or her expected income as an insurance premium.

This is an ingenious way of interpreting and defending the welfare state, or at least two of its central policies—progressive income taxation and transfer payments to those in need. But it is not an adequate account for several reasons. In the first place, the tax-transfer scheme simply is not a solution to the problem that Dworkin himself poses. Although it would somewhat equalize income differentials due to differences in talent, it would at the same time equalize income differentials due to differences in the willingness to bear risk, ambition, and the unpleasantness of tasks. For when the hypothetical insurance scheme that is to be used to determine the extent of redistribution is set up, the income distribution that is used as a baseline will reflect all these factors, not merely differences in natural aptitude. A progressive income tax may be superior to schemes of flat equalization because it allows some scope for different choices regarding risk, leisure, and the amenities of the working environment, but it fails to achieve the goals Dworkin sets.

A more important shortcoming of this argument, however, is that it misunderstands the point of the progressive tax-transfer policy of the welfare state. Although tax-transfer policies lead to a degree of equalization (essentially as a result of transfers), this is more a means to achieve other goals, particularly dignity and self-respect, than an end in itself. . . . Where Dworkin's argument goes wrong is in equating equality of resources, as he articulates it, with the concept of equality underlying the values of self-respect, equal dignity, and equal worth. . . .

. . . We do not distinguish between the person and his or her circumstances in the way that Dworkin suggests. Indeed, we do not draw a rigid line at all; sometimes we impute characteristics to the person that at other times we impute to the person's circumstances. In some contexts we identify ourselves through our relationships with others, which may extend over significant distances in time and space. But in almost all contexts we understand ourselves as essentially embodied beings. Systematically to assign "features of [one's] body or mind or personality" to one's circumstances, as opposed to one's person, would be for us a kind of madness. If we are to attain self-respect and a sense of equal worth, and if we are to live lives that are relatively free of envy, we must be able to do so in the face of significant differences and even inequalities among us. Ultimately, then, it is the extreme narrowness of Dworkin's conception of the person that causes him to miss essential features of the democratic welfare state.

The Welfare State: Ideals and Institutions

I began this paper by suggesting that the starting point of any attempt to understand the democratic welfare state should be to see it as an attempt to solve what I called "Hegel's dilemma." The welfare state must overcome poverty, which involves a kind of moral exile from society, and which results from the normal operation of the market, but it must do so in a way that is compatible with the self-respect of its beneficiaries. In the preceding two sections I argued that two alternate approaches to the welfare state—one focusing on a human right to welfare, and the other focusing on equality of resources—are inadequate. Both fail to grasp the importance of self-respect in a society where people are expected to provide for themselves, and where citizens demand equality not as disembodied wills, but as full persons whose claim to equality transcends otherwise important differences in their natural aptitudes and capacities. In this section I will show how the welfare state attempts to solve Hegel's dilemma by establishing certain institutions and policies, which generally conform to three "institutional principles" of the welfare state: economic management, the universal provision of services, and social insurance. But before doing that, it is necessary to explicate the ideal of moral equality, or equal citizenship, which is fundamental to the democratic welfare state.

Shortly after World War II, T. H. Marshall argued that the welfare state must be seen as part of, or as the current stage in, a long struggle for equal citizenship. Modern, liberal society is distinctive in part because it is based upon the premise of moral equality, that is, that no person is inherently superior, simply as a person, to any other, and thus entitled to differential rights and privileges. By nature, as Locke put it, "all power and jurisdiction is reciprocal, no one having more than another." Basic human equality requires full membership in the community—or citizenship—for all.

In Marshall's account, equal citizenship can be understood in terms of three sorts of rights: civil and legal rights, political rights, and the "social rights of citizenship." He argues that the achievement of these rights took place in three distinct stages. The first stage was the extension of civil rights to the entire population. This extension was, as Marshall argues, a corollary of the abolition of villeinage, as civil rights are simply the rights of free persons. Needless to say, the effective recognition of these rights for all is still on the political agenda, but the principle of equal civil rights was conceded long ago. The second stage was the extension of political rights. This was part of the struggle for democracy, in particular, the right to vote and to hold office. Although the struggle for political equality continues, the triumph of the principle of equal political rights was in large measure the achievement of the nineteenth and early twentieth centuries.

The achievement of the social rights of citizenship constitutes the third stage in the quest for full citizenship for all. These are the rights that the welfare state seeks to guarantee, although some of them, such as the right to a publicly provided education, preceded the development of the welfare state. That these rights are different from most traditional civil rights and, to a lesser extent, political rights has long been recognized. In particular, they do not give rise to duties on the part of individuals generally, but on the part of political society as a whole. And these duties require the provision of specific services or goods. They cannot be discharged by refraining from interference with a protected sphere of individual action, as can many (though not all) of our civil and political rights.

The basis of these rights is in part, but only in part, the need to make our other rights effective. Without the ability to perform certain activities, and without some basic level of economic security, the classical civil rights such as life, liberty, freedom of conscience, are deprived of at least part of their moral significance in a person's life. I say "at least part of" because it is a mistake to denigrate them by saying they are "merely formal," and to suggest that they are of no use or even "a burden to the vast mass of the exploited and oppressed in both the developed and undeveloped worlds."* These rights are of immense value even for those whose positions in society are relatively disadvantaged. These supposedly "merely formal" rights are essential expressions of the moral equality of persons. To see the speciousness of arguments that discount the value of "formal" equality, one need merely consider justifications of apartheid that point to the superior levels of material well-being enjoyed by blacks in South Africa, as opposed to other African countries.

The other basis for these rights is the recognition of what Marshall calls the "equal social worth" of all members of the society. This is a notion that goes beyond the idea of making civil rights effective by providing the resources necessary to their exercise. In addition, it includes the ideal of enabling everyone to achieve full membership in the community, and to participate in what a particular society has come to regard as valued and worthwhile ways of living. It thus includes a concern with social integration, or social solidarity, with promoting enough commonality in the social experiences and ways of life of different sections of the society so that genuine equality of respect will be possible. Equal social worth is closely tied to the idea of self-respect for, as I argued earlier, equality of respect is a necessary condition for self-respect in a democracy.

The ideal of equal social worth requires that there be a "safety net," a minimum level of resources available to everyone, sufficient to enable them to maintain a place in society. This will involve some equalization of circumstances, as Dworkin argues. But even in principle, even as an ideal, it does not require that the only differences in peoples' material well-being be traceable to different choices made under identical circum-

* Anthony Arblaster, "Liberal Values and Socialist Values," in Ralph Miliband and John Sevile, eds., *The Socialist Register* (London: Merlin Press, 1972), p. 98.

stances—particularly when a person's "circumstances" are defined as including the person's body and natural aptitudes. Rather, this ideal anticipates a society in which the bonds of fellowship and mutual respect are as significant as the inevitable differences and inequalities that will remain. As Tawney put it,

> What is repulsive is not that one man should earn more than others, for where community of environment, and a common education and habit of life, have bred a common tradition of respect and consideration, these details of the counting house are forgotten or ignored. It is that some classes should be excluded from the heritage of civilization which others enjoy, and that the fact of human fellowship, which is ultimate and profound, should be obscured by economic contrasts, which are trivial and superficial. What is important is not that all men should receive the same pecuniary income. It is that the surplus resources of society should be so husbanded and applied that it is a matter of minor significance whether they receive it or not.*

The social rights of citizens and the principle of equal social worth are fundamental to the welfare state. To realize them without undermining self-respect, however, requires that the government manage the economy in an attempt to achieve full employment, ensure the universal provision of certain social services, and establish a program of social insurance to meet a wide range of needs and contingencies. Economic management, universal provision, and social insurance may be thought of as a set of "institutional principles" governing the policies of the welfare state. These principles are expressed differently in different contexts, but in general they work to enable people to exercise the social rights of citizenship in a way that is compatible with maintaining their self-respect. Thus, they enable the welfare state to solve, at least to a significant extent, the dilemma Hegel posed. . . .

. . . Even in the absence of cyclical changes in employment and in economic activity, in a dynamic economy jobs will continually disappear. Even if new ones are promptly created, the period of transition will involve hardships for workers and their families. Many will suffer from illness or disabilities that impair their capacity for work, and everyone faces the need to make provision for retirement and old age. There are also certain needs that must be satisfied if one is to be able to participate in the life of the community. An obvious need is education. Although education is, from a narrowly economic viewpoint, a form of capital investment whose returns accrue mainly to the person receiving it, it is so essential to citizenship that it is never entirely left to be provided by the market.

In responding to these contingencies and needs, the welfare state is guided by the principles of universal provision and social insurance. In some areas—education is the obvious example—public provision of a (nearly) universally consumed service enables everyone to receive the service without stigma. Consuming a universally provided service, like enjoying a universally accorded right, does not enable a person to achieve self-respect, since these activities do not involve a performance or an achievement. At the same time, when a need can be met through some form of universal provision, such programs do not threaten the individual's self-respect.

In other areas, where it is necessary to respond to differential needs, the establishment of social insurance enables people to receive differential benefits without violating the idea of reciprocity, which is fundamental to their sense of themselves as moral equals. Two obvious examples are social security and unemployment compensation. Both of these systems are set up as insurance schemes, so that those who collect benefits under them see themselves as (and, to a large extent, are in fact) receiving something to which they have a right just because they have contributed their fair share to provision of those benefits.

The observance of these principles in providing public services may be older than the welfare state itself. What is distinctive about the welfare state is the generalization of services provided on the basis of these principles to cover a wide range of needs.

* R. H. Tawney, *Equality* (New York: Barnes and Noble, 1964), p. 113.

And that generalization is essential if citizens are to protect themselves against the contingencies of illness, disability, old age, and unemployment in a way that enables them to maintain their membership in society and their self-respect.

Economic management, the universal provision of certain services, and social insurance have enabled us to make considerable progress in overcoming the moral breach in civil society that Hegel pointed to. Many of the risks that caused some to lose their effective membership in society have been significantly socialized and their effects ameliorated —particularly the risks of adult unemployment, disability, and old age. Educational opportunities have been significantly broadened, and public education continues to represent a major area of shared social experience for Americans. . . .

JOHN HOSPERS

What Libertarianism Is

John Hospers is Professor Emeritus of Philosophy at the University of Southern California. He ran for president on the Libertarian Party ticket in 1972. (Source: Reprinted from Tibor R. Machan [ed.], The Libertarian Alternative: Essays in Social and Political Philosophy, *Nelson-Hall, 1974.*

QUESTIONS FOR REFLECTION

1. How does Hospers define libertarianism?
2. What conception of rights emerges from Hospers's analysis?
3. What, according to Hospers, is the proper function of government? How does his view compare to Mill's? To Locke's?
4. How does Hospers respond to the charge that libertarianism fails to respond to real human needs? Do you find his answer convincing?

The political philosophy that is called libertarianism (from the Latin *libertas,* liberty) is the doctrine that every person is the owner of his own life, and that no one is the owner of anyone else's life; and that consequently every human being has the right to act in accordance with his own choices, unless those actions infringe on the equal liberty of other human beings to act in accordance with *their* choices.

There are several other ways of stating the same libertarian thesis:

1. *No one is anyone else's master, and no one is anyone else's slave.* Since I am the one to decide how my life is to be conducted, just as you decide about yours, I have no right (even if I had the power) to make you my slave and be your master, nor have you the right to become the master by enslaving me. Slavery is *forced* servitude, and since no one owns the life of anyone else, no one has the right to enslave another. Political theories past and present have traditionally been concerned with who should be the master (usually the king, the dictator, or government bureaucracy) and who should be the slaves, and what the extent of the slavery should be. Libertarianism holds that no one has the right to use force to enslave the life of another, or any portion or aspect of that life.

2. *Other men's lives are not yours to dispose of.* I enjoy seeing operas; but operas are expensive to produce. Opera-lovers often say, "The state (or the city, etc.) should subsidize opera, so that we can all see it. Also it would be for people's betterment, cultural benefit, etc." But what they are advocating is nothing more or less than legalized plunder. They can't pay for the productions themselves, and yet they want to see opera, which involves a large number of people and their labor; so what they are saying in effect is, "Get the money through legalized force. Take a little bit more out of every worker's paycheck every week to pay for the operas we want to see." But I have no right to take by force from the workers' pockets to pay for what I want.

Perhaps it would be better if he *did* go to see opera—then I should try to convince him to go voluntarily. But to take the money from him forcibly, because in my opinion it would be good for *him,* is still seizure of his earnings, which is plunder.

Besides, if I have the right to force him to help pay for my pet projects, hasn't he equally the right to force me to help pay for his? Perhaps he in turn wants the government to subsidize rock-and-roll, or his new car, or a house in the country? If I have the right to milk him, why hasn't he the right to milk me? If I can be a moral cannibal, why can't he too?

We should beware of the inventors of utopias. They would remake the world according to their vision—with the lives and fruits of the labor of *other* human beings. Is it someone's utopian vision that others should build pyramids to beautify the landscape? Very well, then other men should provide the labor; and if he is in a position of political power, and he can't get men to do it voluntarily, then he must *compel* them to "cooperate"—i.e. he must enslave them.

A hundred men might gain great pleasure from beating up or killing just one insignificant human being; but other men's lives are not theirs to dispose of. "In order to achieve the worthy goals of the next five-year-plan, we must forcibly collectivize the peasants . . . "; but other men's lives are not theirs to dispose of. Do you want to occupy, rent-free, the mansion that another man has worked for twenty years to buy? But other men's lives are not yours to dispose of. Do you want operas so badly that everyone is forced to work harder to pay for their subsidization through taxes? But other men's lives are not yours to dispose of. Do you want to have free medical care at the expense of other people, whether they wish to provide it or not? But this would require them to work longer for you whether they want to or not, and other men's lives are not yours to dispose of.

> The freedom to engage in any type of enterprise, to produce, to own and control property, to buy and sell on the free market, is derived from the rights to life, liberty, and property . . . which are stated in the Declaration of Independence . . . [but] when a government guarantees a "right" to an education or parity on farm products or a guaranteed annual income, it is staking a claim on the property of one group of citizens for the sake of another group. In short, it is violating one of the fundamental rights it was instituted to protect.*

3. *No human being should be a nonvoluntary mortgage on the life of another.* I cannot claim your life, your work, or the products of your efforts as mine. The fruit of one man's labor should not be fair game for every freeloader who comes along and demands it as his own. The orchard that has been carefully grown, nurtured, and harvested by its owner should not be ripe for the plucking for any bypasser who has a yen for the ripe fruit. The wealth that some men have produced should not be fair game for looting by government, to be used for whatever purposes its representatives determine, no matter what their motives in so doing may be. The theft of your money by a robber is not justified by the fact that he used it to help his injured mother.

It will already be evident that libertarian doctrine is embedded in a view of the rights of man. Each human being has the right to live his life as he chooses, compatibly with the equal right of all other human beings to live their lives as they choose.

All man's rights are implicit in the above statement. Each man has the right to life: any attempt by others to take it away from him, or even to injure him, violates this right, through the use of coercion against him. Each man has the right to liberty: to conduct his life in accordance with the alternatives open to him without coercive action by others. And every man has the right to property: to work to sustain his life (and the lives of whichever others he chooses to sustain, such as his family) and to retain the fruits of his labor.

People often defend the rights of life and liberty

* William W. Bayes, "What Is Property?" *The Freeman*, July 1970, p. 348.

but denigrate property rights, and yet the right to property is as basic as the other two; indeed, without property rights no other rights are possible. Depriving you of property is depriving you of the means by which you live.

> . . . All that which an individual possesses by right (including his life and property) are morally his to use, dispose of and even destroy, as he sees fit. If I own my life, then it follows that I am free to associate with whom I please and not to associate with whom I please. If I own my knowledge and services, it follows that I may ask any compensation I wish for providing them for another, or I may abstain from providing them at all, if I so choose. If I own my house, it follows that I may decorate it as I please and live in it with whom I please. If I control my own business, it follows that I may charge what I please for my products or services, hire whom I please and not hire whom I please. All that which I own in fact, I may dispose of as I choose to in reality. For anyone to attempt to limit my freedom to do so is to violate my rights.
>
> Where do my rights end? Where yours begin. I may do anything I wish with my own life, liberty and property without your consent; but I may do nothing with your life, liberty and property without your consent. If we recognize the principle of man's rights, it follows that the individual is sovereign of the domain of his own life and property, and is sovereign of no other domain. To attempt to interfere forcibly with another's use, disposal or destruction of his own property is to initiate force against him and to violate his rights.

I have no right to decide how *you* should spend your time or your money. I can make that decision for myself, but not for you, my neighbor. I may deplore your choice of life-style, and I may talk with you about it provided you are willing to listen to me. But I have no right to use force to change it. Nor have I the right to decide how you should spend the money you have earned. I may appeal to you to give it to the Red Cross, and you may prefer to go to prizefights. But that is your decision, and however much I may chafe about it I do not have the right to interfere forcibly with it, for example by robbing you in order to use the money in accordance with *my* choices. (If I have the right to rob you, have you also the right to rob me?)

When I claim a right, I carve out a niche, as it were, in my life, saying in effect, "This activity I must be able to perform without interference from others. For you and everyone else, this is off limits." And so I put up a "no trespassing" sign, which marks off the area of my right. Each individual's right is his "no trespassing" sign in relation to me and others. I may not encroach upon his domain any more than he upon mine, without my consent. Every right entails a duty, true—but the duty is only that of *forbearance*—that is, of *refraining* from violating the other person's right. If you have a right to life, I have no right to take your life; if you have a right to the products of your labor (property), I have no right to take it from you without your consent. The non-violation of these rights will not guarantee you protection against natural catastrophes such as floods and earthquakes, but it will protect you against the aggressive activities *of other men*. And rights, after all, have to do with one's relations to other human beings, not with one's relations to physical nature.

Nor were these rights created by government; governments—some governments, obviously not all—*recognize* and *protect* the rights that individuals already have. Governments regularly forbid homicide and theft; and, at a more advanced stage, protect individuals against such things as libel and breach of contract. . . .

Government is the most dangerous institution known to man. Throughout history it has violated the rights of men more than any individual or group of individuals could do: it has killed people, enslaved them, sent them to forced labor and concentration camps, and regularly robbed and pillaged them of the fruits of their expended labor. Unlike individual criminals, government has the power to arrest and try; unlike individual criminals, it can surround and encompass a person totally, dominating every aspect of one's life, so that one has no recourse from it but to leave the country (and in totalitarian nations even that is prohibited). Government throughout history has a much sorrier record than any individual, even that of a ruthless mass murderer. The signs we see on bumper stickers are chillingly accurate: "Beware: the Government is Armed and Dangerous."

The only proper role of government, according to libertarians, is that of the protector of the citizen against aggression by other individuals. The government, of course, should never initiate aggression; its proper role is as the embodiment of the *retaliatory* use of force against anyone who initiates its use.

If each individual had constantly to defend himself against possible aggressors, he would have to spend a considerable portion of his life in target practice, karate exercises, and other means of self-defenses, and even so he would probably be helpless against groups of individuals who might try to kill, maim, or rob him. He would have little time for cultivating those qualities which are essential to civilized life, nor would improvements in science, medicine, and the arts be likely to occur. The function of government is to take this responsibility off his shoulders: the government undertakes to defend him against aggressors and to punish them if they attack him. When the government is effective in doing this, it enables the citizen to go about his business unmolested and without constant fear for his life. To do this, of course, government must have physical power—the police, to protect the citizen from aggression within its borders, and the armed forces, to protect him from aggressors outside. Beyond that, the government should not intrude upon his life, either to run his business, or adjust his daily activities, or prescribe his personal moral code.

Government, then, undertakes to be the individual's protector; but historically governments have gone far beyond this function. Since they already have the physical power, they have not hesitated to use it for purposes far beyond that which was entrusted to them in the first place. Undertaking initially to protect its citizens against aggression, it has often itself become an aggressor—a far greater aggressor, indeed, than the criminals against whom it was supposed to protect its citizens. Governments have done what no private citizens can do: arrest and imprison individuals without a trial and send them to slave labor camps. Government must have power in order to be effective—and yet the very means by which alone it can be effective make it vulnerable to the abuse of power, leading to managing the lives of individuals and even inflicting terror upon them.

What then should be the function of government? In a word, the *protection of human rights.*

1. *The right to life:* libertarians support all such legislation as will protect human beings against the use of force by others, for example, laws against killing, attempted killing, maiming, beating, and all kinds of physical violence.

2. *The right to liberty:* there should be no laws compromising in any way freedom of speech, of the press, and of peaceable assembly. There should be no censorship of ideas, books, films, or of anything else by government.

3. *The right to property:* libertarians support legislation that protects the property rights of individuals against confiscation, nationalization, eminent domain, robbery, trespass, fraud and misrepresentation, patent and copyright, libel and slander.

Someone has violently assaulted you. Should he be legally liable? Of course. He has violated one of your rights. He has knowingly injured you, and since he has initiated aggression against you he should be made to expiate.

Someone has negligently left his bicycle on the sidewalk where you trip over it in the dark and injure yourself. He didn't do it intentionally; he didn't mean you any harm. Should he be legally liable? Of course; he has, however unwittingly, injured you, and since the injury is caused by him and you are the victim, he should pay.

Someone across the street is unemployed. Should you be taxed extra to pay for his expenses? Not at all. You have not injured him, you are not responsible for the fact that he is unemployed (unless you are a senator or bureaucrat who agitated for further curtailing of business, which legislation passed, with the result that your neighbor was laid off by the curtailed business). You may voluntarily wish to help him out, or better still, try to get him a job to put him on his feet again; but since you have initiated no aggressive act against him, and neither purposely nor accidentally injured him in any way, you should not be legally penalized for the fact of his unemployment. (Actually, it is just such penalties that increase unemployment.)

One man, A, works hard for years and finally earns a high salary as a professional man. A second man, B, prefers not to work at all, and to spend wastefully what money he has (through inheritance), so that after a year or two he has nothing left. At the end of this time he has a long siege of illness and lots of medical bills to pay. He demands that the bills be paid by the government—that is, by the taxpayers of the land, including Mr. A.

But of course B has no such right. He chose to lead his life in a certain way—that was his voluntary decision. One consequence of that choice is that he must depend on charity in case of later need. Mr. A chose not to live that way. (And if everyone lived like Mr. B, on whom would he depend in case of later need?) Each has a right to live in the way he pleases, but each must live with the consequences of his own decision (which, as always, fall primarily on himself). He cannot, in time of need, claim A's beneficence as his right. . . .

Laws may be classified into three types: (1) laws protecting individuals against themselves, such as laws against fornication and other sexual behavior, alcohol, and drugs; (2) laws protecting individuals against aggressions by other individuals, such as laws against murder, robbery, and fraud; (3) laws requiring people to help one another; for example, all laws which rob Peter to pay Paul, such as welfare.

Libertarians reject the first class of laws totally. Behavior which harms no one else is strictly the individual's own affair. Thus, there should be no laws against becoming intoxicated, since whether or not to become intoxicated is the individual's own decision; but there should be laws against driving while intoxicated, since the drunken driver is a threat to every other motorist on the highway (drunken driving falls into type 2). Similarly, there should be no laws against drugs (except the prohibition of sale of drugs to minors) as long as the taking of these drugs poses no threat to anyone else. Drug addiction is a psychological problem to which no present solution exists. Most of the social harm caused by addicts, other than to themselves, is the result of thefts which they perform in order to continue their habit—and then the *legal* crime is the theft, not the addiction. The actual cost of heroin is about ten cents a shot; if it were legalized, the enormous traffic in illegal sale and purchase of it would stop, as well as the accompanying proselytization to get new addicts (to make more money for the pusher) and the thefts performed by addicts who often require eighty dollars a day just to keep up the habit. Addiction would not stop, but the crimes would: it is estimated that 75 percent of the burglaries in New York City today are performed by addicts, and all these crimes could be wiped out at one stroke through the legalization of drugs. (Only when the taking of drugs could be shown to constitute a threat to *others*, should it be prohibited by law. It is only laws protecting people against *themselves* that libertarians oppose.)

Laws should be limited to the second class only: aggression by individuals against other individuals. These are laws whose function is to protect human beings against encroachment by others; and this, as we have seen, is (according to libertarianism) the sole function of government.

Libertarians also reject the third class of laws totally: no one should be forced by law to help others, not even to tell them the time of day if requested, and certainly not to give them a portion of one's weekly paycheck. Governments, in the guise of humanitarianism, have given to some by taking from others (charging a "handling fee" in the process, which, because of the government's waste and inefficiency, sometimes is several hundred percent). And in so doing they have decreased incentive, violated the rights of individuals, and lowered the standard of living of almost everyone.

All such laws constitute what libertarians call *moral cannibalism*. A cannibal in the physical sense is a person who lives off the flesh of other human beings. A *moral* cannibal is one who believes he has a right to live off the "spirit" of other human beings—who believes that he has a moral claim on the productive capacity, time, and effort expended by others.

It has become fashionable to claim virtually everything that one needs or desires as one's *right*. Thus, many people claim that they have a right to a job, the right to free medical care, to free food and clothing, to a decent home, and so on. Now if one asks, apart from any specific context, whether it would be desirable if everyone had these things, one might well say yes. But there is a gimmick attached to each of them: *At whose expense?* Jobs, medical care, education, and so on, don't grow on trees. These are goods and services *produced only by men*. Who, then, is to provide them, and under what conditions?

If you have a right to a job, who is to supply it? Must an employer supply it even if he doesn't want to hire you? What if you are unemployable, or incurably lazy? (If you say "the government must supply it," does that mean that a job must be created for you which no employer needs done, and that you must be kept in it regardless of how much or little you work?) If the employer is forced to supply it at his expense even if he doesn't need you, then isn't *he* being enslaved to that extent? What ever happened to *his* right to conduct his life and his affairs in accordance with his choices?

If you have a right to free medical care, then, since medical care doesn't exist in nature as wild apples do, some people will have to supply it to you for free: that is, they will have to spend their time and money and energy taking care of you whether they want to or not. What ever happened to *their* right to conduct their lives as they see fit? Or do you have a right to violate theirs? Can there be a right to violate rights?

All those who demand this or that as a "free service" are consciously or unconsciously evading the fact that there is in reality no such thing as free services. All man-made goods and services are the result of human expenditure of time and effort. There is no such thing as "something for nothing" in this world. If you demand something free, you are demanding that other men give their time and effort to you without compensation. If they voluntarily choose to do this, there is no problem; but if you demand that they be *forced* to do it, you are interfering with their right not to do it if they so choose. "Swimming in this pool ought to be free!" says the indignant passerby. What he means is that others should build a pool, others should provide the materials, and still others should run it and keep it in functioning order, so that *he* can use it without fee. But what right has he to the expenditure of *their* time and effort? To expect something "for free" is to expect it *to be paid for by others* whether they choose to or not.

Many questions, particularly about economic matters, will be generated by the libertarian account of human rights and the role of government. Should government have no role in assisting the needy, in providing social security, in legislating minimum wages, in fixing prices and putting a ceiling on rents, in curbing monopolies, in erecting tariffs, in guaranteeing jobs, in managing the money supply? To these and all similar questions the libertarian answers with an unequivocal no.

"But then you'd let people go hungry!" comes the rejoinder. This, the libertarian insists, is precisely what would not happen; with the restrictions removed, the economy would flourish as never before. With the controls taken off business, existing enterprises would expand and new ones would spring into existence satisfying more and more consumer needs; millions more people would be gainfully employed instead of subsisting on welfare, and all kinds of research and production, released from the stranglehold of government, would proliferate, fulfilling man's needs and desires as never before. It has always been so whenever government has permitted men to be free traders on a free market. . . .

CHARLES MURRAY

from *Losing Ground: American Social Policy, 1950–1980*

Charles Murray is Bradley Fellow at the Manhattan Institute for Policy Research. (Source: From Losing Ground: American Social Policy, 1950–1980 *by Charles Murray. Copyright © 1984 by Charles Murray. Reprinted by permission of Basic Books, a division of HarperCollins Publishers Inc.)*

QUESTIONS FOR REFLECTION

1. Explain Murray's three laws.
2. Are you convinced that Murray's laws are true? Why or why not?
3. What benefits would accrue, according to Murray, if welfare programs were eliminated altogether?
4. Who might be harmed by eliminating welfare programs, in Murray's view? In your view?

[CHAPTER 16 / THE CONSTRAINTS ON HELPING]

Laws of Social Programs

. . . Let me suggest some characteristics . . . that occur so widely and for such embedded reasons that they suggest laws. That is, no matter how ingenious the design of a social transfer program may be, we cannot—in a free society—design programs that escape their influence. . . .

#1. The Law of Imperfect Selection. Any objective rule that defines eligibility for a social transfer program will irrationally exclude some persons.

It can always be demonstrated that some persons who are excluded from the Food Stamps program are in greater need than some persons who receive Food Stamps. It can always be demonstrated that someone who is technically ineligible for Medicaid really "ought" to be receiving it, given the intent of the legislation.

These inequities, which are observed everywhere, are not the fault of inept writers of eligibility rules, but an inescapable outcome of the task of rule-writing. Eligibility rules must convert the concept of "true need" into objectified elements. The rules constructed from these bits and pieces are necessarily subject to what Herbert Costner has called "epistemic error"—the inevitable gap between quantified measures and the concept they are intended to capture. We have no way of defining "truly needy" precisely—not those who truly need to stop smoking, nor those truly in need of college scholarships or subsidized loans or disability insurance. Any criterion we specify will inevitably include a range of people, some of whom are unequivocally the people we intended to help, others of whom are less so, and still others of whom meet the letter of the eligibility requirement but are much less needy than some persons who do not.

Social welfare policy in earlier times tended to deal with this problem by erring in the direction of exclusion—better to deny help to some truly needy persons than to let a few slackers slip through. Such attitudes depended, however, on the assumption that the greater good was being served. Moral precepts had to be upheld. Whenever a person was inappropriately given help, it was bad for the recipient (undermining his character) and a bad example to the community at large.

When that assumption is weakened or dispensed with altogether, it follows naturally that the Law of Imperfect Selection leads to programs with constantly broadening target populations. If persons are not to blame for their plight, no real harm is done by giving them help they do not fully "need." No moral cost is incurred by permitting some undeserving into the program. A moral cost *is* incurred by excluding a deserving person. No one has a scalpel sharp enough to excise only the undeserving. Therefore it is not just a matter of political expedience to add a new layer to the eligible population rather than to subtract one (though that is often a factor in the actual decision-making process). It is also the morally correct thing to do, given the premises of the argument.

> **#2. The Law of Unintended Rewards.** Any social transfer increases the net value of being in the condition that prompted the transfer.

A deficiency is observed—too little money, too little food, too little academic achievement—and a social transfer program tries to fill the gap—with a welfare payment, Food Stamps, a compensatory education program. An unwanted behavior is observed—drug addiction, crime, unemployability—and the program tries to change that behavior to some other, better behavior—through a drug rehabilitation program, psychotherapy, vocational training. In each case, the program, however unintentionally, *must* be constructed in such a way that it increases the net value of being in the condition that it seeks to change—either by increasing the rewards or by reducing the penalties.

For some people in some circumstances, it is absurd to think in terms of "net value," because they so clearly have no choice at all about the fix they are in or because the net value is still less desirable than virtually any alternative. Paraplegics receiving Medicaid cannot easily be seen as "rewarded" for becoming paraplegics by the existence of free medical care. Poor children in Head Start cannot be seen as rewarded for being poor. Persons who are in the unwanted condition *completely involuntarily* are not affected by the existence of the reward.

But the number of such pure examples is very small. Let us return to the case of the middle-aged worker who loses his job, wants desperately to work, but can find nothing. He receives Unemployment Insurance, hating every penny of it. He would seem to be "completely involuntarily" in his situation and his search for a job unaffected by the existence of Unemployment Insurance. In fact, however, his behavior (unless he is peculiarly irrational) *is* affected by the existence of the Unemployment Insurance. For example, the cushion provided by Unemployment Insurance may lead him to refuse to take a job that requires him to move to another town, whereas he would take the job and uproot his home if he were more desperate. Most people (including me) are glad that his behavior is so affected, that he does not have to leave the home and friends of a lifetime, that he can wait for a job opening nearby. But he is not "completely involuntarily" unemployed in such a case, and the reason he is not is that the Unemployment Insurance has made the condition of unemployment more tolerable.

Our paraplegic anchors one end of the continuum labeled "Degree of Voluntarism in the Conditions that Social Policy Seeks to Change or Make Less Painful," and our unemployed worker is only slightly to one side of him—but he is to one side, not in the same place. The apparent unattractiveness of most of the conditions that social policy seeks to change must not obscure the continuum involved. No one chooses to be a paraplegic, and perhaps no one chooses to be a heroin addict. But the distinction remains: very few heroin addicts developed their addiction by being tied down and forcibly injected with heroin. They may not have chosen to become addicts, but they *did* choose initially to take heroin.

Let us consider the implications in terms of the archetypical social program for helping the chronic unemployed escape their condition, the job-training program.

Imagine that a program is begun that has the most basic and benign inducement of all, the chance to learn a marketable skill. It is open to everybody. By opening it to all, we have circumvented (for the time being) the Law of Unintended Rewards. All may obtain the training, no matter what their job history, so no unintended reward is being given for the condition of chronic unemployment.

On assessing the results, we observe that the ones who enter the program, stick with it, and learn a skill include very few of the hardcore unemployed whom we most wanted to help. The typical "success" stories from our training program are persons with a history of steady employment who wanted to upgrade their earning power. This is admirable. But what about the hardcore unemployed? A considerable number entered the program, but almost all of them dropped out or failed to get jobs once they left. Only a small proportion used the training opportunity as we had hoped. The problem of the hardcore unemployed remains essentially unchanged.

We may continue to circumvent the Law of Unintended Rewards. All we need do is continue the job-training program unchanged. It will still be there, still available to all who want to enroll, but we will do nothing to entice participation. Our theory (should we adopt this stance) is that, as time goes on, we will continue to help at least a few of the hardcore unemployed who are in effect skimmed from the top of the pool. We may even hope that the number skimmed from the top will be larger than the number who enter the pool, so that, given enough time, the population of hardcore unemployed will diminish. But this strategy is a gradualist one and relies on the assumption that other conditions in society are not creating more hardcore unemployed than the program is skimming off.

The alternative is to do something to get more of the hardcore unemployed into the program, and to improve the content so that more of them profit from the training. And once this alternative is taken, the program planner is caught in the trap of unintended rewards. Because we cannot "draft" people into the program or otherwise coerce their participation, our only alternative is to make it more attractive by changing the rules a bit.

Suppose, for example, we find that the reason many did not profit from the earlier program was that they got fired from (or quit) their new jobs within a few days of getting them, and that the reason they did so had to do with the job-readiness problem. The ex-trainee was late getting to work, the boss complained, the ex-trainee reacted angrily and was fired. We observe this to be a common pattern. We know the problem is not that the ex-trainee is lazy or unmotivated, but that he has never been socialized into the discipline of the workplace. He needs more time, more help, more patience than other workers until he develops the needed work habits. Suppose that we try to compensate—for example, by placing our trainees with employers who are being subsidized to hire such persons. The employer accepts lower productivity and other problems in return for a payment to do so (such plans have been tried frequently, with mixed results). Given identical work at identical pay, the ex-trainee is being rewarded for his "credential" of hardcore unemployment. He can get away with behavior that an ordinary worker cannot get away with.

May we still assume that the program is making progress in preparing its trainees for the real-world marketplace? Will the hardcore unemployed modify their unreliable behavior? What will be the effect on morale and self-esteem among those trainees who were succeeding in the program before the change of rules? It is tempting to conclude that the program has already ceased to function effectively for anyone anymore, that the change in rules has done more harm than good. But my proposition is for the moment a more restricted one: The reward for unproductive behavior (both past and present) now exists.

What of the case of a drug addict who is chronically unemployed because (let us assume) of the addiction? It might seem that the unintended reward in such a case is innocuous; it consists of measures to relieve the addict of his addiction, measures for which the nonaddict will have no need or use. If we were dealing with an involuntary disability—our paraplegic again—the argument would be valid. But in the case of drug addiction (or any other behavior that has its rewards), a painless cure generally increases the attractiveness of the behavior. Imagine, for example, a pill that instantly and painlessly relieved dependence on heroin, and the subsequent effects on heroin use.

Thus we are faced with the problem we observed in the thought experiment. The program that seeks to change behavior must offer an inducement that unavoidably either adds to the attraction of, or reduces the penalties of engaging in, the behavior in question. The best-known example in real life is the thirty-and-a-third rule for AFDC recipients. It becomes more advantageous financially to hold a job than not to hold a job (the intended inducement for AFDC recipients to work), but it also becomes more advantageous to be on AFDC (the unintended reward to nonrecipients).

We are now ready to tackle the question of when a social program can reasonably be expected to accomplish net good and when it can reasonably be expected to produce net harm. Again let us think in terms of a continuum. All social programs, I have argued, provide an unintended reward for being in the condition that the program is trying to change or make more tolerable. But some of these unintended rewards are so small that they are of little practical importance. Why then can we not simply bring a bit of care to the design of such programs, making sure that the unintended reward is *always* small? The reason we are not free to do so lies in the third law of social programs:

> **#3. The Law of Net Harm.** The less likely it is that the unwanted behavior will change voluntarily, the more likely it is that a program to induce change will cause net harm.

A social program that seeks to change behavior must do two things. It must induce participation by the persons who are to benefit, as described under the Law of Unintended Rewards. Then it must actually produce the desired change in behavior. It must succeed, and success depends crucially on one factor above all others: The price that the participant is willing to pay.

The more that the individual is willing to accept whatever needs to be done in order to achieve the desired state of affairs, the broader the discretion of the program designers. Thus, expensive health resorts can withhold food from their guests, hospitals can demand that their interns work inhuman schedules, and elite volunteer units in the armed forces can ask their trainees to take risks in training exercises that seem (to the rest of us) suicidal. Such programs need offer no inducement at all except the "thing in itself" that is the *raison d'être* of the program—a shapelier body, a career as a physician, membership in the elite military unit. Similarly, the drug addict who is prepared to sign over to a program a great of deal of control over his own behavior may very well be successful—witness the sometimes impressive success rates of private treatment clinics.

The smaller the price that the participant is willing to pay, the greater the constraints on program design. It makes no difference to an official running a training program for the hardcore unemployed that (for example) the Marine Corps can install exemplary work habits in recruits who come to the Corps no more "job-ready" than the recruits to the job-training program. If the training program tried for one day to use the techniques that the Marine Corps uses, it would lose its participants. Boot camp was not part of the bargain the job trainees struck with the government when they signed on. Instead, the training program must not only induce persons to join the program (which may be fairly easy). It must also induce them to stay in the program, induce them to cooperate with its curriculum, and induce them, finally, to adopt major changes in outlook, habits, and assumptions. The program content must be almost entirely carrot.

There is nothing morally reprehensible in approaches that are constrained to use only positive inducements. The objections are practical.

First, it is guaranteed that success rates will be very low. The technology of changing human behavior depends heavily on the use of negative reinforcement in conjunction with positive reinforcement. The more deeply engrained the behavior to be changed and the more attractions it holds for the person whose behavior is involved, the more important it is that the program have both a full tool kit available to it *and* the participant's willingness to go along with whatever is required. The Marine Corps has both these assets. Social programs to deal with the hardcore unemployed, teenaged mothers, delinquents, and addicts seldom do.

Second, as inducements become large—as they must, if the program is dealing with the most intractable problems—the more attractive they become to people who were not in need of help in the first place. We do not yet know how large they must finally become. We do know from experience, however, that quite generous experimental programs have provided extensive counseling, training, guaranteed jobs, and other supports—and failed. We can only guess at what would be enough—perhaps a matter of years of full-time residential training, followed by guaranteed jobs at double or triple the minimum wage; we do not know. Whatever they are, however, consider their effects on the people not in the program. At this point, it appears that any program that would succeed in helping large numbers of the hardcore unemployed will make hardcore unemployment a highly desirable state to be in.

The conditions that combine to produce net harm are somewhat different in the theoretical and the practical cases, but they come to the same thing. Theoretically, any program that mounts an intervention with sufficient rewards to sustain participation and an effective result will generate so much of the unwanted behavior (in order to become eligible for the program's rewards) that the net effect will be to increase the incidence of the unwanted behavior. In practice, the programs that deal with the most intractable behavior problems have included a package of rewards large enough to induce participation, but not large enough to produce the desired result.

My conclusion is that social programs in a democratic society tend to produce net harm in dealing with the most difficult problems. They will inherently tend to have enough of an inducement to produce bad behavior and not enough of a solution to stimulate good behavior; and the more difficult the problem, the more likely it is that this relationship will prevail. The lesson is not that we can do no good at all, but that we must pick our shots.

[CHAPTER 17 / CHOOSING A FUTURE]

A Proposal for Public Welfare

I begin with the proposition that it is within our resources to do enormous good for some people quickly. We have available to us a program that would convert a large proportion of the younger generation of hardcore unemployed into steady workers making a living wage. The same program would drastically reduce births to single teenage girls. It would reverse the trendline in the breakup of poor families. It would measurably increase the upward socioeconomic mobility of poor families. These improvements would affect some millions of persons.

All these are results that have eluded the efforts of the social programs installed since 1965, yet, from everything we know, there is no real question about whether they would occur under the program I propose. A wide variety of persuasive evidence from our own culture and around the world, from experimental data and longitudinal studies, from theory and practice, suggests that the program would achieve such results.

The proposed program, our final and most ambitious thought experiment, consists of scrapping the entire federal welfare and income-support structure for working-aged persons, including AFDC, Medicaid, Food Stamps, Unemployment Insurance, Worker's Compensation, subsidized housing, disability insurance, and the rest. It would leave the working-aged person with no recourse whatsoever except the job market, family members, friends, and public or private locally funded services. It is the Alexandrian solution: cut the knot, for there is no way to untie it.

It is difficult to examine such a proposal dispassionately. Those who dislike paying for welfare are for it without thinking. Others reflexively imagine bread lines and people starving in the streets. But as a means of gaining fresh perspective on the problem of effective reform, let us consider what this hypothetical society might look like.

A large majority of the population is unaffected. A surprising number of the huge American middle and working classes go from birth to grave without using any social welfare benefits until they receive their first Social Security check. Another portion of the population is technically affected, but the change in income is so small or so sporadic that it makes no difference in quality of life. A third group comprises persons who have to make new arrangements and behave in different ways. Sons and daughters who fail to find work continue to live with their parents or relatives or friends. Teenaged mothers have to rely on support from their parents or the father of the child and perhaps work as well. People laid off from work have to use their own savings or borrow from others to make do until the next job is found. All these changes involve great disruption in expectations and accustomed roles.

Along with the disruptions go other changes in behavior. Some parents do not want their young adult children continuing to live off their income, and become quite insistent about their children learning skills and getting jobs. This attitude is most prevalent among single mothers who have to depend most critically on the earning power of their offspring.

Parents tend to become upset at the prospect of a daughter's bringing home a baby that must be entirely supported on an already inadequate income. Some become so upset that they spend considerable parental energy avoiding such an eventuality. Potential fathers of such babies find themselves under more pressure not to cause such a problem, or to help with its solution if it occurs.

Adolescents who were not job-ready find they are job-ready after all. It turns out that they can work for low wages and accept the discipline of the workplace if the alternative is grim enough. After a few years, many—not all, but many—find that they have acquired salable skills, or that they are at the right place at the right time, or otherwise find that the original entry-level job has gradually been transformed into a secure job paying a decent wage. A few—not a lot, but a few—find that the process leads to affluence.

Perhaps the most rightful, deserved benefit goes to the much larger population of low-income families who have been doing things right all along and have been punished for it: the young man who has taken responsibility for his wife and child even though his friends with the same choice have called him a fool; the single mother who has worked full time and forfeited her right to welfare for very little extra money; the parents who have set an example for their children even as the rules of the game have taught their children that the example is outmoded. For these millions of people, the instantaneous result is that no one makes fun of them any longer. The longer-term result will be that they regain the status that is properly theirs. They will not only be the bedrock upon which the community is founded (which they always have been), they will be recognized as such. The process whereby they regain their position is not magical, but a matter of logic. When it becomes highly dysfunctional for a person to be dependent, status will accrue to being independent, and in fairly short order. Noneconomic rewards will once again reinforce the economic rewards of being a good parent and provider.

The prospective advantages are real and extremely plausible. In fact, if a government program of the traditional sort (one that would "do" something rather than simply get out of the way) could *as plausibly* promise these advantages, its passage would be a foregone conclusion. Congress, yearning for programs that are not retreads of failures, would be prepared to spend billions. Negative side-effects (as long as they were the traditionally acceptable negative side-effects) would be brushed aside as trivial in return for the benefits. For let me be quite clear: I am not suggesting that we dismantle income support for the working-aged to balance the budget or punish welfare cheats. I am hypothesizing, with the advantage of powerful collateral evidence, that the lives of large numbers of poor people would be radically changed for the better.

There is, however, a fourth segment of the

population yet to be considered, those who are pauperized by the withdrawal of government supports and unable to make alternate arrangements: the teenaged mother who has no one to turn to; the incapacitated or the inept who are thrown out of the house; those to whom economic conditions have brought long periods in which there is no work to be had; those with illnesses not covered by insurance. What of these situations?

The first resort is the network of local services. Poor communities in our hypothetical society are still dotted with storefront health clinics, emergency relief agencies, employment services, legal services. They depend for support on local taxes or local philanthropy, and the local taxpayers and philanthropists tend to scrutinize them rather closely. But, by the same token, they also receive considerably more resources than they formerly did. The dismantling of the federal services has poured tens of billions of dollars back into the private economy. Some of that money no doubt has been spent on Mercedes and summer homes on the Cape. But some has been spent on capital investments that generate new jobs. And some has been spent on increased local services to the poor, voluntarily or as decreed by the municipality. In many cities, the coverage provided by this network of agencies is more generous, more humane, more wisely distributed, and more effective in its results than the services formerly subsidized by the federal government.

But we must expect that a large number of people will fall between the cracks. How might we go about trying to retain the advantages of a zero-level welfare system and still address the residual needs?

As we think about the nature of the population still in need, it becomes apparent that their basic problem in the vast majority of the cases is the lack of a job, and this problem is temporary. What they need is something to tide them over while finding a new place in the economy. So our first step is to reinstall the Unemployment Insurance program in more or less its previous form. Properly administered, unemployment insurance makes sense. Even if it is restored with all the defects of current practice, the negative effects of Unemployment Insurance *alone* are relatively minor. Our objective is not to wipe out chicanery or to construct a theoretically unblemished system, but to meet legitimate human needs without doing more harm than good. Unemployment Insurance is one of the least harmful ways of contributing to such ends. Thus the system has been amended to take care of the victims of short-term swings in the economy.

Who is left? We are now down to the hardest of the hard core of the welfare-dependent. They have no jobs. They have been unable to find jobs (or have not tried to find jobs) for a longer period of time than the unemployment benefits cover. They have no families who will help. They have no friends who will help. For some reason, they cannot get help from local services or private charities except for the soup kitchen and a bed in the Salvation Army hall.

What will be the size of this population? We have never tried a zero-level federal welfare system under conditions of late-twentieth-century national wealth, so we cannot do more than speculate. But we may speculate. Let us ask of whom the population might consist and how they might fare.

For any category of "needy" we may name, we find ourselves driven to one of two lines of thought. Either the person is in a category that is going to be at the top of the list of services that localities vote for themselves, and at the top of the list of private services, or the person is in a category where help really is not all that essential or desirable. The burden of the conclusion is not that every single person will be taken care of, but that the extent of resources to deal with needs is likely to be very great—not based on wishful thinking, but on extrapolations from reality.

To illustrate, let us consider the plight of the stereotypical welfare mother—never married, no skills, small children, no steady help from a man. It is safe to say that, now as in the 1950s, there is no one who has less sympathy from the white middle class, which is to be the source of most of the money for the private and local services we envision. Yet this same white middle class is a soft touch for people trying to make it on their own, and a soft touch for "deserving" needy mothers—AFDC was one of the most widely popular of the New Deal welfare measures intended as it was for widows with small children. Thus we may envision two quite different scenarios.

In one scenario, the woman is presenting the local or private service with this proposition: "Help me find a job and day-care for my children, and I will take care of the rest." In effect, she puts herself into the same category as the widow and the deserted wife—identifies herself as one of the most obviously deserving of the deserving poor. Welfare mothers who want to get into the labor force are likely to find a wide range of help. In the other scenario, she asks for an outright and indefinite cash grant—in effect, a private or local version of AFDC—so that she can stay with the children and not hold a job. In the latter case, it is very easy to imagine situations in which she will not be able to find a local service or a private philanthropy to provide the help she seeks. The question we must now ask is: What's so bad about that? If children were always better off being with their mother all day and if, by the act of giving birth, a mother acquired the inalienable right to be with the child, then her situation would be unjust to her and injurious to her children. Neither assertion can be defended, however—especially not in the 1980s, when more mothers of all classes work away from the home than ever before, and even more especially not in view of the empirical record for the children growing up under the current welfare system. Why should the mother be exempted by the system from the pressures that must affect everyone else's decision to work?

As we survey these prospects, important questions remain unresolved. The first of these is why, if federal social transfers are treacherous, should locally mandated transfers be less so? Why should a municipality be permitted to legislate its own AFDC or Food Stamp program if their results are so inherently bad?

Part of the answer lies in conceptions of freedom. I have deliberately avoided raising them—the discussion is about how to help the disadvantaged, not about how to help the advantaged cut their taxes, to which arguments for personal freedom somehow always get diverted. Nonetheless, the point is valid: Local or even state systems leave much more room than a federal system for everyone, donors and recipients alike, to exercise freedom of choice about the kind of system they live under. Laws are more easily made and changed, and people who find them unacceptable have much more latitude in going somewhere more to their liking.

But the freedom of choice argument, while legitimate, is not necessary. We may put the advantages of local systems in terms of the Law of Imperfect Selection. A federal system must inherently employ very crude, inaccurate rules for deciding who gets what kind of help, and the results are as I outlined them in chapter 16. At the opposite extreme—a neighbor helping a neighbor, a family member helping another family member—the law loses its validity nearly altogether. Very fine-grained judgments based on personal knowledge are being made about specific people and changing situations. In neighborhoods and small cities, the procedures can still bring much individualized information to bear on decisions. Even systems in large cities and states can do much better than a national system; a decaying industrial city in the Northeast and a booming sunbelt city of the same size can and probably should adopt much different rules about who gets what and how much.

A final and equally powerful argument for not impeding local systems is diversity. We know much more in the 1980s than we knew in the 1960s about what does not work. We have a lot to learn about what *does* work. Localities have been a rich source of experiments. Marva Collins in Chicago gives us an example of how a school can bring inner-city students up to national norms. Sister Falaka Fattah in Philadelphia shows us how homeless youths can be rescued from the streets. There are numberless such lessons waiting to be learned from the diversity of local efforts. By all means, let a hundred flowers bloom, and if the federal government can play a useful role in lending a hand and spreading the word of successes, so much the better.

The ultimate unresolved question about our proposal to abolish income maintenance for the working-aged is how many people will fall through the cracks. In whatever detail we try to foresee the consequences, the objection may always be raised: We cannot be *sure* that everyone will be taken care of in the degree to which we would wish. But this observation by no means settles the question. If one may point in objection to the child now fed by

Food Stamps who would go hungry, one may also point with satisfaction to the child who would have an entirely different and better future. Hungry children should be fed; there is no argument about that. It is no less urgent that children be allowed to grow up in a system free of the forces that encourage them to remain poor and dependent. If a strategy reasonably promises to remove those forces, after so many attempts to "help the poor" have failed, it is worth thinking about.

But that rationale is too vague. Let me step outside the persona I have employed and put the issue in terms of one last intensely personal hypothetical example. Let us suppose that you, a parent, could know that tomorrow your own child would be made an orphan. You have a choice. You may put your child with an extremely poor family, so poor that your child will be badly clothed and will indeed sometimes be hungry. But you also know that the parents have worked hard all their lives, will make sure your child goes to school and studies, and will teach your child that independence is a primary value. Or you may put your child with a family with parents who have never worked, who will be incapable of overseeing your child's education—but who have plenty of food and good clothes, provided by others. If the choice about where one would put one's own child is as clear to you as it is to me, on what grounds does one justify support of a system that, indirectly but without doubt, makes the other choice for other children? The answer that "What we really want is a world where that choice is not forced upon us" is no answer. We have tried to have it that way. We failed. Everything we know about why we failed tells us that more of the same will not make the dilemma go away.

The Ideal of Opportunity

Billions for equal opportunity, not one cent for equal outcome—such is the slogan to inscribe on the banner of whatever cause my proposals constitute. Their common theme is to make it possible to get as far as one can go on one's merit, hardly a new ideal in American thought.

The ideal itself has never lapsed. What did lapse was the recognition that practical merit exists. Some people are better than others. They deserve more of society's rewards, of which money is only one small part. A principal function of social policy is to make sure they have the opportunity to reap those rewards. Government cannot identify the worthy, but it can protect a society in which the worthy can identify themselves.

I am proposing triage of a sort, triage by self-selection. In triage on the battlefield, the doctor makes the decision—this one gets treatment, that one waits, the other one is made comfortable while waiting to die. In our social triage, the decision is left up to the patient. The patient always has the right to say "I can do X" and get a chance to prove it. Society always has the right to hold him to that pledge. The patient always has the right to fail. Society always has the right to let him.

There is in this stance no lack of compassion but a presumption of respect. People—all people, black or white, rich or poor—may be unequally responsible for what has happened to them in the past, but all are equally responsible for what they do next. Just as in our idealized educational system a student can come back a third, fourth, or fifth time to a course, in our idealized society a person can fail repeatedly and always be qualified for another chance—to try again, to try something easier, to try something different. The options are always open. Opportunity is endless. There is no punishment for failure, only a total absence of rewards. Society—or our idealized society—should be preoccupied with making sure that achievement is rewarded.

There is no shortage of people to be rewarded. Go into any inner-city school and you will find students of extraordinary talent, kept from knowing how good they are by rules we imposed in the name of fairness. Go into any poor community, and you will find people of extraordinary imagination and perseverance, energy and pride, making tortured accommodations to the strange world we created in the name of generosity. The success stories of past generations of poor in this country are waiting to be repeated.

There is no shortage of institutions to provide the rewards. Our schools know how to educate students who want to be educated. Our industries know how to find productive people and reward them. Our police know how to protect people who are ready to cooperate in their own protection. Our system of justice knows how to protect the rights of individuals who know what their rights are. Our philanthropic institutions know how to multiply the effectiveness of people who are already trying to help themselves. In short, American society is very good at reinforcing the investment of an individual in himself. For the affluent and for the middle-class, these mechanisms continue to work about as well as they ever have, and we enjoy their benefits. Not so for the poor. American government, in its recent social policy, has been ineffectual in trying to stage-manage the decision to invest, and it has been unintentionally punitive toward those who would make the decision on their own. It is time to get out of the way. . . .

Affirmative Action

The United States, like many other countries, has a history of racial and sexual discrimination. Unlike many other countries, it also has a history of slavery. Discrimination and slavery have long been recognized as evils. Discrimination, for example, might be defined as making a judgment or decision on the basis of irrelevant factors. Race and sex are almost always irrelevant to decisions about whom to hire, whom to fire, whom to admit to a college or university, and other similar decisions. Kant's categorical imperative requires that we judge similar cases similarly—that we judge a case as if our judgment were universal law. To discriminate is to judge similar cases differently, depending on some irrelevant factor such as race or sex. Discrimination thus directly violates Kant's imperative.

The obligation to eliminate discrimination, therefore, is not controversial. What its elimination requires is. Racial or sexual discrimination, as a violation of Kant's principle, is by its very nature unfair. So, we might think that justice requires making decisions about hiring, firing, admissions, and other matters of economic and political significance in a "color-blind" way, without regard for race, sex, or other irrelevant factors. From another perspective, however, this apparent even-handedness is only apparent, for some of the players in the economic and political game have been harmed by prior discrimination. Setting things right requires, from this point of view, giving those players an advantage to balance the disadvantages they suffer as a result of past injustices. On this conception, then, race, sex, and perhaps other characteristics are no longer irrelevant. The history of discrimination has turned them into relevant factors.

From this perspective have sprung "affirmative-action" programs: programs that give preferences to some people because of their race, sex, ethnic background, or other characteristic. Generally, these programs try to "level the playing field" by granting preference to those who suffer from prior discrimination or are otherwise disadvantaged. Sometimes, the preference is general, of the form "all other things being equal, we prefer people with the following characteristics"; in other cases, there are explicit quotas for people of different groups. Affirmative-action programs have been a source of controversy. In the United States, they have provoked arguments and lawsuits. In other countries, they have provoked riots and bloodshed.

The University of California operated a quota system at its medical school at Davis. It reserved sixteen of the one hundred places in each class at the medical school for members of minority groups. Alan Bakke, a white male, applied and was rejected. He learned, however, that his grades and test scores were higher than those of many students admitted under the minority quota. Bakke sued, claiming that he had been discriminated against on account of his race. In 1978, the Supreme Court decided in Bakke's favor. The Court stopped short of declaring that taking race and similar qualities into account is unacceptable. The Court did, however, decide that quota systems like that operating at the University of California were unconstitutional, amounting themselves to a form of discrimination. Dissenters on the Court decried the decision, maintaining that there is a great moral difference between using a racial classification against a disadvantaged group and using it to benefit that group. In short, the dissenters insisted that race, sex, and other factors are not irrelevant in themselves, though there is a strong presumption of their irrelevance. Prior discrimination and economic disadvantage may, they claimed, make these factors relevant and even require that they be taken into account in decision making.

Following Bakke was a series of decisions on affirmative action in various contexts: education, industry, unions, state government, and others. These decisions are extremely complex. They agree, however, that affirmative-action programs, to be constitutional, must pass strict scrutiny; that is, they must be necessary to achieve a compelling state interest. Racial equality is a compelling state interest, so the crucial question has been, Is this program necessary to achieve it? In the Court's jargon, Is it *narrowly tailored?* The Court has upheld several voluntary race-conscious affirmative-action plans, and even some court-imposed quota systems in cases where there appeared to be ongoing discrimination.

Antonin Scalia and Ronald Dworkin react to the *Bakke* decision in opposite ways: Scalia arguing that the decision makes no sense, and Dworkin arguing that racial preference is justified.

Thomas Sowell, an economist, argues that affirmative action brings about far more harm than good. He traces the history of affirmative action in many societies around the world, contending that it uniformly increases racial tensions. Advocates argue that affirmative-action plans are temporary repairs of harm brought about by prior discrimination. Sowell argues that there is no way to determine how much of the economic position of an individual or a group is due to prior discrimination. Consequently, there is no way to tell when the effects of prior discrimination have been eliminated. Once instituted, therefore, preferences never go away; indeed, they expand to more groups, few of whose claims can be founded on prior discrimination

JUSTICE LEWIS POWELL

majority opinion in *Regents of the University of California* v. *Bakke* (1978)

(Source: Regents of the University of California *v.* Bakke *438 U.S. 265 [1978]. Most legal references have been omitted.)*

QUESTIONS FOR REFLECTION

1. Justice Powell argues that the University of California's racial classification should not simply be viewed as "benign." Why?
2. How did the University of California try to justify its affirmative-action program? Why does Justice Powell reject those arguments?
3. What sort of affirmative-action program does Justice Powell find acceptable? How does it differ from the University of California program?

... Mr. Justice Powell announced the judgment of the Court. ...

I

The Medical School of the University of California at Davis opened in 1968 with an entering class of 50 students. In 1971, the size of the entering class was increased to 100 students, a level at which it remains. No admissions program for disadvantaged or minority students existed when the school opened, and the first class contained three Asians but no blacks, no Mexican-Americans, and no American Indians. Over the next two years, the faculty devised a special admissions program to increase the representation of "disadvantaged" students in each Medical School class. The special program consisted of a separate admissions system operating in coordination with the regular admissions process. ...

The special admissions program operated with a separate committee, a majority of whom were members of minority groups. On the 1973 application form, candidates were asked to indicate whether they wished to be considered as "economically and/or educationally disadvantaged" applicants; on the 1974 form the question was whether they wished to be considered as members of a "minority group," which the Medical School apparently viewed as "Blacks," "Chicanos," "Asians," and "American Indians." If these questions were answered affirmatively, the application was forwarded to the special admissions committee. No formal definition of "disadvantaged" was ever produced, but the chairman of the special committee screened each application to see whether it reflected economic or educational deprivation. Having passed this initial hurdle, the applications then were rated by the special committee in a fashion similar to that used by the general admissions committee, except that special candidates did not have to meet the 2.5 grade point average cutoff applied to regular applicants. About one-fifth of the total number of special applicants were invited for interviews in 1973 and 1974. Following each interview, the special committee assigned each special applicant a benchmark score. The special committee then presented its top choices to the general admissions committee. The latter did not rate or compare the special candidates against the general applicants, but could reject recommended special candidates for failure to meet course requirements or other specific deficiencies. The special committee continued to recommend special applicants until a number prescribed by faculty vote were admitted. While the overall class size was still 50, the prescribed number was 8; in 1973 and 1974, when the class size had doubled to 100, the prescribed number of special admissions also doubled, to 16.

From the year of the increase in class size—1971—through 1974, the special program resulted in the admission of 21 black students, 30 Mexican-Americans, and 12 Asians, for a total of 63 minority students. Over the same period, the regular admissions program produced 1 black, 6 Mexican-Americans, and 37 Asians, for a total of 44 minority students. Although disadvantaged whites applied to the special program in large numbers, none received an offer of admission through that process. Indeed, in 1974, at least, the special committee explicitly considered only "disadvantaged" special applicants who were members of one of the designated minority groups.

Allan Bakke is a white male who applied to the Davis Medical School in both 1973 and 1974. In both years Bakke's application was considered under the general admissions program, and he received an interview. His 1973 interview was with Dr. Theodore C. West, who considered Bakke "a very desirable applicant to [the] medical school." Despite a strong benchmark score of 468 out of 500, Bakke was rejected. His application had come late in the year, and no applicants in the general admissions process with scores below 470 were accepted after Bakke's application was completed. There were four special admissions slots unfilled at that time however, for which Bakke was not considered. After his 1973 rejection, Bakke wrote to Dr. George H. Lowrey, Associate Dean and Chairman of the Admissions Committee, protesting that the special admissions program operated as a racial and ethnic quota.

Bakke's 1974 application was completed early in the year. His student interviewer gave him an overall rating of 94, finding him "friendly, well tempered, conscientious and delightful to speak with." His faculty interviewer was, by coincidence, the same Dr. Lowrey to whom he had written in protest of the special admissions program. Dr. Lowrey found Bakke "rather limited in his approach" to the problems of the medical profession and found disturbing Bakke's "very definite opinions which were based more on his personal viewpoints than upon a study of the total problem." Dr. Lowrey gave Bakke the lowest of his six ratings, an 86; his total was 549 out of 600. Again, Bakke's application was rejected. In neither year did the chairman of the admissions committee, Dr. Lowrey, exercise his discretion to place Bakke on the waiting list. In both years, applicants were admitted under the special program with grade point averages, MCAT scores, and benchmark scores significantly lower than Bakke's. The table on page 546 compares Bakke's science grade point average, overall grade point average, and MCAT scores with the average scores of regular admittees and of special admittees in both 1973 and 1974.

After the second rejection, Bakke filed the instant suit in the Superior Court of California. He sought mandatory, injunctive, and declaratory relief compelling his admission to the Medical School. He alleged that the Medical School's special admissions program operated to exclude him from the school on the basis of his race, in violation of his rights under the Equal Protection Clause of the Fourteenth Amendment, Art. I, *1/8* 21, of the California Constitution, and *1/8* 601 of Title VI of the Civil Rights Act of 1964. The University cross-complained for a declaration that its special admissions program was lawful. . . .

CLASS ENTERING IN 1973

			MCAT (Percentiles)			
	SGPA	OGPA	Verbal	Quanti-tative	Science	Gen. Infor.
Bakke	3.44	3.46	96	94	97	72
Average of regular admittees	3.51	3.49	81	76	83	69
Average of special admittees	2.62	2.88	46	24	35	33

CLASS ENTERING IN 1974

			MCAT (Percentiles)			
	SGPA	OGPA	Verbal	Quanti-tative	Science	Gen. Infor.
Bakke	3.44	3.46	96	94	97	72
Average of regular admittees	3.36	3.29	69	67	82	72
Average of special admittees	2.42	2.62	34	30	37	18

Applicants admitted under the special program also had benchmark scores significantly lower than many students, including Bakke, rejected under the general admissions program, even though the special rating system apparently gave credit for overcoming "disadvantage."

[II . . .]

III

A

. . . The guarantees of the Fourteenth Amendment extend to all persons. Its language is explicit: "No State shall . . . deny to any person within its jurisdiction the equal protection of the laws." It is settled beyond question that the "rights created by the first section of the Fourteenth Amendment are, by its terms, guaranteed to the individual. The rights established are personal rights." The guarantee of equal protection cannot mean one thing when applied to one individual and something else when applied to a person of another color. If both are not accorded the same protection, then it is not equal.

Nevertheless, petitioner argues that the court below erred in applying strict scrutiny to the special admissions program because white males, such as respondent, are not a "discrete and insular minority" requiring extraordinary protection from the majoritarian political process. This rationale, however, has never been invoked in our decisions as a prerequisite to subjecting racial or ethnic distinctions to strict scrutiny. Nor has this Court held that discreteness and insularity constitute necessary preconditions to a holding that a particular classification is invidious. These characteristics may be relevant in deciding whether or not to add new types of classifications to the list of "suspect" categories or whether a particular classification survives close examination. Racial and ethnic classifications, however, are subject to stringent examination without regard to these additional characteristics. We declared as much in the first cases explicitly to recognize racial distinctions as suspect:

> "Distinctions between citizens solely because of their ancestry are by their very nature odious to a free people whose institutions are founded upon the doctrine of equality."
>
> "[A]ll legal restrictions which curtail the civil rights of a single racial group are immediately suspect. That is not to say that all such restrictions are unconstitutional. It is to say that courts must subject them to the most rigid scrutiny."

The Court has never questioned the validity of those pronouncements. Racial and ethnic distinctions of any sort are inherently suspect and thus call for the most exacting judicial examination.

B

This perception of racial and ethnic distinctions is rooted in our Nation's constitutional and demographic history. The Court's initial view of the Fourteenth Amendment was that its "one pervading purpose" was "the freedom of the slave race, the security and firm establishment of that freedom, and the protection of the newly-made freeman and citizen from the oppressions of those who had formerly exercised dominion over him." *Slaughter-House Cases* (1873). The Equal Protection Clause, however, was "[v]irtually strangled in infancy by post-civil-war judicial reactionism." It was relegated to decades of relative desuetude while the Due Process Clause of the Fourteenth Amendment, after a short germinal period, flourished as a cornerstone in the Court's defense of property and liberty of contract. In that cause, the Fourteenth Amendment's "one pervading purpose" was displaced. It was only as the era of substantive due process came to a close that the Equal Protection Clause began to attain a genuine measure of vitality.

By that time it was no longer possible to peg the guarantees of the Fourteenth Amendment to the struggle for equality of one racial minority. During the dormancy of the Equal Protection Clause, the United States had become a Nation of minorities. Each had to struggle—and to some extent struggles still—to overcome the prejudices not of a monolithic majority, but of a "majority" composed of various minority groups of whom it was said—perhaps unfairly in many cases—that a shared characteristic was a willingness to disadvantage other groups. As the Nation filled with the stock of many lands, the reach of the Clause was gradually extended to all ethnic groups seeking protection from official discrimination. The guarantees of equal protection, said the Court in *Yick Wo,* "are universal in their application, to all persons within the territorial jurisdiction, without regard to any differences of race, of color, or of nationality; and the equal protection of the laws is a pledge of the protection of equal laws."

Although many of the Framers of the Fourteenth Amendment conceived of its primary function as bridging the vast distance between members of the Negro race and the white "majority," the Amendment itself was framed in universal terms, without reference to color, ethnic origin, or condition of prior servitude. As this Court recently remarked in interpreting the 1866 Civil Rights Act to extend to claims of racial discrimination against white persons, "the 39th Congress was intent upon establishing in the federal law a broader principle than would have been necessary simply to meet the particular and immediate plight of the newly freed Negro slaves." And that legislation was specifically broadened in 1870 to ensure that "all persons," not merely "citizens," would enjoy equal rights under the law. Indeed, it is not unlikely that among the Framers were many who would have applauded a reading of the Equal Protection Clause that states a principle of universal application and is responsive to the racial, ethnic, and cultural diversity of the Nation.

Over the past 30 years, this Court has embarked upon the crucial mission of interpreting the Equal Protection Clause with the view of assuring to all persons "the protection of equal laws," in a Nation confronting a legacy of slavery and racial discrimination. Because the landmark decisions in this area arose in response to the continued exclusion of Negroes from the mainstream of American society, they could be characterized as involving discrimination by the "majority" white race against the Negro minority. But they need not be read as depending upon that characterization for their results. It suffices to say that "[o]ver the years, this Court has consistently repudiated '[d]istinctions between citizens solely because of their ancestry' as being 'odious to a free people whose institutions are founded upon the doctrine of equality.'"

Petitioner urges us to adopt for the first time a more restrictive view of the Equal Protection Clause and hold that discrimination against members of the white "majority" cannot be suspect if its purpose can be characterized as "benign."* The clock of our liberties, however, cannot be turned back to 1868. It is far too late to argue that the guarantee of equal protection to *all* persons permits the recognition of special wards entitled to a degree of protection greater than that accorded others.† "The Fourteenth Amendment is not directed solely against discrimination due to a 'two-class theory'—that is, based upon differences between 'white' and Negro."

Once the artificial line of a "two-class theory" of the Fourteenth Amendment is put aside, the difficulties entailed in varying the level of judicial review according to a perceived "preferred" status of a particular racial or ethnic minority are intractable. The concepts of "majority" and "minority" necessarily reflect temporary arrangements and political judgments. As observed above, the white "majority" itself is composed of various minority groups, most of which can lay claim to a history of prior discrimination at the hands of the State and private individuals. Not all of these groups can receive preferential treatment and corresponding judicial tolerance of distinctions drawn in terms of race and nationality, for then the only "majority" left would be a new minority of white Anglo-Saxon Protestants. There is no principled basis for deciding which groups would merit "heightened judicial solicitude" and which would not. Courts would be asked to evaluate the extent of the prejudice and consequent harm suffered by various minority groups. Those whose societal injury is thought to exceed some arbitrary level of tolerability then would be entitled to preferential classifications at the expense of individuals belonging to other groups. Those classifications would be free from exacting judicial scrutiny. As these preferences began to have their desired effect, and the consequences of past discrimination were undone, new judicial rankings would be necessary. The kind of variable sociological and politi-

* In the view of Mr. Justice Brennan, Mr. Justice White, Mr. Justice Marshall, and Mr. Justice Blackmun, the pliable notion of "stigma" is the crucial element in analyzing racial classifications. The Equal Protection Clause is not framed in terms of "stigma." Certainly the word has no clearly defined constitutional meaning. It reflects a subjective judgment that is standardless. *All* state-imposed classifications that rearrange burdens and benefits on the basis of race are likely to be viewed with deep resentment by the individuals burdened. The denial to innocent persons of equal rights and opportunities may outrage those so deprived and therefore may be perceived as invidious. These individuals are likely to find little comfort in the notion that the deprivation they are asked to endure is merely the price of membership in the dominant majority and that its imposition is inspired by the supposedly benign purpose of aiding others. One should not lightly dismiss the inherent unfairness of, and the perception of mistreatment that accompanies, a system of allocating benefits and privileges on the basis of skin color and ethnic origin. Moreover, Mr. Justice Brennan, Mr. Justice White, Mr. Justice Marshall, and Mr. Justice Blackmun offer no principle for deciding whether preferential classifications reflect a benign remedial purpose or a malevolent stigmatic classification, since they are willing in this case to accept mere *post hoc* declarations by an isolated state entity—a medical school faculty—unadorned by particularized findings of past discrimination, to establish such a remedial purpose.

† Professor Bickel noted the self-contradiction of that view:

"The lesson of the great decisions of the Supreme Court and the lesson of contemporary history have been the same for at least a generation: discrimination on the basis of race is illegal, immoral, unconstitutional, inherently wrong, and destructive of democratic society. Now this is to be unlearned and we are told that this is not a matter of fundamental principle but only a matter of whose ox is gored. Those for whom racial equality was demanded are to be more equal than others. Having found support in the Constitution for equality, they now claim support for inequality under the same Constitution." A. Bickel, The Morality of Consent 133 (1975).

cal analysis necessary to produce such rankings simply does not lie within the judicial competence—even if they otherwise were politically feasible and socially desirable.

Moreover, there are serious problems of justice connected with the idea of preference itself. First, it may not always be clear that a so-called preference is in fact benign. Courts may be asked to validate burdens imposed upon individual members of a particular group in order to advance the group's general interest. Nothing in the Constitution supports the notion that individuals may be asked to suffer otherwise impermissible burdens in order to enhance the societal standing of their ethnic groups. Second, preferential programs may only reinforce common stereotypes holding that certain groups are unable to achieve success without special protection based on a factor having no relationship to individual worth. Third, there is a measure of inequity in forcing innocent persons in respondent's position to bear the burdens of redressing grievances not of their making.

By hitching the meaning of the Equal Protection Clause to these transitory considerations, we would be holding, as a constitutional principle, that judicial scrutiny of classifications touching on racial and ethnic background may vary with the ebb and flow of political forces. Disparate constitutional tolerance of such classifications well may serve to exacerbate racial and ethnic antagonisms rather than alleviate them. Also, the mutability of a constitutional principle, based upon shifting political and social judgments, undermines the chances for consistent application of the Constitution from one generation to the next, a critical feature of its coherent interpretation. In expounding the Constitution, the Court's role is to discern "principles sufficiently absolute to give them roots throughout the community and continuity over significant periods of time, and to lift them above the level of the pragmatic political judgments of a particular time and place."

If it is the individual who is entitled to judicial protection against classifications based upon his racial or ethnic background because such distinctions impinge upon personal rights, rather than the individual only because of his membership in a particular group, then constitutional standards may be applied consistently. Political judgments regarding the necessity for the particular classification may be weighed in the constitutional balance, but the standard of justification will remain constant. This is as it should be, since those political judgments are the product of rough compromise struck by contending groups within the democratic process. When they touch upon an individual's race or ethnic background, he is entitled to a judicial determination that the burden he is asked to bear on that basis is precisely tailored to serve a compelling governmental interest. The Constitution guarantees that right to every person regardless of his background. . . .

IV

We have held that in "order to justify the use of a suspect classification, a State must show that its purpose or interest is both constitutionally permissible and substantial, and that its use of the classification is 'necessary . . . to the accomplishment' of its purpose or the safeguarding of its interest." The special admissions program purports to serve the purposes of: (i) "reducing the historic deficit of traditionally disfavored minorities in medical schools and in the medical profession," (ii) countering the effects of societal discrimination; (iii) increasing the number of physicians who will practice in communities currently underserved; and (iv) obtaining the educational benefits that flow from an ethnically diverse student body. It is necessary to decide which, if any, of these purposes is substantial enough to support the use of a suspect classification.

A

If petitioner's purpose is to assure within its student body some specified percentage of a particular group merely because of its race or ethnic origin, such a preferential purpose must be rejected not as insubstantial but as facially invalid. Preferring members of any one group for no reason other than race or ethnic origin is discrimination for its own sake. This the Constitution forbids.

B

The State certainly has a legitimate and substantial interest in ameliorating, or eliminating where feasible, the disabling effects of identified discrimination. The line of school desegregation cases, commencing with *Brown*, attests to the importance of this state goal and the commitment of the judiciary to affirm all lawful means toward its attainment. In the school cases, the States were required by court order to redress the wrongs worked by specific instances of racial discrimination. That goal was far more focused than the remedying of the effects of "societal discrimination," an amorphous concept of injury that may be ageless in its reach into the past.

We have never approved a classification that aids persons perceived as members of relatively victimized groups at the expense of other innocent individuals in the absence of judicial, legislative, or administrative findings of constitutional or statutory violations. After such findings have been made, the governmental interest, in preferring members of the injured groups at the expense of others is substantial, since the legal rights of the victims must be vindicated. In such a case, the extent of the injury and the consequent remedy will have been judicially, legislatively, or administratively defined. Also, the remedial action usually remains subject to continuing oversight to assure that it will work the least harm possible to other innocent persons competing for the benefit. Without such findings of constitutional or statutory violations, it cannot be said that the government has any greater interest in helping one individual than in refraining from harming another. Thus, the government has no compelling justification for inflicting such harm. . . .

Hence, the purpose of helping certain groups whom the faculty of the Davis Medical School perceived as victims of "societal discrimination" does not justify a classification that imposes disadvantages upon persons like respondent, who bear no responsibility for whatever harm the beneficiaries of the special admissions program are thought to have suffered. To hold otherwise would be to convert a remedy heretofore reserved for violations of legal rights into a privilege that all institutions throughout the Nation could grant at their pleasure to whatever groups are perceived as victims of societal discrimination. That is a step we have never approved.

C

Petitioner identifies, as another purpose of its program, improving the delivery of health-care services to communities currently underserved. It may be assumed that in some situations a State's interest in facilitating the health care of its citizens is sufficiently compelling to support the use of a suspect classification. But there is virtually no evidence in the record indicating that petitioner's special admissions program is either needed or geared to promote that goal. The court below addressed this failure of proof:

> "The University concedes it cannot assure that minority doctors who entered under the program, all of whom expressed an 'interest' in practicing in a disadvantaged community, will actually do so. It may be correct to assume that some of them will carry out this intention, and that it is more likely they will practice in minority communities than the average white doctor. Nevertheless, there are more precise and reliable ways to identify applicants who are genuinely interested in the medical problems of minorities than by race. An applicant of whatever race who has demonstrated his concern for disadvantaged minorities in the past and who declares that practice in such a community is his primary professional goal would be more likely to contribute to alleviation of the medical shortage than one who is chosen entirely on the basis of race and disadvantage. In short, there is no empirical data to demonstrate that any one race is more selflessly socially oriented or by contrast that another is more selfishly acquisitive."

Petitioner simply has not carried its burden of demonstrating that it must prefer members of particular ethnic groups over all other individuals in order to promote better health-care delivery to deprived citizens. Indeed, petitioner has not shown that its preferential classification is likely to have any significant effect on the problem.

D

The fourth goal asserted by petitioner is the attainment of a diverse student body. This clearly is a constitutionally permissible goal for an institution of higher education. Academic freedom, though not a specifically enumerated constitutional right, long has been viewed as a special concern of the First Amendment. The freedom of a university to make its own judgments as to education includes the selection of its student body. Mr. Justice Frankfurter summarized the "four essential freedoms" that constitute academic freedom:

> "'It is the business of a university to provide that atmosphere which is most conducive to speculation, experiment and creation. It is an atmosphere in which there prevail "the four essential freedoms" of a university—to determine for itself on academic grounds who may teach, what may be taught, how it shall be taught, and who may be admitted to study.'"

Our national commitment to the safeguarding of these freedoms within university communities was emphasized in *Keyishian v. Board of Regents* (1967):

> "Our Nation is deeply committed to safeguarding academic freedom which is of transcendent value to all of us and not merely to the teachers concerned. That freedom is therefore a special concern of the First Amendment. . . . The Nation's future depends upon leaders trained through wide exposure to that robust exchange of ideas which discovers truth 'out of a multitude of tongues, [rather] than through any kind of authoritative selection'."

The atmosphere of "speculation, experiment and creation"—so essential to the quality of higher education—is widely believed to be promoted by a diverse student body. As the Court noted in *Keyishian,* it is not too much to say that the "nation's future depends upon leaders trained through wide exposure" to the ideas and mores of students as diverse as this Nation of many peoples.

Thus, in arguing that its universities must be accorded the right to select those students who will contribute the most to the "robust exchange of ideas," petitioner invokes a countervailing constitutional interest, that of the First Amendment. In this light, petitioner must be viewed as seeking to achieve a goal that is of paramount importance in the fulfillment of its mission.

It may be argued that there is greater force to these views at the undergraduate level than in a medical school where the training is centered primarily on professional competency. But even at the graduate level, our tradition and experience lend support to the view that the contribution of diversity is substantial. In *Sweatt v. Painter,* the Court made a similar point with specific reference to legal education:

> "The law school, the proving ground for legal learning and practice, cannot be effective in isolation from the individuals and institutions with which the law interacts. Few students and no one who has practiced law would choose to study in an academic vacuum, removed from the interplay of ideas and the exchange of views with which the law is concerned."

Physicians serve a heterogeneous population. An otherwise qualified medical student with a particular background—whether it be ethnic, geographic, culturally advantaged or disadvantaged—may bring to a professional school of medicine experiences, outlooks, and ideas that enrich the training of its student body and better equip its graduates to render with understanding their vital service to humanity.

Ethnic diversity, however, is only one element in a range of factors a university properly may consider in attaining the goal of a heterogeneous student body. Although a university must have wide discretion in making the sensitive judgments as to who should be admitted, constitutional limitations protecting individual rights may not be disregarded. Respondent urges—and the courts below have held—that petitioner's dual admissions program is a racial classification that impermissibly infringes his rights under the Fourteenth Amendment. As the interest of diversity is compelling in the context of a university's admissions program, the question remains whether the program's racial classification is necessary to promote this interest.

V

A

It may be assumed that the reservation of a specified number of seats in each class for individuals from the preferred ethnic groups would contribute to the attainment of considerable ethnic diversity in the student body. But petitioner's argument that this is the only effective means of serving the interest of diversity is seriously flawed. In a most fundamental sense the argument misconceives the nature of the state interest that would justify consideration of race or ethnic background. It is not an interest in simple ethnic diversity, in which a specified percentage of the student body is in effect guaranteed to be members of selected ethnic groups, with the remaining percentage an undifferentiated aggregation of students. The diversity that furthers a compelling state interest encompasses a far broader array of qualifications and characteristics of which racial or ethnic origin is but a single though important element. Petitioner's special admissions program, focused *solely* on ethnic diversity, would hinder rather than further attainment of genuine diversity.

Nor would the state interest in genuine diversity be served by expanding petitioner's two-track system into a multitrack program with a prescribed number of seats set aside for each identifiable category of applicants. Indeed, it is inconceivable that a university would thus pursue the logic of petitioner's two-track program to the illogical end of insulating each category of applicants with certain desired qualifications from competition with all other applicants. . . .

B

In summary, it is evident that the Davis special admissions program involves the use of an explicit racial classification never before countenanced by this Court. It tells applicants who are not Negro, Asian, or Chicano that they are totally excluded from a specific percentage of the seats in an entering class. No matter how strong their qualifications, quantitative and extracurricular, including their own potential for contribution to educational diversity, they are never afforded the chance to compete with applicants from the preferred groups for the special admissions seats. At the same time, the preferred applicants have the opportunity to compete for every seat in the class.

The fatal flaw in petitioner's preferential program is its disregard of individual rights as guaranteed by the Fourteenth Amendment. Such rights are not absolute. But when a State's distribution of benefits or imposition of burdens hinges on ancestry or the color of a person's skin, that individual is entitled to a demonstration that the challenged classification is necessary to promote a substantial state interest. Petitioner has failed to carry this burden. For this reason, that portion of the California court's judgment holding petitioner's special admissions program invalid under the Fourteenth Amendment must be affirmed. . . .

ANTONIN SCALIA

The Disease as a Cure

Antonin Scalia is Justice of the United States Supreme Court. (Source: From the Washington University Law Quarterly, *1979, no. 1. Copyright © 1979. Reprinted by permission.)*

QUESTIONS FOR REFLECTION

1. Scalia rejects the justification for affirmative action from rectification or compensation. Why? Do you find his arguments compelling?
2. What harms does affirmative action produce, according to Scalia?

I have grave doubts about the wisdom of where we are going in affirmative action, and in equal protection generally. I find this area an embarrassment to teach. Here, as in some other fields of constitutional law, it is increasingly difficult to pretend to one's students that the decisions of the Supreme Court are tied together by threads of logic and analysis—as opposed to what seems to be the fact that the decisions of each of the justices on the court are tied together by threads of social preference and predisposition. Frankly, I do not have it in me to play the game of distinguishing and reconciling the cases in this utterly confused field.

The chaos in which we find ourselves is exemplified well enough by *Bakke* itself. Four of the justices tell us that both the Constitution and Title VI permit racial preference; four of the justices tell us that whatever the Constitution may permit, Title VI forbids it. And the law of the land, pronounced by the one remaining justice, apparently is that Title VI is no different from the Constitution; governmental racial distinctions of any sort are "odious to a free people" and their validity "inherently suspect"; they must pass "the most exacting judicial examination," and can only be justified by a "compelling" state interest. We later learn that the "compelling" interest at issue in *Bakke* is the enormously important goal of assuring that in medical school—where we are dealing with students in an age range of twenty-two to twenty-eight, or in Bakke's case, thirty-three to thirty-nine—we will expose these impressionable youngsters to a great diversity of people. We want them to work and play with pianists, maybe flute players. We want people from the country, from the city. We want bespectacled chess champions and football players. And, oh yes, we may want some racial minorities, too. If that is all it takes to overcome the presumptions against discrimination by race, we have witnessed an historic trivialization of the Constitution. Justice Powell's opinion, which we must work with as the law of the land, strikes me as an excellent compromise between two committees of the American Bar Association on some insignificant legislative proposal. But it is thoroughly unconvincing as an honest, hard-minded, reasoned analysis of an important provision of the Constitution.

There is, of course, a lot of pretense or self-delusion (you can take your choice) in all that pertains to affirmative action. Does anyone really think, for example, that the situation has changed at Davis? So instead of reserving class places for minority students, the school will open all slots to all applicants, but in choosing among them, will take into account the need for diversity—piano players, football players, people from the country, minority students, etc. When it comes to choosing among these manifold diversities in God's creation, will being a piano player, do you suppose, be regarded as more important than having yellow skin? Or will coming from Oshkosh, Wisconsin, be regarded as more important than having a Spanish surname? It will be very difficult to tell.

Only two results of the *Bakke* decision are certain. First, the judgments that the Davis medical school makes in filling these 100 slots will be effectively unappealable to the courts. (There is no way to establish, for example, that the diversity value of New York City oboists has not been accorded its proper weight.) Second, when all is said and done, it is a safe bet that though there may not be a piano player in the class, there are going to be close to sixteen minority students. And I suspect that Justice Powell's delightful compromise was drafted precisely to achieve these results—just as, it has been charged, the Harvard College "diversity admissions" program, which Mr. Justice Powell's opinion so generously praises, was designed to reduce as inconspicuously as possible the disproportionate number of New York Jewish students that a merit admissions system had produced.

Examples abound to support my suggestion that this area is full of pretense or self-delusion. Affirmative action requirements under Title VI and VII are said repeatedly "not to require the hiring of any unqualified individuals." That gives one a great feeling of equal justice until it is analyzed. Unfortunately, the world of employment applicants does not divide itself merely into "qualified" and "unqualified" individuals. There is a whole range of ability—from unqualified, through minimally qualified, qualified, well qualified, to outstanding. If I cannot get Leontyne Price to sing a concert I have scheduled, I may have to settle for Erma Glatt. La Glatt has a pretty good voice, but not as good as Price. Is she unqualified? Not really—she has sung other concerts with modest success. But she is just not as good as Price. Any system that coerces me to hire her in preference to Price, because of her race, degrades the quality of my product and discriminates on racial grounds against Price. And it is no answer to either of these charges that Glatt is "qualified." To seek to assuage either the employer's demand for quality or the disfavored applicant's demand for equal treatment by saying there is no need to hire any unqualified individuals is a sort of intellectual shell game, which diverts attention from the major issue by firmly responding to a minor one.

But, of course, even the disclaimer of compulsion to hire unqualified individuals loses something when it is translated into practice by the advocates of affirmative action. Consider, for example, the following statement by Professor Edwards: "This is not to say that blacks or women must be thrust into positions for which they are not qualified; however, when the choice is between white males and other qualified or qualifiable individuals, we should open the available positions to those who formerly could not occupy them." Note that what begins with the ritualistic denial of any intent to foster hiring of the unqualified imperceptibly shifts to a call for hiring of the "qualifiable," which surely must be a subcategory of the unqualified. It is typical of the confused level of debate that characterizes this field.

Another example of pretense or self-delusion is the Department of Labor's regulations concerning goals for hiring to overcome "underutilization": "The purpose of a contractor's establishment and use of goals is to insure that he meets his affirmative action obligation. It is not intended and should not be used to discriminate against any applicant or employee because of race, color, religion, sex, or national origin." This is, quite literally, incredible. Once there is established a numerical figure, the failure to meet it will have material, adverse consequences; namely, the substantial risk of cutoff of government contracts and the substantial certainty of disruptive and expensive government investigations. All that we know about human nature and human motivations indicates quite clearly that discrimination often will be produced in an effort to meet or exceed the magic number. I am a businessman who has, let us say, six more jobs to fill, and I am three short of my minority "goal." Reaching the goal will render my government contracts secure and will save thousands of dollars in the expenses necessary to comply with the demands of an equal employment investigation. If I consult my self-interest, which people tend to do, I will hire three minority applicants, even if they are somewhat less qualified than others. When the results that are inevitable are compared with the results that are said to be "intended," one must conclude that the drafter of the regulation is either fooling us or fooling himself. I appreciate, of course, that any antidiscrimination law with teeth in it will generate *some* pressures to favor minority groups. But that is worlds away from the "we-need-three-more-nonwhites" attitude that is the utterly predictable result of so-called "goals."

Judge Wisdom, dissenting in the *Weber* case, makes the following statement: "The Union's duty to bargain in good faith for all its members [an obligation imposed by law] does not prevent it from fairly advancing the national policy against discrimination, even if that requires assisting some of its members more than others." One has to be reminded of the line from *Animal Farm*, to the effect that all animals are created equal but some are more equal than others. And one cannot help but think that a paraphrase of Judge Wisdom's statement would fit very nicely in the mouth of a good old-fashioned racist employer: "We favor all applicants, but we favor white applicants more than others." It is very difficult to take Judge Wisdom's argument as a serious attempt to identify and grapple with the real issue rather than as an elaborate intellectual word game.

Another pretense or self-delusion—perhaps the grandest of all—is the notion that what was involved in the *Weber* case is voluntary private discrimination against whites. As Judge Wisdom put it: "While the government might not be able to require that restorative justice be done, neither should it prevent it." Fancy that! To think that the real issue in *Weber*, and presumably all those "reverse discrimination" cases, is damnable federal regulation: whether the federal government should be able to *prevent* the discrimination against better qualified employees, which Kaiser and thousands of other businesses throughout the country are chomping at the bit to engage in! That is, of course, chimerical. Nobody really believes that Kaiser would have established the challenged program, or the union permitted it, without the "incentive" of federal administrative regulations, which in effect makes the application of what Judge Wisdom calls "restorative justice" a condition for the award of government contracts and for the avoidance of expensive litigation in and out of the courts. To discuss the issue in the fictitious context of voluntarism not only makes any intelligently reasoned decision impossible in the particular case, but poisons the well of legal discourse.

The Restorative Justice Handicapping System

That last quotation concerning "restorative justice" may explain why I feel a bit differently about these issues than, for example, Judge Wisdom or Justice Powell or Justice White. When John Minor Wisdom speaks of "restorative justice," I am reminded of the story about the Lone Ranger and his "faithful Indian companion" Tonto. If you recall the famous radio serial, you know that Tonto never said much, but what he did say was (disguised beneath a Hollywood-Indian dialect) wisdom of an absolutely Solomonic caliber. On one occasion, it seems that the Lone Ranger was galloping along with Tonto, heading eastward, when they saw coming towards them a large band of Mohawk Indians in full war dress. The Lone Ranger reigns in his horse, turns to Tonto, and asks, "Tonto, what should we do?" Tonto says, "Ugh, ride-um west." So they wheel around and gallop off to the west until suddenly they encounter a large band of Sioux heading straight toward them. The Lone Ranger asks, "Tonto, what should we do?" Tonto says, "Ugh, ride-um north." So, they turn around and ride north, and, sure enough, there's a whole tribe of Iroquois headed straight towards them. The Ranger asks, "Tonto, what should we do?" And Tonto says, "Ugh, ride-um south," which they do until they see a war party of Apaches coming right for them. The Lone Ranger says, "Tonto, what should we do?" And Tonto says, "Ugh, what you mean, 'we' white man?"

I have somewhat the same feeling when John Minor Wisdom talks of the evils that "we" whites have done to blacks and that "we" must now make restoration for. My father came to this country when he was a teenager. Not only had he never profited from the sweat of any black man's brow, I don't think he had ever seen a black man. There are, of course, many white ethnic groups that came to this country in great numbers relatively late in its history—Italians, Jews, Irish, Poles—who not only took no part in, and derived no profit from, the major historic suppression of the currently acknowledged minority groups, but were, in fact, themselves the object of discrimination by the dominant Anglo-Saxon majority. If I can recall in my lifetime the obnoxious "White Trade Only" signs in shops in Washington, D.C., others can recall "Irish Need Not Apply" signs in Boston, three or four decades earlier. To be sure, in relatively recent years some or all of these groups have been the beneficiaries of discrimination against blacks, or have themselves practiced discrimination. But to compare their racial debt—I must use that term, since the concept of "restorative justice" implies it; there is no creditor without a debtor—with that of those who plied the slave trade, and who maintained a formal caste system for many years thereafter, is to confuse a mountain with a molehill. Yet curiously enough, we find that in the system of restorative justice established by the Wisdoms and the Powells and the Whites, it is precisely *these* groups that do most of the restoring. It is they who, to a disproportionate degree, are the competitors with the urban blacks and Hispanics for jobs, housing, education—all those things that enable one to scramble to the top of the social heap where one can speak eloquently (and quite safely) of restorative justice.

To remedy this inequity, I have developed a modest proposal, which I call RJHS—the Restorative Justice Handicapping System. I only have applied it thus far to restorative justice for the Negro, since obviously he has been the victim of the most widespread and systematic exploitation in this country; but a similar system could be devised for other creditor-races, creditor-sexes, or minority groups. Under my system each individual in society would be assigned at birth Restorative Justice Handicapping Points, determined on the basis of his or her ancestry. Obviously, the highest number of points must go to what we may loosely call the Aryans—the Powells, the Whites, the Stewarts, the Burgers, and, in fact (curiously enough), the entire composition of the present Supreme Court, with the exception of Justice Marshall. This grouping of north European races obviously played the greatest role in the suppression of the American black. But unfortunately, what was good enough for Nazi Germany is not good enough for our purposes. We must further divide the Aryans into subgroups. As I have suggested, the Irish (having arrived later) probably owe less of a racial debt than the Germans, who in turn surely owe less of a racial debt than the English. It will, to be sure, be difficult to draw precise lines and establish the correct number of handicapping points, but having reviewed the Supreme Court's jurisprudence on abortion, I am convinced that our justices would not shrink from the task.

Of course, the mere identification of the various degrees of debtor-races is only part of the job. One must in addition account for the dilution of bloodlines by establishing, for example, a half-Italian, half-Irish handicapping score. There are those who will scoff at this as a refinement impossible of achievement, but I am confident it can be done, and can even be extended to take account of dilution of blood in creditor-races as well. Indeed, I am informed (though I have not had the stomach to check) that a system to achieve the latter objective is already in place in federal agencies—specifying, for example, how much dilution of blood deprives one of his racial-creditor status as a "Hispanic" under affirmative action programs. Moreover, it should not be forgotten that we have a rich body of statutory and case law from the Old South to which we can turn for guidance in this exacting task.

But I think it unnecessary to describe the Restorative Justice Handicapping System any further. I trust you find it thoroughly offensive, as I do. It, and the racist concept of restorative justice of which it is merely the concrete expression, is fundamentally contrary to the principles that govern, and should govern, our society. I owe no man anything, nor he me, because of the blood that flows in our veins. To go down that road (or I should say to return down that road), even behind a banner as gleaming as restorative justice, is to make a frightening mistake. This is not to say that I have no obligation to my fellow citizens who are black. I assuredly do—not because of their race or because of any special debt that my bloodline owes to theirs, but because they have (many of them) special needs, and they are (all of them) my countrymen and (as I believe) my brothers. This means that I am entirely in favor of according the poor inner-city child, who happens to be black, advantages and preferences not given to my own children because they do not need them. But I am not willing to prefer the son of a prosperous and well-educated black doctor or lawyer—solely because of his race—to the son of a recent refugee from Eastern Europe who is working as a manual laborer to get his family ahead. The affirmative action system now in place will produce the latter result because it is based upon concepts of racial indebtedness and racial entitlement rather than individual worth and individual need; that is to say, because it is racist.

Evil Fruits of a Bad Seed

But I not only question the principle upon which racial affirmative action is based; I even question its effectiveness in achieving the desired goal of advancing a particular race. Professor Edwards, for example, states in one of his pieces that: "The continued existence of long-standing myths about the inherent inability of blacks to perform certain work has also contributed to their exclusion from significant jobs in the employment market." That strikes me as true, but one may well wonder whether the prescribed solution of affirmative action based on race will eliminate the myths rather than assure their perpetuation. When one reads the *Bakke* case, the most striking factual data is the enormous divergence in the average college grades and average test scores of the regular admittees and the special (minority) admittees of the Davis medical school for the years Bakke was rejected. In 1973 they looked like this:

	Grade Point Average		Medical College Admission Test			
	Science	Overall	Verbal	Quantitative	Science	Gen'l Info.
Regular	3.51	3.49	81	76	83	69
Minority	2.62	2.88	46	24	35	33

Do you suppose the "image" of minority groups has been improved by this? I suggest that, to the contrary, the very ability of minority group members to distinguish themselves and their race has been dreadfully impaired. To put the issue to you in its starkest form: If you must select your brain surgeon from among recent graduates of Davis medical school and have nothing to go on but their names and pictures, would you not be well advised—playing the odds—to eliminate all minority group members? It is well known to the public that the outstanding institutions of higher education graduate the best and the brightest principally through the simple device of admitting only the best and the brightest. And it is obvious to the public that (to the extent these schools flunk *anyone* out) the same factor that produced special admissions will also tend to produce special retention and, ultimately, special graduation. Thus, insofar as "public image" is concerned, the immediate and predictable effect of affirmative action is to establish a second-class, "minority" degree, which is a less certain certificate of quality. In other words, we have established within our institutions of higher education (and wherever else racial affirmative action is applied) a regime reminiscent of major league baseball in the years before Jackie Robinson: a separate "league" for minority students, which makes it difficult for the true excellence of the minority star to receive his or her deserved acknowledgment. To be sure, the students' teachers, and those of us who have the opportunity of examining the students' transcripts, can tell who is or is not outstanding. But those members of the public about whom Professor Edwards is concerned—those who judge by generalities, or by "image," if you will—are they likely to think better or worse of minority graduates? The person who was so ignorant as to say "a Negro simply cannot become a truly outstanding doctor" can now plausibly add "—and the fact that he obtained a degree from one of the best medical schools in the country doesn't prove a thing."

In response to this, the advocates of racial affirmative action might say the following: "Even if, as you say, our system cannot give an increased number of minority students a first-class Davis degree —and indeed, even if it may, as you say, make it impossible for *any* minority student to obtain a first-class Davis degree—at least it gives more minority students the concrete benefits of a first-class Davis education." But that is questionable pedagogy. In grammar school, at least, where the politics of race do not yet seem to have permeated pupil assignment within schools, we do not "help" a disadvantaged student by admitting him into a faster group. Why should college and graduate school be different? During the guns-on-campus disturbances at Cornell, one-half of that school's black students were on academic probation. Why? They were neither stupid nor lazy. As a whole their test scores were in the *upper* 25 per cent of all students admitted to college. But the Cornell student body as a whole was in the upper one percent. Was it really "helping" these young men and women, either from the standpoint of their personal intellectual development or from the standpoint of their "image" as minority graduates in later life, to place them in an environment where it was quite probable (as probable as such things can ever be) that they did not belong? It solved the political problems of the school administrators, no doubt. And it may have given the administrators, faculty, and alumni the warm feeling that they were doing their part (at no expense, by and large, to their own children) for "restorative justice." But did it really help these young men and women? With few exceptions, I suspect not.

I could mention other harmful, practical effects of racial affirmative action. It has been suggested, for example, that one consequence is to encourage the location of industries in areas where affirmative action problems are likely to be reduced; that is, away from the inner cities where the game of racial percentages produces significantly higher quotas (or, if you prefer, goals). In any case, it is a fact that statistics show an increase in the economic status of blacks in the years immediately preceding affirmative action and a decline thereafter. Whatever else the program may be, it is not demonstrably effective.

Conclusion

I am, in short, opposed to racial affirmative action for reasons of both principle and practicality. Sex-based affirmative action presents somewhat different constitutional issues, but it seems to me an equally poor idea, for many of the reasons suggested above. I do not, on the other hand, oppose—indeed, I strongly favor—what might be called (but for the coloration that the term has acquired in the context of its past use) "affirmative action programs" of many types of help for the poor and disadvantaged. It may well be that many, or even most, of these benefited by such programs would be members of minority races that the existing programs exclusively favor. I would not care if *all* of them were. The unacceptable vice is simply selecting or rejecting them *on the basis of their race.*

A person espousing the views I have expressed, of course, exposes himself to charges of, at best, insensitivity or, at worst, bigotry. That is one reason these views are not expressed more often, particularly in academia. Beyond an anticipatory denial, I must content myself with the observation that it must be a queer sort of bigotry indeed, since it is shared by many intelligent members of the alleged target group. Some of the most vocal opposition to racial affirmative action comes from minority group members who have seen the value of their accomplishments debased by the suspicion—no, to be frank, the reality—of a lower standard for their group in the universities and the professions. This new racial presumption, imposed upon those who have lifted themselves above the effects of old racial presumptions, is the most evil fruit of a fundamentally bad seed. From racist principles flow racist results.

RONALD DWORKIN

Bakke's Case: Are Quotas Unfair?

QUESTIONS FOR REFLECTION

1. What are the benefits of affirmative-action programs, according to Dworkin? Do you agree?
2. Why, according to Dworkin, does Bakke have no right to a place at the University of California at Davis Medical School? Do you agree?

On October 12, 1977, the Supreme Court heard oral argument in the case of *The Regents of the University of California v. Allan Bakke.* No lawsuit has ever been more widely watched or more thoroughly debated in the national and international press before the Court's decision. Still, some of the most pertinent facts set before the Court have not been clearly summarized.

The medical school of the University of California at Davis has an affirmative action program (called the "task force program") designed to admit more black and other minority students. It sets sixteen places aside for which only members of "educationally and economically disadvantaged minorities" compete. Allan Bakke, white, applied for one of the remaining eighty-four places; he was rejected but, since his test scores were relatively high, the medical school has conceded that it could not prove that he would have been rejected if the sixteen places reserved had been open to him. Bakke sued, arguing that the task force program deprived him of his constitutional rights. The California Supreme Court agreed, and ordered the medical school to admit him. The university appealed to the Supreme Court.

The Davis program for minorities is in certain respects more forthright (some would say cruder) than similar plans now in force in many other American universities and professional schools. Such programs aim to increase the enrollment of black and other minority students by allowing the fact of their race to count affirmatively as part of the case for admitting them. Some schools set a "target" of a particular number of minority places instead of setting aside a flat number of places. But Davis would not fill the number of places set aside unless there were sixteen minority candidates it considered clearly qualified for medical education. The difference is therefore one of administrative strategy and not of principle.

So the constitutional question raised by *Bakke* is of capital importance for higher education in the United States, and a large number of universities and schools have entered briefs *amicus curiae* urging the Court to reverse the California decision. They believe that if they are not free to use explicit racial criteria in their admissions programs, they will be unable to fulfill what they take to be their responsibilities to the nation.

It is often said that affirmative action programs aim to achieve a racially conscious society divided into racial and ethnic groups, each entitled as a group to some proportionable share of resources, careers, or opportunities. That is a perverse description. American society is currently a racially conscious society; this is the inevitable and evident consequence of a history of slavery, repression, and prejudice. Black men and women, boys and girls, are not free to choose for themselves in what roles—or as members of which social groups—others will characterize them. They are black, and no other feature of personality or allegiance or ambition will so thoroughly influence how they will be perceived and treated by others, and the range and character of the lives that will be open to them.

The tiny number of black doctors and other professionals is both a consequence and a continuing cause of American racial consciousness, one link in a long and self-fueling chain reaction. Affirmative action programs use racially explicit criteria because their immediate goal is to increase the number of members of certain races in these professions. But their long-term goal is to *reduce* the degree to which American society is overall a racially conscious society.

The programs rest on two judgments. The first is a judgment of social theory: that the United States will continue to be pervaded by racial divisions as long as the most lucrative, satisfying, and important careers remain mainly the prerogative of members of the white race, while others feel themselves systematically excluded from a professional and social elite. The second is a calculation of strategy: that increasing the number of blacks who are at work in the professions will, in the long run, reduce the sense of frustration and injustice and racial self-consciousness in the black community to the point at which blacks may begin to think of themselves as individuals who can succeed like others through talent and initiative. At that future point the consequences of nonracial admissions programs, whatever these consequences might be, could be accepted with no sense of racial barriers or injustice.

It is therefore the worst possible misunderstanding to suppose that affirmative action programs are designed to produce a balkanized America, divided into racial and ethnic subnations. They use strong measures because weaker ones will fail; but their ultimate goal is to lessen not to increase the importance of race in American social and professional life.

According to the 1970 census, only 2.1 percent of American doctors were black. Affirmative action programs aim to provide more black doctors to serve black patients. This is not because it is desirable that blacks treat blacks and whites treat whites, but because blacks, through no fault of their own, are now unlikely to be well served by whites, and because a failure to provide the doctors they trust will exacerbate rather than reduce the resentment that now leads them to trust only their own. Affirmative action tries to provide more blacks as classmates for white doctors, not because it is desirable that a medical school class reflect the racial makeup of the community as a whole, but because professional association between blacks and whites will decrease the degree to which whites think of blacks as a race rather than as people, and thus the degree to which blacks think of themselves that way. It tries to provide "role models" for future black doctors, not because it is desirable for a black boy or girl to find adult models only among blacks, but because our history has made them so conscious of their race that the success of whites, for now, is likely to mean little or nothing for them.

The history of the campaign against racial injustice since 1954, when the Supreme Court decided *Brown v. Board of Education,* is a history in large part of failure. We have not succeeded in reforming the racial consciousness of our society by racially neutral means. We are therefore obliged to look upon the arguments for affirmative action with sympathy and an open mind. Of course, if Bakke is right that such programs, no matter how effective they may be, violate his constitutional rights, then they cannot be permitted to continue. But we must not forbid them in the name of some mindless maxim, like the maxim that it cannot be right to fight fire with fire, or that the end cannot justify the means. If the strategic claims for affirmative action are cogent, they cannot be dismissed on the ground that racially explicit tests are distasteful. If such tests are distasteful, it can only be for reasons that make the underlying social realities the programs attack more distasteful still.

It is said that, in a pluralistic society, membership in a particular group cannot be used as a criterion of inclusion or exclusion from benefits. But group membership is, as a matter of social reality rather than formal admission standards, part of what determines inclusion or exclusion for us now. If we must choose between a society that is in fact liberal and an illiberal society that scrupulously avoids formal racial criteria, we can hardly appeal to the ideals of liberal pluralism to prefer the latter.

Archibald Cox of Harvard Law School, speaking for the University of California in oral argument, told the Supreme Court that this is the choice the United States must make. As things stand, he said, affirmative action programs are the only effective means of increasing the absurdly small number of black doctors. The California Supreme Court, in approving Bakke's claim, had urged the university to pursue that goal by methods that do not explicitly take race into account. But that is unrealistic. We must distinguish, Cox said, between two interpretations of what the California Court's recommendation means. It might mean that the university should aim at the same immediate goal, of increasing the proportion of black and other minority students in the medical school, by an admissions procedure that on the surface is not racially conscious.

That is a recommendation of hypocrisy. If those who administer the admissions standards, however these are phrased, understand that their immediate goal is to increase the number of blacks in the school, then they will use race as a criterion in making the various subjective judgments the explicit criteria will require, because that will be, given the goal, the only right way to make those judgments. The recommendation might mean, on the other hand, that the school should adopt some non-racially conscious goal, like increasing the number of disadvantaged students of all races, and then hope that that goal will produce an increase in the number of blacks as a by-product. But even if that strategy is less hypocritical (which is far from plain), it will almost certainly fail because no different goal, scrupulously administered in a non-racially conscious way, will significantly increase the number of black medical students.

Cox offered powerful evidence for that conclusion, and it is supported by the recent and comprehensive report of the Carnegie Council on Policy Studies in Higher Education. Suppose, for example, that the medical school sets aside separate places for applicants "disadvantaged" on some racially neutral test, like poverty, allowing only those disadvantaged in that way to compete for these places. If the school selects those from that group who scored best on standard medical school aptitude tests, then it will take almost no blacks, because blacks score relatively low even among the economically disadvantaged. But if the school chooses among the disadvantaged on some basis other than test scores, just so that more blacks will succeed, then it will not be administering the special procedure in a non-racially conscious way.

So Cox was able to put his case in the form of two simple propositions. A racially conscious test for admission, even one that sets aside certain places for qualified minority applicants exclusively, serves goals that are in themselves unobjectionable and even urgent. Such programs are, moreover, the only means that offer any significant promise of achieving these goals. If these programs are halted, then no more than a trickle of black students will enter medical or other professional schools for another generation at least.

If these propositions are sound, then on what ground can it be thought that such programs are either wrong or unconstitutional? We must notice an important distinction between two different sorts of objections that might be made. These programs are intended, as I said, to decrease the importance of race in the United States in the long run. It may be objected, first, that the programs will harm that goal more than they will advance it. There is no way now to prove that that is not so.

Cox conceded in his argument that there are costs and risks in these programs.

Affirmative action programs seem to encourage, for example, a popular misunderstanding, which is that they assume that racial or ethnic groups are entitled to proportionate shares of opportunities, so that Italian or Polish ethnic minorities are, in theory, as entitled to their proportionate shares as blacks or Chicanos or American Indians are entitled to the shares the present programs give them. That is a plain mistake: the programs are not based on the idea that those who are aided are entitled to aid, but only on the strategic hypothesis that helping them is now an effective way of attacking a national problem. Some medical schools may well make that judgment, under certain circumstances, about a white ethnic minority. Indeed it seems likely that some medical schools are even now attempting to help white Appalachian applicants, for example, under programs of regional distribution.

So the popular understanding is wrong, but so long as it persists it is a cost of the program because the attitudes it encourages tend to a degree to make people more rather than less conscious of race. There are other possible costs. It is said, for example, that some blacks find affirmative action degrading; they find that it makes them more rather than less conscious of prejudice against their race as such. This attitude is also based on a misperception, I think, but for a small minority of blacks at least it is a genuine cost.

In the view of the many important universities which have such programs, however, the gains will very probably exceed the losses in reducing racial consciousness overall. This view is hardly so implausible that it is wrong for these universities to seek to acquire the experience that will allow us to judge whether they are right. It would be particularly silly to forbid these experiments if we know that the failure to try will mean, as the evidence shows, that the status quo will almost certainly continue. In any case, this first objection could provide no argument that would justify a decision by the Supreme Court holding the programs unconstitutional. The Court has no business substituting its speculative judgment about the probable consequences of educational policies for the judgment of professional educators.

So the acknowledged uncertainties about the long-term results of such programs could not justify a Supreme Court decision making them illegal. But there is a second and very different form of objection. It may be argued that even if the programs *are* effective in making our society less a society dominated by race, they are nevertheless unconstitutional because they violate the individual constitutional rights of those, like Allan Bakke, who lose places in consequence. In the oral argument Reynold H. Colvin of San Francisco, who is Bakke's lawyer, made plain that his objection takes this second form. Mr. Justice White asked him whether he accepted that the goals affirmative action programs seek are important goals. Colvin acknowledged that they were. Suppose, Justice White continued, that affirmative action programs are, as Cox had argued, the only effective means of seeking such goals. Would Colvin nevertheless maintain that the programs are unconstitutional? Yes, he insisted, they would be, because his client has a constitutional right that the programs be abandoned, no matter what the consequences.

Colvin was wise to put his objections on this second ground; he was wise to claim that his client has rights that do not depend on any judgment about the likely consequences of affirmative action for society as a whole, because if he sustains that claim, then the Court must give him the relief he seeks.

But can he be right? If Allan Bakke has a constitutional right so important that the urgent goals of affirmative action must yield, then this must be because affirmative action violates some fundamental principle of political morality. This is not a case in which what might be called formal or technical law requires a decision one way or the other. There is no language in the Constitution whose plain meaning forbids affirmative action. Only the most naive theories of statutory construction could argue that such a result is required by the language of any earlier Supreme Court decision or of the Civil Rights Act of 1964 or of any other congressional enactment. If Colvin is right, it must be because Allan Bakke has not simply some technical legal right but an important moral right as well.

What could that right be? The popular argument frequently made on editorial pages is that Bakke has a right to be judged on his merit. Or that he has a right to be judged as an individual rather than as a member of a social group. Or that he has a right, as much as any black man, not to be sacrificed or excluded from any opportunity because of his race alone. But these catch phrases are deceptive here, because, as reflection demonstrates, the only genuine principle they describe is the principle that no one should suffer from the prejudice or contempt of others. And that principle is not at stake in this case at all. In spite of popular opinion, the idea that the *Bakke* case presents a conflict between a desirable social goal and important individual rights is a piece of intellectual confusion.

Consider, for example, the claim that individuals applying for places in medical school should be judged on merit, and merit alone. If that slogan means that admissions committees should take nothing into account but scores on some particular intelligence test, then it is arbitrary and, in any case, contradicted by the long-standing practice of every medical school. If it means, on the other hand, that a medical school should choose candidates that it supposes will make the most useful doctors, then everything turns on the judgment of what factors make different doctors useful. The Davis medical school assigned to each regular applicant, as well as to each minority applicant, what it called a "benchmark score." This reflected not only the results of aptitude tests and college grade averages, but a subjective evaluation of the applicant's chances of functioning as an effective doctor, in view of society's present needs for medical service. Presumably the qualities deemed important were different from the qualities that a law school or engineering school or business school would seek, just as the intelligence tests a medical school might use would be different from the tests these other schools would find appropriate.

There is no combination of abilities and skills and traits that constitutes "merit" in the abstract; if quick hands count as "merit" in the case of a prospective surgeon, this is because quick hands will enable him to serve the public better and for no other reason. If a black skin will, as a matter of regrettable fact, enable another doctor to do a different medical job better, then that black skin is by the same token "merit" as well. That argument may strike some as dangerous; but only because they confuse its conclusion—that black skin may be a socially useful trait in particular circumstances—with the very different and despicable idea that one race may be inherently more worthy than another.

Consider the second of the catch phrases I have mentioned. It is said that Bakke has a right to be judged as an "individual," in deciding whether he is to be admitted to medical school and thus to the medical profession, and not as a member of some group that is being judged as a whole. What can that mean? Any admissions procedure must rely on generalizations about groups that are justified only statistically. The regular admissions process at Davis, for example, set a cutoff figure for college grade-point averages. Applicants whose averages fell below that figure were not invited to any interview, and therefore rejected out of hand.

An applicant whose average fell one point below the cutoff might well have had personal qualities of dedication or sympathy that would have been revealed at an interview, and that would have made him or her a better doctor than some applicant whose average rose one point above the line. But the former is excluded from the process on the basis of a decision taken for administrative convenience and grounded in the generalization, unlikely to hold true for every individual, that those with grade averages below the cutoff will not have other qualities sufficiently persuasive. Even the use of standard Medical College Aptitude Tests (MCAT) as part of the admissions procedure requires judging people as part of groups, because it assumes that test scores are a guide to medical intelligence, which is in turn a guide to medical ability. Though this judgment is no doubt true statistically, it hardly holds true for every individual.

Allan Bakke was himself refused admission to two other medical schools, not because of his race but because of his age: these schools thought that a student entering medical school at the age of thirty-three was likely to make less of a contribution to medical care over his career than someone entering at the standard age of twenty-one. Suppose these schools relied, not on any detailed investigation of whether Bakke himself had abilities that would contradict the generalization in his specific case, but on a rule of thumb that allowed only the most cursory look at applicants over (say) the age of thirty. Did these two medical schools violate his right to be judged as an individual rather than as a member of a group?

The Davis medical school permitted whites to apply for the sixteen places reserved for members of "educationally or economically disadvantaged minorities," a phrase whose meaning might well include white ethnic minorities. In fact several whites have applied, though none has been accepted, and the California Court found that the special committee charged with administering the program had decided, in advance, against admitting any. Suppose that decision had been based on the following administrative theory: it is so unlikely that any white doctor can do as much to counteract racial imbalance in the medical professions as a well-qualified and trained black doctor can do that the committee should for reasons of convenience proceed on the presumption no white doctor could. That presumption is, as a matter of fact, more plausible than the corresponding presumption about medical students over the age of thirty, or even the presumption about applicants whose grade-point averages fall below the cutoff line. If the latter presumptions do not deny the alleged right of individuals to be judged as individuals in an admissions procedure, then neither can the former.

Colvin, in oral argument, argued the third of the catch phrases I mentioned. He said that his client had a right not to be excluded from medical school because of his race alone, and this as a statement of constitutional right sounds more plausible than claims about the right to be judged on merit or as an individual. It sounds plausible, however, because it suggests the following more complex principle. Every citizen has a constitutional right that he not suffer disadvantage, at least in the competition for any public benefit, because the race or religion or sect or region or other natural or artificial group to which he belongs is the object of prejudice or contempt.

That is a fundamentally important constitutional right, and it is that right that was systematically violated for many years by racist exclusions and anti-Semitic quotas. Color bars and Jewish quotas were not unfair just because they made race or religion relevant or because they fixed on qualities beyond individual control. It is true that blacks or Jews do not choose to be blacks or Jews. But it is also true that those who score low in aptitude or admissions tests do not choose their levels of intelligence. Nor do those denied admission because they are too old, or because they do not come from a part of the country underrepresented in the school, or because they cannot play basketball well, choose not to have the qualities that made the difference.

Race seems different because exclusions based on race have historically been motivated not by some instrumental calculation, as in the case of intelligence or age or regional distribution or athletic ability, but because of contempt for the excluded race or religion as such. Exclusion by race was in itself an insult, because it was generated by and signaled contempt.

Bakke's claim, therefore, must be made more specific than it is. He says he was kept out of medical school because of his race. Does he mean that he was kept out because his race is the object of prejudice or contempt? That suggestion is absurd. A very high proportion of those who were accepted (and, presumably, of those who run the admissions program) were members of the same race. He therefore means simply that if he had been black he would have been accepted, with no suggestion that this would have been so because blacks are thought more worthy or honorable than whites.

That is true: no doubt he would have been accepted if he were black. But it is also true, and in exactly the same sense, that he would have been accepted if he had been more intelligent, or made a better impression in his interview, or, in the case of other schools, if he had been younger when he decided to become a doctor. Race is not, in *his* case, a different matter from these other factors equally beyond his control. It is not a different matter because in his case race is not distinguished by the special character of public insult. On the contrary, the program presupposes that his race is still widely if wrongly thought to be superior to others.

In the past it made sense to say that an excluded black or Jewish student was being sacrificed because of his race or religion; that meant that his or her exclusion was treated as desirable in itself, not because it contributed to any goal in which he as well as the rest of society might take pride. Allan Bakke is being "sacrificed" because of his race only in a very artificial sense of the word. He is being "sacrificed" in the same artificial sense because of his level of intelligence, since he would have been accepted if he were more clever than he is. In both cases he is being excluded not by prejudice but because of a rational calculation about the socially most beneficial use of limited resources for medical education.

It may now be said that this distinction is too subtle, and that if racial classifications have been and may still be used for malign purposes, then everyone has a flat right that racial classifications not be used at all. This is the familiar appeal to the lazy virtue of simplicity. It supposes that if a line is difficult to draw, or might be difficult to administer if drawn, then there is wisdom in not making the attempt to draw it. There may be cases in which that is wise, but those would be cases in which nothing of great value would as a consequence be lost. If racially conscious admissions policies now offer the only substantial hope for bringing more qualified black and other minority doctors into the profession, then a great loss is suffered if medical schools are not allowed voluntarily to pursue such programs. We should then be trading away a chance to attack certain and present injustice in order to gain protection we may not need against speculative abuses we have other means to prevent. And such abuses cannot, in any case, be worse than the injustice to which we would then surrender.

We have now considered three familiar slogans, each widely thought to name a constitutional right that enables Allan Bakke to stop programs of affirmative action no matter how effective or necessary these might be. When we inspect these slogans, we find that they can stand for no genuine principle except one. This is the important principle that no one in our society should suffer because he is a member of a group thought less worthy of respect, as a group, than other groups. We have different aspects of that principle in mind when we say that individuals should be judged on merit, that they should be judged as individuals, and that they should not suffer disadvantages because of their race. The spirit of that fundamental principle is the spirit of the goal that affirmative action is intended to serve. The principle furnishes no support for those who find, as Bakke does, that their own interests conflict with that goal.

It is regrettable when any citizen's expectations are defeated by new programs serving some more general concern. It is regrettable, for example, when established small businesses fail because new and superior roads are built; in that case people have invested more than Bakke has. And they have more reason to believe their businesses will continue than Bakke had to suppose he could have entered the Davis medical school at thirty-three, even without a task force program.

There is, of course, no suggestion in that program that Bakke shares in any collective or individual guilt for racial injustice in the United States; or that he is any less entitled to concern or respect than any black student accepted in the program. He has been disappointed, and he must have the sympathy due that disappointment, just as any other disappointed applicant—even one with much worse test scores who would not have been accepted in any event—must have sympathy. Each is disappointed because places in medical schools are scarce resources and must be used to provide what the more general society most needs. It is not Bakke's fault that racial justice is now a special need—but he has no right to prevent the most effective measures of securing that justice from being used.

THOMAS SOWELL

"Affirmative Action": A Worldwide Disaster

Thomas Sowell is Senior Research Fellow at the Hoover Institution at Stanford University. (Source: Reprinted from Commentary *[December 1989], by permission; all rights reserved.)*

QUESTIONS FOR REFLECTION

1. What patterns does Sowell find in affirmative-action programs around the world?
2. What are Sowell's responses to arguments from compensation? Do you find them convincing?
3. To what incentives do affirmative-action policies give rise, according to Sowell? How are these incentives harmful, in his view?
4. Some advocates of affirmative action believe that race is a good proxy for disadvantage in general. Sowell disagrees. Why? What evidence does he present?

Arguments for and against "affirmative action" have raged for about twenty years in the United States. Similar arguments have provoked controversy—and even bloodshed—for a longer or a shorter period, in the most disparate societies, scattered around the world. India, Nigeria, Australia, Guyana, Malaysia, Sri Lanka, Pakistan, and Indonesia are just some of the countries where some groups receive official, government-sanctioned preferences over others. While the American phrase "affirmative action" is used in Australia and Canada, other countries have used a variety of other phrases, such as "positive discrimination" (India), "sons of the soil" preferences (Indonesia, Malaysia), "standardization" (Sri Lanka), or "reflecting the federal character" of the country (Nigeria). The same general principle of government apportionment of coveted positions, to supersede the competition of the marketplace or of academia, was of course also embodied in the *numerus clausus* laws used to restrict the opportunities of Jews in prewar Central and Eastern Europe.

The countries with preferential policies have varied enormously in cultural, political, economic, and other ways. The groups receiving preferences have likewise varied greatly, from locally or nationally dominant groups in some countries to the poorest and most abject groups, such as the untouchables of India. Such vast disparities in settings and people make it all the more striking that there are common patterns among these countries—patterns with serious implications for "affirmative-action" policies in the United States. Among these patterns are the following:

1. Preferential programs, even when explicitly and repeatedly defined as "temporary," have tended not only to persist but also to expand in scope, either embracing more groups or spreading to wider realms for the same groups, or both. Even preferential programs established with legally mandated cut-off dates, as in India and Pakistan, have continued far past those dates by subsequent extensions.

2. Within the groups designated by government as recipients of preferential treatment, the benefits have usually gone disproportionately to those members already more fortunate.

3. Group polarization has tended to increase in the wake of preferential programs, with nonpreferred groups reacting adversely, in ways ranging from political backlash to mob violence and civil war.
4. Fraudulent claims of belonging to the designated beneficiary groups have been widespread and have taken many forms in various countries.

In the United States, as in other countries around the world, the empirical consequences of preferential policies have received much less attention than the rationales and goals of such policies. Too often these rationales and goals have been sufficient unto themselves, both in the political arena and in courts of law. Without even an attempt at empirical assessment of costs versus benefits, with no attempt to pinpoint either losers or gainers, discussions of preferential policies are often exercises in assertion, counter-assertion, and accusation. Illusions flourish in such an atmosphere. So do the disappointments and bitterness to which illusions lead.

Foremost among these illusions is the belief that group "disparities" in "representation" are suspect anomalies that can be corrected by having the government temporarily apportion places on the basis of group membership. Every aspect of this belief fails the test of evidence, in country after country. The prime moral illusion is that preferential policies compensate for wrongs suffered. This belief has been supported only by a thin veneer of emotional rhetoric, seldom examined but often reiterated.

I. The Assumptions of "Affirmative Action"

"Temporary" Policies

When U.S. Supreme Court Justice William J. Brennan described the "affirmative-action" plan in the *Weber* case as "a temporary measure," he was echoing a view widely held, not only in the United States but also around the world. Britain's Lord Scarman likewise said:

> We can and for the present must accept the loading of the law in favor of one group at the expense of others, defending it as a temporary expedient in the balancing process which has to be undertaken when and where there is social and economic inequality.

The rhetoric of transience and the reality of persistence and proliferation are both international features of preferential policies. "Affirmative-action" plans initially justified in the United States by the unique historic sufferings of blacks have been successively extended, over the years, to groups that now add up to several times as many people as the black population—and more than half of the total American population. These include not only American Indians, Hispanics, and Asians, but also women. A very similar pattern emerged in India, where official preferences were established more than forty years ago for untouchables, for some tribal groups, and for unspecified "other backward classes." Since then, so many groups have managed to get themselves included under "other backward classes" that they now outnumber the untouchables and the tribal peoples put together.

Even where no new groups are added to those legally entitled to official preferences, new occupations, institutions, and sectors of the society can fall under the coverage of preferential policies. Malays were granted preferential employment in government back in colonial Malaya under the British. After Malaya became independent Malaysia, and especially after the "New Economic Policy" announced in 1969, preferences spread to university admissions, government loans, occupational licenses, and employment in private businesses, both local and foreign-owned. The island nation of Sri Lanka has followed a pattern much like that of Malaysia. Preferences for the Sinhalese have not spread to other groups but have simply become more pronounced and more widespread over time.

Perhaps the classic example of preferences that spread far beyond their initial group and their original rationale have been the preferences in Pakistan. The desperately poor Bengalis of East Pakistan were "underrepresented" in the civil service, the military, business, and the professions. Even the administration of East Pakistan was filled with West Pakistanis. Preferential policies to correct this were advocated in 1949 as "temporary" expedients to be phased out in five to ten years. In reality, however, these policies have lasted decades beyond this time and in 1984 were extended to 1994 by the late President Zia. Not only did preferential quotas spread well beyond people from the East Pakistan region; they persisted long after East Pakistan broke away in 1971 to form the independent nation of Bangladesh. In other words, those who provided the initial rationale for preferential policies have now disappeared by secession but the policies themselves have acquired a political life of their own.

Despite such patterns in these and other countries, the word "temporary" continues to be used in discussions of preferential policies—judicial and scholarly, as well as popular and political. No argument seems to be considered necessary to show that this transience can be enforced, so that the word "temporary" will be something more than political decoration. Indeed, few seem to feel a need to specify whether the dimensions of "temporary" are to be measured in actual units of time or by the attainment of some preconceived social results. If the latter, then the distinction between "temporary" and "eternal" can be wholly illusory in practice. In short, the nebulousness of the concept of "temporary" preference has matched its futility.

Statistical Disparities

Equally nebulous are the assumptions about the statistical "disparities" and "imbalances" that preferential policies are supposed to correct.

The idea that large statistical disparities between groups are unusual—and therefore suspicious—is commonplace, but only among those who have not bothered to study the history of racial, ethnic, and other groups in countries around the world. Among leading scholars who have in fact devoted years of research to such matters, a radically different picture emerges. Donald L. Horowitz of Duke University, at the end of a massive and masterful international study of ethnic groups—a study highly praised in scholarly journals—examined the idea of a society where groups are "proportionately represented" at different levels and in different sectors. He concluded that "few, if any, societies have ever approximated this description."

A worldwide study of military forces and police forces by Cynthia Enloe of Clark University likewise concluded that "militaries fall far short of mirroring, even roughly, the multi-ethnic societies" from which they come. Moreover, just "as one is unlikely to find a police force or a military that mirrors its plural society, so one is unlikely to find a representative bureaucracy." One reason is that "it is common for different groups to rely on different mobility ladders." Some choose the military, some the bureaucracy, and some various parts of the private sector. Even within the military, different branches tend to have very different racial or ethnic compositions—the Afrikaners, for example, being slightly underrepresented in the South African navy and greatly overrepresented in the South African army, though their utter dominance in the government ensures that they cannot be discriminated against in either branch. Powerless minorities have likewise been greatly overrepresented or even dominant in particular branches of the military or the police—the Chinese in Malaysia's air force and among detectives in the police force, for example.

In the private sector as well, it is commonplace for minorities to be overrepresented, or even dominant, in competitive industries where they have no power to prevent others from establishing rival businesses. Jewish prominence in the clothing industry, not only in the United States, but in Argentina and Chile as well, did not reflect any ability to prevent other Americans, Argentines, or Chileans from manufacturing garments, but simply the advantages of the Jews' having brought needle-trade skills and experience with them from Eastern Europe. The fact that Jews owned more than half the clothing stores in mid-19th-century Melbourne likewise reflected that same advantage, rather than any ability to forbid other Australians from selling clothes. In a similar way, German minorities have been dominant as pioneers in piano manufacturing in colonial America, czarist Russia, Australia, France, and England. Italian fishermen, Japanese farmers, and Irish politicians have been among many other minority groups with special success in special fields in various countries, without any ability to keep out others.

Another distinguished scholar who has studied multi-ethnic societies around the world, Myron Weiner of MIT, refers to "the universality of ethnic inequality." He points out that those inequalities are multidimensional:

> All multi-ethnic societies exhibit a tendency for ethnic groups to engage in different occupations, have different levels (and, often, types) of education, receive different incomes, and occupy a different place in the social hierarchy.

Yet the pattern Professor Weiner has seen, after years of research, as a "universality" is routinely assumed to be an *anomaly,* not only by preferential-policy advocates, but also by the intelligentsia, the media, legislators, and judges—all of whom tend to assume, as a *norm,* what Professor Horowitz has found to exist (or even to be approximated) in "few, if any, societies." That what exists widely across the planet is regarded as an anomaly, while what exists virtually nowhere is regarded as a norm, is a tribute to the effectiveness of sheer reiteration in establishing a vision—and of the difficulties of dispelling a prevailing vision by facts.

Some might try to salvage the statistical argument for discrimination by describing discrimination as also being universal. But, to repeat, groups who are in no position to discriminate against anybody have often been overrepresented in coveted positions—the Chinese in Malaysian universities, the Tamils in Sri Lankan universities, the southerners in Nigerian universities, all during the 1960's, and Asians in American universities today being just some of the minorities of whom this has been true. All sorts of other powerless minorities have dominated particular industries or sectors of the economy, the intellectual community, or government employment. Among businessmen, India's Gujaratis in East Africa, the Lebanese in West Africa, the Chinese in Southeast Asia, the Jews in Eastern Europe, and Koreans and Vietnamese in black ghettos across the United States are just some examples. Among high government officials, the Germans were greatly overrepresented in czarist Russia, as were Christians in the Ottoman empire. Among intellectuals, the Scots were as dominant in 18th- and 19th-century Britain as the Jews have been in other parts of Europe. In short, large statistical disparities have been commonplace, both in the presence of discrimination and in its absence. Indeed, large disparities have been commonplace in the utilization of preferential programs designed to reduce disparities.

The intellectual and political *coup* of those who promote the randomness assumption is to put the burden of proof entirely on others. It is not merely the individual employer, for example, who must disprove this assumption in his own particular case in order to escape a charge of discrimination. All who oppose the randomness assumption find themselves confronted with the task of disproving an elusive plausibility, for which no evidence is offered. As for counter-evidence, no enumeration of the myriad ways in which groups are grossly disparate—in age of marriage, alcohol consumption, immigration patterns, performance in sports, performance on tests—can ever be conclusive, even when extended past the point where the patience of the audience is exhausted.

Those viscerally convinced of the pervasiveness of discrimination and its potency as an explanation of social disparities—and convinced also of the effectiveness of preferential policies as a remedy—are little troubled by the logical shakiness of the statistical evidence. That is all the more reason for others to be doubly troubled—not simply because an incorrect policy may be followed but also, and more importantly, because actions ostensibly based on the rule of law are in substance based on visceral convictions, the essence of lynch law. . . .

Assumptions as Law

Flaws in logic or evidence are unfortunate in intellectual speculation but they are far more serious in courts of law, where major penalties may be inflicted on those whose employees or students, for example, do not have a racial or ethnic composition that meets the preconceptions of other people. Some U.S. Supreme Court Justices have repeatedly treated statistical disparities as tantamount to discrimination and assumed the task of restoring groups to where they would have been otherwise. Even where group disparities in "representation" reflect demonstrable performance disparities, these performance disparities themselves have been taken as proof of societal discrimination. Thus, in the *Weber* case, Justice Harry Blackmun declared that there could be "little doubt that any lack of skill" on the part of minority workers competing with Brian Weber "has its roots in purposeful discrimination of the past." In the *Bakke* case, four Justices declared that the failure of minority medical-school applicants to perform as well as Allan Bakke "was due principally to the effects of past discrimination." The Court's task, therefore, was one of "putting minority applicants in the position they would have been in if not for the evil of racial discrimination."

All this presupposes a range of knowledge that no one has ever possessed. Ironically, this sweeping assumption of knowledge has been combined with an apparent ignorance of vast disparities in performance, disparities favoring groups with no power to discriminate against anybody. From such judicial speculation it is only a short step to the idea of restoring groups to where they would have been—and *what* they would have been—but for the offending discrimination.

What would the average Englishman be like today "but for" the Norman conquest? What would the average Japanese be like "but for" the enforced isolation of Japan for two-and-a-half centuries under the Tokugawa shoguns? What would the Middle East be like "but for" the emergence of Islam? In any other context besides preferential-policy issues, the presumption of knowing the answers to such questions would be regarded as ridiculous, even as intellectual speculation, much less as a basis for serious legal action.

To know how one group's employment, education, or other pattern differs statistically from another's is usually easy. What is difficult to know are the many variables determining the interest, skill, and performance of those individuals from various groups who are being considered for particular jobs, roles, or institutions. What is virtually impossible to know are the patterns that would exist in a non-discriminatory world—the deviations from which would indicate the existence and magnitude of discrimination.

Age distribution and geographic distribution are only two very simple factors which can play havoc with the assumption that groups would be evenly or randomly distributed in occupations and institutions, in the absence of discrimination. When one group's median age is a decade younger than another's—not at all uncommon—that alone may be enough to cause the younger group to be statistically "overrepresented" in sports, crime, and entry-level jobs, as well as in those kinds of diseases and accidents that are more prevalent among the young, while the older group is overrepresented in homes for the elderly, in the kinds of jobs requiring long years of experience, and in the kinds of diseases and accidents especially prevalent among older people.

Another very simple factor operating against an even "representation" of groups is that many ethnic groups are distributed geographically in patterns differing from one another. It would be unlikely that American ethnic groups concentrated in cold states like Minnesota and Wisconsin would be as well represented among citrus growers and tennis players as they are on hockey teams and among skiers. It is also unlikely that groups concentrated in land-locked states would be equally represented in maritime activities, or that groups from regions lacking mineral deposits would be as well-represented among miners or in other occupations associated with extractive industries as groups located in Pennsylvania or West Virginia.

Differences in geographic concentrations among racial and ethnic groups are by no means confined to the U.S. In Brazil, people of German and Japanese ancestry are concentrated in the south. In Switzerland, whole regions are predominantly French, German, or Italian. In countries around the world, an overwhelming majority of the Chinese or the Jewish population is heavily concentrated in a few major cities—often in just one city in a given country. Group differences in geographical distribution can reach right down to the neighborhood level or even to particular streets. In Buenos Aires, people of Italian ancestry have concentrated in particular neighborhoods or on particular streets, according to the places of their own or their ancestral origins in Italy. In Bombay, people from different parts of India are likewise concentrated in particular neighborhoods or on particular streets.

Lest the point be misunderstood, while these two simple and obvious factors—age and location—are capable of disrupting the even "representation" that many assume to exist in the absence of discrimination, there are also innumerable other factors, of varying degrees of complexity and influence, that can do the same. Moreover, differences in age and location may play a significant role in explaining *some* socioeconomic differences between *some* groups but not other socioeconomic differences between those groups, or among other groups. The purpose here is not to pinpoint the reasons for intergroup differences—or even to assume that they can all be pinpointed—but rather to show how arbitrary and unfounded is the assumption that groups would be evenly "represented," in the absence of discrimination. Precisely because the known differences among groups are large and multidimensional, the presumption of weighing these differences so comprehensively and accurately as to know where some group would be "but for" discrimination approaches hubris.

Even the more modest goal of knowing the *general direction* of the deviation of a group's position from where it would have been without discrimination is by no means necessarily achievable. What are the "effects" of centuries of injustice, punctuated by recurring outbursts of lethal mass violence, against the overseas Chinese in Southeast Asia or against the Jews in Europe? Both groups are generally more prosperous than their persecutors. Would they have been still more prosperous in the absence of such adversity? Perhaps—but many peoples with a long history of peace, and with prosperity supplied by nature itself, have quietly stagnated. This is not to say that the Jews and the Chinese would have done so. It is only to say that *we do not know and cannot know.* No amount of good intentions will make us omniscient. No fervent invocation of "social justice" will supply the missing knowledge.

Incentives and Results

"Affirmative-action" policies assume not only a level of knowledge that no one has ever possessed but also a degree of control that no one has ever exercised. Proponents of preferential policies have tended to reason in terms of the rationales and goals of such policies—not in terms of the *incentives* these policies create. Yet these incentives acquire a life of their own, independent of—and often counter to—the avowed goals of preferential policies. Nor are these simply isolated "mistakes" that can be "corrected." They are the fruition of fundamental misconceptions of the degree of control that can be maintained over a whole galaxy of complex social interactions.

At the individual level, the potential beneficiary and the potential loser are not mere blocks of wood passively placed where the policy dictates. Nor are they automatons who continue acting as before, except for modifications specified for them by others. Rather, they respond *in their own ways* to preferential policies. One of these ways was exemplified by a question raised by a group activist seeking preferential hiring in India's city of Hyderabad: "Are we not entitled to jobs just because we are not as qualified?" A Nigerian wrote of "the tyranny of skills." The sense of entitlement—independent of skills or performance—has long been an accompaniment of preferential policies, for the most disparate groups in the most disparate societies.

The late South African economist W. H. Hutt pointed out long ago that the most "virulent" white supporters of early racial-preferential policies in the mines were "those who had not troubled to qualify themselves for promotion," and who therefore relied on being white instead. Today, in the Virgin Islands, even schoolchildren excuse their own substandard academic and behavioral performance by pointing out that government jobs will be waiting for them as U.S. citizens—jobs for which their better-behaved and better-performing West Indian classmates are ineligible. In Malaysia, likewise, "Malay students, who sense that their future is assured, feel less pressure to perform," according to a study there. A study of black colleges in the United States similarly noted that even students planning postgraduate study often showed no sense of urgency about needing to be prepared "because they believed that certain rules would simply be set aside for them." In India, even a fervent advocate of the untouchables, and of preferential policies for them, has urged untouchable students in medical and engineering schools to abandon their "indifference."

The disincentives created by group preferences apply to both preferred and non-preferred groups. As W. H. Hutt wrote of the South African "color bar," these racial preferences "have vitiated the efficiency of the non-whites by destroying incentives" and have also "weakened incentives to efficiency on the part of the whites who have been featherbedded." A very similar principle is found in the very different setting of Jamaica, after it became independent and black-run. There it was the whites who faced the disincentives of the non-preferred. Many withdrew from the competition for public office because they "felt that the day of the black man had come and questioned why they had to make the effort if the coveted job or the national honor would go to the blacks, despite their qualifications." The upshot is that preferential policies represent not simply a transfer of benefits from one group to another, but can also represent a net loss, as both groups perform less well as a result.

Those who initiate preferential policies cannot sufficiently control the reactions of either preferred or non-preferred groups to ensure that such policies will have the desired effect, or even move in the desired direction: Counterproductive reactions that reduce national prosperity or social tranquility adversely affect even members of the preferred group, who are also members of the general society. Whether their gains in one role exceed their losses in the other role is an empirical question whose answer depends on the specifics of each situation. One of the clearly undesired and uncontrolled consequences of preferential policies has been a backlash by non-preferred groups. This backlash has ranged from campus racial incidents in the United States to a bloody civil war in Sri Lanka.

Honors

Nowhere is control more illusory than in the awarding of honors, whose very meaning and effect depend upon other people's opinions. Preferential honors for members of particular groups can easily render suspect not only those particular honors but also honors fully merited and awarded after free and open competition. If one-fifth of the honors received by preferred groups are awarded under double standards, the other four-fifths are almost certain to fall under a cloud of suspicion as well, if only because some of those who lost out in the competition would prefer to believe that they were not bested fairly. It is by no means clear that more real honors—which are ultimately other people's opinions—will come to a group preferentially given awards. Preferential honors can in practice mean a moratorium on recognition of the group's achievements, which can be confounded with patronage or pay-offs. This need not inevitably be so. The point is that the matter is out of the control of those who decide award policy, and in the hands of others observing the outcomes and deciding what to make of them.

Honor is more than a sop to personal vanity. It is a powerful incentive which accomplishes many social tasks, including tasks that are too arduous and dangerous to be compensated by money—even inducing individuals in crisis situations to sacrifice their lives for the greater good of others. In more mundane matters, honor and respect from one's colleagues and subordinates are important and sometimes indispensable aids, without which even the most talented and conscientious individuals sometimes cannot fulfill their promise. To jeopardize the respect and recognition of individuals from preferred groups by rewarding "honors" tainted with double standards is not only to downgrade their own achievements but also to downgrade their chances of accomplishing those achievements in the first place. For example, minority faculty members have often complained about a lack of intellectual and research interaction with their collegues, and of being thought of as "affirmative-action" professors. After the media revealed that black students were admitted to the Harvard Medical School with lower qualifications, white patients began to refuse to be examined by such students. The negative effects of tainted honors are by no means limited to academia.

Partial Preferences

The illusion of control includes the belief that preferential policies can be extended *partway* into a process while maintaining equal treatment in the remainder of the process. For example, in the early days of "affirmative action" in the United States, it was sometimes asserted that special efforts to recruit minority employees or minority students would be followed by equal treatment at the actual selection stage and afterward. Special concern for particular groups might also mean only special scrutiny to see that they were treated equally. President John F. Kennedy's Executive Order No. 10,925 required that employers who were government contractors "take affirmative action to ensure that the applicants are employed, and that employees are treated during employment without regard to race, creed, color, or national origin." That is virtually the antithesis of what "affirmative action" has come to mean today, either in the United States or in other countries where the term refers to statistical results viewed precisely *with regard* to race, color, creed, or national origin.

The concept of preferential concern stopping partway into a process is not confined to employment or to the United States. In India, a government minister has urged a small lowering of university-admissions standards for students from scheduled castes (untouchables) and scheduled tribes, with the proviso that "he was recommending relaxation for admission and not for passing or grading." Similar views were once expressed in the United States, where special recruitment programs for minority students quickly led to lower admission standards for them—and this in turn sometimes led to "affirmative grading," to prevent excessive failures by minority students. Double standards in grading may originate with the individual professor or be a result of administrative pressures. Halfway around the world—in Soviet Central Asia—professors are also pressured to give preferential grading to Central Asian students. In Malaysia, preferential grading is virtually institutionalized. As Gordon P. Means puts it:

> Although grading is supposed to be without reference to ethnicity, all grades must be submitted to an evaluation review committee having heavy Malay representation. Individual faculty members report various instances when grades were unilaterally raised, apparently for purposes of "ethnic balance."

Sometimes preferential grading takes the less direct form of creating special or easier subjects for particular groups, such as Maori Studies in New Zealand, Malay Studies in Singapore, or a variety of ethnic studies in the United States.

Whether in employment, education, or other areas, carefully limited or fine-tuned preferences have repeatedly proved to be illusory. Neither time limitations nor other limitations have in fact stopped their persistence and spread.

A wide variety of moral arguments has been used to justify preferential policies. Some of these arguments have little in common, except for being largely unexamined in the excitement of crusading zeal—and being successful politically. Among the reasons given for preferences are that (1) the group is indigenous; (2) the group has been historically wronged; and (3) the group happens to be less well represented in desirable institutions or occupations, for whatever reason, so that this "imbalance" must be "corrected."

Whatever the arguments for preferential policies, these preferences (as we have seen) can long outlive the validity of those arguments, whether the degree of validity be zero or 100 percent, or anywhere in between. A genuinely disadvantaged group can cling to preferences, or seek more, long after their disadvantages have been redressed. The moral question, therefore, is not simply whether particular groups deserve particular benefits for particular periods of time, or until particular social conditions are achieved. The real quesion is whether the *actual consequences of the particular processes* being initiated are likely to be justified, morally or otherwise. . . .

Historical Compensation

The wrongs of history have been invoked by many groups in many countries as a moral claim for contemporary compensation. Much emotional fervor goes into such claims but the question here is about their logic or morality. Assuming for the sake of argument that the historical claims are factually correct, which may not be the case in all countries, to transfer benefits between two groups of living contemporaries because of what happened between two sets of dead people is to raise the question whether any sufferer is in fact being compensated. Only where both wrongs and compensation are viewed as collectivized and inheritable does redressing the wrongs of history have a moral, or even a logical, basis.

The biological continuity of the generations lends plausibility to the notion of group compensation—but only if guilt can be inherited. Otherwise there are simply windfall gains and windfall losses among contemporaries, according to the accident of their antecedents. Moreover, few people would accept this as a general principle to be applied consistently, however much they may advocate it out of compassion (or guilt) over the fate of particular unfortunates. No one would advocate that today's Jews are morally entitled to put today's Germans in concentration camps, in compensation for the Nazi Holocaust. Most people would not only be horrified at any such suggestion but would also regard it as a second act of gross immorality, in no way compensating the first, but simply adding to the sum total of human sins.

Sometimes a more sociological, rather than moral, claim is made that living contemporaries are suffering from the *effects* of past wrongs and that it is these effects which must be offset by compensatory preferences. Tempting as it is to imagine that the contemporary troubles of historically wronged groups are due to those wrongs, this is confusing causation with morality. The contemporary socioeconomic position of groups in a given society often bears no relationship to the historic wrongs they have suffered. Both in Canada and in the United States, the Japanese have significantly higher incomes than the whites, who have a documented history of severe anti-Japanese discrimination in both countries. The same story could be told of the Chinese in Malaysia, Indonesia, and many other countries around the world, of the Jews in countries with virulent anti-Semitism, and a wide variety of other groups in a wide variety of other countries. Among poorer groups as well, the level of poverty often has little correlation with the degree of oppression. No one would claim that the historic wrongs suffered by Puerto Ricans in the United States exceed those suffered by blacks, but the average Puerto Rican income is lower than the average income of blacks.

None of this proves that historic wrongs have no contemporary effects. Rather, it is a statement about the limitations of our knowledge, which is grossly inadequate to the task undertaken and likely to remain so. To pretend to disentangle the innumerable sources of intergroup differences is an exercise in hubris rather than morality.

As one contemporary example of how easy it is to go astray in such efforts, it was repeated for years that the high rate of single-parent, teenage pregnancy among blacks were "a legacy of slavery." Evidence was neither asked nor given. But when serious scholarly research was finally done on this subject, the evidence devastated this widely held belief. The vast majority of black children grew up in two-parent homes, even under slavery itself, and for generations thereafter. The current levels of single-parent, teenage pregnancy are a phenomenon of the last half of the 20th century and are a disaster that has also struck groups with wholly different histories from that of blacks. Passionate commitment to "social justice" can never be a substitute for knowing what you are talking about.

Those who attribute any part of the socioeconomic fate of any group to factors internal to that group are often accused of "blaming the victim." This may sometimes be part of an attempt to salvage the historical-compensation principle but it deserves separate treatment.

"Blame" and "Victims"

The illusion of morality is often confused with the reality of causation. If group A originates in a country where certain scientific and technological skills are widespread and group B originates in a country where they are not, then when they immigrate to the same third country, they are likely to be statistically "represented" to very different degrees in occupations and institutions requiring such skills. There is nothing mysterious about this, in causal terms. But those who wish to attribute this disparity to institutional discrimination are quick to respond to any mention of group B's lesser scientfic-technological background as a case of "blaming the victim." By making the issue *who* is to blame, such arguments evade or preempt the more fundamental question—whether this is a matter of blame in the first place.

Clearly today's living generation—in any group—cannot be *blamed* for the centuries of cultural evolution that went on before they were born, often in lands that they have never seen. Nor can they be blamed for the fact that the accident of birth caused them to inherit one culture rather than another. In causal terms, it would be a staggering coincidence if cultures evolving in radically different historical circumstances were equally effective for all purposes when transplanted to a new society. Blame has nothing to do with it. . . .

"Underrepresentation" and "Life Chances"

Quite aside from claims of historic wrongs, the argument has often been made—on grounds of morality as well as political or social expediency—that the "underrepresentation" of particular groups in desirable roles is an "imbalance" to be "corrected." Majorities have pressed such claims as readily as minorities, in circumstances where their only disadvantages were their own lack of skills or interest, as well as where a plausible case could be made that imposed disabilities have handicapped them.

Among the many unexamined assumptions behind preferential policies is the belief that intergroup friction is a function of the magnitude of income gaps, so that more social harmony can be achieved by reducing these gaps. As with so much that has been said in this area, evidence has been neither asked nor given, while counter-evidence is plentiful, varied, and ignored.

In Bombay, the hosility of the Maharashtrians has been directed primarily at the South Indians, who are somewhat ahead of them economically, rather than against the Gujaratis, who are far ahead of them. Throughout sub-Saharan Africa, there has historically been far more hostility directed by Africans against Asians than against Europeans, who are economically far ahead of both. A similar pattern is found *within* African groups. In Nigeria, for example, the Yoruba were far ahead of the Ibo economically in 1940, while there was a much smaller gap at that time between the Hausa and the Ibo. Yet the hostility and violence between Hausa and Ibo in that era greatly exceeded any friction between either of these groups and the Yoruba. Later, as the Ibos rose, narrowing the gap between themselves and the Yoruba, it was precisely then that Ibo-Yoruba outbreaks of violence occurred.

Advocates of preferential policies often express a related belief, similarly unsupported by evidence, that an even distribution of groups across sectors of the economy tends to reduce social frictions and hostility. Much history suggests the opposite, that (in the words of Professor Horowitz) "the ethnic division of labor is more a shield than a sword."

The utter dominance of particular sectors by particular minority groups has been quietly accepted for generations in many countries—until a specific, organized campaign has been whipped up against the minority, often by members of the majority who are seeking to enter the minority-dominated sector and are finding their competition very formidable. Often majority-group customers or suppliers actually prefer dealing with the minority-run entrepreneurs. Even in the midst of ethnic riots against other groups certain middleman minorities have been spared—the Greeks in the Sudan, Hindus in Burma, Marwaris in Assam. Organized boycotts of minority businessmen have been spearheaded by majority-group business rivals, from Uganda and Kenya to the Philippines and the United States. Contrary to what is widely (and lightly) assumed, neither an even representation of groups nor mass resentment at unevenness is "natural."

Repeatedly, in countries scattered around the world, it has been precisely the rise of newly emerging ethnic competitors—whether in business, government, or the professions—which has produced not only friction with groups already dominant in the sectors concerned but also, and much more importantly, has led the newcomers to whip up their whole group emotionally against the already established group. A Sri Lankan legislator noted this pattern early in that country's inter-ethnic troubles:

> University graduates and people like that are the cause of all the trouble—not the vast mass of the Sinhalese people. It is those men, these middle-class unemployed seeking employment, who are jealous of the fact that a few Tamils occupy seats of office in government—these are the people who have gone round the countryside, rousing the masses and creating this problem.

Halfway around the world a similar charge was made, that "the educated Nigerian is the worst peddler of tribalism." In the very different setting of Hungary in the 1880's, the promotion of anti-Semitism was largely the work of students, intellectuals, and sections of the middle classes, while the Hungarian peasant masses remained relatively unresponsive.

Advocates of preferential policies often see these policies as not only promoting social harmony by reducing gaps in income and "representation," but also as part of a more general attempt to "equalize life chances." Much effort is expended establishing the moral desirability of this goal and the extent to which we currently fall short of it, while little or no effort goes into establishing our *capability* to accomplish such a staggering task. One clue to the magnitude and difficulty of what is being attempted are the various ways in which first-born children excel their siblings. A completely disproportionate number of the famous individuals in history were either first-born or the only child. In more mundane achievements as well, the first-born tend to excel. A study of National Merit Scholarship finalists showed that, even in five-child families, the first-born became finalists more often than all the other siblings combined. The same was true in two-, three-, and four-child families. Such disparities, among people born of the same parents and raised under the same roof, mock presumptions of being able to equalize life chances across broader and deeper differences among people in a large, complex, and, especially, multi-ethnic society.

The abstract moral desirability of a goal cannot preempt the prior question of our capacity to achieve it. This is not even a question of falling short of all that might be hoped for. It is a question of risking counterproductive, disastrous, and even bloody results.

Beneficiaries and Losers

Part of the moral aura surrounding preferential policies is due to the belief that such policies benefit the less fortunate. The losers in this presumed redistribution are seldom specified, though the underlying assumption seems to be that they are the more fortunate.

Empirical evidence for such assumptions is largely lacking and the *a priori* case for believing them is unconvincing. For example, the effects of preferential policies depend on the costs of complementary factors required to use the preferences. These costs can obviously be borne more readily by those who are already more fortunate. Benefits set aside for businessmen of the preferred group are of no use to members of that group who do not happen to own a business, or possess the capital to start one. Preferential admission to medical school is a benefit only to those who have already gone to college. Because preferential benefits tend to be concentrated on more lucrative or prestigious things, they are often within striking distance only for the fortunate few who have already advanced well beyond most other members of the preferred group. In Third World countries, where the great demand is for clerical jobs in the government, the poorer groups in these countries often have difficulty reaching even the modest level of education required for such employment.

Preferential scholarships for Malays in Malaysia are a classic example. Students from families in the lower-income brackets—63 percent of the population—received 14 percent of the university scholarships, while students whose families were in the top 17 percent of the income distribution received more than half of the scholarships. In India, preferential programs for both untouchables and "other backward classes" show the same pattern. In the state of Haryana, 37 different untouchable castes were entitled to preferential scholarships but only 18 actually received any—and just one of these received 65 percent of the scholarships at the graduate levels and 80 percent at the undergraduate level. Similar patterns are found in other parts of the country. In the state of Tamil Nadu, the highest of the so-called "backward classes" (11 percent of the total) received nearly half of all jobs and all university admissions set aside for such classes. The bottom 12 percent received no more than 2 percent of the jobs and university admissions.

In some cases—including the United States—the less fortunate members of a preferred group may actually retrogress while the more fortunate advance under preferential policies. After "affirmative-action" policies took hold in the early 1970's, blacks with little education and little job experience fell further behind the general population—and indeed further behind whites with little education and little job experience. Meanwhile, blacks with college education or substantial job experience advanced economically, both absolutely and relative to whites with the same advantages. Yet another example of the benefits of "affirmative action" to those already more fortunate are the business "set-asides" that give minority entrepreneurs preferential access to government contracts under Section 8(a) of the Small Business Act. Minority businessmen who participate in this program have an average net worth of $160,000. This is not only far higher than the average net worth of the groups they come from, but also higher than the average net worth of Americans in general.

This pattern of simultaneous advance at the top and retrogression at the bottom is not confined to the United States. In India, the era of preferential policies has seen the proportion of untouchables increase significantly among high-level government officials, while the proportion of untouchables who work as landless agricultural laborers has also increased. In Malaysia, the representation of Malays on corporate boards of directors has increased significantly, while the proportion of Malays among the population living below the official poverty level has also increased.

Just as the advocates of preferential policies arbitrarily assume that such policies will benefit the "disadvantaged," so they arbitrarily assume that this will be at the expense of the "privileged." They neither offer evidence of this in advance nor are so impolitic as to collect data on this point after preferential programs have been inaugurated. Such evidence as exists points in the opposite direction. In Bombay, preferential policies to put Maharashtrians into the ranks of business executives had only minor effects on the Gujaratis who were dominant in that occupation, reducing the proportion of Gujarati executives from 52 percent to 44 percent. Among the South Indians, however, their 25-percent representation among Bombay executives was cut in half, to 12 percent. A similar pattern appeared in the very different setting of prewar Hungary, where policies favoring Gentiles had relatively little effect on the Jewish financial and industrial elite but imposed real hardships on the Jewish middle class and lower middle class. In the United States, despite voluminous official statistics on all sorts of racial and ethnic matters, no one seems to have collected data on the actual losers under "affirmative action." It may be significant, however, that those who have protested their losses all the way up to the U.S. Supreme Court have not been named Adams, Cabot, or Rockefeller, but DeFunis, Bakke, and Weber.

II. The Illusion of Compensation

What makes compensation an illusion is not only that sufferers are not in fact compensated, or the effects of historic wrongs redressed—or even accurately identified and separated from innumerable other social factors at work simultaneously. Both the principle of compensation and the particular form of compensation via preferential policies require careful examination.

The Principle of Compensation

Given the mortality of human beings, often the only compensation for historic wrongs that is within the scope of our knowledge and control is purely symbolic compensation—taking from individuals who inflicted no harm and giving to individuals who suffered none. In addition to the moral shakiness and social dangers of such a policy, it also promotes a kind of social irredentism, a set of *a priori* grievances against living people, whether or not they have ever inflicted harm on those who feel aggrieved. In view of the futile but bitter and bloody struggles engendered by territorial irredentism, there is little good to hope for by applying this same principle in a new field.

The factual reality that actual benefits from compensatory preferences tend to be concentrated in the already more fortunate elites among the preferred groups makes the moral case for such policies weaker and the social dangers greater. The more educated, articulate, and more politically sophisticated elites have every incentive to whip up group emotions in favor of more and better preferences, despite the increasing group polarization this may produce, and to be intransigent against any suggestion that any such preferences should ever be reduced or ended. This has been a common pattern in the most disparate countries.

In principle, compensation can take many forms, beginning with a simple transfer of money from one group to another. In practice, however, preferential policies are the form taken in many countries around the world. The implications of that particular form, and of its alternatives, raise still more troubling questions.

The Form of Compensation

If, notwithstanding all philosophic objections to the principle of group compensation, such a policy is in fact chosen, then the particular form of the compensation can make a major difference in the costs and the consequences of compensatory policies. When resources, or the benefits they create, are transferred from group A to group B, this is not necessarily—or even likely—a zero-sum process, in which the value of what is lost by one is the same as the value of what is gained by the other. What is transferred may be subjectively valued differently by the losers and the recipients. There may also be objectively discernible differences in the use of the same resources by the two groups.

Compensatory policies may, in theory, take place through transfers of money, transfers of in-kind benefits, or through differential applications of rules and standards. In Australia, for example, various money and in-kind transfers to the aborigines add up to more than $2,000 annually for every aboriginal man, woman, and child. Such transfers arouse relatively little political opposition or social backlash. Similarly, in the United States, monetary compensation for Japanese Americans interned during World War II aroused relatively little controversy—and even that little controversy quickly subsided, once the decision was made.

Such monetary transfers are less costly to individual members of the majority population the more the majority outnumbers the minority receiving the transfer. Obviously, if group A is 100 times as large as group B, each member of group B can receive $100 at a cost of only one dollar to each member of group A. However, even where the losses sustained by one group are significant, monetary transfers may still be efficient, in the narrowly economic sense that what is lost by one group as a whole is gained by another group, with no direct net loss to society as a whole. Whatever the merits or demerits of the particular transfer on other grounds, it is not inefficient. Politically and socially, the opposition to such transfers is therefore unlikely to be as great as opposition to the same net transfers in forms that cost more to the losers than is gained by the gainers. Preferential policies often cost the losers more than is gained by the gainers. Preferential policies, by definition, involve a differential application of rules and standards to individuals originating in different groups. Even where the preferences are not stated in terms of differential rules or standards, but rather in terms of numerical quotas, "goals," or "targets," differences in the qualifications of the respective pools of applicants can readily make numerical similarities amount to differences in standards. This is a very common result in countries around the world. In Nigeria, programs to have college-student populations reflect "the federal character" of the country—i.e., tribal quotas under regional names—led to a situation where cut-off scores for admission to the same college varied substantially between students from different tribes or regions. In Sri Lanka, demographic "standardization" policies led to similar disparities in qualification requirements for individuals from different regions of the country. In India, attempts to meet quotas for untouchable students led to drastic reductions in the qualifications they needed for admission to various institutions. Where applicant pools in different groups are different in qualifications, numerical quotas are equivalent to different standards. Therefore preferential policies in general, however phrased, are essentially an application of different rules or standards to individuals from different groups. The question then is: what are the effects of transfers between groups in this particular form?

There are many ways in which intergroup transfers through differential standards can become negative-sum processes, in which what is lost by one group exceeds what is gained by another, thus representing a direct loss to society as a whole—as well as causing indirect losses, due to a larger resistance or backlash than if the recipient group had obtained the same value or benefit in some other form. An obvious example is when a particular group, in which 90 percent of the students admitted to college succeed in graduating, loses places to another group in which only 30 percent of the students graduate. Group A must lose 900 graduates, in order for group B to gain 300 graduates. It might be objected that this overstates the net loss, since there may be some marginal benefit simply from having attended college, even without graduating. Offsetting this, however, is the fact that groups with lower qualifications tend to specialize in easier and less remunerative fields, whether in India, Malaysia, the Soviet Union, or the United States. Therefore group A may lose 900 graduates largely concentrated in mathematics, science, and engineering, while group B gains 300 graduates largely concentrated in sociology, education, and ethnic studies.

The *apparent* losses to one group under preferential policies may also far exceed the real losses, thereby further raising the indirect social costs of backlash and turmoil. For example, an observer of India's preferential policies for untouchables (known officially as "scheduled castes") has commented:

> . . . we hear innumerable tales of persons being deprived of appointments in favor of people who ranked lower than they did in the relevant examinations. No doubt this does happen, but if all these people were, in fact, paying the price for appointments to Scheduled Castes, there would be many more SC persons appointed than there actually are. To illustrate: supposing that 300 people qualify for ten posts available. The top nine are appointed on merit but the tenth is reserved, so the authorities go down the list to find an SC applicant. They find one at 140 and he is appointed. Whereupon all 131 between him and the merit list feel aggrieved. He has not taken 131 posts; he has taken one, yet 131 people believe they have paid the price for it. Moreover, the remaining 159 often also resent the situation, believing that their chances were, somehow, lessened by the existence of SC reservations.

Where certain opportunities are rigidly "set aside" for particular groups, in the sense that members of other groups cannot have them, even if these opportunities remain unused, then there is the potential for a maximum of grievance for a minimum of benefit transfer. Admission to medical school in India's state of Gujarat operates on this principle—and has led repeatedly to bloody riots in which many people have died. Reservations or "set-asides" in general tend to provoke strong objections. The first major setback for "affirmative action" in the U.S. Supreme Court was based on objections to reserved-admissions places for minority applicants in the 1978 *Bakke* case. A later major setback occurred in *City of Richmond v. Croson* (1989), where minority business set-asides were struck down by the Supreme Court. Similarly, in India, an exhaustive, scholarly legal study of preferential policies found: "Virtually all of the litigation about compensatory discrimination has involved reservations, even though preferences in the form of provisions of facilities, resources, and protections directly affect a much larger number of recipients." This litigation has been initiated mostly by non-preferred individuals who complain of being adversely affected. In some ultimate sense, non-preferred individuals are just as much adversely affected by preferences in other forms that direct resources away from them and toward preferred groups. But it is preference in the specific form of "reservation" or "set-aside" that seems most to provoke both violence and litigation.

By contrast, resource transfers designed to enable disadvantaged groups to meet standards are accepted while attempts to bring the standards down to them are overwhelmingly rejected. In the United States, preferential policies have repeatedly been rejected in public-opinion polls. However, the same American public has strongly supported "special educational or vocational courses, free of charge, to enable members of minority groups to do better on tests." More than three-fifths of all whites even support "requiring large companies to set up special training programs for members of minority groups." The issue is not simply whether one is for or against the advancement of particular groups or is willing to see transfers of resources for their betterment. The method by which their betterment is attempted matters greatly in terms of whether such efforts have the support or the opposition of others.

III. Replacing Illusions

With all the empirical weaknesses, logical flaws, and social dangers of preferential policies, why have they become so popular and spread so rapidly around the world? One reason is that their *political* attractions are considerable. They offer an immediate response—a quick fix—at relatively little government expense, to the demands of vocal, aroused, and often organized elites, speaking in the name of restive masses. This restiveness of the masses is by no means incidental. Violence has frequently preceded preferences, from the American ghetto riots of the 1960's to the Malay and Indonesian riots against the Chinese at about the same time, to terrorism in India, and massive mob violence against the Tamils in Sri Lanka. This violence by the masses is typically used politically to promote elite purposes via preferential policies. An international study of ethnic conflicts concluded:

> Preferences tend to respond to middle-class aspirations almost entirely. They do little or nothing about the resentments of those who do not aspire to attend secondary school or university, to enter the modern private sector or the bureaucracy, or to become businessmen. Although lower-class resentments are often profound—it is not, after all, the middle class that typically participates in ethnic violence—the resentments may have nothing to do with occupational mobility and preferences do not address them.

Preferential policies, then, are politically attractive as a response, however socially ineffective or counterproductive such policies may later prove to be in practice. At a sufficiently superficial level, the moral attractions of preferential policies are considerable as well. Even in South Africa, moral appeals were made on behalf of a "civilized labor policy"—protecting European workers' customary standard of living from being undercut by Africans and Indians accustomed to living on less—and clergy, intellectuals, and others not personally benefiting joined in support of these policies on that basis. Preferential policies allow intellectuals as well as politicians to be on the side of the angels (as locally defined at the time) at low cost—or rather, at a low down payment, for the real costs come later, and have sometimes been paid in blood.

The last refuge of a failed policy is "the long run," in which it will supposedly be a success. In other words, those who predicted the short run wrongly ask to be trusted with the much harder task of predicting the long run rightly. This argument, used to defend the counterproductive effects of preferential policies, is far less defensible in an international perspective where older preferential policies (as in India or Sri Lanka) have progressed from intergroup political hostility to bloodshed in the streets and deaths by the thousands, while newer programs (as in the United States) are still in the process of increasing group polarization, and the even more recent preferential policies taking shape in Australia and New Zealand are still at the stage of optimistic predictions.

Even the most damning indictment of a policy is almost certain to be met with the response: "But what would you replace it with?" However effective as a political tactic, such a question confuses rather than clarifies. It is like an arbitrary prohibition against saying that the emperor has no clothes, until a complete wardrobe has been designed. The question misconceives policy, and human actions in general, in yet another way: no one who extinguishes a forest fire or removes a cancer has to "replace" it with anything. We are well rid of evils.

This is not to say that none of the aspects of social issues raised during "affirmative-action" controversies should ever be addressed by public policy. The case for public policy in general, or for a particular public policy, must be made on the individual merits of the particular issues raised—but not as a general "replacement" for some discredited policy.

What must be replaced are the social illusions and misconceptions underlying preferential policies, for any alternative policy based on the same illusions and misconceptions will have the same fatal weaknesses in its structure. In some countries and for some purposes social policy may wish to ameliorate the lot of the less fortunate or make it possible for individuals or groups to acquire the knowledge and skills necessary for their own advancement. It is infinitely more important that such efforts be based on facts and logic than that there be one particular scheme selected from innumerable possibilities as the uniquely designated "replacement" for existing policy.

We may or may not be able to agree on what the ideal, or even a viable, policy must be. What we can agree on is far more fundamental: We can agree to *talk sense*. That will mean abandoning a whole vocabulary of political rhetoric which preempts factual questions by arbitrarily calling statistical disparities "discrimination," "exclusion," "segregation," and the like. It will mean confronting issues instead of impugning motives. It will mean specifying goals and defending those specifics, rather than speaking in terms of seeking some nebulously unctuous "change" or "social justice." Perhaps more than anything else, talking sense will mean examining policies in terms of the incentives they create, and the results to which these incentives lead, rather than the hopes they embody. It will mean that evidence takes precedence over assertion and reiteration. . . .

VI. Politics Versus Progress

. . . Could some judicious blend of preferential programs and programs designed to improve the performances of less educated groups work? Here the problem is that the two kinds of programs create incentives that work at cross-purposes, even if their goals are the same. Forcing students to meet higher standards—a painful process for them and their teachers alike—will be made all the more difficult if the students know that these standards are unnecessary for them to reach whatever educational or employment goals they have, or even to be promoted to the next grade. If group-representation statistics are the standard by which institutions will be judged, other standards will be sacrificed for the sake of body count. This is true not only of educational institutions but of other institutions as well.

Political feasibility is the greatest obstacle to new policies with an overriding goal of advancing the less fortunate because time is the key ingredient in such advancement on a large scale. Even in the extreme case of South Africa, where massive transfers of the nation's resources were focused on a small minority of its people, in *addition* to preferential policies pursued in utter disregard of the losses and even tragedies suffered by others as a result, it was decades before the Afrikaner "poor whites" became middle-class. Only in terms of political appearances are preferential policies a "quick fix." The dangers of an actual retrogression among the masses of the beneficiary group cannot be dismissed, either from an analytical or an empirical perspective. Even greater dangers have materialized in countries that have experienced bloodshed in the wake of group polarization brought on by preferential policies.

While current political feasibility may be the touchstone of the professional politician, it cannot be the last word for others. In many countries, what is most politically feasible are policies that further a continued drift in the direction of group polarization and the dangers and disasters this entails. Specific alternative policies will differ for different groups and different countries. What is crucial is that these alternatives be examined in terms of the incentives they create and the results to which such incentives can be expected to lead—regardless of the rationales, aspirations, or symbolism of these policies. Determining in this way what *should* be done is not an exercise in utopianism, for once there is a consensus on what needs to be done, that in itself changes what is politically feasible.

The starting point for rethinking and reform must be a recognition that "affirmative action" has been a failure in the United States and a disaster in other countries that have had such policies longer. Indeed, a growing polarization and increasing numbers of ugly racial incidents (especially on campuses that are strongholds of "affirmative action") may be early warnings that we too may be moving from the stage of mere failure to the stage of social disaster.

Index